Android Studio Giraffe Essentials

Java Edition

Android Studio Giraffe Essentials – Java Edition

ISBN-13: 978-1-951442-75-0

© 2023 Neil Smyth / Payload Media, Inc. All Rights Reserved.

This book is provided for personal use only. Unauthorized use, reproduction and/or distribution strictly prohibited. All rights reserved.

The content of this book is provided for informational purposes only. Neither the publisher nor the author offers any warranties or representation, express or implied, with regard to the accuracy of information contained in this book, nor do they accept any liability for any loss or damage arising from any errors or omissions.

This book contains trademarked terms that are used solely for editorial purposes and to the benefit of the respective trademark owner. The terms used within this book are not intended as infringement of any trademarks.

Rev: 1.0

Contents

Table of Contents

1. Introduction 1
   1.1 Downloading the Code Samples 1
   1.2 Feedback 1
   1.3 Errata 2
   1.4 Download the Color eBook 2
2. Setting up an Android Studio Development Environment 3
   2.1 System requirements 3
   2.2 Downloading the Android Studio package 3
   2.3 Installing Android Studio 4
      2.3.1 Installation on Windows 4
      2.3.2 Installation on macOS 4
      2.3.3 Installation on Linux 5
   2.4 The Android Studio setup wizard 5
   2.5 Installing additional Android SDK packages 6
   2.6 Installing the Android SDK Command-line Tools 9
      2.6.1 Windows 8.1 10
      2.6.2 Windows 10 11
      2.6.3 Windows 11 11
      2.6.4 Linux 11
      2.6.5 macOS 11
   2.7 Android Studio memory management 11
   2.8 Updating Android Studio and the SDK 12
   2.9 Summary 13
3. Creating an Example Android App in Android Studio 15
   3.1 About the Project 15
   3.2 Creating a New Android Project 15
   3.3 Creating an Activity 16
   3.4 Defining the Project and SDK Settings 16
   3.5 Enabling the New Android Studio UI 17
   3.6 Modifying the Example Application 18
   3.7 Modifying the User Interface 19
   3.8 Reviewing the Layout and Resource Files 25
   3.9 Adding Interaction 28
   3.10 Summary 29
4. Creating an Android Virtual Device (AVD) in Android Studio 31
   4.1 About Android Virtual Devices 31
   4.2 Starting the Emulator 33
   4.3 Running the Application in the AVD 34
   4.4 Running on Multiple Devices 35
   4.5 Stopping a Running Application 36
   4.6 Supporting Dark Theme 36

i

Table of Contents

    4.7 Running the Emulator in a Separate Window 37
    4.8 Enabling the Device Frame 40
    4.9 Summary 41

5. Using and Configuring the Android Studio AVD Emulator 43

    5.1 The Emulator Environment 43
    5.2 Emulator Toolbar Options 43
    5.3 Working in Zoom Mode 45
    5.4 Resizing the Emulator Window 45
    5.5 Extended Control Options 45
        5.5.1 Location 46
        5.5.2 Displays 46
        5.5.3 Cellular 46
        5.5.4 Battery 46
        5.5.5 Camera 46
        5.5.6 Phone 46
        5.5.7 Directional Pad 46
        5.5.8 Microphone 46
        5.5.9 Fingerprint 46
        5.5.10 Virtual Sensors 47
        5.5.11 Snapshots 47
        5.5.12 Record and Playback 47
        5.5.13 Google Play 47
        5.5.14 Settings 47
        5.5.15 Help 47
    5.6 Working with Snapshots 47
    5.7 Configuring Fingerprint Emulation 48
    5.8 The Emulator in Tool Window Mode 50
    5.9 Creating a Resizable Emulator 50
    5.10 Summary 51

6. A Tour of the Android Studio User Interface 53

    6.1 The Welcome Screen 53
    6.2 The Menu Bar 54
    6.3 The Main Window 54
    6.4 The Tool Windows 56
    6.5 The Tool Window Menus 59
    6.6 Android Studio Keyboard Shortcuts 59
    6.7 Switcher and Recent Files Navigation 60
    6.8 Changing the Android Studio Theme 61
    6.9 Summary 62

7. Testing Android Studio Apps on a Physical Android Device 63

    7.1 An Overview of the Android Debug Bridge (ADB) 63
    7.2 Enabling USB Debugging ADB on Android Devices 63
        7.2.1 macOS ADB Configuration 64
        7.2.2 Windows ADB Configuration 65
        7.2.3 Linux adb Configuration 66
    7.3 Resolving USB Connection Issues 66
    7.4 Enabling Wireless Debugging on Android Devices 67
    7.5 Testing the adb Connection 69

    7.6 Device Mirroring..69
    7.7 Summary..69
8. **The Basics of the Android Studio Code Editor**..71
    8.1 The Android Studio Editor..71
    8.2 Splitting the Editor Window...74
    8.3 Code Completion..74
    8.4 Statement Completion..76
    8.5 Parameter Information..76
    8.6 Parameter Name Hints..76
    8.7 Code Generation...77
    8.8 Code Folding...78
    8.9 Quick Documentation Lookup..79
    8.10 Code Reformatting..79
    8.11 Finding Sample Code..80
    8.12 Live Templates..80
    8.13 Summary...81
9. **An Overview of the Android Architecture**...83
    9.1 The Android Software Stack..83
    9.2 The Linux Kernel...84
    9.3 Android Runtime – ART..84
    9.4 Android Libraries..84
        9.4.1 C/C++ Libraries..85
    9.5 Application Framework..85
    9.6 Applications..86
    9.7 Summary...86
10. **The Anatomy of an Android App**..87
    10.1 Android Activities...87
    10.2 Android Fragments...87
    10.3 Android Intents...88
    10.4 Broadcast Intents..88
    10.5 Broadcast Receivers..88
    10.6 Android Services...88
    10.7 Content Providers...89
    10.8 The Application Manifest..89
    10.9 Application Resources..89
    10.10 Application Context..89
    10.11 Summary...89
11. **An Overview of Android View Binding**...91
    11.1 Find View by Id...91
    11.2 View Binding 91
    11.3 Converting the AndroidSample project..92
    11.4 Enabling View Binding..92
    11.5 Using View Binding...92
    11.6 Choosing an Option..93
    11.7 View Binding in the Book Examples..93
    11.8 Migrating a Project to View Binding..94
    11.9 Summary...94

iii

12. Understanding Android Application and Activity Lifecycles 97
12.1 Android Applications and Resource Management 97
12.2 Android Process States 97
12.2.1 Foreground Process 98
12.2.2 Visible Process 98
12.2.3 Service Process 98
12.2.4 Background Process 98
12.2.5 Empty Process 99
12.3 Inter-Process Dependencies 99
12.4 The Activity Lifecycle 99
12.5 The Activity Stack 99
12.6 Activity States 100
12.7 Configuration Changes 100
12.8 Handling State Change 101
12.9 Summary 101

13. Handling Android Activity State Changes 103
13.1 New vs. Old Lifecycle Techniques 103
13.2 The Activity and Fragment Classes 103
13.3 Dynamic State vs. Persistent State 105
13.4 The Android Lifecycle Methods 106
13.5 Lifetimes 107
13.6 Foldable Devices and Multi-Resume 108
13.7 Disabling Configuration Change Restarts 108
13.8 Lifecycle Method Limitations 109
13.9 Summary 109

14. Android Activity State Changes by Example 111
14.1 Creating the State Change Example Project 111
14.2 Designing the User Interface 112
14.3 Overriding the Activity Lifecycle Methods 113
14.4 Filtering the Logcat Panel 115
14.5 Running the Application 117
14.6 Experimenting with the Activity 117
14.7 Summary 118

15. Saving and Restoring the State of an Android Activity 119
15.1 Saving Dynamic State 119
15.2 Default Saving of User Interface State 119
15.3 The Bundle Class 120
15.4 Saving the State 121
15.5 Restoring the State 122
15.6 Testing the Application 122
15.7 Summary 122

16. Understanding Android Views, View Groups and Layouts 125
16.1 Designing for Different Android Devices 125
16.2 Views and View Groups 125
16.3 Android Layout Managers 125
16.4 The View Hierarchy 127
16.5 Creating User Interfaces 128

16.6 Summary 128
17. A Guide to the Android Studio Layout Editor Tool 129
17.1 Basic vs. Empty Views Activity Templates 129
17.2 The Android Studio Layout Editor 133
17.3 Design Mode 133
17.4 The Palette 134
17.5 Design Mode and Layout Views 135
17.6 Night Mode 136
17.7 Code Mode 136
17.8 Split Mode 137
17.9 Setting Attributes 138
17.10 Transforms 139
17.11 Tools Visibility Toggles 140
17.12 Converting Views 141
17.13 Displaying Sample Data 142
17.14 Creating a Custom Device Definition 143
17.15 Changing the Current Device 143
17.16 Layout Validation 144
17.17 Summary 145
18. A Guide to the Android ConstraintLayout 147
18.1 How ConstraintLayout Works 147
18.1.1 Constraints 147
18.1.2 Margins 148
18.1.3 Opposing Constraints 148
18.1.4 Constraint Bias 149
18.1.5 Chains 150
18.1.6 Chain Styles 150
18.2 Baseline Alignment 151
18.3 Configuring Widget Dimensions 151
18.4 Guideline Helper 152
18.5 Group Helper 152
18.6 Barrier Helper 152
18.7 Flow Helper 154
18.8 Ratios 155
18.9 ConstraintLayout Advantages 155
18.10 ConstraintLayout Availability 156
18.11 Summary 156
19. A Guide to Using ConstraintLayout in Android Studio 157
19.1 Design and Layout Views 157
19.2 Autoconnect Mode 159
19.3 Inference Mode 159
19.4 Manipulating Constraints Manually 159
19.5 Adding Constraints in the Inspector 161
19.6 Viewing Constraints in the Attributes Window 161
19.7 Deleting Constraints 162
19.8 Adjusting Constraint Bias 163
19.9 Understanding ConstraintLayout Margins 163
19.10 The Importance of Opposing Constraints and Bias 165

19.11 Configuring Widget Dimensions 167
19.12 Design Time Tools Positioning 168
19.13 Adding Guidelines 169
19.14 Adding Barriers 171
19.15 Adding a Group 172
19.16 Working with the Flow Helper 173
19.17 Widget Group Alignment and Distribution 173
19.18 Converting other Layouts to ConstraintLayout 175
19.19 Summary 175

20. Working with ConstraintLayout Chains and Ratios in Android Studio 177

20.1 Creating a Chain 177
20.2 Changing the Chain Style 179
20.3 Spread Inside Chain Style 180
20.4 Packed Chain Style 180
20.5 Packed Chain Style with Bias 180
20.6 Weighted Chain 180
20.7 Working with Ratios 181
20.8 Summary 183

21. An Android Studio Layout Editor ConstraintLayout Tutorial 185

21.1 An Android Studio Layout Editor Tool Example 185
21.2 Preparing the Layout Editor Environment 185
21.3 Adding the Widgets to the User Interface 186
21.4 Adding the Constraints 189
21.5 Testing the Layout 191
21.6 Using the Layout Inspector 191
21.7 Summary 192

22. Manual XML Layout Design in Android Studio 193

22.1 Manually Creating an XML Layout 193
22.2 Manual XML vs. Visual Layout Design 196
22.3 Summary 196

23. Managing Constraints using Constraint Sets 197

23.1 Java Code vs. XML Layout Files 197
23.2 Creating Views 197
23.3 View Attributes 198
23.4 Constraint Sets 198
  23.4.1 Establishing Connections 198
  23.4.2 Applying Constraints to a Layout 198
  23.4.3 Parent Constraint Connections 198
  23.4.4 Sizing Constraints 199
  23.4.5 Constraint Bias 199
  23.4.6 Alignment Constraints 199
  23.4.7 Copying and Applying Constraint Sets 199
  23.4.8 ConstraintLayout Chains 199
  23.4.9 Guidelines 200
  23.4.10 Removing Constraints 200
  23.4.11 Scaling 200
  23.4.12 Rotation 201

23.5 Summary 201

24. An Android ConstraintSet Tutorial..203

24.1 Creating the Example Project in Android Studio 203
24.2 Adding Views to an Activity 203
24.3 Setting View Attributes... 204
24.4 Creating View IDs 205
24.5 Configuring the Constraint Set 206
24.6 Adding the EditText View 207
24.7 Converting Density Independent Pixels (dp) to Pixels (px) 208
24.8 Summary 209

25. A Guide to Using Apply Changes in Android Studio 211

25.1 Introducing Apply Changes 211
25.2 Understanding Apply Changes Options 211
25.3 Using Apply Changes 212
25.4 Configuring Apply Changes Fallback Settings 213
25.5 An Apply Changes Tutorial 213
25.6 Using Apply Code Changes 213
25.7 Using Apply Changes and Restart Activity 214
25.8 Using Run App 214
25.9 Summary 214

26. An Overview and Example of Android Event Handling 215

26.1 Understanding Android Events 215
26.2 Using the android:onClick Resource 215
26.3 Event Listeners and Callback Methods 216
26.4 An Event Handling Example 216
26.5 Designing the User Interface 217
26.6 The Event Listener and Callback Method 217
26.7 Consuming Events 219
26.8 Summary 220

27. Android Touch and Multi-touch Event Handling 221

27.1 Intercepting Touch Events 221
27.2 The MotionEvent Object 221
27.3 Understanding Touch Actions 222
27.4 Handling Multiple Touches 222
27.5 An Example Multi-Touch Application 222
27.6 Designing the Activity User Interface 223
27.7 Implementing the Touch Event Listener 223
27.8 Running the Example Application 226
27.9 Summary 227

28. Detecting Common Gestures Using the Android Gesture Detector Class 229

28.1 Implementing Common Gesture Detection 229
28.2 Creating an Example Gesture Detection Project 230
28.3 Implementing the Listener Class 230
28.4 Creating the GestureDetectorCompat Instance 232
28.5 Implementing the onTouchEvent() Method 233
28.6 Testing the Application 233

28.7 Summary 234

29. Implementing Custom Gesture and Pinch Recognition on Android 235

29.1 The Android Gesture Builder Application 235
29.2 The GestureOverlayView Class 235
29.3 Detecting Gestures 235
29.4 Identifying Specific Gestures 235
29.5 Installing and Running the Gesture Builder Application 235
29.6 Creating a Gestures File 236
29.7 Creating the Example Project 236
29.8 Extracting the Gestures File from the SD Card 236
29.9 Adding the Gestures File to the Project 237
29.10 Designing the User Interface 237
29.11 Loading the Gestures File 238
29.12 Registering the Event Listener 239
29.13 Implementing the onGesturePerformed Method 239
29.14 Testing the Application 240
29.15 Configuring the GestureOverlayView 240
29.16 Intercepting Gestures 241
29.17 Detecting Pinch Gestures 241
29.18 A Pinch Gesture Example Project 241
29.19 Summary 244

30. An Introduction to Android Fragments 245

30.1 What is a Fragment? 245
30.2 Creating a Fragment 245
30.3 Adding a Fragment to an Activity using the Layout XML File 246
30.4 Adding and Managing Fragments in Code 248
30.5 Handling Fragment Events 249
30.6 Implementing Fragment Communication 250
30.7 Summary 251

31. Using Fragments in Android Studio - An Example 253

31.1 About the Example Fragment Application 253
31.2 Creating the Example Project 253
31.3 Creating the First Fragment Layout 253
31.4 Migrating a Fragment to View Binding 255
31.5 Adding the Second Fragment 256
31.6 Adding the Fragments to the Activity 257
31.7 Making the Toolbar Fragment Talk to the Activity 258
31.8 Making the Activity Talk to the Text Fragment 261
31.9 Testing the Application 262
31.10 Summary 263

32. Modern Android App Architecture with Jetpack 265

32.1 What is Android Jetpack? 265
32.2 The "Old" Architecture 265
32.3 Modern Android Architecture 265
32.4 The ViewModel Component 266
32.5 The LiveData Component 266
32.6 ViewModel Saved State 267

32.7 LiveData and Data Binding	267
32.8 Android Lifecycles	268
32.9 Repository Modules	268
32.10 Summary	269

33. An Android ViewModel Tutorial 271

33.1 About the Project	271
33.2 Creating the ViewModel Example Project	271
33.3 Removing Unwanted Project Elements	271
33.4 Designing the Fragment Layout	272
33.5 Implementing the View Model	273
33.6 Associating the Fragment with the View Model	274
33.7 Modifying the Fragment	275
33.8 Accessing the ViewModel Data	276
33.9 Testing the Project	276
33.10 Summary	277

34. An Android Jetpack LiveData Tutorial 279

34.1 LiveData - A Recap	279
34.2 Adding LiveData to the ViewModel	279
34.3 Implementing the Observer	281
34.4 Summary	283

35. An Overview of Android Jetpack Data Binding 285

35.1 An Overview of Data Binding	285
35.2 The Key Components of Data Binding	285
35.2.1 The Project Build Configuration	285
35.2.2 The Data Binding Layout File	286
35.2.3 The Layout File Data Element	287
35.2.4 The Binding Classes	288
35.2.5 Data Binding Variable Configuration	288
35.2.6 Binding Expressions (One-Way)	289
35.2.7 Binding Expressions (Two-Way)	290
35.2.8 Event and Listener Bindings	290
35.3 Summary	291

36. An Android Jetpack Data Binding Tutorial 293

36.1 Removing the Redundant Code	293
36.2 Enabling Data Binding	294
36.3 Adding the Layout Element	295
36.4 Adding the Data Element to Layout File	296
36.5 Working with the Binding Class	297
36.6 Assigning the ViewModel Instance to the Data Binding Variable	298
36.7 Adding Binding Expressions	298
36.8 Adding the Conversion Method	299
36.9 Adding a Listener Binding	299
36.10 Testing the App	300
36.11 Summary	300

37. An Android ViewModel Saved State Tutorial 301

37.1 Understanding ViewModel State Saving	301

37.2 Implementing ViewModel State Saving 301
37.3 Saving and Restoring State 303
37.4 Adding Saved State Support to the ViewModelDemo Project 303
37.5 Summary 305

38. Working with Android Lifecycle-Aware Components 307

38.1 Lifecycle Awareness 307
38.2 Lifecycle Owners 307
38.3 Lifecycle Observers 308
38.4 Lifecycle States and Events 309
38.5 Summary 310

39. An Android Jetpack Lifecycle Awareness Tutorial 311

39.1 Creating the Example Lifecycle Project 311
39.2 Creating a Lifecycle Observer 311
39.3 Adding the Observer 313
39.4 Testing the Observer 313
39.5 Creating a Lifecycle Owner 313
39.6 Testing the Custom Lifecycle Owner 315
39.7 Summary 316

40. An Overview of the Navigation Architecture Component 317

40.1 Understanding Navigation 317
40.2 Declaring a Navigation Host 318
40.3 The Navigation Graph 320
40.4 Accessing the Navigation Controller 321
40.5 Triggering a Navigation Action 321
40.6 Passing Arguments 322
40.7 Summary 322

41. An Android Jetpack Navigation Component Tutorial 323

41.1 Creating the NavigationDemo Project 323
41.2 Adding Navigation to the Build Configuration 323
41.3 Creating the Navigation Graph Resource File 324
41.4 Declaring a Navigation Host 325
41.5 Adding Navigation Destinations 326
41.6 Designing the Destination Fragment Layouts 328
41.7 Adding an Action to the Navigation Graph 329
41.8 Implement the OnFragmentInteractionListener 331
41.9 Adding View Binding Support to the Destination Fragments 332
41.10 Triggering the Action 332
41.11 Passing Data Using Safeargs 333
41.12 Summary 336

42. An Introduction to MotionLayout 337

42.1 An Overview of MotionLayout 337
42.2 MotionLayout 337
42.3 MotionScene 337
42.4 Configuring ConstraintSets 338
42.5 Custom Attributes 339
42.6 Triggering an Animation 341

    42.7 Arc Motion 342
    42.8 Keyframes 342
        42.8.1 Attribute Keyframes 342
        42.8.2 Position Keyframes 343
    42.9 Time Linearity 346
    42.10 KeyTrigger 346
    42.11 Cycle and Time Cycle Keyframes 347
    42.12 Starting an Animation from Code 347

43. An Android MotionLayout Editor Tutorial 349

    43.1 Creating the MotionLayoutDemo Project 349
    43.2 ConstraintLayout to MotionLayout Conversion 349
    43.3 Configuring Start and End Constraints 351
    43.4 Previewing the MotionLayout Animation 354
    43.5 Adding an OnClick Gesture 354
    43.6 Adding an Attribute Keyframe to the Transition 356
    43.7 Adding a CustomAttribute to a Transition 358
    43.8 Adding Position Keyframes 360
    43.9 Summary 362

44. A MotionLayout KeyCycle Tutorial 363

    44.1 An Overview of Cycle Keyframes 363
    44.2 Using the Cycle Editor 367
    44.3 Creating the KeyCycleDemo Project 368
    44.4 Configuring the Start and End Constraints 368
    44.5 Creating the Cycles 370
    44.6 Previewing the Animation 372
    44.7 Adding the KeyFrameSet to the MotionScene 372
    44.8 Summary 374

45. Working with the Floating Action Button and Snackbar 375

    45.1 The Material Design 375
    45.2 The Design Library 375
    45.3 The Floating Action Button (FAB) 375
    45.4 The Snackbar 376
    45.5 Creating the Example Project 377
    45.6 Reviewing the Project 377
    45.7 Removing Navigation Features 378
    45.8 Changing the Floating Action Button 378
    45.9 Adding an Action to the Snackbar 380
    45.10 Summary 380

46. Creating a Tabbed Interface using the TabLayout Component 383

    46.1 An Introduction to the ViewPager2 383
    46.2 An Overview of the TabLayout Component 383
    46.3 Creating the TabLayoutDemo Project 384
    46.4 Creating the First Fragment 385
    46.5 Duplicating the Fragments 386
    46.6 Adding the TabLayout and ViewPager2 387
    46.7 Creating the Pager Adapter 388
    46.8 Performing the Initialization Tasks 389

46.9 Testing the Application 391
46.10 Customizing the TabLayout 392
46.11 Summary 393

47. Working with the RecyclerView and CardView Widgets 395

47.1 An Overview of the RecyclerView 395
47.2 An Overview of the CardView 397
47.3 Summary 398

48. An Android RecyclerView and CardView Tutorial 399

48.1 Creating the CardDemo Project 399
48.2 Modifying the Basic Views Activity Project 399
48.3 Designing the CardView Layout 400
48.4 Adding the RecyclerView 401
48.5 Adding the Image Files 401
48.6 Creating the RecyclerView Adapter 402
48.7 Initializing the RecyclerView Component 404
48.8 Testing the Application 405
48.9 Responding to Card Selections 406
48.10 Summary 407

49. A Layout Editor Sample Data Tutorial 409

49.1 Adding Sample Data to a Project 409
49.2 Using Custom Sample Data 413
49.3 Summary 416

50. Working with the AppBar and Collapsing Toolbar Layouts 417

50.1 The Anatomy of an AppBar 417
50.2 The Example Project 418
50.3 Coordinating the RecyclerView and Toolbar 418
50.4 Introducing the Collapsing Toolbar Layout 420
50.5 Changing the Title and Scrim Color 423
50.6 Summary 424

51. An Android Studio Primary/Detail Flow Tutorial 425

51.1 The Primary/Detail Flow 425
51.2 Creating a Primary/Detail Flow Activity 426
51.3 Adding the Primary/Detail Flow Activity 426
51.4 Modifying the Primary/Detail Flow Template 427
51.5 Changing the Content Model 427
51.6 Changing the Detail Pane 429
51.7 Modifying the ItemDetailFragment Class 430
51.8 Modifying the ItemListFragment Class 431
51.9 Adding Manifest Permissions 432
51.10 Running the Application 432
51.11 Summary 433

52. An Overview of Android Services 435

52.1 Intent Service 435
52.2 Bound Service 435
52.3 The Anatomy of a Service 436
52.4 Controlling Destroyed Service Restart Options 436

| 52.5 Declaring a Service in the Manifest File 436
| 52.6 Starting a Service Running on System Startup 437
| 52.7 Summary 438

53. An Overview of Android Intents 439

    53.1 An Overview of Intents 439
    53.2 Explicit Intents 439
    53.3 Returning Data from an Activity 440
    53.4 Implicit Intents 441
    53.5 Using Intent Filters 442
    53.6 Automatic Link Verification 442
    53.7 Manually Enabling Links 445
    53.8 Checking Intent Availability 446
    53.9 Summary 447

54. Android Explicit Intents – A Worked Example 449

    54.1 Creating the Explicit Intent Example Application 449
    54.2 Designing the User Interface Layout for MainActivity 449
    54.3 Creating the Second Activity Class 450
    54.4 Designing the User Interface Layout for SecondActivity 451
    54.5 Reviewing the Application Manifest File 451
    54.6 Creating the Intent 452
    54.7 Extracting Intent Data 453
    54.8 Launching SecondActivity as a Sub-Activity 454
    54.9 Returning Data from a Sub-Activity 455
    54.10 Testing the Application 455
    54.11 Summary 455

55. Android Implicit Intents – A Worked Example 457

    55.1 Creating the Android Studio Implicit Intent Example Project 457
    55.2 Designing the User Interface 457
    55.3 Creating the Implicit Intent 458
    55.4 Adding a Second Matching Activity 459
    55.5 Adding the Web View to the UI 459
    55.6 Obtaining the Intent URL 460
    55.7 Modifying the MyWebView Project Manifest File 461
    55.8 Installing the MyWebView Package on a Device 462
    55.9 Testing the Application 463
    55.10 Manually Enabling the Link 463
    55.11 Automatic Link Verification 465
    55.12 Summary 467

56. Android Broadcast Intents and Broadcast Receivers 469

    56.1 An Overview of Broadcast Intents 469
    56.2 An Overview of Broadcast Receivers 470
    56.3 Obtaining Results from a Broadcast 471
    56.4 Sticky Broadcast Intents 471
    56.5 The Broadcast Intent Example 472
    56.6 Creating the Example Application 472
    56.7 Creating and Sending the Broadcast Intent 472
    56.8 Creating the Broadcast Receiver 473

Table of Contents

    56.9 Registering the Broadcast Receiver 474
    56.10 Testing the Broadcast Example 475
    56.11 Listening for System Broadcasts 475
    56.12 Summary 476

57. Android Local Bound Services – A Worked Example 477

    57.1 Understanding Bound Services 477
    57.2 Bound Service Interaction Options 477
    57.3 A Local Bound Service Example 477
    57.4 Adding a Bound Service to the Project 478
    57.5 Implementing the Binder 478
    57.6 Binding the Client to the Service 481
    57.7 Completing the Example 482
    57.8 Testing the Application 483
    57.9 Summary 483

58. Android Remote Bound Services – A Worked Example 485

    58.1 Client to Remote Service Communication 485
    58.2 Creating the Example Application 485
    58.3 Designing the User Interface 485
    58.4 Implementing the Remote Bound Service 485
    58.5 Configuring a Remote Service in the Manifest File 487
    58.6 Launching and Binding to the Remote Service 488
    58.7 Sending a Message to the Remote Service 489
    58.8 Summary 490

59. A Basic Overview of Java Threads, Handlers and Executors 491

    59.1 The Application Main Thread 491
    59.2 Thread Handlers 491
    59.3 A Threading Example 491
    59.4 Building the App 492
    59.5 Creating a New Thread 493
    59.6 Implementing a Thread Handler 494
    59.7 Passing a Message to the Handler 496
    59.8 Java Executor Concurrency 496
    59.9 Working with Runnable Tasks 497
    59.10 Shutting down an Executor Service 498
    59.11 Working with Callable Tasks and Futures 498
    59.12 Handling a Future Result 500
    59.13 Scheduling Tasks 501
    59.14 Summary 502

60. Making Runtime Permission Requests in Android 503

    60.1 Understanding Normal and Dangerous Permissions 503
    60.2 Creating the Permissions Example Project 505
    60.3 Checking for a Permission 505
    60.4 Requesting Permission at Runtime 507
    60.5 Providing a Rationale for the Permission Request 508
    60.6 Testing the Permissions App 510
    60.7 Summary 510

61. An Android Notifications Tutorial 511

    61.1 An Overview of Notifications 511
    61.2 Creating the NotifyDemo Project 513
    61.3 Designing the User Interface 513
    61.4 Creating the Second Activity 513
    61.5 Creating a Notification Channel 514
    61.6 Requesting Notification Permission 515
    61.7 Creating and Issuing a Notification 518
    61.8 Launching an Activity from a Notification 520
    61.9 Adding Actions to a Notification 522
    61.10 Bundled Notifications 523
    61.11 Summary 525

62. An Android Direct Reply Notification Tutorial 527
    62.1 Creating the DirectReply Project 527
    62.2 Designing the User Interface 527
    62.3 Requesting Notification Permission 528
    62.4 Creating the Notification Channel 529
    62.5 Building the RemoteInput Object 530
    62.6 Creating the PendingIntent 531
    62.7 Creating the Reply Action 532
    62.8 Receiving Direct Reply Input 534
    62.9 Updating the Notification 535
    62.10 Summary 537

63. Foldable Devices and Multi-Window Support 539
    63.1 Foldables and Multi-Window Support 539
    63.2 Using a Foldable Emulator 540
    63.3 Entering Multi-Window Mode 541
    63.4 Enabling and using Freeform Support 542
    63.5 Checking for Freeform Support 542
    63.6 Enabling Multi-Window Support in an App 542
    63.7 Specifying Multi-Window Attributes 543
    63.8 Detecting Multi-Window Mode in an Activity 544
    63.9 Receiving Multi-Window Notifications 544
    63.10 Launching an Activity in Multi-Window Mode 545
    63.11 Configuring Freeform Activity Size and Position 545
    63.12 Summary 546

64. An Overview of Android SQLite Databases 547
    64.1 Understanding Database Tables 547
    64.2 Introducing Database Schema 547
    64.3 Columns and Data Types 547
    64.4 Database Rows 548
    64.5 Introducing Primary Keys 548
    64.6 What is SQLite? 548
    64.7 Structured Query Language (SQL) 548
    64.8 Trying SQLite on an Android Virtual Device (AVD) 549
    64.9 The Android Room Persistence Library 550
    64.10 Summary 551

65. The Android Room Persistence Library 553

65.1 Revisiting Modern App Architecture 553
65.2 Key Elements of Room Database Persistence 553
    65.2.1 Repository 554
    65.2.2 Room Database 554
    65.2.3 Data Access Object (DAO) 554
    65.2.4 Entities 554
    65.2.5 SQLite Database 554
65.3 Understanding Entities 555
65.4 Data Access Objects 558
65.5 The Room Database 559
65.6 The Repository 560
65.7 In-Memory Databases 561
65.8 Database Inspector 561
65.9 Summary 561

66. An Android TableLayout and TableRow Tutorial 563

66.1 The TableLayout and TableRow Layout Views 563
66.2 Creating the Room Database Project 564
66.3 Converting to a LinearLayout 564
66.4 Adding the TableLayout to the User Interface 565
66.5 Configuring the TableRows 566
66.6 Adding the Button Bar to the Layout 567
66.7 Adding the RecyclerView 568
66.8 Adjusting the Layout Margins 569
66.9 Summary 569

67. An Android Room Database and Repository Tutorial 571

67.1 About the RoomDemo Project 571
67.2 Modifying the Build Configuration 571
67.3 Building the Entity 571
67.4 Creating the Data Access Object 573
67.5 Adding the Room Database 574
67.6 Adding the Repository 575
67.7 Adding the ViewModel 578
67.8 Creating the Product Item Layout 579
67.9 Adding the RecyclerView Adapter 579
67.10 Preparing the Main Activity 581
67.11 Adding the Button Listeners 582
67.12 Adding LiveData Observers 583
67.13 Initializing the RecyclerView 584
67.14 Testing the RoomDemo App 584
67.15 Using the Database Inspector 584
67.16 Summary 585

68. Accessing Cloud Storage using the Android Storage Access Framework 587

68.1 The Storage Access Framework 587
68.2 Working with the Storage Access Framework 588
68.3 Filtering Picker File Listings 588
68.4 Handling Intent Results 589
68.5 Reading the Content of a File 589
68.6 Writing Content to a File 590

- 68.7 Deleting a File 591
- 68.8 Gaining Persistent Access to a File 591
- 68.9 Summary 591

69. An Android Storage Access Framework Example 593
- 69.1 About the Storage Access Framework Example 593
- 69.2 Creating the Storage Access Framework Example 593
- 69.3 Designing the User Interface 593
- 69.4 Adding the Activity Launchers 594
- 69.5 Creating a New Storage File 596
- 69.6 Saving to a Storage File 596
- 69.7 Opening and Reading a Storage File 598
- 69.8 Testing the Storage Access Application 599
- 69.9 Summary 600

70. Video Playback on Android using the VideoView and MediaController Classes 601
- 70.1 Introducing the Android VideoView Class 601
- 70.2 Introducing the Android MediaController Class 602
- 70.3 Creating the Video Playback Example 602
- 70.4 Designing the VideoPlayer Layout 602
- 70.5 Downloading the Video File 603
- 70.6 Configuring the VideoView 603
- 70.7 Adding the MediaController to the Video View 605
- 70.8 Setting up the onPreparedListener 606
- 70.9 Summary 606

71. Android Picture-in-Picture Mode 607
- 71.1 Picture-in-Picture Features 607
- 71.2 Enabling Picture-in-Picture Mode 608
- 71.3 Configuring Picture-in-Picture Parameters 608
- 71.4 Entering Picture-in-Picture Mode 609
- 71.5 Detecting Picture-in-Picture Mode Changes 609
- 71.6 Adding Picture-in-Picture Actions 610
- 71.7 Summary 610

72. An Android Picture-in-Picture Tutorial 613
- 72.1 Adding Picture-in-Picture Support to the Manifest 613
- 72.2 Adding a Picture-in-Picture Button 613
- 72.3 Entering Picture-in-Picture Mode 614
- 72.4 Detecting Picture-in-Picture Mode Changes 615
- 72.5 Adding a Broadcast Receiver 615
- 72.6 Adding the PiP Action 616
- 72.7 Testing the Picture-in-Picture Action 619
- 72.8 Summary 620

73. Android Audio Recording and Playback using MediaPlayer and MediaRecorder 621
- 73.1 Playing Audio 621
- 73.2 Recording Audio and Video using the MediaRecorder Class 622
- 73.3 About the Example Project 623
- 73.4 Creating the AudioApp Project 623
- 73.5 Designing the User Interface 623

Table of Contents

73.6 Checking for Microphone Availability 624
73.7 Initializing the Activity 625
73.8 Implementing the recordAudio() Method 626
73.9 Implementing the stopAudio() Method 626
73.10 Implementing the playAudio() method 627
73.11 Configuring and Requesting Permissions 627
73.12 Testing the Application 629
73.13 Summary 630

74. Working with the Google Maps Android API in Android Studio 631

74.1 The Elements of the Google Maps Android API 631
74.2 Creating the Google Maps Project 632
74.3 Creating a Google Cloud Billing Account 632
74.4 Creating a New Google Cloud Project 633
74.5 Enabling the Google Maps SDK 634
74.6 Generating a Google Maps API Key 635
74.7 Adding the API Key to the Android Studio Project 636
74.8 Testing the Application 636
74.9 Understanding Geocoding and Reverse Geocoding 636
74.10 Adding a Map to an Application 638
74.11 Requesting Current Location Permission 638
74.12 Displaying the User's Current Location 640
74.13 Changing the Map Type 641
74.14 Displaying Map Controls to the User 642
74.15 Handling Map Gesture Interaction 643
    74.15.1 Map Zooming Gestures 643
    74.15.2 Map Scrolling/Panning Gestures 643
    74.15.3 Map Tilt Gestures 643
    74.15.4 Map Rotation Gestures 643
74.16 Creating Map Markers 644
74.17 Controlling the Map Camera 645
74.18 Summary 646

75. Printing with the Android Printing Framework 647

75.1 The Android Printing Architecture 647
75.2 The Print Service Plugins 647
75.3 Google Cloud Print 648
75.4 Printing to Google Drive 648
75.5 Save as PDF 649
75.6 Printing from Android Devices 649
75.7 Options for Building Print Support into Android Apps 650
    75.7.1 Image Printing 650
    75.7.2 Creating and Printing HTML Content 651
    75.7.3 Printing a Web Page 652
    75.7.4 Printing a Custom Document 653
75.8 Summary 653

76. An Android HTML and Web Content Printing Example 655

76.1 Creating the HTML Printing Example Application 655
76.2 Printing Dynamic HTML Content 655
76.3 Creating the Web Page Printing Example 658

| 76.4 Removing the Floating Action Button 658
| 76.5 Removing Navigation Features... 658
| 76.6 Designing the User Interface Layout 660
| 76.7 Accessing the WebView from the Main Activity 660
| 76.8 Loading the Web Page into the WebView.. 661
| 76.9 Adding the Print Menu Option... 662
| 76.10 Summary 664

77. A Guide to Android Custom Document Printing 665

       77.1 An Overview of Android Custom Document Printing 665
              77.1.1 Custom Print Adapters 665
       77.2 Preparing the Custom Document Printing Project... 666
       77.3 Creating the Custom Print Adapter.. 667
       77.4 Implementing the onLayout() Callback Method 668
       77.5 Implementing the onWrite() Callback Method 671
       77.6 Checking a Page is in Range 673
       77.7 Drawing the Content on the Page Canvas 674
       77.8 Starting the Print Job 676
       77.9 Testing the Application 677
       77.10 Summary 677

78. An Introduction to Android App Links... 679

       78.1 An Overview of Android App Links 679
       78.2 App Link Intent Filters 679
       78.3 Handling App Link Intents 680
       78.4 Associating the App with a Website... 680
       78.5 Summary 681

79. An Android Studio App Links Tutorial 683

       79.1 About the Example App 683
       79.2 The Database Schema 683
       79.3 Loading and Running the Project 683
       79.4 Adding the URL Mapping... 685
       79.5 Adding the Intent Filter.. 688
       79.6 Adding Intent Handling Code... 689
       79.7 Testing the App 691
       79.8 Creating the Digital Asset Links File 691
       79.9 Testing the App Link... 692
       79.10 Summary 692

80. An Android Biometric Authentication Tutorial.. 693

       80.1 An Overview of Biometric Authentication... 693
       80.2 Creating the Biometric Authentication Project 693
       80.3 Configuring Device Fingerprint Authentication 694
       80.4 Adding the Biometric Permission to the Manifest File... 694
       80.5 Designing the User Interface 695
       80.6 Adding a Toast Convenience Method 695
       80.7 Checking the Security Settings... 696
       80.8 Configuring the Authentication Callbacks 697
       80.9 Adding the CancellationSignal 698
       80.10 Starting the Biometric Prompt 698

xix

Table of Contents

    80.11 Testing the Project 699
    80.12 Summary 700

81. Creating, Testing, and Uploading an Android App Bundle 701

    81.1 The Release Preparation Process 701
    81.2 Android App Bundles 701
    81.3 Register for a Google Play Developer Console Account 702
    81.4 Configuring the App in the Console 703
    81.5 Enabling Google Play App Signing 704
    81.6 Creating a Keystore File 704
    81.7 Creating the Android App Bundle 705
    81.8 Generating Test APK Files 707
    81.9 Uploading the App Bundle to the Google Play Developer Console 708
    81.10 Exploring the App Bundle 709
    81.11 Managing Testers 710
    81.12 Rolling the App Out for Testing 710
    81.13 Uploading New App Bundle Revisions 711
    81.14 Analyzing the App Bundle File 712
    81.15 Summary 713

82. An Overview of Android In-App Billing 715

    82.1 Preparing a Project for In-App Purchasing 715
    82.2 Creating In-App Products and Subscriptions 715
    82.3 Billing Client Initialization 716
    82.4 Connecting to the Google Play Billing Library 717
    82.5 Querying Available Products 718
    82.6 Starting the Purchase Process 718
    82.7 Completing the Purchase 719
    82.8 Querying Previous Purchases 720
    82.9 Summary 721

83. An Android In-App Purchasing Tutorial 723

    83.1 About the In-App Purchasing Example Project 723
    83.2 Creating the InAppPurchase Project 723
    83.3 Adding Libraries to the Project 723
    83.4 Designing the User Interface 724
    83.5 Adding the App to the Google Play Store 724
    83.6 Creating an In-App Product 725
    83.7 Enabling License Testers 725
    83.8 Initializing the Billing Client 726
    83.9 Querying the Product 728
    83.10 Launching the Purchase Flow 729
    83.11 Handling Purchase Updates 729
    83.12 Consuming the Product 730
    83.13 Restoring a Previous Purchase 731
    83.14 Testing the App 732
    83.15 Troubleshooting 733
    83.16 Summary 734

84. Working with Material Design 3 Theming 735

    84.1 Material Design 2 vs. Material Design 3 735

84.2 Understanding Material Design Theming 735
84.3 Material Design 3 Theming 735
84.4 Building a Custom Theme.. 737
84.5 Summary 738

85. A Material Design 3 Theming and Dynamic Color Tutorial 739
85.1 Creating the ThemeDemo Project 739
85.3 Designing the User Interface 739
85.4 Building a New Theme 741
85.5 Adding the Theme to the Project 742
85.6 Enabling Dynamic Color Support 743
85.7 Previewing Dynamic Colors.. 744
85.8 Summary 745

86. An Overview of Gradle in Android Studio 747
86.1 An Overview of Gradle 747
86.2 Gradle and Android Studio 747
    86.2.1 Sensible Defaults 747
    86.2.2 Dependencies... 747
    86.2.3 Build Variants 748
    86.2.4 Manifest Entries 748
    86.2.5 APK Signing... 748
    86.2.6 ProGuard Support... 748
86.3 The Property and Settings Gradle Build File 748
86.4 The Top-level Gradle Build File... 749
86.5 Module Level Gradle Build Files 750
86.6 Configuring Signing Settings in the Build File... 752
86.7 Running Gradle Tasks from the Command Line 753
86.8 Summary 754

Index 755

Chapter 1

1. Introduction

Fully updated for Android Studio Giraffe and the new UI, this book aims to teach you how to develop Android-based applications using the Java programming language.

This book begins with the basics and outlines how to set up an Android development and testing environment, followed by an overview of areas such as tool windows, the code editor, and the Layout Editor tool. An introduction to the architecture of Android is followed by an in-depth look at the design of Android applications and user interfaces using the Android Studio environment.

Chapters also cover the Android Architecture Components, including view models, lifecycle management, Room database access, the Database Inspector, app navigation, live data, and data binding.

More advanced topics such as intents are also covered, as are touch screen handling, gesture recognition, and the recording and playback of audio. This book edition also covers printing, transitions, and foldable device support.

The concepts of material design are also covered in detail, including the use of floating action buttons, Snackbars, tabbed interfaces, card views, navigation drawers, and collapsing toolbars.

Other key features of Android Studio and Android are also covered in detail, including the Layout Editor, the ConstraintLayout and ConstraintSet classes, MotionLayout Editor, view binding, constraint chains, barriers, and direct reply notifications.

Chapters also cover advanced features of Android Studio, such as App Links, Gradle build configuration, in-app billing, and submitting apps to the Google Play Developer Console.

Assuming you already have some Java programming experience, are ready to download Android Studio and the Android SDK, have access to a Windows, Mac, or Linux system, and have ideas for some apps to develop, you are ready to get started.

1.1 Downloading the Code Samples

The source code and Android Studio project files for the examples contained in this book are available for download at:

https://www.ebookfrenzy.com/retail/giraffejava/index.php

The steps to load a project from the code samples into Android Studio are as follows:

1. From the Welcome to Android Studio dialog, click on the Open button option.

2. In the project selection dialog, navigate to and select the folder containing the project to be imported and click on OK.

1.2 Feedback

We want you to be satisfied with your purchase of this book. If you find any errors in the book, or have any comments, questions or concerns please contact us at *feedback@ebookfrenzy.com*.

1.3 Errata

While we make every effort to ensure the accuracy of the content of this book, it is inevitable that a book covering a subject area of this size and complexity may include some errors and oversights. Any known issues with the book will be outlined, together with solutions, at the following URL:

https://www.ebookfrenzy.com/errata/giraffejava.html

If you find an error not listed in the errata, please let us know by emailing our technical support team at *feedback@ebookfrenzy.com*. They are there to help you and will work to resolve any problems you may encounter.

1.4 Download the Color eBook

Thank you for purchasing the print edition of this book. If you would like to download the color PDF version of this book, please email proof of purchase (for example a receipt, delivery notice or photo of the physical book) to *feedback@ebookfrenzy.com* and we will provide you with a download link for the book in PDF format.

2. Setting up an Android Studio Development Environment

Before any work can begin on developing an Android application, the first step is to configure a computer system to act as the development platform. This involves several steps consisting of installing the Android Studio Integrated Development Environment (IDE), including the Android Software Development Kit (SDK) and the OpenJDK Java development environment.

This chapter will cover the steps necessary to install the requisite components for Android application development on Windows, macOS, and Linux-based systems.

2.1 System requirements

Android application development may be performed on any of the following system types:

- Windows 8/10/11 64-bit

- macOS 10.14 or later running on Intel or Apple silicon

- Chrome OS device with Intel i5 or higher

- Linux systems with version 2.31 or later of the GNU C Library (glibc)

- Minimum of 8GB of RAM

- Approximately 8GB of available disk space

- 1280 x 800 minimum screen resolution

2.2 Downloading the Android Studio package

Most of the work involved in developing applications for Android will be performed using the Android Studio environment. The content and examples in this book were created based on Android Studio Giraffe 2022.3.1 using the Android API 33 SDK (Tiramisu), which, at the time of writing, are the latest stable releases.

Android Studio is, however, subject to frequent updates, so a newer version may have been released since this book was published.

The latest release of Android Studio may be downloaded from the primary download page, which can be found at the following URL:

https://developer.android.com/studio/index.html

If this page provides instructions for downloading a newer version of Android Studio, there may be differences between this book and the software. A web search for "Android Studio Giraffe" should provide the option to download the older version if these differences become a problem. Alternatively, visit the following web page to find Android Studio Giraffe 2022.3.1 in the archives:

https://developer.android.com/studio/archive

2.3 Installing Android Studio

Once downloaded, the exact steps to install Android Studio differ depending on the operating system on which the installation is performed.

2.3.1 Installation on Windows

Locate the downloaded Android Studio installation executable file (named *android-studio-<version>-windows.exe*) in a Windows Explorer window and double-click on it to start the installation process, clicking the *Yes* button in the User Account Control dialog if it appears.

Once the Android Studio setup wizard appears, work through the various screens to configure the installation to meet your requirements in terms of the file system location into which Android Studio should be installed and whether or not it should be made available to other system users. When prompted to select the components to install, ensure that the *Android Studio* and *Android Virtual Device* options are all selected.

Although there are no strict rules on where Android Studio should be installed on the system, the remainder of this book will assume that the installation was performed into *C:\Program Files\Android\Android Studio* and that the Android SDK packages have been installed into the user's *AppData\Local\Android\sdk* sub-folder. Once the options have been configured, click the *Install* button to begin the installation process.

On versions of Windows with a Start menu, the newly installed Android Studio can be launched from the entry added to that menu during the installation. The executable may be pinned to the taskbar for easy access by navigating to the *Android Studio\bin* directory, right-clicking on the *studio64* executable, and selecting the *Pin to Taskbar* menu option (on Windows 11, this option can be found by selecting *Show more options* from the menu).

2.3.2 Installation on macOS

Android Studio for macOS is downloaded as a disk image (.dmg) file. Once the *android-studio-<version>-mac.dmg* file has been downloaded, locate it in a Finder window and double-click on it to open it, as shown in Figure 2-1:

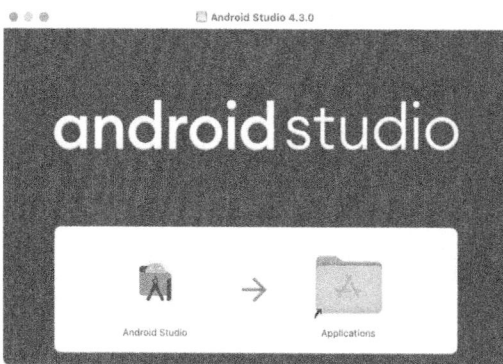

Figure 2-1

To install the package, drag the Android Studio icon and drop it onto the Applications folder. The Android Studio package will then be installed into the Applications folder of the system, a process that will typically take a few seconds to complete.

To launch Android Studio, locate the executable in the Applications folder using a Finder window and double-click on it.

For future, easier access to the tool, drag the Android Studio icon from the Finder window and drop it onto the dock.

2.3.3 Installation on Linux

Having downloaded the Linux Android Studio package, open a terminal window, change directory to the location where Android Studio is to be installed, and execute the following command:

```
tar xvfz /<path to package>/android-studio-<version>-linux.tar.gz
```

Note that the Android Studio bundle will be installed into a subdirectory named *android-studio*. Therefore, assuming that the above command was executed in */home/demo*, the software packages will be unpacked into */home/demo/android-studio*.

To launch Android Studio, open a terminal window, change directory to the *android-studio/bin* sub-directory, and execute the following command:

```
./studio.sh
```

2.4 The Android Studio setup wizard

If you have previously installed an earlier version of Android Studio, the first time this new version is launched, a dialog may appear providing the option to import settings from a previous Android Studio version. If you have settings from a previous version and would like to import them into the latest installation, select the appropriate option and location. Alternatively, indicate that you do not need to import any previous settings and click the OK button to proceed.

If you are installing Android Studio for the first time, the initial dialog that appears once the setup process starts may resemble that shown in Figure 2-2 below:

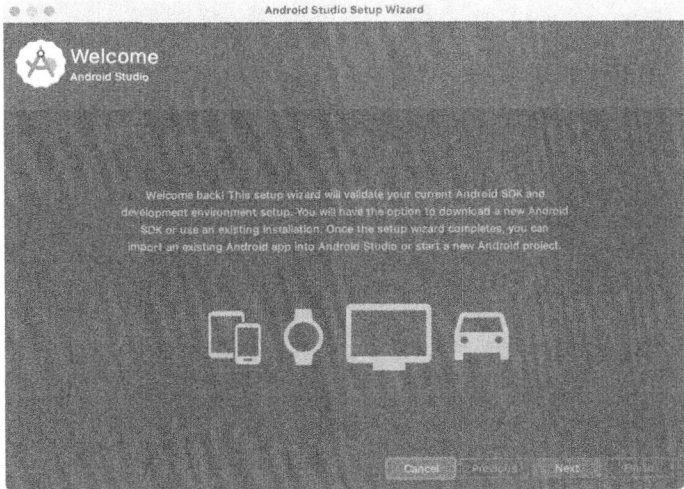

Figure 2-2

If this dialog appears, click the Next button to display the Install Type screen (Figure 2-3). On this screen, select the Standard installation option before clicking Next.

Setting up an Android Studio Development Environment

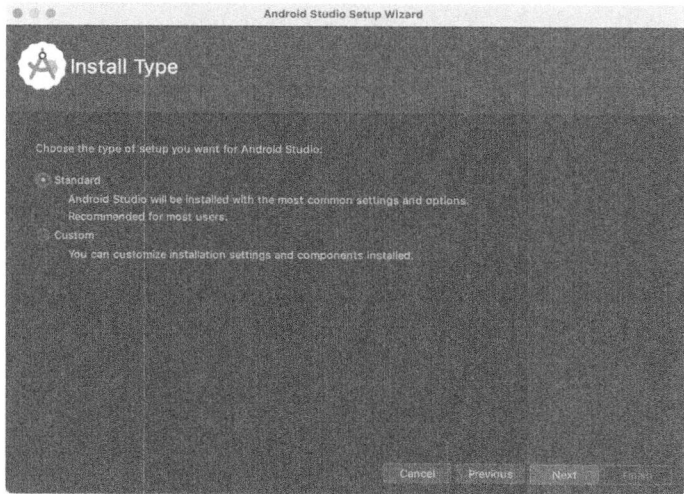

Figure 2-3

On the Select UI Theme screen, select either the Darcula or Light theme based on your preferences. After making a choice, click Next, and review the options in the Verify Settings screen before proceeding to the License Agreement screen. Select each license category and enable the Accept checkbox. Finally, click the Finish button to initiate the installation.

After these initial setup steps have been taken, click the Finish button to display the Welcome to Android Studio screen using your chosen UI theme:

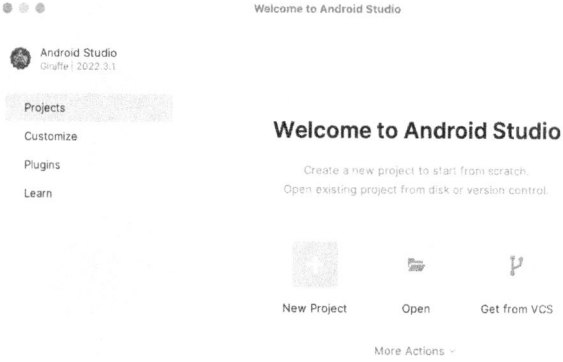

Figure 2-4

2.5 Installing additional Android SDK packages

The steps performed so far have installed the Android Studio IDE and the current set of default Android SDK packages. Before proceeding, it is worth taking some time to verify which packages are installed and to install any missing or updated packages.

Setting up an Android Studio Development Environment

This task can be performed by clicking on the *More Actions* link within the welcome dialog and selecting the *SDK Manager* option from the drop-down menu. Once invoked, the *Android SDK* screen of the Settings dialog will appear as shown in Figure 2-5:

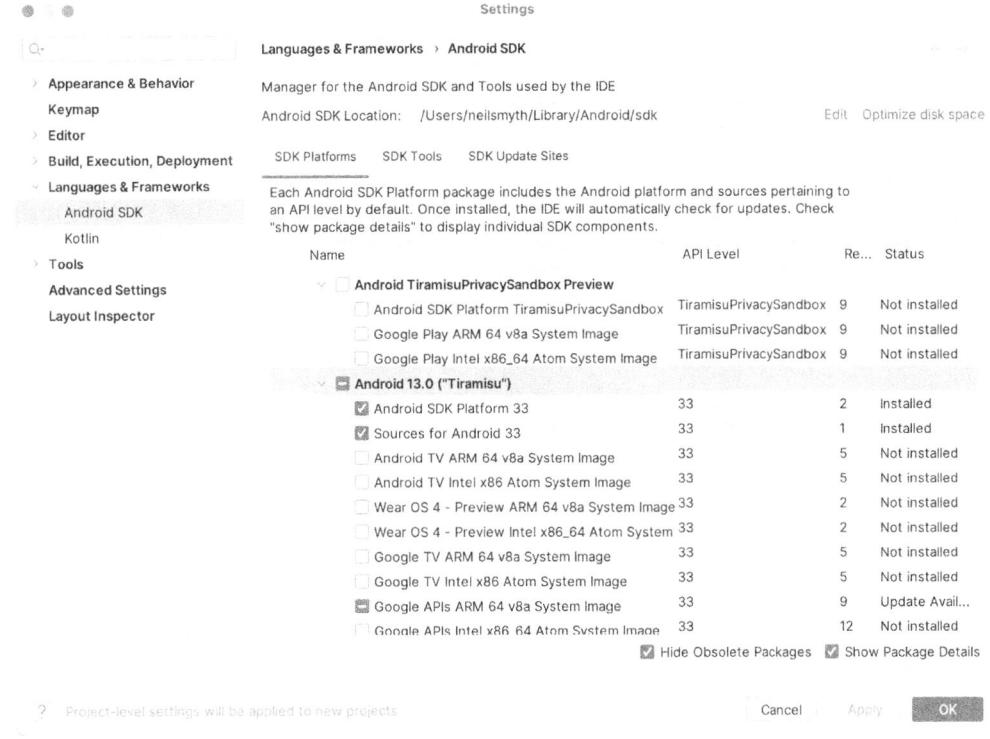

Figure 2-5

Google pairs each release of Android Studio with a maximum supported Application Programming Interface (API) level of the Android SDK. In the case of Android Studio Giraffe, this is Android Tiramisu (API Level 33). This information can be confirmed using the following link:

https://developer.android.com/studio/releases#api-level-support

Immediately after installing Android Studio for the first time, it is likely that only the latest supported version of the Android SDK has been installed. To install older versions of the Android SDK, select the checkboxes corresponding to the versions and click the *Apply* button. The rest of this book assumes that the Android Tiramisu (API Level 33) SDK is installed.

Most of the examples in this book will support older versions of Android as far back as Android 8.0 (Oreo). This ensures that the apps run on a wide range of Android devices. Within the list of SDK versions, enable the checkbox next to Android 8.0 (Oreo) and click the Apply button. Click the OK button to install the SDK in the resulting confirmation dialog. Subsequent dialogs will seek the acceptance of licenses and terms before performing the installation. Click Finish once the installation is complete.

It is also possible that updates will be listed as being available for the latest SDK. To access detailed information about the packages that are ready to be updated, enable the *Show Package Details* option located in the lower right-hand corner of the screen. This will display information similar to that shown in Figure 2-6:

Setting up an Android Studio Development Environment

Name	API Level	Revision	Status
Android TV ARM 64 v8a System Image	33	5	Not installed
Android TV Intel x86 Atom System Image	33	5	Not installed
Google TV ARM 64 v8a System Image	33	5	Not installed
Google TV Intel x86 Atom System Image	33	5	Not installed
Google APIs ARM 64 v8a System Image	33	8	Update Available: 9
Google APIs Intel x86 Atom_64 System Image	33	9	Not installed
Google Play ARM 64 v8a System Image	33	7	Installed

Figure 2-6

The above figure highlights the availability of an update. To install the updates, enable the checkbox to the left of the item name and click the *Apply* button.

In addition to the Android SDK packages, several tools are also installed for building Android applications. To view the currently installed packages and check for updates, remain within the SDK settings screen and select the SDK Tools tab as shown in Figure 2-7:

Figure 2-7

Within the Android SDK Tools screen, make sure that the following packages are listed as *Installed* in the Status column:

- Android SDK Build-tools

- Android Emulator

- Android SDK Platform-tools

- Google Play Services

- Intel x86 Emulator Accelerator (HAXM installer)*

- Google USB Driver (Windows only)

- Layout Inspector image server for API 31 and 34

*Note that the Intel x86 Emulator Accelerator (HAXM installer) cannot be installed on Apple silicon-based Macs.

If any of the above packages are listed as *Not Installed* or requiring an update, select the checkboxes next to those packages and click the *Apply* button to initiate the installation process. If the HAXM emulator settings dialog appears, select the recommended memory allocation:

Setting up an Android Studio Development Environment

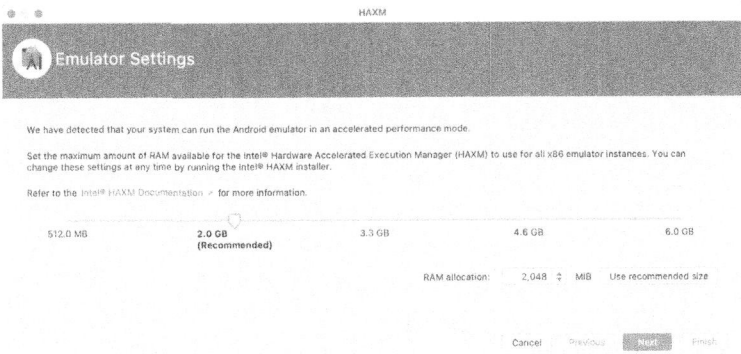

Figure 2-8

Once the installation is complete, review the package list and ensure that the selected packages are listed as *Installed* in the *Status* column. If any are listed as *Not installed,* make sure they are selected and click the *Apply* button again.

2.6 Installing the Android SDK Command-line Tools

Android Studio includes tools that allow some tasks to be performed from your operating system command line. To install these tools on your system, open the SDK Manager, select the SDK Tools tab, and locate the *Android SDK Command-line Tools (latest)* package as shown in Figure 2-9:

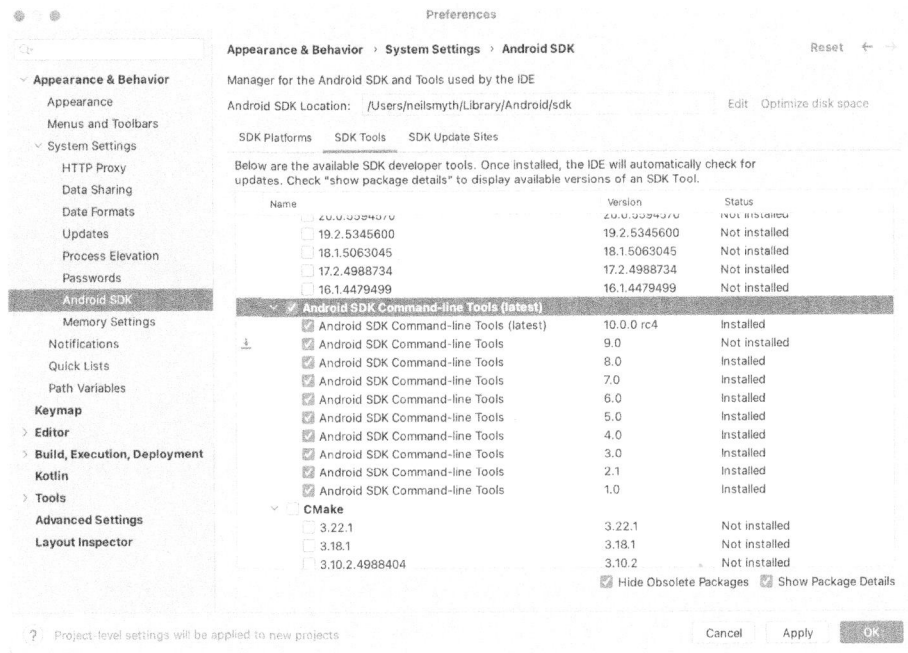

Figure 2-9

If the command-line tools package is not already installed, enable it and click Apply, followed by OK to complete the installation. When the installation completes, click Finish and close the SDK Manager dialog.

For the operating system on which you are developing to be able to find these tools, it will be necessary to add them to the system's *PATH* environment variable.

Setting up an Android Studio Development Environment

Regardless of your operating system, you will need to configure the PATH environment variable to include the following paths (where *<path_to_android_sdk_installation>* represents the file system location into which you installed the Android SDK):

```
<path_to_android_sdk_installation>/sdk/cmdline-tools/latest/bin
<path_to_android_sdk_installation>/sdk/platform-tools
```

You can identify the location of the SDK on your system by launching the SDK Manager and referring to the *Android SDK Location:* field located at the top of the settings panel, as highlighted in Figure 2-10:

Figure 2-10

Once the location of the SDK has been identified, the steps to add this to the PATH variable are operating system dependent:

2.6.1 Windows 8.1

1. On the start screen, move the mouse to the bottom right-hand corner of the screen and select Search from the resulting menu. In the search box, enter Control Panel. When the Control Panel icon appears in the results area, click on it to launch the tool on the desktop.

2. Within the Control Panel, use the Category menu to change the display to Large Icons. From the list of icons, select the one labeled System.

3. In the Environment Variables dialog, locate the Path variable in the System variables list, select it, and click the *Edit…* button. Using the *New* button in the edit dialog, add two new entries to the path. For example, assuming the Android SDK was installed into *C:\Users\demo\AppData\Local\Android\Sdk*, the following entries would need to be added:

```
C:\Users\demo\AppData\Local\Android\Sdk\cmdline-tools\latest\bin
C:\Users\demo\AppData\Local\Android\Sdk\platform-tools
```

4. Click OK in each dialog box and close the system properties control panel.

Open a command prompt window by pressing Windows + R on the keyboard and entering *cmd* into the Run dialog. Within the Command Prompt window, enter:

```
echo %Path%
```

The returned path variable value should include the paths to the Android SDK platform tools folders. Verify that the *platform-tools* value is correct by attempting to run the *adb* tool as follows:

```
adb
```

The tool should output a list of command-line options when executed.

Similarly, check the *tools* path setting by attempting to run the AVD Manager command-line tool (don't worry if the avdmanager tool reports a problem with Java - this will be addressed later):

```
avdmanager
```

If a message similar to the following message appears for one or both of the commands, it is most likely that an

Setting up an Android Studio Development Environment

incorrect path was appended to the Path environment variable:

```
'adb' is not recognized as an internal or external command,
operable program or batch file.
```

2.6.2 Windows 10

Right-click on the Start menu, select Settings from the resulting menu and enter "Edit the system environment variables" into the *Find a setting* text field. In the System Properties dialog, click the *Environment Variables...* button. Follow the steps outlined for Windows 8.1 starting from step 3.

2.6.3 Windows 11

Right-click on the Start icon located in the taskbar and select Settings from the resulting menu. When the Settings dialog appears, scroll down the list of categories and select the "About" option. In the About screen, select *Advanced system settings* from the Related links section. When the System Properties window appears, click the *Environment Variables...* button. Follow the steps outlined for Windows 8.1 starting from step 3.

2.6.4 Linux

This configuration can be achieved on Linux by adding a command to the *.bashrc* file in your home directory (specifics may differ depending on the particular Linux distribution in use). Assuming that the Android SDK bundle package was installed into */home/demo/Android/sdk*, the export line in the *.bashrc* file would read as follows:

```
export PATH=/home/demo/Android/sdk/platform-tools:/home/demo/Android/sdk/cmdline-tools/latest/bin:/home/demo/android-studio/bin:$PATH
```

Note also that the above command adds the *android-studio/bin* directory to the PATH variable. This will enable the *studio.sh* script to be executed regardless of the current directory within a terminal window.

2.6.5 macOS

Several techniques may be employed to modify the $PATH environment variable on macOS. Arguably the cleanest method is to add a new file in the */etc/paths.d* directory containing the paths to be added to $PATH. Assuming an Android SDK installation location of */Users/demo/Library/Android/sdk*, the path may be configured by creating a new file named *android-sdk* in the */etc/paths.d* directory containing the following lines:

```
/Users/demo/Library/Android/sdk/cmdline-tools/latest/bin
/Users/demo/Library/Android/sdk/platform-tools
```

Note that since this is a system directory, it will be necessary to use the *sudo* command when creating the file. For example:

```
sudo vi /etc/paths.d/android-sdk
```

2.7 Android Studio memory management

Android Studio is a large and complex software application with many background processes. Although Android Studio has been criticized in the past for providing less than optimal performance, Google has made significant performance improvements in recent releases and continues to do so with each new version. These improvements include allowing the user to configure the amount of memory used by both the Android Studio IDE and the background processes used to build and run apps. This allows the software to take advantage of systems with larger amounts of RAM.

If you are running Android Studio on a system with sufficient unused RAM to increase these values (this feature is only available on 64-bit systems with 5GB or more of RAM) and find that Android Studio performance appears to be degraded, it may be worth experimenting with these memory settings. Android Studio may also notify you that performance can be increased via a dialog similar to the one shown below:

Setting up an Android Studio Development Environment

Figure 2-11

To view and modify the current memory configuration, select the *File -> Settings...* main menu option (*Android Studio -> Settings...* on macOS) and, in the resulting dialog, select *Appearance & Behavior* followed by the *Memory Settings* option listed under *System Settings* in the left-hand navigation panel, as illustrated in Figure 2-12 below:

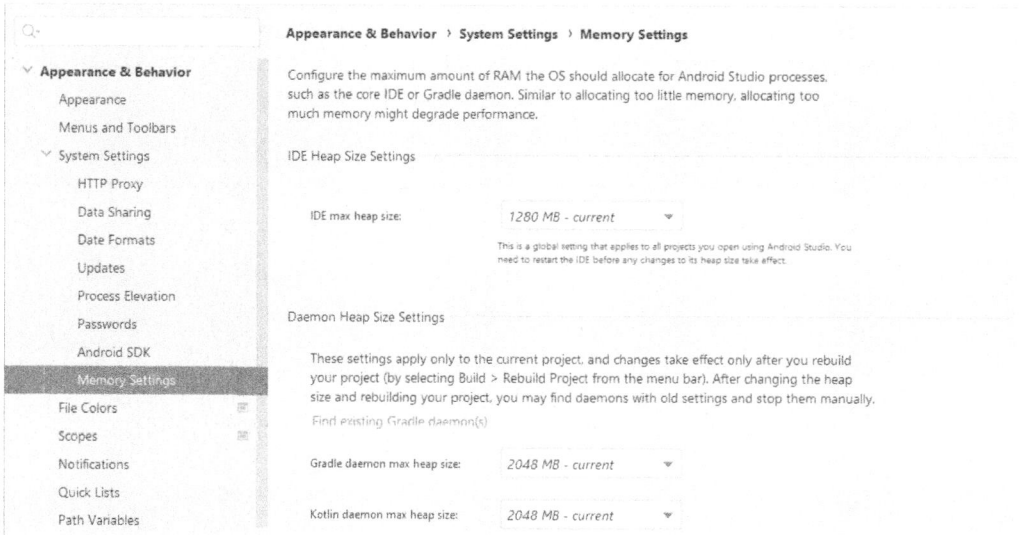

Figure 2-12

When changing the memory allocation, be sure not to allocate more memory than necessary or than your system can spare without slowing down other processes.

The IDE heap size setting adjusts the memory allocated to Android Studio and applies regardless of the currently loaded project. On the other hand, when a project is built and run from within Android Studio, several background processes (referred to as daemons) perform the task of compiling and running the app. When compiling and running large and complex projects, build time could be improved by adjusting the daemon heap settings. Unlike the IDE heap settings, these daemon settings apply only to the current project and can only be accessed when a project is open in Android Studio. To display the SDK Manager from within an open project, select the *Tools -> SDK Manager...* menu option from the main menu.

2.8 Updating Android Studio and the SDK

From time to time, new versions of Android Studio and the Android SDK are released. New versions of the SDK are installed using the Android SDK Manager. Android Studio will typically notify you when an update is ready to be installed.

To manually check for Android Studio updates, use the Help -> Check for Updates... menu option from the Android Studio main window (Android Studio -> Check for Updates... on macOS).

2.9 Summary

Before beginning the development of Android-based applications, the first step is to set up a suitable development environment. This consists of the Android SDKs and Android Studio IDE (which also includes the OpenJDK development environment). This chapter covers the steps necessary to install these packages on Windows, macOS, and Linux.

Chapter 3

3. Creating an Example Android App in Android Studio

The preceding chapters of this book have covered the steps necessary to configure an environment suitable for developing Android applications using the Android Studio IDE. Before moving on to slightly more advanced topics, now is a good time to validate that all required development packages are installed and functioning correctly. The best way to achieve this goal is to create an Android application and compile and run it. This chapter will cover creating an Android application project using Android Studio. Once the project has been created, a later chapter will explore using the Android emulator environment to perform a test run of the application.

3.1 About the Project

The project created in this chapter takes the form of a rudimentary currency conversion calculator (so simple, in fact, that it only converts from dollars to euros and does so using an estimated conversion rate). The project will also use one of the most basic Android Studio project templates. This simplicity allows us to introduce some key aspects of Android app development without overwhelming the beginner by introducing too many concepts, such as the recommended app architecture and Android architecture components, at once. When following the tutorial in this chapter, rest assured that the techniques and code used in this initial example project will be covered in much greater detail later.

3.2 Creating a New Android Project

The first step in the application development process is to create a new project within the Android Studio environment. Begin, therefore, by launching Android Studio so that the "Welcome to Android Studio" screen appears as illustrated in Figure 3-1:

Figure 3-1

Creating an Example Android App in Android Studio

Once this window appears, Android Studio is ready for a new project to be created. To create the new project, click on the *New Project* option to display the first screen of the *New Project* wizard.

3.3 Creating an Activity

The next step is to define the type of initial activity to be created for the application. Options are available to create projects for Phone and Tablet, Wear OS, Television, or Automotive. A range of different activity types is available when developing Android applications, many of which will be covered extensively in later chapters. For this example, however, select the *Phone and Tablet* option from the Templates panel, followed by the option to create an *Empty Views Activity*. The Empty Views Activity option creates a template user interface consisting of a single TextView object.

Figure 3-2

With the Empty Views Activity option selected, click *Next* to continue with the project configuration.

3.4 Defining the Project and SDK Settings

In the project configuration window (Figure 3-3), set the *Name* field to *AndroidSample*. The application name is the name by which the application will be referenced and identified within Android Studio and is also the name that would be used if the completed application were to go on sale in the Google Play store.

The *Package name* uniquely identifies the application within the Android application ecosystem. Although this can be set to any string that uniquely identifies your app, it is traditionally based on the reversed URL of your domain name followed by the application's name. For example, if your domain is *www.mycompany.com*, and the application has been named *AndroidSample*, then the package name might be specified as follows:

`com.mycompany.androidsample`

If you do not have a domain name, you can enter any other string into the Company Domain field, or you may use *example.com* for testing, though this will need to be changed before an application can be published:

`com.example.androidsample`

The *Save location* setting will default to a location in the folder named *AndroidStudioProjects* located in your home directory and may be changed by clicking on the folder icon to the right of the text field containing the current path setting.

Set the minimum SDK setting to API 26 (Oreo; Android 8.0). This minimum SDK will be used in most projects created in this book unless a necessary feature is only available in a more recent version. The objective here is to

Creating an Example Android App in Android Studio

build an app using the latest Android SDK while retaining compatibility with devices running older versions of Android (in this case, as far back as Android 8.0). The text beneath the Minimum SDK setting will outline the percentage of Android devices currently in use on which the app will run. Click on the *Help me choose* button (highlighted in Figure 3-3) to see a full breakdown of the various Android versions still in use:

Figure 3-3

Finally, change the *Language* menu to *Java* and select *Kotlin DSL (build.gradle.kts)* as the build configuration language before clicking *Finish* to create the project.

3.5 Enabling the New Android Studio UI

Android Studio is transitioning to a new, modern user interface that is not enabled by default in the Giraffe version. If your installation of Android Studio resembles Figure 3-4 below, then you will need to enable the new UI before proceeding:

Figure 3-4

Enable the new UI by selecting the *File -> Settings...* menu option (*Android Studio -> Settings...* on macOS) and selecting the New UI option under Appearance and Behavior in the left-hand panel. From the main panel, turn on the *Enable new UI* checkbox before clicking Apply, followed by OK to commit the change:

Creating an Example Android App in Android Studio

Figure 3-5

When prompted, restart Android Studio to activate the new user interface.

3.6 Modifying the Example Application

Once Android Studio has restarted, the main window will reappear using the new UI and containing our AndroidSample project as illustrated in Figure 3-6 below:

Figure 3-6

The newly created project and references to associated files are listed in the *Project* tool window on the left side of the main project window. The Project tool window has several modes in which information can be displayed. By default, this panel should be in *Android* mode. This setting is controlled by the menu at the top of the panel as highlighted in Figure 3-7. If the panel is not currently in Android mode, use the menu to switch mode:

Figure 3-7

3.7 Modifying the User Interface

The user interface design for our activity is stored in a file named *activity_main.xml* which, in turn, is located under *app -> res -> layout* in the Project tool window file hierarchy. Once located in the Project tool window, double-click on the file to load it into the user interface Layout Editor tool, which will appear in the center panel of the Android Studio main window:

Figure 3-8

Creating an Example Android App in Android Studio

In the toolbar across the top of the Layout Editor window is a menu (currently set to *Pixel* in the above figure) which is reflected in the visual representation of the device within the Layout Editor panel. A range of other device options are available by clicking on this menu.

Use the System UI Mode button ( ) to turn Night mode on and off for the device screen layout. To change the orientation of the device representation between landscape and portrait, use the drop-down menu showing the icon.

As we can see in the device screen, the content layout already includes a label that displays a "Hello World!" message. Running down the left-hand side of the panel is a palette containing different categories of user interface components that may be used to construct a user interface, such as buttons, labels, and text fields. However, it should be noted that not all user interface components are visible to the user. One such category consists of *layouts*. Android supports a variety of layouts that provide different levels of control over how visual user interface components are positioned and managed on the screen. Though it is difficult to tell from looking at the visual representation of the user interface, the current design has been created using a ConstraintLayout. This can be confirmed by reviewing the information in the *Component Tree* panel, which, by default, is located in the lower left-hand corner of the Layout Editor panel and is shown in Figure 3-9:

```
Component Tree
  ConstraintLayout
    Ab TextView "Hello World!"
```

Figure 3-9

As we can see from the component tree hierarchy, the user interface layout consists of a ConstraintLayout parent and a TextView child object.

Before proceeding, check that the Layout Editor's Autoconnect mode is enabled. This means that as components are added to the layout, the Layout Editor will automatically add constraints to ensure the components are correctly positioned for different screen sizes and device orientations (a topic that will be covered in much greater detail in future chapters). The Autoconnect button appears in the Layout Editor toolbar and is represented by a U-shaped icon. When disabled, the icon appears with a diagonal line through it (Figure 3-10). If necessary, re-enable Autoconnect mode by clicking on this button.

Figure 3-10

The next step in modifying the application is to add some additional components to the layout, the first of which will be a Button for the user to press to initiate the currency conversion.

The Palette panel consists of two columns, with the left-hand column containing a list of view component categories. The right-hand column lists the components contained within the currently selected category. In Figure 3-11, for example, the Button view is currently selected within the Buttons category:

Creating an Example Android App in Android Studio

Palette		
Common	Button	
Text	ImageButton	
Buttons	ChipGroup	
Widgets	Chip	
Layouts	CheckBox	
Containers	RadioGroup	
Helpers	RadioButton	
Google	ToggleButton	
Legacy	Switch	
	FloatingActionButton	

Figure 3-11

Click and drag the *Button* object from the Buttons list and drop it in the horizontal center of the user interface design so that it is positioned beneath the existing TextView widget:

Figure 3-12

The next step is to change the text currently displayed by the Button component. The panel located to the right of the design area is the Attributes panel. This panel displays the attributes assigned to the currently selected component in the layout. Within this panel, locate the *text* property in the Common Attributes section and change the current value from "Button" to "Convert", as shown in Figure 3-13:

21

Creating an Example Android App in Android Studio

strokeWidth	
cornerRadius	@null
rippleColor	@color/m3_button_rip
text	Convert
🔧 text	
contentDescription	

Figure 3-13

The second text property with a wrench next to it allows a text property to be set, which only appears within the Layout Editor tool but is not shown at runtime. This is useful for testing how a visual component and the layout will behave with different settings without running the app repeatedly.

Just in case the Autoconnect system failed to set all of the layout connections, click on the Infer Constraints button (Figure 3-14) to add any missing constraints to the layout:

Figure 3-14

It is important to explain the warning button in the top right-hand corner of the Layout Editor tool, as indicated in Figure 3-15. This warning indicates potential problems with the layout. For details on any problems, click on the button:

Figure 3-15

When clicked, the Problems tool window (Figure 3-16) will appear, describing the nature of the problems:

Figure 3-16

This tool window is divided into two panels. The left panel (marked A in the above figure) lists issues detected

22

Creating an Example Android App in Android Studio

within the layout file. In our example, only the following problem is listed:

`button <Button>: Hardcoded text`

When an item is selected from the list (B), the right-hand panel will update to provide additional detail on the problem (C). In this case, the explanation reads as follows:

`Hardcoded string "Convert", should use @string resource`

The tool window also includes a preview editor (D), allowing manual corrections to be made to the layout file.

This I18N message informs us that a potential issue exists concerning the future internationalization of the project ("I18N" comes from the fact that the word "internationalization" begins with an "I", ends with an "N" and has 18 letters in between). The warning reminds us that attributes and values such as text strings should be stored as *resources* wherever possible when developing Android applications. Doing so enables changes to the appearance of the application to be made by modifying resource files instead of changing the application source code. This can be especially valuable when translating a user interface to a different spoken language. If all of the text in a user interface is contained in a single resource file, for example, that file can be given to a translator, who will then perform the translation work and return the translated file for inclusion in the application. This enables multiple languages to be targeted without the necessity for any source code changes to be made. In this instance, we are going to create a new resource named *convert_string* and assign to it the string "Convert".

Begin by clicking on the Show Quick Fixes button (E) and selecting the *Extract string resource* option from the menu, as shown in Figure 3-17:

Figure 3-17

After selecting this option, the *Extract Resource* panel (Figure 3-18) will appear. Within this panel, change the resource name field to *convert_string* and leave the resource value set to *Convert* before clicking on the OK button:

Figure 3-18

Creating an Example Android App in Android Studio

The next widget to be added is an EditText widget, into which the user will enter the dollar amount to be converted. From the Palette panel, select the Text category and click and drag a Number (Decimal) component onto the layout so that it is centered horizontally and positioned above the existing TextView widget. With the widget selected, use the Attributes tools window to set the *hint* property to "dollars". Click on the warning icon and extract the string to a resource named *dollars_hint*.

The code written later in this chapter will need to access the dollar value entered by the user into the EditText field. It will do this by referencing the id assigned to the widget in the user interface layout. The default id assigned to the widget by Android Studio can be viewed and changed from within the Attributes tool window when the widget is selected in the layout, as shown in Figure 3-19:

Figure 3-19

Change the id to *dollarText* and, in the Rename dialog, click on the *Refactor* button. This ensures that any references elsewhere within the project to the old id are automatically updated to use the new id:

Figure 3-20

Repeat the steps to set the id of the TextView widget to *textView*, if necessary.

Add any missing layout constraints by clicking on the *Infer Constraints* button. At this point, the layout should resemble that shown in Figure 3-21:

Figure 3-21

3.8 Reviewing the Layout and Resource Files

Before moving on to the next step, we will look at some internal aspects of user interface design and resource handling. In the previous section, we changed the user interface by modifying the *activity_main.xml* file using the Layout Editor tool. In fact, all that the Layout Editor was doing was providing a user-friendly way to edit the underlying XML content of the file. In practice, there is no reason why you cannot modify the XML directly to make user interface changes, and, in some instances, this may actually be quicker than using the Layout Editor tool. In the top right-hand corner of the Layout Editor panel is the View Modes menu button marked A in Figure 3-22 below:

Figure 3-22

By default, the editor will be in *Design* mode, whereby just the visual representation of the layout is displayed.

25

Creating an Example Android App in Android Studio

In *Code* mode, the editor will display the XML for the layout, while in *Split* mode, both the layout and XML are displayed, as shown in Figure 3-23:

Figure 3-23

The button to the left of the View Modes button (marked B in Figure 3-22 above) is used to toggle between Code and Split modes quickly.

As can be seen from the structure of the XML file, the user interface consists of the ConstraintLayout component, which in turn, is the parent of the TextView, Button, and EditText objects. We can also see, for example, that the *text* property of the Button is set to our *convert_string* resource. Although complexity and content vary, all user interface layouts are structured in this hierarchical, XML-based way.

As changes are made to the XML layout, these will be reflected in the layout canvas. The layout may also be modified visually from within the layout canvas panel, with the changes appearing in the XML listing. To see this in action, switch to Split mode and modify the XML layout to change the background color of the ConstraintLayout to a shade of red as follows:

```
<?xml version="1.0" encoding="utf-8"?>
<androidx.constraintlayout.widget.ConstraintLayout xmlns:android="http://schemas.android.com/apk/res/android"
    xmlns:app="http://schemas.android.com/apk/res-auto"
    xmlns:tools="http://schemas.android.com/tools"
    android:layout_width="match_parent"
    android:layout_height="match_parent"
    tools:context=".MainActivity"
    android:background="#ff2438" >
    .
    .
    .
</androidx.constraintlayout.widget.ConstraintLayout>
```

Note that the layout color changes in real-time to match the new setting in the XML file. Note also that a small red square appears in the XML editor's left margin (also called the *gutter*) next to the line containing the color setting. This is a visual cue to the fact that the color red has been set on a property. Clicking on the red square will display a color chooser allowing a different color to be selected:

Creating an Example Android App in Android Studio

Figure 3-24

Before proceeding, delete the background property from the layout file so that the background returns to the default setting.

Finally, use the Project panel to locate the *app -> res -> values -> strings.xml* file and double-click on it to load it into the editor. Currently, the XML should read as follows:

```
<resources>
    <string name="app_name">AndroidSample</string>
    <string name="convert_string">Convert</string>
    <string name="dollars_hint">dollars</string>
</resources>
```

To demonstrate resources in action, change the string value currently assigned to the *convert_string* resource to "Convert to Euros" and then return to the Layout Editor tool by selecting the tab for the layout file in the editor panel. Note that the layout has picked up the new resource value for the string.

There is also a quick way to access the value of a resource referenced in an XML file. With the Layout Editor tool in Split or Code mode, click on the "@string/convert_string" property setting so that it highlights, and then press Ctrl-B on the keyboard (Cmd-B on macOS). Android Studio will subsequently open the *strings.xml* file and take you to the line in that file where this resource is declared. Use this opportunity to revert the string resource to the original "Convert" text and to add the following additional entry for a string resource that will be referenced later in the app code:

```
<resources>
    .
    .
    <string name="convert_string">Convert</string>
    <string name="dollars_hint">dollars</string>
    <string name="no_value_string">No Value</string>
</resources>
```

Resource strings may also be edited using the Android Studio Translations Editor by clicking on the *Open editor* link in the top right-hand corner of the editor window. This will display the Translation Editor in the main panel of the Android Studio window:

Creating an Example Android App in Android Studio

Figure 3-25

This editor allows the strings assigned to resource keys to be edited and for translations for multiple languages to be managed.

3.9 Adding Interaction

The final step in this example project is to make the app interactive so that when the user enters a dollar value into the EditText field and clicks the convert button, the converted euro value appears on the TextView. This involves the implementation of some event handling on the Button widget. Specifically, the Button needs to be configured so that a method in the app code is called when an *onClick* event is triggered. Event handling can be implemented in several ways and is covered in a later chapter entitled *"An Overview and Example of Android Event Handling"*. Return the layout editor to Design mode, select the Button widget in the layout editor, refer to the Attributes tool window, and specify a method named *convertCurrency* as shown below:

Figure 3-26

Next, double-click on the *MainActivity.java* file in the Project tool window (*app -> java -> <package name> -> MainActivity*) to load it into the code editor and add the code for the *convertCurrency* method to the class file so that it reads as follows, noting that it is also necessary to import some additional Android packages:

```
package com.ebookfrenzy.androidsample;

import androidx.appcompat.app.AppCompatActivity;

import android.os.Bundle;
import android.view.View;
import android.widget.EditText;
import android.widget.TextView;
```

```java
    .
    .
import java.util.Locale;

public class MainActivity extends AppCompatActivity {

    @Override
    protected void onCreate(Bundle savedInstanceState) {
        super.onCreate(savedInstanceState);
        setContentView(R.layout.activity_main);
    }

    public void convertCurrency(View view) {

        EditText dollarText = findViewById(R.id.dollarText);
        TextView textView = findViewById(R.id.textView);

        if (!dollarText.getText().toString().equals("")) {

            float dollarValue = Float.parseFloat(dollarText.getText().toString());
            float euroValue = dollarValue * 0.85F;
            textView.setText(String.format(Locale.ENGLISH,"%.2f", euroValue));
        } else {
            textView.setText(R.string.no_value_string);
        }
    }
}
```

The method begins by obtaining references to the EditText and TextView objects by making a call to a method named findViewById, passing through the id assigned within the layout file. A check is then made to ensure that the user has entered a dollar value, and if so, that value is extracted, converted from a String to a floating point value, and converted to euros. Finally, the result is displayed on the TextView widget.

If any of this is unclear, rest assured that these concepts will be covered in greater detail in later chapters. In particular, the topic of accessing widgets from within code using findByViewId and an introduction to an alternative technique referred to as *view binding* will be covered in the chapter entitled *"An Overview of Android View Binding"*.

3.10 Summary

While not excessively complex, several steps are involved in setting up an Android development environment. Having performed those steps, it is worth working through an example to ensure the environment is correctly installed and configured. In this chapter, we have created an example application and then used the Android Studio Layout Editor tool to modify the user interface layout. In doing so, we explored the importance of using resources wherever possible, particularly string values, and briefly touched on layouts. Next, we looked at the underlying XML used to store Android application user interface designs.

Finally, an onClick event was added to a Button connected to a method implemented to extract the user input from the EditText component, convert it from dollars to euros and then display the result on the TextView.

Creating an Example Android App in Android Studio

With the app ready for testing, the steps necessary to set up an emulator for testing purposes will be covered in detail in the next chapter.

4. Creating an Android Virtual Device (AVD) in Android Studio

Although the Android Studio Preview panel allows us to see the layout we are designing, compiling and running an entire app will be necessary to thoroughly test that it works. An Android application may be tested by installing and running it on a physical device or in an Android Virtual Device (AVD) emulator environment. Before an AVD can be used, it must first be created and configured to match the specifications of a particular device model. In this chapter, we will work through creating such a virtual device using the Pixel 4 phone as a reference example.

4.1 About Android Virtual Devices

AVDs are emulators that allow Android applications to be tested without needing to install the application on a physical Android-based device. An AVD may be configured to emulate various hardware features, including screen size, memory capacity, and the presence or otherwise of features such as a camera, GPS navigation support, or an accelerometer. Several emulator templates are installed as part of the standard Android Studio installation, allowing AVDs to be configured for various devices. Custom configurations may be created to match any physical Android device by specifying properties such as processor type, memory capacity, and the size and pixel density of the screen.

An AVD session can appear as a separate window or embedded within the Android Studio window.

New AVDs are created and managed using the Android Virtual Device Manager, which may be used in command-line mode or with a more user-friendly graphical user interface. To create a new AVD, the first step is to launch the AVD Manager. This can be achieved from within the Android Studio environment by clicking the *Device Manager* button in the right-hand tool window bar, as indicated in Figure 4-1:

Figure 4-1

Once opened, the manager will appear as a tool window, as shown in Figure 4-2:

Creating an Android Virtual Device (AVD) in Android Studio

Figure 4-2

If you installed Android Studio for the first time on a computer (as opposed to upgrading an existing Android Studio installation), the installer might have created an initial AVD instance ready for use, as shown in Figure 4-3:

Figure 4-3

If this AVD is present on your system, you can use it to test apps. If no AVD was created, or you would like to create AVDs for different device types, follow the steps in the rest of this chapter.

To add a new AVD, begin by making sure that the Virtual tab is selected before clicking on the *Create device* button to open the *Virtual Device Configuration* dialog:

Figure 4-4

Creating an Android Virtual Device (AVD) in Android Studio

Within the dialog, perform the following steps to create a Pixel 4-compatible emulator:

1. Select the Phone option From the Category panel to display the available Android phone AVD templates.

2. Select the *Pixel 4* device option and click *Next*.

3. On the System Image screen, select the latest version of Android. If the system image has not yet been installed, a *Download* link will be provided next to the Release Name. Click this link to download and install the system image before selecting it. If the image you need is not listed, click on the *x86 Images* (or *ARM images* if you are running a Mac with Apple Silicon) and *Other images* tabs to view alternative lists.

4. Click *Next* to proceed and enter a descriptive name (for example, *Pixel 4 API 33*) into the name field or accept the default name.

5. Click *Finish* to create the AVD.

6. If future modifications to the AVD are necessary, re-open the Device Manager, select the AVD from the list, and click on the pencil icon in the Actions column to edit the settings.

4.2 Starting the Emulator

To test the newly created AVD emulator, select the emulator from the Device Manager and click the launch button (the triangle in the Actions column). The emulator will appear embedded into the main Android Studio window and begin the startup process. The amount of time it takes for the emulator to start will depend on the configuration of both the AVD and the system on which it is running:

Figure 4-5

To hide and show the emulator tool window, click the Running Devices tool window button (marked A above). Click the "x" close button next to the tab (B) to exit the emulator. The emulator tool window can accommodate multiple emulator sessions, with each session represented by a tab. Figure 4-6, for example, shows a tool window with two emulator sessions:

Creating an Android Virtual Device (AVD) in Android Studio

Figure 4-6

To switch between sessions, click on the corresponding tab.

Although the emulator probably defaulted to appearing in portrait orientation, this and other default options can be changed. Within the Device Manager, select the new Pixel 4 entry and click on the pencil icon in the *Actions* column of the device row. In the configuration screen, locate the *Startup orientation* section and change the orientation setting. Exit and restart the emulator session to see this change take effect. More details on the emulator are covered in the next chapter, *"Using and Configuring the Android Studio AVD Emulator"*).

To save time in the next section of this chapter, leave the emulator running before proceeding.

4.3 Running the Application in the AVD

With an AVD emulator configured, the example AndroidSample application created in the earlier chapter can now be compiled and run. With the AndroidSample project loaded into Android Studio, make sure that the newly created Pixel 4 AVD is displayed in the device menu (marked A in Figure 4-7 below), then either click the run button represented by a triangle (B), select the *Run -> Run 'app'* menu option or use the Ctrl-R keyboard shortcut:

Figure 4-7

The device menu (A) may be used to select a different AVD instance or physical device as the run target and also to run the app on multiple devices. The menu also provides access to the Device Manager as well as device connection configuration and troubleshooting options:

Figure 4-8

Once the application is installed and running, the user interface for the first fragment will appear within the emulator (a fragment is a reusable section of an Android project typically consisting of a user interface layout and some code, a topic which will be covered later in the chapter entitled *"An Introduction to Android Fragments"*):

Figure 4-9

Once the run process begins, the Run tool window will appear. The Run tool window will display diagnostic information as the application package is installed and launched. Figure 4-10 shows the Run tool window output from a typical successful application launch:

Figure 4-10

If problems are encountered during the launch process, the Run tool window will provide information to help isolate the problem's cause.

Assuming the application loads into the emulator and runs as expected, we have safely verified that the Android development environment is correctly installed and configured. With the app running, try performing a currency conversion to verify that the app works as intended.

4.4 Running on Multiple Devices

The run target menu shown in Figure 4-8 above includes an option to run the app on multiple emulators and devices in parallel. When selected, this option displays the dialog in Figure 4-11, providing a list of the AVDs configured on the system and any attached physical devices. Enable the checkboxes next to the emulators or devices to be targeted before clicking on the Run button:

Creating an Android Virtual Device (AVD) in Android Studio

Figure 4-11

After clicking the Run button, Android Studio will launch the app on the selected emulators and devices.

4.5 Stopping a Running Application

To stop a running application, click the stop button located in the main toolbar, as shown in Figure 4-12:

Figure 4-12

An app may also be terminated using the Run tool window. Begin by displaying the *Run* tool window using the window bar button that becomes available when the app is running. Once the Run tool window appears, click the stop button highlighted in Figure 4-13 below:

Figure 4-13

4.6 Supporting Dark Theme

To test how an app behaves when dark theme is enabled, open the Settings app within the running Android instance in the emulator, choose the *Display* category, and enable the *Dark theme* option as shown in Figure 4-14:

Creating an Android Virtual Device (AVD) in Android Studio

Figure 4-14

With dark theme enabled, run the AndroidSample app and note that it appears using a dark theme, including a black background and a purple background color on the button, as shown in Figure 4-15:

Figure 4-15

Return to the Settings app and turn off Dark theme mode before continuing.

4.7 Running the Emulator in a Separate Window

So far in this chapter, we have only used the emulator as a tool window embedded within the main Android Studio window. The emulator can be configured to appear in a separate window within the Settings dialog, which can be displayed by clicking on the IDE and Project Settings button located in the Android Studio toolbar, as highlighted in Figure 4-16:

Creating an Android Virtual Device (AVD) in Android Studio

Figure 4-16

Within the Settings dialog, navigate to *Tools -> Emulator* in the side panel, and disable the *Launch in a tool window* option:

Figure 4-17

With the option disabled, click the Apply button followed by OK to commit the change, then exit the current emulator session by clicking on the close button on the tab marked B in Figure 4-5 above.

Run the sample app once again, at which point the emulator will appear as a separate window, as shown below:

Creating an Android Virtual Device (AVD) in Android Studio

Figure 4-18

The choice of standalone or tool window mode is a matter of personal preference. If you prefer the emulator running in a tool window, return to the settings screen and re-enable the *Launch in a tool window* option. Before committing to standalone mode, however, keep in mind that the Running Devices tool window may also be detached from the main Android Studio window from within the tool window Options menu, which is accessed by clicking the button indicated in Figure 4-19:

Figure 4-19

From within the Options menu, select *View Mode -> Float* to detach the tool window from the Android Studio main window:

Creating an Android Virtual Device (AVD) in Android Studio

Figure 4-20

To re-dock the Running Devices tool window, click on the Dock button shown in Figure 4-21:

Figure 4-21

4.8 Enabling the Device Frame

The emulator can be configured to appear with or without the device frame. To change the setting, exit the emulator, open the Device Manager, select the AVD from the list, and click on the pencil icon in the Actions column. In the settings screen, locate and change the Enable Device Frame option:

Figure 4-22

Once the device frame has been enabled, the emulator will appear as shown in Figure 4-23 the next time it is launched:

Figure 4-23

4.9 Summary

A typical application development process follows a cycle of coding, compiling, and running in a test environment. Android applications may be tested on a physical Android device or an Android Virtual Device (AVD) emulator. AVDs are created and managed using the Android Studio Device Manager tool, which may be used as a command-line tool or via a graphical user interface. When creating an AVD to simulate a specific Android device model, the virtual device should be configured with a hardware specification matching that of the physical device.

The AVD emulator session may be displayed as a standalone window or embedded into the main Android Studio user interface.

Chapter 5

5. Using and Configuring the Android Studio AVD Emulator

Before the next chapter explores testing on physical Android devices, this chapter will take some time to provide an overview of the Android Studio AVD emulator and highlight many of the configuration features available to customize the environment in both standalone and tool window modes.

5.1 The Emulator Environment

When launched in standalone mode, the emulator displays an initial splash screen during the loading process. Once loaded, the main emulator window appears, containing a representation of the chosen device type (in the case of Figure 5-1, this is a Pixel 4 device):

Figure 5-1

The toolbar positioned along the right-hand edge of the window provides quick access to the emulator controls and configuration options.

5.2 Emulator Toolbar Options

The emulator toolbar (Figure 5-2) provides access to a range of options relating to the appearance and behavior of the emulator environment.

43

Using and Configuring the Android Studio AVD Emulator

Figure 5-2

Each button in the toolbar has associated with it a keyboard accelerator which can be identified either by hovering the mouse pointer over the button and waiting for the tooltip to appear or via the help option of the extended controls panel.

Though many of the options contained within the toolbar are self-explanatory, each option will be covered for the sake of completeness:

- **Exit / Minimize** – The uppermost 'x' button in the toolbar exits the emulator session when selected, while the '-' option minimizes the entire window.

- **Power** – The Power button simulates the hardware power button on a physical Android device. Clicking and releasing this button will lock the device and turn off the screen. Clicking and holding this button will initiate the device "Power off" request sequence.

- **Volume Up / Down** – Two buttons that control the audio volume of playback within the simulator environment.

- **Rotate Left/Right** – Rotates the emulated device between portrait and landscape orientations.

- **Take Screenshot** – Takes a screenshot of the content displayed on the device screen. The captured image is stored at the location specified in the Settings screen of the extended controls panel, as outlined later in this chapter.

- **Zoom Mode** – This button toggles in and out of zoom mode, details of which will be covered later in this chapter.

- **Back** – Performs the standard Android "Back" navigation to return to a previous screen.

- **Home** – Displays the device's home screen.

- **Overview** – Simulates selection of the standard Android "Overview" navigation, which displays the currently running apps on the device.

- **Fold Device** – Simulates the folding and unfolding of a foldable device. This option is only available if the emulator is running a foldable device system image.

- **Extended Controls** – Displays the extended controls panel, allowing for the configuration of options such as simulated location and telephony activity, battery strength, cellular network type, and fingerprint identification.

5.3 Working in Zoom Mode

The zoom button located in the emulator toolbar switches in and out of zoom mode. When zoom mode is active, the toolbar button is depressed, and the mouse pointer appears as a magnifying glass when hovering over the device screen. Clicking the left mouse button will cause the display to zoom in relative to the selected point on the screen, with repeated clicking increasing the zoom level. Conversely, clicking the right mouse button decreases the zoom level. Toggling the zoom button off reverts the display to the default size.

Clicking and dragging while in zoom mode will define a rectangular area into which the view will zoom when the mouse button is released.

While in zoom mode, the screen's visible area may be panned using the horizontal and vertical scrollbars located within the emulator window.

5.4 Resizing the Emulator Window

The emulator window's size (and the device's corresponding representation) can be changed at any time by clicking and dragging on any of the corners or sides of the window.

5.5 Extended Control Options

The extended controls toolbar button displays the panel illustrated in Figure 5-3. By default, the location settings will be displayed. Selecting a different category from the left-hand panel will display the corresponding group of controls:

Figure 5-3

Using and Configuring the Android Studio AVD Emulator

5.5.1 Location

The location controls allow simulated location information to be sent to the emulator as decimal or sexigesimal coordinates. Location information can take the form of a single location or a sequence of points representing the device's movement, the latter being provided via a file in either GPS Exchange (GPX) or Keyhole Markup Language (KML) format. Alternatively, the integrated Google Maps panel may be used to select single points or travel routes visually.

5.5.2 Displays

In addition to the main display shown within the emulator screen, the Displays option allows additional displays to be added running within the same Android instance. This can be useful for testing apps for dual-screen devices such as the Microsoft Surface Duo. These additional screens can be configured to be any required size and appear within the same emulator window as the main screen.

5.5.3 Cellular

The type of cellular connection being simulated can be changed within the cellular settings screen. Options are available to simulate different network types (CSM, EDGE, HSDPA, etc.) in addition to a range of voice and data scenarios, such as roaming and denied access.

5.5.4 Battery

Various battery state and charging conditions can be simulated on this panel of the extended controls screen, including battery charge level, battery health, and whether the AC charger is currently connected.

5.5.5 Camera

The emulator simulates a 3D scene when the camera is active. This takes the form of the interior of a virtual building through which you can navigate by holding down the Option key (Alt on Windows) while using the mouse pointer and keyboard keys when recording video or before taking a photo within the emulator. This extended configuration option allows different images to be uploaded for display within the virtual environment.

5.5.6 Phone

The phone extended controls provide two straightforward but helpful simulations within the emulator. The first option simulates an incoming call from a designated phone number. This can be particularly useful when testing how an app handles high-level interrupts.

The second option allows the receipt of text messages to be simulated within the emulator session. As in the real world, these messages appear within the Message app and trigger the standard notifications within the emulator.

5.5.7 Directional Pad

A directional pad (D-Pad) is an additional set of controls either built into an Android device or connected externally (such as a game controller) that provides directional controls (left, right, up, down). The directional pad settings allow D-Pad interaction to be simulated within the emulator.

5.5.8 Microphone

The microphone settings allow the microphone to be enabled and virtual headset and microphone connections to be simulated. A button is also provided to launch the Voice Assistant on the emulator.

5.5.9 Fingerprint

Many Android devices are now supplied with built-in fingerprint detection hardware. The AVD emulator makes it possible to test fingerprint authentication without the need to test apps on a physical device containing a fingerprint sensor. Details on configuring fingerprint testing within the emulator will be covered later in this chapter.

5.5.10 Virtual Sensors

The virtual sensors option allows the accelerometer and magnetometer to be simulated to emulate the effects of the physical motion of a device, such as rotation, movement, and tilting through yaw, pitch, and roll settings.

5.5.11 Snapshots

Snapshots contain the state of the currently running AVD session to be saved and rapidly restored, making it easy to return the emulator to an exact state. Snapshots are covered later in this chapter.

5.5.12 Record and Playback

Allows the emulator screen and audio to be recorded and saved in WebM or animated GIF format.

5.5.13 Google Play

If the emulator is running a version of Android with Google Play Services installed, this option displays the current Google Play version. It also provides the option to update the emulator to the latest version.

5.5.14 Settings

The settings panel provides a small group of configuration options. Use this panel to choose a darker theme for the toolbar and extended controls panel, specify a file system location into which screenshots are to be saved, configure OpenGL support levels, and configure the emulator window to appear on top of other windows on the desktop.

5.5.15 Help

The Help screen contains three sub-panels containing a list of keyboard shortcuts, links to access the emulator online documentation, file bugs and send feedback, and emulator version information.

5.6 Working with Snapshots

When an emulator starts for the first time, it performs a *cold boot*, much like a physical Android device when powered on. This cold boot process can take some time to complete as the operating system loads and all the background processes are started. To avoid the necessity of going through this process every time the emulator is started, the system is configured to automatically save a snapshot (referred to as a *quick-boot snapshot*) of the emulator's current state each time it exits. The next time the emulator is launched, the quick-boot snapshot is loaded into memory, and execution resumes from where it left off previously, allowing the emulator to restart in a fraction of the time needed for a cold boot to complete.

The Snapshots screen of the extended controls panel can store additional snapshots at any point during the execution of the emulator. This saves the exact state of the entire emulator allowing the emulator to be restored to the exact point in time that the snapshot was taken. From within the screen, snapshots can be taken using the *Take Snapshot* button (marked A in Figure 5-4). To restore an existing snapshot, select it from the list (B) and click the run button (C) located at the bottom of the screen. Options are also provided to edit (D) the snapshot name and description and to delete (E) the currently selected snapshot:

Using and Configuring the Android Studio AVD Emulator

Figure 5-4

You can also choose whether to start an emulator using either a cold boot, the most recent quick-boot snapshot, or a previous snapshot by making a selection from the run target menu in the main toolbar, as illustrated in Figure 5-5:

Figure 5-5

5.7 Configuring Fingerprint Emulation

The emulator allows up to 10 simulated fingerprints to be configured and used to test fingerprint authentication within Android apps. Configuring simulated fingerprints begins by launching the emulator, opening the Settings app, and selecting the Security option.

Within the Security settings screen, select the fingerprint option. On the resulting information screen, click on

Using and Configuring the Android Studio AVD Emulator

the *Next* button to proceed to the Fingerprint setup screen. Before fingerprint security can be enabled, a backup screen unlocking method (such as a PIN) must be configured. Enter and confirm a suitable PIN and complete the PIN entry process by accepting the default notifications option.

Proceed through the remaining screens until the Settings app requests a fingerprint on the sensor. At this point, display the extended controls dialog, select the *Fingerprint* category in the left-hand panel, and make sure that *Finger 1* is selected in the main settings panel:

Figure 5-6

Click on the *Touch Sensor* button to simulate Finger 1 touching the fingerprint sensor. The emulator will report the successful addition of the fingerprint:

Figure 5-7

To add additional fingerprints, click on the *Add Another* button and select another finger from the extended controls panel menu before clicking on the *Touch Sensor* button again.

5.8 The Emulator in Tool Window Mode

As outlined in the previous chapter (*"Creating an Android Virtual Device (AVD) in Android Studio"*), Android Studio can be configured to launch the emulator in an embedded tool window so that it does not appear in a separate window. When running in this mode, the same controls available in standalone mode are provided in the toolbar, as shown in Figure 5-8:

Figure 5-8

From left to right, these buttons perform the following tasks (details of which match those for standalone mode):

- Power
- Volume Up
- Volume Down
- Rotate Left
- Rotate Right
- Back
- Home
- Overview
- Screenshot
- Snapshots
- Extended Controls

5.9 Creating a Resizable Emulator

In addition to emulators configured to match specific Android device models, Android Studio also provides a resizable AVD that allows you to switch between phone, tablet, and foldable device sizes. To create a resizable emulator, open the Device Manager and click the *Create device* button. Next, select the Resizable device definition illustrated in Figure 5-9, and follow the usual steps to create a new AVD:

Category	Name	Play Store	Size	Resolution	Density
Phone	Resizable (Experimental)		6.0"	1080x2340	420dpi
Tablet	Pixel XL		5.5"	1440x2560	560dpi
Wear OS	Pixel 7 Pro	▷	6.71"	1440x3120	560dpi
Desktop	Pixel 7	▷	6.31"	1080x2400	420dpi
TV	Pixel 6a	▷	6.13"	1080x2400	420dpi
Automotive	Pixel 6 Pro		6.7"	1440x3120	560dpi

Resizable (Experimental)

Size: large
Ratio: long
Density: 420dpi
Folded: 884x2208

This device resizes to:
Phone (1080 x 2340 @ 420dpi)
Foldable (1768 x 2208 @ 420dpi)
Tablet (1920 x 1200 @ 240dpi)
Desktop (1920 x 1080 @ 160dpi)

Figure 5-9

Using and Configuring the Android Studio AVD Emulator

When you run an app on the new emulator within a tool window, the *Display mode* option will appear in the toolbar, allowing you to switch between emulator configurations as shown in Figure 5-10:

Figure 5-10

If the emulator is running in standalone mode, the Display mode option can be found in the side toolbar, as shown below:

Figure 5-11

5.10 Summary

Android Studio contains an Android Virtual Device emulator environment designed to make it easier to test applications without running them on a physical Android device. This chapter has provided a brief tour of the emulator and highlighted key features available to configure and customize the environment to simulate different testing conditions.

Chapter 6

6. A Tour of the Android Studio User Interface

While it is tempting to plunge into running the example application created in the previous chapter, it involves using aspects of the Android Studio user interface, which are best described in advance.

Android Studio is a powerful and feature-rich development environment that is, to a large extent, intuitive to use. That being said, taking the time now to gain familiarity with the layout and organization of the Android Studio user interface will shorten the learning curve in later chapters of the book. With this in mind, this chapter will provide an overview of the various areas and components of the Android Studio environment.

6.1 The Welcome Screen

The welcome screen (Figure 6-1) is displayed any time that Android Studio is running with no projects currently open (open projects can be closed at any time by selecting the *File -> Close Project* menu option). If Android Studio was previously exited while a project was still open, the tool will bypass the welcome screen the next time it is launched, automatically opening the previously active project.

Figure 6-1

In addition to a list of recent projects, the welcome screen provides options for performing tasks such as opening and creating projects, along with access to projects currently under version control. In addition, the *Customize* screen provides options to change the theme and font settings used by both the IDE and the editor. Android Studio plugins may be viewed, installed, and managed using the *Plugins* option.

Additional options are available by selecting the More Actions link or using the menu shown in Figure 6-2 when

A Tour of the Android Studio User Interface

the list of recent projects replaces the More Actions link:

Figure 6-2

6.2 The Menu Bar

The Android Studio main window will appear when a new project is created, or an existing one is opened. When multiple projects are open simultaneously, each will be assigned its own main window. The precise configuration of the window will vary depending on the operating system Android Studio is running on and which tools and panels were displayed the last time the project was open. The appearance, for example, of the main menu bar will differ depending on the host operating system. On macOS, Android Studio follows the standard convention of placing the menu bar along the top edge of the desktop, as illustrated in Figure 6-3:

Figure 6-3

When Android Studio is running on Windows or Linux, however, the main menu is accessed via the button highlighted in Figure 6-4:

Figure 6-4

6.3 The Main Window

Once a project is open, the Android Studio main window will typically resemble that of Figure 6-5:

A Tour of the Android Studio User Interface

Figure 6-5

The various elements of the main window can be summarized as follows:

A – Toolbar – A selection of shortcuts to frequently performed actions. The toolbar buttons provide quick access to a select group of menu bar actions. The toolbar can be customized by right-clicking on the bar and selecting the *Customize Toolbar...* menu option. The toolbar menu shown in Figure 6-6 provides a convenient way to perform tasks such as creating and opening projects and switching between windows when multiple projects are open:

Figure 6-6

B – Navigation Bar – The navigation bar provides a convenient way to move around the files and folders that make up the project. Clicking on an element in the navigation bar will drop down a menu listing the sub-folders and files at that location, ready for selection. Similarly, clicking on a class name displays a menu listing methods contained within that class:

55

A Tour of the Android Studio User Interface

Figure 6-7

Select a method from the list to be taken to the corresponding location within the code editor. You can hide, display, and change the position of this bar using the *View -> Appearance -> Navigation Bar* menu option.

C – Editor Window – The editor window displays the content of the file on which the developer is currently working. When multiple files are open, each file is represented by a tab located along the top edge of the editor, as shown in Figure 6-8:

Figure 6-8

D – Status Bar – The status bar displays informational messages about the project and the activities of Android Studio. Hovering over items in the status bar will display a description of that field. Many fields are interactive, allowing users to click to perform tasks or obtain more detailed status information.

Figure 6-9

The widgets displayed in the status bar can be changed using the *View -> Appearance -> Status Bar Widgets* menu.

E – Project Tool Window – The project tool window provides a hierarchical overview of the project file structure allowing navigation to specific files and folders to be performed. The toolbar can be used to display the project in several different ways. The default setting is the *Android* view which is the mode primarily used in the remainder of this book.

The project tool window is just one of many available tools within the Android Studio environment.

6.4 The Tool Windows

In addition to the project view tool window, Android Studio also includes many other windows, which, when enabled, are displayed *tool window bars* that appear along the left and right edges of the main window and contain buttons for showing and hiding each of the tool windows. Figure 6-10 shows typical tool window bar configurations, though the buttons and their positioning may differ for your Android Studio installation.

A Tour of the Android Studio User Interface

Figure 6-10

Clicking on a button will display the corresponding tool window, while a second click will hide the window. The location of a button in a tool window bar indicates the side of the window against which the window will appear when displayed. These positions can be changed by clicking and dragging the buttons to different locations in other window toolbars.

Android Studio offers a wide range of tool windows, the most commonly used of which are as follows:

- **Project (A)** – The project view provides an overview of the file structure that makes up the project allowing for quick navigation between files. Generally, double-clicking on a file in the project view will cause that file to be loaded into the appropriate editing tool.

- **Resource Manager (B)** - A tool for adding and managing resources and assets within the project, such as images, colors, and layout files.

- **More Tool Windows (C)** - Displays a menu containing additional tool windows not currently displayed in a tool window bar. When a tool window is selected from this menu, it will appear as a button in a tool window bar.

- **Run (D)** – The run tool window becomes available when an application is currently running and provides a view of the results of the run together with options to stop or restart a running process. If an application fails to install and run on a device or emulator, this window typically provides diagnostic information about the problem.

- **Logcat (E)** – The Logcat tool window provides access to the monitoring log output from a running application

57

A Tour of the Android Studio User Interface

and options for taking screenshots and videos of the application and stopping and restarting a process.

- **Problems (F)** - A central location to view all of the current errors or warnings within the project. Double-clicking on an item in the problem list will take you to the problem file and location.

- **App Quality Insights (G)** - Provides access to the cloud-based Firebase app quality and crash analytics platform.

- **Terminal (H)** – Provides access to a terminal window on the system on which Android Studio is running. On Windows systems, this is the Command Prompt interface, while on Linux and macOS systems, this takes the form of a Terminal prompt.

- **Version Control (I)** - This tool window is used when the project files are under source code version control, allowing access to Git repositories and code change history.

- **Notifications (J)** - This tool window is used when the project files are under source code version control, allowing access to Git repositories and code change history.

- **Gradle (K)** – The Gradle tool window provides a view of the Gradle tasks that make up the project build configuration. The window lists the tasks involved in compiling the various elements of the project into an executable application. Right-click on a top-level Gradle task and select the *Open Gradle Config* menu option to load the Gradle build file for the current project into the editor. Gradle will be covered in greater detail later in this book.

- **Device Manager (L)** - Provides access to the Device Manager tool window where physical Android device connections and emulators may be added, removed, and managed.

- **Running Devices (M)** - Contains the AVD emulator if the option has been enabled to run the emulator in a tool window as outlined in the chapter entitled *"Creating an Android Virtual Device (AVD) in Android Studio"*.

- **App Inspection** - Provides access to the Database and Background Task inspectors. The Database Inspector allows you to inspect, query, and modify your app's databases while running. The Background Task Inspector allows background worker tasks created using WorkManager to be monitored and managed.

- **Bookmarks** – The Bookmarks tool window provides quick access to bookmarked files and code lines. For example, right-clicking on a file in the project view allows access to an Add to Bookmarks menu option. Similarly, you can bookmark a line of code in a source file by moving the cursor to that line and pressing the F11 key (F3 on macOS). All bookmarked items can be accessed through this tool window.

- **Build** - The build tool window displays information about the build process while a project is being compiled and packaged and details of any errors encountered.

- **Build Variants** – The build variants tool window provides a quick way to configure different build targets for the current application project (for example, different builds for debugging and release versions of the application or multiple builds to target different device categories).

- **Device File Explorer** – Available via the *View -> Tool Windows -> Device File Explorer* menu, this tool window provides direct access to the filesystem of the currently connected Android device or emulator, allowing the filesystem to be browsed and files copied to the local filesystem.

- **Layout Inspector** - Provides a visual 3D rendering of the hierarchy of components that make up a user interface layout.

- **Structure** – The structure tool provides a high-level view of the structure of the source file currently displayed in the editor. This information includes a list of items such as classes, methods, and variables in the file.

Selecting an item from the structure list will take you to that location in the source file in the editor window.

- **TODO** – As the name suggests, this tool provides a place to review items that have yet to be completed on the project. Android Studio compiles this list by scanning the source files that make up the project to look for comments that match specified TODO patterns. These patterns can be reviewed and changed by opening the Settings dialog and navigating to the *TODO* entry listed under *Editor*.

6.5 The Tool Window Menus

Each tool window has its own toolbar along the top edge. The menu buttons within these toolbars vary from one tool to the next, though all tool windows contain an Options menu (marked A in Figure 6-11):

Figure 6-11

The Options menu allows various aspects of the window to be changed. Figure 6-12, for example, shows the Options menu for the Project tool window. Settings are available, for example, to undock a window and to allow it to float outside of the boundaries of the Android Studio main window, and to move and resize the tool panel:

Figure 6-12

All tool windows also include a far-right button on the toolbar (marked B in Figure 6-11 above), providing an additional way to hide the tool window from view. A search of the items within a tool window can be performed by giving that window focus by clicking on it and then typing the search term (for example, the name of a file in the Project tool window). A search box will appear in the window's toolbar, and items matching the search highlighted.

6.6 Android Studio Keyboard Shortcuts

Android Studio includes many keyboard shortcuts to save time when performing common tasks. A complete keyboard shortcut keymap listing can be viewed and printed from within the Android Studio project window by selecting the *Help -> Keyboard Shortcuts PDF* menu option. You may also list and modify the keyboard shortcuts by opening the Settings dialog and clicking on the Keymap entry, as shown in Figure 6-13 below:

A Tour of the Android Studio User Interface

Figure 6-13

6.7 Switcher and Recent Files Navigation

Another useful mechanism for navigating within the Android Studio main window involves using the *Switcher*. Accessed via the Ctrl-Tab keyboard shortcut, the switcher appears as a panel listing both the tool windows and currently open files (Figure 6-14).

Figure 6-14

Once displayed, the switcher will remain visible as long as the Ctrl key remains depressed. Repeatedly tapping the Tab key while holding down the Ctrl key will cycle through the various selection options while releasing the Ctrl key causes the currently highlighted item to be selected and displayed within the main window.

In addition to the Switcher, the Recent Files panel provides navigation to recently opened files (Figure 6-15). This can be accessed using the Ctrl-E keyboard shortcut (Cmd-E on macOS). Once displayed, either the mouse pointer can be used to select an option, or the keyboard arrow keys can be used to scroll through the file name and tool window options. Pressing the Enter key will select the currently highlighted item:

A Tour of the Android Studio User Interface

Figure 6-15

6.8 Changing the Android Studio Theme

The overall theme of the Android Studio environment may be changed using the Settings dialog. Once the settings dialog is displayed, select the *Appearance & Behavior* option in the left-hand panel, followed by *Appearance*. Then, change the setting of the *Theme* menu before clicking on the *OK* button. The themes available will depend on the platform but usually include options such as Light, IntelliJ, Windows, High Contrast, and Darcula. Figure 6-16 shows an example of the main window with the Dark theme selected:

Figure 6-16

To synchronize the Android Studio theme with the operating system light and dark mode setting, enable the *Sync with OS* option and use the drop-down menu to control which theme to use for each mode:

61

A Tour of the Android Studio User Interface

Figure 6-17

6.9 Summary

The primary elements of the Android Studio environment consist of the welcome screen and main window. Each open project is assigned its own main window, which, in turn, consists of a menu bar, toolbar, editing and design area, status bar, and a collection of tool windows. Tool windows appear on the sides of the main window.

There are very few actions within Android Studio that cannot be triggered via a keyboard shortcut. A keymap of default keyboard shortcuts can be accessed at any time from within the Android Studio main window.

Chapter 7

7. Testing Android Studio Apps on a Physical Android Device

While much can be achieved by testing applications using an Android Virtual Device (AVD), there is no substitute for performing real-world application testing on a physical Android device, and some Android features are only available on physical Android devices.

Communication with both AVD instances and connected Android devices is handled by the *Android Debug Bridge (ADB)*. This chapter explains how to configure the adb environment to enable application testing on an Android device with macOS, Windows, and Linux-based systems.

7.1 An Overview of the Android Debug Bridge (ADB)

The primary purpose of the ADB is to facilitate interaction between a development system, in this case, Android Studio, and both AVD emulators and Android devices to run and debug applications. ADB allows you to connect to devices via WiFi or USB cable.

The ADB consists of a client, a server process running in the background on the development system, and a daemon background process running in either AVDs or real Android devices such as phones and tablets.

The ADB client can take a variety of forms. For example, a client is provided as a command-line tool named *adb* in the Android SDK *platform-tools* sub-directory. Similarly, Android Studio also has a built-in client.

A variety of tasks may be performed using the *adb* command-line tool. For example, active virtual or physical devices may be listed using the *devices* command-line argument. The following command output indicates the presence of an AVD on the system but no physical devices:

```
$ adb devices
List of devices attached
emulator-5554   device
```

7.2 Enabling USB Debugging ADB on Android Devices

Before ADB can connect to an Android device, that device must be configured to allow the connection. On phone and tablet devices running Android 6.0 or later, the steps to achieve this are as follows:

1. Open the Settings app on the device and select the *About tablet* or *About phone* option (on some versions of Android, this can be found on the *System* page of the Settings app).

2. On the *About* screen, scroll down to the *Build number* field (Figure 7-1) and tap it seven times until a message indicates that developer mode has been enabled. If the Build number is not listed on the About screen, it may be available via the *Software information* option. Alternatively, unfold the Advanced section of the list if available.

Wi-Fi MAC address
02:00:00:44:55:66

Build number
PPP2.180412.012

Figure 7-1

3. Return to the main Settings screen and note the appearance of a new option titled Developer options (on newer versions of Android, this option is listed on the System settings screen). Select this option, and on the resulting screen, locate the USB debugging option as illustrated in Figure 7-2:

Debugging

USB debugging
Debug mode when USB is connected

Figure 7-2

4. Enable the USB debugging option and tap the Allow button when confirmation is requested.

The device is now configured to accept debugging connections from adb on the development system over a USB connection. All that remains is to configure the development system to detect the device when it is attached. While this is a relatively straightforward process, the steps differ depending on whether the development system runs Windows, macOS, or Linux. Note that the following steps assume that the Android SDK *platform-tools* directory is included in the operating system PATH environment variable as described in the chapter entitled *"Setting up an Android Studio Development Environment"*.

7.2.1 macOS ADB Configuration

To configure the ADB environment on a macOS system, connect the device to the computer system using a USB cable, open a terminal window, and execute the following command to restart the adb server:

```
$ adb kill-server
$ adb start-server
* daemon not running. starting it now on port 5037 *
* daemon started successfully *
```

Once the server is successfully running, execute the following command to verify that the device has been detected:

```
$ adb devices
List of devices attached
74CE000600000001        offline
```

If the device is listed as *offline*, go to the Android device and check for the dialog shown in Figure 7-3 seeking permission to *Allow USB debugging*. Enable the checkbox next to the option that reads *Always allow from this computer* before clicking OK.

[Figure 7-3 dialog: "Allow USB debugging? The computer's RSA key fingerprint is: 6E:BF:56:13:95:F8:9B:7E:12:CF:C5:67 [ ] Always allow from this computer   CANCEL   OK"]

Figure 7-3

Repeating the *adb devices* command should now list the device as being available:

```
List of devices attached
015d41d4454bf80c        device
```

If the device is not listed, try logging out and back into the macOS desktop and rebooting the system if the problem persists.

7.2.2 Windows ADB Configuration

The first step in configuring a Windows-based development system to connect to an Android device using ADB is to install the appropriate USB drivers on the system. The USB drivers to install will depend on the model of the Android Device. If you have a Google device such as a Pixel phone, installing and configuring the Google USB Driver package on your Windows system will be necessary. Detailed steps to achieve this are outlined on the following web page:

https://developer.android.com/sdk/win-usb.html

For Android devices not supported by the Google USB driver, it will be necessary to download the drivers provided by the device manufacturer. A listing of drivers, together with download and installation information, can be obtained online at:

https://developer.android.com/tools/extras/oem-usb.html

With the drivers installed and the device now being recognized as the correct device type, open a Command Prompt window and execute the following command:

```
adb devices
```

This command should output information about the connected device similar to the following:

```
List of devices attached
HT4CTJT01906        offline
```

If the device is listed as *offline* or *unauthorized*, go to the device display and check for the dialog shown in Figure 7-3 seeking permission to *Allow USB debugging*. Enable the checkbox next to the option that reads *Always allow from this computer* before clicking OK. Repeating the *adb devices* command should now list the device as being ready:

```
List of devices attached
HT4CTJT01906        device
```

If the device is not listed, execute the following commands to restart the ADB server:

```
adb kill-server
adb start-server
```

Testing Android Studio Apps on a Physical Android Device

If the device is still not listed, try executing the following command:

```
android update adb
```

Note that it may also be necessary to reboot the system.

7.2.3 Linux adb Configuration

For this chapter, we will again use Ubuntu Linux as a reference example in configuring adb on Linux to connect to a physical Android device for application testing.

Physical device testing on Ubuntu Linux requires the installation of a package named *android-tools-adb* which, in turn, requires the Android Studio user to be a member of the *plugdev* group. This is the default for user accounts on most Ubuntu versions and can be verified by running the *id* command. If the plugdev group is not listed, run the following command to add your account to the group:

```
sudo usermod -aG plugdev $LOGNAME
```

After the group membership requirement has been met, the *android-tools-adb* package can be installed by executing the following command:

```
sudo apt-get install android-tools-adb
```

Once the above changes have been made, reboot the Ubuntu system. Once the system has restarted, open a Terminal window, start the adb server, and check the list of attached devices:

```
$ adb start-server
* daemon not running. starting it now on port 5037 *
* daemon started successfully *
$ adb devices
List of devices attached
015d41d4454bf80c          offline
```

If the device is listed as *offline* or *unauthorized*, go to the Android device and check for the dialog shown in Figure 7-3 seeking permission to *Allow USB debugging*.

7.3 Resolving USB Connection Issues

If you are unable to successfully connect to the device using the above steps, display the run target menu (Figure 7-4) and select the *Troubleshoot Device Connections* option:

Figure 7-4

Testing Android Studio Apps on a Physical Android Device

The connection assistant will scan for devices and report problems and possible solutions.

7.4 Enabling Wireless Debugging on Android Devices

Follow steps 1 through 3 from section 7.2 above, this time enabling the Wireless Debugging option as shown in Figure 7-5:

Wireless debugging
Debug mode when Wi-Fi is connected

Figure 7-5

Next, tap the above Wireless debugging entry to display the screen shown in Figure 7-6:

Wireless debugging

Use wireless debugging

Device name
sdk_gphone64_arm64

IP address & Port
10.0.2.16:38159

Pair device with QR code
Pair new devices using QR code scanner

Pair device with pairing code
Pair new devices using six digit code

Figure 7-6

If your device has a camera, select *Pair device with QR code*, otherwise select the *Pair device with pairing code* option. Depending on your selection, the Settings app will either start a camera session or display a pairing code, as shown in Figure 7-7:

Pair with device
Wi-Fi pairing code
909814

IP address & Port
10.0.2.16:43967

Cancel

Figure 7-7

Testing Android Studio Apps on a Physical Android Device

With an option selected, return to Android Studio and select the *Pair Devices Using WiFi* option from the run target menu as illustrated in Figure 7-8:

Figure 7-8

In the pairing dialog, select either *Pair using QR code* or *Pair using pairing code* depending on your previous selection in the Settings app on the device:

Figure 7-9

Either scan the QR code using the Android device or enter the pairing code displayed on the device screen into the Android Studio dialog (Figure 7-10) to complete the pairing process:

Figure 7-10

Testing Android Studio Apps on a Physical Android Device

If the pairing process fails, try rebooting both the development system and the Android device and try again.

7.5 Testing the adb Connection

Assuming that the adb configuration has been successful on your chosen development platform, the next step is to try running the test application created in the chapter entitled *"Creating an Example Android App in Android Studio"* on the device. Launch Android Studio, open the AndroidSample project, and verify that the device appears in the device selection menu as highlighted in Figure 7-11:

Figure 7-11

Select the device from the list and click the run button to install and run the app.

7.6 Device Mirroring

Device mirroring allows you to run an app on a physical device while viewing the display within Android Studio's Running Devices tool window. In other words, although your app is running on a physical device, it appears within Android Studio in the same way as an AVD instance.

With a device connected to Android Studio, display the *Running Devices* tool window and click the *Device Mirror settings* link to display the Settings dialog. Within the Settings dialog, enable the mirroring of physical Android devices and click on *OK*. On returning to the main window, Android Studio will mirror the display of the physical device in the Running Devices tool window.

7.7 Summary

While the Android Virtual Device emulator provides an excellent testing environment, it is essential to remember that there is no real substitute for ensuring an application functions correctly on a physical Android device.

By default, however, the Android Studio environment is not configured to detect Android devices as a target testing device. It is necessary, therefore, to perform some steps to load applications directly onto an Android device from within the Android Studio development environment via a USB cable or over a WiFi network. The exact steps to achieve this goal differ depending on the development platform. In this chapter, we have covered those steps for Linux, macOS, and Windows-based platforms.

Chapter 8

8. The Basics of the Android Studio Code Editor

Developing applications for Android involves a considerable amount of programming work which, by definition, involves typing, reviewing, and modifying lines of code. Unsurprisingly, most of a developer's time spent using Android Studio will typically involve editing code within the editor window.

The modern code editor must go far beyond the basics of typing, deleting, cutting, and pasting. Today the usefulness of a code editor is generally gauged by factors such as the amount by which it reduces the typing required by the programmer, ease of navigation through large source code files, and the editor's ability to detect and highlight programming errors in real-time as the code is being written. As will become evident in this chapter, these are just a few areas in which the Android Studio editor excels.

While not an exhaustive overview of the features of the Android Studio editor, this chapter aims to provide a guide to the tool's key features. Experienced programmers will find that some of these features are common to most code editors today, while a number are unique to this editing environment.

8.1 The Android Studio Editor

The Android Studio editor appears in the center of the main window when a Java, Kotlin, XML, or other text-based file is selected for editing. Figure 8-1, for example, shows a typical editor session with a Java source code file loaded:

Figure 8-1

The Basics of the Android Studio Code Editor

The elements that comprise the editor window can be summarized as follows:

A – Document Tabs – Android Studio can hold multiple files open for editing at anytime. As each file is opened, it is assigned a document tab displaying the file name in the tab bar along the editor window's top edge. A small drop-down menu will appear in the far right-hand corner of the tab bar when there is insufficient room to display all of the tabs. Clicking on this menu will drop down a list of additional open files. A wavy red line underneath a file name in a tab indicates that the code in the file contains one or more errors that need to be addressed before the project can be compiled and run.

Switching between files is a matter of clicking on the corresponding tab or using the Alt-Left and Alt-Right keyboard shortcuts. Navigation between files may also be performed using the Switcher mechanism (accessible via the Ctrl-Tab keyboard shortcut).

To detach an editor panel from the Android Studio main window so that it appears in a separate window, click on the tab and drag it to an area on the desktop outside the main window. To return the editor to the main window, click on the file tab in the separated editor window and drag and drop it onto the original editor tab bar in the main window.

B – The Editor Gutter Area - The gutter area is used by the editor to display informational icons and controls. Some typical items in this gutter area are debugging breakpoint markers, controls to fold and unfold blocks of code, bookmarks, change markers, and line numbers. Line numbers are switched on by default but may be disabled by right-clicking in the gutter and selecting the *Appearance -> Show Line Numbers* menu option.

C – Code Structure Location - This bar at the bottom of the editor displays the cursor's current position as it relates to the overall structure of the code. In the following figure, for example, the bar indicates that the convertCurrency method is currently being edited and that this method is contained within the MainActivity class:

Figure 8-2

Double-clicking an element within the bar will move the cursor to the corresponding location within the code file. For example, double-clicking on the convertCurrency entry will move the cursor to the top of the convertCurrency method within the source code. Similarly, clicking on the MainActivity entry displays a list of available code navigation points for selection:

Figure 8-3

D – The Editor Area – The main area where the user reviews, enters, and edits the code. Later sections of this chapter will cover the key features of the editing area in detail.

E – The Validation and Marker Sidebar – Android Studio incorporates a feature called "on-the-fly code analysis". This essentially means that as you are typing code, the editor analyzes the code to check for warnings and syntax errors. The indicators at the top of the validation sidebar will update in real-time to indicate the number of errors and warnings found as code is added. Clicking on this indicator will display a popup containing a summary of the issues found with the code in the editor, as illustrated in Figure 8-4:

Figure 8-4

The up and down arrows move between the error locations within the code. A green check mark indicates that no warnings or errors have been detected.

The sidebar also displays markers at the locations where issues have been detected using the same color coding. Hovering the mouse pointer over a marker when the line of code is visible in the editor area will display a popup containing a description of the issue:

Figure 8-5

Hovering the mouse pointer over a marker for a line of code that is currently scrolled out of the viewing area of the editor will display a "lens" overlay containing the block of code where the problem is located (Figure 8-6) allowing it to be viewed without the necessity to scroll to that location in the editor:

Figure 8-6

It is also worth noting that the lens overlay is not limited to warnings and errors in the sidebar. Hovering over any part of the sidebar will result in a lens appearing containing the code present at that location within the source file.

F – The Status Bar – Though the status bar is part of the main window, as opposed to the editor, it does contain some information about the currently active editing session. This information includes the current position of the cursor in terms of lines and characters and the encoding format of the file (UTF-8, ASCII, etc.). Clicking on these values in the status bar allows the corresponding setting to be changed. For example, clicking on the line number displays the Go to Line:Column dialog. Use the *View -> Appearance -> Status Bar Widgets* menu option to add and remove widgets. For example, the Memory Indicator is a helpful widget if you are experiencing performance problems with Android Studio.

Having provided an overview of the elements that comprise the Android Studio editor, the remainder of this chapter will explore the key features of the editing environment in more detail.

The Basics of the Android Studio Code Editor

8.2 Splitting the Editor Window

By default, the editor will display a single panel showing the content of the currently selected file. A useful feature when working simultaneously with multiple source code files is the ability to split the editor into multiple panes. To split the editor, right-click on a file tab within the editor window and select either the Split Right or Split Down menu option. Figure 8-7, for example, shows the splitter in action with the editor split into three panels:

Figure 8-7

The orientation of a split panel may be changed at any time by right-clicking on the corresponding tab and selecting the Change Splitter Orientation menu option. Repeat these steps to unsplit a single panel, this time selecting the Unsplit option from the menu. All split panels may be removed by right-clicking on any tab and selecting the Unsplit All menu option.

Window splitting may be used to display different files or to provide multiple windows onto the same file, allowing different areas of the same file to be viewed and edited concurrently.

8.3 Code Completion

The Android Studio editor has a considerable amount of built-in knowledge of Java programming syntax and the classes and methods that make up the Android SDK, as well as knowledge of your own code base. As code is typed, the editor scans what is being typed and, where appropriate, makes suggestions with regard to what might be needed to complete a statement or reference. When the editor detects a completion suggestion, a panel containing a list of suggestions will appear. In Figure 8-8, for example, the editor is suggesting possibilities for the beginning of a String declaration:

```
public class MainActivity extends AppCompatActivity {

    Stri
    © String java.lang
    © StrictMath java.lang
    © StringBuffer java.lang
```

Figure 8-8

If none of the auto-completion suggestions are correct, keep typing, and the editor will continue to refine the suggestions where appropriate. To accept the topmost suggestion, press the Enter or Tab key on the keyboard. To select a different suggestion, use the arrow keys to move up and down the list, again using the Enter or Tab key to select the highlighted item.

Completion suggestions can be manually invoked using the Ctrl-Space keyboard sequence. This can be useful when changing a word or declaration in the editor. When the cursor is positioned over a word in the editor, that word will automatically highlight. Pressing Ctrl-Space will display a list of alternate suggestions. Press the Tab key to replace the current word with the highlighted item in the suggestion list.

In addition to the real-time auto-completion feature, the Android Studio editor also offers a Smart Completion system. Smart completion is invoked using the Shift-Ctrl-Space keyboard sequence and, when selected, will provide more detailed suggestions based on the current context of the code. Pressing the Shift-Ctrl-Space shortcut sequence a second time will provide more suggestions from a broader range of possibilities.

Code completion can be a matter of personal preference for many programmers. In recognition of this fact, Android Studio provides a high level of control over the auto-completion settings. These can be viewed and modified by opening the Settings dialog and choosing *Editor -> General -> Code Completion* from the settings panel, as shown in Figure 8-9:

Figure 8-9

The Basics of the Android Studio Code Editor

8.4 Statement Completion

Another form of auto-completion provided by the Android Studio editor is statement completion. This can be used to automatically fill out the parentheses and braces for items such as methods and loop statements. Statement completion is invoked using the *Shift-Ctrl-Enter* (*Shift-Cmd-Enter* on macOS) keyboard sequence. Consider, for example, the following code:

```
myMethod()
```

Having typed this code into the editor, triggering statement completion will cause the editor to add the braces to the method automatically:

```
myMethod() {

}
```

8.5 Parameter Information

It is also possible to ask the editor to provide information about the argument parameters a method accepts. With the cursor positioned between the brackets of a method call, the Ctrl-P (Cmd-P on macOS) keyboard sequence will display the parameters known to be accepted by that method, with the most likely suggestion highlighted in bold:

String format, Object... args

Locale l, String format, Object... args

no usages
String myButtonText = mystring.format()

Figure 8-10

8.6 Parameter Name Hints

The code editor may be configured to display parameter name hints within method calls. Figure 8-11, for example, highlights the parameter name hints within the calls to the *make()* and *setAction()* methods of the Snackbar class:

```
binding.fab.setOnClickListener(new View.OnClickListener() {
    @Override
    public void onClick(View view) {
        displayMessage("Fab clicked");
        Snackbar.make(view, text: "Replace with your own action", duration: Snackbar.LENGTH_LONG)
                .setAction( text: "My Action", actionOnClickListener).show();
    }
```

Figure 8-11

The settings for this mode may be configured by opening the Settings dialog and navigating to *Editor -> Inlay Hints -> Java* in the side panel. Turn on or off the Parameter names option on the resulting screen for your chosen programming language. To adjust the hint settings, click on the *Exclude list...* link and make any necessary adjustments.

The Basics of the Android Studio Code Editor

8.7 Code Generation

In addition to completing code as it is typed, the editor can, under certain conditions, also generate code for you. The list of available code generation options shown in Figure 8-12 can be accessed using the Alt-Insert (Cmd-N on macOS) keyboard shortcut when the cursor is at the location in the file where the code is to be generated.

Figure 8-12

For example, consider a situation where we want to be notified when an Activity in our project is about to be destroyed by the operating system. As outlined in a later chapter of this book, this can be achieved by overriding the *onStop()* lifecycle method of the Activity superclass. To have Android Studio generate a stub method for this, select the *Override Methods...* option from the code generation list and select the *onStop()* method from the resulting list of available methods:

Figure 8-13

77

The Basics of the Android Studio Code Editor

Having selected the method to override, clicking on OK will generate the stub method at the current cursor location in the Java source file as follows:

```
@Override
protected void onStop() {
    super.onStop();
}
```

8.8 Code Folding

Once a source code file reaches a certain size, even the most carefully formatted and well-organized code can become overwhelming and challenging to navigate. Android Studio takes the view that it is not always necessary to have the content of every code block visible at all times. Code navigation can be made easier by using the code folding feature of the Android Studio editor. Code folding is controlled using disclosure arrows that appear at the beginning of each code block in a source file when the mouse pointer hovers in the gutter area. Figure 8-14, for example, highlights the disclosure arrow for a method declaration that is not currently folded:

Figure 8-14

Clicking on this marker will fold the statement such that only the signature line is visible, as shown in Figure 8-15:

Figure 8-15

To unfold a collapsed section of code, click on the disclosure arrow in the editor gutter. To see the hidden code without unfolding it, hover the mouse pointer over the "{…}" indicator, as shown in Figure 8-16. The editor will then display the lens overlay containing the folded code block:

Figure 8-16

All of the code blocks in a file may be folded or unfolded using the Ctrl-Shift-Plus and Ctrl-Shift-Minus keyboard sequences (Cmd-Shift-Plus and Cmd-Shift-Minus on macOS).

The Basics of the Android Studio Code Editor

By default, the Android Studio editor will automatically fold some code when a source file is opened. To configure the conditions under which this happens, navigate to the *Editor -> General -> Code Folding* entry in the Settings dialog (Figure 8-17):

Figure 8-17

8.9 Quick Documentation Lookup

Context-sensitive Java and Android documentation can be accessed by placing the cursor over the declaration for which documentation is required and pressing the Ctrl-Q keyboard shortcut (Ctrl-J on macOS). This will display a popup containing the relevant reference documentation for the item. Figure 8-18, for example, shows the documentation for the Android FloatingActionButton class.

Figure 8-18

8.10 Code Reformatting

In general, the Android Studio editor will automatically format code in terms of indenting, spacing, and nesting of statements and code blocks as they are added. In situations where lines of code need to be reformatted (a common occurrence, for example, when cutting and pasting sample code from a website), the editor provides a

79

source code reformatting feature which, when selected, will automatically reformat code to match the prevailing code style.

Press the Ctrl-Alt-L (Cmd-Opt-L on macOS) keyboard shortcut sequence to reformat the source code. To display the Reformat Code dialog (Figure 8-19) use the Ctrl-Alt-Shift-L (Cmd-Opt-Shift-L on macOS). This dialog provides the option to reformat only the currently selected code, the entire source file currently active in the editor, or only code that has changed as a result of a source code control update:

Figure 8-19

The full range of code style preferences can be changed by opening the Settings dialog and choosing Code Style in the side panel to access a list of supported programming and markup languages. Selecting a language will provide access to a vast array of formatting style options, all of which may be modified from the Android Studio default to match your preferred code style. To configure the settings for the Rearrange code option in the above dialog, for example, unfold the Code Style section, select Java and, from the Java settings, select the Arrangement tab.

8.11 Finding Sample Code

The Android Studio editor provides a way to access sample code relating to the currently highlighted entry within the code listing. This feature can be helpful for learning how a particular Android class or method is used. To find sample code, highlight a method or class name in the editor, right-click on it, and select the *Find Sample Code* menu option. If sample code is available, the Find Sample Code panel will appear with a list of matching samples. Selecting a sample from the list will load the corresponding code into the right-hand panel.

8.12 Live Templates

As you write Android code, you will find that there are common constructs that are used frequently. For example, a common requirement is to display a popup message to the user using the Android Toast class. Live templates are a collection of common code constructs that can be entered into the editor by typing the initial characters followed by a special key (set to the Tab key by default) to insert template code. To experience this in action, type toast in the code editor followed by the Tab key, and Android Studio will insert the following code at the cursor position ready for editing:

```
Toast.makeText(, "", Toast.LENGTH_SHORT).show();
```

To list and edit existing templates, change the special key, or add your own templates, open the Settings dialog and select Live Templates from the Editor section of the left-hand navigation panel:

The Basics of the Android Studio Code Editor

Figure 8-20

Add, remove, duplicate, or reset templates using the buttons marked A in Figure 8-20 above. To modify a template, select it from the list (B) and change the settings in the panel marked C.

8.13 Summary

The Android Studio editor goes to great lengths to reduce the typing needed to write code and make that code easier to read and navigate. This chapter covered key editor features, including code completion, code generation, editor window splitting, code folding, reformatting, documentation lookup, and live templates.

Chapter 9

9. An Overview of the Android Architecture

So far, in this book, steps have been taken to set up an environment suitable for developing Android applications using Android Studio. An initial step has also been taken into the application development process by creating an Android Studio application project.

However, before delving further into the practical matters of Android application development, it is essential to understand some of the more abstract concepts of both the Android SDK and Android development in general. Gaining a clear understanding of these concepts now will provide a sound foundation on which to build further knowledge.

Starting with an overview of the Android architecture in this chapter and continuing in the following few chapters of this book, the goal is to provide a detailed overview of the fundamentals of Android development.

9.1 The Android Software Stack

Android is structured as a software stack comprising applications, an operating system, a runtime environment, middleware, services, and libraries. This architecture can best be represented visually, as Figure 9-1 outlines. Each layer of the stack, and the corresponding elements within each layer, are tightly integrated and carefully tuned to provide the optimal application development and execution environment for mobile devices. The remainder of this chapter will work through the different layers of the Android stack, starting at the bottom with the Linux Kernel.

Figure 9-1

9.2 The Linux Kernel

Positioned at the bottom of the Android software stack, the Linux Kernel provides a level of abstraction between the device hardware and the upper layers of the Android software stack. The kernel provides preemptive multitasking, low-level core system services such as memory, process, and power management, and a network stack and device drivers for hardware such as the device display, WiFi, and audio.

The original Linux kernel was developed in 1991 by Linus Torvalds. It was combined with a set of tools, utilities, and compilers developed by Richard Stallman at the Free Software Foundation to create a complete operating system called GNU/Linux. Various Linux distributions have been derived from these basic underpinnings, such as Ubuntu and Red Hat Enterprise Linux.

However, it is important to note that Android uses only the Linux kernel. That said, it is worth noting that the Linux kernel was originally developed for use in traditional desktop and server computer systems. In fact, Linux is now most widely deployed in mission-critical enterprise server environments. It is a testament to both the power of today's mobile devices and the efficiency and performance of the Linux kernel that we find this software at the heart of the Android software stack.

9.3 Android Runtime – ART

When an Android app is built within Android Studio, it is compiled into an intermediate bytecode format (DEX format). When the application is subsequently loaded onto the device, the Android Runtime (ART) uses a process referred to as Ahead-of-Time (AOT) compilation to translate the bytecode down to the native instructions required by the device processor. This format is known as Executable and Linkable Format (ELF).

Each time the application is subsequently launched, the ELF executable version is run, resulting in faster application performance and improved battery life.

This contrasts with the Just-in-Time (JIT) compilation approach used in older Android implementations, whereby the bytecode was translated within a virtual machine (VM) each time the application was launched.

9.4 Android Libraries

In addition to a set of standard Java development libraries (providing support for such general-purpose tasks as string handling, networking, and file manipulation), the Android development environment also includes the Android Libraries. These are a set of Java-based libraries that are specific to Android development. Examples of libraries in this category include the application framework libraries in addition to those that facilitate user interface building, graphics drawing, and database access.

A summary of some key core Android libraries available to the Android developer is as follows:

- **android.app** – Provides access to the application model and is the cornerstone of all Android applications.
- **android.content** – Facilitates content access, publishing, and messaging between applications and application components.
- **android.database** – Used to access data published by content providers and includes SQLite database management classes.
- **android.graphics** – A low-level 2D graphics drawing API including colors, points, filters, rectangles, and canvases.
- **android.hardware** – Presents an API providing access to hardware such as the accelerometer and light sensor.
- **android.opengl** – A Java interface to the OpenGL ES 3D graphics rendering API.

An Overview of the Android Architecture

- **android.os** – Provides applications with access to standard operating system services, including messages, system services, and inter-process communication.

- **android.media** – Provides classes to enable playback of audio and video.

- **android.net** – A set of APIs providing access to the network stack. Includes *android.net.wifi*, which provides access to the device's wireless stack.

- **android.print** – Includes a set of classes that enable content to be sent to configured printers from within Android applications.

- **android.provider** – A set of convenience classes that provide access to standard Android content provider databases such as those maintained by the calendar and contact applications.

- **android.text** – Used to render and manipulate text on a device display.

- **android.util** – A set of utility classes for performing tasks such as string and number conversion, XML handling and date and time manipulation.

- **android.view** – The fundamental building blocks of application user interfaces.

- **android.widget** - A rich collection of pre-built user interface components such as buttons, labels, list views, layout managers, radio buttons etc.

- **android.webkit** – A set of classes intended to allow web-browsing capabilities to be built into applications.

Having covered the Java-based libraries in the Android runtime, it is now time to turn our attention to the C/C++-based libraries in this layer of the Android software stack.

9.4.1 C/C++ Libraries

The Android runtime core libraries outlined in the preceding section are Java-based and provide the primary APIs for Android developers. It is important to note, however, that the core libraries do not perform much of the actual work and are, in fact, essentially Java "wrappers" around a set of C/C++-based libraries. When making calls, for example, to the *android.opengl* library to draw 3D graphics on the device display, the library ultimately makes calls to the *OpenGL ES* C++ library, which, in turn, works with the underlying Linux kernel to perform the drawing tasks.

C/C++ libraries are included to fulfill a broad and diverse range of functions, including 2D and 3D graphics drawing, Secure Sockets Layer (SSL) communication, SQLite database management, audio and video playback, bitmap and vector font rendering, display subsystem and graphic layer management and an implementation of the standard C system library (libc).

In practice, the typical Android application developer will access these libraries solely through the Java-based Android core library APIs. If direct access to these libraries is needed, this can be achieved using the Android Native Development Kit (NDK), the purpose of which is to call the native methods of non-Java or Kotlin programming languages (such as C and C++) from within Java code using the Java Native Interface (JNI).

9.5 Application Framework

The Application Framework is a set of services that collectively form the environment in which Android applications run and are managed. This framework implements the concept that Android applications are constructed from reusable, interchangeable, and replaceable components. This concept is taken a step further in that an application can also *publish* its capabilities along with any corresponding data so that other applications can find and reuse them.

An Overview of the Android Architecture

The Android framework includes the following key services:

- **Activity Manager** – Controls all aspects of the application lifecycle and activity stack.

- **Content Providers** – Allows applications to publish and share data with other applications.

- **Resource Manager** – Provides access to non-code embedded resources such as strings, color settings, and user interface layouts.

- **Notifications Manager** – Allows applications to display alerts and notifications to the user.

- **View System** – An extensible set of views used to create application user interfaces.

- **Package Manager** – The system by which applications can find information about other applications currently installed on the device.

- **Telephony Manager** – Provides information to the application about the telephony services available on the device, such as status and subscriber information.

- **Location Manager** – Provides access to the location services allowing an application to receive updates about location changes.

9.6 Applications

Located at the top of the Android software stack are the applications. These comprise the native applications provided with the particular Android implementation (for example, web browser and email applications) and the third-party applications installed by the user after purchasing the device.

9.7 Summary

A good Android development knowledge foundation requires an understanding of the overall architecture of Android. Android is implemented as a software stack architecture consisting of a Linux kernel, a runtime environment, corresponding libraries, an application framework, and a set of applications. Applications are predominantly written in Java or Kotlin and compiled into bytecode format within the Android Studio build environment. When the application is subsequently installed on a device, this bytecode is compiled down by the Android Runtime (ART) to the native format used by the CPU. The key goals of the Android architecture are performance and efficiency, both in application execution and in the implementation of reuse in application design.

Chapter 10

10. The Anatomy of an Android App

Regardless of your prior programming experiences, be it Windows, macOS, Linux, or even iOS based, the chances are good that Android development is quite unlike anything you have encountered before.

Therefore, this chapter's objective is to provide an understanding of the high-level concepts behind the architecture of Android applications. In doing so, we will explore in detail the various components that can be used to construct an application and the mechanisms that allow these to work together to create a cohesive application.

10.1 Android Activities

Those familiar with object-oriented programming languages such as Java, Kotlin, C++, or C# will be familiar with the concept of encapsulating elements of application functionality into classes that are then instantiated as objects and manipulated to create an application. This is still true since Android applications are written in Java and Kotlin. Android, however, also takes the concept of reusable components to a higher level.

Android applications are created by combining one or more components known as *Activities*. An activity is a single, standalone module of application functionality that usually correlates directly to a single user interface screen and its corresponding functionality. An appointment application might, for example, have an activity screen that displays appointments set up for the current day. An appointment application might have an activity screen that displays appointments set up for the current day. The application might also utilize a second activity consisting of a screen where the user may enter new appointments.

Activities are intended as fully reusable and interchangeable building blocks that can be shared amongst different applications. An existing email application may contain an activity for composing and sending an email message. A developer might be writing an application that is also required to send an email message. Rather than develop an email composition activity specifically for the new application, the developer can use the activity from the existing email application.

Activities are created as subclasses of the Android *Activity* class and must be implemented so as to be entirely independent of other activities in the application. In other words, a shared activity cannot rely on being called at a known point in a program flow (since other applications may use the activity in unanticipated ways), and one activity cannot directly call methods or access instance data of another activity. This, instead, is achieved using *Intents* and *Content Providers*.

By default, an activity cannot return results to the activity from which it was invoked. If this functionality is required, the activity must be started explicitly as a *sub-activity* of the originating activity.

10.2 Android Fragments

As described above, an activity typically represents a single user interface screen within an app. One option is constructing the activity using a single user interface layout and one corresponding activity class file. A better alternative, however, is to break the activity into different sections. Each section is a *fragment* consisting of part of the user interface layout and a matching class file (declared as a subclass of the Android Fragment class). In this scenario, an activity becomes a container into which one or more fragments are embedded.

Fragments provide an efficient alternative to having each user interface screen represented by a separate activity. Instead, an app can have a single activity that switches between fragments, each representing a different app screen.

10.3 Android Intents

Intents are the mechanism by which one activity can launch another and implement the flow through the activities that make up an application. Intents consist of a description of the operation to be performed and, optionally, the data on which it is to be performed.

Intents can be *explicit*, in that they request the launch of a specific activity by referencing the activity by class name, or *implicit* by stating either the type of action to be performed or providing data of a specific type on which the action is to be performed. In the case of implicit intents, the Android runtime will select the activity to launch that most closely matches the criteria specified by the Intent using a process referred to as *Intent Resolution*.

10.4 Broadcast Intents

Another type of Intent, the *Broadcast Intent*, is a system-wide intent sent out to all applications that have registered an "interested" *Broadcast Receiver*. The Android system, for example, will typically send out Broadcast Intents to indicate changes in device status, such as the completion of system start-up, connection of an external power source to the device, or the screen being turned on or off.

A Broadcast Intent can be *normal* (asynchronous) in that it is sent to all interested Broadcast Receivers at more or less the same time or *ordered* in that it is sent to one receiver at a time where it can be processed and then either aborted or allowed to be passed to the next Broadcast Receiver.

10.5 Broadcast Receivers

Broadcast Receivers are the mechanism by which applications can respond to Broadcast Intents. A Broadcast Receiver must be registered by an application and configured with an *Intent Filter* to indicate the types of broadcast it is interested in. When a matching intent is broadcast, the receiver will be invoked by the Android runtime regardless of whether the application that registered the receiver is currently running. The receiver then has 5 seconds to complete required tasks (such as launching a Service, making data updates, or issuing a notification to the user) before returning. Broadcast Receivers operate in the background and do not have a user interface.

10.6 Android Services

Android Services are processes that run in the background and do not have a user interface. They can be started and managed from activities, Broadcast Receivers, or other Services. Android Services are ideal for situations where an application needs to continue performing tasks but does not necessarily need a user interface to be visible to the user. Although Services lack a user interface, they can still notify the user of events using notifications and *toasts* (small notification messages that appear on the screen without interrupting the currently visible activity) and are also able to issue Intents.

The Android runtime gives Services a higher priority than many other processes and will only be terminated as a last resort by the system to free up resources. If the runtime needs to kill a Service, however, it will be automatically restarted as soon as adequate resources become available. A Service can reduce the risk of termination by declaring itself as needing to run in the *foreground*. This is achieved by making a call to *startForeground()*. This is only recommended for situations where termination would be detrimental to the user experience (for example, if the user is listening to audio being streamed by the Service).

Example situations where a Service might be a practical solution include, as previously mentioned, the streaming of audio that should continue when the application is no longer active or a stock market tracking application that needs to notify the user when a share hits a specified price.

10.7 Content Providers

Content Providers implement a mechanism for the sharing of data between applications. Any application can provide other applications with access to its underlying data by implementing a Content Provider, including the ability to add, remove and query the data (subject to permissions). Access to the data is provided via a Universal Resource Identifier (URI) defined by the Content Provider. Data can be shared as a file or an entire SQLite database.

The native Android applications include several standard Content Providers allowing applications to access data such as contacts and media files. The Content Providers currently available on an Android system may be located using a *Content Resolver*.

10.8 The Application Manifest

The Application Manifest file is the glue that pulls together the various elements that comprise an application. Within this XML-based file, the application outlines the activities, services, broadcast receivers, data providers, and permissions that comprise the complete application.

10.9 Application Resources

In addition to the manifest file and the Dex files containing the byte code, an Android application package typically contains a collection of *resource files*. These files contain resources such as strings, images, fonts, and colors that appear in the user interface, together with the XML representation of the user interface layouts. These files are stored in the */res* sub-directory of the application project's hierarchy by default.

10.10 Application Context

When an application is compiled, a class named *R* is created containing references to the application resources. The application manifest file and these resources combine to create what is known as the *Application Context*. This context, represented by the Android *Context* class, may be used in the application code to gain access to the application resources at runtime. In addition, a wide range of methods may be called on an application's context to gather information and change the application's environment at runtime.

10.11 Summary

A number of different elements can be brought together to create an Android application. In this chapter, we have provided a high-level overview of Activities, Fragments, Services, Intents, and Broadcast Receivers and an overview of the manifest file and application resources.

Maximum reuse and interoperability are promoted by creating individual, standalone functionality modules in the form of activities and intents while implementing content providers to achieve data sharing between applications.

While activities are focused on areas where the user interacts with the application (an activity essentially equating to a single user interface screen and often made up of one or more fragments), background processing is typically handled by Services and Broadcast Receivers.

The components that make up the application are outlined for the Android runtime system in a manifest file which, combined with the application's resources, represents the application's context.

Much has been covered in this chapter that is likely new to the average developer. Rest assured, however, that extensive exploration and practical use of these concepts will be made in subsequent chapters to ensure a solid knowledge foundation on which to build your own applications.

11. An Overview of Android View Binding

An essential part of developing Android apps involves the interaction between the code and the views that make up the user interface layouts. This chapter will look at the options available for gaining access to layout views in code, emphasizing an option known as view binding. Once the basics of view bindings have been covered, the chapter will outline how to convert the AndroidSample project to use this approach.

11.1 Find View by Id

As outlined in the chapter entitled *"The Anatomy of an Android Application"*, all of the resources that make up an application are compiled into a class named *R*. Amongst those resources are those that define layouts. Within the R class is a subclass named *layout*, which contains the layout resources, including the views that make up the user interface. Most apps will need to implement interaction between the code and these views, for example, when reading the value entered into the EditText view or changing the content displayed on a TextView.

Before the introduction of Android Studio 3.6, the most common option for gaining access to a view from within the app code involved writing code to manually find a view based on its id via the *findViewById()* method. For example:

```
TextView exampleView = findViewById(R.id.exampleView);
```

With the reference obtained, the view's properties can then be accessed. For example:

```
exampleView.setText("Hello");
```

While finding views by id is still a viable option, it has some limitations, the most significant disadvantage of *findViewById()* being that it is possible to obtain a reference to a view that has not yet been created within the layout, leading to a null pointer exception when an attempt is made to access the view's properties.

Since Android Studio 3.6, an alternative way of accessing views from the app code has been available in the form of *view binding*.

11.2 View Binding

When view binding is enabled in an app module, Android Studio automatically generates a binding class for each layout file. The layout views can be accessed from within the code using this binding class without using *findViewById()*.

The name of the binding class generated by Android Studio is based on the layout file name converted to so-called "camel case" with the word "Binding" appended to the end. For the *activity_main.xml* file, for example, the binding class will be called ActivityMainBinding.

Android Studio Giraffe is inconsistent in using view bindings within project templates. For example, the Empty Views Activity template used when we created the AndroidSample project does not use view bindings. The Basic Views Activity template, on the other hand, is implemented using view binding. If you use a template that does not use view binding, it is important to know how to add it to your project.

An Overview of Android View Binding

11.3 Converting the AndroidSample project

In the remainder of this chapter, we will practice migrating to view bindings by converting the AndroidSample project to use view binding instead of *findViewById()*.

Begin by launching Android Studio and opening the AndroidSample project created in the chapter entitled *"Creating an Example Android App in Android Studio"*.

11.4 Enabling View Binding

To use view binding, some changes must first be made to the *build.gradle.kts* file for each module in which view binding is needed. In the case of the AndroidSample project, this will require a slight change to the *Gradle Scripts -> build.gradle.kts (Module: app)* file. Load this file into the editor, locate the *android* section and add an entry to enable the *viewBinding* property as follows:

```
plugins {
    id("com.android.application")
}

android {

    buildFeatures {
        viewBinding = true
    }
.
.
```

Once this change has been made, click on the Sync Now link at the top of the editor panel, then use the Build menu to clean and rebuild the project to ensure the binding class is generated. The next step is to use the binding class within the code.

11.5 Using View Binding

The first step in this process is to "inflate" the view binding class to access the root view within the layout. This root view will then be used as the content view for the layout.

The logical place to perform these tasks is within the *onCreate()* method of the activity associated with the layout. A typical *onCreate()* method will read as follows:

```
@Override
protected void onCreate(Bundle savedInstanceState) {
    super.onCreate(savedInstanceState);
    setContentView(R.layout.activity_main);
}
```

To switch to using view binding, the view binding class will need to be imported and the class modified as follows. Note that since the layout file is named *activity_main.xml*, we can surmise that the binding class generated by Android Studio will be named ActivityMainBinding. Note that if you used a domain other than *com.example* when creating the project, the import statement below would need to be changed to reflect this:

.
.

~~import android.widget.EditText;~~
~~import android.widget.TextView;~~

An Overview of Android View Binding

```
.
.
import com.example.androidsample.databinding.ActivityMainBinding;
.
.
public class MainActivity extends AppCompatActivity {

    private ActivityMainBinding binding;
.
.
@Override
protected void onCreate(Bundle savedInstanceState) {
    super.onCreate(savedInstanceState);
    setContentView(R.layout.activity_main);
    binding = ActivityMainBinding.inflate(getLayoutInflater());
    View view = binding.getRoot();
    setContentView(view);
}
```

Now that we have a reference to the binding, we can access the views by name as follows:

```
public void convertCurrency(View view) {

    EditText dollarText = findViewById(R.id.dollarText);
    TextView textView = findViewById(R.id.textView);

    if (!binding.dollarText.getText().toString().equals("")) {

        Float dollarValue = Float.valueOf(
                    binding.dollarText.getText().toString());
        Float euroValue = dollarValue * 0.85F;
        binding.textView.setText(String.format(Locale.ENGLISH,"%.2f",
                                    euroValue));
    } else {
        binding.textView.setText(R.string.no_value_string);
    }
}
```

Compile and run the app and verify that the currency conversion process works as before.

11.6 Choosing an Option

Notwithstanding their failure to adopt view bindings in the Empty Views Activity project template, Google strongly recommends using view binding wherever possible. Therefore, view binding should be used when developing your own projects.

11.7 View Binding in the Book Examples

Any chapters in this book that rely on a project template that does not implement view binding will first be migrated. Instead of replicating the steps every time a migration needs to be performed, however, these chapters

An Overview of Android View Binding

will refer you back here to refresh your memory (don't worry, after a few chapters, the necessary changes will become second nature). To help with the process, the following section summarizes the migration steps more concisely.

11.8 Migrating a Project to View Binding

The process for converting a project module to use view binding involves the following steps:

1. Edit the module-level Gradle build script file listed in the Project tool window as *Gradle Scripts -> build.gradle.kts (Module :app)* where *<project name>* is the name of the project (for example AndroidSample).

2. Locate the *android* section of the file and add an entry to enable the *viewBinding* property as follows:

```
android {

    buildFeatures {
        viewBinding = true
    }
.
.
```

3. Click on the *Sync Now* link at the top of the editor to resynchronize the project with these new build settings.

4. Edit the *MainActivity.java* file and modify it to read as follows (where *<reverse domain>* represents the domain name used when the project was created and *<project name>* is replaced by the lowercase name of the project, for example, *androidsample*) and *<binding name>* is the name of the binding for the corresponding layout resource file (for example, the binding for *activity_main.xml* is ActivityMainBinding).

```
.
.
import android.view.View;

import com.<reverse domain>.<project name>.databinding.<binding name>;

public class MainActivity extends AppCompatActivity {

    private <binding name> binding;

    @Override
    protected void onCreate(Bundle savedInstanceState) {
        super.onCreate(savedInstanceState);
        setContentView(R.layout.activity_main);
        binding = <binding name>.inflate(getLayoutInflater());
        View view = binding.getRoot();
        setContentView(view);
    }
}
```

5. Access views by name as properties of the binding object.

11.9 Summary

Before the introduction of Android Studio 3.6, access to layout views from within the code of an app involved using the *findViewById()* method. An alternative is now available in the form of view bindings. View bindings consist of classes Android Studio automatically generates for each XML layout file. These classes contain bindings to each view in the corresponding layout, providing a safer option than the *findViewById()* method. However, as of Android Studio Giraffe, view bindings are not enabled by default in some project templates. Additional steps are required to enable and configure support within each project module manually.

Chapter 12

12. Understanding Android Application and Activity Lifecycles

In earlier chapters, we learned that Android applications run within processes and comprise multiple components in the form of activities, services, and broadcast receivers. This chapter aims to expand on this knowledge by looking at the lifecycle of applications and activities within the Android runtime system.

Regardless of the fanfare about how much memory and computing power resides in the mobile devices of today compared to the desktop systems of yesterday, it is important to keep in mind that these devices are still considered to be "resource constrained" by the standards of modern desktop and laptop-based systems, particularly in terms of memory. As such, a key responsibility of the Android system is to ensure that these limited resources are managed effectively and that the operating system and the applications running on it remain responsive to the user at all times. To achieve this, Android is given complete control over the lifecycle and state of the processes in which the applications run and the individual components that comprise those applications.

An important factor in developing Android applications, therefore, is to understand Android's application and activity lifecycle management models of Android, and how an application can react to the state changes likely to be imposed upon it during its execution lifetime.

12.1 Android Applications and Resource Management

The operating system views each running Android application as a separate process. If the system identifies that resources on the device are reaching capacity, it will take steps to terminate processes to free up memory.

When determining which process to terminate to free up memory, the system considers both the *priority* and *state* of all currently running processes, combining these factors to create what is referred to by Google as an *importance hierarchy*. Processes are then terminated, starting with the lowest priority and working up the hierarchy until sufficient resources have been liberated for the system to function.

12.2 Android Process States

Processes host applications, and applications are made up of components. Within an Android system, the current state of a process is defined by the highest-ranking active component within the application it hosts. As outlined in Figure 12-1, a process can be in one of the following five states at any given time:

Understanding Android Application and Activity Lifecycles

Figure 12-1

12.2.1 Foreground Process

These processes are assigned the highest level of priority. At any one time, there are unlikely to be more than one or two foreground processes active, which are usually the last to be terminated by the system. A process must meet one or more of the following criteria to qualify for foreground status:

- Hosts an activity with which the user is currently interacting.
- Hosts a Service connected to the activity with which the user is interacting.
- Hosts a Service that has indicated, via a call to *startForeground()*, that termination would disrupt the user experience.
- Hosts a Service executing either its *onCreate()*, *onResume()*, or *onStart()* callbacks.
- Hosts a Broadcast Receiver that is currently executing its *onReceive()* method.

12.2.2 Visible Process

A process containing an activity that is visible to the user but is not the activity with which the user is interacting is classified as a "visible process". This is typically the case when an activity in the process is visible to the user, but another activity, such as a partial screen or dialog, is in the foreground. A process is also eligible for visible status if it hosts a Service that is, itself, bound to a visible or foreground activity.

12.2.3 Service Process

Processes that contain a Service that has already been started and is currently executing.

12.2.4 Background Process

A process that contains one or more activities that are not currently visible to the user and does not host a Service that qualifies for *Service Process* status. Processes that fall into this category are at high risk of termination if additional memory needs to be freed for higher-priority processes. Android maintains a dynamic list of background processes, terminating processes in chronological order such that processes that were the least recently in the foreground are killed first.

12.2.5 Empty Process

Empty processes no longer contain active applications and are held in memory, ready to serve as hosts for newly launched applications. This is analogous to keeping the doors open and the engine running on a bus in anticipation of passengers arriving. Such processes are considered the lowest priority and are the first to be killed to free up resources.

12.3 Inter-Process Dependencies

Determining the highest priority process is more complex than outlined in the preceding section because processes can often be interdependent. As such, when determining the priority of a process, the Android system will also consider whether the process is in some way serving another process of higher priority (for example, a service process acting as the content provider for a foreground process). As a basic rule, the Android documentation states that a process can never be ranked lower than another process that it is currently serving.

12.4 The Activity Lifecycle

As we have previously determined, the state of an Android process is primarily determined by the status of the activities and components that make up the application it hosts. It is important to understand, therefore, that these activities also transition through different states during the execution lifetime of an application. The current state of an activity is determined, in part, by its position in something called the Activity Stack.

12.5 The Activity Stack

The runtime system maintains an *Activity Stack* for each application running on an Android device. When an application is launched, the first of the application's activities to be started is placed onto the stack. When a second activity is started, it is placed on the top of the stack, and the previous activity is *pushed* down. The activity at the top of the stack is called the *active* (or *running*) activity. When the active activity exits, it is *popped* off the stack by the runtime and the activity located immediately beneath it in the stack becomes the current active activity. For example, the activity at the top of the stack might exit because the task for which it is responsible has been completed. Alternatively, the user may have selected a "Back" button on the screen to return to the previous activity, causing the current activity to be popped off the stack by the runtime system and destroyed. A visual representation of the Android Activity Stack is illustrated in Figure 12-2.

As shown in the diagram, new activities are pushed onto the top of the stack when they are started. The current active activity is located at the top of the stack until it is either pushed down the stack by a new activity or popped off the stack when it exits or the user navigates to the previous activity. If resources become constrained, the runtime will kill activities, starting with those at the bottom of the stack.

The Activity Stack is what is referred to in programming terminology as a Last-In-First-Out (LIFO) stack in that the last item to be pushed onto the stack is the first to be popped off.

Figure 12-2

12.6 Activity States

An activity can be in one of several states during the course of its execution within an application:

- **Active / Running** – The activity is at the top of the Activity Stack, is the foreground task visible on the device screen, has focus, and is currently interacting with the user. This is the least likely activity to be terminated in the event of a resource shortage.

- **Paused** – The activity is visible to the user but does not currently have focus (typically because the current *active* activity partially obscures this activity). Paused activities are held in memory, remain attached to the window manager, retain all state information, and can quickly be restored to active status when moved to the top of the Activity Stack.

- **Stopped** – The activity is currently not visible to the user (in other words, it is obscured on the device display by other activities). As with paused activities, it retains all state and member information but is at higher risk of termination in low-memory situations.

- **Killed** – The runtime system has terminated the activity to free up memory and is no longer present on the Activity Stack. Such activities must be restarted if required by the application.

12.7 Configuration Changes

So far in this chapter, we have looked at two causes for the change in the state of an Android activity, namely the movement of an activity between the foreground and background and the termination of an activity by the runtime system to free up memory. In fact, there is a third scenario in which the state of an activity can dramatically change, which involves a change to the device configuration.

By default, any configuration change that impacts the appearance of an activity (such as rotating the orientation of the device between portrait and landscape or changing a system font setting) will cause the activity to be destroyed and recreated. The reasoning behind this is that such changes affect resources such as the layout of the user interface, and destroying and recreating impacted activities is the quickest way for an activity to respond to the configuration change. It is, however, possible to configure an activity so that the system does not restart it in response to specific configuration changes.

12.8 Handling State Change

It should be clear from this chapter that an application and, by definition, the components contained therein will transition through many states during its lifespan. Of particular importance is the fact that these state changes (up to and including complete termination) are imposed upon the application by the Android runtime subject to the user's actions and the availability of resources on the device.

In practice, however, these state changes are not imposed entirely without notice, and an application will, in most circumstances, be notified by the runtime system of the changes and given the opportunity to react accordingly. This will typically involve saving or restoring both internal data structures and user interface state, thereby allowing the user to switch seamlessly between applications and providing at least the appearance of multiple concurrently running applications.

Android provides two ways to handle the changes to the lifecycle states of the objects within an app. One approach involves responding to state change method calls from the operating system and is covered in detail in the next chapter entitled *"Handling Android Activity State Changes"*.

A new approach that Google recommends involves the lifecycle classes included with the Jetpack Android Architecture components, introduced in *"Modern Android App Architecture with Jetpack"* and explained in more detail in the chapter entitled *"Working with Android Lifecycle-Aware Components"*.

12.9 Summary

Mobile devices are typically considered to be resource constrained, particularly in terms of onboard memory capacity. Consequently, a prime responsibility of the Android operating system is to ensure that applications, and the operating system in general, remain responsive to the user.

Applications are hosted on Android within processes. Each application, in turn, comprises components in the form of activities and Services.

The Android runtime system has the power to terminate both processes and individual activities to free up memory. Process state is considered by the runtime system when deciding whether a process is a suitable candidate for termination. The state of a process largely depends upon the status of the activities hosted by that process.

The key message of this chapter is that an application moves through various states during its execution lifespan and has very little control over its destiny within the Android runtime environment. Those processes and activities not directly interacting with the user run a higher risk of termination by the runtime system. An essential element of Android application development, therefore, involves the ability of an application to respond to state change notifications from the operating system.

13. Handling Android Activity State Changes

Based on the information outlined in the chapter entitled *"Understanding Android Application and Activity Lifecycles"* it is now evident that the activities and fragments that make up an application pass through various different states during the application's lifespan. The Android runtime system imposes the change from one state to the other and is, therefore, largely beyond the control of the activity itself. That does not, however, mean that the app cannot react to those changes and take appropriate actions.

The primary objective of this chapter is to provide a high-level overview of how an activity may be notified of a state change and outline the areas where it is advisable to save or restore state information. Having covered this information, the chapter will touch briefly on *activity lifetimes*.

13.1 New vs. Old Lifecycle Techniques

Until recently, there was a standard way to build lifecycle awareness into an app. This approach is covered in this chapter and involves implementing a set of methods (one for each lifecycle state) within an activity or fragment instance that the operating system calls when the lifecycle status of that object changes. This approach has remained unchanged since the early years of the Android operating system, and while still a viable option today, it does have some limitations, which will be explained later in this chapter.

With the introduction of the lifecycle classes with the Jetpack Android Architecture Components, a better approach to lifecycle handling is now available. This modern approach to lifecycle management (together with the Jetpack components and architecture guidelines) will be covered in detail in later chapters. It is still essential, however, to understand the traditional lifecycle methods for a couple of reasons. First, as an Android developer, you will not be completely insulated from the traditional lifecycle methods and will still use some of them. More importantly, understanding the older way of handling lifecycles will provide a sound foundation for learning the new approach later in the book.

13.2 The Activity and Fragment Classes

With few exceptions, an application's activities and fragments are created as subclasses of the Android AppCompatActivity class and Fragment classes, respectively.

Consider, for example, the *AndroidSample* project created in *"Creating an Example Android App in Android Studio"* and subsequently converted to use view binding. Load this project into the Android Studio environment and locate the *MainActivity.java* file (located in *app -> java -> <your domain> -> androidsample*). Having located the file, double-click on it to load it into the editor, where it should read as follows:

```
package com.example.androidsample;

import androidx.appcompat.app.AppCompatActivity;
import android.view.View;
import android.os.Bundle;

import java.util.Locale;
```

```
import com.example.androidsample.databinding.ActivityMainBinding;

public class MainActivity extends AppCompatActivity {

    private ActivityMainBinding binding;

    @Override
    protected void onCreate(Bundle savedInstanceState) {
        super.onCreate(savedInstanceState);
        binding = ActivityMainBinding.inflate(getLayoutInflater());
        View view = binding.getRoot();
        setContentView(view);
    }

    public void convertCurrency(View view) {

        if (!binding.dollarText.getText().toString().equals("")) {

            float dollarValue = Float.parseFloat(
                    binding.dollarText.getText().toString());
            float euroValue = dollarValue * 0.85F;
            binding.textView.setText(
                    String.format(Locale.ENGLISH,"%.2f", euroValue));
        } else {
            binding.textView.setText(R.string.no_value_string);
        }
    }
}
```

When the project was created, we instructed Android Studio also to create an initial activity named *MainActivity.java* As is evident from the above code, the MainActivity class is a subclass of the AppCompatActivity class.

A review of the reference documentation for the AppCompatActivity class would reveal that it is itself a subclass of the Activity class. This can be verified within the Android Studio editor using the *Hierarchy* tool window. With the *MainActivity.java* file loaded into the editor, click on AppCompatActivity in the *class* declaration line and press the *Ctrl-H* keyboard shortcut. The hierarchy tool window will subsequently appear, displaying the class hierarchy for the selected class. As illustrated in Figure 13-1, AppCompatActivity is subclassed from the FragmentActivity class, which is itself ultimately a subclass of the Activity class:

Figure 13-1

The Activity and Fragment classes contain a range of methods intended to be called by the Android runtime to notify the object when its state is changing. For this chapter, we will refer to these as the *lifecycle methods*. An activity or fragment class needs to *override* these methods and implement the necessary functionality to react accordingly to state changes.

One such method is named *onCreate()*, and, turning once again to the above code fragment, we can see that this method has already been overridden and implemented for us in the *MainActivity* class. In a later section, we will explore *onCreate()* and the other relevant lifecycle methods of the Activity and Fragment classes.

13.3 Dynamic State vs. Persistent State

A key objective of lifecycle management is ensuring that the state of the activity is saved and restored at appropriate times. When talking about *state* in this context, we mean the data currently being held within the activity and the appearance of the user interface. The activity might, for example, maintain a data model in memory that needs to be saved to a database, content provider, or file. Because it persists from one invocation of the application to another, such state information is referred to as the *persistent state*.

The appearance of the user interface (such as text entered into a text field but not yet committed to the application's internal data model) is referred to as the *dynamic state* since it is typically only retained during a single invocation of the application (and also referred to as *user interface state* or *instance state*).

Understanding the differences between these two states is important because the ways they are saved and the reasons for doing so differ.

The purpose of saving the persistent state is to avoid data loss that may result from an activity being killed by the runtime system while in the background. On the other hand, the dynamic state is saved and restored for slightly more complex reasons.

Consider, for example, that an application contains an activity (which we will refer to as *Activity A*) containing a text field and some radio buttons. During the course of using the application, the user enters some text into the text field and makes a selection from the radio buttons. However, before performing an action to save these changes, the user switches to another activity, causing *Activity A* to be pushed down the Activity Stack and placed into the background. After some time, the runtime system ascertains that memory is low and kills Activity A to free up resources. However, as far as the user is concerned, *Activity A* was placed in the background and is ready to be moved to the foreground at any time. On returning *Activity A* to the foreground, the user would reasonably expect the entered text and radio button selections to have been retained. In this scenario, however, a new instance of *Activity A* will have been created, and if the dynamic state is not saved and restored, the previous user input is lost.

Therefore, the primary purpose of saving dynamic state is to give the perception of seamless switching between foreground and background activities, regardless of the fact that activities may have been killed and restarted without the user's knowledge.

The mechanisms for saving persistent and dynamic states will become more apparent in the following sections of this chapter.

13.4 The Android Lifecycle Methods

As previously explained, the Activity and Fragment classes contain several lifecycle methods which act as event handlers when the state of an instance changes. The primary methods supported by the Android Activity and Fragment class are as follows:

- **onCreate(Bundle savedInstanceState)** – The method called when the activity is first created and the ideal location for most initialization tasks to be performed. The method is passed an argument in the form of a *Bundle* object that may contain dynamic state information (typically relating to the state of the user interface) from a prior invocation of the activity.

- **onRestart()** – Called when the activity is about to restart after having previously been stopped by the runtime system.

- **onStart()** – Always called immediately after the call to the *onCreate()* or *onRestart()* methods. This method indicates to the activity that it is about to become visible to the user. This call will be followed by a call to *onResume()* if the activity moves to the top of the activity stack, or *onStop()* if it is pushed down the stack by another activity.

- **onResume()** – Indicates that the activity is now at the top of the activity stack and is the activity with which the user is currently interacting.

- **onPause()** – Indicates that a previous activity is about to become the foreground activity. This call will be followed by a call to either the *onResume()* or *onStop()* method, depending on whether the activity moves back to the foreground or becomes invisible to the user. Steps may be taken within this method to store *persistent state* information not yet saved by the app. To avoid delays in switching between activities, time-consuming operations such as storing data to a database or performing network operations should be avoided within this method. This method should also ensure that any CPU-intensive tasks, such as animation, are stopped.

- **onStop()** – The activity is no longer visible to the user. The two possible scenarios following this call are a call to *onRestart()* if the activity moves to the foreground again or *onDestroy()* if the activity is terminated.

- **onDestroy()** – The activity is about to be destroyed, either voluntarily because the activity has completed its tasks and has called the *finish()* method or because the runtime is terminating it either to release memory or due to a configuration change (such as the orientation of the device changing). It is important to note that a call will not always be made to *onDestroy()* when an activity is terminated.

- **onConfigurationChanged()** – Called when a configuration change occurs for which the activity has indicated it is not to be restarted. The method is passed a Configuration object outlining the new device configuration, and it is then the responsibility of the activity to react to the change.

The following lifecycle methods only apply to the Fragment class:

- **onAttach()** - Called when the fragment is assigned to an activity.

- **onCreateView()** - Called to create and return the fragment's user interface layout view hierarchy.

- **onViewCreated()** - Called after *onCreateView()* returns.

- **onViewStatusRestored()** - The fragment's saved view hierarchy has been restored.

In addition to the lifecycle methods outlined above, there are two methods intended specifically for saving and restoring the *dynamic state* of an activity:

- **onRestoreInstanceState(Bundle savedInstanceState)** – This method is called immediately after a call to the *onStart()* method if the activity restarts from a previous invocation in which the state was saved. As with *onCreate()*, this method is passed a Bundle object containing the previous state data. This method is typically used when it makes more sense to restore a previous state after the initialization of the activity has been performed in *onCreate()* and *onStart()*.

- **onSaveInstanceState(Bundle outState)** - Called before an activity is destroyed so that the current *dynamic state* (usually relating to the user interface) can be saved. The method is passed the Bundle object into which the state should be saved and which is subsequently passed through to the *onCreate()* and *onRestoreInstanceState()* methods when the activity is restarted. Note that this method is only called when the runtime ascertains that dynamic state needs to be saved.

When overriding the above methods, it is important to remember that, except for *onRestoreInstanceState()* and *onSaveInstanceState()*, the method implementation must include a call to the corresponding method in the superclass. For example, the following method overrides the *onRestart()* method but also includes a call to the superclass instance of the method:

```
protected void onRestart() {
      super.onRestart();
      Log.i(TAG, "onRestart");
}
```

Failure to make this superclass call in method overrides will result in the runtime throwing an exception during execution. While calls to the superclass in the *onRestoreInstanceState()* and *onSaveInstanceState()* methods are optional (they can, for example, be omitted when implementing custom save and restoration behavior) there are considerable benefits to using them, a subject that will be covered in the chapter entitled *"Saving and Restoring the State of an Android Activity"*.

13.5 Lifetimes

The final topic to be covered involves an outline of the *entire*, *visible*, and *foreground* lifetimes through which an activity or fragment will transition during execution:

- **Entire Lifetime** – The term "entire lifetime" is used to describe everything that takes place between the initial call to the *onCreate()* method and the call to *onDestroy()* before the object terminates.

- **Visible Lifetime** – Covers the periods of execution between the call to *onStart()* and *onStop()*. During this period, the activity or fragment is visible to the user though it may not be the object with which the user is currently interacting.

- **Foreground Lifetime** – Refers to the periods of execution between calls to the *onResume()* and *onPause()* methods.

It is important to note that an activity or fragment may pass through the *foreground* and *visible* lifetimes multiple times during the course of the *entire* lifetime.

The concepts of lifetimes and lifecycle methods are illustrated in Figure 13-2:

Figure 13-2

13.6 Foldable Devices and Multi-Resume

As discussed previously, an activity is considered to be in the resumed state when it has moved to the foreground and is the activity with which the user is currently interacting. On standard devices, an app can have one activity in the resumed state at any one time and all other activities are likely to be in the paused or stopped state.

For some time now, Android has included multi-window support, allowing multiple activities to appear simultaneously in either split-screen or freeform configurations. Although initially used primarily on large-screen tablet devices, this feature is likely to become more popular with the introduction of foldable devices.

On devices running Android 10 and on which multi-window support is enabled (as will be the case for most foldable devices), it will be possible for multiple app activities to be in the resumed state at the same time (a concept referred to as *multi-resume*) allowing those visible activities to continue functioning (for example streaming content or updating visual data) even when another activity currently has focus. Although multiple activities can be in the resumed state, only one of these activities will be considered the *topmost resumed activity* (in other words, the activity with which the user most recently interacted).

An activity can be notified that it has gained or lost the topmost resumed status by implementing the *onTopResumedActivityChanged()* callback method.

13.7 Disabling Configuration Change Restarts

As previously outlined, an activity may indicate that it is not to be restarted in the event of certain configuration changes. This is achieved by adding an *android:configChanges* directive to the activity element within the project manifest file. The following manifest file excerpt, for example, indicates that the activity should not be restarted in the event of configuration changes relating to orientation or device-wide font size:

```
<activity android:name=".MainActivity"
          android:configChanges="orientation|fontScale"
```

```
android:label="@string/app_name">
```

13.8 Lifecycle Method Limitations

As discussed at the start of this chapter, lifecycle methods have been in use for many years and, until recently, were the only mechanism available for handling lifecycle state changes for activities and fragments. There are, however, areas for improvement in this approach.

One issue with the lifecycle methods is that they do not provide an easy way for an activity or fragment to discover its current lifecycle state at any given point during app execution. Instead, the object must track the state internally or wait for the next lifecycle method call.

Also, the methods do not provide a simple way for one object to observe the lifecycle state changes of other objects within an app. This is a serious consideration since a lifecycle state change in a given activity or fragment can impact many other objects within an app.

The lifecycle methods are also only available on subclasses of the Fragment and Activity classes. Therefore, it is impossible to build custom classes that are genuinely lifecycle aware.

Finally, the lifecycle methods result in most lifecycle handling code being written within the activity or fragment, which can lead to complex and error-prone code. Ideally, much of this code should reside in the other classes impacted by the state change. For example, an app that streams video might include a class designed specifically to manage the incoming stream. If the app needs to pause the stream when the main activity is stopped, the code to do so should reside in the streaming class, not the main activity.

All these problems and more are resolved using lifecycle-aware components, a topic that will be covered starting with the chapter entitled *"Modern Android App Architecture with Jetpack"*.

13.9 Summary

All activities are derived from the Android Activity class, which, in turn, contains several lifecycle methods that are designed to be called by the runtime system when the state of an activity changes. Similarly, the Fragment class contains several comparable methods. By overriding these methods, activities and fragments can respond to state changes and, where necessary, take steps to save and restore the current state of the activity and the application. Lifecycle state can be thought of as taking two forms. The persistent state refers to data that needs to be stored between application invocations (for example, to a file or database). Dynamic state, on the other hand, relates instead to the current appearance of the user interface.

Although lifecycle methods have some limitations that can be avoided using lifecycle-aware components, understanding these methods is essential to fully understand the new approaches to lifecycle management covered later in this book.

In this chapter, we have highlighted the lifecycle methods available to activities and covered the concept of activity lifetimes. In the next chapter, entitled *"Android Activity State Changes by Example"*, we will implement an example application that puts much of this theory into practice.

14. Android Activity State Changes by Example

The previous chapters have discussed in detail the different states and lifecycles of the activities comprising an Android application. In this chapter, we will put the theory of handling activity state changes into practice by creating an example application. The purpose of this example application is to provide a real-world demonstration of an activity as it passes through various states within the Android runtime. In the next chapter, entitled *"Saving and Restoring the State of an Android Activity"*, the example project constructed in this chapter will be extended to demonstrate the saving and restoration of dynamic activity state.

14.1 Creating the State Change Example Project

The first step in this exercise is to create a new project. Launch Android Studio and, if necessary, close any currently open projects using the *File -> Close Project* menu option so that the Welcome screen appears.

Select the *New Project* option from the welcome screen and, within the resulting new project dialog, choose the Empty Views Activity template before clicking on the Next button.

Enter StateChange into the Name field and specify *com.ebookfrenzy.statechange* as the package name. Before clicking on the Finish button, change the Minimum API level setting to API 26: Android 8.0 (Oreo) and the Language menu to Java. Upon completing the project creation process, the *StateChange* project should be listed in the Project tool window located along the left-hand edge of the Android Studio main window. Use the steps outlined in section 11.8 Migrating a Project to View Binding to convert the project to use view binding.

The next action to take involves the design of the user interface for the activity. This is stored in a file named *activity_main.xml* which should already be loaded into the Layout Editor tool. If it is not, navigate to it in the Project tool window where it can be found in the *app -> res -> layout* folder. Once located, double-clicking on the file will load it into the Android Studio Layout Editor tool.

Figure 14-1

14.2 Designing the User Interface

With the user interface layout loaded into the Layout Editor tool, it is time to design the user interface for the example application. Instead of the "Hello World!" TextView currently in the user interface design, the activity requires an EditText view. Select the TextView object in the Component Tree panel and press the Delete key on the keyboard to remove it from the design.

From the Palette located on the left side of the Layout Editor, select the *Text* category and, from the list of text components, click and drag a *Plain Text* component over to the layout canvas. Move the component to the center of the display so that the center guidelines appear and drop it into place so that the layout resembles that of Figure 14-2.

Figure 14-2

When using the EditText widget, it is necessary to specify an *input type* for the view. This defines the type of text or data the user will enter. For example, if the input type is set to *Phone*, the user will be restricted to entering numerical digits into the view. Alternatively, if the input type is set to *TextCapCharacters,* the input will default to upper-case characters. Input type settings may also be combined.

For this example, we will use the default input type to support general text input. To choose a different setting in the future, select the EditText widget in the layout and locate the inputType entry within the Attributes tool window. Next, click the flag icon to the left of the current setting to open the list of options, as shown in Figure 14-3 below. The Type menu provides options to restrict the input to text, numbers, dates and times, and phone numbers. The Variations menu provides additional options for the currently selected input type. For example, a variation is available for the text input type for email addresses as input.

Once a type and variation have been chosen, the input type may be customized further using the list of flag checkboxes:

Android Activity State Changes by Example

[Figure: Attributes panel showing EditText properties with Type: text, Variation: text, various Flags checkboxes (textAutoComplete, textAutoCorrect, textCapCharacters, textCapSentences, textCapWords, textEnableTextConversio..., textImeMultiLine, textMultiLine, textNoSuggestions), inputType: text, text: Name]

Figure 14-3

Remaining in the Attributes tool window, change the view's id to *editText* and click on the Refactor button in the resulting dialog.

By default, the EditText displays text which reads "Name". Remaining within the Attributes panel, delete this from the *text* property field so that the view is blank within the layout.

Before continuing, click the *Infer Constraints* button in the layout editor toolbar to add any missing constraints.

14.3 Overriding the Activity Lifecycle Methods

At this point, the project contains a single activity named *MainActivity*, derived from the Android *AppCompatActivity* class. The source code for this activity is contained within the *MainActivity.java* file, which should already be open in an editor session and represented by a tab in the editor tab bar. If the file is no longer open, navigate to it in the Project tool window panel (*app -> java -> com.ebookfrenzy.statechange -> MainActivity*) and double-click on it to load the file into the editor.

So far, the only lifecycle method overridden by the activity is the *onCreate()* method which has been implemented to call the superclass instance of the method before setting up the user interface for the activity. We will now modify this method to output a diagnostic message in the Android Studio Logcat panel each time it executes. For this, we will use the *Log* class, which requires that we import *android.util.Log* and declare a tag that will enable us to filter these messages in the log output:

```
package com.ebookfrenzy.statechange;
    .
    .
import android.util.Log;
import androidx.annotation.NonNull;
import android.view.View;

public class MainActivity extends AppCompatActivity {
```

113

Android Activity State Changes by Example

```java
    private ActivityMainBinding binding;
    private static final String TAG = "StateChange";

    @Override
    protected void onCreate(Bundle savedInstanceState) {
        super.onCreate(savedInstanceState);
        binding = ActivityMainBinding.inflate(getLayoutInflater());
        View view = binding.getRoot();
        setContentView(view);

        Log.i(TAG, "onCreate");
    }
}
```

The next task is to override more methods, each containing a corresponding log call. These override methods may be added manually or generated using the *Alt-Insert* keyboard shortcut as outlined in the chapter entitled *"The Basics of the Android Studio Code Editor"*. Note that the Log calls will still need to be added manually if the methods are being auto-generated:

```java
@Override
protected void onStart() {
    super.onStart();
    Log.i(TAG, "onStart");
}

@Override
protected void onResume() {
    super.onResume();
    Log.i(TAG, "onResume");
}

@Override
protected void onPause() {
    super.onPause();
    Log.i(TAG, "onPause");
}

@Override
protected void onStop() {
    super.onStop();
    Log.i(TAG, "onStop");
}

@Override
protected void onRestart() {
    super.onRestart();
```

```
        Log.i(TAG, "onRestart");
}

@Override
protected void onDestroy() {
    super.onDestroy();
    Log.i(TAG, "onDestroy");
}

@Override
protected void onSaveInstanceState(@NonNull Bundle outState) {
    super.onSaveInstanceState(outState);
    Log.i(TAG, "onSaveInstanceState");
}

@Override
protected void onRestoreInstanceState(@NonNull Bundle savedInstanceState) {
    super.onRestoreInstanceState(savedInstanceState);
    Log.i(TAG, "onRestoreInstanceState");
}
```

14.4 Filtering the Logcat Panel

The purpose of the code added to the overridden methods in *MainActivity.java* is to output logging information to the *Logcat* tool window, which is displayed using the button shown in Figure 14-4:

Figure 14-4

The Logcat tool window can be configured to display all events relating to the device or emulator session or restricted to those events that relate to the currently selected app. The output can also be restricted to only those log events that match a specified filter.

When displayed while the current app is running, the Logcat tool window will appear as shown in Figure 14-5 below:

Android Activity State Changes by Example

Figure 14-5

The menu marked A in the above figure allows you to select the device or emulator for which log output will be displayed. This output appears in the output panel marked C. The log output can be filtered by entering options into the field marked B. The default key setting, *package:mine*, restricts the output to log messages generated by the current app package (in this case com.ebookfrenzy.statechange). Leaving this field blank will allow log output from the selected device or emulator to be displayed, including diagnostic messages generated by the operating system. Keys may also be combined to filter the output further. For example, we can configure the Logcat panel to display only messages associated with our StateChange tag as follows:

```
package:mine tag:StateChange
```

We can exclude output by prefixing the key with a minus (-) sign. In addition to the StateChange tag, we might have diagnostic messages using a different tag. To filter the log so that output from this second tag is excluded, we could enter the following key options:

```
package:mine tag:StateChange -tag:OtherTag
```

In addition to your own tag values, it is also possible to select from a range of predefined diagnostic tags built into Android. Logcat will display a list of matching tags as you type into the filter field, as shown in Figure 14-6:

Figure 14-6

Alternatively, use Ctrl-Space to access a complete list of filtering suggestions.

The *level* key may be used to control which messages are displayed based on severity. To filter out all messages except error messages, the following key would be used:

```
level:error
```

In addition to *error*, the Logcat panel supports *verbose*, *info*, *warn*, and *assert* level settings.

Logcat also supports multiple log panels, each with its own filter settings. To add another panel, click on the +

button marked D in Figure 14-5 above. Switch between different panels using the corresponding tabs, or display them side-by-side by right-clicking on the currently displayed panel and selecting either the *Split-Right* or *Split-Down* menu option to arrange the panels horizontally or vertically. To rename a panel, right-click on the tab and select the *Rename Tab* option. Before proceeding, close all but one Logcat panel and configure the filter as follows:

```
package:mine tag:StateChange
```

14.5 Running the Application

For optimal results, the application should be run on a physical Android device or emulator. With the device configured and connected to the development computer, click on the run button in the Android Studio toolbar as shown in Figure 14-7 below:

Figure 14-7

Select the physical Android device or emulator from the *Choose Device* dialog if it appears (assuming you have not already configured it as the default target). After Android Studio has built the application and installed it on the device, it should start up and be running in the foreground.

A review of the Logcat panel should indicate which methods have so far been triggered:

Figure 14-8

14.6 Experimenting with the Activity

With the diagnostics working, it is time to exercise the application to understand the activity lifecycle state changes. To begin with, consider the initial sequence of log events in the Logcat panel:

```
onCreate
onStart
onResume
```

Clearly, the initial state changes are exactly as outlined in *"Understanding Android Application and Activity Lifecycles"*. Note, however, that a call was not made to *onRestoreInstanceState()* since the Android runtime detected that there was no state to restore in this situation.

Tap on the Home icon in the bottom status bar on the device display and note the sequence of method calls reported in the log as follows:

```
onPause
```

Android Activity State Changes by Example

```
onStop
onSaveInstanceState
```

In this case, the runtime has noticed that the activity is no longer in the foreground, is not visible to the user, and has stopped the activity, but not without providing an opportunity for the activity to save the dynamic state. Depending on whether the runtime ultimately destroyed the activity or restarted it, the activity will either be notified it has been restarted via a call to *onRestart()* or will go through the creation sequence again when the user returns to the activity.

As outlined in *"Understanding Android Application and Activity Lifecycles"*, the destruction and recreation of an activity can be triggered by making a configuration change to the device, such as rotating from portrait to landscape. To see this in action, rotate the device while the *StateChange* application is in the foreground. When using the emulator, device rotation may be simulated using the rotation button located in the emulator toolbar. To complete the rotation, it may also be necessary to tap on the rotation button. This appears at the bottom of the device or emulator screen, as shown in Figure 14-9:

Figure 14-9

The resulting sequence of method calls in the log should read as follows:

```
onPause
onStop
onSaveInstanceState
onDestroy
onCreate
onStart
onRestoreInstanceState
onResume
```

Clearly, the runtime system has allowed the activity to save the state before being destroyed and restarted.

14.7 Summary

The adage that a picture is worth a thousand words holds just as true for examples when learning a new programming paradigm. In this chapter, we created an example Android application to demonstrate the different lifecycle states an activity will likely pass through. While developing the project in this chapter, we also looked at a mechanism for generating diagnostic logging information from within an activity.

In the next chapter, we will extend the *StateChange* example project to demonstrate how to save and restore an activity's dynamic state.

15. Saving and Restoring the State of an Android Activity

If the previous few chapters have achieved their objective, it should now be clearer as to the importance of saving and restoring the state of a user interface at particular points in the lifetime of an activity.

In this chapter, we will extend the example application created in *"Android Activity State Changes by Example"* to demonstrate the steps involved in saving and restoring state when the runtime system destroys and recreates an activity.

A key component of saving and restoring dynamic state involves using the Android SDK *Bundle* class, a topic that will also be covered in this chapter.

15.1 Saving Dynamic State

As we have learned, an activity can save dynamic state information via a call from the runtime system to the activity's implementation of the *onSaveInstanceState()* method. Passed through as an argument to the method is a reference to a Bundle object into which the method must store any dynamic data that needs to be saved. The Bundle object is then stored by the runtime system on behalf of the activity and subsequently passed through as an argument to the activity's *onCreate()* and *onRestoreInstanceState()* methods if and when they are called. The data can then be retrieved from the Bundle object within these methods and used to restore the state of the activity.

15.2 Default Saving of User Interface State

In the previous chapter, the diagnostic output from the *StateChange* example application showed that an activity goes through several state changes when the device on which it is running is rotated sufficiently to trigger an orientation change.

Launch the *StateChange* application once again and enter some text into the EditText field before performing the device rotation (on devices or emulators running Android 9 or later, it may be necessary to tap the rotation button in the status bar to complete the rotation). Having rotated the device, the following state change sequence should appear in the Logcat window:

```
onPause
onStop
onSaveInstanceState
onDestroy
onCreate
onStart
onRestoreInstanceState
onResume
```

Clearly, this has resulted in the activity being destroyed and re-created. A review of the user interface of the running application, however, should show that the text entered into the EditText field has been preserved. Given that the activity was destroyed and recreated and we did not add any specific code to ensure the text was saved and restored, this behavior requires some explanation.

Saving and Restoring the State of an Android Activity

In fact, most view widgets included with the Android SDK already implement the behavior necessary to save and restore state when an activity is restarted automatically. The only requirement to enable this behavior is for the *onSaveInstanceState()* and *onRestoreInstanceState()* override methods in the activity to include calls to the equivalent methods of the superclass:

```
@Override
protected void onSaveInstanceState(@NonNull Bundle outState) {
    super.onSaveInstanceState(outState);
}

@Override
protected void onRestoreInstanceState(@NonNull Bundle savedInstanceState) {
    super.onRestoreInstanceState(savedInstanceState);
}
```

The automatic saving of state for a user interface view can be disabled in the XML layout file by setting the *android:saveEnabled* property to *false*. The automatic state saving for a user interface view can be turned off in the XML layout file by setting the android:saveEnabled property to false. For this example, we will disable the automatic state-saving mechanism for the EditText view in the user interface layout and then add code to the application to manually save and restore the view's state.

To configure the EditText view such that state will not be saved and restored if the activity is restarted, edit the *activity_main.xml* file so that the entry for the view reads as follows (note that the XML can be edited by switching the Layout Editor to Code view mode as outlined in *"Creating an Example Android App in Android Studio"*):

```
<EditText
    android:id="@+id/editText"
    android:layout_width="wrap_content"
    android:layout_height="wrap_content"
    android:ems="10"
    android:inputType="text"
    android:saveEnabled="false"
    app:layout_constraintBottom_toBottomOf="parent"
    app:layout_constraintEnd_toEndOf="parent"
    app:layout_constraintStart_toStartOf="parent"
    app:layout_constraintTop_toTopOf="parent" />
```

After making the change, run the application, enter text, and rotate the device to verify that the text is no longer saved and restored.

15.3 The Bundle Class

For situations where state needs to be saved beyond the default functionality provided by the user interface view components, the Bundle class provides a container for storing data using a *key-value pair* mechanism. The *keys* take the form of string values, while the *values* associated with those *keys* can be a primitive value or any object that implements the Android *Parcelable* interface. A wide range of classes already implements the Parcelable interface. Custom classes may be made "parcelable" by implementing the set of methods defined in the Parcelable interface, details of which can be found in the Android documentation at:

https://developer.android.com/reference/android/os/Parcelable.html

Saving and Restoring the State of an Android Activity

The Bundle class also contains a set of methods that can be used to get and set key-value pairs for various data types, including both primitive types (including Boolean, char, double, and float values) and objects (such as Strings and CharSequences).

For this example, having disabled the automatic saving of text for the EditText view, we need to ensure that the text entered into the EditText field by the user is saved into the Bundle object and subsequently restored. This will demonstrate how to manually save and restore state within an Android application and will be achieved using the *putCharSequence()* and *getCharSequence()* methods of the Bundle class, respectively.

15.4 Saving the State

The first step in extending the *StateChange* application is to make sure that the text entered by the user is extracted from the EditText component within the *onSaveInstanceState()* method of the *MainActivity* activity and then saved as a key-value pair into the Bundle object.

To extract the text from the EditText object, we must first identify that object in the user interface. Clearly, this involves bridging the gap between the Java code for the activity (contained in the *MainActivity.java* source code file) and the XML representation of the user interface (contained within the *activity_main.xml* resource file). To extract the text entered into the EditText component, we need to gain access to that user interface object.

Each component within a user interface has associated with it a unique identifier. By default, the Layout Editor tool constructs the id for a newly added component from the object type. If more than one view of the same type is contained in the layout, the type name is followed by a sequential number (though this can, and should, be changed to something more meaningful by the developer). As can be seen by checking the *Component Tree* panel within the Android Studio main window when the *activity_main.xml* file is selected and the Layout Editor tool displayed, the EditText component has been assigned the id *editText*:

Figure 15-1

We can now obtain the text that the editText view contains via the object's *getText()* method, which, in turn, returns the current text:

```
CharSequence userText = binding.editText.getText();
```

Finally, we can save the text using the Bundle object's *putCharSequence()* method, passing through the key (this can be any string value, but in this instance, we will declare it as "savedText") and the *userText* object as arguments:

```
outState.putCharSequence("savedText", userText);
```

Bringing this all together gives us a modified *onSaveInstanceState()* method in the *MainActivity.java* file that reads as follows:

```
package com.ebookfrenzy.statechange;
.
.
.
public class MainActivity extends AppCompatActivity {
.
.
```

```
    protected void onSaveInstanceState(@NonNull Bundle outState) {
        super.onSaveInstanceState(outState);
        Log.i(TAG, "onSaveInstanceState");

        CharSequence userText = binding.editText.getText();
        outState.putCharSequence("savedText", userText);
    }
```

Now that steps have been taken to save the state, the next phase is to restore it when needed.

15.5 Restoring the State

The saved dynamic state can be restored in those lifecycle methods that are passed the Bundle object as an argument. This leaves the developer with the choice of using either *onCreate()* or *onRestoreInstanceState()*. The method to use will depend on the nature of the activity. In instances where state is best restored after the activity's initialization tasks have been performed, the *onRestoreInstanceState()* method is generally more suitable. For this example, we will add code to the *onRestoreInstanceState()* method to extract the saved state from the Bundle using the "savedText" key. We can then display the text on the editText component using the object's *setText()* method:

```
@Override
protected void onRestoreInstanceState(@NonNull Bundle savedInstanceState) {
    super.onRestoreInstanceState(savedInstanceState);
    Log.i(TAG, "onRestoreInstanceState");

    CharSequence userText =
            savedInstanceState.getCharSequence("savedText");

    binding.editText.setText(userText);
}
```

15.6 Testing the Application

All that remains is once again to build and run the *StateChange* application. Once running and in the foreground, touch the EditText component and enter some text before rotating the device to another orientation. Whereas the text changes were previously lost, the new text is retained within the editText component thanks to the code we have added to the activity in this chapter.

Having verified that the code performs as expected, comment out the *super.onSaveInstanceState()* and *super.onRestoreInstanceState()* calls from the two methods, re-launch the app and note that the text is still preserved after a device rotation. The default save and restoration system has essentially been replaced by a custom implementation, thereby providing a way to dynamically and selectively save and restore state within an activity.

15.7 Summary

The saving and restoration of dynamic state in an Android application is a matter of implementing the appropriate code in the appropriate lifecycle methods. For most user interface views, this is handled automatically by the Activity superclass. In other instances, this typically consists of extracting values and settings within the *onSaveInstanceState()* method and saving the data as key-value pairs within the Bundle object passed through to the activity by the runtime system.

State can be restored in either the *onCreate()* or the *onRestoreInstanceState()* methods of the activity by extracting values from the Bundle object and updating the activity based on the stored values.

In this chapter, we have used these techniques to update the *StateChange* project so that the Activity retains changes through the destruction and subsequent recreation of an activity.

Chapter 16

16. Understanding Android Views, View Groups and Layouts

With the possible exception of listening to streaming audio, a user's interaction with an Android device is primarily visual and tactile. All of this interaction occurs through the user interfaces of the applications installed on the device, including both the built-in applications and any third-party applications installed by the user. Therefore, it should come as no surprise that a critical element of developing Android applications involves designing and creating user interfaces.

This chapter covers the Android user interface structure, including an overview of the elements that can be combined to make up a user interface: Views, View Groups, and Layouts.

16.1 Designing for Different Android Devices

The term "Android device" covers many tablet and smartphone products with different screen sizes and resolutions. As a result, application user interfaces must now be carefully designed to ensure correct presentation on as wide a range of display sizes as possible. A key part of this is ensuring that the user interface layouts resize correctly when run on different devices. This can largely be achieved through careful planning and using the layout managers outlined in this chapter.

It is also essential to remember that most Android-based smartphones and tablets can be held by the user in both portrait and landscape orientations. A well-designed user interface should be able to adapt to such changes and make sensible layout adjustments to utilize the available screen space in each orientation.

16.2 Views and View Groups

Every item in a user interface is a subclass of the Android *View* class (to be precise *android.view.View*). The Android SDK provides a set of pre-built views that can be used to construct a user interface. Typical examples include standard items such as the Button, CheckBox, ProgressBar, and TextView classes. Such views are also referred to as *widgets* or *components*. For requirements not met by the widgets supplied with the SDK, new views may be created by subclassing and extending an existing class or creating an entirely new component by building directly on top of the View class.

A view can also comprise multiple other views (otherwise known as a *composite view*). Such views are subclassed from the Android *ViewGroup* class (*android.view.ViewGroup*), which is itself a subclass of *View*. An example of such a view is the RadioGroup, which is intended to contain multiple RadioButton objects such that only one can be in the "on" position at any one time. Regarding structure, composite views consist of a single parent view (derived from the ViewGroup class and otherwise known as a *container view* or *root element*) capable of containing other views (known as *child views*).

Another category of ViewGroup-based container view is that of the layout manager.

16.3 Android Layout Managers

In addition to the widget style views discussed in the previous section, the SDK also includes a set of views referred to as *layouts*. Layouts are container views (and, therefore, subclassed from ViewGroup) designed to control how child views are positioned on the screen.

Understanding Android Views, View Groups and Layouts

The Android SDK includes the following layout views that may be used within an Android user interface design:

- **ConstraintLayout** – Introduced in Android 7, this layout manager is recommended for most layout requirements. ConstraintLayout allows the positioning and behavior of the views in a layout to be defined by simple constraint settings assigned to each child view. The flexibility of this layout allows complex layouts to be quickly and easily created without the necessity to nest other layout types inside each other, resulting in improved layout performance. ConstraintLayout is also tightly integrated into the Android Studio Layout Editor tool. Unless otherwise stated, this is the layout of choice for most of examples in this book.

- **LinearLayout** – Positions child views in a single row or column depending on the orientation selected. A *weight* value can be set on each child to specify how much of the layout space that child should occupy relative to other children.

- **TableLayout** – Arranges child views into a grid format of rows and columns. Each row within a table is represented by a *TableRow* object child, which, in turn, contains a view object for each cell.

- **FrameLayout** – The purpose of the FrameLayout is to allocate an area of the screen, typically to display a single view. If multiple child views are added, they will, by default, appear on top of each other and be positioned in the top left-hand corner of the layout area. Alternate positioning of individual child views can be achieved by setting gravity values on each child. For example, setting a *center_vertical* gravity value on a child will cause it to be positioned in the vertical center of the containing FrameLayout view.

- **RelativeLayout** – The RelativeLayout allows child views to be positioned relative to each other and the containing layout view through the specification of alignments and margins on child views. For example, child *View A* may be configured to be positioned in the vertical and horizontal center of the containing RelativeLayout view. *View B*, on the other hand, might also be configured to be centered horizontally within the layout view but positioned 30 pixels above the top edge of *View A*, thereby making the vertical position *relative* to that of *View A*. The RelativeLayout manager can be helpful when designing a user interface that must work on various screen sizes and orientations.

- **AbsoluteLayout** – Allows child views to be positioned at specific X and Y coordinates within the containing layout view. Using this layout is discouraged since it lacks the flexibility to respond to screen size and orientation changes.

- **GridLayout** – A GridLayout instance is divided by invisible lines that form a grid containing rows and columns of cells. Child views are then placed in cells and may be configured to cover multiple cells horizontally and vertically, allowing a wide range of layout options to be quickly and easily implemented. Gaps between components in a GridLayout may be implemented by placing a special type of view called a *Space* view into adjacent cells or setting margin parameters.

- **CoordinatorLayout** – Introduced as part of the Android Design Support Library with Android 5.0, the CoordinatorLayout is designed specifically for coordinating the appearance and behavior of the app bar across the top of an application screen with other view elements. When creating a new activity using the Basic Views Activity template, the parent view in the main layout will be implemented using a CoordinatorLayout instance. This layout manager will be covered in greater detail, starting with the chapter *"Working with the Floating Action Button and Snackbar"*.

When considering layouts in the user interface for an Android application, it is worth keeping in mind that, as outlined in the next section, these can be nested within each other to create a user interface design of just about any necessary level of complexity.

16.4 The View Hierarchy

Each view in a user interface represents a rectangular area of the display. A view is responsible for what is drawn in that rectangle and responding to events within that part of the screen (such as a touch event).

A user interface screen is comprised of a view hierarchy with a *root view* positioned at the top of the tree and child views positioned on branches below. The child of a container view appears on top of its parent view and is constrained to appear within the bounds of the parent view's display area. Consider, for example, the user interface illustrated in Figure 16-1:

Figure 16-1

In addition to the visible button and checkbox views, the user interface actually includes a number of layout views that control how the visible views are positioned. Figure 16-2 shows an alternative view of the user interface, this time highlighting the presence of the layout views in relation to the child views:

Figure 16-2

Understanding Android Views, View Groups and Layouts

As was previously discussed, user interfaces are constructed in the form of a view hierarchy with a root view at the top. This being the case, we can also visualize the above user interface example in the form of the view tree illustrated in Figure 16-3:

Figure 16-3

The view hierarchy diagram gives probably the clearest overview of the relationship between the various views that make up the user interface shown in Figure 16-1. When a user interface is displayed to the user, the Android runtime walks the view hierarchy, starting at the root view and working down the tree as it renders each view.

16.5 Creating User Interfaces

With a clearer understanding of the concepts of views, layouts and the view hierarchy, the following few chapters will focus on the steps involved in creating user interfaces for Android activities. In fact, there are three different approaches to user interface design: using the Android Studio Layout Editor tool, handwriting XML layout resource files or writing Java code, each of which will be covered.

16.6 Summary

Each element within a user interface screen of an Android application is a view that is ultimately subclassed from the *android.view.View* class. Each view represents a rectangular area of the device display and is responsible both for what appears in that rectangle and for handling events that take place within the view's bounds. Multiple views may be combined to create a single *composite view*. The views within a composite view are children of a *container view* which is generally a subclass of *android.view.ViewGroup* (which is itself a subclass of *android.view.View*). A user interface is comprised of views constructed in the form of a view hierarchy.

The Android SDK includes a range of pre-built views that can be used to create a user interface. These include basic components such as text fields and buttons, in addition to a range of layout managers that can be used to control the positioning of child views. If the supplied views do not meet a specific requirement, custom views may be created, either by extending or combining existing views, or by subclassing *android.view.View* and creating an entirely new class of view.

User interfaces may be created using the Android Studio Layout Editor tool, handwriting XML layout resource files or by writing Java code. Each of these approaches will be covered in the chapters that follow.

Chapter 17

17. A Guide to the Android Studio Layout Editor Tool

It is challenging to think of an Android application concept that does not require some form of user interface. Most Android devices come equipped with a touch screen and keyboard (either virtual or physical), and taps and swipes are the primary interaction between the user and the application. Invariably these interactions take place through the application's user interface.

A well-designed and implemented user interface, an essential factor in creating a successful and popular Android application, can vary from simple to highly complex, depending on the design requirements of the individual application. Regardless of the level of complexity, the Android Studio Layout Editor tool significantly simplifies the task of designing and implementing Android user interfaces.

17.1 Basic vs. Empty Views Activity Templates

As outlined in the chapter entitled *"The Anatomy of an Android Application"*, Android applications comprise one or more activities. An activity is a standalone module of application functionality that usually correlates directly to a single user interface screen. As such, when working with the Android Studio Layout Editor, we are invariably work on the layout for an activity.

When creating a new Android Studio project, several templates are available to be used as the starting point for the user interface of the main activity. The most basic templates are the Basic Views Activity and Empty Views Activity templates. Although these seem similar at first glance, there are considerable differences between the two options. To see these differences within the layout editor, use the View Options menu to enable Show System UI, as shown in Figure 17-1 below:

Figure 17-1

The Empty Views Activity template creates a single layout file consisting of a ConstraintLayout manager instance containing a TextView object, as shown in Figure 17-2:

Figure 17-2

The Basic Views Activity, on the other hand, consists of multiple layout files. The top-level layout file has a CoordinatorLayout as the root view, a configurable app bar (which contains a toolbar) that appears across the top of the device screen (marked A in Figure 17-3), and a floating action button (the email button marked B). In addition to these items, the *activity_main.xml* layout file contains a reference to a second file named *content_main.xml* containing the content layout (marked C):

Figure 17-3

The Basic Views Activity contains layouts for two screens containing a button and a text view. This template aims to demonstrate how to implement navigation between multiple screens within an app. If an unmodified app using the Basic Views Activity template were to be run, the first of these two screens would appear (marked A in Figure 17-4). Pressing the Next button would navigate to the second screen (B), which, in turn, contains a button to return to the first screen:

A Guide to the Android Studio Layout Editor Tool

Figure 17-4

This app behavior uses of two Android features referred to as *fragments* and *navigation*, which will be covered starting with the chapters entitled *"An Introduction to Android Fragments"* and *"An Overview of the Navigation Architecture Component"* respectively.

The *content_main.xml* file contains a special fragment, known as a Navigation Host Fragment which allows different content to be switched in and out of view depending on the settings configured in the *res -> layout -> nav_graph.xml* file. In the case of the Basic Views Activity template, the *nav_graph.xml* file is configured to switch between the user interface layouts defined in the *fragment_first.xml* and *fragment_second.xml* files based on the Next and Previous button selections made by the user.

The Empty Views Activity template is helpful if you need neither a floating action button nor a menu in your activity and do not need the special app bar behavior provided by the CoordinatorLayout, such as options to make the app bar and toolbar collapse from view during certain scrolling operations (a topic covered in the chapter entitled *"Working with the AppBar and Collapsing Toolbar Layouts"*). However, the Basic Views Activity is helpful because it provides these elements by default. In fact, it is often quicker to create a new activity using the Basic Views Activity template and delete the elements you do not require than to use the Empty Views Activity template and manually implement behavior such as collapsing toolbars, a menu, or a floating action button.

Since not all of the examples in this book require the features of the Basic Views Activity template, however, most of the examples in this chapter will use the Empty Views Activity template unless the example requires one or other of the features provided by the Basic Views Activity template.

For future reference, if you need a menu but not a floating action button, use the Basic Views Activity and follow these steps to delete the floating action button:

1. Double-click on the main *activity_main.xml* layout file in the Project tool window under *app -> res -> layout* to load it into the Layout Editor. With the layout loaded into the Layout Editor tool, select the floating action button and tap the keyboard *Delete* key to remove the object from the layout.

2. Locate and edit the Java code for the activity (located under *app -> java -> <package name> -> <activity class name>* and remove the floating action button code from the onCreate method as follows:

131

A Guide to the Android Studio Layout Editor Tool

```
@Override
protected void onCreate(Bundle savedInstanceState) {
    super.onCreate(savedInstanceState);

    binding = ActivityMainBinding.inflate(getLayoutInflater());
    setContentView(binding.getRoot());

    setSupportActionBar(binding.toolbar);

    NavController navController = Navigation.findNavController(this, R.id.nav_host_fragment_content_main);
    appBarConfiguration = new AppBarConfiguration.Builder(navController.getGraph()).build();
    NavigationUI.setupActionBarWithNavController(this, navController, appBarConfiguration);

    binding.fab.setOnClickListener(new View.OnClickListener() {
        @Override
        public void onClick(View view) {
            Snackbar.make(view, "Replace with your own action", Snackbar.LENGTH_LONG)
                    .setAction("Action", null).show();
        }
    });
}
```

(The `binding.fab.setOnClickListener(...)` block above is struck through.)

If you need a floating action button but no menu, use the Basic Views Activity template and follow these steps:

1. Edit the main activity class file and delete the *onCreateOptionsMenu* and *onOptionsItemSelected* methods.

2. Select the *res -> menu* item in the Project tool window and tap the keyboard *Delete* key to remove the folder and corresponding menu resource files from the project.

If you need to use the Basic Views Activity template but need neither the navigation features nor the second content fragment, follow these steps:

1. Within the Project tool window, navigate to and double-click on the *app -> res -> navigation -> nav_graph.xml* file to load it into the navigation editor.

2. Within the editor, select the SecondFragment entry in the graph panel and tap the keyboard delete key to remove it from the graph.

3. Locate and delete the *SecondFragment.java* (*app -> java -> <package name> -> SecondFragment*) and *fragment_second.xml* (*app -> res -> layout -> fragment_second.xml*) files.

4. The final task is to remove some code from the FirstFragment class so that the Button view no longer navigates to the now non-existent second fragment when clicked. Locate the *FirstFragment.java* file, double-click on it to load it into the editor, and remove the code from the *onViewCreated()* method so that it reads as follows:

```
public void onViewCreated(@NonNull View view, Bundle savedInstanceState) {
    super.onViewCreated(view, savedInstanceState);
```

```
        binding.buttonFirst.setOnClickListener(new View.OnClickListener() {
            @Override
            public void onClick(View view) {
                NavHostFragment.findNavController(FirstFragment.this)
                        .navigate(R.id.action_FirstFragment_to_SecondFragment);
            }
        });
    }
```

17.2 The Android Studio Layout Editor

As demonstrated in previous chapters, the Layout Editor tool provides a "what you see is what you get" (WYSIWYG) environment in which views can be selected from a palette and then placed onto a canvas representing the display of an Android device. Once a view has been placed on the canvas, it can be moved, deleted, and resized (subject to the constraints of the parent view). Moreover, various properties relating to the selected view may be modified using the Attributes tool window.

Under the surface, the Layout Editor tool constructs an XML resource file containing the definition of the user interface that is being designed. As such, the Layout Editor tool operates in three distinct modes: Design, Code, and Split.

17.3 Design Mode

In design mode, the user interface can be visually manipulated by directly working with the view palette and the graphical representation of the layout. Figure 17-5 highlights the key areas of the Android Studio Layout Editor tool in design mode:

Figure 17-5

A – Palette – The palette provides access to the range of view components the Android SDK provides. These are grouped into categories for easy navigation. Items may be added to the layout by dragging a view component from the palette and dropping it at the desired position on the layout.

B – Device Screen – The device screen provides a visual "what you see is what you get" representation of the user interface layout as it is being designed. This layout allows direct design manipulation by allowing views to be selected, deleted, moved, and resized. The device model represented by the layout can be changed anytime using a menu in the toolbar.

C – Component Tree – As outlined in the previous chapter (*"Understanding Android Views, View Groups and Layouts"*), user interfaces are constructed using a hierarchical structure. The component tree provides a visual overview of the hierarchy of the user interface design. Selecting an element from the component tree will cause the corresponding view in the layout to be selected. Similarly, selecting a view from the device screen layout will select that view in the component tree hierarchy.

D – Attributes – All of the component views listed in the palette have associated with them a set of attributes that can be used to adjust the behavior and appearance of that view. The Layout Editor's attributes panel provides access to the attributes of the currently selected view in the layout allowing changes to be made.

E – Toolbar – The Layout Editor toolbar provides quick access to a wide range of options, including, amongst other options, the ability to zoom in and out of the device screen layout, change the device model currently displayed, rotate the layout between portrait and landscape and switch to a different Android SDK API level. The toolbar also has a set of context-sensitive buttons which will appear when relevant view types are selected in the device screen layout.

F – Mode Switching Controls – These three buttons provide a way to switch back and forth between the Layout Editor tool's Design, Code, and Split modes.

G - Zoom and Pan Controls - This control panel allows you to zoom in and out of the design canvas, grab the canvas, and pan around to find obscured areas when zoomed in.

17.4 The Palette

The Layout Editor palette is organized into two panels designed to make it easy to locate and preview view components for addition to a layout design. The category panel (marked A in Figure 17-6) lists the different categories of view components supported by the Android SDK. When a category is selected from the list, the second panel (B) updates to display a list of the components that fall into that category:

Figure 17-6

A Guide to the Android Studio Layout Editor Tool

To add a component from the palette onto the layout canvas, select the item from the component list or the preview panel, drag it to the desired location on the canvas, and drop it into place.

A search for a specific component within the selected category may be initiated by clicking the search button (marked C in Figure 17-6 above) in the palette toolbar and typing in the component name. As characters are typed, matching results will appear in the component list panel. If you are unsure of the component's category, select the All Results category before or during the search operation.

17.5 Design Mode and Layout Views

By default, the layout editor will appear in Design mode, as shown in Figure 17-5 above. This mode provides a visual representation of the user interface. Design mode can be selected at any time by clicking on the View Modes button, as shown in Figure 17-7:

Figure 17-7

When the Layout Editor tool is in Design mode, the layout can be viewed in two ways. The view shown in Figure 17-5 above is the Design view and shows the layout and widgets as they will appear in the running app. A second mode, the Blueprint view, can be shown instead of or concurrently with the Design view. The toolbar menu in Figure 17-8 provides options to display the Design, Blueprint, or both views. Settings are also available to adjust for color blindness. A fifth option, *Force Refresh Layout*, causes the layout to rebuild and redraw. This can be useful when the layout enters an unexpected state or is not accurately reflecting the current design settings:

Figure 17-8

Whether to display the layout view, design view, or both is a matter of personal preference. A good approach is to begin with both displayed as shown in Figure 17-9:

Figure 17-9

17.6 Night Mode

To view the layout in night mode during the design work, select the menu shown in Figure 17-10 below and change the setting to *Night*:

Figure 17-10

The mode menu also includes options for testing dynamic colors, a topic covered in the chapter *"A Material Design 3 Theming and Dynamic Color Tutorial"*.

17.7 Code Mode

It is important to remember when using the Android Studio Layout Editor tool that all it is doing is providing a user-friendly approach to creating XML layout resource files. The underlying XML can be viewed and directly edited during the design process by selecting Code from the View Modes menu shown in Figure 17-7 above.

Figure 17-11 shows the Android Studio Layout Editor tool in Code mode, allowing changes to be made to the user interface declaration by modifying the XML:

A Guide to the Android Studio Layout Editor Tool

```
activity_main.xml
<?xml version="1.0" encoding="utf-8"?>
<androidx.constraintlayout.widget.ConstraintLayout xmlns:android="http://schemas.android.com/apk/res/android"
    xmlns:app="http://schemas.android.com/apk/res-auto"
    xmlns:tools="http://schemas.android.com/tools"
    android:layout_width="match_parent"
    android:layout_height="match_parent"
    tools:context=".MainActivity">

    <TextView
        android:layout_width="wrap_content"
        android:layout_height="wrap_content"
        android:text="Hello World!"
        app:layout_constraintBottom_toBottomOf="parent"
        app:layout_constraintEnd_toEndOf="parent"
```

Figure 17-11

17.8 Split Mode

In Split mode, the editor shows the Design and Code views side-by-side, allowing the user interface to be modified visually using the design canvas and making changes directly to the XML declarations. Split mode can be selected either using the View Modes menu or using the Editor and Preview button shown below:

Figure 17-12

Any changes to the XML are automatically reflected in the design canvas and vice versa. Figure 17-13 shows the editor in Split mode:

Figure 17-13

137

17.9 Setting Attributes

The Attributes panel provides access to all available settings for the currently selected component. Figure 17-14, for example, shows some of the attributes for the TextView widget:

Figure 17-14

The Attributes tool window is divided into the following different sections.

- **id** - Contains the id property, which defines the name by which the currently selected object will be referenced in the app's source code.

- **Declared Attributes** - Contains all of the properties already assigned a value.

- **Layout** - The settings that define how the currently selected view object is positioned and sized relative to the screen and other objects in the layout.

- **Transforms** - Contains controls allowing the currently selected object to be rotated, scaled, and offset.

- **Common Attributes** - A list of attributes that commonly need to be changed for the class of view object currently selected.

- **All Attributes** - A complete list of all the attributes available for the currently selected object.

A search for a specific attribute may also be performed by selecting the search button in the toolbar of the attributes tool window and typing in the attribute name.

Some attributes contain a narrow button to the right of the value field. This indicates that the Resources dialog is available to assist in selecting a suitable property value. To display the dialog, click on the button. The appearance of this button changes to reflect whether or not the corresponding property value is stored in a resource file or hard-coded. If the value is stored in a resource file, the button to the right of the text property field will be filled in to indicate that the value is not hard-coded, as highlighted in Figure 17-15 below:

Figure 17-15

Attributes for which a finite number of valid options are available will present a drop-down menu (Figure 17-16) from which a selection may be made.

Figure 17-16

A dropper icon can be clicked to display the color selection palette. Similarly, when a flag icon appears, it can be clicked to display a list of options available for the attribute, while an image icon opens the resource manager panel allowing images and other resource types to be selected for the attribute.

17.10 Transforms

The transforms panel within the Attributes tool window (Figure 17-17) provides a set of controls and properties that control visual aspects of the currently selected object in terms of rotation, alpha (used to fade a view in and out), scale (size), and translation (offset from current position):

Figure 17-17

The panel contains a visual representation of the view, which updates as properties are changed. These changes are also reflected in the view within the layout canvas.

17.11 Tools Visibility Toggles

When reviewing the content of an Android Studio XML layout file in Code mode, you will notice that many attributes that define how a view appears and behaves begin with the *android:* prefix. This indicates that the attributes are set within the *android* namespace and will take effect when the app is run. The following excerpt from a layout file, for example, sets a variety of attributes on a Button view:

```
<Button
    android:id="@+id/button"
    android:layout_width="wrap_content"
    android:layout_height="wrap_content"
    android:text="Button"
    .
    .
    .
```

In addition to the android namespace, Android Studio also provides a *tools* namespace. When attributes are set within this namespace, they only take effect within the layout editor preview. While designing a layout, you might find it helpful for an EditText view to display some text but require the view to be blank when the app runs. To achieve this, you would set the text property of the view using the tools namespace as follows:

```
<EditText
    android:id="@+id/editTextTextPersonName"
    android:layout_width="wrap_content"
    android:layout_height="wrap_content"
    android:ems="10"
    android:inputType="textPersonName"
    tools:text="Sample Text"
    .
    .
    .
```

A tool attribute of this type is set in the Attributes tool window by entering the value into the property fields marked by the wrench icon, as shown in Figure 17-18:

Figure 17-18

Tools attributes are particularly useful for changing the visibility of a view during the design process. A layout may contain a view that is programmatically displayed and hidden when the app runs, depending on user actions. To simulate the hiding of the view, the following tools attribute could be added to the view XML declaration:

```
tools:visibility="invisible"
```

Although the view will no longer be visible when using the invisible setting, it is still present in the layout and occupies the same space it did when it was visible. To make the layout behave as though the view no longer exists, the visibility attribute should be set to *gone* as follows:

```
tools:visibility="gone"
```

In both examples above, the visibility settings only apply within the layout editor and will have no effect in the running app. To control visibility in both the layout editor and running app, the same attribute would be set using the *android* namespace:

A Guide to the Android Studio Layout Editor Tool

```
android:visibility="gone"
```

While these visibility tools attributes are useful, having to manually edit the XML layout file is a cumbersome process. To make it easier to change these settings, Android Studio provides a set of toggles within the layout editor Component Tree panel. To access these controls, click in the margin to the right of the corresponding view in the panel. Figure 17-19, for example, shows the tools visibility toggle controls for a Button view named myButton:

Figure 17-19

These toggles control the visibility of the corresponding view for both the android and tools namespaces and provide *not set*, *visible*, *invisible* and *gone* options. When conflicting attributes are set (for example, an android namespace toggle is set to visible while the tools value is set to invisible), the tools namespace takes precedence within the layout preview. When a toggle selection is made, Android Studio automatically adds the appropriate attribute to the XML view element in the layout file.

In addition to the visibility toggles in the Component Tree panel, the layout editor also includes the *tools visibility and position* toggle button shown highlighted in Figure 17-20 below:

Figure 17-20

This button toggles the current tools visibility settings. If the Button view shown above currently has the tools visibility attribute set to *gone*, for example, toggling this button will make it visible. This makes it easy to quickly check the layout behavior as the view is added to and removed from the layout. This toggle is also useful for checking that the views in the layout are correctly constrained, a topic covered in the chapter entitled *"A Guide to Using ConstraintLayout in Android Studio"*.

17.12 Converting Views

Changing a view in a layout from one type to another (such as converting a TextView to an EditText) can be performed easily within the Android Studio layout editor by right-clicking on the view either within the screen layout or Component tree window and selecting the *Convert view...* menu option (Figure 17-21):

Figure 17-21

Once selected, a dialog containing a list of compatible view types to which the selected object is eligible for conversion will appear. Figure 17-22, for example, shows the types to which an existing TextView view may be converted:

Figure 17-22

This technique is also helpful in converting layouts from one type to another (for example, converting a ConstraintLayout to a LinearLayout).

17.13 Displaying Sample Data

When designing layouts in Android Studio, situations will arise where the content to be displayed within the user interface will not be available until the app is completed and running. This can sometimes make it difficult to assess how the layout will appear at app runtime from within the layout editor. To address this issue, the layout editor allows sample data to be specified, which will populate views within the layout editor with sample images and data. This sample data only appears within the layout editor and is not displayed when the app runs. Sample data may be configured either by directly editing the XML for the layout or visually using the design-time helper by right-clicking on the widget in the design area and selecting the *Set Sample Data* menu option. The design-time helper panel will display a range of preconfigured options for sample data to be displayed on the selected view item, including combinations of text and images in various configurations. Figure 17-23, for example, shows the sample data options displayed when selecting sample data to appear in a RecyclerView list:

Figure 17-23

Alternatively, custom text and images may be provided for display during the layout design process. An example of using sample data within the layout editor is included in a later chapter entitled *"A Layout Editor Sample Data Tutorial"*. Since sample data is implemented as a *tools* attribute, the visibility of the data within the preview can be controlled using the toggle button highlighted in Figure 17-20 above.

17.14 Creating a Custom Device Definition

The device menu in the Layout Editor toolbar (Figure 17-24) provides a list of pre-configured device types, which, when selected, will appear as the device screen canvas. In addition to the pre-configured device types, any AVD instances previously configured within the Android Studio environment will also be listed within the menu. To add additional device configurations, display the device menu, select the *Add Device Definition* option and follow the steps outlined in the chapter entitled *"Creating an Android Virtual Device (AVD) in Android Studio"*.

Figure 17-24

17.15 Changing the Current Device

As an alternative to the device selection menu, the current device format may be changed by selecting the *Custom* option from the device menu, clicking on the resize handle located next to the bottom right-hand corner of the device screen (Figure 17-25), and dragging to select an alternate device display format. As the screen resizes, markers will appear indicating the various size options and orientations available for selection:

Figure 17-25

17.16 Layout Validation

The layout validation option allows the user interface layout to be previewed simultaneously on a range of Pixel-sized screens. To access the layout validation tool window, click on the tab on the right-hand edge of the Android Studio main window or use the Tool Window menu in the bottom left-hand corner of the window. Once loaded, the panel will appear as shown in Figure 17-26, with the layout rendered on multiple device screen configurations:

Figure 17-26

17.17 Summary

A key part of developing Android applications involves the creation of the user interface. This is performed within the Android Studio environment using the Layout Editor tool, which operates in three modes. In Design mode, view components are selected from a palette, positioned on a layout representing an Android device screen, and configured using a list of attributes. The underlying XML representing the user interface layout can be directly edited in Code mode. Split mode, on the other hand, allows the layout to be created and modified both visually and via direct XML editing. These modes combine to provide an extensive and intuitive user interface design environment.

The layout validation panel allows user interface layouts to be quickly previewed on various device screen sizes.

18. A Guide to the Android ConstraintLayout

As discussed in the chapter entitled *"Understanding Android Views, View Groups and Layouts"*, Android provides several layout managers to design user interfaces. With Android 7, Google introduced a layout that addressed many of the shortcomings of the older layout managers. This layout, called ConstraintLayout, combines a simple, expressive, and flexible layout system with powerful features built into the Android Studio Layout Editor tool to ease the creation of responsive user interface layouts that adapt automatically to different screen sizes and changes in device orientation.

This chapter will outline the basic concepts of ConstraintLayout, while the next chapter will provide a detailed overview of how constraint-based layouts can be created using ConstraintLayout within the Android Studio Layout Editor tool.

18.1 How ConstraintLayout Works

In common with all other layouts, ConstraintLayout manages the positioning and sizing behavior of the visual components (also referred to as widgets) it contains. It does this based on the constraint connections set on each child widget.

To fully understand and use ConstraintLayout, it is essential to gain an appreciation of the following key concepts:

- Constraints
- Margins
- Opposing Constraints
- Constraint Bias
- Chains
- Chain Styles
- Guidelines
- Groups
- Barriers
- Flow

18.1.1 Constraints

Constraints are sets of rules that dictate how a widget is aligned and distanced relative to other widgets, the sides of the containing ConstraintLayout, and special elements called *guidelines*. Constraints also dictate how the user interface layout of an activity will respond to changes in device orientation or when displayed on devices of differing screen sizes. To be adequately configured, a widget must have sufficient constraint connections such that its position can be resolved by the ConstraintLayout layout engine in both the horizontal and vertical planes.

18.1.2 Margins

A margin is a form of constraint that specifies a fixed distance. Consider a Button object that needs to be positioned near the top right-hand corner of the device screen. This might be achieved by implementing margin constraints from the top and right-hand edges of the Button connected to the corresponding sides of the parent ConstraintLayout, as illustrated in Figure 18-1:

Figure 18-1

As indicated in the above diagram, each of these constraint connections has associated with it a margin value dictating the fixed distances of the widget from two sides of the parent layout. Under this configuration, regardless of screen size or the device orientation, the Button object will always be positioned 20 and 15 device-independent pixels (dp) from the top and right-hand edges of the parent ConstraintLayout, respectively, as specified by the two constraint connections.

While the above configuration will be acceptable for some situations, it does not provide any flexibility in terms of allowing the ConstraintLayout layout engine to adapt the position of the widget to respond to device rotation and to support screens of different sizes. To add this responsiveness to the layout, it is necessary to implement opposing constraints.

18.1.3 Opposing Constraints

Two constraints operating along the same axis on a single widget are considered *opposing constraints*. In other words, a widget with constraints on both its left and right-hand sides is considered to have horizontally opposing constraints. Figure 18-2, for example, illustrates the addition of both horizontally and vertically opposing constraints to the previous layout:

Figure 18-2

The key point to understand here is that once opposing constraints are implemented on a particular axis, the positioning of the widget becomes percentage rather than coordinate-based. Instead of being fixed at 20dp from the top of the layout, for example, the widget is now positioned at 30% from the top. In different orientations and when running on larger or smaller screens, the Button will always be in the same location relative to the dimensions of the parent layout.

It is now important to understand that the layout outlined in Figure 18-2 has been implemented using not only opposing constraints, but also by applying *constraint bias*.

18.1.4 Constraint Bias

It has now been established that a widget in a ConstraintLayout can potentially be subject to opposing constraint connections. By default, opposing constraints are equal, resulting in the corresponding widget being centered along the axis of opposition. Figure 18-3, for example, shows a widget centered within the containing ConstraintLayout using opposing horizontal and vertical constraints:

Widget Centered by Opposing Constraints

Figure 18-3

To allow for the adjustment of widget position in the case of opposing constraints, the ConstraintLayout implements a feature known as *constraint bias*. Constraint bias allows the positioning of a widget along the axis of opposition to be biased by a specified percentage in favor of one constraint. Figure 18-4, for example, shows the previous constraint layout with a 75% horizontal bias and 10% vertical bias:

Widget Offset using Constraint Bias

Figure 18-4

The next chapter, entitled *"A Guide to Using ConstraintLayout in Android Studio"*, will cover these concepts in greater detail and explain how these features have been integrated into the Android Studio Layout Editor tool.

A Guide to the Android ConstraintLayout

In the meantime, however, a few more areas of the ConstraintLayout class need to be covered.

18.1.5 Chains

ConstraintLayout chains provide a way for the layout behavior of two or more widgets to be defined as a group. Chains can be declared in either the vertical or horizontal axis and configured to define how the widgets in the chain are spaced and sized.

Widgets are chained when connected by bi-directional constraints. Figure 18-5, for example, illustrates three widgets chained in this way:

Figure 18-5

The first element in the chain is the *chain head* which translates to the top widget in a vertical chain or, in the case of a horizontal chain, the left-most widget. The layout behavior of the entire chain is primarily configured by setting attributes on the chain head widget.

18.1.6 Chain Styles

The layout behavior of a ConstraintLayout chain is dictated by the *chain style* setting applied to the chain head widget. The ConstraintLayout class currently supports the following chain layout styles:

- **Spread Chain** – The widgets within the chain are distributed evenly across the available space. This is the default behavior for chains.

Figure 18-6

- **Spread Inside Chain** – The widgets within the chain are spread evenly between the chain head and the last widget. The head and last widgets are not included in the distribution of spacing.

Figure 18-7

- **Weighted Chain** – Allows the space taken up by each widget in the chain to be defined via weighting properties.

A Guide to the Android ConstraintLayout

Figure 18-8

- **Packed Chain** – The widgets that make up the chain are packed together without spacing. A bias may be applied to control the horizontal or vertical positioning of the chain relative to the parent container.

Figure 18-9

18.2 Baseline Alignment

So far, this chapter has only referred to constraints that dictate alignment relative to the sides of a widget (typically referred to as side constraints). A common requirement, however, is for a widget to be aligned relative to the content that it displays rather than the boundaries of the widget itself. To address this need, ConstraintLayout provides *baseline alignment* support.

For example, assume that the previous theoretical layout from Figure 18-1 requires a TextView widget to be positioned 40dp to the left of the Button. In this case, the TextView needs to be *baseline aligned* with the Button view. This means that the text within the Button needs to be vertically aligned with the text within the TextView. The additional constraints for this layout would need to be connected as illustrated in Figure 18-10:

Figure 18-10

The TextView is now aligned vertically along the baseline of the Button and positioned 40dp horizontally from the Button object's left-hand edge.

18.3 Configuring Widget Dimensions

Controlling the dimensions of a widget is a key element of the user interface design process. The ConstraintLayout provides three options that can be set on individual widgets to manage sizing behavior. These settings are configured individually for height and width dimensions:

- **Fixed** – The widget is fixed to specified dimensions.

- **Match Constraint** – Allows the widget to be resized by the layout engine to satisfy the prevailing constraints.

151

Also referred to as the *AnySize* or MATCH_CONSTRAINT option.

- **Wrap Content** – The widget's size is dictated by its content (i.e., text or graphics).

18.4 Guideline Helper

Guidelines are special elements available within the ConstraintLayout that provide an additional target to which constraints may be connected. Multiple guidelines may be added to a ConstraintLayout instance which may, in turn, be configured in horizontal or vertical orientations. Once added, constraint connections may be established from widgets in the layout to the guidelines. This is particularly useful when multiple widgets must be aligned along an axis. In Figure 18-11, for example, three Button objects contained within a ConstraintLayout are constrained along a vertical guideline:

Figure 18-11

18.5 Group Helper

This feature of ConstraintLayout allows widgets to be placed into logical groups, and the visibility of those widgets controlled as a single entity. A Group is a list of references to other widgets in a layout. Once defined, changing the visibility attribute (visible, invisible, or gone) of the group instance will apply the change to all group members. This makes hiding and showing multiple widgets with a single attribute change easy. A single layout may contain multiple groups, and a widget can belong to more than one group. If a conflict occurs between groups, the last group to be declared in the XML file takes priority.

18.6 Barrier Helper

Rather like guidelines, barriers are virtual views that can be used to constrain views within a layout. As with guidelines, a barrier can be vertical or horizontal, and one or more views may be constrained to it (to avoid confusion, these will be referred to as *constrained views*). Unlike guidelines, where the guideline remains at a fixed position within the layout, however, the position of a barrier is defined by a set of so-called *reference views*. Barriers were introduced to address an issue that occurs with some frequency involving overlapping views. Consider, for example, the layout illustrated in Figure 18-12 below:

A Guide to the Android ConstraintLayout

Figure 18-12

The key points to note about the above layout are that the width of View 3 is set to match constraint mode, and the left-hand edge of the view is connected to the right-hand edge of View 1. As currently implemented, an increase in width of View 1 will have the desired effect of reducing the width of View 3:

Figure 18-13

A problem arises, however, if View 2 increases in width instead of View 1:

Figure 18-14

Because View 3 is only constrained by View 1, it does not resize to accommodate the increase in width of View

153

2, causing the views to overlap.

A solution to this problem is to add a vertical barrier and assign Views 1 and 2 as the barrier's *reference views* so that they control the barrier position. The left-hand edge of View 3 will then be constrained relative to the barrier, making it a *constrained view*.

Now when either View 1 or View 2 increases in width, the barrier will move to accommodate the widest of the two views, causing the width of View 3 to change relative to the new barrier position:

Figure 18-15

When working with barriers, there is no limit to the number of reference and constrained views that can be associated with a single barrier.

18.7 Flow Helper

The ConstraintLayout Flow helper allows groups of views to be displayed in a flowing grid-style layout. As with the Group helper, Flow contains references to the views it is responsible for positioning and provides various configuration options, including vertical and horizontal orientations, wrapping behavior (including the maximum number of widgets before wrapping), spacing, and alignment properties. Chain behavior may also be applied to a Flow layout, including spread, spread inside, and packed options.

Figure 18-16 represents the layout of five uniformly sized buttons positioned using a Flow helper instance in horizontal mode with no wrap settings:

Figure 18-16

Figure 18-17 shows the same buttons in a horizontal flow configuration with wrapping set to occur after every third widget:

Figure 18-17

Figure 18-18, on the other hand, shows the buttons with wrapping set to chain mode using spread inside (the effects of which are only visible on the second row since the first row is full). The configuration also has the gap attribute set to add spacing between buttons:

Figure 18-18

As a final demonstration of the flexibility of the Flow helper, Figure 18-19 shows five buttons of varying sizes configured in horizontal, packed chain mode with wrapping after each third widget. In addition, the grid content has been right-aligned by setting a horizontal-bias value of 1.0 (a value of 0.0 would cause left-alignment while 0.5 would center-align the grid content):

Figure 18-19

18.8 Ratios

The dimensions of a widget may be defined using ratio settings. A widget could, for example, be constrained using a ratio setting such that, regardless of any resizing behavior, the width is always twice the height dimension.

18.9 ConstraintLayout Advantages

ConstraintLayout provides a level of flexibility that allows many of the features of older layouts to be achieved with a single layout instance where it would previously have been necessary to nest multiple layouts. This can avoid the problems inherent in layout nesting by allowing so-called "flat" or "shallow" layout hierarchies to be designed, leading both to less complex layouts and improved user interface rendering performance at runtime.

ConstraintLayout was also implemented to address the wide range of Android device screen sizes available today. The flexibility of ConstraintLayout makes it easier for user interfaces to be designed that respond and adapt to the device on which the app is running.

Finally, as will be demonstrated in the chapter entitled *"A Guide to Using ConstraintLayout in Android Studio"*, the Android Studio Layout Editor tool has been enhanced specifically for ConstraintLayout-based user interface design.

18.10 ConstraintLayout Availability

Although introduced with Android 7, ConstraintLayout is provided as a separate support library from the main Android SDK and is compatible with older Android versions as far back as API Level 9 (Gingerbread). This allows apps that use this layout to run on devices running much older versions of Android.

18.11 Summary

ConstraintLayout is a layout manager introduced with Android 7. It is designed to ease the creation of flexible layouts that adapt to the size and orientation of the many Android devices on the market. ConstraintLayout uses constraints to control the alignment and positioning of widgets relative to the parent ConstraintLayout instance, guidelines, barriers, and the other widgets in the layout. ConstraintLayout is the default layout for newly created Android Studio projects and is recommended when designing user interface layouts. This simple yet flexible approach to layout management allows complex and responsive user interfaces to be easily implemented.

Chapter 19

19. A Guide to Using ConstraintLayout in Android Studio

As mentioned more than once in previous chapters, Google has made significant changes to the Android Studio Layout Editor tool, many of which were made solely to support user interface layout design using ConstraintLayout. Now that the basic concepts of ConstraintLayout have been outlined in the previous chapter, this chapter will explore these concepts in more detail while also outlining how the Layout Editor tool allows ConstraintLayout-based user interfaces to be designed and implemented.

19.1 Design and Layout Views

The chapter entitled *"A Guide to the Android Studio Layout Editor Tool"* explained that the Android Studio Layout Editor tool provides two ways to view the user interface layout of an activity in the form of Design and Layout (also known as blueprint) views. These views of the layout may be displayed individually or, as in Figure 19-1, side-by-side:

Figure 19-1

The Design view (positioned on the left in the above figure) presents a "what you see is what you get" representation of the layout, wherein the layout appears as it will within the running app. On the other hand, the Layout view displays a blueprint style of view where shaded outlines represent the widgets. As shown in Figure 19-1 above, the Layout view also displays the constraint connections (in this case, opposing constraints used to center a button within the layout). These constraints are also overlaid onto the Design view when a specific widget in the layout is selected or when the mouse pointer hovers over the design area, as illustrated in Figure 19-2:

Figure 19-2

The appearance of constraint connections in both views can be changed using the View Options menu shown in Figure 19-3:

Figure 19-3

In addition to the two modes of displaying the user interface layout, the Layout Editor tool provides three ways of establishing the constraints required for a specific layout design.

19.2 Autoconnect Mode

Autoconnect, as the name suggests, automatically establishes constraint connections as items are added to the layout. Autoconnect mode may be turned on and off using the toolbar button indicated in Figure 19-4:

Figure 19-4

Autoconnect mode uses algorithms to decide the best constraints to establish based on the widget's position and the widget's proximity to both the sides of the parent layout and other elements. If any of the automatic constraint connections fail to provide the desired behavior, these may be changed manually, as outlined later in this chapter.

19.3 Inference Mode

Inference mode uses a heuristic approach involving algorithms and probabilities to automatically implement constraint connections after widgets have already been added to the layout. This mode is usually used when the Autoconnect feature has been turned off, and objects have been added to the layout without any constraint connections. This allows the layout to be designed by dragging and dropping objects from the palette onto the layout canvas and making size and positioning changes until the layout appears as required. Essentially, this involves "painting" the layout without worrying about constraints. Inference mode may also be used during the design process to fill in missing constraints within a layout.

Constraints are automatically added to a layout when the *Infer constraints* button (Figure 19-5) is clicked:

Figure 19-5

As with Autoconnect mode, there is always the possibility that the Layout Editor tool will infer incorrect constraints, though these may be modified and corrected manually.

19.4 Manipulating Constraints Manually

The third option for implementing constraint connections is to do so manually. When doing so, it will be helpful to understand the various handles that appear around a widget within the Layout Editor tool. Consider, for example, the widget shown in Figure 19-6:

Figure 19-6

The spring-like lines (A) represent established constraint connections leading from the sides of the widget to the targets. The small square markers (B) in each corner of the object are resizing handles which, when clicked and dragged, serve to resize the widget. The small circle handles (C) located on each side of the widget are the side constraint anchors. To create a constraint connection, click on the handle and drag the resulting line to the element to which the constraint is to be connected (such as a guideline or the side of either the parent layout or another widget), as outlined in Figure 19-7. When connecting to the side of another widget, drag the line to the side constraint handle of that widget and release the line when the widget and handle are highlighted:

Figure 19-7

If the constraint line is dragged to a widget and released but not attached to a constraint handle, the layout editor will display a menu containing a list of the sides to which the constraint may be attached. In Figure 19-8, for example, the constraint can be attached to the top or bottom edge of the destination button widget:

Figure 19-8

An additional marker indicates the anchor point for baseline constraints whereby the content within the widget (as opposed to outside edges) is used as the alignment point. To display this marker, right-click on the widget and select the *Show Baseline* menu option. To establish a constraint connection from a baseline constraint handle, hover the mouse pointer over the handle until it highlights before clicking and dragging to the target (such as the baseline anchor of another widget, as shown in Figure 19-9).

Figure 19-9

To hide the baseline anchors, right-click on the widget again and select the *Hide Baseline* menu option.

19.5 Adding Constraints in the Inspector

Constraints may also be added to a view within the Android Studio Layout Editor tool using the *Inspector* panel in the Attributes tool window, as shown in Figure 19-10. The square in the center represents the currently selected view, and the areas around the square the constraints, if any, applied to the corresponding sides of the view:

Figure 19-10

The absence of a constraint on the side of the view is represented by a dotted line leading to a blue circle containing a plus sign (as is the case with the view's bottom edge in the above figure). To add a constraint, click on this blue circle, and the layout editor will add a constraint connected to what it considers the most appropriate target within the layout.

19.6 Viewing Constraints in the Attributes Window

A list of constraints configured on the currently selected widget can be viewed by displaying the Constraints section of the Attributes tool window, as shown in Figure 19-11 below:

Figure 19-11

Clicking on a constraint in the list will select that constraint within the design layout.

19.7 Deleting Constraints

To delete an individual constraint, select the constraint either within the design layout or the Attributes tool window so that it highlights (in Figure 19-12, for example, the right-most constraint has been selected) and tap the keyboard delete key. The constraint will then be removed from the layout.

Figure 19-12

Another option is to hover the mouse pointer over the constraint anchor while holding down the Ctrl (Cmd on macOS) key and clicking on the anchor after it turns red:

Figure 19-13

Alternatively, remove all of the constraints on a widget by right-clicking on it and selecting the *Clear Constraints of Selection* menu option.

To remove all of the constraints from every widget in a layout, use the toolbar button highlighted in Figure 19-14:

Figure 19-14

19.8 Adjusting Constraint Bias

The previous chapter outlined the concept of using bias settings to favor one opposing constraint over another. Bias within the Android Studio Layout Editor tool is adjusted using the *Inspector* located in the Attributes tool window and shown in Figure 19-15. The two sliders indicated by the arrows in the figure are used to control the bias of the currently selected widget's vertical and horizontal opposing constraints.

Figure 19-15

19.9 Understanding ConstraintLayout Margins

Constraints can be used with margins to implement fixed gaps between a widget and another element (such as another widget, a guideline, or the side of the parent layout). Consider, for example, the horizontal constraints applied to the Button object in Figure 19-16:

Figure 19-16

As currently configured, horizontal constraints run to the left and right edges of the parent ConstraintLayout. As such, the widget has opposing horizontal constraints indicating that the ConstraintLayout layout engine has some discretion in terms of the actual positioning of the widget at runtime. This allows the layout some flexibility to accommodate different screen sizes and device orientations. The horizontal bias setting can also control the widget's position right up to the right-hand side of the layout. Figure 19-17, for example, shows the same button with 100% horizontal bias applied:

Figure 19-17

ConstraintLayout margins can appear at the end of constraint connections and represent a fixed gap into which the widget cannot be moved, even when adjusting bias or responding to layout changes elsewhere in the activity. In Figure 19-18, the right-hand constraint now includes a 50dp margin into which the widget cannot be moved even though the bias is still set at 100%.

Figure 19-18

Existing margin values on a widget can be modified from within the Inspector. As shown in Figure 19-19, a drop-down menu is being used to change the right-hand margin on the currently selected widget to 16dp. Alternatively, clicking on the current value also allows a number to be typed into the field.

Figure 19-19

The default margin for new constraints can be changed at any time using the option in the toolbar highlighted in Figure 19-20:

Figure 19-20

19.10 The Importance of Opposing Constraints and Bias

As discussed in the previous chapter, opposing constraints, margins, and bias form the cornerstone of responsive layout design in Android when using the ConstraintLayout. When a widget is constrained without opposing constraint connections, those constraints are essentially margin constraints. This is indicated visually within the Layout Editor tool by solid straight lines accompanied by margin measurements, as shown in Figure 19-21.

Figure 19-21

The above constraints fix the widget at that position. The result is that if the device is rotated to landscape orientation, the widget will no longer be visible since the vertical constraint pushes it beyond the top edge of the device screen (as is the case in Figure 19-22). A similar problem will arise if the app is run on a device with a smaller screen than that used during the design process.

Figure 19-22

When opposing constraints are implemented, the constraint connection is represented by the jagged spring-like line (the spring metaphor is intended to indicate that the position of the widget is not fixed to absolute X and Y coordinates):

Figure 19-23

In the above layout, vertical and horizontal bias settings have been configured such that the widget will always be positioned 90% of the distance from the bottom and 35% from the left-hand edge of the parent layout. When rotated, therefore, the widget is still visible and positioned in the same location relative to the dimensions of the screen:

Figure 19-24

When designing a responsive and adaptable user interface layout, it is important to consider bias and opposing constraints when manually designing a user interface layout and correcting automatically created constraints.

19.11 Configuring Widget Dimensions

The inner dimensions of a widget within a ConstraintLayout can also be configured using the Inspector. As outlined in the previous chapter, widget dimensions can be set to wrap content, fixed, or match constraint modes. The prevailing settings for each dimension on the currently selected widget are shown within the square representing the widget in the Inspector, as illustrated in Figure 19-25:

Figure 19-25

The above figure sets the horizontal and vertical dimensions to wrap content mode (indicated by the inward-pointing chevrons). The inspector uses the following visual indicators to represent the three dimension modes:

Fixed Size	⊢―⊣
Match Constraint	⊢⋀⋀⊣
Wrap Content	>>>

Table 19-1

To change the current setting, click on the indicator to cycle through the three settings.

In addition, a widget's size can be expanded horizontally or vertically to the maximum amount allowed by the constraints and other widgets in the layout using the Expand Horizontally and Expand Vertically options. These are accessible by right-clicking on a widget within the layout and selecting the Organize option from the resulting menu (Figure 19-26). When used, the currently selected widget will increase in size horizontally or vertically to fill the available space around it.

Figure 19-26

19.12 Design Time Tools Positioning

The chapter entitled *"A Guide to the Android Studio Layout Editor Tool"* introduced the concept of the *tools* namespace and explained how it can be used to set visibility attributes that only take effect within the layout editor. Behind the scenes, Android Studio also uses tools attributes to hold widgets in position when placed on the layout without constraints. Imagine, for example, a Button placed onto the layout while autoconnect mode is disabled. While the widget will appear to be in the correct position within the preview canvas, when the app is run, it will appear in the top left-hand corner of the screen. This is because the widget has no constraints to tell the ConstraintLayout parent where to position it.

The widget appears to be in the correct location in the layout editor because Android Studio has set absolute X and Y positioning tools attributes to keep it in the correct location until constraints can be added. Within the XML layout file, this might read as follows:

```
<Button
    android:id="@+id/button4"
    android:layout_width="wrap_content"
    android:layout_height="wrap_content"
    android:text="Button"
    tools:layout_editor_absoluteX="111dp"
    tools:layout_editor_absoluteY="88dp" />
```

Once adequate constraints have been added to the widget, the layout editor will remove these tools attributes. A useful technique to quickly identify which widgets lack constraints without waiting until the app runs is to click on the button highlighted in Figure 19-27 to toggle tools position visibility. Any widgets that jump to the top left-hand corner are not fully constrained and are being held in place by temporary tools absolute X and Y positioning attributes.

A Guide to Using ConstraintLayout in Android Studio

Figure 19-27

19.13 Adding Guidelines

Guidelines provide additional elements to which constraints may be anchored. Guidelines are added by right-clicking on the layout and selecting either the *Vertical Guideline* or *Horizontal Guideline* menu option or using the toolbar menu options as shown in Figure 19-28:

Figure 19-28

Alternatively, horizontal and vertical Guidelines may be dragged from the Helpers section of the Palette and dropped either onto the layout canvas or Component Tree panel as indicated by the arrows in Figure 19-29:

Figure 19-29

169

A Guide to Using ConstraintLayout in Android Studio

Once added, a guideline will appear as a dashed line in the layout and may be moved by clicking and dragging the line. To establish a constraint connection to a guideline, click on the constraint handler of a widget and drag it to the guideline before releasing. In Figure 19-30, the left sides of two Buttons are connected by constraints to a vertical guideline.

The position of a vertical guideline can be specified as an absolute distance from either the left or the right of the parent layout (or the top or bottom for a horizontal guideline). For example, the vertical guideline in the figure below is positioned at 97dp from the left-hand edge of the parent:

Figure 19-30

Alternatively, the guideline may be positioned as a percentage of the overall width or height of the parent layout. To switch between these three modes, select the guideline and click on the circle at the bottom or end of the guideline (depending on whether the guideline is vertical or horizontal). Figure 19-31, for example, shows a guideline positioned based on percentage:

Figure 19-31

19.14 Adding Barriers

Barriers are added by right-clicking on the layout and selecting either the *Vertical* or *Horizontal Barrier* option from the *Add helpers* menu or using the toolbar menu options, as shown in Figure 19-28. Alternatively, locate the Barrier types in the Helpers section of the Palette and drag and drop them either onto the layout canvas or the Component Tree panel.

Once a barrier has been added to the layout, it will appear as an entry in the Component Tree panel:

Figure 19-32

To add views as reference views (in other words, the views that control the position of the barrier), drag the widgets from within the Component Tree onto the barrier entry. In Figure 19-33, for example, widgets named textView2 and textView3 have been assigned as the reference widgets for the barrier:

Figure 19-33

After the reference views have been added, the barrier needs to be configured to specify the direction of the barrier relative to those views. This is the *barrier direction* setting and is defined within the Attributes tool window when the barrier is selected in the Component Tree panel:

Figure 19-34

A Guide to Using ConstraintLayout in Android Studio

The following figure shows a layout containing a barrier declared with textView1 and textView2 acting as the reference views and textview3 as the constrained view. Since the barrier is pushing from the end of the reference views towards the constrained view, the barrier direction has been set to *end*:

Figure 19-35

19.15 Adding a Group

To add a Group to a layout, right-click on the layout and select the *Group* option from the Add *helpers* menu or use the toolbar menu options shown in Figure 19-28. Alternatively, locate the Group item in the Helpers section of the Palette and drag and drop it either onto the layout canvas or Component Tree panel.

To add widgets to the group, select them in the Component Tree and drag and drop them onto the Group entry. Figure 19-36, for example, shows three selected widgets being added to a group:

Figure 19-36

Any widgets referenced by the group will appear italicized beneath the group entry in the Component Tree, as shown in Figure 19-37. To remove a widget from the group, select it and tap the keyboard delete key:

Figure 19-37

Once widgets have been assigned to the group, use the Constraints section of the Attributes tool window to modify the visibility setting:

Figure 19-38

19.16 Working with the Flow Helper

Flow helpers may be added using either the menu or Palette, as outlined previously for the other helpers. As with the Group helper (Figure 19-36), widgets are added to a Flow instance by dragging them within the Component Tree onto the Flow entry. Having added a Flow helper and assigned widgets to it, select it in the Component Tree and use the Common Attributes section of the Attribute tool window to configure the flow layout behavior:

Figure 19-39

19.17 Widget Group Alignment and Distribution

The Android Studio Layout Editor tool provides a range of alignment and distribution actions that can be performed when two or more widgets are selected in the layout. Shift-click on each of the widgets to be included in the action, right-click on the layout and make a selection from the many options displayed in the Align menu:

A Guide to Using ConstraintLayout in Android Studio

Figure 19-40

As shown in Figure 19-41 below, these options are also accessible via the Align button located in the Layout Editor toolbar:

Figure 19-41

Similarly, the Pack menu (Figure 19-42) can be used to collectively reposition the selected widgets so that they are packed tightly together, either vertically or horizontally. It achieves this by changing the widgets' absolute x and y coordinates but does not apply any constraints. The two distribution options in the Pack menu, on the other hand, move the selected widgets so that they are spaced evenly apart in either vertical or horizontal axis and apply constraints between the views to maintain this spacing:

A Guide to Using ConstraintLayout in Android Studio

Figure 19-42

19.18 Converting other Layouts to ConstraintLayout

For existing user interface layouts that use one or more of the other Android layout classes (such as RelativeLayout or LinearLayout), the Layout Editor tool provides an option to convert the user interface to use the ConstraintLayout.

The Component Tree panel is displayed beneath the Palette when the Layout Editor tool is open and in Design mode. To convert a layout to ConstraintLayout, locate it within the Component Tree, right-click on it, and select the *Convert <current layout> to Constraint Layout* menu option:

Figure 19-43

When this menu option is selected, Android Studio will convert the selected layout to a ConstraintLayout and use inference to establish constraints designed to match the layout behavior of the original layout type.

19.19 Summary

A redesigned Layout Editor tool combined with ConstraintLayout makes designing complex user interface layouts with Android Studio a relatively fast and intuitive process. This chapter has covered the concepts of constraints, margins, and bias in more detail while also exploring how ConstraintLayout-based design has been integrated into the Layout Editor tool.

Chapter 20

20. Working with ConstraintLayout Chains and Ratios in Android Studio

The previous chapters have introduced the key features of the ConstraintLayout class and outlined the best practices for ConstraintLayout-based user interface design within the Android Studio Layout Editor. Although the concepts of ConstraintLayout chains and ratios were outlined in the chapter entitled *"A Guide to the Android ConstraintLayout"*, we have not yet addressed how to use these features within the Layout Editor. Therefore, this chapter's focus is to provide practical steps on how to create and manage chains and ratios when using the ConstraintLayout class.

20.1 Creating a Chain

Chains may be implemented by adding a few lines to an activity's XML layout resource file or by using some chain-specific features of the Layout Editor.

Consider a layout consisting of three Button widgets constrained to be positioned in the top-left, top-center, and top-right of the ConstraintLayout parent, as illustrated in Figure 20-1:

Figure 20-1

To represent such a layout, the XML resource layout file might contain the following entries for the button widgets:

```
<Button
    android:id="@+id/button1"
    android:layout_width="wrap_content"
    android:layout_height="wrap_content"
    android:layout_marginStart="8dp"
    android:layout_marginTop="16dp"
    android:text="Button"
    app:layout_constraintHorizontal_bias="0.5"
    app:layout_constraintStart_toStartOf="parent"
    app:layout_constraintTop_toTopOf="parent" />

<Button
    android:id="@+id/button2"
    android:layout_width="wrap_content"
    android:layout_height="wrap_content"
```

Working with ConstraintLayout Chains and Ratios in Android Studio

```
        android:layout_marginEnd="8dp"
        android:layout_marginStart="8dp"
        android:layout_marginTop="16dp"
        android:text="Button"
        app:layout_constraintHorizontal_bias="0.5"
        app:layout_constraintEnd_toStartOf="@+id/button3"
        app:layout_constraintStart_toEndOf="@+id/button1"
        app:layout_constraintTop_toTopOf="parent" />

<Button
        android:id="@+id/button3"
        android:layout_width="wrap_content"
        android:layout_height="wrap_content"
        android:layout_marginEnd="8dp"
        android:layout_marginTop="16dp"
        android:text="Button"
        app:layout_constraintHorizontal_bias="0.5"
        app:layout_constraintEnd_toEndOf="parent"
        app:layout_constraintTop_toTopOf="parent" />
```

As currently configured, there are no bi-directional constraints to group these widgets into a chain. To address this, additional constraints need to be added from the right-hand side of button1 to the left side of button2 and from the left side of button3 to the right side of button2 as follows:

```
<Button
        android:id="@+id/button1"
        android:layout_width="wrap_content"
        android:layout_height="wrap_content"
        android:layout_marginStart="8dp"
        android:layout_marginTop="16dp"
        android:text="Button"
        app:layout_constraintHorizontal_bias="0.5"
        app:layout_constraintStart_toStartOf="parent"
        app:layout_constraintTop_toTopOf="parent"
        app:layout_constraintEnd_toStartOf="@+id/button2" />

<Button
        android:id="@+id/button2"
        android:layout_width="wrap_content"
        android:layout_height="wrap_content"
        android:layout_marginEnd="8dp"
        android:layout_marginStart="8dp"
        android:layout_marginTop="16dp"
        android:text="Button"
        app:layout_constraintHorizontal_bias="0.5"
        app:layout_constraintEnd_toStartOf="@+id/button3"
        app:layout_constraintStart_toEndOf="@+id/button1"
```

```
        app:layout_constraintTop_toTopOf="parent" />

<Button
    android:id="@+id/button3"
    android:layout_width="wrap_content"
    android:layout_height="wrap_content"
    android:layout_marginEnd="8dp"
    android:layout_marginTop="16dp"
    android:text="Button"
    app:layout_constraintHorizontal_bias="0.5"
    app:layout_constraintEnd_toEndOf="parent"
    app:layout_constraintTop_toTopOf="parent"
    app:layout_constraintStart_toEndOf="@+id/button2" />
```

With these changes, the widgets now have bi-directional horizontal constraints configured. This constitutes a ConstraintLayout chain represented visually within the Layout Editor by chain connections, as shown in Figure 20-2 below. Note that the chain has defaulted to the *spread* chain style in this configuration.

Figure 20-2

A chain may also be created by right-clicking on one of the views and selecting the *Chains -> Create Horizontal Chain* or *Chains -> Create Vertical Chain* menu options.

20.2 Changing the Chain Style

If no chain style is configured, the ConstraintLayout will default to the spread chain style. The chain style can be altered by right-clicking any of the widgets in the chain and selecting the *Cycle Chain Mode* menu option. Each time the menu option is clicked, the style will switch to another setting in the order of spread, spread inside, and packed.

Alternatively, the style may be specified in the Attributes tool window unfolding the *layout_constraints* property and changing either the *horizontal_chainStyle* or *vertical_chainStyle* property depending on the orientation of the chain:

Figure 20-3

20.3 Spread Inside Chain Style

Figure 20-4 illustrates the effect of changing the chain style to the *spread inside* chain style using the above techniques:

Figure 20-4

20.4 Packed Chain Style

Using the same technique, changing the chain style property to *packed* causes the layout to change, as shown in Figure 20-5:

Figure 20-5

20.5 Packed Chain Style with Bias

The positioning of the packed chain may be influenced by applying a bias value. The bias can be between 0.0 and 1.0, with 0.5 representing the parent's center. Bias is controlled by selecting the chain head widget and assigning a value to the *layout_constraintHorizontal_bias* or *layout_constraintVertical_bias* attribute in the Attributes panel. Figure 20-6 shows a packed chain with a horizontal bias setting of 0.2:

Figure 20-6

20.6 Weighted Chain

The final area of chains to explore involves weighting the individual widgets to control how much space each widget in the chain occupies within the available space. A weighted chain may only be implemented using the spread chain style, and any widget within the chain that responds to the weight property must have the corresponding dimension property (height for a vertical chain and width for a horizontal chain) configured for *match constraint* mode. Match constraint mode for a widget dimension may be configured by selecting the widget, displaying the Attributes panel, and changing the dimension to *match_constraint* (equivalent to 0dp). In Figure 20-7, for example, the *layout_width* constraint for a button has been set to *match_constraint (0dp)* to indicate that the width of the widget is to be determined based on the prevailing constraint settings:

Figure 20-7

Assuming that the spread chain style has been selected and all three buttons have been configured such that the width dimension is set to match the constraints, the widgets in the chain will expand equally to fill the available space:

Figure 20-8

The amount of space occupied by each widget relative to the other widgets in the chain can be controlled by adding weight properties to the widgets. Figure 20-9 shows the effect of setting the *layout_constraintHorizontal_weight* property to 4 on button1, and to 2 on both button2 and button3:

Figure 20-9

As a result of these weighting values, button1 occupies half of the space (4/8), while button2 and button3 each occupy one-quarter (2/8) of the space.

20.7 Working with Ratios

ConstraintLayout ratios allow one widget dimension to be sized relative to the widget's other dimension (also referred to as aspect ratio). For example, an aspect ratio setting could be applied to an ImageView to ensure that its width is always twice its height.

Working with ConstraintLayout Chains and Ratios in Android Studio

A dimension ratio constraint is configured by setting the constrained dimension to match constraint mode and configuring the *layout_constraintDimensionRatio* attribute on that widget to the required ratio. This ratio value may be specified as a float value or a *width:height* ratio setting. The following XML excerpt, for example, configures a ratio of 2:1 on an ImageView widget:

```
<ImageView
        android:layout_width="0dp"
        android:layout_height="100dp"
        android:id="@+id/imageView"
        app:layout_constraintDimensionRatio="2:1" />
```

The above example demonstrates how to configure a ratio when only one dimension is set to *match constraint*. A ratio may also be applied when both dimensions are set to match constraint mode. This involves specifying the ratio preceded with either an H or a W to indicate which of the dimensions is constrained relative to the other.

Consider, for example, the following XML excerpt for an ImageView object:

```
<ImageView
    android:layout_width="0dp"
    android:layout_height="0dp"
    android:id="@+id/imageView"
    app:layout_constraintBottom_toBottomOf="parent"
    app:layout_constraintRight_toRightOf="parent"
    app:layout_constraintLeft_toLeftOf="parent"
    app:layout_constraintTop_toTopOf="parent"
    app:layout_constraintDimensionRatio="W,1:3" />
```

In the above example, the height will be defined subject to the constraints applied to it. In this case, constraints have been configured such that it is attached to the top and bottom of the parent view, essentially stretching the widget to fill the entire height of the parent. On the other hand, the width dimension has been constrained to be one-third of the ImageView's height dimension. Consequently, whatever size screen or orientation the layout appears on, the ImageView will always be the same height as the parent and the width one-third of that height.

The same results may also be achieved without manually editing the XML resource file. Whenever a widget dimension is set to match constraint mode, a ratio control toggle appears in the Inspector area of the property panel. Figure 20-10, for example, shows the layout width and height attributes of a button widget set to match constraint mode and 100dp respectively, and highlights the ratio control toggle in the widget sizing preview:

Figure 20-10

By default, the ratio sizing control is toggled off. Clicking on the control enables the ratio constraint and displays an additional field where the ratio may be changed:

Figure 20-11

20.8 Summary

Both chains and ratios are powerful features of the ConstraintLayout class intended to provide additional options for designing flexible and responsive user interface layouts within Android applications. As outlined in this chapter, the Android Studio Layout Editor has been enhanced to make it easier to use these features during the user interface design process.

Chapter 21

21. An Android Studio Layout Editor ConstraintLayout Tutorial

The easiest and most productive way to design a user interface for an Android application is to use the Android Studio Layout Editor tool. This chapter will provide an overview of how to create a ConstraintLayout-based user interface using this approach. The exercise included in this chapter will also be used as an opportunity to outline the creation of an activity starting with a "bare-bones" Android Studio project.

Having covered the use of the Android Studio Layout Editor, the chapter will also introduce the Layout Inspector tool.

21.1 An Android Studio Layout Editor Tool Example

The first step in this phase of the example is to create a new Android Studio project. Launch Android Studio and close any previously opened projects by selecting the *File -> Close Project* menu option.

Select the *New Project* option from the welcome screen, select the Empty Views Activity template, and click Next. Enter *LayoutSample* into the Name field and specify *com.ebookfrenzy.layoutsample* as the package name. Before clicking the Finish button, change the Minimum API level setting to API 26: Android 8.0 (Oreo) and the Language menu to Java.

21.2 Preparing the Layout Editor Environment

Locate and double-click on the *activity_main.xml* layout file in the *app -> res -> layout* folder to load it into the Layout Editor tool. Since this tutorial aims to gain experience with the use of constraints, turn off the Autoconnect feature using the button located in the Layout Editor toolbar. Once disabled, the button will appear with a line through it, as is the case in Figure 21-1:

Figure 21-1

If the default margin value to the right of the Autoconnect button is not set to 8dp, click on it and select 8dp from the resulting panel.

The user interface design will also use the ImageView object to display an image. Before proceeding, this image should be added to the project, ready for use later in the chapter. This file is named *GalaxyS23.webp* and can be found in the *project_icons* folder of the sample code download available from the following URL:

https://www.ebookfrenzy.com/retail/giraffejava/index.php

An Android Studio Layout Editor ConstraintLayout Tutorial

Within Android Studio, display the Resource Manager tool window (*View -> Tool Windows -> Resource Manager*). Locate the *GalaxyS23.webp* image in the file system navigator for your operating system and drag and drop the image onto the Resource Manager tool window. In the resulting dialog, click *Next*, followed by the *Import* button, to add the image to the project. The image should now appear in the Resource Manager, as shown in Figure 21-2 below:

Figure 21-2

The image will also appear in the *res -> drawables* section of the Project tool window:

Figure 21-3

21.3 Adding the Widgets to the User Interface

From within the *Common* palette category, drag an ImageView object into the center of the display view. Note that horizontal and vertical dashed lines appear, indicating the center axes of the display. When centered, release the mouse button to drop the view into position. Once placed within the layout, the Resources dialog will appear, seeking the image to be displayed within the view. In the search bar at the top of the dialog, enter "galaxy" to locate the *galaxys6.png* resource, as illustrated in Figure 21-4.

An Android Studio Layout Editor ConstraintLayout Tutorial

Figure 21-4

Select the image and click OK to assign it to the ImageView object. If necessary, adjust the size of the ImageView using the resize handles and reposition it in the center of the layout. At this point, the layout should match Figure 21-5:

Figure 21-5

Click and drag a TextView object from the *Common* section of the palette and position it to appear above the ImageView, as illustrated in Figure 21-6.

Using the Attributes panel, unfold the *textAppearance* attribute entry in the Common Attributes section, change the *textSize* property to 24sp, the *textAlignment* setting to center, and the text to "Samsung Galaxy S23".

Figure 21-6

Next, add three Button widgets along the bottom of the layout and set the text attributes of these views to "Buy Now", "Pricing", and "Details". The completed layout should now match Figure 21-7:

Figure 21-7

At this point, the widgets are not sufficiently constrained for the layout engine to be able to position and size the widgets at runtime. Were the app to run now, all of the widgets would be positioned in the top left-hand corner of the display.

With the widgets added to the layout, use the device rotation menu located in the Layout Editor toolbar (indicated by the arrow in Figure 21-8) to view the user interface in landscape orientation:

Figure 21-8

The absence of constraints results in a layout that fails to adapt to the change in device orientation, leaving the content off-center and with part of the image and all three buttons positioned beyond the screen's viewable area. Some work still needs to be done to make this a responsive user interface.

21.4 Adding the Constraints

Constraints are the key to creating layouts that adapt to device orientation changes and different screen sizes. Begin by rotating the layout back to portrait orientation and selecting the TextView widget above the ImageView. With the widget selected, establish constraints from the left, right and top sides of the TextView to the corresponding sides of the parent ConstraintLayout, as shown in Figure 21-9. Set the spacing on the top constraint to 16:

Figure 21-9

With the TextView widget constrained, select the ImageView instance and establish opposing constraints on the left and right sides, each connected to the corresponding sides of the parent layout. Next, establish a constraint connection from the top of the ImageView to the bottom of the TextView and from the bottom of the ImageView to the top of the center Button widget. If necessary, click and drag the ImageView to remain positioned in the vertical center of the layout.

With the ImageView still selected, use the Inspector in the attributes panel to change the top and bottom margins on the ImageView to 24 and 8, respectively, and to change both the widget height and width dimension properties to *match_constraint* so that the widget will resize to match the constraints. These settings will allow the layout engine to enlarge and reduce the size of the ImageView when necessary to accommodate layout changes:

Figure 21-11 shows the currently implemented constraints for the ImageView relative to the other elements in the layout:

Figure 21-11

The final task is to add constraints to the three Button widgets. For this example, the buttons will be placed in a chain. Begin by turning on Autoconnect within the Layout Editor by clicking the toolbar button highlighted in Figure 21-1.

Next, click on the Buy Now button and then shift-click on the other two buttons to select all three. Right-click on the Buy Now button and select the *Chains -> Create Horizontal Chain* menu option from the resulting menu. By default, the chain will be displayed using the spread style, which is the correct behavior for this example.

Finally, establish a constraint between the bottom of the Buy Now button and the bottom of the layout with a margin of 8. Repeat this step for the remaining buttons.

On completion of these steps, the buttons should be constrained as outlined in Figure 21-12:

Figure 21-12

21.5 Testing the Layout

With the constraints added to the layout, rotate the screen into landscape orientation and verify that the layout adapts to accommodate the new screen dimensions.

While the Layout Editor tool provides a good visual environment in which to design user interface layouts, when it comes to testing, there is no substitute for testing the running app. Launch the app on a physical Android device or emulator session and verify that the user interface reflects the layout created in the Layout Editor. Figure 21-13, for example, shows the running app in landscape orientation:

Figure 21-13

The user interface design is now complete. Designing a more complex user interface layout is a continuation of the steps outlined above. Drag and drop views onto the display, position, constrain and set properties as needed.

21.6 Using the Layout Inspector

The hierarchy of components comprising a user interface layout may be viewed using the Layout Inspector tool. The app must be running on a device or emulator running Android API 29 or later to access this information. Once the app is running, select the *Tools -> Layout Inspector* menu option, followed by the process to be inspected using the menu marked A in Figure 21-14 below).

Once the inspector loads, the leftmost panel (A) shows the hierarchy of components that make up the user

An Android Studio Layout Editor ConstraintLayout Tutorial

interface layout. The center panel (B) visually represents the layout design. Clicking on a widget in the visual layout will cause that item to highlight in the hierarchy list, making it easy to find where a visual component is situated relative to the overall layout hierarchy.

The right-most panel (marked C in Figure 21-14) contains all the property settings for the currently selected component, allowing for an in-depth analysis of the component's internal configuration. Where appropriate, the value cell will contain a link to the location of the property setting within the project source code.

Figure 21-14

To view the layout in 3D, click on the button labeled D. This displays an "exploded" representation of the hierarchy so that it can be rotated and inspected. This can be useful for tasks such as identifying obscured views:

Figure 21-15

Click and drag the rendering to rotate it in three dimensions, using the slider indicated by the arrow above to increase the spacing between the layers. Click the button marked E again to return to the 2D view.

21.7 Summary

The Layout Editor tool in Android Studio has been tightly integrated with the ConstraintLayout class. This chapter has worked through creating an example user interface intended to outline how a ConstraintLayout-based user interface can be implemented using the Layout Editor tool to add widgets and set constraints. This chapter also introduced the Live Layout Inspector tool, which is useful for analyzing the structural composition of a user interface layout.

22. Manual XML Layout Design in Android Studio

While the design of layouts using the Android Studio Layout Editor tool greatly improves productivity, it is still possible to create XML layouts by manually editing the underlying XML. This chapter will introduce the basics of the Android XML layout file format.

22.1 Manually Creating an XML Layout

The structure of an XML layout file is quite straightforward and follows the hierarchical approach of the view tree. The first line of an XML resource file should ideally include the following standard declaration:

```
<?xml version="1.0" encoding="utf-8"?>
```

This declaration should be followed by the root element of the layout, typically a container view such as a layout manager. This is represented by opening and closing tags and any properties that need to be set on the view. The following XML, for example, declares a ConstraintLayout view as the root element and sets *match_parent* attributes such that it fills all the available space of the device display:

```
<?xml version="1.0" encoding="utf-8"?>
<androidx.constraintlayout.widget.ConstraintLayout
    xmlns:android="http://schemas.android.com/apk/res/android"
    xmlns:app="http://schemas.android.com/apk/res-auto"
    xmlns:tools="http://schemas.android.com/tools"
    android:layout_width="match_parent"
    android:layout_height="match_parent"
    android:paddingLeft="16dp"
    android:paddingRight="16dp"
    android:paddingTop="16dp"
    android:paddingBottom="16dp"
    tools:context=".MainActivity">
</androidx.constraintlayout.widget.ConstraintLayout>
```

In the above example, the layout element is also configured with padding on each side of 16dp (density-independent pixels). Any specification of spacing in an Android layout must be specified using one of the following units of measurement:

- **in** – Inches.

- **mm** – Millimeters.

- **pt** – Points (1/72 of an inch).

- **dp** – Density-independent pixels. An abstract unit of measurement based on the physical density of the device display relative to a 160dpi display baseline.

- **sp** – Scale-independent pixels. Similar to dp but scaled based on the user's font preference.

Manual XML Layout Design in Android Studio

- **px** – Actual screen pixels. Use is not recommended since different displays will have different pixels per inch. Use *dp* in preference to this unit.

Any children that need to be added to the ConstraintLayout parent must be *nested* within the opening and closing tags. In the following example, a Button widget has been added as a child of the ConstraintLayout:

```
<?xml version="1.0" encoding="utf-8"?>
<androidx.constraintlayout.widget.ConstraintLayout
    xmlns:android="http://schemas.android.com/apk/res/android"
    xmlns:app="http://schemas.android.com/apk/res-auto"
    xmlns:tools="http://schemas.android.com/tools"
    android:layout_width="match_parent"
    android:layout_height="match_parent"
    tools:context=".MainActivity">

    <Button
        android:text="My Button"
        android:layout_width="wrap_content"
        android:layout_height="wrap_content"
        android:id="@+id/button" />

</androidx.constraintlayout.widget.ConstraintLayout>
```

As currently implemented, the button has no constraint connections. At runtime, therefore, the button will appear in the top left-hand corner of the screen (though indented 16dp by the padding assigned to the parent layout). If opposing constraints are added to the sides of the button, however, it will appear centered within the layout:

```
<Button
    android:text="My Button"
    android:layout_width="wrap_content"
    android:layout_height="wrap_content"
    android:id="@+id/button"
    app:layout_constraintBottom_toBottomOf="parent"
    app:layout_constraintEnd_toEndOf="parent"
    app:layout_constraintStart_toStartOf="parent"
    app:layout_constraintTop_toTopOf="parent" />
```

To add a second widget to the layout, embed it within the body of the ConstraintLayout element. The following modification, for example, adds a TextView widget to the layout:

```
<?xml version="1.0" encoding="utf-8"?>
<androidx.constraintlayout.widget.ConstraintLayout
    xmlns:android="http://schemas.android.com/apk/res/android"
    xmlns:app="http://schemas.android.com/apk/res-auto"
    xmlns:tools="http://schemas.android.com/tools"
    android:layout_width="match_parent"
    android:layout_height="match_parent"
    android:paddingLeft="16dp"
    android:paddingTop="16dp"
```

```
    android:paddingRight="16dp"
    android:paddingBottom="16dp"
    tools:context=".MainActivity">

    <Button
        android:text="@string/button_string"
        android:layout_width="wrap_content"
        android:layout_height="wrap_content"
        android:id="@+id/button"
        app:layout_constraintBottom_toBottomOf="parent"
        app:layout_constraintEnd_toEndOf="parent"
        app:layout_constraintStart_toStartOf="parent"
        app:layout_constraintTop_toTopOf="parent" />

    <TextView
        android:text="My Text"
        android:layout_width="wrap_content"
        android:layout_height="wrap_content"
        android:id="@+id/textView" />

</androidx.constraintlayout.widget.ConstraintLayout>
```

Once again, the absence of constraints on the newly added TextView will cause it to appear in the top left-hand corner of the layout at runtime. The following modifications add opposing constraints connected to the parent layout to center the widget horizontally, together with a constraint connecting the bottom of the TextView to the top of the button:

```
<TextView
    android:text="My Text"
    android:layout_width="wrap_content"
    android:layout_height="wrap_content"
    android:id="@+id/textView"
    android:layout_marginTop="8dp"
    android:layout_marginBottom="8dp"
    app:layout_constraintBottom_toTopOf="@+id/button"
    app:layout_constraintEnd_toEndOf="parent"
    app:layout_constraintStart_toStartOf="parent"
    app:layout_constraintTop_toTopOf="parent" />
```

Also, note that the Button and TextView views have several attributes declared. Both views have been assigned IDs and configured to display text strings represented by string resources named *button_string* and *text_string*, respectively. Additionally, the *wrap_content* height and width properties have been declared on both objects so that they are sized to accommodate the content (in this case, the text referenced by the string resource value).

Viewed from within the Preview panel of the Layout Editor in Design mode, the above layout will be rendered as shown in Figure 22-1:

Figure 22-1

22.2 Manual XML vs. Visual Layout Design

When to write XML manually as opposed to using the Layout Editor tool in design mode is a matter of personal preference. There are, however, advantages to using design mode.

First, design mode will generally be quicker because it avoids the need to type XML lines. Additionally, design mode avoids the need to learn the intricacies of the various property values of the Android SDK view classes. Rather than continually referring to the Android documentation to find the correct keywords and values, most properties can be located by referring to the Attributes panel.

All the advantages of design mode aside, it is important to remember that the two approaches to user interface design are in no way mutually exclusive. As an application developer, you will likely create user interfaces within design mode while performing fine-tuning and layout tweaks of the design by directly editing the generated XML resources. Both views of the interface design are displayed side-by-side within the Android Studio environment, making it easy to work seamlessly on both the XML and the visual layout.

22.3 Summary

The Android Studio Layout Editor tool provides a visually intuitive method for designing user interfaces. Using a drag-and-drop paradigm combined with a set of property editors, the tool provides considerable productivity benefits to the application developer.

User interface designs may also be implemented by manually writing the XML layout resource files, the format of which is well-structured and easily understood.

The fact that the Layout Editor tool generates XML resource files means that these two approaches to interface design can be combined to provide a "best of both worlds" approach to user interface development.

23. Managing Constraints using Constraint Sets

Until this point in the book, all user interface design tasks have been performed using the Android Studio Layout Editor tool, either in text or design mode. An alternative to writing XML resource files or using the Android Studio Layout Editor is to write Java code to directly create, configure and manipulate the view objects comprising an Android activity's user interface. This chapter will explore some advantages and disadvantages of writing Java code to create a user interface before describing key concepts such as view properties and the creation and management of layout constraints.

In the next chapter, an example project will be created and used to demonstrate some of the typical steps involved in this approach to Android user interface creation.

23.1 Java Code vs. XML Layout Files

There are several advantages to using XML resource files to design a user interface instead of writing Java code. In fact, Google goes to considerable lengths in the Android documentation to extol the virtues of XML resources over Java code. As discussed in the previous chapter, one key advantage of the XML approach is using the Android Studio Layout Editor tool, which generates XML resources. A second advantage is that once an application has been created, changes to user interface screens can be made by modifying the XML file, thereby avoiding recompiling the application. Also, even when-hand writing XML layouts, it is possible to get instant feedback on the appearance of the user interface using the preview feature of the Android Studio Layout Editor tool. To test the appearance of a Java-created user interface, the developer will inevitably cycle through a loop of writing code, compiling, and testing to complete the design work.

Regarding the strengths of the Java coding approach to layout creation, the most significant advantage that Java has over XML resource files comes into play when dealing with dynamic user interfaces. XML resource files are inherently most useful when defining static layouts, which are unlikely to change significantly from one invocation of an activity to the next. Java code, on the other hand, is ideal for creating user interfaces dynamically at run-time. This is particularly useful when the user interface may appear differently each time the activity executes, subject to external factors.

Knowledge of working with user interface components in Java code can also be useful when dynamic changes to a static XML resource-based layout must be performed in real-time as the activity is running.

Finally, some developers prefer to write Java code than to use layout tools and XML, regardless of the advantages offered by the latter approaches.

23.2 Creating Views

As previously established, the Android SDK includes a toolbox of view classes to meet most basic user interface design needs. The creation of a view in Java is a matter of creating instances of these classes, passing through as an argument a reference to the activity with which that view is to be associated.

The first view (typically a container view to which additional child views can be added) is displayed to the user via a call to the *setContentView()* activity method. Additional views may be added to the root view via calls to the object's *addView()* method.

When working with Java code to manipulate views contained in XML layout resource files, it is necessary to obtain the ID of the view. The same rule holds true for views created in Java. As such, it is necessary to assign an ID to any view for which certain types of access will be required in subsequent Java code. This is achieved via a call to the *setId()* method of the view object in question. In later code, the ID for a view may be obtained via the object's *getId()* method.

23.3 View Attributes

Each view class has associated with it a range of *attributes*. These property settings are set directly on the view instances and generally define how the view object will appear or behave. Examples of attributes are the text that appears on a Button object or the background color of a ConstraintLayout view. Each view class within the Android SDK has a pre-defined set of methods that allow the user to *set* and *get* these property values. The Button class, for example, has a *setText()* method, which can be called from within Java code to set the text displayed on the button to a specific string value. On the other hand, the background color of a ConstraintLayout object can be set with a call to the object's *setBackgroundColor()* method.

23.4 Constraint Sets

While property settings are internal to view objects and dictate how a view appears and behaves, *constraint sets* control how a view appears relative to its parent view and other sibling views. Every ConstraintLayout instance has associated with it a set of constraints that define how its child views are positioned and constrained.

The key to working with constraint sets in Java code is the *ConstraintSet* class. This class contains a range of methods that allow tasks such as creating, configuring, and applying constraints to a ConstraintLayout instance. In addition, the current constraints for a ConstraintLayout instance may be copied into a ConstraintSet object and applied to other layouts (with or without modifications).

A ConstraintSet instance is created just like any other Java object:

```
ConstraintSet set = new ConstraintSet();
```

Once a constraint set has been created, methods can be called on the instance to perform a wide range of tasks.

23.4.1 Establishing Connections

The *connect()* method of the ConstraintSet class is used to establish constraint connections between views. The following code configures a constraint set in which the left-hand side of a Button view is connected to the right-hand side of an EditText view with a margin of 70dp:

```
set.connect(button1.getId(), ConstraintSet.LEFT,
            editText1.getId(), ConstraintSet.RIGHT, 70);
```

23.4.2 Applying Constraints to a Layout

Once the constraint set is configured, it must be applied to a ConstraintLayout instance before it will take effect. A constraint set is applied via a call to the *applyTo()* method, passing through a reference to the layout object to which the settings are to be applied:

```
set.applyTo(myLayout);
```

23.4.3 Parent Constraint Connections

Connections between a child view and its parent ConstraintLayout may also be established by referencing the ConstraintSet.PARENT_ID constant. In the following example, the constraint set is configured to connect the top edge of a Button view to the top of the parent layout with a margin of 100dp:

```
set.connect(button1.getId(), ConstraintSet.TOP,
            ConstraintSet.PARENT_ID, ConstraintSet.TOP, 100);
```

23.4.4 Sizing Constraints

Several methods are available for controlling the sizing behavior of views. The following code, for example, sets the horizontal size of a Button view to *wrap_content* and the vertical size of an ImageView instance to a maximum of 250dp:

```
set.constrainWidth(button1.getId(), ConstraintSet.WRAP_CONTENT);
set.constrainMaxHeight(imageView1.getId(), 250);
```

23.4.5 Constraint Bias

As outlined in the chapter entitled *"A Guide to Using ConstraintLayout in Android Studio"*, when a view has opposing constraints, it is centered along the axis of the constraints (i.e., horizontally or vertically). This centering can be adjusted by applying a bias along the particular constraint axis. When using the Android Studio Layout Editor, this is achieved using the controls in the Attributes tool window. When working with a constraint set, however, bias can be added using the *setHorizontalBias()* and *setVerticalBias()* methods, referencing the view ID and the bias as a floating point value between 0 and 1.

The following code, for example, constrains the left and right-hand sides of a Button to the corresponding sides of the parent layout before applying a 25% horizontal bias:

```
set.connect(button1.getId(), ConstraintSet.LEFT,
            ConstraintSet.PARENT_ID, ConstraintSet.LEFT, 0);
set.connect(button1.getId(), ConstraintSet.RIGHT,
            ConstraintSet.PARENT_ID, ConstraintSet.RIGHT, 0);
set.setHorizontalBias(button1.getId(), 0.25f);
```

23.4.6 Alignment Constraints

Alignments may also be applied using a constraint set. The full set of alignment options available with the Android Studio Layout Editor may also be configured using a constraint set via the *centerVertically()* and *centerHorizontally()* methods, both of which take various arguments depending on the alignment being configured. In addition, the *center()* method may be used to center a view between two other views.

In the code below, button2 is positioned so that it is aligned horizontally with button1:

```
set.centerHorizontally(button2.getId(), button1.getId());
```

23.4.7 Copying and Applying Constraint Sets

The current constraint set for a ConstraintLayout instance may be copied into a constraint set object using the *clone()* method. The following line of code, for example, copies the constraint settings from a ConstraintLayout instance named *myLayout* into a constraint set object:

```
set.clone(myLayout);
```

Once copied, the constraint set may be applied directly to another layout or, as in the following example, modified before being applied to the second layout:

```
ConstraintSet set = new ConstraintSet();
set.clone(myLayout);
set.constrainWidth(button1.getId(), ConstraintSet.WRAP_CONTENT);
set.applyTo(mySecondLayout);
```

23.4.8 ConstraintLayout Chains

Vertical and horizontal chains may also be created within a constraint set using the *createHorizontalChain()* and *createVerticalChain()* methods. The syntax for using these methods is as follows:

```
createHorizontalChain(int leftId, int leftSide, int rightId,
```

```
            int rightSide, int[] chainIds, float[] weights, int style);
```

Based on the above syntax, the following example creates a horizontal spread chain that starts with button1 and ends with button4. In between these views are button2 and button3 with weighting set to zero for both:

```
int[] chainViews = {button2.getId(), button3.getId()};
float[] chainWeights = {0, 0};

set.createHorizontalChain(button1.getId(), ConstraintSet.LEFT,
                          button4.getId(), ConstraintSet.RIGHT,
                          chainViews, chainWeights,
                          ConstraintSet.CHAIN_SPREAD);
```

A view can be removed from a chain by passing the ID of the view to be removed through to either the *removeFromHorizontalChain()* or *removeFromVerticalChain()* methods. A view may be added to an existing chain using either the *addToHorizontalChain()* or *addToVerticalChain()* methods. In both cases, the methods take as arguments the IDs of the views between which the new view is to be inserted as follows:

```
set.addToHorizontalChain(newViewId, leftViewId, rightViewId);
```

23.4.9 Guidelines

Guidelines are added to a constraint set using the *create()* method and then positioned using the *setGuidelineBegin()*, *setGuidelineEnd()*, or *setGuidelinePercent()* methods. In the following code, a vertical guideline is created and positioned 50% across the width of the parent layout. The left side of a button view is then connected to the guideline with no margin:

```
set.create(R.id.myGuideline, ConstraintSet.VERTICAL_GUIDELINE);
set.setGuidelinePercent(R.id.myGuideline, 0.5f);

set.connect(button.getId(), ConstraintSet.LEFT,
            R.id.myGuideline, ConstraintSet.RIGHT, 0);

set.applyTo(layout);
```

23.4.10 Removing Constraints

A constraint may be removed from a view in a constraint set using the *clear()* method, passing through as arguments the view ID and the anchor point for which the constraint is to be removed:

```
set.clear(button.getId(), ConstraintSet.LEFT);
```

Similarly, all of the constraints on a view may be removed in a single step by referencing only the view in the *clear()* method call:

```
set.clear(button.getId());
```

23.4.11 Scaling

The scale of a view within a layout may be adjusted using the ConstraintSet *setScaleX()* and *setScaleY()* methods which take as arguments the view on which the operation is to be performed together with a float value indicating the scale. In the following code, a button object is scaled to twice its original width and half the height:

```
set.setScaleX(myButton.getId(), 2f);
set.setScaleY(myButton.getId(), 0.5f);
```

23.4.12 Rotation

A view may be rotated on either the X or Y axis using the *setRotationX()* and *setRotationY()* methods, respectively, both of which must be passed the ID of the view to be rotated and a float value representing the degree of rotation to be performed. The pivot point on which the rotation is to take place may be defined via a call to the *setTransformPivot()*, *setTransformPivotX()*, and *setTransformPivotY()* methods. The following code rotates a button view 30 degrees on the Y axis using a pivot point located at point 500, 500:

```
set.setTransformPivot(button.getId(), 500, 500);
set.setRotationY(button.getId(), 30);
set.applyTo(layout);
```

Having covered the theory of constraint sets and user interface creation from within Java code, the next chapter will work through creating an example application to put this theory into practice. For more details on the ConstraintSet class, refer to the reference guide at the following URL:

https://developer.android.com/reference/androidx/constraintlayout/widget/ConstraintSet

23.5 Summary

As an alternative to writing XML layout resource files or using the Android Studio Layout Editor tool, Android user interfaces may also be dynamically created in Java code.

Creating layouts in Java code consists of creating instances of view classes and setting attributes on those objects to define required appearance and behavior.

How a view is positioned and sized relative to its ConstraintLayout parent view and any sibling views are defined using constraint sets. A constraint set is represented by an instance of the ConstraintSet class, which, once created, can be configured using a wide range of method calls to perform tasks such as establishing constraint connections, controlling view sizing behavior, and creating chains.

With the basics of the ConstraintSet class covered in this chapter, the next chapter will work through a tutorial that puts these features to practical use.

Chapter 24

24. An Android ConstraintSet Tutorial

The previous chapter introduced the basic concepts of creating and modifying user interface layouts in Java code using the ConstraintLayout and ConstraintSet classes. This chapter will put these concepts into practice by creating an example layout created entirely in Java code and without using the Android Studio Layout Editor tool.

24.1 Creating the Example Project in Android Studio

Launch Android Studio and select the *New Project* option from the welcome screen and, within the resulting new project dialog, choose the Empty Views Activity template before clicking on the Next button.

Enter *JavaLayout* into the Name field and specify *com.ebookfrenzy.javalayout* as the package name. Before clicking on the Finish button, change the Minimum API level setting to API 26: Android 8.0 (Oreo) and the Language menu to Java.

Once the project has been created, the *MainActivity.java* file should automatically load into the editing panel. As we have come to expect, Android Studio has created a template activity and overridden the *onCreate()* method, providing an ideal location for Java code to be added to create a user interface.

24.2 Adding Views to an Activity

The *onCreate()* method is currently designed to use a resource layout file for the user interface. Begin, therefore, by deleting this line from the method:

```
@Override
protected void onCreate(Bundle savedInstanceState) {
        super.onCreate(savedInstanceState);
        setContentView(R.layout.activity_main);
}
```

The next modification is to add a ConstraintLayout object with a single Button view child to the activity. This involves the creation of new instances of the ConstraintLayout and Button classes. The Button view then needs to be added as a child to the ConstraintLayout view, which, in turn, is displayed via a call to the *setContentView()* method of the activity instance:

```
package com.ebookfrenzy.javalayout;

import androidx.appcompat.app.AppCompatActivity;

import android.os.Bundle;
import androidx.constraintlayout.widget.ConstraintLayout;
import android.widget.Button;
import android.widget.EditText;
```

203

An Android ConstraintSet Tutorial

```
public class MainActivity extends AppCompatActivity {

    @Override
    protected void onCreate(Bundle savedInstanceState) {
        super.onCreate(savedInstanceState);
        configureLayout();
    }

    private void configureLayout() {
        Button myButton = new Button(this);
        ConstraintLayout myLayout = new ConstraintLayout(this);
        myLayout.addView(myButton);
        setContentView(myLayout);
    }
}
```

When new instances of user interface objects are created in this way, the constructor methods must be passed the context within which the object is being created, which, in this case, is the current activity. Since the above code resides within the activity class, the context is referenced by the standard *this* keyword:

```
Button myButton = new Button(this);
```

Once the above additions have been made, compile and run the application (either on a physical device or an emulator). Once launched, the visible result will be a button containing no text appearing in the top left-hand corner of the ConstraintLayout view, as shown in Figure 24-1:

Figure 24-1

24.3 Setting View Attributes

For this exercise, we need the background of the ConstraintLayout view to be blue and the Button view to display text that reads "Press Me" on a yellow background. These tasks can be achieved by setting attributes on the views in the Java code as outlined in the following code fragment. To allow the text on the button to be easily translated to other languages, it will be added as a String resource. Within the Project tool window, locate the *app -> res -> values -> strings.xml* file and modify it to add a resource value for the "Press Me" string:

```
<resources>
    <string name="app_name">JavaLayout</string>
    <string name="press_me">Press Me</string>
</resources>
```

Although this is the recommended way to handle strings directly referenced in code, many subsequent code

An Android ConstraintSet Tutorial

samples will directly enter strings into the code to avoid repetition of this step throughout the remainder of the book.

Once the string is stored as a resource, it can be accessed from within the code as follows:

```
getString(R.string.press_me);
```

With the string resource created, add code to the *configureLayout()* method to set the button text and color attributes:

```
.
.
import android.graphics.Color;

public class MainActivity extends AppCompatActivity {

    private void configureLayout() {
        Button myButton = new Button(this);
        myButton.setText(getString(R.string.press_me));
        myButton.setBackgroundColor(Color.YELLOW);

        ConstraintLayout myLayout = new ConstraintLayout(this);
        myLayout.setBackgroundColor(Color.BLUE);

        myLayout.addView(myButton);
        setContentView(myLayout);
    }
}
```

When the application is compiled and run, the layout will reflect the property settings such that the layout will appear with a blue background, and the button will display the assigned text on a yellow background.

24.4 Creating View IDs

When the layout is complete, it will consist of a Button and an EditText view. Before these views can be referenced within the methods of the ConstraintSet class, they must be assigned unique view IDs. The first step in this process is to create a new resource file containing these ID values.

Right-click on the *app -> res -> values* folder, select the *New -> Values Resource File* menu option, and name the new resource file *id.xml*. With the resource file created, edit it so that it reads as follows:

```
<?xml version="1.0" encoding="utf-8"?>
<resources>
    <item name="myButton" type="id" />
    <item name="myEditText" type="id" />
</resources>
```

At this point in the tutorial, only the Button has been created, so edit the *configureLayout()* method to assign the corresponding ID to the object:

```
private void configureLayout() {
    Button myButton = new Button(this);
    myButton.setText(getString(R.string.press_me));
    myButton.setBackgroundColor(Color.YELLOW);
```

205

```
    myButton.setId(R.id.myButton);
```
.
.

24.5 Configuring the Constraint Set

Without constraints, the ConstraintLayout view has placed the Button view in the display's top left corner. To instruct the layout view to place the button in a different location, in this case, centered both horizontally and vertically, it will be necessary to create a ConstraintSet instance, initialize it with the appropriate settings and apply it to the parent layout.

For this example, the button needs to be configured so that the width and height are constrained to the size of the text it displays and the view centered within the parent layout. Edit the *configureLayout()* method once more to make these changes:

.
.
```
import androidx.constraintlayout.widget.ConstraintSet;
```
.
.
```
private void configureLayout() {
    Button myButton = new Button(this);
    myButton.setText(getString(R.string.press_me));
    myButton.setBackgroundColor(Color.YELLOW);
    myButton.setId(R.id.myButton);

    ConstraintLayout myLayout = new ConstraintLayout(this);
    myLayout.setBackgroundColor(Color.BLUE);

    myLayout.addView(myButton);
    setContentView(myLayout);

    ConstraintSet set = new ConstraintSet();

    set.constrainHeight(myButton.getId(),
            ConstraintSet.WRAP_CONTENT);
    set.constrainWidth(myButton.getId(),
            ConstraintSet.WRAP_CONTENT);

    set.connect(myButton.getId(), ConstraintSet.START,
            ConstraintSet.PARENT_ID, ConstraintSet.START, 0);
    set.connect(myButton.getId(), ConstraintSet.END,
            ConstraintSet.PARENT_ID, ConstraintSet.END, 0);
    set.connect(myButton.getId(), ConstraintSet.TOP,
            ConstraintSet.PARENT_ID, ConstraintSet.TOP, 0);
    set.connect(myButton.getId(), ConstraintSet.BOTTOM,
            ConstraintSet.PARENT_ID, ConstraintSet.BOTTOM, 0);
```

```
    set.applyTo(myLayout);
}
```

With the initial constraints configured, compile and run the application and verify that the Button view now appears in the center of the layout:

Figure 24-2

24.6 Adding the EditText View

The next item to be added to the layout is the EditText view. The first step is to create the EditText object, assign the ID as declared in the *id.xml* resource file and add it to the layout. The code changes to achieve these steps now need to be made to the *configureLayout()* method as follows:

```
private void configureLayout() {
    Button myButton = new Button(this);
    myButton.setText(getString(R.string.press_me));
    myButton.setBackgroundColor(Color.YELLOW);
    myButton.setId(R.id.myButton);

    EditText myEditText = new EditText(this);
    myEditText.setId(R.id.myEditText);

    ConstraintLayout myLayout = new ConstraintLayout(this);
    myLayout.setBackgroundColor(Color.BLUE);

    myLayout.addView(myButton);
    myLayout.addView(myEditText);

    setContentView(myLayout);
    .
    .
}
```

The EditText widget is intended to be sized subject to the content it displays, centered horizontally within the layout, and positioned 70dp above the existing Button view. Add code to the *configureLayout()* method so that

An Android ConstraintSet Tutorial

it reads as follows:

```
.
.
set.connect(myButton.getId(), ConstraintSet.START,
            ConstraintSet.PARENT_ID, ConstraintSet.START, 0);
set.connect(myButton.getId(), ConstraintSet.END,
            ConstraintSet.PARENT_ID, ConstraintSet.END, 0);
set.connect(myButton.getId(), ConstraintSet.TOP,
            ConstraintSet.PARENT_ID, ConstraintSet.TOP, 0);
set.connect(myButton.getId(), ConstraintSet.BOTTOM,
            ConstraintSet.PARENT_ID, ConstraintSet.BOTTOM, 0);

set.constrainHeight(myEditText.getId(),
                    ConstraintSet.WRAP_CONTENT);
set.constrainWidth(myEditText.getId(),
                    ConstraintSet.WRAP_CONTENT);

set.connect(myEditText.getId(), ConstraintSet.START,
            ConstraintSet.PARENT_ID, ConstraintSet.START, 0);
set.connect(myEditText.getId(), ConstraintSet.END,
            ConstraintSet.PARENT_ID, ConstraintSet.END, 0);
set.connect(myEditText.getId(), ConstraintSet.BOTTOM,
            myButton.getId(), ConstraintSet.TOP, 70);

set.applyTo(myLayout);
```

A test run of the application should show the EditText field centered above the button with a margin of 70dp.

24.7 Converting Density Independent Pixels (dp) to Pixels (px)

The next task in this exercise is to set the width of the EditText view to 200dp. As outlined in the chapter entitled *"An Android Studio Layout Editor ConstraintLayout Tutorial"*, when setting sizes and positions in user interface layouts, it is better to use density independent-pixels (dp) rather than pixels (px). To set a position using dp, it is necessary to convert a dp value to a px value at runtime, considering the density of the device display. In order, therefore, to set the width of the EditText view to 200dp, the following code needs to be added to the class:

```
package com.ebookfrenzy.javalayout;
.
.
import android.content.res.Resources;
import android.util.TypedValue;

public class MainActivity extends AppCompatActivity {

    private int convertToPx(int value) {
        Resources r = getResources();
        return (int) TypedValue.applyDimension(
                TypedValue.COMPLEX_UNIT_DIP, value,
```

```
                r.getDisplayMetrics());
    }

    private void configureLayout() {
        Button myButton = new Button(this);
        myButton.setText(getString(R.string.press_me));
        myButton.setBackgroundColor(Color.YELLOW);
        myButton.setId(R.id.myButton);

        EditText myEditText = new EditText(this);
        myEditText.setId(R.id.myEditText);

        int px = convertToPx(200);
        myEditText.setWidth(px);
.
.
.
}
```

Compile and run the application one more time and note that the width of the EditText view has changed, as illustrated in Figure 24-3:

Figure 24-3

24.8 Summary

The example activity created in this chapter has created a similar user interface (the change in background color and view type notwithstanding) as that created in the earlier *"Manual XML Layout Design in Android Studio"* chapter. If nothing else, this chapter should have provided an appreciation of the level to which the Android Studio Layout Editor tool and XML resources shield the developer from many of the complexities of creating Android user interface layouts.

An Android ConstraintSet Tutorial

There are, however, instances where it makes sense to create a user interface in Java. For example, this approach is most useful when creating dynamic user interface layouts.

Chapter 25

25. A Guide to Using Apply Changes in Android Studio

Now that some of the basic concepts of Android development using Android Studio have been covered, this is a good time to introduce the Android Studio Apply Changes feature. As all experienced developers know, every second spent waiting for an app to compile and run is better spent writing and refining code.

25.1 Introducing Apply Changes

In early versions of Android Studio, each time a change to a project needed to be tested, Android Studio would recompile the code, convert it to Dex format, generate the APK package file, and install it on the device or emulator. Having performed these steps, the app would finally be launched and ready for testing. Even on a fast development system, this process takes considerable time to complete. It is not uncommon for it to take a minute or more for this process to complete for a large application.

Apply Changes, in contrast, allows many code and resource changes within a project to be reflected nearly instantaneously within the app while it is already running on a device or emulator session.

Consider, for example, an app being developed in Android Studio which has already been launched on a device or emulator. If changes are made to resource settings or the code within a method, Apply Changes will push the updated code and resources to the running app and dynamically "swap" the changes. The changes are then reflected in the running app without the need to build, deploy and relaunch the entire app. This often allows changes to be tested in a fraction of the time without Apply Changes.

25.2 Understanding Apply Changes Options

Android Studio provides three options for applying changes to a running app in the form of *Run App*, *Apply Changes and Restart Activity* and *Apply Code Changes*. These options can be summarized as follows:

- **Run App** - Stops the currently running app and restarts it. If no changes have been made to the project since it was last launched, this option will restart the app. If, on the other hand, changes have been made to the project, Android Studio will rebuild and re-install the app onto the device or emulator before launching it.

- **Apply Code Changes** - This option can be used when the only changes made to a project involve modifications to the body of existing methods or when a new class or method has been added. When selected, the changes will be applied to the running app without needing to restart the app or the currently running activity. This mode cannot, however, be used when changes have been made to any project resources, such as a layout file. Other restrictions include removing methods, changing a method signature, renaming classes, and other structural code changes. It is also impossible to use this option when changes have been made to the project manifest.

- **Apply Changes and Restart Activity** - When selected, this mode will dynamically apply any code or resource changes made within the project and restart the activity without re-installing or restarting the app. Unlike the Apply Code changes option, this can be used when changes have been made to the code and resources of the project. However, the same restrictions involving some structural code changes and manifest modifications apply.

A Guide to Using Apply Changes in Android Studio

25.3 Using Apply Changes

When a project has been loaded into Android Studio but is not yet running on a device or emulator, it can be launched as usual using either the run (marked A in Figure 25-1) or debug (B) button located in the toolbar:

Figure 25-1

After the app has launched and is running, a stop button (marked A in Figure 25-2) will appear, and the *Apply Changes and Restart Activity* (B) and *Apply Code Changes* (C) buttons will be enabled:

Figure 25-2

If the changes cannot be applied when one of the Apply Changes buttons is selected, Android Studio will display a message indicating the failure and an explanation. Figure 25-3, for example, shows the message displayed by Android Studio when the *Apply Code Changes* option is selected after a change has been made to a resource file:

> ⓘ Changes were not applied. Modifying resources requires an activity restart.
>
> Apply changes and restart activity

Figure 25-3

In this situation, the solution is to use the *Apply Changes and Restart Activity* option (for which a link is provided). Similarly, the following message will appear when an attempt to apply changes that involve the removal of a method is made:

> ⓘ Changes were not applied. Removing a method requires an app restart.
>
> Reinstall and restart app

Figure 25-4

In this case, the only option is to click on the *Run App* button to re-install and restart the app. As an alternative to manually selecting the correct option, Android Studio may be configured to automatically fall back to performing a Run App operation.

25.4 Configuring Apply Changes Fallback Settings

The Apply Changes fallback settings are located in the Android Studio Settings dialog. Within the Settings dialog, select the *Build, Execution, Deployment* entry in the left-hand panel, followed by *Deployment*, as shown in Figure 25-5:

Figure 25-5

Once the required options have been enabled, click on Apply, followed by the OK button to commit the changes and dismiss the dialog. After these defaults have been enabled, Android Studio will automatically re-install and restart the app when necessary.

25.5 An Apply Changes Tutorial

Launch Android Studio, select the New Project option from the welcome screen, and choose the Basic Views Activity template within the resulting new project dialog before clicking the Next button.

Enter *ApplyChanges* into the Name field and specify *com.ebookfrenzy.applychanges* as the package name. Before clicking the Finish button, change the Minimum API level setting to API 26: Android 8.0 (Oreo) and the Language menu to Java.

25.6 Using Apply Code Changes

Begin by clicking the run button and selecting an emulator or physical device as the run target. After clicking the run button, track the time before the example app appears on the device or emulator.

Once running, click on the action button (the button displaying an envelope icon in the screen's lower right-hand corner). Note that a Snackbar instance appears, displaying text which reads "Replace with your own action", as shown in Figure 25-6:

Figure 25-6

Once the app is running, the Apply Changes buttons should have been enabled, indicating that certain project changes can be applied without reinstalling and restarting the app. To see this in action, edit the *MainActivity.java* file, locate the *onCreate* method, and modify the action code so that a different message is displayed when the action button is selected:

```
binding.fab.setOnClickListener(new View.OnClickListener() {
    @Override
    public void onClick(View view) {
        Snackbar.make(view, "Apply Changes is Amazing!", Snackbar.LENGTH_LONG)
                .setAction("Action", null).show();
    }
});
```

With the code change implemented, click the *Apply Code Changes* button and note that a message appears within a few seconds indicating the app has been updated. Tap the action button and note that the new message is now displayed in the Snackbar.

25.7 Using Apply Changes and Restart Activity

Any resource change will require the use of the *Apply Changes and Restart Activity* option. Within Android Studio, select the *app -> res -> layout -> fragment_first.xml* layout file. With the Layout Editor tool in Design mode, select the default TextView component and change the text property in the attributes tool window to "Hello Android".

Ensure that the fallback options outlined in *"Configuring Apply Changes Fallback Settings"* above are turned off before clicking on the *Apply Code Changes* button. Note that the request fails because this change involves project resources. Click on the *Apply Changes and Restart Activity* button and verify that the activity restarts and displays the new text on the TextView widget.

25.8 Using Run App

As previously described, removing a method requires the complete re-installation and restart of the running app. To experience this, edit the *MainActivity.java* file and add a new method after the *onCreate* method as follows:

```
public void demoMethod() {
}
```

Use the *Apply Code Changes* button and confirm that the changes are applied without re-installing the app.

Next, delete the new method and verify that clicking on either of the two Apply Changes buttons will result in the request failing. The only way to run the app after such a change is to click the Run App button.

25.9 Summary

Apply Changes is a feature of Android Studio designed to significantly accelerate the code, build and run cycle performed when developing an app. The Apply Changes feature can push updates to the running application, in many cases, without reinstalling or restarting the app. Apply Changes provides several different levels of support depending on the nature of the modification being applied to the project.

Chapter 26

26. An Overview and Example of Android Event Handling

Much has been covered in the previous chapters relating to the design of user interfaces for Android applications. However, an area that has yet to be covered involves how a user's interaction with the user interface triggers the underlying activity to perform a task. In other words, from the previous chapters, we know how to create a user interface containing a button view but not how to make something happen within the application when the user touches it.

Therefore, this chapter's primary objective is to provide an overview of event handling in Android applications together with an Android Studio-based example project.

26.1 Understanding Android Events

Android events can take various forms but are usually generated in response to an external action. The most common form of events, particularly for devices such as tablets and smartphones, involve some form of interaction with the touch screen. Such events fall into the category of *input events*.

The Android framework maintains an *event queue* into which events are placed as they occur. Events are then removed from the queue on a first-in, first-out (FIFO) basis. In the case of an input event, such as a touch on the screen, the event is passed to the view positioned at the location on the screen where the touch took place. In addition to the event notification, the view is also passed a range of information (depending on the event type) about the nature of the event, such as the coordinates of the point of contact between the user's fingertip and the screen.

To handle an event that has been passed, the view must have an *event listener* in place. The Android View class, from which all user interface components are derived, contains a range of event listener interfaces, each containing an abstract declaration for a callback method. To be able to respond to an event of a particular type, a view must register the appropriate event listener and implement the corresponding callback. For example, if a button is to respond to a *click* event (the equivalent of the user touching and releasing the button view as though clicking on a physical button), it must both register the *View.onClickListener* event listener (via a call to the target view's *setOnClickListener()* method) and implement the corresponding *onClick()* callback method. If a "click" event is detected on the screen at the location of the button view, the Android framework will call the *onClick()* method of that view when that event is removed from the event queue. It is, of course, within the implementation of the onClick() callback method that any tasks or other methods called in response to the button click should be performed.

26.2 Using the android:onClick Resource

Before exploring event listeners in more detail, it is worth noting that a shortcut is available when all that is required is for a callback method to be called when a user "clicks" on a button view in the user interface. Consider a user interface layout containing a button view named *button1* with the requirement that when the user touches the button, a method called *buttonClick()* declared in the activity class is called. All that is required to implement this behavior is to write the *buttonClick()* method (which takes as an argument a reference to the view that triggered the click event) and add a single line to the declaration of the button view in the XML file. For example:

```xml
<Button
    android:id="@+id/button1"
    android:layout_width="wrap_content"
    android:layout_height="wrap_content"
    android:onClick="buttonClick"
    android:text="Click me" />
```

This provides a simple way to capture click events. It does not, however, provide the range of options offered by event handlers, which is the topic of the rest of this chapter. As outlined in later chapters, the onClick property also has limitations in layouts involving fragments. When working within Android Studio Layout Editor, the onClick property can be found and configured in the Attributes panel when a suitable view type is selected in the device screen layout.

26.3 Event Listeners and Callback Methods

In the example activity outlined later in this chapter, the steps involved in registering an event listener and implementing the callback method will be covered in detail. Before doing so, however, it is worth taking some time to outline the event listeners available in the Android framework and the callback methods associated with each one.

- **onClickListener** – Used to detect click style events whereby the user touches and then releases an area of the device display occupied by a view. Corresponds to the *onClick()* callback method, which is passed a reference to the view that received the event as an argument.

- **onLongClickListener** – Used to detect when the user maintains the touch over a view for an extended period. Corresponds to the *onLongClick()* callback method, which is passed as an argument the view that received the event.

- **onTouchListener** – Used to detect any contact with the touch screen, including individual or multiple touches and gesture motions. Corresponding with the *onTouch()* callback, this topic will be covered in greater detail in the chapter entitled *"Android Touch and Multi-touch Event Handling"*. The callback method is passed as arguments the view that received the event and a MotionEvent object.

- **onCreateContextMenuListener** – Listens for the creation of a context menu as the result of a long click. Corresponds to the *onCreateContextMenu()* callback method. The callback is passed the menu, the view that received the event and a menu context object.

- **onFocusChangeListener** – Detects when focus moves away from the current view due to interaction with a trackball or navigation key. Corresponds to the *onFocusChange()* callback method, which is passed the view that received the event and a Boolean value to indicate whether focus was gained or lost.

- **onKeyListener** – Used to detect when a key on a device is pressed while a view has focus. Corresponds to the *onKey()* callback method. It is passed as arguments the view that received the event, the KeyCode of the physical key that was pressed, and a KeyEvent object.

26.4 An Event Handling Example

In the remainder of this chapter, we will create an Android Studio project designed to demonstrate the implementation of an event listener and corresponding callback method to detect when the user has clicked on a button. The code within the callback method will update a text view to indicate that the event has been processed.

Select the *New Project* option from the welcome screen and, within the resulting new project dialog, choose the Empty Views Activity template before clicking the Next button.

An Overview and Example of Android Event Handling

Enter *EventExample* into the Name field and specify *com.ebookfrenzy.eventexample* as the package name. Before clicking on the Finish button, change the Minimum API level setting to API 26: Android 8.0 (Oreo) and the Language menu to Java. Using the steps outlined in section *11.8 Migrating a Project to View Binding*, convert the project to use view binding.

26.5 Designing the User Interface

The user interface layout for the *MainActivity* class in this example will consist of a ConstraintLayout, a Button, and a TextView, as illustrated in Figure 26-1.

Figure 26-1

Locate and select the *activity_main.xml* file created by Android Studio (located in the Project tool window under *app -> res -> layouts*) and double-click on it to load it into the Layout Editor tool.

Ensure that Autoconnect is enabled, then drag a Button widget from the palette and move it so that it is positioned in the horizontal center of the layout and beneath the existing TextView widget. When correctly positioned, drop the widget into place so that the autoconnect system adds appropriate constraints.

Select the "Hello World!" TextView widget and use the Attributes panel to set the ID to *statusText*. Repeat this step to change the ID of the Button widget to *myButton*.

Add any missing constraints by clicking on the *Infer Constraints* button in the layout editor toolbar.

With the Button widget selected, use the Attributes panel to set the text property to Press Me. Extract the text string on the button to a resource named *press_me*.

With the user interface layout completed, the next step is registering the event listener and callback method.

26.6 The Event Listener and Callback Method

For this example, an *onClickListener* needs to be registered for the *myButton* view. This is achieved by calling the *setOnClickListener()* method of the button view, passing through a new *onClickListener* object as an argument, and implementing the *onClick()* callback method. Since this task only needs to be performed when the activity is created, a good location is the *onCreate()* method of the MainActivity class.

217

An Overview and Example of Android Event Handling

If the *MainActivity.java* file is already open within an editor session, select it by clicking on the tab in the editor panel. Alternatively, locate it within the Project tool window by navigating to (*app -> java -> com.ebookfrenzy. eventexample -> MainActivity*) and double-click on it to load it into the code editor. Once loaded, locate the template *onCreate()* method and modify it to obtain a reference to the button view, register the event listener, and implement the *onClick()* callback method:

```
package com.ebookfrenzy.eventexample;

import androidx.appcompat.app.AppCompatActivity;

import android.os.Bundle;
import android.view.View;
import android.widget.Button;

public class MainActivity extends AppCompatActivity {

    @Override
    protected void onCreate(Bundle savedInstanceState) {
        super.onCreate(savedInstanceState);
        binding = ActivityMainBinding.inflate(getLayoutInflater());
        View view = binding.getRoot();
        setContentView(view);

        binding.myButton.setOnClickListener(
                new Button.OnClickListener() {
                    public void onClick(View v) {

                    }
                }
        );
    }
    .
    .
}
```

The above code has registered the event listener on the button and implemented the *onClick()* method. If the application were to be run at this point, however, there would be no indication that the event listener installed on the button was working since there is, as yet, no code implemented within the body of the *onClick()* callback method. The goal for the example is to have a message appear on the TextView when the button is clicked, so some further code changes need to be made:

```
@Override
protected void onCreate(Bundle savedInstanceState) {
    super.onCreate(savedInstanceState);
    binding = ActivityMainBinding.inflate(getLayoutInflater());
    View view = binding.getRoot();
    setContentView(view);
```

An Overview and Example of Android Event Handling

```java
        binding.myButton.setOnClickListener(
                new Button.OnClickListener() {
                    public void onClick(View v) {
                        binding.statusText.setText("Button clicked");
                    }
                }
        );
}
```

Complete this tutorial phase by compiling and running the application on either an AVD emulator or a physical Android device. On touching and releasing the button view (otherwise known as "clicking"), the text view should change to display the "Button clicked" text.

26.7 Consuming Events

The detection of standard clicks (as opposed to long clicks) on views is a straightforward case of event handling. The example will now be extended to include the detection of long click events, which occur when the user clicks and holds a view on the screen and, in doing so, cover the topic of event consumption.

Consider the code for the *onClick()* method in the above section of this chapter. The callback is declared as *void* and, as such, does not return a value to the Android framework after it has finished executing.

On the other hand, the code assigned to the *onLongClickListener* is required to return a Boolean value to the Android framework. The purpose of this return value is to indicate to the Android runtime whether or not the callback has consumed the event. If the callback returns a true value, the framework discards the event. If, on the other hand, the callback returns a false value, the Android framework will consider the event still to be active and pass it along to the next matching event listener registered on the same view.

As with many programming concepts, this is best demonstrated with an example. The first step is to add an event listener and callback method for long clicks to the button view in the example activity:

```java
@Override
protected void onCreate(Bundle savedInstanceState) {
    .
    .
        binding.myButton.setOnLongClickListener(
                new Button.OnLongClickListener() {
                    public boolean onLongClick(View v) {
                        binding.statusText.setText("Long button click");
                        return true;
                    }
                }
        );
    }
}
```

When a long click is detected, the *onLongClick()* callback method will display "Long button click" on the text view. Note, however, that the callback method returns a *true* value to indicate that it has consumed the event. Run the application and press and hold the Button view until the "Long button click" text appears in the text view. On releasing the button, the text view displays the "Long button click" text indicating that the onClick listener code was not called.

Next, modify the code so that the onLongClick listener now returns a *false* value:

```
button.setOnLongClickListener(
    new Button.OnLongClickListener() {
        public boolean onLongClick(View v) {
            TextView myTextView = findViewById(R.id.myTextView);
            myTextView.setText("Long button click");
            return false;
        }
    }
);
```

Once again, compile and run the application and perform a long click on the button until the long click message appears. However, after releasing the button this time, note that the onClick listener is also triggered, and the text changes to "Button clicked". This is because the *false* value returned by the *onLongClick* listener code indicated to the Android framework that the event was not consumed by the method and was eligible to be passed on to the next registered listener on the view. In this case, the runtime ascertained that the onClickListener on the button was also interested in events of this type and subsequently called the *onClick* listener code.

26.8 Summary

A user interface is of little practical use if the views it contains do not do anything in response to user interaction. Android bridges the gap between the user interface and the back-end code of the application through the concepts of event listeners and callback methods. The Android View class defines a set of event listeners which can be registered on view objects. Each event listener also has associated with it a callback method.

When an event takes place on a view in a user interface, that event is placed into an event queue and handled on a first-in, first-out basis by the Android runtime. If the view on which the event took place has registered a listener that matches the type of event, the corresponding callback method is called. This code then performs any tasks required by the activity before returning. Some callback methods are required to return a Boolean value to indicate whether the event needs to be passed on to other event listeners registered on the view or discarded by the system.

Now that the basics of event handling have been covered, the next chapter will explore touch events with a particular emphasis on handling multiple touches.

Chapter 27

27. Android Touch and Multi-touch Event Handling

Most Android-based devices use a touch screen as the primary interface between the user and the device. The previous chapter introduced how a touch on the screen translates into an action within a running Android application. There is, however, much more to touch event handling than responding to a single finger tap on a view object. Most Android devices can, for example, detect more than one touch at a time. Nor are touches limited to a single point on the device display. Touches can be dynamic as the user slides one or more contact points across the screen's surface.

An application can also interpret touches as a gesture. Consider, for example, that a horizontal swipe is typically used to turn the page of an eBook or how a pinching motion can zoom in and out of an image displayed on the screen.

An application can also interpret touches as a *gesture*. Consider, for example, that a horizontal swipe is typically used to turn the page of an eBook or how a pinching motion can zoom in and out of an image displayed on the screen.

This chapter will explain the handling of touches that involve motion and explore the concept of intercepting multiple concurrent touches. The topic of identifying distinct gestures will be covered in the next chapter.

27.1 Intercepting Touch Events

A view object can intercept touch events by registering an onTouchListener event listener and implementing the corresponding onTouch() callback method. The following code, for example, ensures that any touches on a ConstraintLayout view instance named *myLayout* result in a call to the *onTouch()* method:

```
binding.myLayout.setOnTouchListener(
     new ConstraintLayout.OnTouchListener() {
          public boolean onTouch(View v, MotionEvent m) {
               // Perform tasks here
               return true;
          }
     }
);
```

As indicated in the code example, the *onTouch()* callback is required to return a Boolean value indicating to the Android runtime system whether or not the event should be passed on to other event listeners registered on the same view or discarded. The method is passed both a reference to the view on which the event was triggered and an object of type *MotionEvent*.

27.2 The MotionEvent Object

The MotionEvent object passed through to the *onTouch()* callback method is the key to obtaining information about the event. Information within the object includes the location of the touch within the view and the type of action performed. The MotionEvent object is also the key to handling multiple touches.

27.3 Understanding Touch Actions

An important aspect of touch event handling involves identifying the type of action the user performed. The type of action associated with an event can be obtained by making a call to the *getActionMasked()* method of the MotionEvent object, which was passed through to the *onTouch()* callback method. When the first touch on a view occurs, the MotionEvent object will contain an action type of ACTION_DOWN together with the coordinates of the touch. When that touch is lifted from the screen, an ACTION_UP event is generated. Any motion of the touch between the ACTION_DOWN and ACTION_UP events will be represented by ACTION_MOVE events.

When more than one touch is performed simultaneously on a view, the touches are referred to as *pointers*. In a multi-touch scenario, pointers begin and end with event actions of type ACTION_POINTER_DOWN and ACTION_POINTER_UP, respectively. To identify the index of the pointer that triggered the event, the *getActionIndex()* callback method of the MotionEvent object must be called.

27.4 Handling Multiple Touches

The chapter entitled *"An Overview and Example of Android Event Handling"* began exploring event handling within the narrow context of a single-touch event. In practice, most Android devices can respond to multiple consecutive touches (though it is important to note that the number of simultaneous touches that can be detected varies depending on the device).

As previously discussed, each touch in a multi-touch situation is considered by the Android framework to be a *pointer*. Each pointer, in turn, is referenced by an *index* value and assigned an *ID*. The current number of pointers can be obtained via a call to the *getPointerCount()* method of the current MotionEvent object. The ID for a pointer at a particular index in the list of current pointers may be obtained via a call to the MotionEvent *getPointerId()* method. For example, the following code excerpt obtains a count of pointers and the ID of the pointer at index 0:

```
public boolean onTouch(View v, MotionEvent m) {
        int pointerCount = m.getPointerCount();
        int pointerId = m.getPointerId(0);
        return true;
}
```

Note that the pointer count will always be greater than or equal to 1 when the *onTouch* listener is triggered (since at least one touch must have occurred for the callback to be triggered).

A touch on a view, particularly one involving motion across the screen, will generate a stream of events before the point of contact with the screen is lifted. An application will likely need to track individual touches over multiple touch events. While the ID of a specific touch gesture will not change from one event to the next, it is important to remember that the index value will change as other touch events come and go. When working with a touch gesture over multiple events, the ID value must be used as the touch reference to ensure the same touch is being tracked. When calling methods that require an index value, this should be obtained by converting the ID for a touch to the corresponding index value via a call to the *findPointerIndex()* method of the *MotionEvent* object.

27.5 An Example Multi-Touch Application

The example application created in the remainder of this chapter will track up to two touch gestures as they move across a layout view. As the events for each touch are triggered, the coordinates, index, and ID for each touch will be displayed on the screen.

Select the *New Project* option from the welcome screen and, within the resulting new project dialog, choose the

Android Touch and Multi-touch Event Handling

Empty Views Activity template before clicking on the Next button.

Enter *MotionEvent* into the Name field and specify *com.ebookfrenzy.motionevent* as the package name. Before clicking the Finish button, change the Minimum API level setting to API 26: Android 8.0 (Oreo) and the Language menu to Java.

Adapt the project to use view binding as outlined in section *11.8 Migrating a Project to View Binding*.

27.6 Designing the Activity User Interface

The user interface for the application's sole activity is to consist of a ConstraintLayout view containing two TextView objects. Within the Project tool window, navigate to *app -> res -> layout* and double-click on the *activity_main.xml* layout resource file to load it into the Android Studio Layout Editor tool.

Select and delete the default "Hello World!" TextView widget and then, with autoconnect enabled, drag and drop a new TextView widget so that it is centered horizontally and positioned at the 16dp margin line on the top edge of the layout:

Figure 27-1

Drag a second TextView widget and position and constrain it so that a 32dp margin distances it from the bottom of the first widget:

Figure 27-2

Using the Attributes tool window, change the IDs for the TextView widgets to *textView1* and *textView2*, respectively. Change the text displayed on the widgets to read "Touch One Status" and "Touch Two Status" and extract the strings to resources using the warning button in the top right-hand corner of the Layout Editor.

27.7 Implementing the Touch Event Listener

To receive touch event notification, it will be necessary to register a touch listener on the layout view within the *onCreate()* method of the *MainActivity* activity class. Select the *MainActivity.java* tab from the Android Studio editor panel to display the source code. Within the *onCreate()* method, add code to register the touch listener and implement code which, in this case, is going to call a second method named *handleTouch()* to which is passed the MotionEvent object:

```
package com.ebookfrenzy.motionevent;

import androidx.appcompat.app.AppCompatActivity;
import androidx.constraintlayout.widget.ConstraintLayout;

import android.os.Bundle;
import android.view.MotionEvent;
import android.view.View;
```

Android Touch and Multi-touch Event Handling

```java
import com.ebookfrenzy.motionevent.databinding.ActivityMainBinding;

public class MainActivity extends AppCompatActivity {

    private ActivityMainBinding binding;

    @Override
    protected void onCreate(Bundle savedInstanceState) {
        super.onCreate(savedInstanceState);
        binding = ActivityMainBinding.inflate(getLayoutInflater());
        View view = binding.getRoot();
        setContentView(view);

        binding.activityMain.setOnTouchListener(
            new ConstraintLayout.OnTouchListener() {
                public boolean onTouch(View v, MotionEvent m) {
                    handleTouch(m);
                    return true;
                }
            }
        );
    }
}
```

When we designed the user interface, the parent ConstraintLayout was not assigned an ID that would allow us to access it via the view binding mechanism. Since this layout component is the topmost component in the UI layout hierarchy, we have been able to reference it using the *root* binding property in the code above.

Before testing the application, the final task is to implement the *handleTouch()* method called by the listener. The code for this method reads as follows:

```java
void handleTouch(MotionEvent m) {

    int pointerCount = m.getPointerCount();

    for (int i = 0; i < pointerCount; i++)
    {
        int x = (int) m.getX(i);
        int y = (int) m.getY(i);
        int id = m.getPointerId(i);
        int action = m.getActionMasked();
        int actionIndex = m.getActionIndex();
        String actionString;

        switch (action)
        {
            case MotionEvent.ACTION_DOWN:
                actionString = "DOWN";
                break;
```

Android Touch and Multi-touch Event Handling

```
            case MotionEvent.ACTION_UP:
                actionString = "UP";
                break;
            case MotionEvent.ACTION_POINTER_DOWN:
                actionString = "PNTR DOWN";
                break;
            case MotionEvent.ACTION_POINTER_UP:
                actionString = "PNTR UP";
                break;
            case MotionEvent.ACTION_MOVE:
                actionString = "MOVE";
                break;
            default:
                actionString = "";
        }

        String touchStatus = "Action: " + actionString + " Index: " + actionIndex
  + " ID: " + id + " X: " + x + " Y: " + y;

        if (id == 0)
            binding.textView1.setText(touchStatus);
        else
            binding.textView2.setText(touchStatus);
    }
}
```

Before compiling and running the application, it is worth taking the time to walk through this code systematically to highlight the tasks performed.

The code begins by obtaining references to the two TextView objects in the user interface and identifying how many pointers are currently active on the view:

```
TextView textView1 = findViewById(R.id.textView1);
TextView textView2 = findViewById(R.id.textView2);

int pointerCount = m.getPointerCount();
```

Next, the *pointerCount* variable initiates a for loop, which performs tasks for each active pointer. The first few lines of the loop obtain the X and Y coordinates of the touch together with the corresponding event ID, action type, and action index. Lastly, a string variable is declared:

```
for (int i = 0; i < pointerCount; i++)
{
    int x = (int) m.getX(i);
    int y = (int) m.getY(i);
    int id = m.getPointerId(i);
    int action = m.getActionMasked();
    int actionIndex = m.getActionIndex();
    String actionString;
```

225

Android Touch and Multi-touch Event Handling

Since action types equate to integer values, a *switch* statement is used to convert the action type to a more meaningful string value, which is stored in the previously declared *actionString* variable:

```
switch (action)
{
    case MotionEvent.ACTION_DOWN:
        actionString = "DOWN";
        break;
    case MotionEvent.ACTION_UP:
        actionString = "UP";
        break;
    case MotionEvent.ACTION_POINTER_DOWN:
        actionString = "PNTR DOWN";
        break;
    case MotionEvent.ACTION_POINTER_UP:
        actionString = "PNTR UP";
        break;
    case MotionEvent.ACTION_MOVE:
        actionString = "MOVE";
        break;
    default:
        actionString = "";
}
```

Finally, the string message is constructed using the *actionString* value, the action index, touch ID, and X and Y coordinates. The ID value is then used to decide whether the string should be displayed on the first or second TextView object:

```
String touchStatus = "Action: " + actionString + " Index: "
        + actionIndex + " ID: " + id + " X: " + x + " Y: " + y;

if (id == 0)
    binding.textView1.setText(touchStatus);
else
    binding.textView2.setText(touchStatus);
```

27.8 Running the Example Application

Compile and run the application and, once launched, experiment with single and multiple touches on the screen and note that the text views update to reflect the events as illustrated in Figure 27-3. When running on an emulator, multiple touches may be simulated by holding down the Ctrl (Cmd on macOS) key while clicking the mouse button (note that simulating multiple touches may not work if the emulator is running in a tool window):

> 10:28
>
> Action: PNTR UP Index: 0 ID: 0 X: 764.94507 Y: 691.9358
>
> Action: UP Index: 0 ID: 1 X: 313.9673 Y: 1454.9509

Figure 27-3

27.9 Summary

Activities receive notifications of touch events by registering an onTouchListener event listener and implementing the onTouch() callback method, which, in turn, is passed a MotionEvent object when called by the Android runtime. This object contains information about the touch, such as the type of touch event, the coordinates of the touch, and a count of the number of touches currently in contact with the view.

When multiple touches are involved, each point of contact is referred to as a pointer, with each assigned an index and an ID. While the index of a touch can change from one event to another, the ID will remain unchanged until the touch ends.

This chapter has worked through creating an example Android application designed to display the coordinates and action type of up to two simultaneous touches on a device display.

Having covered touches in general, the next chapter (entitled *"Detecting Common Gestures Using the Android Gesture Detector Class"*) will look further at touchscreen event handling through gesture recognition.

Chapter 28

28. Detecting Common Gestures Using the Android Gesture Detector Class

The term "gesture" defines a contiguous sequence of interactions between the touch screen and the user. A typical gesture begins at the point that the screen is first touched and ends when the last finger or pointing device leaves the display surface. When correctly harnessed, gestures can be implemented to communicate between the user and the application. Swiping motions to turn the pages of an eBook or a pinching movement involving two touches to zoom in or out of an image are prime examples of how gestures can interact with an application.

The Android SDK provides mechanisms for the detection of both common and custom gestures within an application. Common gestures involve interactions such as a tap, double tap, long press, or a swiping motion in either a horizontal or a vertical direction (referred to in Android nomenclature as a *fling*).

This chapter explores using the Android GestureDetector class to detect common gestures performed on the display of an Android device. The next chapter, *"Implementing Custom Gesture and Pinch Recognition on Android"*, will cover detecting more complex, custom gestures such as circular motions and pinches.

28.1 Implementing Common Gesture Detection

When a user interacts with the display of an Android device, the *onTouchEvent()* method of the currently active application is called by the system and passed MotionEvent objects containing data about the user's contact with the screen. This data can be interpreted to identify if the motion on the screen matches a common gesture such as a tap or a swipe. This can be achieved with minimal programming effort by using the Android GestureDetectorCompat class. This class is designed to receive motion event information from the application and trigger method calls based on the type of common gesture, if any, detected.

The basic steps in detecting common gestures are as follows:

1. Declaration of a class which implements the GestureDetector.OnGestureListener interface including the required *onFling()*, *onDown()*, *onScroll()*, *onShowPress()*, *onSingleTapUp()* and *onLongPress()* callback methods. Note that this can be either an entirely new or an enclosing activity class. If double-tap gesture detection is required, the class must also implement the GestureDetector.OnDoubleTapListener interface and include the corresponding *onDoubleTap()* method.

2. Creation of an instance of the Android GestureDetectorCompat class, passing through an instance of the class created in step 1 as an argument.

3. An optional call to the *setOnDoubleTapListener()* method of the GestureDetectorCompat instance to enable double tap detection if required.

4. Implementation of the *onTouchEvent()* callback method on the enclosing activity, which, in turn, must call the *onTouchEvent()* method of the GestureDetectorCompat instance, passing through the current motion event object as an argument to the method.

Detecting Common Gestures Using the Android Gesture Detector Class

Once implemented, the result is a set of methods within the application code that will be called when a gesture of a particular type is detected. The code within these methods can then be implemented to perform any tasks that need to be performed in response to the corresponding gesture.

In the remainder of this chapter, we will work through creating an example project intended to put the above steps into practice.

28.2 Creating an Example Gesture Detection Project

This project aims to detect the full range of common gestures currently supported by the GestureDetectorCompat class and to display status information to the user indicating the type of gesture that has been detected.

Select the *New Project* option from the welcome screen and, within the resulting new project dialog, choose the Empty Views Activity template before clicking on the Next button.

Enter *CommonGestures* into the Name field and specify *com.ebookfrenzy.commongestures* as the package name. Before clicking the Finish button, change the Minimum API level setting to API 26: Android 8.0 (Oreo) and the Language menu to Java.

Adapt the project to use view binding as outlined in section *11.8 Migrating a Project to View Binding*.

Once the new project has been created, navigate to the *app -> res -> layout -> activity_main.xml* file in the Project tool window and double-click on it to load it into the Layout Editor tool.

Within the Layout Editor tool, select the "Hello, World!" TextView component and, in the Attributes tool window, enter *gestureStatusText* as the ID. Finally, set the textSize to 20sp and enable the bold textStyle:

Figure 28-1

28.3 Implementing the Listener Class

As previously outlined, it is necessary to create a class that implements the GestureDetector.OnGestureListener interface and, if double tap detection is required, the GestureDetector.OnDoubleTapListener interface. While this can be an entirely new class, it is also perfectly valid to implement this within the current activity class. Therefore, we will modify the MainActivity class to implement these listener interfaces for this example. Edit the *MainActivity.java* file so that it reads as follows:

```
package com.ebookfrenzy.commongestures;

import android.view.GestureDetector;
.
.
.
public class MainActivity extends AppCompatActivity
        implements GestureDetector.OnGestureListener,
```

Detecting Common Gestures Using the Android Gesture Detector Class

```
        GestureDetector.OnDoubleTapListener
{
    .
    .
    .
}
```

Declaring that the class implements the listener interfaces mandates that the corresponding methods also be implemented in the class:

```
package com.ebookfrenzy.commongestures;
    .
    .
    .
import android.view.MotionEvent;

public class MainActivity extends AppCompatActivity
        implements GestureDetector.OnGestureListener,
        GestureDetector.OnDoubleTapListener {
    .
    .

    @Override
    public boolean onDown(MotionEvent event) {
        binding.gestureStatusText.setText ("onDown");
        return true;
    }

    @Override
    public boolean onFling(MotionEvent event1, MotionEvent event2,
                           float velocityX, float velocityY) {
        binding.gestureStatusText.setText("onFling");
        return true;
    }

    @Override
    public void onLongPress(MotionEvent event) {
        binding.gestureStatusText.setText("onLongPress");
    }

    @Override
    public boolean onScroll(MotionEvent e1, MotionEvent e2,
                            float distanceX, float distanceY) {
        binding.gestureStatusText.setText("onScroll");
        return true;
    }

    @Override
    public void onShowPress(MotionEvent event) {
        binding.gestureStatusText.setText("onShowPress");
```

Detecting Common Gestures Using the Android Gesture Detector Class

```
    }

    @Override
    public boolean onSingleTapUp(MotionEvent event) {
        binding.gestureStatusText.setText("onSingleTapUp");
        return true;
    }

    @Override
    public boolean onDoubleTap(MotionEvent event) {
        binding.gestureStatusText.setText("onDoubleTap");
        return true;
    }

    @Override
    public boolean onDoubleTapEvent(MotionEvent event) {
        binding.gestureStatusText.setText("onDoubleTapEvent");
        return true;
    }

    @Override
    public boolean onSingleTapConfirmed(MotionEvent event) {
        binding.gestureStatusText.setText("onSingleTapConfirmed");
        return true;
    }
    .
    .
    .
}
```

Note that many of these methods return *true*. This indicates to the Android Framework that the method has consumed the event and does not need to be passed to the next event handler in the stack.

28.4 Creating the GestureDetectorCompat Instance

With the activity class now updated to implement the listener interfaces, the next step is to create an instance of the GestureDetectorCompat class. Since this only needs to be performed once at the point that the activity is created, the best place for this code is in the *onCreate()* method. Since we also want to detect double taps, the code also needs to call the *setOnDoubleTapListener()* method of the GestureDetectorCompat instance:

```
package com.ebookfrenzy.commongestures;
    .
    .
import androidx.core.view.GestureDetectorCompat;

public class MainActivity extends AppCompatActivity
        implements GestureDetector.OnGestureListener,
        GestureDetector.OnDoubleTapListener {
```

```
    private ActivityMainBinding binding;
    private GestureDetectorCompat gDetector;

    @Override
    protected void onCreate(Bundle savedInstanceState) {
        super.onCreate(savedInstanceState);
        binding = ActivityMainBinding.inflate(getLayoutInflater());
        View view = binding.getRoot();
        setContentView(view);

        this.gDetector = new GestureDetectorCompat(this,this);
        gDetector.setOnDoubleTapListener(this);
    }
    .
    .
}
```

28.5 Implementing the onTouchEvent() Method

If the application were to be compiled and run at this point, nothing would happen if gestures were performed on the device display. This is because no code has been added to intercept touch events and to pass them through to the GestureDetectorCompat instance. To achieve this, it is necessary to override the *onTouchEvent()* method within the activity class and implement it such that it calls the *onTouchEvent()* method of the GestureDetectorCompat instance. Remaining in the *MainActivity.java* file, therefore, implement this method so that it reads as follows:

```
@Override
public boolean onTouchEvent(MotionEvent event) {
        this.gDetector.onTouchEvent(event);
        // Be sure to call the superclass implementation
        return super.onTouchEvent(event);
}
```

28.6 Testing the Application

Compile and run the application on either a physical Android device or an AVD emulator. Once launched, experiment with swipes, presses, scrolling motions, and double and single taps. Note that the text view updates to reflect the events as illustrated in Figure 28-2:

Figure 28-2

28.7 Summary

Any physical contact between the user and the touchscreen display of a device can be considered a "gesture". Lacking the physical keyboard and mouse pointer of a traditional computer system, gestures are widely used as a method of interaction between the user and the application. While a gesture can comprise just about any sequence of motions, there is a widely used set of gestures with which users of touchscreen devices have become familiar. Some of these so-called "common gestures" can be easily detected within an application by using the Android Gesture Detector classes. In this chapter, the use of this technique has been outlined both in theory and through the implementation of an example project.

Having covered common gestures in this chapter, the next chapter will look at detecting a wider range of gesture types, including the ability to design and detect your own gestures.

29. Implementing Custom Gesture and Pinch Recognition on Android

The previous chapter covered the detection of what is referred to as "common gestures" from within an Android application. In practice, however, a gesture can conceivably involve just about any sequence of touch motions on the display of an Android device. In recognition of this, the Android SDK allows custom gestures of just about any nature to be defined by the application developer and used to trigger events when performed by the user. This is a multi-stage process, the details of which are the topic of this chapter.

29.1 The Android Gesture Builder Application

The Android SDK allows developers to design custom gestures stored in a gesture file bundled with an Android application package. These custom gesture files are most easily created using the Gesture Builder application. Creating a gestures file involves launching the Gesture Builder application on a physical device or emulator and "drawing" the gestures that will need to be detected by the application. Once the gestures have been designed, the file containing the gesture data can be downloaded and added to the application project. Within the application code, the file is loaded into an instance of the *GestureLibrary* class, which can be used to search for matches to any gestures the user performs on the device display.

29.2 The GestureOverlayView Class

To facilitate the detection of gestures within an application, the Android SDK provides the GestureOverlayView class. This transparent view can be placed over other views in the user interface to detect gestures.

29.3 Detecting Gestures

Gestures are detected by loading the gestures file created using the Gesture Builder app and then registering a *GesturePerformedListener* event listener on an instance of the GestureOverlayView class. The enclosing class is then declared to implement both the *OnGesturePerformedListener* interface and the corresponding *onGesturePerformed* callback method required by that interface. If the listener detects a gesture, the Android runtime system triggers a call to the onGesturePerformed callback method.

29.4 Identifying Specific Gestures

When a gesture is detected, the *onGesturePerformed* callback method is called and passed as arguments a reference to the GestureOverlayView object on which the gesture was detected, together with a Gesture object containing information about the gesture.

With access to the Gesture object, the GestureLibrary can compare the detected gesture to those contained in the gestures file previously loaded into the application. The GestureLibrary reports the probability that the gesture performed by the user matches an entry in the gestures file by calculating a *prediction score* for each gesture. A prediction score of 1.0 or greater is generally accepted as a good match between a gesture stored in the file and that performed by the user on the device display.

29.5 Installing and Running the Gesture Builder Application

The easiest way to create a gestures file is to use an app allowing gesture motions to be captured and saved. Although Google originally provided an app for this purpose, it has not been maintained adequately for use on more recent versions of Android. Fortunately, an alternative is available in the form of the Gesture Builder Tool app, which is available from the Google Play Store at the following URL:

https://play.google.com/store/apps/details?id=migueldp.runeforge

29.6 Creating a Gestures File

Once the Gesture Builder Tool has loaded, click on the *Create New Gesture* button at the bottom of the device screen and "draw" a gesture using a circular motion on the gray canvas, as illustrated in Figure 29-1. Assuming that the gesture appears as required (represented by the yellow line on the device screen), click on the save button to add the gesture to the gestures file, entering "Circle Gesture" when prompted for a name:

Figure 29-1

After the gesture has been saved, the Gesture Builder Tool will display a list of currently defined gestures that will consist solely of the new *Circle Gesture*.

29.7 Creating the Example Project

Select the *New Project* option from the welcome screen and, within the resulting new project dialog, choose the Empty Views Activity template before clicking on the Next button.

Enter *CustomGestures* into the Name field and specify *com.ebookfrenzy.customgestures* as the package name. Before clicking the Finish button, change the Minimum API level setting to API 26: Android 8.0 (Oreo) and the Language menu to Java. Adapt the project to use view binding as outlined in section *11.8 Migrating a Project to View Binding*.

29.8 Extracting the Gestures File from the SD Card

As each gesture was created within the Gesture Builder application, it was added to a file named *gesture.txt*, located in the storage of the emulator or device on which the app was running. However, before this file can be added to an Android Studio project, it must be copied off the device storage and saved to the local file system. This is most easily achieved using the Android Studio Device File Explorer tool window. Display this tool using the *View -> Tool Windows -> Device File Explorer* menu option. Once displayed, select the device or emulator

Implementing Custom Gesture and Pinch Recognition on Android

on which the gesture file was created from the drop-down menu, then navigate through the filesystem to the following folder:

`/storage/emulated/0/Android/data/migueldp.runeforge/files/gestures.txt`

Locate the *gesture.txt* file in this folder, right-click on it, select the *Save As...* menu option, and save the file to a temporary location as a file named *gestures*.

Figure 29-2

Once the gestures file has been created and pulled from the device storage, it can be added to an Android Studio project as a resource file.

29.9 Adding the Gestures File to the Project

Within the Android Studio Project tool window, locate and right-click on the *res* folder (located under *app*) and select *New -> Directory* from the resulting menu. In the New Directory dialog, enter *raw* as the folder name and tap the keyboard enter key. Using the appropriate file explorer utility for your operating system type, locate the *gestures* file previously pulled from the device storage and copy and paste it into the new *raw* folder in the Project tool window.

29.10 Designing the User Interface

This example application calls for a user interface consisting of a ConstraintLayout view with a GestureOverlayView layered on it to intercept any gestures the user performs. Locate the *app -> res -> layout -> activity_main.xml* file, double-click on it to load it into the Layout Editor tool, and select and delete the default TextView widget.

Switch the layout editor Code mode and modify the XML so that it reads as follows:

```xml
<?xml version="1.0" encoding="utf-8"?>
<androidx.constraintlayout.widget.ConstraintLayout
    xmlns:android="http://schemas.android.com/apk/res/android"
    xmlns:app="http://schemas.android.com/apk/res-auto"
    xmlns:tools="http://schemas.android.com/tools"
```

237

```
        android:layout_width="match_parent"
        android:layout_height="match_parent"
        tools:context=".MainActivity" >

    <android.gesture.GestureOverlayView
        android:id="@+id/gOverlay"
        android:layout_width="0dp"
        android:layout_height="0dp"
        app:layout_constraintBottom_toBottomOf="parent"
        app:layout_constraintEnd_toEndOf="parent"
        app:layout_constraintStart_toStartOf="parent"
        app:layout_constraintTop_toTopOf="parent" />

</androidx.constraintlayout.widget.ConstraintLayout>
```

29.11 Loading the Gestures File

Now that the gestures file has been added to the project, the next step is to write some code to load the file when the activity starts. For this project, the code to achieve this will be added to the MainActivity class as follows:

```
package com.ebookfrenzy.customgestures;
.
.
import android.gesture.GestureLibraries;
import android.gesture.GestureLibrary;
import android.gesture.GestureOverlayView;
import android.gesture.GestureOverlayView.OnGesturePerformedListener;

public class MainActivity extends AppCompatActivity
        implements OnGesturePerformedListener {

    private ActivityMainBinding binding;
    private GestureLibrary gLibrary;

    @Override
    protected void onCreate(Bundle savedInstanceState) {
        super.onCreate(savedInstanceState);
        binding = ActivityMainBinding.inflate(getLayoutInflater());
        View view = binding.getRoot();
        setContentView(view);

        gestureSetup();
    }

    private void gestureSetup() {
        gLibrary =
                GestureLibraries.fromRawResource(this,
                        R.raw.gestures);
```

```
        if (!gLibrary.load()) {
            finish();
        }
    }
.
.
.
}
```

In addition to some necessary import directives, the above code also creates a *GestureLibrary* instance named *gLibrary* and then loads into it the contents of the *gesture* file located in the *raw* resources folder. The activity class has also been modified to implement the *OnGesturePerformedListener* interface, which requires adding the onGesturePerformed callback method (which will be created later in this chapter).

29.12 Registering the Event Listener

For the activity to receive a notification that the user has performed a gesture on the screen, it is necessary to register the *OnGesturePerformedListener* event listener on the *gLayout* view, a reference to which can be obtained using the *findViewById* method as outlined in the following code fragment:

```
private void gestureSetup() {
    gLibrary =
            GestureLibraries.fromRawResource(this,
                    R.raw.gestures);
    if (!gLibrary.load()) {
        finish();
    }

    GestureOverlayView gOverlay = findViewById(R.id.gOverlay);
    gOverlay.addOnGesturePerformedListener(this);
}
```

29.13 Implementing the onGesturePerformed Method

All that remains before an initial test run of the application can be performed is to implement the *OnGesturePerformed* callback method. This is the method that will be called when a gesture is performed on the GestureOverlayView instance:

```
package com.ebookfrenzy.customgestures;
.
.
.
import android.gesture.Prediction;
import android.widget.Toast;
import android.gesture.Gesture;
import java.util.ArrayList;

public class MainActivity extends AppCompatActivity implements
OnGesturePerformedListener {

    private GestureLibrary gLibrary;
.
.
```

```
    public void onGesturePerformed(GestureOverlayView overlay, Gesture
            gesture) {
        ArrayList<Prediction> predictions =
                gLibrary.recognize(gesture);

        if (predictions.size() > 0 && predictions.get(0).score > 1.0)
        {

            String action = predictions.get(0).name;

            Toast.makeText(this, action, Toast.LENGTH_SHORT).show();
        }
    }
.
.
.
}
```

When the Android runtime detects a gesture on the gesture overlay view object, the *onGesturePerformed* method is called. Passed through as arguments are a reference to the GestureOverlayView object on which the gesture was detected together with an object of type *Gesture*. The Gesture class is designed to hold the information that defines a specific gesture (essentially a sequence of timed points on the screen depicting the path of the strokes that comprise a gesture).

The Gesture object is passed through to the *recognize()* method of our *gLibrary* instance to compare the current gesture with each gesture loaded from the *gesture* file. Once this task is complete, the *recognize()* method returns an ArrayList object containing a Prediction object for each comparison performed. The list is ranked in order from the best match (at position 0 in the array) to the worst. Contained within each prediction object is the name of the corresponding gesture from the *gesture* file and a prediction score indicating how closely it matches the current gesture.

The code in the above method, therefore, takes the prediction at position 0 (the closest match), makes sure it has a score of greater than 1.0, and then displays a Toast message (an Android class designed to display notification pop-ups to the user) displaying the name of the matching gesture.

29.14 Testing the Application

Build and run the application on an emulator or a physical Android device and perform the circle gesture on the display. When performed, the toast notification should appear containing the name of the detected gesture. Note that when a gesture is recognized, it is outlined on the display with a bright yellow line, while gestures about which the overlay is uncertain appear as a faint yellow line. While useful during development, this is probably not ideal for a real-world application. Therefore, there is still some more configuration work to do.

29.15 Configuring the GestureOverlayView

By default, the GestureOverlayView is configured to display yellow lines during gestures. The color that draws recognized and unrecognized gestures can be defined via the *android:gestureColor* and *android:uncertainGestureColor* attributes. For example, to hide the gesture lines, modify the *activity_main.xml* file in the example project as follows:

```
<android.gesture.GestureOverlayView
    android:id="@+id/gOverlay"
```

```
        android:layout_width="0dp"
        android:layout_height="0dp"
        app:layout_constraintBottom_toBottomOf="parent"
        app:layout_constraintEnd_toEndOf="parent"
        app:layout_constraintStart_toStartOf="parent"
        app:layout_constraintTop_toTopOf="parent"
        android:gestureColor="#00000000"
        android:uncertainGestureColor="#00000000" />
```

On re-running the application, gestures should now be invisible (since they are drawn in white on the white background of the ConstraintLayout view).

29.16 Intercepting Gestures

The GestureOverlayView is, as previously described, a transparent overlay that may be positioned over the top of other views. This leads to the question of whether events intercepted by the gesture overlay should be passed on to the underlying views when a gesture has been recognized. This is controlled via the *android:eventsInterceptionEnabled* property of the GestureOverlayView instance. When set to true, the gesture events are not passed to the underlying views when a gesture is recognized. This can be a particularly useful setting when gestures are being performed over a view that might be configured to scroll in response to certain gestures. Setting this property to *true* will avoid gestures also being interpreted as instructions to the underlying view to scroll in a particular direction.

29.17 Detecting Pinch Gestures

Before moving on from touch handling in general and gesture recognition in particular, the last topic of this chapter is handling pinch gestures. While it is possible to create and detect a wide range of gestures using the steps outlined in the previous sections of this chapter, it is, in fact, not possible to detect a pinching gesture (where two fingers are used in a stretching and pinching motion, typically to zoom in and out of a view or image) using the techniques discussed so far.

The simplest method for detecting pinch gestures is to use the Android *ScaleGestureDetector* class. In general terms, detecting pinch gestures involves the following three steps:

1. Declaration of a new class which implements the SimpleOnScaleGestureListener interface, including the required *onScale()*, *onScaleBegin()*, and *onScaleEnd()* callback methods.

2. Creation of an instance of the ScaleGestureDetector class, passing through an instance of the class created in step 1 as an argument.

3. Implementing the *onTouchEvent()* callback method on the enclosing activity, which, in turn, calls the *onTouchEvent()* method of the ScaleGestureDetector class.

In the remainder of this chapter, we will create an example designed to demonstrate the implementation of pinch gesture recognition.

29.18 A Pinch Gesture Example Project

Select the *New Project* option from the welcome screen and, within the resulting new project dialog, choose the Empty Views Activity template before clicking on the Next button.

Enter *PinchExample* into the Name field and specify *com.ebookfrenzy.pinchexample* as the package name. Before clicking on the Finish button, change the Minimum API level setting to API 26: Android 8.0 (Oreo) and the Language menu to Java. Convert the project to use view binding by following the steps in *11.8 Migrating a*

Implementing Custom Gesture and Pinch Recognition on Android

Project to View Binding.

Within the *activity_main.xml* file, select the default TextView object and use the Attributes tool window to set the ID to *myTextView*.

Locate and load the *MainActivity.java* file into the Android Studio editor and modify the file as follows:

```
package com.ebookfrenzy.pinchexample;
.
.
import android.view.MotionEvent;
import android.view.ScaleGestureDetector;
import android.view.ScaleGestureDetector.SimpleOnScaleGestureListener;

public class MainActivity extends AppCompatActivity {

    private ActivityMainBinding binding;
    ScaleGestureDetector scaleGestureDetector;

    @Override
    protected void onCreate(Bundle savedInstanceState) {
        super.onCreate(savedInstanceState);
        binding = ActivityMainBinding.inflate(getLayoutInflater());
        View view = binding.getRoot();
        setContentView(view);

        scaleGestureDetector =
                new ScaleGestureDetector(this,
                        new MyOnScaleGestureListener());
    }

    @Override
    public boolean onTouchEvent(MotionEvent event) {
        scaleGestureDetector.onTouchEvent(event);
        return true;
    }

    public class MyOnScaleGestureListener extends
            SimpleOnScaleGestureListener {

        @Override
        public boolean onScale(ScaleGestureDetector detector) {

            float scaleFactor = detector.getScaleFactor();

            if (scaleFactor > 1) {
                binding.myTextView.setText("Zooming In");
```

Implementing Custom Gesture and Pinch Recognition on Android

```
        } else {
            binding.myTextView.setText("Zooming Out");
        }
        return true;
    }

    @Override
    public boolean onScaleBegin(ScaleGestureDetector detector) {
        return true;
    }

    @Override
    public void onScaleEnd(ScaleGestureDetector detector) {

    }
}
.
.
.
}
```

The code declares a new class named MyOnScaleGestureListener, extending the Android SimpleOnScaleGestureListener class. This interface requires that three methods (*onScale()*, *onScaleBegin()*, and *onScaleEnd()*) be implemented. In this instance, the *onScale()* method identifies the scale factor and displays a message on the text view indicating the type of pinch gesture detected.

Within the *onCreate()* method, a new *ScaleGestureDetector* instance is created, passing through a reference to the enclosing activity and an instance of our new *MyOnScaleGestureListener* class as arguments. Finally, an *onTouchEvent()* callback method is implemented for the activity, which calls the corresponding *onTouchEvent()* method of the *ScaleGestureDetector* object, passing through the MotionEvent object as an argument.

Compile and run the application on an emulator or physical Android device and perform pinching gestures on the screen, noting that the text view displays either the zoom-in or zoom-out message depending on the pinching motion. Pinching gestures may be simulated within the emulator in stand-alone mode by holding down the Ctrl (or macOS Cmd) key and clicking and dragging the mouse pointer, as shown in Figure 29-3:

Figure 29-3

29.19 Summary

A gesture is the motion of points of contact on a touch screen involving one or more strokes and can be used as a method of communication between the user and the application. Android allows gestures to be designed using the Gesture Builder application. Once created, gestures can be saved to a gestures file and loaded into an activity at application runtime using the GestureLibrary.

Gestures can be detected on areas of the display by overlaying existing views with instances of the transparent *GestureOverlayView* class and implementing an *OnGesturePerformedListener* event listener. Using the GestureLibrary, a ranked list of matches between a gesture performed by the user and the gestures stored in a gestures file may be generated, using a prediction score to decide whether a gesture is a close enough match.

Pinch gestures may be detected by implementing the ScaleGestureDetector class, an example of which was also provided in this chapter.

30. An Introduction to Android Fragments

As you progress through the chapters of this book, it will become increasingly evident that many of the design concepts behind the Android system were conceived to promote the reuse of and interaction between the different elements that make up an application. One such area that will be explored in this chapter involves using Fragments.

This chapter will provide an overview of the basics of fragments in terms of what they are and how they can be created and used within applications. The next chapter will work through a tutorial designed to show fragments in action when developing applications in Android Studio, including the implementation of communication between fragments.

30.1 What is a Fragment?

A fragment is a self-contained, modular section of an application's user interface and corresponding behavior that can be embedded within an activity. Fragments can be assembled to create an activity during the application design phase and added to or removed from an activity during application runtime to create a dynamically changing user interface.

Fragments may only be used as part of an activity and cannot be instantiated as standalone application elements. However, a fragment can be considered a functional "sub-activity" with its own lifecycle similar to that of a full activity.

Fragments are stored in the form of XML layout files. They may be added to an activity by placing appropriate <fragment> elements in the activity's layout file or through code within the activity's class implementation.

30.2 Creating a Fragment

The two components that make up a fragment are an XML layout file and a corresponding Java class. The XML layout file for a fragment takes the same format as a layout for any other activity layout and can contain any combination and complexity of layout managers and views. The following XML layout, for example, is for a fragment consisting of a ConstraintLayout with a red background containing a single TextView with a white foreground:

```
<?xml version="1.0" encoding="utf-8"?>
<androidx.constraintlayout.widget.ConstraintLayout
    xmlns:android="http://schemas.android.com/apk/res/android"
    xmlns:app="http://schemas.android.com/apk/res-auto"
    xmlns:tools="http://schemas.android.com/tools"
    android:id="@+id/constraintLayout"
    android:layout_width="match_parent"
    android:layout_height="match_parent"
    android:background="@android:color/holo_red_dark"
    tools:context=".FragmentOne">
```

An Introduction to Android Fragments

```
    <TextView
        android:id="@+id/textView1"
        android:layout_width="wrap_content"
        android:layout_height="wrap_content"
        android:text="My First Fragment"
        android:textAppearance="@style/TextAppearance.AppCompat.Large"
        android:textColor="@color/white"
        app:layout_constraintBottom_toBottomOf="parent"
        app:layout_constraintEnd_toEndOf="parent"
        app:layout_constraintStart_toStartOf="parent"
        app:layout_constraintTop_toTopOf="parent" />
</androidx.constraintlayout.widget.ConstraintLayout>
```

The corresponding class to go with the layout must be a subclass of the Android *Fragment* class. This class should, at a minimum, override the *onCreateView()* method, which is responsible for loading the fragment layout. For example:

```
package com.example.myfragmentdemo;

import android.os.Bundle;
import android.view.LayoutInflater;
import android.view.View;
import android.view.ViewGroup;
import androidx.fragment.app.Fragment;

public class FragmentOne extends Fragment {

    @Override
    public View onCreateView(LayoutInflater inflater,
            ViewGroup container,
             Bundle savedInstanceState) {
        // Inflate the layout for this fragment
        binding = FragmentTextBinding.inflate(inflater, container, false);
        return binding.getRoot();
    }
}
```

In addition to the *onCreateView()* method, the class may also override the standard lifecycle methods.

Once the fragment layout and class have been created, the fragment is ready to be used within application activities.

30.3 Adding a Fragment to an Activity using the Layout XML File

Fragments may be incorporated into an activity by writing Java code or embedding the fragment into the activity's XML layout file. Regardless of the approach used, a key point to be aware of is that when the support library is being used for compatibility with older Android releases, any activities using fragments must be implemented as a subclass of *FragmentActivity* instead of the *AppCompatActivity* class:

```
package com.example.myfragmentdemo;
```

```
import android.os.Bundle;
import androidx.fragment.app.FragmentActivity;
import android.view.Menu;

public class MainActivity extends FragmentActivity {
.
.
```

Fragments are embedded into activity layout files using the FragmentContainerView class. The following example layout embeds the fragment created in the previous section of this chapter into an activity layout:

```
<?xml version="1.0" encoding="utf-8"?>
<androidx.constraintlayout.widget.ConstraintLayout
    xmlns:android="http://schemas.android.com/apk/res/android"
    xmlns:app="http://schemas.android.com/apk/res-auto"
    xmlns:tools="http://schemas.android.com/tools"
    android:layout_width="match_parent"
    android:layout_height="match_parent"
    tools:context=".MainActivity">

    <androidx.fragment.app.FragmentContainerView
        android:id="@+id/fragment2"
        android:name="com.ebookfrenzy.myfragmentdemo.FragmentOne"
        android:layout_width="0dp"
        android:layout_height="wrap_content"
        android:layout_marginStart="32dp"
        android:layout_marginEnd="32dp"
        app:layout_constraintBottom_toBottomOf="parent"
        app:layout_constraintEnd_toEndOf="parent"
        app:layout_constraintStart_toStartOf="parent"
        app:layout_constraintTop_toTopOf="parent"
        tools:layout="@layout/fragment_one" />
</androidx.constraintlayout.widget.ConstraintLayout>
```

The key properties within the <fragment> element are *android:name*, which must reference the class associated with the fragment, and *tools:layout*, which must reference the XML resource file containing the fragment's layout.

Once added to the layout of an activity, fragments may be viewed and manipulated within the Android Studio Layout Editor tool. Figure 30-1, for example, shows the above layout with the embedded fragment within the Android Studio Layout Editor:

An Introduction to Android Fragments

Figure 30-1

30.4 Adding and Managing Fragments in Code

The ease of adding a fragment to an activity via the activity's XML layout file comes at the cost of the activity not being able to remove the fragment at runtime. To achieve full dynamic control of fragments during runtime, those activities must be added via code. This has the advantage that the fragments can be added, removed, and even made to replace one another dynamically while the application is running.

When using code to manage fragments, the fragment will still consist of an XML layout file and a corresponding class. The difference comes when working with the fragment within the hosting activity. There is a standard sequence of steps when adding a fragment to an activity using code:

1. Create an instance of the fragment's class.

2. Pass any additional intent arguments through to the class instance.

3. Obtain a reference to the fragment manager instance.

4. Call the *beginTransaction()* method on the fragment manager instance. This returns a fragment transaction instance.

5. Call the *add()* method of the fragment transaction instance, passing through as arguments the resource ID of the view that is to contain the fragment and the fragment class instance.

6. Call the *commit()* method of the fragment transaction.

The following code, for example, adds a fragment defined by the FragmentOne class so that it appears in the container view with an ID of LinearLayout1:

```
FragmentOne firstFragment = new FragmentOne();
firstFragment.setArguments(getIntent().getExtras());

FragmentManager fragManager = getSupportFragmentManager();
FragmentTransaction transaction = fragManager.beginTransaction();
```

```
transaction.add(R.id.LinearLayout1, firstFragment);
transaction.commit();
```

The above code breaks down each step into a separate statement for clarity. The last four lines can, however, be abbreviated into a single line of code as follows:

```
getSupportFragmentManager().beginTransaction()
        .add(R.id.LinearLayout1, firstFragment).commit();
```

Once added to a container, a fragment may subsequently be removed via a call to the *remove()* method of the fragment transaction instance, passing through a reference to the fragment instance that is to be removed:

```
transaction.remove(firstFragment);
```

Similarly, one fragment may be replaced with another by a call to the *replace()* method of the fragment transaction instance. This takes as arguments the ID of the view containing the fragment and an instance of the new fragment. The replaced fragment may also be placed on what is referred to as the *back* stack so that it can be quickly restored if the user navigates back to it. This is achieved by making a call to the *addToBackStack()* method of the fragment transaction object before making the *commit()* method call:

```
FragmentTwo secondFragment = new FragmentTwo();
transaction.replace(R.id.LinearLayout1, secondFragment);
transaction.addToBackStack(null);
transaction.commit();
```

30.5 Handling Fragment Events

As previously discussed, a fragment is like a sub-activity with its layout, class, and lifecycle. The view components (such as buttons and text views) within a fragment can generate events like regular activity. This raises the question of which class receives an event from a view in a fragment, the fragment itself, or the activity in which the fragment is embedded. The answer to this question depends on how the event handler is declared.

In the chapter entitled *"An Overview and Example of Android Event Handling"*, two approaches to event handling were discussed. The first method involved configuring an event listener and callback method within the activity's code. For example:

```
binding.button.setOnClickListener(
        new Button.OnClickListener() {
                public void onClick(View v) {
                        // Code to be performed when
                        // the button is clicked
                }
        }
);
```

In the case of intercepting click events, the second approach involved setting the *android:onClick* property within the XML layout file:

```
<Button
    android:id="@+id/button1"
    android:layout_width="wrap_content"
    android:layout_height="wrap_content"
    android:onClick="onClick"
    android:text="Click me" />
```

The general rule for events generated by a view in a fragment is that if the event listener were declared in the

An Introduction to Android Fragments

fragment class using the event listener and callback method approach, the event would be handled first by the fragment. However, if the *android:onClick* resource is used, the event will be passed directly to the activity containing the fragment.

30.6 Implementing Fragment Communication

Once one or more fragments are embedded within an activity, the chances are good that some form of communication will need to take place between the fragments and the activity and between one fragment and another. Good practice dictates that fragments do not communicate directly with one another. All communication should take place via the encapsulating activity.

To communicate with a fragment, the activity must identify the fragment object via the ID assigned to it. Once this reference has been obtained, the activity can call the public methods of the fragment object.

Communicating in the other direction (from fragment to activity) is a little more complicated. In the first instance, the fragment must define a listener interface, which is then implemented within the activity class. For example, the following code declares a ToolbarListener interface on a fragment named ToolbarFragment. The code also declares a variable in which a reference to the activity will later be stored:

```
public class ToolbarFragment extends Fragment {

        ToolbarListener activityCallback;

        public interface ToolbarListener {
            public void onButtonClick(int position, String text);
        }
.
.
.
}
```

The above code dictates that any class that implements the ToolbarListener interface must also implement a callback method named *onButtonClick* which, in turn, accepts an integer and a String as arguments.

Next, the *onAttach()* method of the fragment class needs to be overridden and implemented. This method is called automatically by the Android system when the fragment has been initialized and associated with an activity. The method is passed a reference to the activity in which the fragment is contained. The method must store a local reference to this activity and verify that it implements the ToolbarListener interface:

```
@Override
public void onAttach(Context context) {
    super.onAttach(context);

    try {
       activityCallback = (ToolbarListener) activity;
    } catch (ClassCastException e) {
       throw new ClassCastException(activity.toString()
              + " must implement ToolbarListener");
    }
}
```

Upon execution of this example, a reference to the activity will be stored in the local *activityCallback* variable, and an exception will be thrown if that activity does not implement the ToolbarListener interface.

The next step is to call the callback method of the activity from within the fragment. When and how this happens depends entirely on the circumstances under which the activity needs to be contacted by the fragment. The following code, for example, calls the callback method on the activity when a button is clicked:

```
public void buttonClicked (View view) {
   activityCallback.onButtonClick(arg1, arg2);
}
```

All that remains is to modify the activity class to implement the ToolbarListener interface. For example:

```
public class MainActivity extends FragmentActivity
            implements ToolbarFragment.ToolbarListener {

   public void onButtonClick(String arg1, int arg2) {
       // Implement code for callback method
   }
   .
   .
   .
}
```

As we can see from the above code, the activity declares that it implements the ToolbarListener interface of the ToolbarFragment class and then proceeds to implement the *onButtonClick()* method as required by the interface.

30.7 Summary

Fragments provide a powerful mechanism for creating reusable modules of user interface layout and application behavior, which, once created, can be embedded in activities. A fragment consists of a user interface layout file and a class. Fragments may be utilized in an activity by adding the fragment to the activity's layout file or writing code to manage the fragments at runtime. Fragments added to an activity in code can be removed and replaced dynamically at runtime. All communication between fragments should be performed via the activity within which the fragments are embedded.

Having covered the basics of fragments in this chapter, the next chapter will work through a tutorial designed to reinforce the techniques outlined in this chapter.

31. Using Fragments in Android Studio - An Example

As outlined in the previous chapter, fragments provide a convenient mechanism for creating reusable modules of application functionality consisting of both sections of a user interface and the corresponding behavior. Once created, fragments can be embedded within activities.

Having explored the general theory of fragments in the previous chapter, this chapter aims to create an example Android application using Android Studio designed to demonstrate the actual steps involved in creating and using fragments and implementing communication between one fragment and another within an activity.

31.1 About the Example Fragment Application

The application created in this chapter will consist of a single activity and two fragments. The user interface for the first fragment will contain a toolbar consisting of an EditText view, a SeekBar, and a Button, all contained within a ConstraintLayout view. The second fragment will consist solely of a TextView object within a ConstraintLayout view.

The two fragments will be embedded within the main activity of the application and communication implemented such that when the button in the first fragment is pressed, the text entered into the EditText view will appear on the TextView of the second fragment using a font size dictated by the position of the SeekBar in the first fragment.

Since this application is intended to work on earlier versions of Android, we will need to use the appropriate Android support library.

31.2 Creating the Example Project

Select the *New Project* option from the welcome screen and, within the resulting new project dialog, choose the Empty Views Activity template before clicking on the Next button.

Enter *FragmentExample* into the Name field and specify *com.ebookfrenzy.fragmentexample* as the package name. Before clicking the Finish button, change the Minimum API level setting to API 26: Android 8.0 (Oreo) and the Language menu to Java. Modify the project to use view binding using the steps outlined in *11.8 Migrating a Project to View Binding*.

Return to the *Gradle Scripts -> build.gradle.kts (Module :app)* file and add the following directive to the *dependencies* section (keeping in mind that a more recent version of the library may now be available):

```
implementation 'androidx.navigation:navigation-fragment:2.5.2'
```

31.3 Creating the First Fragment Layout

The next step is to create the user interface for the first fragment used within our activity.

This user interface will consist of an XML layout file and a fragment class. While these could be added manually, it is quicker to ask Android Studio to create them for us. Within the project tool window, locate the *app -> java -> com.ebookfrenzy.fragmentexample* entry and right-click on it. From the resulting menu, select the *New ->*

Using Fragments in Android Studio - An Example

Fragment -> Gallery... option to display the dialog shown in Figure 31-1 below:

Figure 31-1

Select the *Fragment (Blank)* template before clicking the Next button. On the subsequent screen, name the fragment *ToolbarFragment* with a layout file named *fragment_toolbar*:

Figure 31-2

Load the *fragment_toolbar.xml* file into the layout editor using Design mode. Next, right-click on the FrameLayout entry in the Component Tree panel and select the *Convert FrameLayout to ConstraintLayout* menu option, accepting the default settings in the confirmation dialog. Change the id from to *constraintLayout*. Ensure that Autoconnect mode is enabled, then select and delete the default TextView and add Plain Text, Seekbar, and Button widgets to the layout so that their positions match those shown in Figure 31-3. Finally, change the view ids to *editText1*, *seekBar1*, and *button1*, respectively.

Change the text on the button to read "Change Text", extract the text to a string resource named *change_text*, and remove the Name text from the EditText view. Finally, set the *layout_width* property of the Seekbar to *match_constraint* with margins set to 16dp on the left and right edges.

Using Fragments in Android Studio - An Example

Use the *Infer constraints* toolbar button to add any missing constraints, at which point the layout should match that shown in Figure 31-3 below:

Figure 31-3

31.4 Migrating a Fragment to View Binding

As with the Empty Views Activity template, Android Studio does not enable view binding support when new fragments are added to a project. Therefore, we will need to perform this migration before moving to the next step of this tutorial. Begin by editing the *ToolbarFragment.java* file and importing the binding for the fragment as follows:

```
import com.ebookfrenzy.fragmentexample.databinding.FragmentToolbarBinding;
```

Next, locate the *onCreateView()* method and make the following declarations and changes (which also include adding the *onDestroyView()* method to ensure that the binding reference is removed when the fragment is destroyed):

.
.

private FragmentToolbarBinding binding;

```
@Override
public View onCreateView(LayoutInflater inflater, ViewGroup container,
                        Bundle savedInstanceState) {
    // Inflate the layout for this fragment
    return inflater.inflate(R.layout.fragment_toolbar, container, false);
    binding = FragmentToolbarBinding.inflate(inflater, container, false);
    return binding.getRoot();
}
```

```
@Override
public void onDestroyView() {
    super.onDestroyView();
    binding = null;
}
```

Once these changes are complete, the fragment is ready to use view binding.

255

Using Fragments in Android Studio - An Example

31.5 Adding the Second Fragment

Repeating the steps to create the toolbar fragment, add another empty fragment named TextFragment with a layout file named *fragment_text*. Once again, convert the FrameLayout container to a ConstraintLayout (changing the id to *constraintLayout2*) and remove the default TextView.

Drag a drop a TextView widget from the palette and position it in the center of the layout, using the *Infer constraints* button to add any missing constraints. Change the id of the TextView to *textView2*, the text to read "Fragment Two" and modify the *textSize* attribute to 24sp.

On completion, the layout should match that shown in Figure 31-4:

Figure 31-4

Repeat the steps performed in the previous section to migrate the TextFragment class to use view binding as follows:

.
.
```
import com.ebookfrenzy.fragmentexample.databinding.FragmentTextBinding;
```
.
.
```
private FragmentTextBinding binding;

@Override
public View onCreateView(LayoutInflater inflater, ViewGroup container,
                        Bundle savedInstanceState) {
    // Inflate the layout for this fragment
    return inflater.inflate(R.layout.fragment_text, container, false);
    binding = FragmentTextBinding.inflate(inflater, container, false);
    return binding.getRoot();
}

@Override
public void onDestroyView() {
```

```
        super.onDestroyView();
        binding = null;
}
```

31.6 Adding the Fragments to the Activity

The main activity for the application has associated with it an XML layout file named *activity_main.xml*. For this example, the fragments will be added to the activity using the <fragment> element within this file. Using the Project tool window, navigate to the *app -> res -> layout* section of the *FragmentExample* project and double-click on the *activity_main.xml* file to load it into the Android Studio Layout Editor tool.

With the Layout Editor tool in Design mode, select and delete the default TextView object from the layout and select the *Common* category in the palette. Drag the *FragmentContainerView* component from the list of views and drop it onto the layout so that it is centered horizontally and positioned such that the dashed line appears, indicating the top layout margin:

Figure 31-5

On dropping the fragment onto the layout, a dialog will appear displaying a list of Fragments available within the current project, as illustrated in Figure 31-6:

Figure 31-6

Select the ToolbarFragment entry from the list and click OK to dismiss the Fragments dialog. Once added, click the red warning button in the top right-hand corner of the layout editor to display the Problems tool window. An *unknown fragments* message will indicate that the Layout Editor tool needs to know which fragment to display during the preview session. Select the Unknown fragment item, then click on the *Pick Layout...* link in the right-hand panel as shown in Figure 31-7:

Figure 31-7

Using Fragments in Android Studio - An Example

In the resulting dialog (Figure 31-8), select the *fragment_toolbar* entry and then click OK:

Figure 31-8

With the fragment selected, change the *layout_width* property to *match_constraint* so that it occupies the full width of the screen. Click and drag another *FragmentContainerView* entry from the palette and position it so that it is centered horizontally and located beneath the bottom edge of the first fragment. When prompted, select the *TextFragment* entry from the fragment dialog before clicking OK. Display the Problems tool window and repeat the previous steps, this time selecting the *fragment_text* layout. Use the *Infer constraints* button to establish any missing layout constraints.

Note that the fragments are now visible in the layout, as demonstrated in Figure 31-9:

Figure 31-9

Before proceeding to the next step, select the TextFragment instance in the layout and, within the Attributes tool window, change the ID of the fragment to *text_fragment*.

31.7 Making the Toolbar Fragment Talk to the Activity

When the user touches the button in the toolbar fragment, the fragment class will need to extract the text from the EditText view and the current value of the SeekBar and send them to the text fragment. As outlined in *"An*

Using Fragments in Android Studio - An Example

Introduction to Android Fragments", fragments should not communicate with each other directly, instead using the activity in which they are embedded as an intermediary.

The first step in this process is ensuring that the toolbar fragment responds to the clicked button. We also need to implement some code to keep track of the value of the SeekBar view. For this example, we will implement these listeners within the ToolbarFragment class. Select the *ToolbarFragment.java* file and modify it so that it reads as shown in the following listing:

```
package com.ebookfrenzy.fragmentexample;
.
.
import androidx.annotation.NonNull;
import androidx.annotation.Nullable;
import android.content.Context;
import android.widget.SeekBar;

public class ToolbarFragment extends Fragment implements
                              SeekBar.OnSeekBarChangeListener {

    private static int seekvalue = 10;
.
.
@Override
    public void onViewCreated(@NonNull View view,
                 @Nullable Bundle savedInstanceState) {
        super.onViewCreated(view, savedInstanceState);

        binding.seekBar1.setOnSeekBarChangeListener(this);
        binding.button1.setOnClickListener(new View.OnClickListener() {
            public void onClick(View v) {
                buttonClicked(v);
            }
        });
    }

    public void buttonClicked (View view) {

    }

    @Override
    public void onProgressChanged(SeekBar seekBar, int progress,
                                  boolean fromUser) {
        seekvalue = progress;
    }

    @Override
    public void onStartTrackingTouch(SeekBar arg0) {
```

Using Fragments in Android Studio - An Example

```
        }

        @Override
        public void onStopTrackingTouch(SeekBar arg0) {

        }
}
```

Before moving on, we need to take some time to explain the above code changes. First, the class is declared as implementing the OnSeekBarChangeListener interface. This is because the user interface contains a SeekBar instance, and the fragment needs to receive notifications when the user slides the bar to change the font size. Implementation of the OnSeekBarChangeListener interface requires that the *onProgressChanged()*, *onStartTrackingTouch()*, and *onStopTrackingTouch()* methods be implemented. These methods have been implemented, but only the *onProgressChanged()* method is required to perform a task, in this case, storing the new value in a variable named seekvalue, which was declared at the start of the class. Also declared is a variable to store a reference to the EditText object.

The *onViewCreated()* method has been added to set up an onClickListener on the button, which is configured to call a method named *buttonClicked()* when a click event is detected. This method is also then implemented, though it does not do anything at this point.

The next phase of this process is to set up the listener that will allow the fragment to call the activity when the button is clicked. This follows the mechanism outlined in the previous chapter:

```
public class ToolbarFragment extends Fragment
    implements SeekBar.OnSeekBarChangeListener {

        private static int seekvalue = 10;
        private FragmentToolbarBinding binding;
        ToolbarListener activityCallback;

        public interface ToolbarListener {
            public void onButtonClick(int position, String text);
        }

        @Override
        public void onAttach(Context context) {
            super.onAttach(context);
            try {
                activityCallback = (ToolbarListener) context;
            } catch (ClassCastException e) {
                throw new ClassCastException(context.toString()
                    + " must implement ToolbarListener");
            }
        }
.
.
        public void buttonClicked (View view) {
```

```
        activityCallback.onButtonClick(seekvalue,
            binding.editText1.getText().toString());
    }
.
.
.
}
```

The above implementation will result in a method named *onButtonClick()* belonging to the activity class being called when the user clicks the button. All that remains, therefore, is to declare that the activity class implements the newly created ToolbarListener interface and to implement the *onButtonClick()* method.

Since the Android Support Library is being used for fragment support in earlier Android versions, the activity also needs to be changed to subclass from *FragmentActivity* instead of *AppCompatActivity*. Bringing these requirements together results in the following modified *MainActivity.java* file:

```
package com.ebookfrenzy.fragmentexample;

import androidx.appcompat.app.AppCompatActivity;
import androidx.fragment.app.FragmentActivity;
import android.os.Bundle;

public class MainActivity extends FragmentActivity implements ToolbarFragment.ToolbarListener {
.
.
    public void onButtonClick(int fontsize, String text) {

    }
}
```

With the code changes as they currently stand, the toolbar fragment will detect when the user clicks the button and call a method on the activity passing through the content of the EditText field and the current setting of the SeekBar view. It is now the job of the activity to communicate with the Text Fragment and to pass along these values so that the fragment can update the TextView object accordingly.

31.8 Making the Activity Talk to the Text Fragment

As *"An Introduction to Android Fragments"* outlined, an activity can communicate with a fragment by obtaining a reference to the fragment class instance and then calling public methods on the object. As such, within the TextFragment class, we will now implement a public method named *changeTextProperties()* which takes as arguments an integer for the font size and a string for the new text to be displayed. The method will then use these values to modify the TextView object. Within the Android Studio editing panel, locate and modify the *TextFragment.java* file to add this new method:

```
package com.ebookfrenzy.fragmentexample;
.
.
.
public class TextFragment extends Fragment {
.
```

```
    public void changeTextProperties(int fontsize, String text)
    {
        binding.textView2.setTextSize(fontsize);
        binding.textView2.setText(text);
    }
}
```

When the TextFragment fragment was placed in the activity's layout, it was given an ID of *text_fragment*. Using this ID, it is now possible for the activity to obtain a reference to the fragment instance and call the *changeTextProperties()* method on the object. Edit the *MainActivity.java* file and modify the *onButtonClick()* method as follows:

```
public void onButtonClick(int fontsize, String text) {

    TextFragment textFragment =
    (TextFragment)
        getSupportFragmentManager().findFragmentById(R.id.text_fragment);

    textFragment.changeTextProperties(fontsize, text);
}
```

31.9 Testing the Application

With the coding for this project now complete, the last remaining task is to run the application. When the application is launched, the main activity will start and will, in turn, create and display the two fragments. When the user touches the button in the toolbar fragment, the *onButtonClick()* method of the activity will be called by the toolbar fragment and passed the text from the EditText view and the current value of the SeekBar. The activity will then call the *changeTextProperties()* method of the second fragment, which will modify the TextView to reflect the new text and font size:

Figure 31-10

31.10 Summary

The goal of this chapter was to work through creating an example project to demonstrate the steps involved in using fragments within an Android application. Topics covered included using the Android Support Library for compatibility with Android versions predating the introduction of fragments, including fragments within an activity layout, and implementing inter-fragment communication.

32. Modern Android App Architecture with Jetpack

For many years, Google did not recommend a specific approach to building Android apps other than to provide tools and development kits while letting developers decide what worked best for a particular project or individual programming style. That changed in 2017 with the introduction of the Android Architecture Components, which, in turn, became part of Android Jetpack when it was released in 2018.

This chapter provides an overview of the concepts of Jetpack, Android app architecture recommendations, and some key architecture components. Once the basics have been covered, these topics will be covered in more detail and demonstrated through practical examples in later chapters.

32.1 What is Android Jetpack?

Android Jetpack consists of Android Studio, the Android Architecture Components, the Android Support Library, and a set of guidelines recommending how an Android App should be structured. The Android Architecture Components are designed to make it quicker and easier to perform common tasks when developing Android apps while also conforming to the key principle of the architectural guidelines.

While all Android Architecture Components will be covered in this book, this chapter will focus on the key architectural guidelines and the ViewModel, LiveData, and Lifecycle components while introducing Data Binding and Repositories.

Before moving on, it is important to understand that the Jetpack approach to app development is optional. While highlighting some of the shortcomings of other techniques that have gained popularity over the years, Google stopped short of completely condemning those approaches to app development. Google is taking the position that while there is no right or wrong way to develop an app, there is a recommended way.

32.2 The "Old" Architecture

In the chapter entitled *"Creating an Example Android App in Android Studio"*, an Android project was created consisting of a single activity that contained all of the code for presenting and managing the user interface together with the back-end logic of the app. Until the introduction of Jetpack, the most common architecture followed this paradigm with apps consisting of multiple activities (one for each screen within the app), with each activity class to some degree mixing user interface and back-end code.

This approach led to a range of problems related to the lifecycle of an app (for example, an activity is destroyed and recreated each time the user rotates the device leading to the loss of any app data that had not been saved to some form of persistent storage) as well as issues such as inefficient navigation involving launching a new activity for each app screen accessed by the user.

32.3 Modern Android Architecture

At the most basic level, Google now advocates single-activity apps where different screens are loaded as content within the same activity.

Modern architecture guidelines also recommend separating different areas of responsibility within an app into entirely separate modules (a concept referred to as "separation of concerns"). One of the keys to this approach is the ViewModel component.

32.4 The ViewModel Component

The purpose of ViewModel is to separate the user interface-related data model and logic of an app from the code responsible for displaying and managing the user interface and interacting with the operating system. When designed this way, an app will consist of one or more UI Controllers, such as an activity, together with ViewModel instances responsible for handling the data those controllers need.

The ViewModel only knows about the data model and corresponding logic. It knows nothing about the user interface and does not attempt to directly access or respond to events relating to views within the user interface. When a UI controller needs data to display, it asks the ViewModel to provide it. Similarly, when the user enters data into a view within the user interface, the UI controller passes it to the ViewModel for handling.

This separation of responsibility addresses the issues relating to the lifecycle of UI controllers. Regardless of how often the UI controller is recreated during the lifecycle of an app, the ViewModel instances remain in memory, thereby maintaining data consistency. For example, a ViewModel used by an activity will remain in memory until the activity finishes, which, in the single activity app, is not until the app exits.

Figure 32-1

32.5 The LiveData Component

Consider an app that displays real-time data, such as the current price of a financial stock. The app could use a stock price web service to continuously update the data model within the ViewModel with the latest information. This real-time data is of use only if it is displayed to the user promptly. There are only two ways that the UI controller can ensure that the latest data is displayed in the user interface. One option is for the controller to continuously check with the ViewModel to determine if the data has changed since it was last displayed. However, the problem with this approach is that it could be more efficient. To maintain the real-time nature of the data feed, the UI controller would have to run on a loop, continuously checking for the data to change.

A better solution would be for the UI controller to receive a notification when a specific data item within a ViewModel changes. This is made possible by using the LiveData component. LiveData is a data holder that allows a value to become *observable*. In basic terms, an observable object can notify other objects when changes to its data occur, thereby solving the problem of ensuring that the user interface always matches the data within the ViewModel.

This means, for example, that a UI controller interested in a ViewModel value can set up an observer, which will, in turn, be notified when that value changes. In our hypothetical application, for example, the stock price would be wrapped in a LiveData object within the ViewModel, and the UI controller would assign an observer to the value, declaring a method to be called when the value changes. When triggered by data change, this method will read the updated value from the ViewModel and use it to update the user interface.

Figure 32-2

A LiveData instance may also be declared as mutable, allowing the observing entity to update the underlying value held within the LiveData object. The user might, for example, enter a value in the user interface that needs to overwrite the value stored in the ViewModel.

Another of the key advantages of using LiveData is that it is aware of the *lifecycle state* of its observers. If, for example, an activity contains a LiveData observer, the corresponding LiveData object will know when the activity's lifecycle state changes and respond accordingly. If the activity is paused (perhaps the app is put into the background), the LiveData object will stop sending events to the observer. Suppose the activity has just started or resumes after being paused. In that case, the LiveData object will send a LiveData event to the observer so that the activity has the most up-to-date value. Similarly, the LiveData instance will know when the activity is destroyed and remove the observer to free up resources.

So far, we've only talked about UI controllers using observers. In practice, however, an observer can be used within any object that conforms to the Jetpack approach to lifecycle management.

32.6 ViewModel Saved State

Android allows the user to place an active app in the background and return to it after performing other tasks on the device (including running other apps). When a device runs low on resources, the operating system will rectify this by terminating background app processes, starting with the least recently used app. However, when the user returns to the terminated background app, it should appear in the same state as when it was placed in the background, regardless of whether it was terminated. In terms of the data associated with a ViewModel, this can be implemented using the ViewModel Saved State module. This module allows values to be stored in the app's *saved state* and restored in case of system-initiated process termination. This topic will be covered later in the *"An Android ViewModel Saved State Tutorial"* chapter.

32.7 LiveData and Data Binding

Android Jetpack includes the Data Binding Library, which allows data in a ViewModel to be mapped directly to specific views within the XML user interface layout file. In the AndroidSample project created earlier, code had to be written to obtain references to the EditText and TextView views and to set and get the text properties to reflect data changes. Data binding allows the LiveData value stored in the ViewModel to be referenced directly within the XML layout file avoiding the need to write code to keep the layout views updated.

Figure 32-3

Data binding will be covered in greater detail, starting with the chapter *"An Overview of Android Jetpack Data Binding"*.

32.8 Android Lifecycles

The duration from when an Android component is created to the point that it is destroyed is called the *lifecycle*. During this lifecycle, the component will change between different lifecycle states, usually under the operating system's control and in response to user actions. An activity, for example, will begin in the *initialized* state before transitioning to the *created* state. Once the activity runs, it will switch to the *started* state, from which it will cycle through various states, including *created*, *started*, *resumed*, and *destroyed*.

Many Android Framework classes and components allow other objects to access their current state. *Lifecycle observers* may also be used so that an object receives a notification when the lifecycle state of another object changes. The ViewModel component uses this technique behind the scenes to identify when an observer has restarted or been destroyed. This functionality is not limited to Android framework and architecture components. It may also be built into any other classes using a set of lifecycle components included with the architecture components.

Objects that can detect and react to lifecycle state changes in other objects are said to be *lifecycle-aware*. In contrast, objects that provide access to their lifecycle state are called *lifecycle owners*. The chapter entitled *"Working with Android Lifecycle-Aware Components"* will cover Lifecycles in greater detail.

32.9 Repository Modules

If a ViewModel obtains data from one or more external sources (such as databases or web services, it is important to separate the code involved in handling those data sources from the ViewModel class. Failure to do this would, after all, violate the separation of concerns guidelines. To avoid mixing this functionality with the ViewModel, Google's architecture guidelines recommend placing this code in a separate *Repository* module.

A repository is not an Android architecture component but a Java class created by the app developer that is responsible for interfacing with the various data sources. The class then provides an interface to the ViewModel, allowing that data to be stored in the model.

Figure 32-4

32.10 Summary

Until recently, Google has tended not to recommend any particular approach to structuring an Android app. That has now changed with the introduction of Android Jetpack, consisting of tools, components, libraries, and architecture guidelines. Google now recommends that an app project be divided into separate modules, each responsible for a particular area of functionality, otherwise known as "separation of concerns".

In particular, the guidelines recommend separating the view data model of an app from the code responsible for handling the user interface. In addition, the code responsible for gathering data from data sources such as web services or databases should be built into a separate repository module instead of being bundled with the view model.

Android Jetpack includes the Android Architecture Components, designed to make developing apps that conform to the recommended guidelines easier. This chapter has introduced the ViewModel, LiveData, and Lifecycle components. These will be covered in more detail, starting with the next chapter. Other architecture components not mentioned in this chapter will be covered later in the book.

Chapter 33

33. An Android ViewModel Tutorial

The previous chapter introduced the fundamental concepts of Android Jetpack and outlined the basics of modern Android app architecture. Jetpack defines a set of recommendations describing how an Android app project should be structured while providing a set of libraries and components that make it easier to conform to these guidelines to develop reliable apps with less coding and fewer errors.

To help reinforce and clarify the information provided in the previous chapter, this chapter will step through creating an example app project that uses the ViewModel component. The next chapter will further enhance this example by including LiveData and data binding support.

33.1 About the Project

In the chapter entitled *"Creating an Example Android App in Android Studio"*, a project named AndroidSample was created in which all of the code for the app was bundled into the main Activity class file. In the following chapter, an AVD emulator was created and used to run the app. While the app was running, we experienced first-hand the problems that occur when developing apps in this way when the data displayed on a TextView widget was lost during a device rotation.

This chapter will implement the same currency converter app, using the ViewModel component and following the Google app architecture guidelines to avoid Activity lifecycle complications.

33.2 Creating the ViewModel Example Project

When the AndroidSample project was created, the Empty Views Activity template was chosen as the basis for the project. However, the Basic Views Template template will be used for this project.

Select the *New Project* option from the welcome screen and, within the resulting new project dialog, choose the *Basic Views Activity* template before clicking on the Next button.

Enter *ViewModelDemo* into the Name field and specify *com.ebookfrenzy.viewmodeldemo* as the package name. Before clicking on the Finish button, change the Minimum API level setting to API 26: Android 8.0 (Oreo) and the Language menu to Java.

33.3 Removing Unwanted Project Elements

As outlined in the *"A Guide to the Android Studio Layout Editor Tool"*, the Basic Views Activity template includes features not required by all projects. Before adding the ViewModel to the project, we first need to remove the navigation features, the second content fragment, and the floating action button as follows:

1. Double-click on the *activity_main.xml* layout file in the Project tool window, select the floating action button, and tap the keyboard delete key to remove the object from the layout.

2. Edit the *MainActivity.java* file and remove the floating action button code from the onCreate method as follows:

```
@Override
protected void onCreate(Bundle savedInstanceState) {
    .
    .
```

271

An Android ViewModel Tutorial

~~binding.fab.setOnClickListener(new View.OnClickListener() {~~
~~@Override~~
~~public void onClick(View view) {~~
~~Snackbar.make(view, "Replace with your own action", Snackbar.LENGTH_LONG)~~
~~.setAnchorView(R.id.fab)~~
~~.setAction("Action", null).show();~~
~~}~~
~~});~~
}

3. Within the Project tool window, navigate to and double-click on the *app -> res -> navigation -> nav_graph.xml* file to load it into the navigation editor.

4. Within the editor, select the SecondFragment entry in the graph panel and tap the keyboard delete key to remove it from the graph.

5. Locate and delete the *SecondFragment.java* and *fragment_second.xml* files.

6. The final task is to remove some code from the FirstFragment class so that the Button view no longer navigates to the now non-existent second fragment when clicked. Edit the *FirstFragment.java* file and remove the code from the *onViewCreated()* method so that it reads as follows:

```
public void onViewCreated(@NonNull View view, Bundle savedInstanceState) {
    super.onViewCreated(view, savedInstanceState);
```

~~binding.buttonFirst.setOnClickListener(new View.OnClickListener() {~~
~~@Override~~
~~public void onClick(View view) {~~
~~NavHostFragment.findNavController(FirstFragment.this)~~
~~.navigate(R.id.action_FirstFragment_to_SecondFragment);~~
~~}~~
~~});~~
}

33.4 Designing the Fragment Layout

The next step is to design the layout of the fragment. First, locate the *fragment_first.xml* file in the Project tool window and double-click on it to load it into the layout editor. Once the layout has loaded, select and delete the existing Button, TextView, and ConstraintLayout components. Next, right-click on the NestedScrollView instance in the Component Tree panel and select the *Convert NestedScrollView to ConstraintLayout* menu option as shown in Figure 33-1, and accept the default settings in the resulting dialog:

An Android ViewModel Tutorial

Figure 33-1

Select the converted ConstraintLayout component and use the Attributes tool window to change the id to *constraintLayout*.

Add a new TextView, position it in the center of the layout, and change the id to *resultText*. Next, drag a Number (Decimal) view from the palette and position it above the existing TextView. With the view selected in the layout, refer to the Attributes tool window and change the id to *dollarText*.

Drag a Button widget onto the layout to position it below the TextView, and change the text attribute to read "Convert". With the button still selected, change the id property to *convertButton*. At this point, the layout should resemble that illustrated in Figure 33-2 (note that the three views have been constrained using a vertical chain):

Figure 33-2

Finally, click on the warning icon in the top right-hand corner of the layout editor and convert the hard-coded strings to resources.

33.5 Implementing the View Model

With the user interface layout completed, the data model for the app needs to be created within the view model. Begin by locating the *com.ebookfrenzy.viewmodeldemo* entry in the Project tool window, right-clicking on it, and selecting the *New -> Java Class* menu option. Name the new class MainViewModel and press the keyboard enter key. Edit the new class file so that it reads as follows:

```
package com.ebookfrenzy.viewmodeldemo.ui.main;

import androidx.lifecycle.ViewModel;

public class MainViewModel extends ViewModel {

    private static final Float rate = 0.74F;
    private String dollarText = "";
    private Float result = 0F;

    public void setAmount(String value) {
        this.dollarText = value;
        result = Float.parseFloat(dollarText)*rate;
    }

    public Float getResult()
    {
        return result;
    }
}
```

The class declares variables to store the current dollar string value and the converted amount together with getter and setter methods to provide access to those data values. When called, the *setAmount()* method takes the current dollar amount as an argument and stores it in the local *dollarText* variable. The dollar string value is converted to a floating point number, multiplied by a fictitious exchange rate, and the resulting euro value is stored in the *result* variable. The *getResult()* method, on the other hand, returns the current value assigned to the *result* variable.

33.6 Associating the Fragment with the View Model

There needs to be some way for the fragment to obtain a reference to the ViewModel to access the model and observe data changes. A Fragment or Activity maintains references to the ViewModels on which it relies for data using an instance of the ViewModelProvider class.

A ViewModelProvider instance is created using the ViewModelProvider class from within the Fragment. When called, the class initializer is passed a reference to the current Fragment or Activity and returns a ViewModelProvider instance as follows:

```
ViewModelProvider viewModelProvider = new ViewModelProvider(this);
```

Once the ViewModelProvider instance has been created, an index value can be used to request a specific ViewModel class. The provider will then either create a new instance of that ViewModel class or return an existing instance, for example:

```
ViewModel viewModel = viewModelProvider.get(MainViewModel.class);
```

Edit the *FirstFragment.java* file and override the *onCreate()* method to set up the ViewModelProvider:

.
.

```
import androidx.lifecycle.ViewModelProvider;
```

An Android ViewModel Tutorial

```
import androidx.annotation.Nullable;
.
.
public class FirstFragment extends Fragment {

    private MainViewModel viewModel;
.
.
  @Override
    public void onCreate(@Nullable Bundle savedInstanceState) {
        super.onCreate(savedInstanceState);
        viewModel = new ViewModelProvider(this).get(MainViewModel.class);
    }
.
.
```

With access to the model view, code can now be added to the Fragment to begin working with the data model.

33.7 Modifying the Fragment

The fragment class needs to be updated to react to button clicks and interact with the data values stored in the ViewModel. The class will also need references to the three views in the user interface layout to react to button clicks, extract the current dollar value, and display the converted currency amount.

In the chapter entitled *"Creating an Example Android App in Android Studio"*, the onClick property of the Button widget was used to designate the method to be called when the user clicks the button. Unfortunately, this property can only call methods on an Activity and cannot be used to call a method in a Fragment. To overcome this limitation, we must add some code to the Fragment class to set up an onClick listener on the button. This can be achieved in the *onViewCreated()* lifecycle method in the *FirstFragment.java* file as outlined below:

```
.
.
public class MainFragment extends Fragment {

    private MainViewModel viewModel;
.
.
    @Override
    public void onViewCreated(@NonNull View view, @Nullable Bundle savedInstanceState) {
        super.onViewCreated(view, savedInstanceState);

        binding.convertButton.setOnClickListener(v -> {

        });
    }
.
.
}
```

275

An Android ViewModel Tutorial

With the listener added, any code placed within the *onClick()* method will be called whenever the user clicks the button.

33.8 Accessing the ViewModel Data

When the button is clicked, the *onClick()* method needs to read the current value from the EditText view, confirm that the field is not empty, and then call the *setAmount()* method of the ViewModel instance. The method will then need to call the ViewModel's *getResult()* method and display the converted value on the TextView widget.

Since LiveData has yet to be used in the project, it will also be necessary to get the latest result value from the ViewModel each time the Fragment is created.

Remaining in the *FirstFragment.java* file, implement these requirements as follows in the *onViewCreated()* method:

.
.
```
import java.util.Locale;
```
.
.
```
@Override
public void onViewCreated(@NonNull View view, @Nullable Bundle savedInstanceState) {
    super.onViewCreated(view, savedInstanceState);

    binding.resultText.setText(String.format(Locale.ENGLISH,"%.2f",
            viewModel.getResult()));

        binding.convertButton.setOnClickListener(v -> {
            if (!binding.dollarText.getText().toString().equals("")) {
                viewModel.setAmount(String.format(Locale.ENGLISH,"%s",
                        binding.dollarText.getText()));
                binding.resultText.setText(String.format(Locale.ENGLISH,"%.2f",
                        viewModel.getResult()));
            } else {
                binding.resultText.setText("No Value");
            }
        });
}
```

33.9 Testing the Project

With this project development phase completed, build and run the app on the simulator or a physical device, enter a dollar value, and click the Convert button. The converted amount should appear on the TextView, indicating that the UI controller and ViewModel re-structuring is working as expected.

When the original AndroidSample app was run, rotating the device caused the value displayed on the *resultText* TextView widget to be lost. Repeat this test now with the ViewModelDemo app and note that the current euro value is retained after the rotation. This is because the ViewModel remained in memory as the Fragment was destroyed and recreated, and code was added to the *onViewCreated()* method to update the TextView with the result data value from the ViewModel each time the Fragment re-started.

While this is an improvement on the original AndroidSample app, much more can be done to simplify the project by using LiveData and data binding, both of which are the topics of the next chapters.

33.10 Summary

In this chapter, we revisited the AndroidSample project created earlier in the book and created a new version of the project structured to comply with the Android Jetpack architectural guidelines. The example project also demonstrated the use of ViewModels to separate data handling from user interface-related code. Finally, the chapter showed how the ViewModel approach avoids problems handling Fragment and Activity lifecycles.

Chapter 34

34. An Android Jetpack LiveData Tutorial

The previous chapter began building an app to conform to the recommended Jetpack architecture guidelines. These initial steps involved implementing the data model for the app user interface within a ViewModel instance.

This chapter will further enhance the app design using the LiveData architecture component. Once LiveData support has been added to the project in this chapter, the next chapters (starting with *"An Overview of Android Jetpack Data Binding"*) will use the Jetpack Data Binding library to eliminate even more code from the project.

34.1 LiveData - A Recap

LiveData was previously introduced in the *"Modern Android App Architecture with Jetpack"* chapter. As described earlier, the LiveData component can be used as a wrapper around data values within a view model. Once contained in a LiveData instance, those variables become observable to other objects within the app, typically UI controllers such as Activities and Fragments. This allows the UI controller to receive a notification whenever the underlying LiveData value changes. An observer is set up by creating an instance of the Observer class and defining an *onChange()* method to be called when the LiveData value changes. Once the Observer instance has been created, it is attached to the LiveData object via a call to the LiveData object's *observe()* method.

LiveData instances can be declared mutable using the MutableLiveData class, allowing both the ViewModel and UI controller to change the underlying data value.

34.2 Adding LiveData to the ViewModel

Launch Android Studio, open the ViewModelDemo project created in the previous chapter, and open the *MainViewModel.java* file, which should currently read as follows:

```
package com.ebookfrenzy.viewmodeldemo;

import androidx.lifecycle.ViewModel;

public class MainViewModel extends ViewModel {

    private static final Float rate = 0.74F;
    private String dollarText = "";
    private Float result = 0F;

    public void setAmount(String value) {
        this.dollarText = value;
        result = Float.parseFloat(dollarText)*rate;
    }

    public Float getResult()
    {
```

An Android Jetpack LiveData Tutorial

```
        return result;
    }
}
```

This stage in the chapter aims to wrap the *result* variable in a MutableLiveData instance (the object will need to be mutable so that the value can be changed each time the user requests a currency conversion). Begin by modifying the class so that it now reads as follows, noting that an additional package needs to be imported when making use of LiveData:

```
package com.ebookfrenzy.viewmodeldemo;

import androidx.lifecycle.MutableLiveData;
import androidx.lifecycle.ViewModel;

public class MainViewModel extends ViewModel {

    private static final Float rate = 0.74F;
    private String dollarText = "";
    private Float result = 0F;
    final private MutableLiveData<Float> result = new MutableLiveData<>();

    public void setAmount(String value) {
        this.dollarText = value;
        result = Float.parseFloat(dollarText)*rate;
    }

    public Float getResult()
    {
        return result;
    }
}
```

Now that the result variable is contained in a mutable LiveData instance, both the *setAmount()* and *getResult()* methods must be modified. In the case of the *setAmount()* method, a value can no longer be assigned to the result variable using the assignment (=) operator. Instead, the LiveData *setValue()* method must be called, passing through the new value as an argument. As currently implemented, the *getResult()* method is declared to return a Float value and must be changed to return a MutableLiveData object. Making these remaining changes results in the following class file:

```
package com.ebookfrenzy.viewmodeldemo;

import androidx.lifecycle.MutableLiveData;
import androidx.lifecycle.ViewModel;

public class MainViewModel extends ViewModel {

    private static final Float rate = 0.74F;
    private String dollarText = "";
    final private MutableLiveData<Float> result = new MutableLiveData<>();
```

```
    public void setAmount(String value) {
        this.dollarText = value;
        result = Float.parseFloat(dollarText)*rate;
        result.setValue(Float.parseFloat(dollarText)*rate);
    }

    public Float getResult()
    public MutableLiveData<Float> getResult()
    {
        return result;
    }
}
```

34.3 Implementing the Observer

Now that the conversion result is contained within a LiveData instance, the next step is configuring an observer within the UI controller, which, in this example, is the FirstFragment class. Locate the *FirstFragment.java* class (*app -> java -> <package name> -> FirstFragment*), double-click on it to load it into the editor, and modify the *onViewCreated()* method to create a new Observer instance named *resultObserver*:

```
package com.ebookfrenzy.viewmodeldemo;

import androidx.lifecycle.Observer;
    .
    .
    .
@Override
public void onViewCreated(@NonNull View view, @Nullable Bundle
savedInstanceState) {
    super.onViewCreated(view, savedInstanceState);

    binding.resultText.setText(String.format(Locale.ENGLISH,"%.2f",
            viewModel.getResult()));

    final Observer<Float> resultObserver = new Observer<Float>() {
        @Override
        public void onChanged(@Nullable final Float result) {
            binding.resultText.setText(String.format(Locale.ENGLISH,
                    "%.2f", result));
        }
    };
    .
    .
    .
}
```

The *resultObserver* instance declares the *onChanged()* method which, when called, is passed the current result value, which it then converts to a string and displays on the resultText TextView object. The next step is to add the observer to the result LiveData object, a reference that can be obtained via a call to the *getResult()* method of the ViewModel object. Since updating the result TextView is now the responsibility of the *onChanged()* callback

An Android Jetpack LiveData Tutorial

method, the existing lines of code to perform this task can now be deleted:

```
@Override
public void onViewCreated(@NonNull View view, @Nullable Bundle
savedInstanceState) {
    super.onViewCreated(view, savedInstanceState);

    binding.resultText.setText(String.format(Locale.ENGLISH,"%.2f",
            viewModel.getResult()));

    final Observer<Float> resultObserver = new Observer<Float>() {
        @Override
        public void onChanged(@Nullable final Float result) {
            binding.resultText.setText(String.format(Locale.ENGLISH,
                    "%.2f", result));
        }
    };

    viewModel.getResult().observe(getViewLifecycleOwner(), resultObserver);

    binding.convertButton.setOnClickListener(v -> {
        if (!binding.dollarText.getText().toString().equals("")) {
            viewModel.setAmount(String.format(Locale.ENGLISH,"%s",
                    binding.dollarText.getText()));
            binding.resultText.setText(String.format(Locale.ENGLISH,"%.2f",
                    viewModel.getResult()));
        } else {
            binding.resultText.setText("No Value");
        }
    });
}
```

Compile and run the app, enter a value into the dollar field, click on the Convert button, and verify that the converted euro amount appears on the TextView. This confirms that the observer received notification that the result value had changed and called the *onChanged()* method to display the latest data.

Note in the above implementation of the *onViewCreated()* method that the line of code responsible for displaying the current result value each time the method was called was removed. This was originally put in place to ensure that the displayed value was recovered if the Fragment was recreated for any reason. Because LiveData monitors the lifecycle status of its observers, this step is no longer necessary. When LiveData detects that the UI controller was recreated, it automatically triggers any associated observers and provides the latest data. Verify this by rotating the device while a euro value is displayed on the TextView object and confirming that the value is not lost.

Before moving on to the next chapter, close the project, copy the ViewModelDemo project folder, and save it as ViewModelDemo_LiveData to be used later when saving the ViewModel state.

34.4 Summary

This chapter demonstrated the use of the Android LiveData component to ensure that the data displayed to the user always matches that stored in the ViewModel. This relatively simple process consisted of wrapping a ViewModel data value within a LiveData object and setting up an observer within the UI controller subscribed to the LiveData value. Each time the LiveData value changes, the observer is notified, and the *onChanged()* method is called and passed the updated value.

Adding LiveData support to the project has gone some way towards simplifying the design of the project. Additional and significant improvements are also possible using the Data Binding Library, details of which will be covered in the next chapter.

Chapter 35

35. An Overview of Android Jetpack Data Binding

In the chapter entitled *"Modern Android App Architecture with Jetpack"*, we introduced the concept of Android Data Binding. We explained how it is used to directly connect the views in a user interface layout to the methods and data located in other objects within an app without the need to write code. This chapter will provide more details on data binding, emphasizing how data binding is implemented within an Android Studio project. The tutorial in the next chapter (*"An Android Jetpack Data Binding Tutorial"*) will provide a practical example of data binding in action.

35.1 An Overview of Data Binding

The Android Jetpack Data Binding Library provides data binding support, primarily providing a simple way to connect the views in a user interface layout to the data stored within the app's code (typically within ViewModel instances). Data binding also provides a convenient way to map user interface controls, such as Button widgets, to event and listener methods within other objects, such as UI controllers and ViewModel instances.

Data binding becomes particularly powerful when used in conjunction with the LiveData component. Consider, for example, an EditText view bound to a LiveData variable within a ViewModel using data binding. When connected in this way, any changes to the data value in the ViewModel will automatically appear within the EditText view, and when using two-way binding, any data typed into the EditText will automatically be used to update the LiveData value. Perhaps most impressive is that this can be achieved with no code beyond that necessary to initially set up the binding.

Connecting an interactive view, such as a Button widget, to a method within a UI controller traditionally required that the developer write code to implement a listener method to be called when the button is clicked. Data binding makes this as simple as referencing the method to be called within the Button element in the layout XML file.

35.2 The Key Components of Data Binding

An Android Studio project is not configured for data binding support by default. Several elements must be combined before an app can begin using data binding. These involve the project build configuration, the layout XML file, data binding classes, and the use of the data binding expression language. While this may appear overwhelming at first, when taken separately, these are quite simple steps that, once completed, are more than worthwhile in terms of saved coding effort. Each element will be covered in detail in the remainder of this chapter. Once these basics have been covered, the next chapter will work through a detailed tutorial demonstrating these steps.

35.2.1 The Project Build Configuration

Before a project can use data binding, it must be configured to use the Android Data Binding Library and to enable support for data binding classes and the binding syntax. Fortunately, this can be achieved with just a few lines added to the module level *build.gradle.kts* file (the one listed as *build.gradle.kts (Module: app)* under *Gradle Scripts* in the Project tool window). The following lists a partial build file with data binding enabled:

```
android {
    
    buildFeatures {
        dataBinding = true
    }
    .
    .
```

35.2.2 The Data Binding Layout File

As we have seen in previous chapters, the user interfaces for an app are typically contained within an XML layout file. Before the views contained within one of these layout files can take advantage of data binding, the layout file must be converted to a *data binding layout file*.

As outlined earlier in the book, XML layout files define the hierarchy of components in the layout, starting with a top-level or *root view*. Invariably, this root view takes the form of a layout container such as a ConstraintLayout, FrameLayout, or LinearLayout instance, as is the case in the *fragment_main.xml* file for the ViewModelDemo project:

```
<?xml version="1.0" encoding="utf-8"?>
<androidx.constraintlayout.widget.ConstraintLayout
    xmlns:android="http://schemas.android.com/apk/res/android"
    xmlns:app="http://schemas.android.com/apk/res-auto"
    xmlns:tools="http://schemas.android.com/tools"
    android:id="@+id/main"
    android:layout_width="match_parent"
    android:layout_height="match_parent"
    tools:context=".ui.main.MainFragment">
    .
    .
</androidx.constraintlayout.widget.ConstraintLayout>
```

To use data binding, the layout hierarchy must have a *layout* component as the root view, which, in turn, becomes the parent of the current root view.

In the case of the above example, this would require that the following changes be made to the existing layout file:

```
<?xml version="1.0" encoding="utf-8"?>

<layout xmlns:app="http://schemas.android.com/apk/res-auto"
    xmlns:tools="http://schemas.android.com/tools"
    xmlns:android="http://schemas.android.com/apk/res/android">

        <androidx.constraintlayout.widget.ConstraintLayout
            xmlns:android="http://schemas.android.com/apk/res/android"
            xmlns:app="http://schemas.android.com/apk/res-auto"
            xmlns:tools="http://schemas.android.com/tools"
            android:id="@+id/main"
            android:layout_width="match_parent"
```

```
            android:layout_height="match_parent"
            tools:context=".ui.main.MainFragment">
.
.
        </androidx.constraintlayout.widget.ConstraintLayout>
</layout>
```

35.2.3 The Layout File Data Element

The data binding layout file needs some way to declare the classes within the project to which the views in the layout are to be bound (for example, a ViewModel or UI controller). Having declared these classes, the layout file will need a variable name to reference those instances within binding expressions.

This is achieved using the *data* element, an example of which is shown below:

```
<?xml version="1.0" encoding="utf-8"?>

<layout xmlns:app="http://schemas.android.com/apk/res-auto"
    xmlns:tools="http://schemas.android.com/tools"
    xmlns:android="http://schemas.android.com/apk/res/android">

    <data>
        <variable
            name="myViewModel"
            type="com.ebookfrenzy.myapp.ui.main.MainViewModel" />
    </data>

    <androidx.constraintlayout.widget.ConstraintLayout
        android:id="@+id/main"
        android:layout_width="match_parent"
        android:layout_height="match_parent"
        tools:context=".ui.main.MainFragment">
.
.
</layout>
```

The above data element declares a new variable named *myViewModel* of type MainViewModel (note that it is necessary to declare the full package name of the MyViewModel class when declaring the variable).

The data element can import other classes that may then be referenced within binding expressions elsewhere in the layout file. For example, if you have a class containing a method that needs to be called on a value before it is displayed to the user, the class could be imported as follows:

```
<data>
        <import type="com.ebookfrenzy.MyFormattingTools" />
        <variable
            name="viewModel"
            type="com.ebookfrenzy.myapp.ui.main.MainViewModel" />
    </data>
```

An Overview of Android Jetpack Data Binding

35.2.4 The Binding Classes

For each class referenced in the *data* element within the binding layout file, Android Studio will automatically generate a corresponding *binding class*. This subclass of the Android ViewDataBinding class will be named based on the layout filename using word capitalization and the *Binding* suffix. Therefore, the binding class for a layout file named *fragment_main.xml* file will be named *FragmentMainBinding*. The binding class contains the bindings specified within the layout file and maps them to the variables and methods within the bound objects.

Although the binding class is generated automatically, code must be written to create an instance of the class based on the corresponding data binding layout file. Fortunately, this can be achieved by making use of the DataBindingUtil class.

The initialization code for an Activity or Fragment will typically set the content view or "inflate" the user interface layout file. This means that the code opens the layout file, parses the XML, and creates and configures all of the view objects in memory. In the case of an existing Activity class, the code to achieve this can be found in the *onCreate()* method and will read as follows:

```
setContentView(R.layout.activity_main);
```

In the case of a Fragment, this takes place in the *onCreateView()* method:

```
return inflater.inflate(R.layout.fragment_main, container, false);
```

All that is needed to create the binding class instances within an Activity class is to modify this initialization code as follows:

```
ActivityMainBinding binding;

binding = DataBindingUtil.setContentView(this, R.layout.activity_main, false);
```

In the case of a Fragment, the code would read as follows:

```
FragmentMainBinding binding;

binding = DataBindingUtil.inflate(
        inflater, R.layout.fragment_main, container, false);

binding.setLifecycleOwner(this);
View view = binding.getRoot();
return view;
```

35.2.5 Data Binding Variable Configuration

As outlined above, the data binding layout file contains the *data* element, which contains *variable* elements consisting of variable names and the class types to which the bindings are to be established. For example:

```
<data>
    <variable
        name="viewModel"
        type="com.ebookfrenzy.viewmodeldemo.ui.main.MainViewModel" />
    <variable
            name="uiController"
            type="com.ebookfrenzy.viewmodeldemo_databinding.ui.main.MainFragment"
/>
</data>
```

An Overview of Android Jetpack Data Binding

In the above example, the first variable knows that it will be binding to an instance of a ViewModel class of type MainViewModel but has yet to be connected to an actual MainViewModel object instance. This requires the additional step of assigning the MainViewModel instance used within the app to the variable declared in the layout file. This is performed via a call to the *setVariable()* method of the data binding instance, a reference to which was obtained in the previous chapter:

```
MainViewModel mViewModel = new ViewModelProvider(this).get(MainViewModel.class);
binding.setVariable(viewModel, mViewModel);
```

The second variable in the above data element references a UI controller class in the form of a Fragment named MainFragment. In this situation, the code within a UI controller (be it an Activity or Fragment) would need to assign itself to the variable as follows:

```
binding.setVariable(uiController, this);
```

35.2.6 Binding Expressions (One-Way)

Binding expressions define how a particular view interacts with bound objects. For example, a binding expression on a Button might declare which method on an object is called in response to a click. Alternatively, a binding expression might define which data value stored in a ViewModel is to appear within a TextView and how it is to be presented and formatted.

Binding expressions use a declarative language that allows logic and access to other classes and methods to decide how bound data is used. Expressions can, for example, include mathematical expressions, method calls, string concatenations, access to array elements, and comparison operations. In addition, all standard Java language libraries are imported by default, so many things that can be achieved in Java can also be performed in a binding expression. As already discussed, the data element may also be used to import custom classes to add more capability to expressions.

A binding expression begins with an @ symbol followed by the expression enclosed in curly braces ({}).

Consider, for example, a ViewModel instance containing a variable named *result*. Assume that this class has been assigned to a variable named *viewModel* within the data binding layout file and needs to be bound to a TextView object so that the view always displays the latest result value. If this value were stored as a String object, this would be declared within the layout file as follows:

```
<TextView
    android:id="@+id/resultText"
    android:layout_width="wrap_content"
    android:layout_height="wrap_content"
    android:text="@{viewModel.result}"
    app:layout_constraintBottom_toBottomOf="parent"
    app:layout_constraintEnd_toEndOf="parent"
    app:layout_constraintStart_toStartOf="parent"
    app:layout_constraintTop_toTopOf="parent" />
```

In the above XML, the *text* property is set to the value stored in the *result* LiveData property of the viewModel object.

Consider, however, that the result is stored within the model as a Float value instead of a String. That being the case, the above expression would cause a compilation error. Clearly, the Float value must be converted to a string before the TextView can display it. To resolve issues such as this, the binding expression can include the necessary steps to complete the conversion using the standard Java language classes:

```
android:text="@{String.valueOf(viewModel.result)}"
```

An Overview of Android Jetpack Data Binding

When running the app after making this change, it is important to be aware that the following warning may appear in the Android Studio console:

```
warning: myViewModel.result.getValue() is a boxed field but needs to be un-boxed to execute String.valueOf(viewModel.result.getValue()).
```

Values in Java can take the form of primitive values such as the *boolean* type (referred to as being *unboxed*) or wrapped in a Java object such as the *Boolean* type and accessed via reference to that object (i.e., *boxed*). The unboxing process involves unwrapping the primitive value from the object.

To avoid this message, wrap the offending operation in a *safeUnbox()* call as follows:

```
android:text="@{String.valueOf(safeUnbox(myViewModel.result))}"
```

String concatenation may also be used. For example, to include the word "dollars" after the result string value, the following expression would be used:

```
android:text='@{String.valueOf(safeUnbox(myViewModel.result)) + " dollars"}'
```

Note that since the appended result string is wrapped in double quotes, the expression is now encapsulated with single quotes to avoid syntax errors.

The expression syntax also allows ternary statements to be declared. In the following expression, the view will display different text depending on whether or not the result value is greater than 10.

```
@{myViewModel.result > 10 ? "Out of range" : "In range"}
```

Expressions may also be constructed to access specific elements in a data array:

```
@{myViewModel.resultsArray[3]}
```

35.2.7 Binding Expressions (Two-Way)

The type of expression covered so far is called *one-way binding*. In other words, the layout is constantly updated as the corresponding value changes, but changes to the value from within the layout do not update the stored value.

A *two-way binding*, on the other hand, allows the data model to be updated in response to changes in the layout. An EditText view, for example, could be configured with a two-way binding so that when the user enters a different value, that value is used to update the corresponding data model value. When declaring a two-way expression, the syntax is similar to a one-way expression except that it begins with @=. For example:

```
android:text="@={myViewModel.result}"
```

35.2.8 Event and Listener Bindings

Binding expressions may also trigger method calls in response to events on a view. A Button view, for example, can be configured to call a method when clicked. In the chapter entitled *"Creating an Example Android App in Android Studio"*, for example, the onClick property of a button was configured to call a method within the app's main activity named *convertCurrency()*. Within the XML file, this was represented as follows:

```
android:onClick="convertCurrency"
```

The *convertCurrency()* method was declared along the following lines:

```
public void convertCurrency(View view) {
    .
    .
    .
}
```

Note that this type of method call is always passed a reference to the view on which the event occurred. The same effect can be achieved in data binding using the following expression (assuming the layout has been bound to a class with a variable name of *uiController*):

```
android:onClick="@{uiController::convertCurrency}"
```

Another option, and one which provides the ability to pass parameters to the method, is referred to as a *listener binding*. The following expression uses this approach to call a method on the same viewModel instance with no parameters:

```
android:onClick='@{() -> myViewModel.methodOne()}'
```

The following expression calls a method that expects three parameters:

```
android:onClick='@{() -> myViewModel.methodTwo(viewModel.result, 10, "A String")}'
```

Binding expressions provide a rich and flexible language to bind user interface views to data and methods in other objects. This chapter has only covered the most common use cases. To learn more about binding expressions, review the Android documentation online at:

```
https://developer.android.com/topic/libraries/data-binding/expressions
```

35.3 Summary

Android data bindings provide a system for creating connections between the views in a user interface layout and the data and methods of other objects within the app architecture without writing code. Once some initial configuration steps have been performed, data binding involves using binding expressions within the view elements of the layout file. These binding expressions can be either one-way or two-way and may also be used to bind methods to be called in response to events such as button clicks within the user interface.

Chapter 36

36. An Android Jetpack Data Binding Tutorial

So far in this book, we have covered the basic concepts of modern Android app architecture and looked in more detail at the ViewModel and LiveData components. The concept of data binding was also covered in the previous chapter and will now be used in this chapter to modify the ViewModelDemo app further.

36.1 Removing the Redundant Code

If you still need to, copy the ViewModelDemo project folder and save it as ViewModelDemo_LiveData for the next chapter. Once copied, open the original ViewModelDemo project, ready to implement data binding.

Before implementing data binding within the ViewModelDemo app, the power of data binding will be demonstrated by deleting all of the code within the project that will no longer be needed by the end of this chapter.

Launch Android Studio, open the ViewModelDemo project, edit the *FirstFragment.java* file, and modify the code as follows:

```
package com.ebookfrenzy.viewmodeldemo;
.
.
import android.arch.lifecycle.Observer;
.
.
public class MainFragment extends Fragment {

    private MainViewModel viewModel;
.
.
    @Override
    public void onViewCreated(@NonNull View view,
                   @Nullable Bundle savedInstanceState) {
        super.onViewCreated(view, savedInstanceState);

        final Observer<Float> resultObserver = new Observer<Float>() {
            @Override
            public void onChanged(@Nullable final Float result) {
                binding.resultText.setText(String.format(Locale.ENGLISH,
                        "%.2f", result));
            }
        };
```

293

An Android Jetpack Data Binding Tutorial

```
            viewModel.getResult().observe(getViewLifecycleOwner(), resultObserver);

        binding.convertButton.setOnClickListener(v -> {
            if (!binding.dollarText.getText().toString().equals("")) {
                viewModel.setAmount(String.format(Locale.ENGLISH, "%s",
                        binding.dollarText.getText()));
            } else {
                binding.resultText.setText("No Value");
            }
        });
    }
.
.
```

Next, edit the *MainViewModel.java* file and continue deleting code as follows (note also the conversion of the *dollarText* variable to LiveData):

```
package com.ebookfrenzy.viewmodeldemo;

import android.arch.lifecycle.MutableLiveData;
import android.arch.lifecycle.ViewModel;

public class  MainViewModel extends ViewModel {

    private static final Float rate = 0.74F;
    final public MutableLiveData<String> dollarValue = new MutableLiveData<>();
    private String dollarText = "";
    final private public MutableLiveData<Float> result = new MutableLiveData<>();

    public void setAmount(String value) {
        this.dollarText = value;
        result.setValue(Float.valueOf(dollarText)*rate);
    }

    public MutableLiveData<Float> getResult()
    {
        return result;
    }
}
```

Though we'll add a few additional lines of code in implementing data binding, data binding has significantly reduced the amount of code that needs to be written.

36.2 Enabling Data Binding

The first step in using data binding is to enable it within the Android Studio project. This involves adding a new property to the *Gradle Scripts -> build.gradle.kts (Module :app)* file.

Within the *build.gradle.kts* file, add the element below to enable data binding within the project:

An Android Jetpack Data Binding Tutorial

```
plugins {
    id("com.android.application")
}

android {
    .
    .
    buildFeatures {
        viewBinding = true
        dataBinding = true
    }
    .
    .
    .
}
```

Once the entry has been added, a bar will appear across the top of the editor screen containing a *Sync Now* link. Click this to resynchronize the project with the new build configuration settings.

36.3 Adding the Layout Element

As described in *"An Overview of Android Jetpack Data Binding"*, the layout hierarchy must have a layout component as the root view to use data binding. This requires that the following changes be made to the *fragment_first.xml* layout file (*app -> res -> layout -> fragment_first.xml*). Open this file in the layout editor tool, switch to Code mode, and make these changes:

```xml
<?xml version="1.0" encoding="utf-8"?>

<layout xmlns:app="http://schemas.android.com/apk/res-auto"
    xmlns:tools="http://schemas.android.com/tools"
    xmlns:android="http://schemas.android.com/apk/res/android">

        <androidx.constraintlayout.widget.ConstraintLayout
            xmlns:android="http://schemas.android.com/apk/res/android"
            xmlns:app="http://schemas.android.com/apk/res-auto"
            xmlns:tools="http://schemas.android.com/tools"
            android:id="@+id/main"
            android:layout_width="match_parent"
            android:layout_height="match_parent"
            tools:context=".FirstFragment">
    .
    .
        </androidx.constraintlayout.widget.ConstraintLayout>
</layout>
```

Once these changes have been made, switch back to Design mode and note that the new root view, though invisible in the layout canvas, is now listed in the component tree, as shown in Figure 36-1:

An Android Jetpack Data Binding Tutorial

```
Component Tree
  <layout>
    constraintLayout
      Ab dollarText
      Ab resultText "TextView"
      convertButton "@string/convert_string"
```

Figure 36-1

Build and run the app to verify that adding the layout element has not changed the user interface appearance. When building the project, you may encounter an error that reads in part:

```
Duplicate class kotlin.collections.jdk8.CollectionsJDK8Kt found in modules kotlin-stdlib
```

This error is caused by a bug in the Android Studio build toolchain and can be resolved by making the following changes to the *build.gradle.kts (Module: app)* file:

```
dependencies {
    .
    .
    implementation(platform("org.jetbrains.kotlin:kotlin-bom:1.8.0"))
    .
    .
}
```

36.4 Adding the Data Element to Layout File

The next step in converting the layout file to a data binding layout file is to add the *data* element. For this example, the layout will be bound to MainViewModel, so edit the *fragment_first.xml* file to add the data element as follows:

```xml
<?xml version="1.0" encoding="utf-8"?>

<layout xmlns:app="http://schemas.android.com/apk/res-auto"
    xmlns:tools="http://schemas.android.com/tools"
    xmlns:android="http://schemas.android.com/apk/res/android">

    <data>
        <variable
            name="myViewModel"
            type="com.ebookfrenzy.viewmodeldemo.MainViewModel" />
    </data>

    <androidx.constraintlayout.widget.ConstraintLayout
        android:id="@+id/main"
        android:layout_width="match_parent"
        android:layout_height="match_parent"
        tools:context=".FirstFragment">
```

```
.
.
</layout>
```

Build and rerun the app to ensure these changes take effect.

36.5 Working with the Binding Class

The next step is to modify the *FirstFragment.java* file code to inflate the data binding. This is best achieved by rewriting the *onCreateView()* method:

```
.
.
import androidx.databinding.DataBindingUtil;

import com.ebookfrenzy.viewmodeldemo.R;
.
.
public class MainFragment extends Fragment {
.
.
    public View onCreateView(@NonNull LayoutInflater inflater, @Nullable ViewGroup container,
                             @Nullable Bundle savedInstanceState) {
        binding = FragmentMainBinding.inflate(inflater, container, false);

        binding = DataBindingUtil.inflate(
                inflater, R.layout.fragment_first, container, false);
        binding.setLifecycleOwner(this);
        return binding.getRoot();
    }
.
.
}
```

The old code inflated the *fragment_first.xml* layout file (in other words, created the layout containing all of the view objects) and returned a reference to the root view (the top-level layout container). The Data Binding Library contains a utility class that provides a special inflation method which, in addition to constructing the UI, also initializes and returns an instance of the layout's data binding class. The new code calls this method and stores a reference to the binding class instance in a variable:

```
binding = DataBindingUtil.inflate(
            inflater, R.layout.fragment_first, container, false);
```

The binding object must only remain in memory for as long as the fragment is present. To ensure that the instance is destroyed when the fragment goes away, the current fragment is declared as the lifecycle owner for the binding object.

```
binding.lifecycleOwner = this;
return binding.getRoot;
```

An Android Jetpack Data Binding Tutorial

36.6 Assigning the ViewModel Instance to the Data Binding Variable

At this point, the data binding knows it will be binding to an instance of a class of type MainViewModel but has yet to be connected to an actual MainViewModel object. This requires the additional step of assigning the MainViewModel instance used within the app to the viewModel variable declared in the layout file. Add this code to the *onViewCreated()* method in the FirstFragment.java file as follows:

```
.
.
import static com.ebookfrenzy.viewmodeldemo.BR.myViewModel;
.
.
@Override
public void onViewCreated(@NonNull View view, @Nullable Bundle savedInstanceState) {
    super.onViewCreated(view, savedInstanceState);
    binding.setVariable(myViewModel, viewModel);
}
```

If Android Studio reports myViewModel as undefined, rebuild the project using the *Build -> Make Project* menu option to force the class to be generated. With these changes made, the next step is to insert some binding expressions into the view elements of the data binding layout file.

36.7 Adding Binding Expressions

The first binding expression will bind the resultText TextView to the result value within the model view. Edit the *fragment_first.xml* file, locate the resultText element, and modify the text property so that the element reads as follows:

```
<TextView
    android:id="@+id/resultText"
    android:layout_width="wrap_content"
    android:layout_height="wrap_content"
    android:text="TextView"
    android:text='@{safeUnbox(myViewModel.result) == 0.0 ? "Enter value" : String.valueOf(safeUnbox(myViewModel.result)) + " euros"}'
    app:layout_constraintBottom_toBottomOf="parent"
    app:layout_constraintEnd_toEndOf="parent"
    app:layout_constraintStart_toStartOf="parent"
    app:layout_constraintTop_toTopOf="parent" />
```

The expression begins by checking if the result value is currently zero and, if it is, displays a message instructing the user to enter a value. However, if the result is not zero, the value is converted to a string and concatenated with the word "euros" before being displayed to the user.

The result value only requires a one-way binding in that the layout does not ever need to update the value stored in the ViewModel. The *dollarValue* EditText view, on the other hand, needs to use two-way binding so that the data model can be updated with the latest value entered by the user and to allow the current value to be redisplayed in the view in the event of a lifecycle event such as that triggered by a device rotation. The *dollarText* element should now be declared as follows:

```
<EditText
    android:id="@+id/dollarText"
```

298

```
        android:layout_width="wrap_content"
        android:layout_height="wrap_content"
        android:layout_marginTop="96dp"
        android:ems="10"
        android:importantForAutofill="no"
        android:inputType="numberDecimal"
        android:text="@={myViewModel.dollarValue}"
        app:layout_constraintEnd_toEndOf="parent"
        app:layout_constraintHorizontal_bias="0.502"
        app:layout_constraintStart_toStartOf="parent"
        app:layout_constraintTop_toTopOf="parent" />
```

Now that these initial binding expressions have been added, a method must be written to perform the conversion when the user clicks on the Button widget.

36.8 Adding the Conversion Method

When the Convert button is clicked, it will call a method on the ViewModel to perform the conversion calculation and place the euro value in the *result* LiveData variable. Add this method now within the *MainViewModel.java* file:

.
.
```
public class  MainViewModel extends ViewModel {

    private static final Float usd_to_eu_rate = 0.74F;
    final public MutableLiveData<String> dollarValue = new MutableLiveData<>();
    final public MutableLiveData<Float> result = new MutableLiveData<>();

    public void convertValue() {
        if ((dollarValue.getValue() != null) &&
                        (!dollarValue.getValue().equals(""))) {
            result.setValue(Float.parseFloat(dollarValue.getValue())
                                              * rate);
        } else {
            result.setValue(0F);
        }
    }
}
```

Note that a zero value is assigned to the *result* LiveData variable in the absence of a valid dollar value. This ensures that the binding expression assigned to the *resultText* TextView displays the "Enter value" message if no value has been entered by the user.

36.9 Adding a Listener Binding

The final step before testing the project is to add a listener binding expression to the Button element within the layout file to call the *convertValue()* method when the button is clicked. Edit the *fragment_first.xml* file in Code mode once again, locate the *convertButton* element, and add an onClick entry as follows:

```
<Button
```

```
        android:id="@+id/convertButton"
        android:layout_width="wrap_content"
        android:layout_height="wrap_content"
        android:onClick="@{() -> myViewModel.convertValue()}"
        android:text="@string/convert_text"
        app:layout_constraintBottom_toBottomOf="parent"
        app:layout_constraintEnd_toEndOf="parent"
        app:layout_constraintHorizontal_bias="0.5"
        app:layout_constraintStart_toStartOf="parent"
        app:layout_constraintTop_toBottomOf="@+id/resultText" />
```

36.10 Testing the App

Compile and run the app and test that entering a value into the dollar field and clicking on the Convert button displays the correct result on the TextView (together with the "euros" suffix) and that the "Enter value" prompt appears if a conversion is attempted while the dollar field is empty. Also, verify that information displayed in the user interface is retained through a device rotation.

36.11 Summary

The primary goal of this chapter has been to work through the steps involved in setting up a project to use data binding and to demonstrate the use of one-way, two-way, and listener binding expressions. The chapter also provided a practical example of how much code writing is saved by using data binding in conjunction with LiveData to connect the user interface views with the back-end data and logic of the app.

37. An Android ViewModel Saved State Tutorial

The preservation and restoration of app state is about presenting the user with continuity in appearance and behavior after an app is placed in the background. Users expect to be able to switch from one app to another and, on returning to the original app, find it in the exact state it was in before the switch took place.

As outlined in the chapter entitled *"Understanding Android Application and Activity Lifecycles"*, when the user places an app in the background, that app becomes eligible for termination by the operating system if resources become constrained. When the user attempts to return the terminated app to the foreground, Android relaunches the app in a new process. Since this is all invisible to the user, it is the app's responsibility to restore itself to the same state it was in when it was originally placed in the background instead of presenting itself in its "initial launch" state. In the case of ViewModel-based apps, much of this behavior can be achieved using the ViewModel *Saved State* module.

37.1 Understanding ViewModel State Saving

As outlined in the previous chapters, the ViewModel brings many benefits to app development, including UI state restoration in the event of configuration changes such as a device rotation. To see this in action, run the ViewModelDemo app (or, if you still need to create the project, load into Android Studio the *ViewModelDemo_LiveData* project from the sample code download accompanying the book).

Once running, enter a dollar value and convert it to euros. With both the dollar and euro values displayed, rotate the device or emulator and note that both values are still visible once the app has responded to the orientation change.

Unfortunately, this behavior does not extend to the termination of a background app process. With the app still running, tap the device home button to place the ViewModelDemo app in the background, then terminate it by opening the Terminal tool window and running the following command (where *<package name>* is the name you used when the project was created, for example, *com.ebookfrenzy.viewmodeldemo*):

```
adb shell am kill <package name>
```

If the *adb* command is not found, refer to the chapter *"Setting up an Android Studio Development Environment"* for steps to set up your Android Studio environment.

Once the app has been terminated, return to the device or emulator and select the app from the launcher (do not re-run the app from within Android Studio). Once the app appears, it will do so as if it was just launched, with the last dollar and euro values lost. From the user's perspective, however, the app was restored from the background and should still have contained the original data. In this case, the app has failed to provide the continuity that users have come to expect from Android apps.

37.2 Implementing ViewModel State Saving

Basic ViewModel state saving is made possible through the introduction of the ViewModel Saved State library. This library extends the ViewModel class to include support for maintaining state through the termination and subsequent relaunch of a background process.

An Android ViewModel Saved State Tutorial

The key to saving state is the SavedStateHandle class which is used to save and restore the state of a view model instance. A SavedStateHandle object contains a key-value map that allows data values to be saved and restored by referencing corresponding keys.

To support state saving, a different kind of ViewModel subclass needs to be declared, in this case containing a constructor which can receive a SavedStateHandle instance. Once declared, ViewModel instances of this type can be created by including a SavedStateViewModelFactory object at creation time. Consider the following code excerpt from a standard ViewModel declaration:

```
package com.ebookfrenzy.viewmodeldemo.ui.main;

import androidx.lifecycle.ViewModel;
import androidx.lifecycle.MutableLiveData;

public class MainViewModel extends ViewModel {
.
.
}
```

The code to create an instance of this class would likely resemble the following:

```
private MainViewModel mViewModel;

mViewModel = new ViewModelProvider(this).get(MainViewModel.class);
```

A ViewModel subclass designed to support saved state, on the other hand, would need to be declared as follows:

```
package com.ebookfrenzy.viewmodeldemo.ui.main;

import android.util.Log;

import androidx.lifecycle.ViewModel;
import androidx.lifecycle.MutableLiveData;
import androidx.lifecycle.SavedStateHandle;

public class MainViewModel extends ViewModel {

    private SavedStateHandle savedStateHandle;

    public MainViewModel(SavedStateHandle savedStateHandle) {
        this.savedStateHandle = savedStateHandle;
    }
.
.
}
```

When instances of the above ViewModel are created, the *ViewModelProvider* class initializer must be passed a SavedStateViewModelFactory instance as follows:

```
SavedStateViewModelFactory factory =
        new SavedStateViewModelFactory(getActivity().getApplication(),this);
```

An Android ViewModel Saved State Tutorial

```
mViewModel = new ViewModelProvider(this).get(MainViewModel.class);
```

37.3 Saving and Restoring State

An object or value can be saved from within the ViewModel by passing it through to the *set()* method of the SavedStateHandle instance, providing the key string by which it is to be referenced when performing a retrieval:

```
private static final String NAME_KEY = "Customer Name";


savedStateHandle.set(NAME_KEY, customerName);
```

When used with LiveData objects, a previously saved value may be restored using the *getLiveData()* method of the SavedStateHandle instance, once again referencing the corresponding key as follows:

```
MutableLiveData<String> restoredName = savedStateHandle.getLiveData(NAME_KEY);
```

To restore a normal (non-LiveData) object, use the SavedStateHandle *get()* method:

```
String restoredName = savedStateHandle.get(NAME_KEY);
```

Other useful SavedStateHandle methods include the following:

- **contains(String key)** - Returns a boolean value indicating whether the saved state contains a value for the specified key.

- **remove(String key)** - Removes the value and key from the saved state. Returns the value that was removed.

- **keys()** - Returns a String set of all keys contained within the saved state.

37.4 Adding Saved State Support to the ViewModelDemo Project

With the basics of ViewModel Saved State covered, the ViewModelDemo app can be extended to include this support. Begin by loading the ViewModelDemo_LiveData project created in *"An Android Jetpack LiveData Tutorial"* into Android Studio (a copy of the project is also available in the sample code download), opening the *build.gradle.kts (Module :app)* file and adding the Saved State library dependencies (checking, as always, if more recent library versions are available):

```
.
.
dependencies {
.
.
    implementation ("androidx.savedstate:savedstate:1.2.1")
    implementation ("androidx.lifecycle:lifecycle-viewmodel-savedstate:2.6.1")
.
.
}
```

Next, modify the *MainViewModel.java* file so the constructor accepts and stores a SavedStateHandle instance. Also, import androidx.lifecycle.SavedStateHandle, declare a key string constant and modify the *result* LiveData variable so that the value is now obtained from the saved state in the constructor:

```
package com.ebookfrenzy.viewmodeldemo.ui.main;


import androidx.lifecycle.ViewModel;
import androidx.lifecycle.MutableLiveData;
import androidx.lifecycle.SavedStateHandle;
```

An Android ViewModel Saved State Tutorial

```java
public class MainViewModel extends ViewModel {

    private static final String RESULT_KEY = "Euro Value";
    private static final Float rate = 0.74F;
    private String dollarText = "";
    final private SavedStateHandle savedStateHandle;
    final private MutableLiveData<Float> result = new MutableLiveData<>();

    public MainViewModel(SavedStateHandle savedStateHandle) {
        this.savedStateHandle = savedStateHandle;
        result = savedStateHandle.getLiveData(RESULT_KEY);
    }
.
.
.
}
```

Remaining within the *MainViewModel.java* file, modify the *setAmount()* method to include code to save the result value each time a new euro amount is calculated:

```java
public void setAmount(String value) {
    this.dollarText = value;
    result.setValue(Float.valueOf(dollarText) * rate);
    Float convertedValue = Float.parseFloat(dollarText) * rate;
    result.setValue(convertedValue);
    savedStateHandle.set(RESULT_KEY, convertedValue);
}
```

With the changes to the ViewModel complete, open the *FirstFragment.java* file and make the following alterations to include a Saved State factory instance during the ViewModel creation process:

```java
.
.
import androidx.lifecycle.SavedStateViewModelFactory;
.
.
@Override
public void onCreate(@Nullable Bundle savedInstanceState) {
    super.onCreate(savedInstanceState);

    SavedStateViewModelFactory factory =
            new SavedStateViewModelFactory(
                    getActivity().getApplication(), this);

    mViewModel = new ViewModelProvider(this, factory).get(MainViewModel.class);
    // TODO: Use the ViewModel
}
```

With the screen UI populated with dollar and euro values, place the app into the background, terminate it using the *adb* tool, and then relaunch it from the device or emulator screen. After restarting, the previous currency amounts should still be visible in the TextView and EditText components, confirming that the state was successfully saved and restored.

37.5 Summary

A well-designed app should always present the user with the same state when brought forward from the background, regardless of whether the operating system terminated the process containing the app in the interim. When working with ViewModels, this can be achieved by taking advantage of the ViewModel Saved State module. This involves modifying the ViewModel constructor to accept a SavedStateHandle instance which, in turn, can be used to save and restore data values via a range of method calls. When the ViewModel instance is created, it must be passed a SavedStateViewModelFactory instance. Once these steps have been implemented, the app will automatically save and restore state during a background termination.

38. Working with Android Lifecycle-Aware Components

The earlier chapter, *"Understanding Android Application and Activity Lifecycles"* described the use of lifecycle methods to track lifecycle state changes within a UI controller such as an activity or fragment. One of the main problems with these methods is that they place the burden of handling lifecycle changes onto the UI controller. On the surface, this might seem like the logical approach since the UI controller is, after all, the object going through the state change. However, the fact is that the code typically impacted by the state change invariably resides in other classes within the app. This led to complex code appearing in the UI controller that needed to manage and manipulate other objects in response to changes in the lifecycle state. This scenario is best avoided when following the Android architectural guidelines.

A much cleaner and more logical approach would be for the objects within an app to be able to observe the lifecycle state of other objects and to be responsible for taking any necessary actions in response to the changes. For example, the class responsible for tracking a user's location could observe the lifecycle state of a UI controller and suspend location updates when the controller enters a paused state. Tracking would then be restarted when the controller enters the resumed state. This is made possible by the classes and interfaces provided by the Lifecycle package bundled with the Android architecture components.

This chapter will introduce the terminology and key components that enable lifecycle awareness to be built into Android apps.

38.1 Lifecycle Awareness

An object is said to be *lifecycle-aware* if it can detect and respond to changes in the lifecycle state of other objects within an app. Some Android components, LiveData being a prime example, are already lifecycle-aware. Configuring any class to be lifecycle-aware is also possible by implementing the LifecycleObserver interface within the class.

38.2 Lifecycle Owners

Lifecycle-aware components can only observe the status of objects that are *lifecycle owners*. Lifecycle owners implement the LifecycleOwner interface and are assigned a companion *Lifecycle object* responsible for storing the current state of the component and providing state information to *lifecycle observers*. Most standard Android Framework components (such as activity and fragment classes) are lifecycle owners. Custom classes may also be configured as lifecycle owners using the LifecycleRegistry class and implementing the LifecycleObserver interface. For example:

```
public class SampleOwner implements LifecycleOwner {

    private LifecycleRegistry lifecycleRegistry;

    @Override
    protected void onCreate(Bundle savedInstanceState) {
        super.onCreate(savedInstanceState);
```

```
        lifecycleRegistry = new LifecycleRegistry(this);
    }

    @NonNull
    @Override
    public Lifecycle getLifecycle() {
        return lifecycleRegistry;
    }
}
```

Unless the lifecycle owner is a subclass of another lifecycle-aware component, the class will need to trigger lifecycle state changes via calls to methods of the LifecycleRegistry class. The *markState()* method can be used to trigger a lifecycle state change passing through the new state value:

```
public void resuming() {
    lifecycleRegistry.markState(Lifecycle.State.RESUMED);
}
```

The above call will also result in a call to the corresponding event handler. Alternatively, the LifecycleRegistry *handleLifecycleEvent()* method may be called and passed the lifecycle event to be triggered (which will also result in the lifecycle state changing). For example:

```
lifecycleRegistry.handleLifecycleEvent(Lifecycle.Event.ON_START);
```

38.3 Lifecycle Observers

To observe the state of a lifecycle owner, a lifecycle-aware component must implement the DefaultLifecycleObserver interface and override methods for any lifecycle change events it needs to observe.

```
public class SampleObserver implements DefaultLifecycleObserver {
    // Lifecycle event methods overrides go here
}
```

An instance of this observer class is then created and added to the list of observers maintained by the Lifecycle object.

```
getLifecycle().addObserver(new SampleObserver());
```

An observer may be removed from the Lifecycle object anytime if it no longer needs to track the lifecycle state.

Figure 38-1 illustrates the relationship between the key elements that provide lifecycle awareness:

Figure 38-1

38.4 Lifecycle States and Events

When the status of a lifecycle owner changes, the assigned Lifecycle object will be updated with the new state. At any given time, a lifecycle owner will be in one of the following five states:

- Lifecycle.State.INITIALIZED
- Lifecycle.State.CREATED
- Lifecycle.State.STARTED
- Lifecycle.State.RESUMED
- Lifecycle.State.DESTROYED

The Lifecycle object will trigger events on any observers added to the list as the component transitions through the different states. The following event methods are available to be overridden within the lifecycle observer:

- onCreate()
- onResume()
- onPause()
- onStop()
- onStart()
- onDestroy()

The following code, for example, overrides the DefaultLifecycleObserver *onResume()* method:

```
@Override
public void onResume(@NonNull LifecycleOwner owner) {
    // Perform tasks in response to Resume status event
}
```

The flowchart in Figure 38-2 illustrates the sequence of state changes for a lifecycle owner and the lifecycle events that will be triggered on observers between each state transition:

Figure 38-2

38.5 Summary

This chapter has introduced the basics of lifecycle awareness and the classes and interfaces of the Android Lifecycle package included with Android Jetpack. The package contains several classes and interfaces for creating lifecycle owners, observers, and lifecycle-aware components. A lifecycle owner has assigned to it a Lifecycle object that maintains a record of the owner's state and a list of subscribed observers. When the owner's state changes, the observer is notified via lifecycle event methods to respond to the change.

The next chapter will create an Android Studio project that demonstrates how to work with and create lifecycle-aware components, including the creation of both lifecycle observers and owners and the handling of lifecycle state changes and events.

39. An Android Jetpack Lifecycle Awareness Tutorial

The previous chapter provided an overview of lifecycle awareness and outlined the key classes and interfaces that make this possible within an Android app project. This chapter will build on this knowledge base by building an Android Studio project to highlight lifecycle awareness in action.

39.1 Creating the Example Lifecycle Project

Select the *New Project* quick start option from the welcome screen and, within the resulting new project dialog, choose the Empty Views Activity template before clicking on the Next button.

Enter *LifecycleDemo* into the Name field and specify *com.ebookfrenzy.lifecycledemo* as the package name. Before clicking on the Finish button, change the Minimum API level setting to API 26: Android 8.0 (Oreo) and the Language menu to Java.

39.2 Creating a Lifecycle Observer

As previously discussed, activities and fragments already implement the LifecycleOwner interface and are ready to be observed by other objects. To see this in practice, the next step in this tutorial is to add a new class to the project that will be able to observe the MainActivity instance.

To add the new class, right-click on a*pp -> java -> com.ebookfrenzy.lifecycledemo* in the Project tool window and select *New -> Java Class...* from the resulting menu. In the New Class dialog, name the class DemoObserver and press the keyboard Return key to create the *DemoObserver.java* file. The new file should automatically open in the editor, where it will read as follows:

```
package com.ebookfrenzy.lifecycledemo;

public class DemoObserver {
}
```

Remaining in the editor, modify the class file to declare that it will be implementing the DefaultLifecycleObserver interface:

```
package com.ebookfrenzy.lifecycledemo;

import androidx.lifecycle.DefaultLifecycleObserver;

public class DemoObserver implements DefaultLifecycleObserver {

}
```

The next step is to override the lifecycle methods of the DefaultLifecycleObserver class. For this example, all events will be handled, each outputting a message to the Logcat panel displaying the event type. Update the observer class as outlined in the following listing:

```
package com.ebookfrenzy.lifecycledemo;
```

```java
import android.util.Log;

import androidx.annotation.NonNull;
import androidx.lifecycle.LifecycleOwner;
    .
    .
    .
public class DemoObserver implements DefaultLifecycleObserver {

    private String LOG_TAG = "DemoObserver";

    @Override
    public void onCreate(@NonNull LifecycleOwner owner) {
        Log.i(LOG_TAG, "onCreate");
    }

    @Override
    public void onResume(@NonNull LifecycleOwner owner) {
        Log.i(LOG_TAG, "onResume");
    }

    @Override
    public void onPause(@NonNull LifecycleOwner owner) {
        Log.i(LOG_TAG, "onPause");
    }

    @Override
    public void onStart(@NonNull LifecycleOwner owner) {
        Log.i(LOG_TAG, "onStart");
    }

    @Override
    public void onStop(@NonNull LifecycleOwner owner) {
        Log.i(LOG_TAG, "onStop");
    }

    @Override
    public void onDestroy(@NonNull LifecycleOwner owner) {
        Log.i(LOG_TAG, "onDestroy");
    }
}
```

With the DemoObserver class completed, the next step is to add it as an observer on the MainActivity class.

An Android Jetpack Lifecycle Awareness Tutorial

39.3 Adding the Observer

Observers are added to lifecycle owners via calls to the *addObserver()* method of the owner's Lifecycle object, a reference to which is obtained via a call to the *getLifecycle()* method. Edit the *MainActivity.java* class file and edit the *onCreate()* method to add an observer:

.
.
```
import com.ebookfrenzy.lifecycledemo.DemoObserver;
```
.
.
```
@Override
public void onViewCreated(@NonNull View view, @Nullable Bundle savedInstanceState) {
    super.onViewCreated(view, savedInstanceState);

    getLifecycle().addObserver(new DemoObserver());
}
```

With the observer class created and added to the lifecycle owner's Lifecycle object, the app is ready to be tested.

39.4 Testing the Observer

Since the DemoObserver class outputs diagnostic information to the Logcat console, it will be easier to see the output if a filter is configured to display only the DemoObserver messages. Using the steps outlined previously in *"Android Activity State Changes by Example"*, display the Logcat panel and enter the following keys into the filter field:

```
package:mine tag:DemoObserver
```

On successful launch of the app, the Logcat output should indicate the following lifecycle state changes and events:

```
onCreate
onStart
onResume
```

With the app still running, perform a device rotation to trigger the destruction and recreation of the activity, generating the following additional output:

```
onPause
onStop
onDestroy
onCreate
onStart
onResume
```

Before moving to the next section in this chapter, take some time to compare the output from the app with the flow chart in Figure 38-2 of the previous chapter.

39.5 Creating a Lifecycle Owner

The final task in this chapter is to create a custom lifecycle owner class and demonstrate how to trigger events and modify the lifecycle state from within that class.

Add a new class by right-clicking on the *app -> java -> com.ebookfrenzy.lifecycledemo* entry in the Project tool

An Android Jetpack Lifecycle Awareness Tutorial

window and selecting the *New -> Java Class...* menu option. Name the class DemoOwner in the Create Class dialog before tapping the keyboard Return key. With the new *DemoOwner.java* file loaded into the code editor, modify it as follows:

```
package com.ebookfrenzy.lifecycledemo;

import androidx.lifecycle.Lifecycle;
import androidx.lifecycle.LifecycleOwner;
import androidx.lifecycle.LifecycleRegistry;

import androidx.annotation.NonNull;

public class DemoOwner implements LifecycleOwner {
}
```

The class will need a LifecycleRegistry instance initialized with a reference to itself and a *getLifecycle()* method configured to return the LifecycleRegistry instance. Declare a variable to store the LifecycleRegistry reference, a constructor to initialize the LifecycleRegistry instance, and add the *getLifecycle()* method:

```
public class DemoOwner implements LifecycleOwner {

    private final LifecycleRegistry lifecycleRegistry;

    public DemoOwner() {
        lifecycleRegistry = new LifecycleRegistry(this);
    }

    @NonNull
    @Override
    public Lifecycle getLifecycle() {
        return lifecycleRegistry;
    }
}
```

Next, the class must notify the registry of lifecycle state changes. This can be achieved by marking the state with the *markState()* method of the LifecycleRegistry object or by triggering lifecycle events using the *handleLifecycleEvent()* method. What constitutes a state change within a custom class will depend on the purpose of the class. For this example, we will add some methods that trigger lifecycle events when called:

```
.
.
private final LifecycleRegistry lifecycleRegistry;
.
.
    public void startOwner() {
        lifecycleRegistry.handleLifecycleEvent(Lifecycle.Event.ON_START);
    }

    public void stopOwner() {
        lifecycleRegistry.handleLifecycleEvent(Lifecycle.Event.ON_STOP);
```

```
    }

    @NonNull
    @Override
    public Lifecycle getLifecycle() {
        return lifecycleRegistry;
    }
```
.
.

The last change within the DemoOwner class is to add the DemoObserver class as the observer. This call will be made by adding the following constructor to the class:

```
public DemoOwner() {
    lifecycleRegistry = new LifecycleRegistry(this);
    getLifecycle().addObserver(new DemoObserver());
}
```

Load the *MainActivity.java* file into the code editor, locate the *onCreate()* method, and add code to create an instance of the DemoOwner class and to call the *startOwner()* and *stopOwner()* methods. Note also that the call to add the DemoObserver as an observer has been removed. Although a single observer can be used with multiple owners, it is removed in this case to avoid duplicated and confusing output within the Logcat tool window:

.
.

```
import com.ebookfrenzy.lifecycledemo.DemoOwner;
```
.
.

```
private DemoOwner demoOwner;
```
.
.

```
@Override
public void onViewCreated(@NonNull View view, @Nullable Bundle savedInstanceState) {
    super.onViewCreated(view, savedInstanceState);

    demoOwner = new DemoOwner();
    demoOwner.startOwner();
    demoOwner.stopOwner();
    getLifecycle().addObserver(new DemoObserver());
}
```

39.6 Testing the Custom Lifecycle Owner

Build and run the app one final time, refer to the Logcat tool window, and confirm that the observer detected the create, start, and stop lifecycle events in the following order:

```
onCreate
onStart
onStop
```

An Android Jetpack Lifecycle Awareness Tutorial

Note that the "created" state changes were triggered even though code was not added to the DemoOwner class to do this manually. These were triggered automatically when the owner instance was first created and when the ON_STOP event was handled.

39.7 Summary

This chapter has provided a practical demonstration of implementing lifecycle awareness within an Android app, including creating a lifecycle observer and designing and implementing a basic lifecycle owner class.

Chapter 40

40. An Overview of the Navigation Architecture Component

Very few Android apps today consist of just a single screen. In reality, most apps comprise multiple screens through which the user navigates using screen gestures, button clicks, and menu selections. Before the introduction of Android Jetpack, implementing navigation within an app was largely a manual coding process with no easy way to view and organize potentially complex navigation paths. However, this situation has improved considerably with the introduction of the Android Navigation Architecture Component combined with support for navigation graphs in Android Studio.

40.1 Understanding Navigation

Every app has a home screen that appears after the app has launched and after any splash screen has appeared (a splash screen being the app branding screen that appears temporarily while the app loads). The user will typically perform tasks from this home screen, resulting in other screens appearing. These screens will usually take the form of other activities and fragments within the app. For example, a messaging app may have a home screen listing current messages from which users can navigate to another screen to access a contact list or a settings screen. The contacts list screen, in turn, might allow the user to navigate to other screens where new users can be added or existing contacts updated. Graphically, the app's *navigation graph* might be represented as shown in Figure 40-1:

Figure 40-1

Each screen that makes up an app, including the home screen, is referred to as a *destination* and is usually a fragment or activity. The Android navigation architecture uses a *navigation stack* to track the user's path through the destinations within the app. When the app first launches, the home screen is the first destination placed onto the stack and becomes the *current destination*. When the user navigates to another destination, that screen

An Overview of the Navigation Architecture Component

becomes the current destination and is *pushed* onto the stack above the home destination. As the user navigates to other screens, they are also pushed onto the stack. Figure 40-2, for example, shows the current state of the navigation stack for the hypothetical messaging app after the user has launched the app and is navigating to the "Add Contact" screen:

Figure 40-2

As the user navigates back through the screens using the system back button, each destination is *popped* off the stack until the home screen is once again the only destination on the stack. In Figure 40-3, the user has navigated back from the Add Contact screen, popping it off the stack and making the Contacts List screen the current destination:

Figure 40-3

All of the work involved in navigating between destinations and managing the navigation stack is handled by a *navigation controller*, represented by the NavController class.

Adding navigation to an Android project using the Navigation Architecture Component is a straightforward process involving a navigation host, navigation graph, navigation actions, and minimal code writing to obtain a reference to, and interact with, the navigation controller instance.

40.2 Declaring a Navigation Host

A navigation host is a special fragment (NavHostFragment) embedded into the user interface layout of an activity and serves as a placeholder for the destinations through which the user will navigate. Figure 40-4, for example, shows a typical activity screen and highlights the area represented by the navigation host fragment:

An Overview of the Navigation Architecture Component

Figure 40-4

A NavHostFragment can be placed into an activity layout within the Android Studio layout editor either by dragging and dropping an instance from the Containers section of the palette or by manually editing the XML as follows:

```
<?xml version="1.0" encoding="utf-8"?>
<FrameLayout xmlns:android="http://schemas.android.com/apk/res/android"
    xmlns:app="http://schemas.android.com/apk/res-auto"
    xmlns:tools="http://schemas.android.com/tools"
    android:id="@+id/container"
    android:layout_width="match_parent"
    android:layout_height="match_parent"
    tools:context=".MainActivity" >

    <androidx.fragment.app.FragmentContainerView
        android:id="@+id/demo_nav_host_fragment"
        android:name="androidx.navigation.fragment.NavHostFragment"
        android:layout_width="match_parent"
        android:layout_height="match_parent"
        app:defaultNavHost="true"
        app:navGraph="@navigation/navigation_graph" />

</FrameLayout>
```

The points of note in the above navigation host fragment element are the reference to the NavHostFragment in the *name* property, the setting of *defaultNavHost* to true, and the assignment of the file containing the navigation graph to the *navGraph* property.

When the activity launches, this navigation host fragment is replaced by the home destination designated in the navigation graph. As the user navigates through the app screens, the host fragment will be replaced by the appropriate fragment for the destination.

An Overview of the Navigation Architecture Component

40.3 The Navigation Graph

A navigation graph is an XML file that contains the destinations that will be included in the app navigation. In addition to these destinations, the file contains navigation actions that define navigation between destinations and optional arguments for passing data from one destination to another. Android Studio includes a navigation graph editor that can be used to design graphs and implement actions either visually or by manually editing the XML.

Figure 40-5 shows the Android Studio navigation graph editor in Design mode:

Figure 40-5

The destinations list (A) lists all destinations within the graph. Selecting a destination from the list will locate and select the corresponding destination in the graph (particularly useful for locating specific destinations in a large graph). The navigation graph panel (B) contains a dialog for each destination representing the user interface layout. In this example, this graph contains two destinations named mainFragment and secondFragment. Arrows between destinations (C) represent navigation action connections. Actions are added by hovering the mouse pointer over the edge of the origin until a circle appears, then clicking and dragging from the circle to the destination. The Attributes panel (D) allows the properties of the currently selected destination or action connection to be viewed and modified. In the above figure, the attributes for the action are displayed. New destinations are added by clicking on the button marked E and selecting options from a menu. Options are available to add existing fragments or activities as destinations or to create new blank fragment destinations. The Component Tree panel (F) provides a hierarchical overview of the navigation graph.

The underlying XML for the navigation graph can be viewed and modified by switching the editor into Code mode. The following XML listing represents the navigation graph for the destinations and action connection shown in Figure 40-5 above:

```
<?xml version="1.0" encoding="utf-8"?>
<navigation xmlns:android="http://schemas.android.com/apk/res/android"
    xmlns:app="http://schemas.android.com/apk/res-auto"
    xmlns:tools="http://schemas.android.com/tools"
    android:id="@+id/navigation_graph"
    app:startDestination="@id/mainFragment">

    <fragment
        android:id="@+id/mainFragment"
```

```
            android:name="com.ebookfrenzy.navigationdemo.ui.main.MainFragment"
            android:label="fragment_main"
            tools:layout="@layout/fragment_main" >
            <action
                android:id="@+id/mainToSecond"
                app:destination="@id/secondFragment" />
    </fragment>
    <fragment
            android:id="@+id/secondFragment"
            android:name="com.ebookfrenzy.navigationdemo.SecondFragment"
            android:label="fragment_second"
            tools:layout="@layout/fragment_second" >
    </fragment>
</navigation>
```

Navigation graphs can also be split over multiple files to improve organization and promote reuse. When structured in this way, *nested graphs* are embedded into *root graphs*. To create a nested graph, shift-click on the destinations to be nested, right-click over the first destination and select the *Move to Nested Graph -> New Graph* menu option. The nested graph will then appear as a new node in the graph. Double-click on the nested graph node to load the graph file into the editor to access the nested graph.

40.4 Accessing the Navigation Controller

Navigating from one destination to another usually occurs in response to an event within an app, such as a button click or menu selection. Before a navigation action can be triggered, the code must first obtain a reference to the navigation controller instance. This requires a call to the *findNavController()* method of the Navigation or NavHostFragment classes. The following code, for example, can be used to access the navigation controller of an activity. Note that for the code to work, the activity must contain a navigation host fragment:

```
NavController controller =
        Navigation.findNavController(activity, R.id.demo_nav_host_fragment);
```

In this case, the method call is passed a reference to the activity and the id of the NavHostFragment embedded in the activity's layout.

Alternatively, the navigation controller associated with any view may be identified by passing that view to the method:

```
NavController controller = Navigation.findNavController(binding.button);
```

The final option finds the navigation controller for a fragment by calling the *findNavController()* method of the NavHostFragment class, passing through a reference to the fragment:

```
NavController controller = NavHostFragment.findNavController(fragment);
```

40.5 Triggering a Navigation Action

Once the navigation controller has been found, a navigation action is triggered by calling the controller's *navigate()* method and passing through the resource id of the action to be performed. For example:

```
controller.navigate(R.id.goToContactsList);
```

The id of the action is defined within the Attributes panel of the navigation graph editor when an action connection is selected.

40.6 Passing Arguments

Data may be passed from one destination to another during a navigation action by using arguments declared within the navigation graph file. An argument consists of a name, type, and an optional default value and may be added manually within the XML or using the Attributes panel when an action arrow or destination is selected within the graph. In Figure 40-6, for example, an integer argument named *contactsCount* has been declared with a default value of 0:

> Arguments   + −
>
> a contactsCount: integer (0)

Figure 40-6

Once added, arguments are placed within the XML element of the receiving destination, for example:

```
<fragment
    android:id="@+id/secondFragment"
    android:name="com.ebookfrenzy.navigationdemo.SecondFragment"
    android:label="fragment_second"
    tools:layout="@layout/fragment_second" >
    <argument
        android:name="contactsCount"
        android:defaultValue=0
        app:type="integer" />
</fragment>
```

The Navigation Architecture Component provides two techniques for passing data between destinations. One approach involves placing the data into a Bundle object that is passed to the destination during an action, where it is then unbundled and the arguments extracted.

The main drawback to this particular approach is that it is not "type safe". In other words, if the receiving destination treats an argument as a different type than it was declared (for example, treating a string as an integer) this error will not be caught by the compiler and will likely cause problems at runtime.

A better option, which is used in this book, is *safeargs*. Safeargs is a plugin for the Android Studio Gradle build system which automatically generates special classes that allow arguments to be passed in a type-safe way. The safeargs approach to argument passing will be described and demonstrated in the next chapter (*"An Android Jetpack Navigation Component Tutorial"*).

40.7 Summary

Navigation within the context of an Android app user interface refers to the ability of a user to move back and forth between different screens. Once time-consuming to implement and difficult to organize, Android Studio and the Navigation Architecture Component now make it easier to implement and manage navigation within Android app projects.

The different screens within an app are referred to as destinations and are usually represented by fragments or activities. All apps have a home destination, including the screen displayed when the app first loads. The content area of this layout is replaced by a navigation host fragment which is swapped out for other destination fragments as the user navigates the app. The navigation path is defined by the navigation graph file consisting of destinations and the actions that connect them together with any arguments to be passed between destinations. Navigation is handled by navigation controllers, which, in addition to managing the navigation stack, provide methods to initiate navigation actions from within app code.

41. An Android Jetpack Navigation Component Tutorial

The previous chapter described the Android Jetpack Navigation Component and how it integrates with the navigation graphing features of Android Studio to provide an easy way to implement navigation between the screens of an Android app. In this chapter, a new Android Studio project will be created that uses these navigation features to implement an example app containing multiple screens. In addition to demonstrating the use of the Android Studio navigation graph editor, the example project will also implement the passing of data between origin and destination screens using type-safe arguments.

41.1 Creating the NavigationDemo Project

Select the *New Project* option from the welcome screen and, within the resulting new project dialog, choose the Empty Views Activity template before clicking on the Next button.

Enter *NavigationDemo* into the Name field and specify *com.ebookfrenzy.navigationdemo* as the package name. Before clicking on the Finish button, change the Minimum API level setting to API 26: Android 8.0 (Oreo) and the Language menu to Java.

41.2 Adding Navigation to the Build Configuration

A new Empty Views Activity project does not include the Navigation component libraries in the build configuration files by default. Before performing any other tasks, therefore, the first step is to modify the app level *build.gradle.kts* file. Locate this file in the Project tool window (*Gradle Scripts -> build.gradle.kts (Module :app)*), double-click on it to load it into the code editor, and modify the dependencies section to add the navigation libraries. Also, take this opportunity to enable view binding for this module:

```
android {

    buildFeatures {
        viewBinding = true
    }
.
.
dependencies {
    implementation ("androidx.navigation:navigation-fragment:2.6.0")
    implementation ("androidx.navigation:navigation-ui:2.6.0")
    implementation(platform("org.jetbrains.kotlin:kotlin-bom:1.8.0"))
.
.
}
```

Note that newer versions of these libraries may have been released since this book was published. After adding the navigation dependencies to the file, click on the *Sync Now* link to resynchronize the build configuration for the project.

41.3 Creating the Navigation Graph Resource File

With the navigation libraries added to the build configuration, the navigation graph resource file can now be added to the project. As outlined in *"An Overview of the Navigation Architecture Component"*, this is an XML file containing the fragments and activities through which the user will be able to navigate, together with the actions to perform the transitions and any data to be passed between destinations.

Within the Project tool window, locate the *res* folder (*app -> res*), right-click on it, and select the *New ->Android Resource File* menu option:

Figure 41-1

After selecting the menu item, the New Resource File dialog will appear. In this dialog, name the file *navigation_graph* and change the Resource type menu to Navigation as outlined in Figure 41-2 before clicking on the OK button to create the file.

Figure 41-2

After the navigation graph resource file has been added to the project, it will appear in the main panel, ready for adding new destinations. Switch the editor to Code mode and review the XML for the graph before any destinations are added:

```
<?xml version="1.0" encoding="utf-8"?>
<navigation xmlns:android="http://schemas.android.com/apk/res/android"
    xmlns:app="http://schemas.android.com/apk/res-auto"
    android:id="@+id/navigation_graph">

</navigation>
```

Switch back to Design mode within the editor and note that the Host section of the Destinations panel indicates that no navigation host fragments have been detected within the project:

An Android Jetpack Navigation Component Tutorial

Hosts

No NavHostFragments found

This nav graph must be referenced from a NavHostFragment in a layout in order to be accessible.

Using Navigation Component ↗

Figure 41-3

Before adding any destinations to the navigation graph, the next step is to add a navigation host fragment to the project.

41.4 Declaring a Navigation Host

For this project, the navigation host fragment will be contained within the user interface layout of the main activity. First, locate the main activity layout file in the Project tool window (*app -> res -> layout -> activity_main.xml*), load it into the layout editor tool, and delete the default TextView component.

With the layout editor in Design mode, drag a NavHostFragment element from the Containers section of the Palette and drop it onto the container area of the activity layout, as indicated by the arrow in Figure 41-4:

Figure 41-4

Select the *navigation_graph.xml* file created in the previous section from the resulting Navigation Graphs dialog and click on the OK button.

With the newly added NavHostFragment instance selected in the layout, use the Attributes tool window to change the element's ID to *demo_nav_host_fragment* before clicking on the *Infer constraints* button.

Switch the layout editor to Code mode and review the XML file. Note that the editor has correctly configured the navigation graph property to reference the *navigation_graph.xml* file and that the *defaultNavHost* property has been set to *true*:

An Android Jetpack Navigation Component Tutorial

```xml
<?xml version="1.0" encoding="utf-8"?>
<androidx.constraintlayout.widget.ConstraintLayout
    xmlns:android="http://schemas.android.com/apk/res/android"
    xmlns:app="http://schemas.android.com/apk/res-auto"
    xmlns:tools="http://schemas.android.com/tools"
    android:layout_width="match_parent"
    android:layout_height="match_parent"
    tools:context=".MainActivity">

    <androidx.fragment.app.FragmentContainerView
        android:id="@+id/demo_nav_host_fragment"
        android:name="androidx.navigation.fragment.NavHostFragment"
        android:layout_width="409dp"
        android:layout_height="729dp"
        app:defaultNavHost="true"
        app:layout_constraintBottom_toBottomOf="parent"
        app:layout_constraintEnd_toEndOf="parent"
        app:layout_constraintStart_toStartOf="parent"
        app:layout_constraintTop_toTopOf="parent"
        app:navGraph="@navigation/navigation_graph" />
</androidx.constraintlayout.widget.ConstraintLayout>
```

Return to the *navigation_graph.xml* file and confirm that the NavHostFragment instance has been detected (it may be necessary to close and reopen the file before the change appears):

Figure 41-5

41.5 Adding Navigation Destinations

Remaining in the navigation graph, it is time to add the first destination. Click on the new destination button as shown in Figure 41-6 to select or create a destination:

Figure 41-6

An Android Jetpack Navigation Component Tutorial

Next, select the *Create new destination* option from the menu. In the resulting dialog, select the Fragment (Blank) template, name the new fragment *FirstFragment* and the layout *fragment_first* before clicking on the Finish button. After a short delay while the project rebuilds, the new fragment will appear as a destination within the graph, as shown in Figure 41-7:

Figure 41-7

The home icon above the destination node indicates this is the *start destination*. This means the destination will be the first displayed when the NavHostFragment activity is created. To change the start destination to another, select that node in the graph and click on the home button in the toolbar.

Review the XML content of the navigation graph by switching the editor to Code mode:

```
<?xml version="1.0" encoding="utf-8"?>
<navigation xmlns:android="http://schemas.android.com/apk/res/android"
    xmlns:app="http://schemas.android.com/apk/res-auto"
    xmlns:tools="http://schemas.android.com/tools"
    android:id="@+id/navigation_graph"
    app:startDestination="@id/firstFragment">

    <fragment
        android:id="@+id/firstFragment"
        android:name="com.ebookfrenzy.navigationdemo.FirstFragment"
        android:label="fragment_first"
        tools:layout="@layout/fragment_first" />
</navigation>
```

Before any navigation can be performed, the graph needs at least one more destination. Repeat the above steps to add a fragment named *SecondFragment* with the layout file named *fragment_second*. The new fragment will appear as another destination within the graph, as shown in Figure 41-8:

327

An Android Jetpack Navigation Component Tutorial

Figure 41-8

41.6 Designing the Destination Fragment Layouts

Before adding actions to navigate between destinations, now is a good time to add some user interface components to the two destination fragments in the graph. Begin by double-clicking on the firstFragment destination so that the *fragment_first.xml* file loads into the layout editor, then select and delete the default TextView instance. Within the Component Tree panel, right-click on the FrameLayout entry and select the *Convert from FrameLayout to ConstraintLayout* menu option, accepting the default settings in the resulting conversion dialog:

Figure 41-9

Using the Attributes tool window, change the ID of the ConstraintLayout to *constraintLayout*, then drag and drop Button and Plain Text EditText widgets onto the layout so that it resembles that shown in Figure 41-10 below:

Figure 41-10

Once the views are correctly positioned, click on the *Infer constraints* button in the toolbar to add any missing constraints to the layout. Select the EditText view and use the Attributes tool window to delete the default "Name" text and change the widget's ID to *userText*. Next, change the button text property to read "Navigate" and extract it to a string resource.

Return to the *navigation_graph.xml* file and double-click on the secondFragment destination to load the *fragment_second.xml* file into the layout editor. Select and delete the default TextView instance and repeat the above steps to convert the FrameLayout to a ConstraintLayout, changing the id to *constraintLayout2*. Next, drag and drop a new TextView widget to position it in the center of the layout and click on the *Infer constraints* button to add any missing constraints. With the new TextView selected, use the Attributes panel to change the ID to *argText*.

41.7 Adding an Action to the Navigation Graph

Now that the two destinations have been added to the graph and the corresponding user interface layouts are designed, the project needs a way for the user to navigate from the first fragment to the second. This will be achieved by adding an action to the graph, which can then be referenced from within the app code.

To establish an action connection with the first fragment as the origin and the second fragment as the destination, open the navigation graph and hover the mouse pointer over the vertical center of the right-hand edge of the firstFragment destination so that a circle appears as highlighted in Figure 41-11:

An Android Jetpack Navigation Component Tutorial

Figure 41-11

Click within the circle and drag the resulting line to the secondFragment destination:

Figure 41-12

Release the line to establish the action connection between the origin and destination, at which point the line will change into an arrow, as shown in Figure 41-13:

Figure 41-13

An action connection may be deleted anytime by selecting it and pressing the keyboard Delete key. With the arrow selected, review the properties available within the Attributes tool window and change the ID to *mainToSecond*. This is the ID by which the action will be referenced within the code. Switch the editor to Code mode and note that the action is now included within the XML:

```
<?xml version="1.0" encoding="utf-8"?>
<navigation xmlns:android="http://schemas.android.com/apk/res/android"
    xmlns:app="http://schemas.android.com/apk/res-auto"
    xmlns:tools="http://schemas.android.com/tools"
    android:id="@+id/navigation_graph"
    app:startDestination="@id/firstFragment">

    <fragment
        android:id="@+id/firstFragment"
```

```
            android:name="com.ebookfrenzy.navigationdemo.FirstFragment"
            android:label="fragment_first"
            tools:layout="@layout/fragment_first" >
            <action
                android:id="@+id/mainToSecond"
                app:destination="@id/secondFragment" />
    </fragment>
    <fragment
        android:id="@+id/secondFragment"
        android:name="com.ebookfrenzy.navigationdemo.SecondFragment"
        android:label="fragment_second"
        tools:layout="@layout/fragment_second" />
</navigation>
```

41.8 Implement the OnFragmentInteractionListener

Before adding code to trigger the action, the MainActivity class must be modified to implement the OnFragmentInteractionListener interface. This interface was generated within the Fragment classes when the blank fragments were created within the navigation graph editor. To conform to the interface, the activity needs a method named *onFragmentInteraction()* to implement communication between the fragment and the activity.

Edit the *MainActivity.java* file and modify it so that it reads as follows:

.
.
```
import android.net.Uri;
```
.
.
```
public class MainActivity extends AppCompatActivity implements SecondFragment.
OnFragmentInteractionListener {

    @Override
    protected void onCreate(Bundle savedInstanceState) {
        super.onCreate(savedInstanceState);
        setContentView(R.layout.activity_main);
    }

    @Override
    public void onFragmentInteraction(Uri uri) {
    }
}
```

If Android Studio reports that OnFragmentInteractionListener is undefined (some versions of Android Studio add it automatically, while others do not), edit the *SecondFragment.java* file and add the following:

.
.
```
import android.net.Uri;
```
.
.

```
public interface OnFragmentInteractionListener {
    // TODO: Update argument type and name
    void onFragmentInteraction(Uri uri);
}
```

41.9 Adding View Binding Support to the Destination Fragments

Since we will access some views in the fragment layouts, we must modify the current code to enable view binding support. Begin by editing the *FirstFragment.java* file and making the following changes:

```
    .
    .
import com.ebookfrenzy.navigationdemo.databinding.FragmentFirstBinding;
    .
    .
public class FirstFragment extends Fragment {

    private FragmentFirstBinding binding;
    .
    .
    @Nullable
    @Override
    public View onCreateView(@NonNull LayoutInflater inflater, @Nullable ViewGroup container,
                             @Nullable Bundle savedInstanceState) {
        return inflater.inflate(R.layout.fragment_first, container, false);

        binding = FragmentFirstBinding.inflate(inflater, container, false);
        return binding.getRoot();
    }

    @Override
    public void onDestroyView() {
        super.onDestroyView();
        binding = null;
    }
```

Repeat the above steps for the *SecondFragment.java* file, referencing FragmentSecondBinding.

41.10 Triggering the Action

Now that the action has been added to the navigation graph, the next step is to add some code within the first fragment to trigger the action when the Button widget is clicked. Locate the *FirstFragment.java* file, load it into the code editor, and override the *onViewCreated()* method to obtain a reference to the button instance and to configure an onClickListener instance to be called when the user clicks the button:

An Android Jetpack Navigation Component Tutorial

```
.
import androidx.annotation.NonNull;
import androidx.annotation.Nullable;
import android.widget.Button;
import androidx.navigation.Navigation;
.
.
public class FirstFragment extends Fragment  {
.
.
    @Override
    public void onViewCreated(@NonNull View view,
                       @Nullable Bundle savedInstanceState) {
        super.onViewCreated(view, savedInstanceState);

        binding.button.setOnClickListener(new View.OnClickListener() {
            @Override
            public void onClick(View view) {
                Navigation.findNavController(view).navigate(
                        R.id.mainToSecond);
            }
        });
    }
}
```

The above code obtains a reference to the navigation controller and calls the *navigate()* method on that instance, passing through the resource ID of the navigation action as an argument.

Compile and run the app and verify that clicking the button in the first fragment transitions to the second fragment.

As an alternative to this approach to setting up a listener, the Navigation class also includes a method named *createNavigateOnClickListener()* which provides a more efficient way of setting up a listener and navigating to a destination. The same result can be achieved, therefore, using the following single line of code to initiate the transition:

```
binding.button.setOnClickListener(Navigation.createNavigateOnClickListener(
                          R.id.mainToSecond, null));
```

41.11 Passing Data Using Safeargs

The next objective is to pass the text entered into the EditText view in the first fragment to the second fragment, where it will be displayed on the TextView widget. As outlined in the previous chapter, the Android Navigation component supports two approaches to passing data. This chapter will make use of type-safe argument passing.

The first step in using safeargs is to add the safeargs plugin to the Gradle build configuration. Using the Project tool window, locate and edit the project-level *build.gradle.kts* file (*Gradle Scripts -> build.gradle.kts (Project: NavigationDemo)*) to add the plugin dependency as follows (once again, keeping in mind that a more recent version may now be available):

```
// Top-level build file where you can add configuration options common to all sub-projects/modules.
```

```
buildscript {
    dependencies {
        classpath("androidx.navigation:navigation-safe-args-gradle-plugin:2.6.0")
    }
}

plugins {
    .
    .
```

Next, edit the module level *build.gradle.kts* file (*Gradle Scripts -> build.gradle.kts (Module :app)*) to apply the plugin as follows and resync the project:

```
plugins {
    id("com.android.application")
    id ("androidx.navigation.safeargs")
    .
    .
}

android {
    .
    .
```

The next step is to define any arguments that will be received by the destination, which, in this case, is the second fragment. Edit the navigation graph, select the secondFragment destination, and locate the Arguments section within the Attributes tool window. Click on the + button (highlighted in Figure 41-14) to add a new argument to the destination:

Figure 41-14

After the + button has been clicked, a dialog will appear into which the argument name, type, and default value need to be entered. Name the argument *message*, set the type to *String*, enter *No Message* into the default value field, and click the Add button:

An Android Jetpack Navigation Component Tutorial

Figure 41-15

The newly configured argument will appear in the secondFragment element of the *navigation_graph.xml* file as follows:

```
<fragment
    android:id="@+id/secondFragment"
    android:name="com.ebookfrenzy.navigationdemo.SecondFragment"
    android:label="fragment_second"
    tools:layout="@layout/fragment_second" >
    <argument
        android:name="message"
        app:argType="string"
        android:defaultValue="No Message" />
</fragment>
```

The next step is to add code to the *FirstFragment.java* file to extract the text from the EditText view and pass it to the second fragment during the navigation action. This will involve using some special navigation classes generated automatically by the safeargs plugin. Currently, the navigation involves the FirstFragment class, the SecondFragment class, a navigation action named *mainToSecond*, and an argument named *message*.

When the project is built, the safeargs plugin will generate the following additional classes that can be used to pass and receive arguments during navigation.

- **FirstFragmentDirections** - This class represents the origin for the navigation action (named using the class name of the navigation origin with "Directions" appended to the end) and provides access to the action object.

- **ActionMainToSecond** - The class representing the action used to perform the transition (named based on the ID assigned to the action within the navigation graph file prefixed with "Action"). This class contains a setter method for each argument configured on the destination. For example, since the second fragment destination contains an argument named *message*, the class includes a method named *setMessage()*. Once configured, an instance of this class is then passed to the *navigate()* method of the navigation controller to navigate to the destination.

- **SecondFragmentArgs** - The class used in the destination fragment to access the arguments passed from the origin (named using the class name of the navigation destination with "Args" appended to the end). This class includes a getter method for each of the arguments passed to the destination (i.e., *getMessage()*)

Using these classes, the *onClickListener* code within the *onViewCreated()* method of the *FirstFragment.java* file can be modified as follows to extract the current text from the EditText widget, apply it to the action and initiate the transition to the second fragment:

```
binding.button.setOnClickListener(view1 -> {

    FirstFragmentDirections.MainToSecond action =
            FirstFragmentDirections.mainToSecond();

    action.setMessage(binding.userText.getText().toString());
    Navigation.findNavController(view1).navigate(action);
});
```

The above code obtains a reference to the action object, sets the message argument string using the *setMessage()* method, and then calls the *navigate()* method of the navigation controller, passing through the action object. If Android Studio reports FirstFragmentDirections as undefined, rebuild the project using the *Build -> Make Project* menu option to generate the class.

All that remains is to modify the *SecondFragment.java* class file to receive the argument after the navigation has been performed and display it on the TextView widget. For this example, the code to achieve these tasks will be added using an *onStart()* lifecycle method. Edit the *SecondFragment.java* file and add this method so that it reads as follows:

```
@Override
public void onStart() {
    super.onStart();

    SecondFragmentArgs args = SecondFragmentArgs.fromBundle(getArguments());
    String message = args.getMessage();
    binding.argText.setText(message);
}
```

The code in the above method begins by obtaining a reference to the TextView widget. Next, the *fromBundle()* method of the SecondFragmentArgs class is called to extract the SecondFragmentArgs object received from the origin. Since the argument in this example was named *message* in the *navigation_graph.xml* file, the corresponding *getMessage()* method is called on the args object to obtain the string value. This string is then displayed on the TextView widget.

Compile and run the app and enter some text before clicking on the Button widget. When the second fragment destination appears, the TextView should display the text entered in the first fragment, indicating that the data was successfully passed between navigation destinations.

41.12 Summary

This chapter has provided a practical example of implementing Android app navigation using the Navigation Architecture Component and the Android Studio navigation graph editor. Topics covered included the creation of a navigation graph containing both existing and new destination fragments, embedding a navigation host fragment within an activity layout, writing code to trigger navigation events, and passing arguments between destinations using the safeargs plugin.

Chapter 42

42. An Introduction to MotionLayout

The MotionLayout class provides an easy way to add animation effects to the views of a user interface layout. This chapter will begin by providing an overview of MotionLayout and introduce the concepts of MotionScenes, Transitions, and Keyframes. Once these basics have been covered, the next two chapters (entitled *"An Android MotionLayout Editor Tutorial"* and *"A MotionLayout KeyCycle Tutorial"*) will provide additional detail and examples of MotionLayout animation in action through the creation of example projects.

42.1 An Overview of MotionLayout

MotionLayout is a layout container, the primary purpose of which is to animate the transition of views within a layout from one state to another. MotionLayout could, for example, animate the motion of an ImageView instance from the top left-hand corner of the screen to the bottom right-hand corner over a specified time. In addition to the position of a view, other attribute changes may also be animated, such as the color, size, or rotation angle. These state changes can also be interpolated (such that a view moves, rotates, and changes size throughout the animation).

The motion of a view using MotionLayout may be performed in a straight line between two points or implemented to follow a path comprising intermediate points at different positions between the start and end points. MotionLayout also supports using touches and swipes to initiate and control animation.

MotionLayout animations are declared entirely in XML and do not typically require writing code. These XML declarations may be implemented manually in the Android Studio code editor, visually using the MotionLayout editor, or combining both approaches.

42.2 MotionLayout

When implementing animation, the ConstraintLayout container typically used in a user interface must first be converted to a MotionLayout instance (a task which can be achieved by right-clicking on the ConstraintLayout in the layout editor and selecting the *Convert to MotionLayout* menu option). MotionLayout also requires at least version 2.0.0 of the ConstraintLayout library.

Unsurprisingly since it is a subclass of ConstraintLayout, MotionLayout supports all of the layout features of the ConstraintLayout. Therefore, a user interface layout can be similarly designed when using MotionLayout for views that do not require animation.

For views that are to be animated, two ConstraintSets are declared, defining the appearance and location of the view at the start and end of the animation. A *transition* declaration defines *keyframes* to apply additional effects to the target view between these start and end states and click and swipe handlers used to start and control the animation.

The start and end ConstraintSets and the transitions are declared within a MotionScene XML file.

42.3 MotionScene

As we have seen in earlier chapters, an XML layout file contains the information necessary to configure the appearance and layout behavior of the static views presented to the user, and this is still the case when using MotionLayout. For non-static views (in other words, the views that will be animated), those views are still declared within the layout file, but the start, end, and transition declarations related to those views are stored in a separate XML file referred to as the MotionScene file (so called because all of the declarations are defined

An Introduction to MotionLayout

within a MotionScene element). This file is imported into the layout XML file and contains the start and end ConstraintSets and Transition declarations (a single file can contain multiple ConstraintSet pairs and Transition declarations, allowing different animations to be targeted to specific views within the user interface layout).

The following listing shows a template for a MotionScene file:

```xml
<?xml version="1.0" encoding="utf-8"?>
<MotionScene
    xmlns:android="http://schemas.android.com/apk/res/android"
    xmlns:motion="http://schemas.android.com/apk/res-auto">

    <Transition
        motion:constraintSetEnd="@+id/end"
        motion:constraintSetStart="@id/start"
        motion:duration="1000">
        <KeyFrameSet>
        </KeyFrameSet>
    </Transition>

    <ConstraintSet android:id="@+id/start">
    </ConstraintSet>

    <ConstraintSet android:id="@+id/end">
    </ConstraintSet>
</MotionScene>
```

In the above XML, ConstraintSets named *start* and *end* (though any name can be used) have been declared, which, at this point, are yet to contain any constraint elements. The Transition element defines that these ConstraintSets represent the animation start and end points and contain an empty KeyFrameSet element ready to be populated with additional animation keyframe entries. The Transition element also includes a millisecond duration property to control the running time of the animation.

ConstraintSets do not have to imply the motion of a view. It is possible to have the start and end sets declare the same location on the screen and then use the transition to animate other property changes, such as scale and rotation angle.

ConstraintSets do not have to imply the motion of a view. It is possible, for example, to have the start and end sets declare the same location on the screen and then use the transition to animate other property changes, such as scale and rotation angle.

42.4 Configuring ConstraintSets

The ConstraintSets in the MotionScene file allow the full set of ConstraintLayout settings to be applied to a view regarding positioning, sizing, and relation to the parent and other views. In addition, the following attributes may also be included within the ConstraintSet declarations:

- alpha
- visibility
- elevation
- rotation

- rotationX
- rotationY
- translationX
- translationY
- translationZ
- scaleX
- scaleY

For example, to rotate the view by 180° during the animation, the following could be declared within the start and end constraints:

```
<ConstraintSet android:id="@+id/start">
    <Constraint
.
.
        motion:layout_constraintStart_toStartOf="parent"
        android:rotation="0">
    </Constraint>
</ConstraintSet>

<ConstraintSet android:id="@+id/end">
    <Constraint
.
.
        motion:layout_constraintBottom_toBottomOf="parent"
        android:rotation="180">
    </Constraint>
</ConstraintSet>
```

The above changes tell MotionLayout that the view is to start at 0° and then, during the animation, rotate a full 180° before coming to rest upside-down.

42.5 Custom Attributes

In addition to the standard attributes listed above, it is possible to specify a range of *custom attributes* (declared using CustomAttribute). In fact, just about any property available on the view type can be specified as a custom attribute for inclusion in an animation. To identify the attribute's name, find the getter/setter name from the documentation for the target view class, remove the get/set prefix, and lower the case of the first remaining character. For example, to change the background color of a Button view in code, we might call the *setBackgroundColor()* setter method as follows:

```
myButton.setBackgroundColor(Color.RED)
```

When setting this attribute in a constraint set or keyframe, the attribute name will be *backgroundColor*. In addition to the attribute name, the value must also be declared using the appropriate type from the following list of options:

- **motion:customBoolean** - Boolean attribute values.

An Introduction to MotionLayout

- **motion:customColorValue** - Color attribute values.
- **motion:customDimension** - Dimension attribute values.
- **motion:customFloatValue** - Floating point attribute values.
- **motion:customIntegerValue** - Integer attribute values.
- **motion:customStringValue** - String attribute values

For example, a color setting will need to be assigned using the *customColorValue* type:

```
<CustomAttribute
    motion:attributeName="backgroundColor"
    motion:customColorValue="#43CC76" />
```

The following excerpt from a MotionScene file, for example, declares start and end constraints for a view in addition to changing the background color from green to red:

```
.
.
    <ConstraintSet android:id="@+id/start">
        <Constraint
            android:layout_width="wrap_content"
            android:layout_height="wrap_content"
            motion:layout_editor_absoluteX="21dp"
            android:id="@+id/button"
            motion:layout_constraintTop_toTopOf="parent"
            motion:layout_constraintStart_toStartOf="parent" >
            <CustomAttribute
                motion:attributeName="backgroundColor"
                motion:customColorValue="#33CC33" />
        </Constraint>
    </ConstraintSet>

    <ConstraintSet android:id="@+id/end">
        <Constraint
            android:layout_width="wrap_content"
            android:layout_height="wrap_content"
            motion:layout_editor_absoluteY="21dp"
            android:id="@+id/button"
            motion:layout_constraintEnd_toEndOf="parent"
            motion:layout_constraintBottom_toBottomOf="parent" >
            <CustomAttribute
                motion:attributeName="backgroundColor"
                motion:customColorValue="#F80A1F" />
        </Constraint>
    </ConstraintSet>
.
.
```

42.6 Triggering an Animation

Without some event to tell MotionLayout to start the animation, none of the settings in the MotionScene file will affect the layout (except that the view will be positioned based on the setting in the start ConstraintSet).

The animation can be configured to start in response to either screen tap (OnClick) or swipe motion (OnSwipe) gesture. The OnClick handler causes the animation to start and run until completion, while OnSwipe will synchronize the animation to move back and forth along the timeline to match the touch motion. The OnSwipe handler will also respond to "flinging" motions on the screen. The OnSwipe handler also provides options to configure how the animation reacts to dragging in different directions and the side of the target view to which the swipe is to be anchored. This allows, for example, left-ward dragging motions to move a view in the corresponding direction while preventing an upward motion from causing a view to move sideways (unless, of course, that is the required behavior).

The OnSwipe and OnClick declarations are contained within the Transition element of a MotionScene file. In both cases, the view id must be specified. For example, to implement an OnSwipe handler responding to downward drag motions anchored to the bottom edge of a view named *button*, the following XML would be placed in the Transition element:

```xml
<Transition
    motion:constraintSetEnd="@+id/end"
    motion:constraintSetStart="@id/start"
    motion:duration="1000">
  <KeyFrameSet>
  </KeyFrameSet>
   <OnSwipe
       motion:touchAnchorId="@+id/button"
       motion:dragDirection="dragDown"
       motion:touchAnchorSide="bottom" />
</Transition>
```

Alternatively, to add an OnClick handler to the same button:

```xml
<OnClick motion:targetId="@id/button"
     motion:clickAction="toggle" />
```

In the above example, the action has been set to *toggle* mode. This mode and the other available options can be summarized as follows:

- **toggle** - Animates to the opposite state. For example, if the view is currently at the transition start point, it will transition to the end point, and vice versa.

- **jumpToStart** - Changes immediately to the start state without animation.

- **jumpToEnd** - Changes immediately to the end state without animation.

- **transitionToStart** - Transitions with animation to the start state.

- **transitionToEnd** - Transitions with animation to the end state.

42.7 Arc Motion

By default, a movement of view position will travel in a straight line between the start and end points. To change the motion to an arc path, use the *pathMotionArc* attribute as follows within the start constraint, configured with either a *startHorizontal* or *startVertical* setting to define whether the arc is to be concave or convex:

```
<ConstraintSet android:id="@+id/start">
    <Constraint
        android:layout_width="wrap_content"
        android:layout_height="wrap_content"
        motion:layout_editor_absoluteX="21dp"
        android:id="@+id/button"
        motion:layout_constraintTop_toTopOf="parent"
        motion:layout_constraintStart_toStartOf="parent"
        motion:pathMotionArc="startVertical" >
```

Figure 42-1 illustrates startVertical and startHorizontal arcs in comparison to the default straight line motion:

Figure 42-1

42.8 Keyframes

All of the ConstraintSet attributes outlined so far only apply to the start and end points of the animation. In other words, if the rotation property were set to 180° on the end point, the rotation would begin when the animation starts and complete when the end point is reached. It is not, therefore, possible to configure the rotation to reach the full 180° at a point 50% of the way through the animation and then rotate back to the original orientation by the end. Fortunately, this type of effect is available using Keyframes.

Keyframes are used to define intermediate points during the animation at which state changes are to occur. Keyframes could, for example, be declared such that the background color of a view is to have transitioned to blue at a point 50% of the way through the animation, green at the 75% point, and then back to the original color by the end of the animation. Keyframes are implemented within the Transition element of the MotionScene file embedded into the KeyFrameSet element.

MotionLayout supports several types of Keyframe which can be summarized as follows:

42.8.1 Attribute Keyframes

Attribute Keyframes (declared using KeyAttribute) allow view attributes to be changed at intermediate points in the animation timeline. KeyAttribute supports the attributes listed above for ConstraintSets combined with the ability to specify where the change will take effect in the animation timeline. For example, the following

An Introduction to MotionLayout

Keyframe declaration will gradually cause the button view to double in size horizontally (scaleX) and vertically (scaleY), reaching full size at 50% through the timeline. For the remainder of the timeline, the view will decrease in size to its original dimensions:

```
<Transition
    motion:constraintSetEnd="@+id/end"
    motion:constraintSetStart="@id/start"
    motion:duration="1000">
  <KeyFrameSet>
      <KeyAttribute
          motion:motionTarget="@+id/button"
          motion:framePosition="50"
          android:scaleX="2.0" />
      <KeyAttribute
          motion:motionTarget="@+id/button"
          motion:framePosition="50"
          android:scaleY="2.0" />
  </KeyFrameSet>
```

42.8.2 Position Keyframes

Position keyframes (KeyPosition) modify the path followed by a view as it moves between the start and end locations. By placing key positions at different points on the timeline, a path of just about any level of complexity can be applied to an animation. Positions are declared using x and y coordinates combined with the corresponding points in the transition timeline. These coordinates must be declared relative to one of the following coordinate systems:

- **parentRelative** - The x and y coordinates are relative to the parent container where the coordinates are specified as a percentage (represented as a value between 0.0 and 1.0):

Figure 42-2

- **deltaRelative** - Instead of relative to the parent, the x and y coordinates are relative to the start and end positions. For example, the start point is (0, 0) the end point (1, 1). Keep in mind that the x and y coordinates can be negative values):

Figure 42-3

- **pathRelative** - The x and y coordinates are relative to the path, where the straight line between the start and end points serves as the graph's X-axis. Once again, coordinates are represented as a percentage (0.0 to 1.0). This is similar to the deltaRelative coordinate space but takes into consideration the angle of the path. Once again coordinates may be negative:

Figure 42-4

As an example, the following ConstraintSets declare start and end points on either side of a device screen. By

An Introduction to MotionLayout

default, a view transition using these points would move in a straight line across the screen, as illustrated in Figure 42-5:

Figure 42-5

Suppose, however, that the view is required to follow a path similar to that shown in Figure 42-6 below:

Figure 42-6

To achieve this, keyframe position points could be declared within the transition as follows:

```
<KeyPosition
    motion:motionTarget="@+id/button"
    motion:framePosition="25"
    motion:keyPositionType="pathRelative"
    motion:percentY="0.3"
    motion:percentX="0.25"/>

<KeyPosition
    motion:motionTarget="@+id/button"
    motion:framePosition="75"
    motion:keyPositionType="pathRelative"
    motion:percentY="-0.3"
    motion:percentX="0.75"/>
```

The above elements create keyframe position points 25% and 75% through the path using the pathRelative coordinate system. The first position is placed at coordinates (0.25, 0.3) and the second at (0.75, -0.3). These position keyframes can be visualized as illustrated in Figure 42-7 below:

Figure 42-7

42.9 Time Linearity

Without additional settings, the animations outlined above will be performed at a constant speed. To vary the animation speed (for example, so that it accelerates and then decelerates), the transition easing attribute (transitionEasing) can be used within a ConstraintSet or Keyframe.

For complex easing requirements, the linearity can be defined by plotting points on a cubic Bézier curve, for example:

-
-

```
motion:layout_constraintBottom_toBottomOf="parent"
motion:transitionEasing="cubic(0.2, 0.7, 0.3, 1)"
android:rotation="360">
```

-
-

If you are unfamiliar with Bézier curves, consider using the curve generator online at the following URL:

https://cubic-bezier.com/

For most requirements, however, easing can be specified using the built-in *standard*, *accelerate* and *decelerate* values:

-
-

```
motion:layout_constraintBottom_toBottomOf="parent"
motion:transitionEasing="decelerate"
android:rotation="360">
```

-
-

42.10 KeyTrigger

The trigger keyframe (KeyTrigger) allows a method on a view to be called when the animation reaches a specified frame position within the animation timeline. This also takes into consideration the direction of the

An Introduction to MotionLayout

animations. For example, different methods can be called depending on whether the animation runs forward or backward. Consider a button that is to be made visible when the animation moves beyond 20% of the timeline. The KeyTrigger would be implemented within the KeyFrameSet of the Transition element as follows using the *onPositiveCross* property:

.
.

```
<KeyFrameSet>
    <KeyTrigger
        motion:framePosition="20"
        motion:onPositiveCross="show"
        motion:motionTarget="@id/button"/>
```

.
.

Similarly, if the same button is to be hidden when the animation is reversed and drops below 10%, a second key trigger could be added using the *onNegativeCross* property:

```
<KeyTrigger
    motion:framePosition="10"
    motion:onNegativeCross="show"
    motion:motionTarget="@id/button2"/>
```

If the animation is using toggle action, use the *onCross* property:

```
<KeyTrigger
    motion:framePosition="10"
    motion:onCross="show"
    motion:motionTarget="@id/button2"/>
```

42.11 Cycle and Time Cycle Keyframes

While position keyframes can be used to add intermediate state changes into the animation, this would quickly become cumbersome if large numbers of repetitive positions and changes needed to be implemented. For situations where state changes need to be performed repetitively with predictable changes, MotionLayout includes the Cycle and Time Cycle keyframes. The chapter entitled *"A MotionLayout KeyCycle Tutorial"* will cover this topic in detail.

42.12 Starting an Animation from Code

So far in this chapter, we have only looked at controlling an animation using the OnSwipe and OnClick handlers. It is also possible to start an animation from within code by calling methods on the MotionLayout instance. The following code, for example, runs the transition from start to end with a duration of 2000ms for a layout named *motionLayout*:

```
motionLayout.setTransitionDuration(2000);
motionLayout.transitionToEnd();
```

In the absence of additional settings, the start and end states used for the animation will be those declared in the Transition declaration of the MotionScene file. To use specific start and end constraint sets, reference them by id in a call to the *setTransition()* method of the MotionLayout instance:

```
motionLayout.setTransition(R.id.myStart, R.id.myEnd);
motionLayout.transitionToEnd();
```

To monitor the state of an animation while it is running, add a transition listener to the MotionLayout instance

An Introduction to MotionLayout

as follows:

```
motionLayout.setTransitionListener(transitionListener);

MotionLayout.TransitionListener transitionListener =
                    new MotionLayout.TransitionListener() {
    @Override
    public void onTransitionStarted(MotionLayout motionLayout,
                                int startId, int endId) {
        // Called when the transition starts
    }

    @Override
    public void onTransitionChange(MotionLayout motionLayout, int startId,
                              int endId, float progress) {
        // Called each time a property changes. Track progress value to find
        // current position
    }

    @Override
    public void onTransitionCompleted(MotionLayout motionLayout, int currentId) {
        // Called when the transition is complete
    }

    @Override
    public void onTransitionTrigger(MotionLayout motionLayout, int triggerId,
                               boolean positive, float progress) {
        // Called when a trigger keyframe threshold is crossed
    }
};
```

Summary

MotionLayout is a subclass of ConstraintLayout designed specifically to add animation effects to the views in user interface layouts. MotionLayout works by animating the transition of a view between two states defined by start and end constraint sets. Additional animation effects may be added between these start and end points using keyframes.

Animations may be triggered via OnClick or OnSwipe handlers or programmatically via method calls on the MotionLayout instance.

Chapter 43

43. An Android MotionLayout Editor Tutorial

Now that the basics of MotionLayout have been covered, this chapter will provide an opportunity to try out MotionLayout in an example project. In addition to continuing to explore the main features of MotionLayout, this chapter will also introduce the MotionLayout editor and explore how it can be used to construct and modify MotionLayout animations visually.

The project created in this chapter will use start and end ConstraintSets, gesture handlers, and Attribute and Position Keyframes.

43.1 Creating the MotionLayoutDemo Project

Click the *New Project* button in the welcome screen and choose the Empty Views Activity template within the resulting new project dialog before clicking the Next button.

Enter *MotionLayoutDemo* into the Name field and specify *com.ebookfrenzy.motionlayoutdemo* as the package name. Before clicking on the Finish button, change the Minimum API level setting to API 26: Android 8.0 (Oreo) and the Language menu to Java.

43.2 ConstraintLayout to MotionLayout Conversion

Android Studio will have placed a ConstraintLayout container as the parent view within the *activity_main.xml* layout file. The next step is to convert this container to a MotionLayout instance. Within the Component Tree, right-click on the ConstraintLayout entry and select the *Convert to MotionLayout* menu option:

Figure 43-1

An Android MotionLayout Editor Tutorial

After making the selection, click the *Convert* button in the confirmation dialog. Once the conversion is complete, the MotionLayout editor will appear within the main Android Studio window, as illustrated in Figure 43-2:

Figure 43-2

As part of the conversion process, Android Studio will create a new folder named *res -> xml* and place within it a MotionLayout scene file named *activity_main_scene.xml*:

Figure 43-3

This file contains a top-level MotionScene element containing the ConstraintSet and Transition entries that will define the animations within the main layout. By default, the file will contain empty elements for the start and end constraint sets and an initial transition:

```xml
<?xml version="1.0" encoding="utf-8"?>
<MotionScene
    xmlns:android="http://schemas.android.com/apk/res/android"
    xmlns:motion="http://schemas.android.com/apk/res-auto">

    <Transition
        motion:constraintSetEnd="@+id/end"
        motion:constraintSetStart="@id/start"
        motion:duration="1000">
```

```
        <KeyFrameSet>
        </KeyFrameSet>
    </Transition>

    <ConstraintSet android:id="@+id/start">
    </ConstraintSet>

    <ConstraintSet android:id="@+id/end">
    </ConstraintSet>
</MotionScene>
```

Any changes made within the MotionLayout editor will be stored within this file. Similarly, this file may be edited directly to implement and modify animation settings outside the MotionLayout editor.

The animations will be implemented primarily using the MotionLayout editor interface in this tutorial. However, we will review how these changes are reflected in the underlying MotionScene file at each stage. As we progress through the chapter, it will become clear that the MotionScene XML syntax is simple and easy to learn.

The first phase of this tutorial will demonstrate the use of MotionLayout to animate a Button object, including motion (including following a path), rotation, and size scaling.

43.3 Configuring Start and End Constraints

With the *activity_main.xml* file loaded into the MotionLayout editor, make sure that the Motion Layout box (marked E in Figure 43-5 below) is selected, then delete the default TextView before dragging and dropping a Button view from the palette to the top left-hand corner of the layout canvas as shown in Figure 43-4:

Figure 43-4

With the button selected, use the Attributes tool window to change the id to *myButton*.

As outlined in the previous chapter, MotionLayout animation is primarily a case of specifying how a view transitions between two states. Therefore, the first step in implementing animation is to specify the constraints that define these states.

For this example, the start point will be the top center of the layout view. To configure these constraints, select the *start* constraint set entry in the editor window (marked A in Figure 43-5):

An Android MotionLayout Editor Tutorial

Figure 43-5

When the *start* box is selected, all constraint and layout changes will be made to the start point constraint set. To return to the standard constraints and properties for the entire layout, click on the Motion Layout box (E).

Next, select the *myButton* entry within the ConstraintSet list (B). Note that the Source column shows that the button is positioned based on constraints within the layout file. Instead, we want the button positioned based on the start constraint set. With the myButton entry still selected, click on the Edit button (C) and select *Create Constraint* from the menu, after which the button entry will indicate that the view is to be positioned based on the start constraint set:

Figure 43-6

The start constraint set must position the button at the top of the layout with an 8dp offset and centered horizontally. With myButton still selected, use the Attributes tool window to set constraints on the top, left, and right sides of the view as follows:

Figure 43-7

An Android MotionLayout Editor Tutorial

Select the end constraint set entry (marked D in Figure 43-5 above) and repeat the steps to create a new constraint, this time placing the button in the horizontal center of the layout but with an 8p offset from the bottom edge of the layout:

Figure 43-8

With the start and end constraints configured, open the *activity_main_scene.xml* file and note that the constraints have been added to the file:

```xml
<?xml version="1.0" encoding="utf-8"?>
<MotionScene
    xmlns:android="http://schemas.android.com/apk/res/android"
    xmlns:motion="http://schemas.android.com/apk/res-auto">
.
.
.
    <ConstraintSet android:id="@+id/start">
        <Constraint
            android:id="@+id/myButton"
            android:layout_width="wrap_content"
            android:layout_height="wrap_content"
            motion:layout_constraintTop_toTopOf="parent"
            android:layout_marginTop="8dp"
            motion:layout_constraintStart_toStartOf="parent"
            motion:layout_constraintEnd_toEndOf="parent" />
    </ConstraintSet>

    <ConstraintSet android:id="@+id/end">
        <Constraint
            android:id="@+id/myButton"
            android:layout_width="wrap_content"
            android:layout_height="wrap_content"
            motion:layout_constraintStart_toStartOf="parent"
            motion:layout_constraintEnd_toEndOf="parent"
            motion:layout_constraintBottom_toBottomOf="parent"
            android:layout_marginBottom="8dp" />
    </ConstraintSet>
```

353

An Android MotionLayout Editor Tutorial

```
</MotionScene>
```

Note also that the Transition element has already been preconfigured to animate the transition between the start and end points over 1000 milliseconds. Although we have yet to add an action to initiate the transition, previewing the animation from within the MotionLayout editor is still possible.

43.4 Previewing the MotionLayout Animation

To preview the animation without building and running the app, select the transition arrow within the MotionLayout editor marked A in Figure 43-9 below. This will display the animation timeline panel (marked B):

Figure 43-9

To test the animation, click on the slider (C) and drag it along the timeline. As the slider moves, the button in the layout canvas will move along the dashed path line (D). Use the toolbar button (E) to perform a full animation to repeat the animation continuously at different speeds (either forwards, backward or toggling back and forth).

43.5 Adding an OnClick Gesture

Although a simple MotionLayout animation transition has been created, we still need a way to start the animation from within the running app. This can be achieved by assigning either a click or swipe handler. For this example, we will configure the animation to start when the user clicks the button. Within the MotionLayout editor, pause the timeline animation if it runs on a loop setting. Next, select the Transition arrow (marked A in Figure 43-9 above), locate the OnClick attribute section in the Attributes tool window and click on the + button indicated by the arrow in Figure 43-10 below:

An Android MotionLayout Editor Tutorial

Figure 43-10

An empty row will appear in the OnClick panel for the first property. For the property name, enter *targetId*; for the value field, enter the button's id (*@id/myButton*). In the next empty row, enter *app:clickAction* into the property name field. In the value field, click the down arrow to display a menu of valid options:

Figure 43-11

For this example, select the toggle action. This will cause the view to animate to the opposite position when clicked. Once these settings have been entered, they should match those shown in Figure 43-12:

Figure 43-12

Once again, open the *activity_main_scene.xml* file and review the OnClick property defined within the Transition entry:

.
.

```
<Transition
    motion:constraintSetEnd="@+id/end"
    motion:constraintSetStart="@id/start"
```

355

An Android MotionLayout Editor Tutorial

```
        motion:duration="1000">
    <KeyFrameSet>
    </KeyFrameSet>
        <OnClick motion:targetId="@id/myButton"
            motion:clickAction="toggle" />
</Transition>
```

•
•

Compile and run the app on a device or emulator and confirm that clicking on the button causes it to transition back and forth between the start and end points as defined in the MotionScene file.

43.6 Adding an Attribute Keyframe to the Transition

So far, the example project is only animating the motion of the button view from one location on the screen to another. Attribute keyframes (KeyAttribute) provide a way to specify points within the transition timeline at which other attribute changes are to have taken effect. A KeyAttribute could, for example, be defined such that the view must have increased in size by 50% by the time the view has moved 30% through the timeline. For this example, we will add a rotation effect positioned at the mid-point of the animation.

Begin by opening the *activity_main.xml* file in the MotionLayout Editor, selecting the transition connector arrow to display the timeline, then click on the button highlighted in Figure 43-13:

Figure 43-13

From the menu, select the *KeyAttribute* option:

Figure 43-14

Once selected, the dialog shown in Figure 43-15 will appear. Within the dialog, make sure the ID option is selected and that myButton is referenced. In the position field, enter 50 (this is specified as a percentage where 0 is the start point and 100 is the end). Finally, select the rotation entry from the Attribute drop-down menu before clicking on the Add button:

Figure 43-15

Once the KeyAttribute has been added, a row will appear within the timeline for the attribute. Click on the row to highlight it, then click on the disclosure arrow on the far left edge of the row to unfold the attribute transition graph. Note that a small diamond marker appears in the timeline (as indicated in Figure 43-16 below), indicating the location of the key. The graph indicates the linearity of the effect. In this case, the button will rotate steadily up to the specified number of degrees, reaching maximum rotation at the location of the keyframe. The button will then rotate back to 0 degrees by the time it reaches the end point:

Figure 43-16

To change the properties of a KeyAttribute, select it in the timeline and then refer to the Attributes tool window. Within the KeyAttribute panel, change the rotation property to 360 degrees:

Figure 43-17

An Android MotionLayout Editor Tutorial

Check that the attribute works by moving the slider back and forth and watching the button rotate as it traverses the animation path in the layout canvas. Refer to the *activity_main_scene.xml* file, which should appear as follows:

-
-
```
<Transition
    motion:constraintSetEnd="@+id/end"
    motion:constraintSetStart="@id/start"
    motion:duration="1000">
    <KeyFrameSet>
        <KeyAttribute
            motion:motionTarget="@+id/myButton"
            motion:framePosition="50"
            android:rotation="360" />
    </KeyFrameSet>
    <OnClick motion:targetId="@id/myButton"
        motion:clickAction="toggle" />
</Transition>
```
-
-

Test the animation using the transition slider or by compiling and running the app and verify that the button now rotates during the animation.

43.7 Adding a CustomAttribute to a Transition

The KeyAttribute property is limited to built-in effects such as resizing and rotation. Additional changes are also possible by declaring CustomAttributes. Unlike KeyAttributes, which are stored in the Transition element, CustomAttributes are located in the start and end constraint sets. As such, these attributes can only be declared to take effect at start and end points (in other words, you cannot specify an attribute keyframe at a position partway through a transition timeline).

For this example, we will configure the button to gradually change color from red to green. Begin by selecting the start box marked A in Figure 43-18, followed by the myButton view constraint set (B):

Figure 43-18

Referring to the Attributes tool window, click on the + button in the CustomAttributes section as highlighted below:

> Transforms

> View Transition

∨ CustomAttributes

Use + to add custom attribute for easy access

Figure 43-19

In the resulting dialog (Figure 43-20), change the attribute type to *Color* and enter *backgroundColor* into the Attribute Name field. Finally, set the value to #F80A1F:

Data Type	Color
Attribute Name	backgroundColor
Value	#F80A1F

Cancel OK

Figure 43-20

Click on OK to commit the changes, then select the end constraint set (marked C in Figure 43-18 above) and repeat the steps to add a custom attribute, this time specifying #33CC33 as the RGB value for the color.

Using the timeline slider or running the app, make sure the button changes color during the animation.

The addition of these CustomAttributes will be reflected in the *activity_main_scene.xml* file as follows:

```
.
.
    <ConstraintSet android:id="@+id/start">
        <Constraint
.
.
            <CustomAttribute
                motion:attributeName="backgroundColor"
                motion:customColorValue="#F80A1F"  />
        </Constraint>
    </ConstraintSet>

    <ConstraintSet android:id="@+id/end">
        <Constraint
.
```

An Android MotionLayout Editor Tutorial

```
            <CustomAttribute
                motion:attributeName="backgroundColor"
                motion:customColorValue="#33CC33" />
        </Constraint>
    </ConstraintSet>
```

43.8 Adding Position Keyframes

The final task for this tutorial is to add two position keyframes (KeyPosition) to the animation path to introduce some lateral movement into the animation. With the transition timeline visible in the MotionLayout editor, click on the button to create a keyframe as highlighted in Figure 43-13 above, and select the KeyPosition option from the menu, as shown in Figure 43-21 below:

Figure 43-21

In the resulting dialog, set the properties as illustrated in Figure 43-22:

Figure 43-22

Click on the Add button to commit the change, then repeat the above steps to add a second position keyframe configured as follows:

- **Position:** 75
- **Type:** parentRelative
- **PercentX:** 0.85
- **PercentY:** 0.75

On completion of these changes, the following keyframe entries will have been added to the transition element in the *activity_main_scene.xml* file:

```
<KeyFrameSet>
.
.
    <KeyPosition
        motion:motionTarget="@+id/myButton"
        motion:framePosition="25"
        motion:keyPositionType="parentRelative"
        motion:percentX="0.15"
        motion:percentY="0.25" />
    <KeyPosition
        motion:motionTarget="@+id/myButton"
        motion:framePosition="75"
        motion:keyPositionType="parentRelative"
        motion:percentX="0.85"
        motion:percentY="0.75" />
</KeyFrameSet>
.
.
```

Test the app one last time and verify that the button now follows the path shown below while still rotating and changing color:

Figure 43-23

An Android MotionLayout Editor Tutorial

Position keyframes are represented by diamond-shaped markers on the dotted line representing the motion path within the preview canvas as indicated in Figure 43-24 (if the markers are not visible, make sure that the Button view is selected in the preview):

Figure 43-24

To visually adjust the position of a keyframe, click on the marker and drag it to a new position. As the marker moves, the Motion Layout editor will display a grid together with the current x and y coordinates:

Figure 43-25

43.9 Summary

This chapter has introduced the MotionLayout editor built into Android Studio and explored how it can be used to add animation to the user interface of an Android app without having to write XML declarations manually. Examples covered in this chapter included the conversion of a ConstraintLayout container to MotionLayout, creating start and end constraint sets and transitions in the MotionScene file, and adding an OnClick handler. The animation previewer, custom attributes, and position keyframes were also covered.

Chapter 44

44. A MotionLayout KeyCycle Tutorial

The previous chapters introduced and demonstrated the concepts of integrating animation into Android app user interfaces using the MotionLayout container combined with the features of the Android Studio MotionLayout editor. The chapter entitled *"An Introduction to MotionLayout"* briefly mentioned the cycle (KeyCycle) and time cycle (KeyTimeCycle) keyframes and explained how these can be used to implement animations involving large numbers of repetitive state changes.

This chapter will cover cycle keyframes in more detail before demonstrating how to make them in an example project using Android Studio and the Cycle Editor.

44.1 An Overview of Cycle Keyframes

Position keyframes can add intermediate state changes to the animation timeline. While this works well for small numbers of state changes, it would be cumbersome to implement in larger quantities. To make a button shake 50 times when tapped to indicate that an error occurred, for example, would involve manually creating 100 position keyframes to perform small clockwise and anti-clockwise rotations. Similarly, implementing a bouncing effect on a view as it moves across the screen would be equally time-consuming.

For situations where state changes need to be performed repetitively, MotionLayout includes the Cycle and Time Cycle keyframes. Both perform the same tasks, except that KeyCycle frames are based on frame positions within an animation path, while KeyTimeCycles are time-based in cycles per second (Hz).

Using these KeyCycle frames, the animation timeline is essentially divided into subsections (called *cycles*), each containing one or more waves that define how a property of a view is to be modified throughout the timeline. The following information is required when creating a KeyCycle cycle:

- **target view** - The id of the view on which the changes will be made.
- **frame position** - The position in the timeline at which the cycle is to start.
- **wave period** - The number of waves to be included in the cycle.
- **attribute** - The property of the view to be modified by the waves.
- **wave offset** - Offsets the cycle by the specified amount from the keyframe baseline.
- **wave shape** - The shape of the wave (sin, cos, sawtooth, square, triangle, bounce or reverse sawtooth)

Consider the following cycle keyframe set:

```
<KeyFrameSet>
    <KeyCycle
        motion:framePosition="0"
        motion:motionTarget="@+id/button"
        motion:wavePeriod="1"
        motion:waveOffset="0dp"
```

```xml
            motion:waveShape="sin"
            android:translationY="50dp"/>

    <KeyCycle
        motion:framePosition="25"
        motion:motionTarget="@+id/button"
        motion:wavePeriod="1"
        motion:waveOffset="0dp"
        motion:waveShape="sin"
        android:translationY="50dp"/>

    <KeyCycle
        motion:framePosition="50"
        motion:motionTarget="@+id/button"
        motion:wavePeriod="1"
        motion:waveOffset="0dp"
        motion:waveShape="sin"
        android:translationY="50dp"/>

    <KeyCycle
        motion:framePosition="75"
        motion:motionTarget="@+id/button"
        motion:wavePeriod="1"
        motion:waveOffset="0dp"
        motion:waveShape="sin"
        android:translationY="50dp"/>

    <KeyCycle
        motion:framePosition="100"
        motion:motionTarget="@+id/button"
        motion:wavePeriod="1"
        motion:waveOffset="0dp"
        motion:waveShape="sin"
        android:translationY="50dp"/>
</KeyFrameSet>
```

The above keyframe set divides the timeline into four equal cycles. Each cycle is configured to contain a sin wave shape which adjusts the translationY property of a button 50dp. This animation will cause the button to oscillate vertically multiple times within the specified range when executed. This keyframe set can be visualized as shown in Figure 44-1, where the five dots represent the keyframe positions:

Figure 44-1

As currently implemented, each cycle contains a single wave. Suppose we need four waves within the last cycle instead of these evenly distributed waves. This can easily be achieved by increasing the *wavePeriod* property for the last KeyCycle element as follows:

.
.

```
<KeyCycle
    motion:framePosition="75"
    motion:motionTarget="@+id/button"
    motion:wavePeriod="4"
    motion:waveOffset="0dp"
    motion:waveShape="sin"
    android:translationY="50dp"/>
```

.
.

After making this change, the frame set can be rendered in wave form as follows:

Figure 44-2

So far, the examples in this chapter have been using sin waves. Several other wave shapes are available when working with cycle keyframes in MotionLayout. Figure 44-3, for example, illustrates the effect of changing the waveShape property for all the cycle keyframes to the sawtooth wave shape:

A MotionLayout KeyCycle Tutorial

Figure 44-3

In addition to *sin* and *sawtooth*, MotionLayout also supports *triangle*, *square*, *bounce*, and *reverseSawtooth* wave shapes.

In the above examples, each cycle moves the button within the same range along the Y-axis. However, suppose we need the second cycle to move the button a greater distance along the positive Y-axis. This involves adjusting the *waveOffset* property of the second cycle as follows:

```
<KeyCycle
        motion:framePosition="25"
        motion:target="@+id/button"
        motion:wavePeriod="1"
        motion:waveOffset="100dp"
        motion:waveShape="sin"
        android:translationY="50dp"/>
```

By making this change, we end up with a timeline that resembles Figure 44-4:

Figure 44-4

The movement of the button during the second cycle will now range between approximately 0 and 150dp on the Y-axis. If we still need the lower end of the range to match the other waves, we can, of course, add 100dp to the translationY value:

```
<KeyCycle
        motion:framePosition="25"
        motion:target="@+id/button"
        motion:wavePeriod="1"
        motion:waveOffset="100dp"
        motion:waveShape="sin"
        android:translationY="150dp"/>
```

This change now gives us the following waveform:

Figure 44-5

44.2 Using the Cycle Editor

Although not particularly complicated, getting the exact cycle configuration you need can take some time by directly editing XML KeyCycle entries in the MotionScene file. In recognition, the Android engineers at Google have developed the Cycle Editor. This separate Java-based utility is not yet part of Android Studio. The Cycle Editor allows you to design and test cycle keyframe sets visually.

The Cycle Editor tool is a Java archive (jar) file requiring the Java runtime to be installed on your development system.

Once you have Java installed, the *CycleEditor.jar* file can be downloaded from the following URL:

https://github.com/googlesamples/android-ConstraintLayoutExamples/releases/download/1.0/CycleEditor.jar

Once downloaded, open a command prompt or terminal window, change directory to the location of the jar file, and run the following command:

```
java -jar CycleEditor.jar
```

Once the tool has loaded, the screen shown in Figure 44-6 will appear:

Figure 44-6

A MotionLayout KeyCycle Tutorial

The panel marked A in the above figure displays the XML for the keyframe set and can be edited directly or using the controls in panel B. Panel C displays the rendering of the cycles in wave form. Unfortunately, this is not redrawn in real time as changes are made. Instead, it must be refreshed by selecting the *File -> parse xml* menu option. The panel marked D will show a live rendering of the cycle animations when the *play* button in panel B is clicked. The Examples menu provides access to a collection of example keyframe sets that can be used both for learning purposes and as the basis for your own animations.

The remainder of this chapter will create a sample project that implements a KeyCycle-based animation effect to demonstrate the use of the Cycle Keyframe and the Cycle Editor.

44.3 Creating the KeyCycleDemo Project

Select the *New Project* option from the welcome screen and, within the resulting new project dialog, choose the Empty Views Activity template before clicking on the Next button.

Enter *KeyCycleDemo* into the Name field and specify *com.ebookfrenzy.keycycledemo* as the package name. Before clicking on the Finish button, change the Minimum API level setting to API 26: Android 8.0 (Oreo) and the Language menu to Java.

With the layout editor in Design mode and the *activity_main.xml* file open, right-click on the ConstraintLayout entry and select the *Convert to MotionLayout* menu option:

Figure 44-7

After making the selection, click the *Convert* button in the confirmation dialog.

44.4 Configuring the Start and End Constraints

This tutorial aims to animate a button's movement from one side of the device screen to the other, including KeyCycle effects that cause the view to also move up and down along the Y-axis. The first step is to configure the start and end constraints.

With the *activity_main.xml* file loaded into the MotionLayout editor, select and delete the default TextView widget. Make sure the Motion Layout box (marked E in Figure 44-9 below) is selected before dragging and dropping a Button view from the palette so that it is centered vertically and positioned along the left-hand edge of the layout canvas:

Figure 44-8

To configure the constraints for the start point, select the *start* constraint set entry in the editor window (marked A in Figure 44-9):

Figure 44-9

Next, select the *button* entry within the ConstraintSet list (B). With the button entry still selected, click the edit button (C) and select *Create Constraint* from the menu.

With the button still selected, use the Attributes tool window to set constraints on the top, left, and bottom sides of the view as follows:

Figure 44-10

A MotionLayout KeyCycle Tutorial

Select the *end* constraint set entry (marked D in Figure 44-9 above) and repeat the steps to create a new constraint, this time with constraints on the top, bottom, and right-hand edges of the button:

Figure 44-11

44.5 Creating the Cycles

The next step is to use the Cycle Editor to generate the cycle keyframes for the animation. With the Cycle Editor running, refer to the control panel shown in Figure 44-12 below:

Figure 44-12

Using the menu marked A, change the property to be modified from *rotation* to *translationY*.

Next, use the KeyCycle control (B) to select cycle 0 so that changes made elsewhere in the panel will be applied to the first cycle. Move the Period slider to 1 and the translationY slider to 60 as shown in Figure 44-13 (refer to the XML panel to see the precise setting for the translationY value as you move the slider):

Figure 44-13

Select the *File -> Parse XML* menu option to see the changes in the graph. Using the values listed in Table 44-1, configure the settings for KeyFrames 1 through 4 (keeping in mind that you have already configured the settings in the KeyCycle 0 column):

A MotionLayout KeyCycle Tutorial

	KeyCycle 0	KeyCycle 1	KeyCycle 2	KeyCycle 3	KeyCycle 4
Position	0	25	50	75	100
Period	1	2	3	2	1
translationY	60	60	150	60	60

Table 44-1

On completion of these changes, the keyframe set XML should read as follows:

```
<KeyFrameSet>
    <KeyCycle
        motion:framePosition="0"
        motion:motionTarget="@+id/button"
        motion:wavePeriod="1"
        motion:waveOffset="0dp"
        motion:waveShape="sin"
        android:translationY="60dp"/>

    <KeyCycle
        motion:framePosition="25"
        motion:motionTarget="@+id/button"
        motion:wavePeriod="2"
        motion:waveOffset="0dp"
        motion:waveShape="sin"
        android:translationY="60dp"/>

    <KeyCycle
        motion:framePosition="50"
        motion:motionTarget="@+id/button"
        motion:wavePeriod="3"
        motion:waveOffset="0dp"
        motion:waveShape="sin"
        android:translationY="150dp"/>

    <KeyCycle
        motion:framePosition="75"
        motion:motionTarget="@+id/button"
        motion:wavePeriod="2"
        motion:waveOffset="0dp"
        motion:waveShape="sin"
        android:translationY="60dp"/>

    <KeyCycle
        motion:framePosition="100"
        motion:motionTarget="@+id/button"
        motion:wavePeriod="1"
```

A MotionLayout KeyCycle Tutorial

```
        motion:waveOffset="0dp"
        motion:waveShape="sin"
        android:translationY="60dp"/>
</KeyFrameSet>
```

To view the graph with the new cycles, select the *File -> Parse XML* menu option to refresh the wave pattern, which should now appear as illustrated in Figure 44-14:

Figure 44-14

44.6 Previewing the Animation

The cycle-based animation may now be previewed from within the Cycle Editor tool. Start the animation by clicking the *play* button (marked A in Figure 44-15). To combine the cycles with horizontal movement, change the second menu (B) from *Stationary* to *West to East*. Also, take some time to experiment with the time and linearity settings (C and D).

Figure 44-15

44.7 Adding the KeyFrameSet to the MotionScene

Within the Cycle Editor, highlight and copy only the *KeyCycle* elements from the XML panel and paste them into the Transition section of the *res -> xml -> activity_main_scene.xml* file within Android Studio so that they are placed between the existing KeyFrameSet markers. Note also the increased duration setting and the addition of an OnClick handler to initiate the animation:

```
<Transition
    motion:constraintSetEnd="@+id/end"
    motion:constraintSetStart="@id/start"
    motion:duration="7000">
    <KeyFrameSet>
        <KeyCycle
            motion:framePosition="0"
            motion:motionTarget="@+id/button"
            motion:wavePeriod="1"
            motion:waveOffset="0dp"
            motion:waveShape="sin"
            android:translationY="60dp"/>
```

```
    <KeyCycle
        motion:framePosition="25"
```
.
.
```
</KeyFrameSet>

<OnClick motion:targetId="@id/button"
        motion:clickAction="toggle" />
```
.
.

Before proceeding, check that each *target* property is correctly declared. At the time of writing, the Cycle Editor was using the outdated *motion:target* tag. For example:

`motion:target="@+id/button"`

This will need to be changed for each of the five KeyCycle entries to read as follows:

`motion:`**`motionTarget`**`="@+id/button"`

Once these changes have been made, compile and run the app on a device or emulator and click the button to start and view the animation.

Note that the KeyCycle wave formation can also be viewed within the Android Studio MotionLayout editor, as shown in Figure 44-16 below:

Figure 44-16

KeyCycle frame sets are not limited to one per animation. For example, add the following KeyFrameSet to the Transition section of the *activity_main_scene.xml* file to add some rotation effects to the button as it moves:

```
<KeyFrameSet>
    <KeyCycle
        motion:framePosition="0"
        motion:motionTarget="@+id/button"
        motion:wavePeriod="1"
        motion:waveOffset="0dp"
        motion:waveShape="sin"
        android:translationY="60dp"
        android:rotation="45"/>

    <KeyCycle
        motion:framePosition="25"
        motion:motionTarget="@+id/button"
```

```xml
        motion:wavePeriod="2"
        motion:waveOffset="0dp"
        motion:waveShape="sin"
        android:translationY="60dp"
        android:rotation="80"/>

    <KeyCycle
        motion:framePosition="50"
        motion:motionTarget="@+id/button"
        motion:wavePeriod="3"
        motion:waveOffset="0dp"
        motion:waveShape="sin"
        android:translationY="150dp"
        android:rotation="45"/>

    <KeyCycle
        motion:framePosition="75"
        motion:motionTarget="@+id/button"
        motion:wavePeriod="2"
        motion:waveOffset="0dp"
        motion:waveShape="sin"
        android:translationY="60dp"
        android:rotation="80"/>

    <KeyCycle
        motion:framePosition="100"
        motion:motionTarget="@+id/button"
        motion:wavePeriod="1"
        motion:waveOffset="0dp"
        motion:waveShape="sin"
        android:translationY="60dp"
        android:rotation="45"/>
</KeyFrameSet>
```

44.8 Summary

Cycle keyframes provide a useful way to build frame animations that involve potentially large numbers of state changes that match wave patterns. As this chapter outlines, generating these cycle keyframes can be eased significantly using the Cycle Editor application.

45. Working with the Floating Action Button and Snackbar

One of the objectives of this chapter is to provide an overview of the concepts of material design. Originally introduced as part of Android 5.0, material design is a set of design guidelines that dictate how the Android user interface, and that of the apps running on Android, appear and behave.

As part of implementing the material design concepts, Google also introduced the Android Design Support Library. This library contains several components that allow many of the key features of material design to be built into Android applications. Two of these components, the floating action button and the Snackbar, will also be covered in this chapter before introducing many of the other components in subsequent chapters.

45.1 The Material Design

The principles of material design define the overall appearance of the Android environment. Material design was created by the Android team at Google and dictates that the elements that make up the user interface of Android and the apps that run on it appear and behave in a certain way in terms of behavior, shadowing, animation, and style. One of the tenets of the material design is that the elements of a user interface appear to have physical depth and a sense that items are constructed in layers of physical material. A button, for example, appears to be raised above the surface of the layout where it resides through shadowing effects. Pressing the button causes the button to flex and lift as though made of a thin material that ripples when released.

Material design also dictates the layout and behavior of many standard user interface elements. A key example is how the app bar located at the top of the screen should appear and how it should behave in relation to scrolling activities taking place within the main content of the activity.

Material design covers a wide range of areas, from recommended color styles to how objects are animated. A full description of the material design concepts and guidelines can be found online at the following link and is recommended reading for all Android developers:

https://material.io/design/introduction

45.2 The Design Library

Many of the building blocks needed to implement Android applications that adopt material design principles are contained within the Android Design Support Library. This library contains a collection of user interface components that can be included in Android applications to implement much of the look, feel, and behavior of material design. Two of the components from this library, the floating action button and Snackbar, will be covered in this chapter, while others will be introduced in later chapters.

45.3 The Floating Action Button (FAB)

The floating action button appears to float above the surface of the user interface of an app. It generally promotes the most common action within a user interface screen. A floating action button could be placed on a screen to allow the user to add an entry to a list of contacts or to send an email from within the app. Figure 45-1, for example, highlights the floating action button that allows the user to add a new contact within the standard Android Contacts app:

Working with the Floating Action Button and Snackbar

Figure 45-1

Several rules should be followed when using floating action buttons to conform with the material design guidelines. Floating action buttons must be circular and can be either 56 x 56dp (Default) or 40 x 40dp (Mini) in size. The button should be positioned a minimum of 16dp from the edge of the screen on phones and 24dp on desktops and tablet devices. Regardless of the size, the button must contain an interior icon that is 24x24dp in size, and it is recommended that each user interface screen have only one floating action button.

Floating action buttons can be animated or designed to morph into other items when touched. For example, a floating action button could rotate when tapped or morph into another element, such as a toolbar or panel listing related actions.

45.4 The Snackbar

The Snackbar component provides a way to present the user with information as a panel at the bottom of the screen, as shown in Figure 45-2. Snackbar instances contain a brief text message and an optional action button that will perform a task when tapped by the user. Once displayed, a Snackbar will either timeout automatically or can be removed manually by the user via a swiping action. During the appearance of the Snackbar, the app will continue to function and respond to user interactions normally.

Figure 45-2

In the remainder of this chapter, an example application will be created that uses the basic features of the floating action button and Snackbar to add entries to a list of items.

45.5 Creating the Example Project

Select the *New Project* option from the welcome screen and, within the resulting new project dialog, choose the Basic Views Activity template before clicking on the Next button.

Enter *FabExample* into the Name field and specify *com.ebookfrenzy.fabexample* as the package name. Before clicking on the Finish button, change the Minimum API level setting to API 26: Android 8.0 (Oreo) and the Language menu to Java.

45.6 Reviewing the Project

Since the Basic Views Activity template was selected, the activity contains four layout files. The *activity_main.xml* file consists of a CoordinatorLayout manager containing entries for an app bar, a Material toolbar, and a floating action button.

The *content_main.xml* file represents the layout of the content area of the activity and contains a NavHostFragment instance. This file is embedded into the *activity_main.xml* file via the following include directive:

```
<include layout="@layout/content_main" />
```

The floating action button element within the *activity_main.xml* file reads as follows:

```
<com.google.android.material.floatingactionbutton.FloatingActionButton
    android:id="@+id/fab"
    android:layout_width="wrap_content"
    android:layout_height="wrap_content"
    android:layout_gravity="bottom|end"
    android:layout_marginEnd="@dimen/fab_margin"
    android:layout_marginBottom="16dp"
    app:srcCompat="@android:drawable/ic_dialog_email" />
```

This declares that the button is to appear in the bottom right-hand corner of the screen with margins represented by the *fab_margin* identifier in the *values/dimens.xml* file (which, in this case, is set to 16dp). The XML further declares that the interior icon for the button is to take the form of the standard drawable built-in email icon.

The blank template has also configured the floating action button to display a Snackbar instance when tapped by the user. The code to implement this can be found in the *onCreate()* method of the *MainActivity.java* file and reads as follows:

```
binding.fab.setOnClickListener(new View.OnClickListener() {
    @Override
    public void onClick(View view) {
        Snackbar.make(view, "Replace with your own action", Snackbar.LENGTH_LONG)
                .setAction("Action", null).show();
    }
});
```

The code accesses the floating action button via the view binding and adds an onClickListener handler to be called when the button is tapped. This method displays a Snackbar instance configured with a message but no actions.

When the project is compiled and run, the floating action button will appear at the bottom of the screen, as shown in Figure 45-3:

Figure 45-3

Tapping the floating action button will trigger the onClickListener handler method causing the Snackbar to appear at the bottom of the screen:

Figure 45-4

45.7 Removing Navigation Features

As *"A Guide to the Android Studio Layout Editor Tool"* outlines, the Basic Views Activity template contains multiple fragments and buttons to navigate from one fragment to the other. These features are unnecessary for this tutorial and will cause problems later if not removed. Before moving ahead with the tutorial, modify the project as follows:

1. Within the Project tool window, navigate to and double-click on the *app -> res -> navigation -> nav_graph.xml* file to load it into the navigation editor.

2. Select the SecondFragment entry in the Component Tree panel within the editor and tap the keyboard delete key to remove it from the graph.

3. Locate and delete the *SecondFragment.java* (app -> java -> <package name> -> SecondFragment) and *fragment_second.xml* (app -> res -> layout -> fragment_second.xml) files.

4. Locate the *FirstFragment.java* file, double-click on it to load it into the editor, and remove the code from the *onViewCreated()* method so that it reads as follows:

```
binding.buttonFirst.setOnClickListener(new View.OnClickListener() {
    @Override
    public void onClick(View view) {
        NavHostFragment.findNavController(FirstFragment.this)
                .navigate(R.id.action_FirstFragment_to_SecondFragment);
    }
});
```

45.8 Changing the Floating Action Button

Since the objective of this example is to configure the floating action button to add entries to a list, the email icon currently displayed on the button needs to be changed to something more indicative of the action being performed. The icon that will be used for the button is named *ic_add_entry.png* and can be found in the *project_icons* folder of the sample code download available from the following URL:

https://www.ebookfrenzy.com/retail/giraffejava/index.php

Locate this image in the file system navigator for your operating system and copy the image file. Right-click on the *app -> res -> drawable* entry in the Project tool window and select Paste from the menu to add the file to the folder:

```
v ⌐ res
    v ⌐ drawable
        ⌐ ic_add_entry.png
        </> ic_launcher_background.xml
        </> ic_launcher_foreground.xml
```

Figure 45-5

Next, edit the *activity_main.xml* file and change the image source for the icon from *@android:drawable/ic_dialog_email* to *@drawable/ic_add_entry* as follows:

```
<com.google.android.material.floatingactionbutton.FloatingActionButton
    android:id="@+id/fab"
    android:layout_width="wrap_content"
    android:layout_height="wrap_content"
    android:layout_gravity="bottom|end"
    android:layout_margin="@dimen/fab_margin"
    android:layout_marginBottom="16dp"
    app:srcCompat="@drawable/ic_add_entry" />
```

Within the layout preview, the interior icon for the button will have changed to a plus sign.

We can also make the floating action button do just about anything when clicked by adding code to the OnClickListener. The following changes to the *MainActivity.java* file, for example, calls a method named *displayMessage()* to display a toast message each time the button is clicked:

```
.
.
import android.widget.Toast;
.
.
binding.fab.setOnClickListener(new View.OnClickListener() {
    @Override
    public void onClick(View view) {
        displayMessage("Fab clicked");
        Snackbar.make(view, "Replace with your own action", Snackbar.LENGTH_LONG)
                .setAction("Action", null).show();
    }
});
.
.
```

379

Working with the Floating Action Button and Snackbar

```
public void displayMessage(String message) {
    Toast.makeText(this,message,Toast.LENGTH_SHORT).show();
}
```

45.9 Adding an Action to the Snackbar

An action may also be added to the Snackbar, which performs a task when tapped by the user. Edit the *MainActivity.java* file and modify the Snackbar creation code to add an action titled "My Action" configured with an onClickListener named *actionOnClickListener* which, in turn, displays a toast message:

```
binding.fab.setOnClickListener(new View.OnClickListener() {
    @Override
    public void onClick(View view) {
        Snackbar.make(view, "Replace with your own action", Snackbar.LENGTH_LONG)
                .setAction("My Action", actionOnClickListener).show();
    }
});
```

Within the *MainActivity.java* file, add the listener handler:

```
View.OnClickListener actionOnClickListener = new View.OnClickListener() {
    @Override
    public void onClick(View view) {
        displayMessage("Action clicked");
        Snackbar.make(view, "Action Complete", Snackbar.LENGTH_LONG)
                .setAction("Action", null).show();
    }
};
```

Run the app and tap the floating action button, at which point both the toast message and Snackbar should appear. While the Snackbar is visible, tap the My Action button in the Snackbar and verify that the text on the Snackbar changes to "Action Complete":

Figure 45-6

45.10 Summary

Before working through an example project that uses these features, this chapter has provided a general overview of material design, the floating action button, and the Snackbar.

The floating action button and the Snackbar are part of Android's material design approach to user interface implementation. The floating action button provides a way to promote the most common action within a particular screen of an Android application. The Snackbar provides a way for an application to present information to the user and allow the user to act upon it.

46. Creating a Tabbed Interface using the TabLayout Component

The previous chapter outlined the concept of material design in Android. It introduced two of the components provided by the design support library in the form of the floating action button and the Snackbar. This chapter will demonstrate how to use another of the design library components, the TabLayout, which can be combined with the ViewPager class to create a tab-based interface within an Android activity.

46.1 An Introduction to the ViewPager2

Although not part of the design support library, ViewPager2 is a useful companion class when used with the TabLayout component to implement a tabbed user interface. The primary role of ViewPager2 is to allow the user to flip through different pages of information where a layout fragment most typically represents each page. The fragments associated with ViewPager2 are managed by an instance of the FragmentStateAdapter class.

At a minimum, the pager adapter assigned to ViewPager2 must implement two methods. The first, named *getItemCount()*, must return the total number of page fragments to be displayed to the user. The second method, *createFragment()*, is passed a page number and must return the corresponding fragment object ready to be presented to the user.

46.2 An Overview of the TabLayout Component

As previously discussed, TabLayout is one of the components introduced in material design and is included in the design support library. The purpose of the TabLayout is to present the user with a row of tabs that can be selected to display different pages to the user. The tabs can be fixed or scrollable, whereby the user can swipe left or right to view more tabs than will currently fit on the display. The information displayed on a tab can be text-based, an image, or a combination of text and images. Figure 46-1, for example, shows the tab bar for an app consisting of four tabs displaying images:

Figure 46-1

Figure 46-2, on the other hand, shows a TabLayout configuration consisting of four tabs displaying text in a scrollable configuration:

Figure 46-2

The remainder of this chapter will work through creating an example project that demonstrates the TabLayout component together with a ViewPager2 and four fragments.

46.3 Creating the TabLayoutDemo Project

Select the *New Project* option from the welcome screen and, within the resulting new project dialog, choose the Basic Views Activity template before clicking on the Next button.

Enter *TabLayoutDemo* into the Name field and specify *com.ebookfrenzy.tablayoutdemo* as the package name. Before clicking on the Finish button, change the Minimum API level setting to API 26: Android 8.0 (Oreo) and the Language menu to Java.

Once the project has been created, load the *content_main.xml* file into the Layout Editor tool, select the NavHostFragment object, and then delete it. Since we will not be using the navigation features of the Basic Views Activity template, edit the *MainActivity.java* file and modify the onCreate() method to remove the navigation code:

```
@Override
protected void onCreate(Bundle savedInstanceState) {
    super.onCreate(savedInstanceState);

    binding = ActivityMainBinding.inflate(getLayoutInflater());
    setContentView(binding.getRoot());

    setSupportActionBar(binding.toolbar);

    NavController navController =
         Navigation.findNavController(this, R.id.nav_host_fragment_content_main);
    appBarConfiguration =
         new AppBarConfiguration.Builder(navController.getGraph()).build();
    NavigationUI.setupActionBarWithNavController(this, navController,
appBarConfiguration);

    binding.fab.setOnClickListener(new View.OnClickListener() {
        @Override
        public void onClick(View view) {
            Snackbar.make(view, "Replace with your own action", Snackbar.LENGTH_LONG)
                    .setAction("Action", null).show();
        }
    });
}
```

Finally, delete the *onSupportNavigateUp()* method:

```
@Override
public boolean onSupportNavigateUp() {
    NavController navController = Navigation.findNavController(this, R.id.nav_host_fragment_content_main);
    return NavigationUI.navigateUp(navController, appBarConfiguration)
            || super.onSupportNavigateUp();
}
```

46.4 Creating the First Fragment

Each tab on the TabLayout will display a different fragment when selected. Create the first of these fragments by right-clicking on the *app -> java -> com.ebookfrenzy.tablayoutdemo* entry in the Project tool window and selecting the *New -> Fragment -> Fragment (Blank)* option. In the resulting dialog, enter *Tab1Fragment* into the *Fragment Name:* field and *fragment_tab1* into the *Fragment Layout Name:* field. Click on the *Finish* button to create the new fragment:

Figure 46-3

Edit the *Tab1Fragment.java* file, and if Android Studio has not added one automatically, add an OnFragmentInteractionListener interface declaration as follows:

.
.
.
```
import android.net.Uri;
```
.
.
```
    public interface OnFragmentInteractionListener {
        // TODO: Update argument type and name
        void onFragmentInteraction(Uri uri);
    }
```
.
.
.

Load the newly created *fragment_tab1.xml* file (located under *app -> res -> layout*) into the Layout Editor tool, right-click on the FrameLayout entry in the Component Tree panel, and select the *Convert FrameLayout to ConstraintLayout* menu option. In the resulting dialog, verify that all conversion options are selected before clicking on OK. Change the ID of the layout to *constraintLayout*.

Once the layout has been converted to a ConstraintLayout, delete the TextView from the layout. From the Palette, locate the TextView widget and drag and drop it so it is positioned in the center of the layout. Edit the object's text property to read "Tab 1 Fragment", extract the string to a resource named *tab_1_fragment*, and click the *Infer Constraints* toolbar button. At this point, the layout should match that of Figure 46-4:

Creating a Tabbed Interface using the TabLayout Component

Figure 46-4

46.5 Duplicating the Fragments

So far, the project contains one of the four required fragments. It would be quicker to duplicate the first fragment instead of creating the remaining three fragments using the previous steps. Each fragment consists of a layout XML file and a Java class file, each needing to be duplicated.

Right-click on the *fragment_tab1.xml* file in the Project tool window and select the Copy option from the resulting menu. Right-click on the *layout* entry, this time selecting the Paste option. Name the new layout file *fragment_tab2.xml* in the resulting dialog before clicking the OK button. Edit the new *fragment_tab2.xml* file and change the text on the Text View to "Tab 2 Fragment", following the usual steps to extract the string to a resource named *tab_2_fragment*.

To duplicate the Tab1Fragment class file, right-click on the class listed under *app -> java -> com.ebookfrenzy.tablayoutdemo* and select Copy. Right-click on the *com.ebookfrenzy.tablayoutdemo* entry and select Paste. In the Copy Class dialog, enter Tab2Fragment into the *New name:* field and click OK.

Edit the new *Tab2Fragment.java* file and modify the *onCreateView()* method to inflate the *fragment_tab2* layout file:

```
@Override
public View onCreateView(LayoutInflater inflater, ViewGroup container,
                    Bundle savedInstanceState) {
    // Inflate the layout for this fragment
    return inflater.inflate(R.layout.fragment_tab2, container, false);
}
```

Perform the above duplication steps twice to create the fragment layout and class files for the remaining two fragments. On completion of these steps, the project structure should match that of Figure 46-5:

```
    v ⌂ app
      > ⌂ manifests
      v ⌂ java
        v ⌂ com.ebookfrenzy.tablayoutdemo
            © FirstFragment
            © MainActivity
            © SecondFragment
            © Tab1Fragment
            © Tab2Fragment
            © Tab3Fragment
            © Tab4Fragment
            © TabPagerAdapter
        > ⌂ com.ebookfrenzy.tablayoutdemo (androidTest)
        > ⌂ com.ebookfrenzy.tablayoutdemo (test)
      v ⌂ res
        > ⌂ drawable
        v ⌂ layout
            </> activity_main.xml
            </> content_main.xml
            </> fragment_first.xml
            </> fragment_second.xml
            </> fragment_tab1.xml
            </> fragment_tab2.xml
            </> fragment_tab3.xml
            </> fragment_tab4.xml
```

Figure 46-5

46.6 Adding the TabLayout and ViewPager2

With the fragment creation process now complete, the next step is to add the TabLayout and ViewPager2 to the main activity layout file. Edit the *activity_main.xml* file and add these elements as outlined in the following XML listing. Note that the TabLayout component is embedded into the AppBarLayout element while the ViewPager2 is placed after the AppBarLayout:

```xml
<?xml version="1.0" encoding="utf-8"?>
<androidx.coordinatorlayout.widget.CoordinatorLayout xmlns:android="http://
schemas.android.com/apk/res/android"
    xmlns:app="http://schemas.android.com/apk/res-auto"
    xmlns:tools="http://schemas.android.com/tools"
    android:layout_width="match_parent"
    android:layout_height="match_parent"
    tools:context=".MainActivity">

    <com.google.android.material.appbar.AppBarLayout
        android:layout_width="match_parent"
        android:layout_height="wrap_content"
        android:theme="@style/Theme.TabLayoutDemo.AppBarOverlay">

        <androidx.appcompat.widget.Toolbar
            android:id="@+id/toolbar"
            android:layout_width="match_parent"
            android:layout_height="?attr/actionBarSize"
```

```xml
            android:background="?attr/colorPrimary"
            app:popupTheme="@style/Theme.TabLayoutDemo.PopupOverlay" />

        <com.google.android.material.tabs.TabLayout
            android:id="@+id/tabLayout"
            android:layout_width="match_parent"
            android:layout_height="wrap_content"
            app:tabMode="fixed"
            app:tabGravity="fill"/>

    </com.google.android.material.appbar.AppBarLayout>

    <androidx.viewpager2.widget.ViewPager2
        android:id="@+id/view_pager"
        android:layout_width="match_parent"
        android:layout_height="match_parent"
        app:layout_behavior="@string/appbar_scrolling_view_behavior" />

    <include layout="@layout/content_main" />

    <com.google.android.material.floatingactionbutton.FloatingActionButton
        android:id="@+id/fab"
        android:layout_width="wrap_content"
        android:layout_height="wrap_content"
        android:layout_gravity="bottom|end"
        android:layout_marginEnd="@dimen/fab_margin"
        android:layout_marginBottom="16dp"
        app:srcCompat="@android:drawable/ic_dialog_email" />

</androidx.coordinatorlayout.widget.CoordinatorLayout>
```

46.7 Creating the Pager Adapter

This example will use the ViewPager2 approach to handling the fragments assigned to the TabLayout tabs, with ViewPager2 added to the layout resource file, a new class which subclasses FragmentStateAdapter needs to be added to the project to manage the fragments that will be displayed when the user selects the tab items.

Add a new class to the project by right-clicking on the *com.ebookfrenzy.tablayoutdemo* entry in the Project tool window and selecting the *New -> Java Class* menu option. In the new class dialog, enter *TabPagerAdapter* into the *Name:* field, select the Class item in the list, and press the keyboard Return key.

Edit the *TabPagerAdapter.java* file so that it reads as follows:

```java
package com.ebookfrenzy.tablayoutdemo;

import androidx.annotation.NonNull;
import androidx.fragment.app.*;
import androidx.viewpager2.adapter.FragmentStateAdapter;
```

Creating a Tabbed Interface using the TabLayout Component

```
public class TabPagerAdapter extends FragmentStateAdapter {

    int tabCount;

    public TabPagerAdapter(@NonNull FragmentActivity fragmentActivity, int numberOfTabs) {
        super(fragmentActivity);
        this.tabCount = numberOfTabs;
    }

    @NonNull
    @Override
    public Fragment createFragment(int position) {
        switch (position) {
            case 0:
                return new Tab1Fragment();
            case 1:
                return new Tab2Fragment();
            case 2:
                return new Tab3Fragment();
            case 3:
                return new Tab4Fragment();
            default:
                return null;
        }
    }

    @Override
    public int getItemCount() {
        return tabCount;
    }
}
```

The class is declared as extending the FragmentStateAdapter class, and a constructor is implemented, allowing the number of pages required to be passed to the class when an instance is created. The *createFragment()* method will be called when a specific page is required. A switch statement is used to identify the page number being requested and to return a corresponding fragment instance. Finally, the *getItemCount()* method returns the count value passed through when the object instance was created.

46.8 Performing the Initialization Tasks

The remaining tasks involve initializing the TabLayout, ViewPager2, and TabPagerAdapter instances and declaring the main activity class as implementing fragment interaction listeners for each of the four tab fragments. Edit the *MainActivity.java* file so that it reads as follows:

```
package com.ebookfrenzy.tablayoutdemo;
.
.
.
import android.net.Uri;
```

Creating a Tabbed Interface using the TabLayout Component

```
import com.google.android.material.tabs.TabLayoutMediator;
.
.
public class MainActivity extends AppCompatActivity implements
        Tab1Fragment.OnFragmentInteractionListener,
        Tab2Fragment.OnFragmentInteractionListener,
        Tab3Fragment.OnFragmentInteractionListener,
        Tab4Fragment.OnFragmentInteractionListener {

    @Override
    protected void onCreate(Bundle savedInstanceState) {
.
.
        configureTabLayout();
    }

    protected void configureTabLayout() {

        for (int i = 0; i < 4; i++) {
            binding.tabLayout.addTab(binding.tabLayout.newTab());
        }

        final TabPagerAdapter adapter = new TabPagerAdapter
                (this, binding.tabLayout.getTabCount());
        binding.viewPager.setAdapter(adapter);

        new TabLayoutMediator(binding.tabLayout, binding.viewPager,
                (tab, position) -> tab.setText("Tab " + (position + 1) +
                        " Item")).attach();
    }

    @Override
    public void onFragmentInteraction(Uri uri) {
    }
.
.
}
```

The code begins by creating four tabs and adding them to the TabLayout instance as follows:

```
for (int i = 0; i < 4; i++) {
    binding.tabLayout.addTab(binding.tabLayout.newTab());
}
```

Next, an instance of the TabPagerAdapter class is created. Note that the code to create the TabPagerAdapter instance passes through the number of tabs assigned to the TabLayout component. The TabPagerAdapter instance is then assigned as the adapter for the ViewPager2 instance:

Creating a Tabbed Interface using the TabLayout Component

```
final TabPagerAdapter adapter = new TabPagerAdapter
        (this, binding.tabLayout.getTabCount());
binding.viewPager.setAdapter(adapter);
```

Finally, an instance of the TabLayoutMediator class is used to connect the TabLayout with the ViewPager2 object:

```
new TabLayoutMediator(binding.tabLayout, binding.viewPager,
        (tab, position) -> tab.setText("Tab " + (position + 1) + " Item")).
attach();
```

This class ensures that the TabLayout tabs remain synchronized with the currently selected fragment. This process involves ensuring that the correct text is displayed on each tab. In this case, the text is configured to read "Tab <n> Item" where <n> is replaced by the number of the currently selected tab.

46.9 Testing the Application

Compile and run the app on a device or emulator and make sure that selecting a tab causes the corresponding fragment to appear in the content area of the screen:

Figure 46-6

When building the project, you may encounter an error that reads in part:

```
Duplicate class kotlin.collections.jdk8.CollectionsJDK8Kt found in modules
kotlin-stdlib
```

This error is caused by a bug in the Android Studio build toolchain and can be resolved by making the following changes to the *build.gradle.kts (Module: app)* file:

```
dependencies {
.
.
    implementation(platform("org.jetbrains.kotlin:kotlin-bom:1.8.0"))
```

        .
        .
}

46.10 Customizing the TabLayout

The TabLayout in this example project is configured using *fixed* mode. This mode works well for a limited number of tabs with short titles. A greater number of tabs or longer titles can quickly become a problem when using fixed mode, as illustrated by Figure 46-7:

Figure 46-7

To fit the tabs into the available display width, the TabLayout has used multiple lines of text. Even so, the second line is truncated, making it impossible to see the full title. The best solution to this problem is to switch the TabLayout to scrollable mode. In this mode, the titles appear in full-length, single-line format allowing the user to swipe to scroll horizontally through the available items, as demonstrated in Figure 46-8:

Figure 46-8

To switch a TabLayout to scrollable mode, change the *app:tabMode* property in the *activity_main.xml* layout resource file from "fixed" to "scrollable":

```
<android.support.design.widget.TabLayout
    android:id="@+id/tabLayout"
    android:layout_width="match_parent"
    android:layout_height="wrap_content"
    app:tabMode="scrollable"
    app:tabGravity="fill"/>
</android.support.design.widget.AppBarLayout>
```

When in fixed mode, the TabLayout may be configured to control how the tab items are displayed to take up the available space on the screen. This is controlled via the *app:tabGravity* property, the results of which are more noticeable on wider displays such as tablets in landscape orientation. When set to "fill", for example, the items will be distributed evenly across the width of the TabLayout, as shown in Figure 46-9:

Figure 46-9

Changing the property value to "center" will cause the items to be positioned relative to the center of the tab bar:

Figure 46-10

46.11 Summary

TabLayout is one of the components introduced in the Android material design implementation. The purpose of the TabLayout component is to present a series of tab items that display different content to the user when selected. The tab items can display text, images, or a combination. When combined with the ViewPager2 class and fragments, tab layouts can be created relatively easily, with each tab item selection displaying a different fragment.

Chapter 47

47. Working with the RecyclerView and CardView Widgets

The RecyclerView and CardView widgets work together to provide scrollable lists of information to the user in which the information is presented as individual cards. Details of both classes will be covered in this chapter before working through the design and implementation of an example project.

47.1 An Overview of the RecyclerView

Much like the ListView class outlined in the chapter entitled *"Working with the Floating Action Button and Snackbar"*, the RecyclerView's purpose is to allow information to be presented to the user as a scrollable list. The RecyclerView, however, provides several advantages over the ListView. In particular, the RecyclerView is significantly more efficient in managing the views that make up a list, reusing existing views that makeup list items as they scroll off the screen instead of creating new ones (hence the name "recycler"). This increases the performance and reduces the resources a list uses, a feature of particular benefit when presenting large amounts of data to the user.

Unlike the ListView, the RecyclerView also provides a choice of three built-in layout managers to control how the list items are presented to the user:

- **LinearLayoutManager** – The list items are presented as horizontal or vertical scrolling lists.

Figure 47-1

- **GridLayoutManager** – The list items are presented in grid format. This manager is best used when the list items are of uniform size.

Figure 47-2

- **StaggeredGridLayoutManager** - The list items are presented in a staggered grid format. This manager is best

Working with the RecyclerView and CardView Widgets

used when the list items are of different sizes.

Figure 47-3

For situations where none of the three built-in managers provide the necessary layout, custom layout managers may be implemented by subclassing the RecyclerView.LayoutManager class.

Each list item displayed in a RecyclerView is created as an instance of the ViewHolder class. The ViewHolder instance contains everything necessary for the RecyclerView to display the list item, including the information to be displayed and the view layout used to display the item.

As with the ListView, the RecyclerView depends on an adapter to act as the intermediary between the RecyclerView instance and the data to be displayed to the user. The adapter is created as a subclass of the RecyclerView.Adapter class and must, at a minimum, implement the following methods, which will be called at various points by the RecyclerView object to which the adapter is assigned:

- **getItemCount()** – This method must return a count of the number of items to be displayed in the list.

- **onCreateViewHolder()** – This method creates and returns a ViewHolder object initialized with the view that is to be used to display the data. This view is typically created by inflating the XML layout file.

- **onBindViewHolder()** – This method is passed the ViewHolder object created by the *onCreateViewHolder()* method together with an integer value indicating the list item that is about to be displayed. Contained within the ViewHolder object is the layout assigned by the *onCreateViewHolder()* method. The *onBindViewHolder()* method is responsible for populating the views in the layout with the text and graphics corresponding to the specified item and returning the object to the RecyclerView, where it will be presented to the user.

Adding a RecyclerView to a layout is a matter of adding the appropriate element to the XML content layout file of the activity in which it is to appear. For example:

```xml
<?xml version="1.0" encoding="utf-8"?>
<androidx.constraintlayout.widget.ConstraintLayout
    xmlns:android="http://schemas.android.com/apk/res/android"
    xmlns:app="http://schemas.android.com/apk/res-auto"
    xmlns:tools="http://schemas.android.com/tools"
    android:layout_width="match_parent"
    android:layout_height="match_parent"
    app:layout_behavior="@string/appbar_scrolling_view_behavior"
    tools:context=".MainActivity"
    tools:showIn="@layout/activity_card_demo">

    <androidx.recyclerview.widget.RecyclerView
        android:id="@+id/recycler_view"
```

```xml
        android:layout_width="0dp"
        android:layout_height="0dp"
        app:layout_constraintBottom_toBottomOf="parent"
        app:layout_constraintEnd_toEndOf="parent"
        app:layout_constraintStart_toStartOf="parent"
        app:layout_constraintTop_toTopOf="parent"
        tools:listItem="@layout/card_layout" />

</androidx.constraintlayout.widget.ConstraintLayout>
    .
    .
```

The RecyclerView has been embedded into the CoordinatorLayout of a main activity layout file along with the AppBar and Toolbar in the above example. This provides some additional features, such as configuring the Toolbar and AppBar to scroll off the screen when the user scrolls up within the RecyclerView (a topic covered in more detail in the chapter entitled *"Working with the AppBar and Collapsing Toolbar Layouts"*).

47.2 An Overview of the CardView

The CardView class is a user interface view that allows information to be presented in groups using a card metaphor. Cards are usually presented in lists using a RecyclerView instance and may be configured to appear with shadow effects and rounded corners. Figure 47-4, for example, shows three CardView instances configured to display a layout consisting of an ImageView and two TextViews:

Figure 47-4

The user interface layout to be presented with a CardView instance is defined within an XML layout resource file and loaded into the CardView at runtime. The CardView layout can contain a layout of any complexity using the standard layout managers such as RelativeLayout and LinearLayout. The following XML layout file represents a card view layout consisting of a RelativeLayout and a single ImageView. The card is configured to be elevated to create a shadowing effect and to appear with rounded corners:

```xml
<?xml version="1.0" encoding="utf-8"?>
    <androidx.cardview.widget.CardView
        xmlns:card_view="http://schemas.android.com/apk/res-auto"
        xmlns:android="http://schemas.android.com/apk/res/android"
        android:id="@+id/card_view"
        android:layout_width="match_parent"
        android:layout_height="wrap_content"
        android:layout_margin="5dp"
```

Working with the RecyclerView and CardView Widgets

```
        card_view:cardCornerRadius="12dp"
        card_view:cardElevation="3dp"
        card_view:contentPadding="4dp">

        <RelativeLayout
            android:layout_width="match_parent"
            android:layout_height="wrap_content"
            android:padding="16dp" >

            <ImageView
                android:layout_width="100dp"
                android:layout_height="100dp"
                android:id="@+id/item_image"
                android:layout_alignParentLeft="true"
                android:layout_alignParentTop="true"
                android:layout_marginRight="16dp" />
        </RelativeLayout>
</androidx.cardview.widget.CardView>
```

When combined with the RecyclerView to create a scrollable list of cards, the *onCreateViewHolder()* method of the recycler view inflates the layout resource file for the card, assigns it to the ViewHolder instance and returns it to the RecyclerView instance.

47.3 Summary

This chapter has introduced the Android RecyclerView and CardView components. The RecyclerView provides a resource-efficient way to display scrollable lists of views within an Android app. The CardView is useful when presenting groups of data (such as a list of names and addresses) in the form of cards. As previously outlined and demonstrated in the tutorial contained in the next chapter, RecyclerView and CardView are particularly useful when combined.

48. An Android RecyclerView and CardView Tutorial

This chapter will create an example project that uses both the CardView and RecyclerView components to create a scrollable list of cards. The completed app will display a list of cards containing images and text. In addition to displaying the list of cards, the project will be implemented such that selecting a card causes messages to be displayed to the user indicating which card was tapped.

48.1 Creating the CardDemo Project

Select the *New Project* option from the welcome screen and, within the resulting new project dialog, choose the Basic Views Activity template before clicking on the Next button.

Enter *CardDemo* into the Name field and specify *com.ebookfrenzy.carddemo* as the package name. Before clicking on the Finish button, change the Minimum API level setting to API 26: Android 8.0 (Oreo) and the Language menu to Java.

48.2 Modifying the Basic Views Activity Project

Since the Basic Views Activity was selected, the layout includes a floating action button which is not required for this project. Load the *activity_main.xml* layout file into the Layout Editor tool, select the floating action button, and tap the keyboard delete key to remove the object from the layout. Edit the *MainActivity.java* file and remove the floating action button and navigation controller code from the onCreate method as follows:

```java
@Override
protected void onCreate(Bundle savedInstanceState) {
    super.onCreate(savedInstanceState);

    binding = ActivityMainBinding.inflate(getLayoutInflater());
    setContentView(binding.getRoot());

    setSupportActionBar(binding.toolbar);

    NavController navController =
            Navigation.findNavController(this, R.id.nav_host_fragment_content_main);
    appBarConfiguration =
            new AppBarConfiguration.Builder(navController.getGraph()).build();
    NavigationUI.setupActionBarWithNavController(this, navController,
            appBarConfiguration);

    binding.fab.setOnClickListener(new View.OnClickListener() {
        @Override
        public void onClick(View view) {
            Snackbar.make(view, "Replace with your own action", Snackbar.LENGTH_
```

An Android RecyclerView and CardView Tutorial

```
 LONG)
                        .setAction("Action", null).show();
         }
    });
}
```

Also, remove the *onSupportNavigateUp()* method, then open the *content_main.xml* file and delete the *nav_host_fragment_content_main* object from the layout so that only the ConstraintLayout parent remains.

48.3 Designing the CardView Layout

The layout of the views contained within the cards will be defined within a separate XML layout file. Within the Project tool window, right-click on the *app -> res -> layout* entry and select the *New -> Layout Resource File* menu option. In the New Resource Dialog, enter *card_layout* into the *File name:* field and *androidx.cardview.widget.CardView* into the root element field before clicking on the *OK* button.

Load the *card_layout.xml* file into the Layout Editor tool, switch to Code mode, and modify the layout so that it reads as follows:

```xml
<?xml version="1.0" encoding="utf-8"?>
<androidx.cardview.widget.CardView
    xmlns:android="http://schemas.android.com/apk/res/android"
    xmlns:app="http://schemas.android.com/apk/res-auto"
    android:layout_width="match_parent"
    android:layout_height="wrap_content"
    android:id="@+id/card_view"
    android:layout_margin="5dp"
    app:cardBackgroundColor="#80B3EF"
    app:cardCornerRadius="12dp"
    app:cardElevation="3dp"
    app:contentPadding="4dp" >

    <androidx.constraintlayout.widget.ConstraintLayout
        android:id="@+id/relativeLayout"
        android:layout_width="match_parent"
        android:layout_height="wrap_content"
        android:padding="16dp">

        <ImageView
            android:id="@+id/itemImage"
            android:layout_width="100dp"
            android:layout_height="100dp"
            app:layout_constraintLeft_toLeftOf="parent"
            app:layout_constraintStart_toStartOf="parent"
            app:layout_constraintTop_toTopOf="parent" />

        <TextView
            android:id="@+id/itemTitle"
            android:layout_width="236dp"
```

```
            android:layout_height="39dp"
            android:layout_marginStart="16dp"
            android:textSize="30sp"
            app:layout_constraintLeft_toRightOf="@+id/itemImage"
            app:layout_constraintStart_toEndOf="@+id/itemImage"
            app:layout_constraintTop_toTopOf="parent" />

        <TextView
            android:id="@+id/itemDetail"
            android:layout_width="236dp"
            android:layout_height="16dp"
            android:layout_marginStart="16dp"
            android:layout_marginTop="8dp"
            app:layout_constraintLeft_toRightOf="@+id/itemImage"
            app:layout_constraintStart_toEndOf="@+id/itemImage"
            app:layout_constraintTop_toBottomOf="@+id/itemTitle" />
    </androidx.constraintlayout.widget.ConstraintLayout>
</androidx.cardview.widget.CardView>
```

48.4 Adding the RecyclerView

Select the *content_main.xml* layout file and drag a RecyclerView object from the *Containers* section of the palette onto the layout so that it is positioned in the center of the screen, where it should automatically resize to fill the entire screen. Use the *Infer constraints* toolbar button to add any missing layout constraints to the view. Using the Attributes tool window, change the ID of the RecyclerView instance to *recyclerView* and the layout_width and layout_height properties to *match_constraint*.

48.5 Adding the Image Files

In addition to the two TextViews, the card layout contains an ImageView on which the Recycler adapter has been configured to display images. Before the project can be tested, these images must be added. The images that will be used for the project are named *android_image_<n>.jpg* and can be found in the *project_icons* folder of the sample code download available from the following URL:

https://www.ebookfrenzy.com/retail/giraffejava/index.php

Locate these images in the file system navigator for your operating system and select and copy the eight images. Right click on the *app -> res -> drawable* entry in the Project tool window and select Paste to add the files to the folder:

Figure 48-1

48.6 Creating the RecyclerView Adapter

As outlined in the previous chapter, the RecyclerView needs to have an adapter to handle the creation of the list items. Add this new class to the project by right-clicking on the *app -> java -> com.ebookfrenzy.carddemo* entry in the Project tool window and selecting the *New -> Java Class* menu option. In the new class dialog, enter *RecyclerAdapter* into the *Name* field and select *Class* from the list before tapping the Return keyboard key to create the new Java class file.

Edit the new *RecyclerAdapter.java* file to add some import directives and to declare that the class now extends *RecyclerView.Adapter*. Rather than create a separate class to provide the data to be displayed, some basic arrays will also be added to the adapter to act as the data for the app:

```
package com.ebookfrenzy.carddemo;

import android.view.LayoutInflater;
import android.view.View;
import android.view.ViewGroup;
import android.widget.ImageView;
import android.widget.TextView;

import androidx.annotation.NonNull;
import androidx.recyclerview.widget.RecyclerView;

public class RecyclerAdapter extends RecyclerView.Adapter<RecyclerAdapter.ViewHolder> {

    final private String[] titles = {"Chapter One",
            "Chapter Two",
            "Chapter Three",
            "Chapter Four",
            "Chapter Five",
            "Chapter Six",
            "Chapter Seven",
            "Chapter Eight"};

    final private String[] details = {"Item one details",
            "Item two details", "Item three details",
            "Item four details", "Item five details",
            "Item six details", "Item seven details",
            "Item eight details"};

    final private int[] images = { R.drawable.android_image_1,
                    R.drawable.android_image_2,
                    R.drawable.android_image_3,
                    R.drawable.android_image_4,
                    R.drawable.android_image_5,
                    R.drawable.android_image_6,
                    R.drawable.android_image_7,
```

```
                              R.drawable.android_image_8 };
}
```

Within the RecyclerAdapter class, we now need our own implementation of the ViewHolder class configured to reference the view elements in the *card_layout.xml* file. Remaining within the *RecyclerAdapter.java*, file implement this class as follows:

```
public class RecyclerAdapter extends RecyclerView.Adapter<RecyclerAdapter.
ViewHolder> {
.
.
    static class ViewHolder extends RecyclerView.ViewHolder {

        ImageView itemImage;
        TextView itemTitle;
        TextView itemDetail;

        ViewHolder(View itemView) {
            super(itemView);
            itemImage = itemView.findViewById(R.id.itemImage);
            itemTitle = itemView.findViewById(R.id.itemTitle);
            itemDetail = itemView.findViewById(R.id.itemDetail);
        }
    }
}
```

The ViewHolder class contains an ImageView and two TextView variables together with a constructor method that initializes those variables with references to the three view items in the *card_layout.xml* file.

The next item to be added to the *RecyclerAdapter.java* file is the implementation of the *onCreateViewHolder()* method:

```
@NonNull
@Override
public ViewHolder onCreateViewHolder(ViewGroup viewGroup, int i) {
    View v = LayoutInflater.from(viewGroup.getContext())
                .inflate(R.layout.card_layout, viewGroup, false);
    return new ViewHolder(v);
}
```

This method will be called by the RecyclerView to obtain a ViewHolder object. It inflates the view hierarchy *card_layout.xml* file and creates an instance of our ViewHolder class initialized with the view hierarchy before returning it to the RecyclerView.

The purpose of the *onBindViewHolder()* method is to populate the view hierarchy within the ViewHolder object with the data to be displayed. It is passed the ViewHolder object and an integer value indicating the list item that is to be displayed. This method should now be added, using the item number as an index into the data arrays. This data is then displayed on the layout views using the references created in the constructor method of the ViewHolder class:

```
@Override
public void onBindViewHolder(ViewHolder viewHolder, int i) {
```

```
        viewHolder.itemTitle.setText(titles[i]);
        viewHolder.itemDetail.setText(details[i]);
        viewHolder.itemImage.setImageResource(images[i]);
}
```

The final requirement for the adapter class is an implementation of the *getItem()* method which, in this case, returns the number of items in the *titles* array:

```
@Override
public int getItemCount() {
    return titles.length;
}
```

48.7 Initializing the RecyclerView Component

At this point, the project consists of a RecyclerView instance, an XML layout file for the CardView instances and an adapter for the RecyclerView. The last step before testing the progress so far is to initialize the RecyclerView with a layout manager, create an instance of the adapter and assign that instance to the RecyclerView object. For the purposes of this example, the RecyclerView will be configured to use the LinearLayoutManager layout option.

There is a slight complication here because we need to be able to use view binding to access the recyclerView component from within the MainActivity class. The problem is that recyclerView is contained within the *content_main.xml* layout file which is, in turn, included in the *activity_main.xml* file. To be able to reach down into the *content_main.xml* file, we need to assign it an id at the point that it is included. To do this, edit the *activity_main.xml* file and modify the *include* element so that it reads as follows:

.
.
```
    <include
        android:id="@+id/contentMain"
        layout="@layout/content_main" />
```
.
.

With an id assigned to the included file, the recyclerView component can be accessed using the following binding:

```
binding.contentMain.recyclerView
```

Now edit the *MainActivity.java* file and modify the *onCreate()* method to implement the initialization code:

```
package com.ebookfrenzy.carddemo;
.
.
import androidx.recyclerview.widget.LinearLayoutManager;
import androidx.recyclerview.widget.RecyclerView;
.
.
public class MainActivity extends AppCompatActivity {

    private RecyclerView recyclerView;
    private RecyclerView.LayoutManager layoutManager;
```

```
    private RecyclerView.Adapter adapter;
.
.
    @Override
    protected void onCreate(Bundle savedInstanceState) {
.
.
        setSupportActionBar(toolbar);

        layoutManager = new LinearLayoutManager(this);
        binding.contentMain.recyclerView.setLayoutManager(layoutManager);

        adapter = new RecyclerAdapter();
        binding.contentMain.recyclerView.setAdapter(adapter);
    }
.
.
}
```

48.8 Testing the Application

Compile and run the app on a physical device or emulator session and scroll through the different card items in the list:

Figure 48-2

When building the project, you may encounter an error that reads in part:

```
Duplicate class kotlin.collections.jdk8.CollectionsJDK8Kt found in modules
kotlin-stdlib
```

This error is caused by a bug in the Android Studio build toolchain and can be resolved by making the following changes to the *build.gradle.kts (Module: app)* file:

An Android RecyclerView and CardView Tutorial

```
dependencies {
    .
    .
    implementation(platform("org.jetbrains.kotlin:kotlin-bom:1.8.0"))
    .
    .
    .
}
```

48.9 Responding to Card Selections

The last phase of this project is to make the cards in the list selectable so that clicking on a card triggers an event within the app. For this example, the cards will be configured to present a message on the display when tapped by the user. To respond to clicks, the ViewHolder class needs to be modified to assign an onClickListener on each item view. Edit the *RecyclerAdapter.java* file and modify the ViewHolder class declaration so that it reads as follows:

```
.
.
import com.google.android.material.snackbar.Snackbar;
.
.
class ViewHolder extends RecyclerView.ViewHolder{

    ImageView itemImage;
    TextView itemTitle;
    TextView itemDetail;

    ViewHolder(View itemView) {
        super(itemView);
        itemImage = itemView.findViewById(R.id.item_image);
        itemTitle = itemView.findViewById(R.id.item_title);
        itemDetail = itemView.findViewById(R.id.item_detail);

        itemView.setOnClickListener(new View.OnClickListener() {
            @Override public void onClick(View v) {

            }
        });
    }
}
```

Within the body of the onClick handler, code can now be added to display a message indicating that the card has been clicked. Given that the actions performed as a result of a click will likely depend on which card was tapped, it is also important to identify the selected card. This information can be obtained via a call to the *getAdapterPosition()* method of the *RecyclerView.ViewHolder* class. Remaining within the *RecyclerAdapter.java* file, add code to the *onClick* handler so it reads as follows:

```
@override
public void onClick(View v) {
```

406

An Android RecyclerView and CardView Tutorial

```
        int position = getAdapterPosition();

        Snackbar.make(v, "Click detected on item " + (position + 1),
                Snackbar.LENGTH_LONG)
                .setAction("Action", null).show();
        }
});
```

The last task is to enable the material design ripple effect that appears when items are tapped within Android applications. This involves the addition of some properties to the declaration of the CardView instance in the *card_layout.xml* file as follows:

```
<?xml version="1.0" encoding="utf-8"?>
<androidx.cardview.widget.CardView
    xmlns:android="http://schemas.android.com/apk/res/android"
    xmlns:card_view="http://schemas.android.com/apk/res-auto"
    android:layout_width="match_parent"
    android:layout_height="match_parent"
    android:id="@+id/card_view"
    android:layout_margin="5dp"
    app:cardBackgroundColor="#80B3EF"
    app:cardCornerRadius="12dp"
    app:cardElevation="3dp"
    app:contentPadding="4dp"
    android:foreground="?selectableItemBackground"
    android:clickable="true" >
```

Run the app once again and verify that tapping a card in the list triggers both the standard ripple effect at the point of contact and the appearance of a Snackbar reporting the number of the selected item.

48.10 Summary

This chapter has worked through the steps involved in combining the CardView and RecyclerView components to display a scrollable list of card-based items. The example also covered the detection of clicks on list items, including the identification of the selected item and the enabling of the ripple effect visual feedback on the tapped CardView instance.

Chapter 49

49. A Layout Editor Sample Data Tutorial

The CardDemo project created in the previous chapter has provided a good example of how it can be difficult to assess from within the layout editor exactly how a user interface is going to appear until the completed app is tested. This is a problem that frequently occurs when the content to be displayed in a user interface is only generated or acquired once the user has the app installed and running.

For some time now, the Android Studio layout editor has provided the ability to specify simple attributes that are active only when the layout is being designed. A design-time only string resource could, for example, be assigned to a TextView within the layout editor that would not appear when the app runs. This capability has been extended significantly with the introduction of sample data support within the Android Studio layout editor and will be used in this chapter to improve the layout editor experience in the CardDemo project.

49.1 Adding Sample Data to a Project

During the design phase of the user interface layout, the RecyclerView instance (Figure 49-1) bears little resemblance to the running app tested at the end of the previous chapter:

Figure 49-1

In the *"Modern Android App Architecture with Jetpack"* chapter earlier in the book the concept of sample data was introduced. To demonstrate sample data in use, the project will now be modified so that the fully populated cards appear within the RecyclerView from within the layout editor. Before doing that, however, it is worth noting that the layout editor has a collection of preconfigured sample data templates that can be used when designing user interfaces. To see some of these in action, load the *content_main.xml* layout file into the layout editor and select the RecyclerView instance. Right-click on the RecyclerView and select the *Set Sample Data* menu option to display the Design-time View Attributes panel:

A Layout Editor Sample Data Tutorial

Figure 49-2

Change the template to the Email Client option and the item count to 12 and note that the RecyclerView changes to display data from the template:

Figure 49-3

These templates can be useful for displaying sample data without any additional work and will often provide enough to complete the layout design. For this example, however, sample data is going to be used to display the cards within the RecyclerView as they are intended to appear in the running app. With the *content_main.xml* file still loaded in the layout editor, switch to Code mode and locate the RecyclerView element which should read as follows:

```
<androidx.recyclerview.widget.RecyclerView
    android:id="@+id/recyclerView"
    android:layout_width="0dp"
    android:layout_height="0dp"
    app:layout_constraintBottom_toBottomOf="parent"
    app:layout_constraintEnd_toEndOf="parent"
    app:layout_constraintStart_toStartOf="parent"
    app:layout_constraintTop_toTopOf="parent"
    tools:itemCount="12"
    tools:listitem="@layout/recycler_view_item" />
```

A Layout Editor Sample Data Tutorial

Note the two special *tools* properties currently configured to display 12 items in the list, each using a layout contained within a file named *recycler_view_item.xml*. The layout editor provides a range of tools options that may be configured within a layout file. Though coverage of all of these settings is beyond the scope of this book, a full description of each can be found at the following URL:

https://developer.android.com/studio/write/tool-attributes#toolssample_resources

The *recycler_view_item.xml* file referenced above was generated automatically by the layout editor when the sample data template was selected and can be found in the project tool window.

Switch back to Design mode and, with the RecyclerView selected, use the Design-time View Attributes panel to switch the template back to the default settings. The *recycler_view_item.xml* file will be removed from the project along with the two *tools* property lines within the *content_main.xml* XML file (if Android Studio fails to remove the lines they may be deleted manually from within the Code view).

To switch to using the card layout for the sample data display, add a *listitem* property to reference the *card_layout.xml* file. With the RecyclerView selected in the layout, search for the *listitem* property in the Attributes tool window and enter *@layout/card_layout* into the property field as illustrated in Figure 49-4:

Figure 49-4

Note the card layout is now appearing for each list item, though without any images and using sample text data:

Figure 49-5

The next step is to display some images and different text on the views within the card layout. This can either

A Layout Editor Sample Data Tutorial

take the form of template sample data provided by the layout editor, or custom sample data added specifically for this project. Load the *card_layout.xml* file into the layout editor, select the ImageView and display the Design-time View Attributes panel as outlined earlier in the chapter. From the srcCompat menu, select the built-in backgrounds/scenic image set as illustrated in Figure 49-6 below:

Figure 49-6

Next, right-click on the *itemTitle* TextView object, select the *Set Sample Data* menu option and, in the Design-time attributes panel, select the *cities* text option. Repeat this step for the *itemDetail* view, this time selecting the *full_names* option as shown in Figure 49-7:

Figure 49-7

Open the *content_main.xml* file in Design mode and note that the RecyclerView is now using the built-in images and sample text data:

412

Figure 49-8

49.2 Using Custom Sample Data

The final step in this chapter is to demonstrate the use of custom sample data and images within the layout editor. This requires the creation of a sample data directory and the addition of some text and image files. Within the Project tool window, right-click on the *app* entry and select the *New -> Sample Data Directory* menu option, at which point a new directory named *sampledata* will appear within the Project tool window. If the new folder is not visible, switch the Project tool window from Android to Project mode and find the folder under *CardDemo -> app* as shown in Figure 49-9:

Figure 49-9

Right-click on the *sampledata* directory, create a directory named *images* and copy and paste the Android images into the new folder using the same steps outlined in the previous chapter. In the *card_layout.xml* file, display the Design-time View Attributes panel for the ImageView once again, this time clicking the Browse link and selecting the newly added Android images in the *Resources* dialog (if the *images* folder does not appear try rebuilding the project):

A Layout Editor Sample Data Tutorial

Figure 49-10

Right-click once again on the *sampledata* directory, select the *New -> File* option, name the file *chapters*, and enter the following content:

```
Chapter One
Chapter Two
Chapter Three
Chapter Four
Chapter Five
Chapter Six
Chapter Seven
Chapter Eight
```

Next, create a second text file named *items* with the following content:

```
Item one details
Item two details
Item three details
Item four details
Item five details
Item six details
Item seven details
Item eight details
```

With the sample data text files created, all that remains is to reference them in the view elements of the *card_layout.xml* file as follows:

```
<TextView
    android:id="@+id/itemTitle"
    android:layout_width="236dp"
    android:layout_height="39dp"
    android:layout_marginStart="16dp"
    android:textSize="30sp"
    app:layout_constraintLeft_toRightOf="@+id/itemImage"
```

```
        app:layout_constraintStart_toEndOf="@+id/itemImage"
        app:layout_constraintTop_toTopOf="parent"
        tools:text="@sample/chapters" />

<TextView
        android:id="@+id/itemDetail"
        android:layout_width="236dp"
        android:layout_height="16dp"
        android:layout_marginStart="16dp"
        android:layout_marginTop="8dp"
        app:layout_constraintLeft_toRightOf="@+id/itemImage"
        app:layout_constraintStart_toEndOf="@+id/itemImage"
        app:layout_constraintTop_toBottomOf="@+id/itemTitle"
        tools:text="@sample/items" />
```

Rebuild the app and return to the layout design in the *content_main.xml* file where the custom sample data and images should now be displayed within the RecyclerView list:

Figure 49-11

Instead of having two separate text files and a reference to the image set, another option is to declare the sample data within a JSON file. For example:

```
{
  "mydata": [
    {
      "chapter" : "Chapter One",
      "details": "Item one details",
      "image": "@sample/images"
    },
    {
```

```
        "chapter" : "Chapter Two",
        "details": "Item two details",
        "image": "@sample/images"
    },
    .
    .
    .
}
```

Assuming the above was contained within a file named *chapterdata.json*, the sample data would then be referenced within the view XML elements as follows:

.

```
<ImageView
    .
    .
    tools:src="@sample/chapterdata.json/mydata/image" />
<TextView
    .
    .
    tools:text="@sample/chapterdata.json/mydata/chapter" />

<TextView
    .
    .
    tools:text="@sample/chapterdata.json/mydata/details" />
    .
    .
```

49.3 Summary

This chapter has demonstrated the use of sample data within the layout editor to provide a more realistic representation of how the user interface will appear at runtime. The steps covered in this tutorial included the use of both pre-existing sample data templates and the integration of custom sample data.

Chapter 50

50. Working with the AppBar and Collapsing Toolbar Layouts

In this chapter, we will explore how the app bar within an activity layout can be customized and made to react to the scrolling events occurring within other screen views. Using the CoordinatorLayout in conjunction with the AppBarLayout and CollapsingToolbarLayout containers, the app bar can be configured to display an image and to animate in and out of view. For example, an upward scrolling motion on a list can be configured so that the app bar recedes from view and reappears when a downward scrolling motion is performed.

Beginning with an overview of the elements that can comprise an app bar, this chapter will work through various examples of app bar configuration.

50.1 The Anatomy of an AppBar

The app bar is the area that appears at the top of the display when an app is running and can be configured to contain various items, including the status bar, toolbar, tab bar, and a flexible space area. Figure 50-1, for example, shows an app bar containing a status bar, toolbar, and tab bar:

Figure 50-1

A blank background color can fill the flexible space area, or as shown in Figure 50-2, an image displayed on an ImageView object:

Figure 50-2

As will be demonstrated in the remainder of this chapter, if the main content area of the activity user interface layout contains scrollable content, the elements of the app bar can be configured to expand and contract as the content on the screen is scrolled.

50.2 The Example Project

For this example, changes will be made to the CardDemo project created in the earlier chapter entitled *"An Android RecyclerView and CardView Tutorial"*. Begin by launching Android Studio and loading this project.

Once the project has loaded, run the app and note when scrolling the list upwards that the toolbar remains visible, as shown in Figure 50-3:

Figure 50-3

The first step is to make configuration changes so the toolbar contracts during an upward scrolling motion and then expands on a downward scroll.

50.3 Coordinating the RecyclerView and Toolbar

Load the *activity_main.xml* file into the Layout Editor tool, switch to Code mode, and review the XML layout design, the hierarchy of which is represented by the diagram in Figure 50-4:

Figure 50-4

At the top level of the hierarchy is the CoordinatorLayout, which, as the name suggests, coordinates the interactions between the various child view elements it contains. As highlighted in *"Working with the Floating*

Working with the AppBar and Collapsing Toolbar Layouts

Action Button and Snackbar" for example, the CoordinatorLayout automatically slides the floating action button upwards to accommodate the appearance of a Snackbar when it appears, then moves the button back down after the bar is dismissed.

The CoordinatorLayout can similarly be used to cause elements of the app bar to slide in and out of view based on the scrolling action of certain views within the view hierarchy. One element within the layout hierarchy shown in Figure 50-4 is the ConstraintLayout. To achieve this coordinated behavior, it is necessary to set properties on the element on which scrolling takes place and the elements with which the scrolling is to be coordinated.

On the scrolling element (in this case, the RecyclerView), the *android:layout_behavior* property must be set to *appbar_scrolling_view_behavior*. Within the *content_main.xml* file, locate the top-level ConstraintLayout element and note that this property has been set by default:

```
<androidx.constraintlayout.widget.ConstraintLayout
    xmlns:android="http://schemas.android.com/apk/res/android"
    xmlns:app="http://schemas.android.com/apk/res-auto"
    xmlns:tools="http://schemas.android.com/tools"
    android:layout_width="match_parent"
    android:layout_height="match_parent"
    app:layout_behavior="@string/appbar_scrolling_view_behavior" >
```

Next, open the *activity_main.xml* file in the layout editor, switch to Code mode, and locate the AppBarLayout element. Note that the only child of AppBarLayout in the view hierarchy is the Toolbar. To make the toolbar react to the scroll events occurring in the RecyclerView, the *app:layout_scrollFlags* property must be set on this element. The value assigned to this property will depend on the nature of the interaction required and must consist of one or more of the following:

- **scroll** – Indicates that the view is to be scrolled off the screen. If this is not set, the view will remain pinned at the top of the screen during scrolling events.

- **enterAlways** – When used with the *scroll* option, an upward scrolling motion will cause the view to retract. Any downward scrolling motion in this mode will cause the view to reappear.

- **enterAlwaysCollapsed** – When set on a view, that view will not expand from the collapsed state until the downward scrolling motion reaches the limit of the list. If the *minHeight* property is set, the view will appear during the initial scrolling motion but only until the minimum height is reached. It will then remain at that height and will not expand fully until the top of the list is reached. Note that this option only works when used with both the *enterAlways* and *scroll* options. For example:

```
app:layout_scrollFlags="scroll|enterAlways|enterAlwaysCollapsed"
android:minHeight="20dp"
```

- **exitUntilCollapsed** – When set, the view will collapse during an upward scrolling motion until the minHeight threshold is met. At that point, it will remain at that height until the scroll direction changes.

For this example, the *scroll* and *enterAlways* options will be set on the Toolbar as follows:

```
<com.google.android.material.appbar.MaterialToolbar
    android:id="@+id/toolbar"
    android:layout_width="match_parent"
    android:layout_height="?attr/actionBarSize"
    app:layout_scrollFlags="scroll|enterAlways" />
```

With the appropriate properties set, rerun the app and make an upward scrolling motion in the RecyclerView list. This should cause the toolbar to collapse out of view (Figure 50-5). A downward scrolling motion should cause the toolbar to reappear.

Figure 50-5

50.4 Introducing the Collapsing Toolbar Layout

The CollapsingToolbarLayout container enhances the standard toolbar by providing a greater range of options and control over the collapsing of the app bar and its children in response to coordinated scrolling actions. The CollapsingToolbarLayout class is intended to be added as a child of the AppBarLayout. It provides features such as automatically adjusting the font size of the toolbar title as the toolbar collapses and expands. A *parallax* mode allows designated content in the app bar to fade from view as it collapses, while a *pin* mode allows elements of the app bar to remain in a fixed position during the contraction.

A *scrim* option is also available to designate the color to which the toolbar should transition during the collapse sequence.

To see these features in action, the app bar contained in the *activity_main.xml* file will be modified to use the CollapsingToolbarLayout class together with the addition of an ImageView to demonstrate the effect of parallax mode better. The new view hierarchy that makes use of the CollapsingToolbarLayout is represented by the diagram in Figure 50-6:

Figure 50-6

Load the *activity_main.xml* file into the Layout Editor tool in Code mode and modify the layout so that it reads as follows:

```xml
<?xml version="1.0" encoding="utf-8"?>
<androidx.coordinatorlayout.widget.CoordinatorLayout xmlns:android="http://schemas.android.com/apk/res/android"
    xmlns:app="http://schemas.android.com/apk/res-auto"
    xmlns:tools="http://schemas.android.com/tools"
    android:layout_width="match_parent"
    android:layout_height="match_parent"
    android:fitsSystemWindows="true"
    tools:context=".MainActivity">

    <com.google.android.material.appbar.AppBarLayout
        android:layout_width="match_parent"
        android:layout_height="wrap_content"
        android:fitsSystemWindows="true">

        <com.google.android.material.appbar.CollapsingToolbarLayout
            android:id="@+id/collapsing_toolbar"
            android:layout_width="match_parent"
            android:layout_height="match_parent"
            app:layout_scrollFlags="scroll|enterAlways"
            android:fitsSystemWindows="true"
            app:expandedTitleMarginBottom="30dp"
            app:expandedTitleMarginStart="15dp"
            app:expandedTitleMarginEnd="64dp">

            <ImageView
                android:id="@+id/backdrop"
                android:layout_width="match_parent"
                android:layout_height="200dp"
                android:scaleType="centerCrop"
                android:fitsSystemWindows="true"
                app:layout_collapseMode="parallax"
                android:src="@drawable/appbar_image" />

            <com.google.android.material.appbar.MaterialToolbar
                android:id="@+id/toolbar"
                android:layout_width="match_parent"
                android:layout_height="?attr/actionBarSize"
                app:layout_scrollFlags="scroll|enterAlways"
                app:layout_collapseMode="pin" />
        </com.google.android.material.appbar.CollapsingToolbarLayout>

    </com.google.android.material.appbar.AppBarLayout>

    <include
```

Working with the AppBar and Collapsing Toolbar Layouts

```
        android:id="@+id/contentMain"
        layout="@layout/content_main" />
```

`</androidx.coordinatorlayout.widget.CoordinatorLayout>`

Using the file system navigator for your operating system, locate the *appbar_image.jpg* image file in the *project_icons* folder of the code sample download for the book and copy it. Right-click on the *app -> res -> drawable* entry in the Project tool window and select *Paste* from the resulting menu.

When run, the app bar should appear as illustrated in Figure 50-7:

Figure 50-7

Scrolling the list upwards will cause the app bar to collapse gradually. During the contraction, the image will fade to the color defined by the scrim property while the title text font size reduces at a corresponding rate until only the toolbar is visible:

Figure 50-8

The toolbar has remained visible during the initial stages of the scrolling motion (the toolbar will also recede from view if the upward scrolling motion continues) as the flexible area collapses because the toolbar element in the *activity_main.xml* file was configured to use pin mode:

`app:layout_collapseMode="pin"`

Had the collapse mode been set to parallax, the toolbar would have retracted along with the image view.

Continuing the upward scrolling motion will cause the toolbar also to collapse, leaving only the status bar visible:

Working with the AppBar and Collapsing Toolbar Layouts

Figure 50-9

Since the scroll flags property for the CollapsingToolbarLayout element includes the enterAlways option, a downward scrolling motion will cause the app bar to expand again.

To fix the toolbar in place so that it no longer recedes from view during the upward scrolling motion, replace *enterAlways* with *exitUntilCollapsed* in the *layout_scrollFlags* property of the CollapsingToolbarLayout element in the *activity_main.xml* file as follows:

```
<com.google.android.material.appbar.CollapsingToolbarLayout
    android:id="@+id/collapsing_toolbar"
    android:layout_width="match_parent"
    android:layout_height="match_parent"
    app:layout_scrollFlags="scroll|exitUntilCollapsed"
    android:fitsSystemWindows="true"
    app:expandedTitleMarginBottom="30dp"
    app:expandedTitleMarginStart="15dp"
    app:expandedTitleMarginEnd="64dp">
```

50.5 Changing the Title and Scrim Color

As a final task, edit the *MainActivity.java* file and add some code to the *onCreate()* method to change the title text on the collapsing layout manager instance and to set a different scrim color (note that the scrim color may also be set within the layout resource file):

```
package com.ebookfrenzy.carddemo;
.
.
import com.google.android.material.appbar.CollapsingToolbarLayout;
import android.graphics.Color;
.
.
.
    @Override
    protected void onCreate(Bundle savedInstanceState) {
        super.onCreate(savedInstanceState);

        binding = ActivityMainBinding.inflate(getLayoutInflater());
        setContentView(binding.getRoot());
```

423

```
        setSupportActionBar(binding.toolbar);

        binding.collapsingToolbar.setTitle("My Toolbar Title");
        binding.collapsingToolbar.setContentScrimColor(Color.GREEN);

        layoutManager = new LinearLayoutManager(this);
        binding.contentMain.recyclerView.setLayoutManager(layoutManager);

        adapter = new RecyclerAdapter();
        binding.contentMain.recyclerView.setAdapter(adapter);
    }
```

·
·

Run the app one last time and note that the new title appears in the app bar and that scrolling now causes the toolbar to transition to green as it retracts from view.

50.6 Summary

The app bar at the top of most Android apps can consist of several elements, including a toolbar, tab layout, and image view. When embedded in a CoordinatorLayout parent, several different options are available to control how the app bar behaves in response to scrolling events in the main content of the activity. For greater control over this behavior, the CollapsingToolbarLayout manager provides a range of additional levels of control over how the app bar content expands and contracts relative to scrolling activity.

Chapter 51

51. An Android Studio Primary/Detail Flow Tutorial

This chapter will explain the concept of the Primary/Detail user interface design before exploring, in detail, the elements that make up the Primary/Detail Flow template included with Android Studio. An example application will then be created that demonstrates the steps involved in modifying the template to meet the specific needs of the application developer.

51.1 The Primary/Detail Flow

A primary/detail flow is an interface design concept whereby a list of items (referred to as the *primary list*) is displayed to the user. On selecting an item from the list, additional information relating to that item is then presented to the user within a *detail* pane. An email application might, for example, consist of a primary list of received messages consisting of the address of the sender and the subject of the message. Upon selection of a message from the primary list, the body of the email message would appear within the detail pane.

On tablet sized Android device displays in landscape orientation, the primary list appears in a narrow vertical panel along the left-hand edge of the screen. The remainder of the display is devoted to the detail pane in an arrangement referred to as *two-pane mode*. Figure 51-1, for example, shows the primary/detail, two-pane arrangement with primary items listed and the content of item one displayed in the detail pane:

Figure 51-1

On smaller, phone sized Android devices, the primary list takes up the entire screen and the detail pane appears on a separate screen which appears when a selection is made from the primary list. In this mode, the detail screen includes an action bar entry to return to the primary list. Figure 51-2 for example, illustrates both the primary and detail screens for the same item list on a 4" phone screen:

Figure 51-2

51.2 Creating a Primary/Detail Flow Activity

In the next section of this chapter, the different elements that comprise the Primary/Detail Flow template will be covered in some detail. This is best achieved by creating a project using the Primary/Detail Views Flow template to use while working through the information. This project will subsequently be used as the basis for the tutorial at the end of the chapter.

Select the *New Project* option from the welcome screen and, within the resulting new project dialog, choose the No Activity template before clicking on the Next button.

Enter *PrimaryDetailFlow* into the Name field and specify *com.ebookfrenzy.primarydetailflow* as the package name. Before clicking on the Finish button, change the Minimum API level setting to API 26: Android 8.0 (Oreo) and the Language menu to Java.

51.3 Adding the Primary/Detail Flow Activity

In the Project tool window, right-click on the *app -> java -> com.ebookfrenzy.primarydetailflow* entry and select the *New -> Activity -> Primary/Detail Views Flow* menu option. In the new activity dialog (Figure 51-3), make sure the Launcher Activity checkbox is enabled before clicking the Finish button:

An Android Studio Primary/Detail Flow Tutorial

Figure 51-3

51.4 Modifying the Primary/Detail Flow Template

While the structure of the Primary/Detail Flow template can appear confusing at first, as will become evident, much of the functionality provided by the template can remain unchanged for many primary/detail implementation requirements.

In the rest of this chapter, the *PrimaryDetailFlow* project will be modified such that the primary list displays a list of website names and the detail pane altered to contain a WebView object instead of the current TextView. When a website is selected by the user, the corresponding web page will subsequently load and display in the detail pane.

51.5 Changing the Content Model

The content for the example as it currently stands is defined by the *PlaceholderContent* class file. Begin, therefore, by selecting the *PlaceholderContent.java* file (located in the Project tool window in the *app -> java -> com.ebookfrenzy.primarydetailflow -> placeholder* folder) and reviewing the code. At the bottom of the file is a declaration for a class named *PlaceholderItem* which is currently able to store three String objects representing content and details strings and an ID. The updated project, on the other hand, will need each item object to contain an ID string, a string for the website name, and a string for the corresponding URL of the website. To add these features, modify the *PlaceholderItem* class so that it reads as follows:

```
public static class PlaceholderItem {
    public String id;
    public String website_name;
    public String website_url;

    public PlaceholderItem(String id, String website_name,
        String website_url)
    {
        this.id = id;
```

An Android Studio Primary/Detail Flow Tutorial

```
            this.website_name = website_name;
            this.website_url = website_url;
    }

    @Override
    public String toString() {
        return website_name;
    }
}
```

Note that the encapsulating PlaceholderContent class currently contains a *for* loop that adds 25 items by making multiple calls to methods named *createPlaceholderItem()* and *makeDetails()*. Much of this code will no longer be required and should be deleted from the class as follows:

```
public static final Map<String, PlaceholderItem> ITEM_MAP = new HashMap<String, PlaceholderItem>();

private static final int COUNT = 25;

static {
    // Add some sample items.
    for (int i = 1; i <= COUNT; i++) {
        addItem(createPlaceholderItem(i));
    }
}

private static void addItem(PlaceholderItem item) {
    ITEMS.add(item);
    ITEM_MAP.put(item.id, item);
}

private static PlaceholderItem createPlaceholderItem(int position) {
    return new PlaceholderItem(String.valueOf(position), "Item " + position, makeDetails(position));
}

private static String makeDetails(int position) {
    StringBuilder builder = new StringBuilder();
    builder.append("Details about Item: ").append(position);
    for (int i = 0; i < position; i++) {
        builder.append("\nMore details information here.");
    }
    return builder.toString();
}
```

This code needs to be modified to initialize the data model with the required website data:

```
public static final Map<String, PlaceholderItem> ITEM_MAP =
        new HashMap<String, PlaceholderItem>();
```

```
static {
    // Add 3 sample items.
     addItem(new PlaceholderItem("1", "eBookFrenzy",
             "https://www.ebookfrenzy.com"));
     addItem(new PlaceholderItem("2", "Amazon",
             "https://www.amazon.com"));
     addItem(new PlaceholderItem("3", "New York Times",
             "https://www.nytimes.com"));
}
```

The code now takes advantage of the modified PlaceholderItem class to store an ID, website name and URL for each item.

51.6 Changing the Detail Pane

The layout for the detail pane (the screen that is displayed when the user selects an item from the primary list) is contained within the *activity_item_detail.xml* file which, in turn, contains a FrameContainerView instance which is used to display the actual detail pane content. If the app is displaying in single-pane mode, the frame container will display the layout contained in the *fragment_item_detail.xml* file, while multi-pane mode will display the *fragment_item_detail.xml* (sw600dp) layout.

The template layout provided by Android Studio for the *fragment_item_detail.xml* comprises a Coordinator layout containing an app bar, toolbar, floating action button, and a text view. For this example, all we need to display is a WebView, so open this file and delete all of the views from the layout with the exception of the *item_detail_container* view. The easiest way to do this is to select all of the unwanted views in the Component Tree as shown in below before tapping the keyboard delete key:

Figure 51-4

Drag a WebView object from the Widgets section of the Palette and drop it onto the center of the layout canvas and change the id to *website_detail*.

Next, edit the *fragment_item_detail.xml* (sw600dp) file and delete the default TextView instance before dragging and dropping a WebView onto the layout, once again changing the id to *website_detail*. The layout for both files should now resemble Figure 51-5:

An Android Studio Primary/Detail Flow Tutorial

Figure 51-5

51.7 Modifying the ItemDetailFragment Class

At this point the user interface detail pane has been modified but the corresponding Java class is still designed for working with a TextView object instead of a WebView. Load the source code for this class by double-clicking on the *ItemDetailFragment.java* file in the Project tool window.

To load the web page URL corresponding to the currently selected item only a few lines of code need to be changed. Once this change has been made, the code should read as follows:

```
.
.
import android.webkit.WebResourceRequest;
import android.webkit.WebView;
import android.webkit.WebViewClient;
.
.
public class ItemDetailFragment extends Fragment {
.
.
    @Override
    public View onCreateView(LayoutInflater inflater, ViewGroup container,
                        Bundle savedInstanceState) {

        binding = FragmentItemDetailBinding.inflate(inflater, container, false);
        View rootView = binding.getRoot();

        mToolbarLayout = rootView.findViewById(R.id.toolbar_layout);
        mTextView = binding.ItemDetail;

        updateContent();
        rootView.setOnDragListener(dragListener);
        return rootView;
    }
```

```
    private void updateContent() {
        if (mItem != null) {
            binding.websiteDetail.setWebViewClient(new WebViewClient(){
                @Override
                public boolean shouldOverrideUrlLoading(
                        WebView view, WebResourceRequest request) {
                    return super.shouldOverrideUrlLoading(
                            view, request);
                }
            });
            binding.websiteDetail.loadUrl(mItem.website_url);
        }
    }
.
.
.
}
```

In the above code, changes are made to delete references to the toolbar layout and item detail text elements which were previously removed from the *fragment_item_detail.xml* file.

Next, *updateContent()* is modified to access the *website_detail* view (this was formally the TextView but is now a WebView) and extract the URL of the website from the selected item. An instance of the WebViewClient class is created and assigned the *shouldOverrideUrlLoading()* callback method. This method is implemented so as to force the system to use the WebView instance to load the page instead of the Chrome browser.

51.8 Modifying the ItemListFragment Class

A minor change also needs to be made to the *ItemListFragment.java* file to make sure that the website names appear in the primary list. Edit this file, locate the *onBindViewHolder()* method and modify the *setText()* method call to reference the website name as follows:

```
@Override
public void onBindViewHolder(final ViewHolder holder, int position) {
    holder.mIdView.setText(mValues.get(position).id);
    holder.mContentView.setText(mValues.get(position).website_name);
.
.
        // identify the id of the content
        ClipData.Item clipItem = new ClipData.Item(mValues.get(position).id);
        ClipData dragData = new ClipData(
                ((PlaceholderContent.PlaceholderItem) v.getTag()).website_name,
                new String[]{ClipDescription.MIMETYPE_TEXT_PLAIN},
                clipItem
        );
.
.
```

51.9 Adding Manifest Permissions

The final step is to add internet permission to the application via the manifest file. This will enable the WebView object to access the internet and download web pages. Navigate to, and load the *AndroidManifest.xml* file in the Project tool window (*app -> manifests*), and double-click on it to load it into the editor. Once loaded, add the appropriate permission line to the file:

```
<?xml version="1.0" encoding="utf-8"?>
<manifest xmlns:android="http://schemas.android.com/apk/res/android"
    package="com.ebookfrenzy.PrimaryDetailflow" >

    <uses-permission android:name="android.permission.INTERNET" />

    <application
        android:allowBackup="true"
.
.
```

51.10 Running the Application

Compile and run the application on a suitably configured emulator or an attached Android device. Depending on the size of the display, the application will appear either in small screen or two-pane mode. Regardless, the primary list should appear primed with the names of the three websites defined in the content model. Selecting an item should cause the corresponding website to appear in the detail pane as illustrated in two-pane mode in Figure 51-6:

Figure 51-6

Note that the build may fail with the following error:

```
Duplicate class kotlin.collections.jdk8.CollectionsJDK8Kt found in modules
jetified-kotlin-stdlib-1.8.0
```

To correct this error, edit the *build.gradle (Module: app)* file, add the following dependency, and sync and rebuilt the project:

```
dependencies {
.
.
    implementation(platform('org.jetbrains.kotlin:kotlin-bom:1.8.0'))
```

51.11 Summary

A primary/detail user interface consists of a primary list of items which, when selected, displays additional information about that selection within a detail pane. The Primary/Detail Flow is a template provided with Android Studio that allows a primary/detail arrangement to be created quickly and with relative ease. As demonstrated in this chapter, with minor modifications to the default template files, a wide range of primary/detail based functionality can be implemented with minimal coding and design effort.

52. An Overview of Android Services

The Android Service class is designed to allow applications to initiate and perform background tasks. Unlike broadcast receivers, which are intended to perform a task quickly and then exit, services are designed to perform tasks that take a long time to complete (such as downloading a file over an internet connection or streaming music to the user) but do not require a user interface.

This chapter will provide an overview of the services available, including *bound* and *intent services*. Once these basics have been covered, subsequent chapters will work through some examples of services in action.

52.1 Intent Service

As previously outlined, services run by default within the same main thread as the component from which they are launched. As such, any CPU-intensive tasks that need to be performed by the service should occur within a new thread, thereby avoiding impacting the performance of the calling application.

The *JobIntentService* class is a convenience class (subclassed from the Service class) that sets up a worker thread for handling background tasks and handles each request asynchronously. Once the service has handled all queued requests, it exits. All that is required when using the JobIntentService class is to implement the *onHandleWork()* method, containing the code to be executed for each request.

For services that do not require synchronous processing of requests, JobIntentService is the recommended option. However, services requiring synchronous handling of requests will need to subclass from the Service class and manually implement and manage threading to handle any CPU-intensive tasks efficiently.

52.2 Bound Service

A bound service allows a launching component to interact with and receive results from the service. This interaction can also occur across process boundaries through the implementation of interprocess communication (IPC). An activity might, for example, start a service to handle audio playback. The activity will, in all probability, include a user interface providing controls to the user to pause playback or skip to the next track. Similarly, the service will likely need to communicate information to the calling activity to indicate that the current audio track has ended and provide details of the next track that is about to start playing.

A component (referred to in this context as a *client*) starts and *binds* to a bound service via a call to the *bindService()* method. Also, multiple components may bind to a service simultaneously. When a client no longer requires the service binding, a call should be made to the *unbindService()* method. When the last bound client unbinds from a service, the Android runtime system will terminate the service. It is important to remember that a bound service may also be started via a call to *startService()*. Once started, components may then bind to it via *bindService()* calls. When a bound service is launched via a call to *startService()*, it will continue to run even after the last client unbinds from it.

A bound service must include an implementation of the *onBind()* method, which is called both when the service is initially created and when other clients subsequently bind to the running service. The purpose of this method is to return to binding clients an object of type *IBinder* containing the information needed by the client to communicate with the service.

When implementing the communication between a client and a bound service, the recommended technique depends on whether the client and service reside in the same or different processes and whether or not the service is private to the client. Local communication can be achieved by extending the Binder class and returning an instance from the *onBind()* method. Interprocess communication, on the other hand, requires Messenger and Handler implementation. Details of both of these approaches will be covered in later chapters.

52.3 The Anatomy of a Service

As has already been mentioned, a service must be created as a subclass of the Android Service class (more specifically, *android.app.Service*) or a sub-class thereof (such as *android.app.IntentService*). As part of the subclassing procedure, one or more of the following superclass callback methods must be overridden, depending on the exact nature of the service being created:

- **onStartCommand()** – This method is called when another component starts the service via a call to the *startService()* method. This method does not need to be implemented for bound services.

- **onBind()** – Called when a component binds to the service via a call to the *bindService()* method. When implementing a bound service, this method must return an *IBinder* object facilitating communication with the client.

- **onCreate()** – Intended as a location to perform initialization tasks, this method is called immediately before the call to either *onStartCommand()* or the *first* call to the *onBind()* method.

- **onDestroy()** – Called when the service is being destroyed.

- **onHandleWork()** – Applies only to JobIntentService subclasses. This method is called to handle the processing for the service. It is executed in a separate thread from the main application.

Note that the IntentService class includes its own implementations of the *onStartCommand()* and *onBind()* callback methods, so these do not need to be implemented in subclasses.

52.4 Controlling Destroyed Service Restart Options

The *onStartCommand()* callback method is required to return an integer value to define what should happen with regard to the service if the Android runtime system destroys it. Possible return values for these methods are as follows:

- **START_NOT_STICKY** – Indicates to the system that the service should not be restarted if it is destroyed unless there are pending intents awaiting delivery.

- **START_STICKY** – Indicates that the service should be restarted as soon as possible after it has been destroyed if the destruction occurred after the *onStartCommand()* method returned. If no pending intents are waiting to be delivered, the *onStartCommand()* callback method is called with a NULL intent value. The intent being processed when the service was destroyed is discarded.

- **START_REDELIVER_INTENT** – Indicates that if the service was destroyed after returning from the *onStartCommand()* callback method, the service should be restarted with the current intent redelivered to the *onStartCommand()* method followed by any pending intents.

52.5 Declaring a Service in the Manifest File

For a service to be usable, it must first be declared within a manifest file. This involves embedding an appropriately configured <service> element into an existing <application> entry. At a minimum, the <service> element must contain a property declaring the class name of the service, as illustrated in the following XML fragment:

```
<application
```

```
            android:icon="@mipmap/ic_launcher"
            android:label="@string/app_name" >
            <activity
                android:label="@string/app_name"
                android:name=".MainActivity" >
                <intent-filter>
                  <action android:name="android.intent.action.MAIN" />
                  <category android:name="android.intent.category.LAUNCHER" />
                </intent-filter>
            </activity>
            <service android:name=".MyService>
            </service>
    </application>
</manifest>
```

By default, services are declared public in that they can be accessed by components outside the application package in which they reside. To make a service private, the *android:exported* property must be declared as *false* within the <service> element of the manifest file. For example:

```
<service android:name="MyService"
            android:exported="false">
</service>
```

When working with JobIntentService, the manifest Service declaration must also request the BIND_JOB_SERVICE permission as follows:

```
<service
    android:name=".MyJobIntentService"
    android:permission="android.permission.BIND_JOB_SERVICE" />
```

As previously discussed, services run within the same process as the calling component by default. To force a service to run within its own process, add an *android:process* property to the <service> element, declaring a name for the process prefixed with a colon (:):

```
<service android:name=".MyService"
    android:exported="false"
    android:process=":myprocess">
</service>
```

The colon prefix indicates that the new process is private to the local application. If the process name begins with a lowercase letter instead of a colon, however, the process will be global and available for use by other components.

Finally, using the same intent filter mechanisms outlined for activities, a service may also advertise capabilities to other applications running on the device. For more details on intent filters, refer to the chapter *"An Overview of Android Intents"*.

52.6 Starting a Service Running on System Startup

Given the background nature of services, it is not uncommon for a service to need to be started when an Android-based system first boots up. This can be achieved by creating a broadcast receiver with an intent filter configured to listen for the system *android.intent.action.BOOT_COMPLETED* intent. When such an intent is detected, the broadcast receiver would invoke the necessary service and then return. Note that, to function, such a broadcast receiver must request the *android.permission.RECEIVE_BOOT_COMPLETED* permission.

52.7 Summary

Android services are a powerful mechanism that allows applications to perform tasks in the background. A service, once launched, will continue to run regardless of whether the calling application is the foreground task or not and even if the component that initiated the service is destroyed.

Services are subclassed from the Android Service class. Bound services provide a communication interface to other client components and generally run until the last client unbinds from the service.

By default, services run locally within the same process and main thread as the calling application. A new thread should, therefore, be created within the service to handle CPU-intensive tasks. Remote services may be started within a separate process by making a minor configuration change to the corresponding <service> entry in the application manifest file.

The IntentService class (a subclass of the Android Service class) provides a convenient mechanism for handling asynchronous service requests within a separate worker thread.

Chapter 53

53. An Overview of Android Intents

By this stage of the book, it should be clear that Android applications comprise one or more activities, among other things. However, an area that has yet to be covered in extensive detail is the mechanism by which one activity can trigger the launch of another activity. As outlined briefly in the chapter entitled *"The Anatomy of an Android Application"*, this is achieved primarily using *Intents*.

Before working through some Android Studio-based example implementations of intents in the following chapters, this chapter aims to provide an overview of intents in the form of *explicit intents* and *implicit intents*, together with an introduction to *intent filters*.

53.1 An Overview of Intents

Intents (*android.content.Intent*) are the messaging system by which one activity can launch another activity. An activity can, for example, issue an intent to request the launch of another activity contained within the same application. Intents also go beyond this concept by allowing an activity to request the services of any other appropriately registered activity on the device for which permissions are configured. Consider, for example, an activity contained within an application that requires a web page to be loaded and displayed to the user. Rather than the application having to contain a second activity to perform this task, the code can send an intent to the Android runtime requesting the services of any activity that has registered the ability to display a web page. The runtime system will match the request to available activities on the device and either launch the activity that matches or, in the event of multiple matches, allow the user to decide which activity to use.

Intents also allow data transfer from the sending to the receiving activity. In the previously outlined scenario, for example, the sending activity would need to send the URL of the web page to be displayed to the second activity. Similarly, the receiving activity may be configured to return data to the sending activity when the required tasks are completed.

Though not covered until later chapters, it is also worth highlighting that, in addition to launching activities, intents are also used to launch and communicate with services and broadcast receivers.

Intents are categorized as either *explicit* or *implicit*.

53.2 Explicit Intents

An *explicit intent* requests the launch of a specific activity by referencing the target activity's component name (which is the class name). This approach is most common when launching an activity residing in the same application as the sending activity (since the class name is known to the developer).

An explicit intent is issued by creating an instance of the Intent class, passing through the activity context and the component name of the activity to be launched. A call is then made to the *startActivity()* method, passing the intent object as an argument. For example, the following code fragment issues an intent for the activity with the class name ActivityB to be launched:

```
Intent i = new Intent(this, ActivityB.class);
startActivity(i);
```

Data may be transmitted to the receiving activity by adding it to the intent object before it is started via calls to the *putExtra()* method of the intent object. Data must be added in the form of key-value pairs. The following code extends the previous example to add String and integer values with the keys "myString" and "myInt"

An Overview of Android Intents

respectively, to the intent:

```
Intent i = new Intent(this, ActivityB.class);
i.putExtra("myString", "This is a message for ActivityB");
i.putExtra("myInt", 100);

startActivity(i);
```

The target activity receives the data as part of a Bundle object which can be obtained via a call to *getIntent()*. *getExtras()*. The *getIntent()* method of the Activity class returns the intent that started the activity, while the *getExtras()* method (of the Intent class) returns a Bundle object containing the data. For example, to extract the data values passed to ActivityB:

```
Bundle extras = getIntent().getExtras();
if (extras != null) {
    String myString = extras.getString("myString");
    int myInt = extras.getInt("myInt");
}
```

When using intents to launch other activities within the same application, those activities must be listed in the application manifest file. The following *AndroidManifest.xml* contents are correctly configured for an application containing activities named ActivityA and ActivityB:

```
<?xml version="1.0" encoding="utf-8"?>
<manifest xmlns:android="http://schemas.android.com/apk/res/android"
    package="com.ebookfrenzy.intent1.intent1" >

    <application
        android:icon="@mipmap/ic_launcher"
        android:label="@string/app_name" >
        <activity
            android:label="@string/app_name"
            android:name="com.ebookfrenzy.intent1.intent1.ActivityA" >
            <intent-filter>
              <action android:name="android.intent.action.MAIN" />
              <category android:name="android.intent.category.LAUNCHER" />
            </intent-filter>
        </activity>
        <activity
            android:name="ActivityB"
            android:label="ActivityB" >
        </activity>
    </application>
</manifest>
```

53.3 Returning Data from an Activity

As the example in the previous section stands, while data is transferred to ActivityB, there is no way for data to be returned to the first activity (which we will call ActivityA). This can, however, be achieved by launching ActivityB as a *sub-activity* of ActivityA. An activity is started as a sub-activity by creating an ActivityResultLauncher instance. An ActivityResultLauncher instance is created by a call to the *registerForActivityResult()* method and is

An Overview of Android Intents

passed a callback handler in the form of a lambda. This handler will be called and passed return data when the sub-activity returns. Once an ActivityResultLauncher instance has been created, it can be called with an intent parameter to launch the sub-activity. The code to create an ActivityResultLauncher instance typically reads as follows:

```
ActivityResultLauncher<Intent> startForResult = registerForActivityResult(
        new ActivityResultContracts.StartActivityForResult(),
        new ActivityResultCallback<ActivityResult>() {
            @Override
            public void onActivityResult(ActivityResult result) {
                if (result.getResultCode() == Activity.RESULT_OK) {
                    Intent data = result.getData();
                    // Code to handle returned data
                }
            }
        });
```

Once the launcher is ready, it can be called and passed the intent to be launched as follows:

```
Intent i = new Intent(this, ActivityB.class);
.
.
.
startForResult.launch(i);
```

To return data to the parent activity, the sub-activity must implement the *finish()* method, the purpose of which is to create a new intent object containing the data to be returned and then call the *setResult()* method of the enclosing activity, passing through a *result code* and the intent containing the return data. The result code is typically *RESULT_OK,* or *RESULT_CANCELED,* but it may also be a custom value subject to the developer's requirements. If a sub-activity crashes, the parent activity will receive a *RESULT_CANCELED* result code.

The following code, for example, illustrates the code for a typical sub-activity *finish()* method:

```
public void finish() {
        Intent data = new Intent();

        data.putExtra("returnString1", "Message to parent activity");
        setResult(RESULT_OK, data);
        super.finish();
}
```

53.4 Implicit Intents

Unlike explicit intents, which reference the class name of the activity to be launched, implicit intents identify the activity to be launched by specifying the action to be performed and the type of data to be handled by the receiving activity. For example, an action type of ACTION_VIEW accompanied by the URL of a web page in the form of a URI object will instruct the Android system to search for and, subsequently, launch a web browser-capable activity. The following implicit intent will, when executed on an Android device, result in the designated web page appearing in a web browser activity:

```
Intent intent = new Intent(Intent.ACTION_VIEW,
        Uri.parse("https://www.ebookfrenzy.com"));

startActivity(intent);
```

An Overview of Android Intents

When an activity issues the above implicit intent, the Android system will search for activities on the device that have registered the ability to handle ACTION_VIEW requests on HTTP scheme data using a process referred to as *intent resolution*. Before the system launches an activity using an implicit intent, the user must either verify or enable that activity. If neither of these conditions has been met, the activity will not be launched by the intent. Before exploring these two options, we first need to talk about intent filters.

53.5 Using Intent Filters

Intent filters are the mechanism by which activities "advertise" supported actions and data handling capabilities to the Android intent resolution process. These declarations also include the settings required to perform the link verification process. The following *AndroidManifest.xml* file illustrates a configuration for an activity named *WebActivity* within an app named *MyWebView* with an appropriately configured intent filter:

```xml
<?xml version="1.0" encoding="utf-8"?>
.
.
    <application
        android:allowBackup="true"
        android:icon="@mipmap/ic_launcher"
        android:label="@string/app_name"
        android:roundIcon="@mipmap/ic_launcher_round"
        android:supportsRtl="true"
        android:theme="@style/Theme.MyWebView">
        <activity
            android:name="WebActivity"
            android:exported="true">
            <intent-filter android:autoVerify="true">
                <action android:name="android.intent.action.VIEW" />
                <category android:name="android.intent.category.BROWSABLE" />
                <category android:name="android.intent.category.DEFAULT" />
                <data android:scheme="https" />
                <data android:host="www.ebookfrenzy.com"/>
            </intent-filter>
        </activity>
    </application>
</manifest>
```

This manifest file configures the WebActivity activity to be launched in response to an implicit intent from another activity when the intent contains the *https://www.ebookfrenzy.com* URL. The following code, for example, would launch the WebActivity activity (assuming that the MyWebView app has been verified or enabled by the user as a support link):

```
Intent intent = new Intent(Intent.ACTION_VIEW,
        Uri.parse("https://www.ebookfrenzy.com"));

startActivity(intent);
```

53.6 Automatic Link Verification

Using a web link to launch an activity on an Android device is considered a potential security hazard. To minimize this risk, the link used to launch an intent must either be automatically verified or manually added as a

An Overview of Android Intents

supported link on the device by the user. To enable automatic verification, the corresponding intent declaration in the target activity must set autoVerify to true as follows:

```
<intent-filter android:autoVerify="true">
  .
  .
</intent-filter>
```

Next, the link URL must be associated with the website on which the app link is based. This is achieved by creating a Digital Assets Link file named *assetlinks.json* and installing it within the website's *.well-known* folder.

A digital asset link file comprises a *relation* statement granting permission for a target app to be launched using the website's link URLs and a target statement declaring the companion app package name and SHA-256 certificate fingerprint for that project. A typical asset link file might, for example, read as follows:

```
[{
  "relation": ["delegate_permission/common.handle_all_urls"],
  "target": {
    "namespace": "android_app",
    "package_name": "com.ebookfrenzy.mywebview",
    "sha256_cert_fingerprints":
    ["<your certificate fingerprint here>"]
  }
}]
```

Note that you can either create this file manually or generate it using the online tool available at the following URL:

https://developers.google.com/digital-asset-links/tools/generator

When working with Android, the namespace value is always set to "android_app", while the package name corresponds to the app package to be launched by the intent. Finally, the certificate fingerprint is the hash code used to build the app. When you are testing an app, this will be the debug certificate contained within the *debug.keystore* file. On Windows systems, Android Studio stores this file at the following location:

```
\Users\<your user name>\.android\debug.keystore
```

On macOS and Linux systems, the file can be found at:

```
$HOME/.android/debug.keystore
```

Once you have located the file, the SHA 256 fingerprint can be obtained by running the following command in a terminal or command prompt window:

```
keytool -list -v -keystore <path to debug.keystore file here>
```

When prompted for a password, enter "android" after which output will appear, including the SHA 256 fingerprint:

```
Certificate fingerprints:
         SHA1: 11:E8:66:11:B6:94:3D:AA:7E:50:63:99:77:B8:6A:90:FF:B6:9C:6D
         SHA256: 7F:EE:E3:C8:38:41:C3:EA:11:56:83:94:2A:4C:D2:EA:A0:69:F8:96:D1:17
:77:02:46:EC:AD:6E:3C:64:A9:29
```

When you are ready to build your app's release version, you must ensure you add the release SHA 256 fingerprint to the asset file. Details on generating release keystore files are covered in the chapter entitled *"Creating, Testing, and Uploading an Android App Bundle"*. Once you have a release keystore file, run the above keytool command

An Overview of Android Intents

to access the fingerprint.

Once you have placed the digital asset file in the correct location on the website, install the app on a device or emulator and wait 30 seconds for the link to be verified. To check the verification status, run the following at a command or terminal prompt:

```
adb shell pm get-app-links --user cur com.example.mywebview
```

The resulting output should include confirmation that the link has been verified:

```
com.example.mywebview:
    ID: 0e399bca-bf58-4cfc-8c7b-d1a6c3b065ec
    Signatures: [7F:EE:E3:C8:38:41:C3:EA:11:56:83:94:2A:4C:D2:EA:A0:69:F8:96:D1:1
7:77:02:46:EC:AD:6E:3C:64:A9:29]
    Domain verification state:
      www.ebookfrenzy.com: verified
    User 0:
      Verification link handling allowed: true
      Selection state:
        Disabled:
          www.ebookfrenzy.com
```

You can also check the status from within the Settings app on the device or emulator using the following steps:

1. Launch the Settings app.

2. Select *Apps* from the main list.

3. Locate and select your app from the list of installed apps.

4. On the settings page for your app, choose the *Open by Default* option.

Choose the Open by Default option on your app's settings page.

Once displayed, the page should indicate that a link has been verified, as shown in Figure 53-1:

Figure 53-1

To review which links have been verified, tap on the info button indicated by the arrow in the above figure to display the following panel:

Figure 53-2

The *assetlinks.json* file can contain multiple digital asset links, allowing a single website to be associated with more than one app. If you cannot use auto link verification, add code to your app to prompt the user to enable the link manually.

53.7 Manually Enabling Links

Where it is not possible to auto-verify links using the steps outlined above, the only option is to request that the user manually enable app links. This involves launching the Open by Default screen of the Settings app for the target app where the user can enable the link.

Since the sudden appearance of the Open by Default screen may be confusing to the average user, it is recommended that an explanatory dialog be displayed before launching the Settings app.

To provide the user with the option to enable a link manually, the following code needs to be executed before attempting to launch the intent:

```
.
.
// Code here to display a dialog explaining that the link needs to be enabled
.
.
Intent intent = new Intent(
        Settings.ACTION_APP_OPEN_BY_DEFAULT_SETTINGS,
        Uri.parse("package:com.ebookfrenzy.mywebview"));

startActivity(intent);
```

The above example code will display the Open by Default settings screen for our target MyWebView app, where the user can click on the Add Link button:

Figure 53-3

Once clicked, a dialog will appear initialized with the link passed in the intent. This can be enabled by setting the checkbox as shown in Figure 53-4:

Figure 53-4

53.8 Checking Intent Availability

It is generally unwise to assume that an activity will be available for a particular intent, especially since the absence of a matching action typically results in the application crashing. Fortunately, it is possible to identify the availability of an activity for a specific intent before it is sent to the runtime system. The following method can be used to identify the availability of an activity for a specified intent action type:

```
public static boolean isIntentAvailable(Context context, String action) {
    final PackageManager packageManager = context.getPackageManager();
    final Intent intent = new Intent(action);
    List<ResolveInfo> list =
```

```
            packageManager.queryIntentActivities(intent,
                   PackageManager.MATCH_DEFAULT_ONLY);
    return list.size() > 0;
}
```

53.9 Summary

Intents are the messaging mechanism by which one Android activity can launch another. An explicit intent references a specific activity to be launched by referencing the receiving activity by class name. Explicit intents are typically, though not exclusively, used when launching activities within the same application. An implicit intent specifies the action to be performed and the type of data to be handled and lets the Android runtime find a matching activity to launch. Implicit intents are generally used when launching activities that reside in different applications.

When working with implicit intents, security restrictions require the user to automatically verify or manually enable the app containing the intent activity target before launching the intent. Automatic verification involves the placement of a Digital Assets Link file on the website corresponding to the link URL.

An activity can send data to the receiving activity by bundling data into the intent object as key-value pairs. Data can only be returned from an activity if it is started as a sub-activity of the sending activity.

Activities advertise capabilities to the Android intent resolution process by specifying intent filters in the application manifest file. Both sending and receiving activities must also request appropriate permissions to perform tasks such as accessing the device contact database or the internet.

Having covered the theory of intents, the next few chapters will work through creating some examples in Android Studio that put both explicit and implicit intents into action.

Chapter 54

54. Android Explicit Intents – A Worked Example

The chapter entitled *"An Overview of Android Intents"* covered the theory of using intents to launch activities. This chapter will put that theory into practice by creating an example application.

The example Android Studio application project created in this chapter will demonstrate the use of an explicit intent to launch an activity, including the transfer of data between sending and receiving activities. The next chapter (*"Android Implicit Intents – A Worked Example"*) will demonstrate using implicit intents.

54.1 Creating the Explicit Intent Example Application

Select the *New Project* option from the welcome screen and, within the resulting new project dialog, choose the Empty Views Activity template before clicking on the Next button.

Enter *ExplicitIntent* into the Name field and specify *com.ebookfrenzy.explicitintent* as the package name. Before clicking on the Finish button, change the Minimum API level setting to API 26: Android 8.0 (Oreo) and the Language menu to Java. Using the steps outlined in section *11.8 Migrating a Project to View Binding*, convert the project to use view binding.

54.2 Designing the User Interface Layout for MainActivity

The user interface for MainActivity will consist of a ConstraintLayout view containing EditText (Plain Text), TextView, and Button views named *editText1*, *textView1*, and *button1*, respectively. Using the Project tool window, locate the *activity_main.xml* resource file for MainActivity (under *app -> res -> layout*) and double-click on it to load it into the Android Studio Layout Editor tool. Select the default "Hello World!" TextView and use the Attributes tool window to assign an ID of *textView1*.

Drag a Button object from the palette and position it to be horizontally centered and located beneath the bottom edge of the TextView. Change the text property to read "Send Text" and configure the *onClick* property to call a method named *sendText*.

Next, add a Plain Text object to be centered horizontally and positioned above the top edge of the TextView. Using the Attributes tool window, remove the "Name" string assigned to the text property and set the ID to *editText1*. With the layout completed, click on the toolbar *Infer constraints* button to add appropriate constraints:

Figure 54-1

Finally, click the red warning button in the top right-hand corner of the Layout Editor window and use the resulting panel to extract the "Send Text" string to a resource named *send_text*. Once the layout is complete, the user interface should resemble that illustrated in Figure 54-2:

Figure 54-2

54.3 Creating the Second Activity Class

When the "Send Text" button is touched by the user, an intent will be issued requesting that a second activity be launched into which the user can enter a response. The next step, therefore, is to create the second activity. Within the Project tool window, right-click on the *com.ebookfrenzy.explicitintent* package name located in *app -> java* and select the *New -> Activity -> Empty Views Activity* menu option to display the *New Android Activity* dialog as shown in Figure 54-3:

Figure 54-3

Enter *SecondActivity* into the Activity Name and Title fields, name the layout file *activity_second,* and change the Language menu to Java. Since this activity will not be started when the application is launched (it will instead be launched via an intent by MainActivity when the button is pressed), ensure the *Launcher Activity* option is disabled before clicking the Finish button.

54.4 Designing the User Interface Layout for SecondActivity

The elements required for the second activity's user interface are a Plain Text EditText, TextView, and Button view. With these requirements in mind, load the *activity_second.xml* layout into the Layout Editor tool, and add the views.

During the design process, note that the *onClick* property on the button view has been configured to call a method named *returnText*, and the TextView and EditText views have been assigned IDs *textView2* and *editText2*, respectively. Once completed, the layout should resemble Figure 54-4. Note that the text on the button ("Return Text") has been extracted to a string resource named *return_text*.

With the layout complete, click on the Infer constraints toolbar button to add the necessary constraints to the layout:

Figure 54-4

54.5 Reviewing the Application Manifest File

For MainActivity to be able to launch SecondActivity using an intent, an entry for SecondActivity needs to be present in the *AndroidManifest.xml* file. Locate this file within the Project tool window (*app -> manifests*), double-click on it to load it into the editor, and verify that Android Studio has automatically added an entry for the activity:

```
<?xml version="1.0" encoding="utf-8"?>
<manifest xmlns:android="http://schemas.android.com/apk/res/android"
    xmlns:tools="http://schemas.android.com/tools">

    <application
```

Android Explicit Intents – A Worked Example

```xml
        android:allowBackup="true"
        android:dataExtractionRules="@xml/data_extraction_rules"
        android:fullBackupContent="@xml/backup_rules"
        android:icon="@mipmap/ic_launcher"
        android:label="@string/app_name"
        android:roundIcon="@mipmap/ic_launcher_round"
        android:supportsRtl="true"
        android:theme="@style/Theme.ExplicitIntent"
        tools:targetApi="31">
        <activity
            android:name=".SecondActivity"
            android:exported="false" />
        <activity
            android:name=".MainActivity"
            android:exported="true">
            <intent-filter>
                <action android:name="android.intent.action.MAIN" />

                <category android:name="android.intent.category.LAUNCHER" />
            </intent-filter>
        </activity>
    </application>

</manifest>
```

With the second activity created and listed in the manifest file, it is time to write some code in the MainActivity class to issue the intent.

54.6 Creating the Intent

The objective for MainActivity is to create and start an intent when the user touches the "Send Text" button. As part of the intent creation process, the question string entered by the user into the EditText view will be added to the intent object as a key-value pair. When the user interface layout was created for MainActivity, the button object was configured to call a method named *sendText()* when "clicked" by the user. This method now needs to be added to the MainActivity class *MainActivity.java* source file as follows:

```java
package com.ebookfrenzy.explicitintent;
.
.
import android.content.Intent;
.
.
public class MainActivity extends AppCompatActivity {

    public void sendText(View view) {

        Intent i = new Intent(this, SecondActivity.class);
```

Android Explicit Intents – A Worked Example

```
        String myString = binding.editText1.getText().toString();
        i.putExtra("qString", myString);
        startActivity(i);
    }
}
```

The code for the *sendText()* method follows the techniques outlined in *"An Overview of Android Intents"*. First, a new Intent instance is created, passing through the current activity and the class name of SecondActivity as arguments. Next, the text entered into the EditText object is added to the intent object as a key-value pair, and the intent started via a call to *startActivity()*, passing through the intent object as an argument.

Compile and run the application and touch the "Send Text" button to launch SecondActivity. Return to the MainActivity screen using either the back button (located in the toolbar along the bottom of the display) or by swiping right from the edge of the screen on newer Android versions.

54.7 Extracting Intent Data

Now that SecondActivity is being launched from MainActivity, the next step is to extract the String data value included in the intent and assign it to the TextView object in the SecondActivity user interface. This involves adding some code to the *onCreate()* method of SecondActivity in the *SecondActivity.java* source file in addition to adapting the activity to use view binding:

```
package com.ebookfrenzy.explicitintent;

import androidx.appcompat.app.AppCompatActivity;
import android.os.Bundle;
import android.content.Intent;
import android.view.View;

import com.ebookfrenzy.explicitintent.databinding.ActivitySecondBinding;

public class SecondActivity extends AppCompatActivity {

    private ActivitySecondBinding binding;

    public void onCreate(Bundle savedInstanceState) {
        super.onCreate(savedInstanceState);
        setContentView(R.layout.SecondActivity);

        binding = ActivitySecondBinding.inflate(getLayoutInflater());
        View view = binding.getRoot();
        setContentView(view);

        Bundle extras = getIntent().getExtras();
        if (extras == null) {
            return;
        }
```

453

```
        String qString = extras.getString("qString");
        binding.textView2.setText(qString);
    }
}
```

Compile and run the application either within an emulator or on a physical Android device. Enter some text into the text box in MainActivity before touching the "Send Text" button. The message should now appear on the TextView component in the SecondActivity user interface.

54.8 Launching SecondActivity as a Sub-Activity

For SecondActivity to be able to return data to MainActivity, SecondActivity must be started as a *sub-activity* of MainActivity. This means we need to call *registerForActivityResult()* and declare a callback handler to be called when SecondActivity returns. This callback will extract the data returned by SecondActivty and display it on textView1.

The call to *registerForActivityResult()* returns an ActivtyResultLauncher instance which can be called from within *sendText()* to launch the intent. Edit the *MainActivity.java* file so that it reads as follows:

```
.
.
import android.app.Activity;
import androidx.activity.result.ActivityResult;
import androidx.activity.result.ActivityResultCallback;
import androidx.activity.result.ActivityResultLauncher;
import androidx.activity.result.contract.ActivityResultContracts;
.
.
public class MainActivity extends AppCompatActivity {
.
.

    ActivityResultLauncher<Intent> startForResult = registerForActivityResult(
            new ActivityResultContracts.StartActivityForResult(),
            new ActivityResultCallback<ActivityResult>() {
                @Override
                public void onActivityResult(ActivityResult result) {
                    if (result.getResultCode() == Activity.RESULT_OK) {
                        Intent data = result.getData();
                        String returnString =
                                data.getExtras().getString("returnData");
                        binding.textView1.setText(returnString);
                    }
                }
            });

    public void sendText(View view) {

        Intent i = new Intent(this, SecondActivity.class);
```

```
            String myString = binding.editText1.getText().toString();
            i.putExtra("qString", myString);
            startActivity(i);
            startForResult.launch(i);
    }
```

54.9 Returning Data from a Sub-Activity

SecondActivity is now launched as a sub-activity of MainActivity, which has, in turn, been modified to handle data returned from SecondActivity. All that remains is to modify *SecondActivity.java* to implement the *finish()* method and to add a method named *returnText()*. The *finish()* method is triggered when an activity exits (for example, when the user selects the back button on the device):

```
public void returnText(View view) {
            finish();
}

@Override
public void finish() {
        Intent data = new Intent();

        String returnString = binding.editText2.getText().toString();
        data.putExtra("returnData", returnString);

        setResult(RESULT_OK, data);
        super.finish();
}
```

The *finish()* method creates a new intent, adds the return data as a key-value pair, and then calls the *setResult()* method, passing through a result code and the intent object. The *returnText()* method calls the *finish()* method.

Open the *activity_second.xml* file, select the button widget, and configure the onClick attribute to call the *returnText()* method.

54.10 Testing the Application

Compile and run the application, enter a question into the text field on MainActivity, and touch the "Send Text" button. When SecondActivity appears, enter the text to the EditText view and use either the back button or the "Return Text" button to return to MainActivity where the response should appear in the text view object.

54.11 Summary

Having covered the basics of intents in the previous chapter, the goal of this chapter was to work through the creation of an application project in Android Studio designed to demonstrate the use of explicit intents together with the concepts of data transfer between a parent activity and sub-activity.

The next chapter will use an example to demonstrate implicit intents in action.

55. Android Implicit Intents – A Worked Example

This chapter will create an example application in Android Studio designed to demonstrate a practical implementation of implicit intents. The goal will be to create and send an intent requesting that the content of a particular web page be loaded and displayed to the user. Since the example application itself will not contain an activity capable of performing this task, an implicit intent will be issued so that the Android intent resolution algorithm can be engaged to identify and launch a suitable activity from another application. This will likely be an activity from the Chrome web browser bundled with the Android operating system.

Having successfully launched the built-in browser, a new project will be created with an activity capable of displaying web pages. This will be installed onto the device or emulator to demonstrate implicit intents and link verification.

55.1 Creating the Android Studio Implicit Intent Example Project

Select the *New Project* option from the welcome screen and, within the resulting new project dialog, choose the Empty Views Activity template before clicking on the Next button.

Enter *ImplicitIntent* into the Name field and specify *com.ebookfrenzy.implicitintent* as the package name. Since this example will use features only available in recent Android versions, change the Minimum API level setting to API 31: Android 12.0 (S) and the Language menu to Java before clicking the Finish button.

55.2 Designing the User Interface

The user interface for the *MainActivity* class is straightforward, consisting solely of a ConstraintLayout and two Button objects. Within the Project tool window, locate the *app -> res -> layout -> activity_main.xml* file and double-click on it to load it into the Layout Editor tool.

Delete the default TextView and, with Autoconnect mode enabled, position Button widgets within the layout so that it appears as shown below:

Figure 55-1

Android Implicit Intents – A Worked Example

Set the text on the buttons to Show Web Page and Enable Links and extract the text to string resources.

Select each Button and use the Attributes tool window to configure the onClick property to call methods named *showWebPage* and *enableLink*, respectively.

55.3 Creating the Implicit Intent

As outlined above, the implicit intent will be created and issued from within a method named *showWebPage()*, which, in turn, needs to be implemented in the *MainActivity* class, the code for which resides in the *MainActivity.java* source file. Locate this file in the Project tool window and double-click on it to load it into an editing pane. Once loaded, modify the code to add the *showWebPage()* and *enableLink()* methods together with a few requisite imports:

```
package com.ebookfrenzy.implicitintent;

import androidx.appcompat.app.AppCompatActivity;
import android.os.Bundle;
import android.net.Uri;
import android.content.Intent;
import android.view.View;

public class MainActivity extends AppCompatActivity {

    @Override
    protected void onCreate(Bundle savedInstanceState) {
        super.onCreate(savedInstanceState);
        setContentView(R.layout.activity_implicit_intent);
    }

    public void showWebPage(View view) {
        Intent intent = new Intent(Intent.ACTION_VIEW,
                Uri.parse("https://www.ebookfrenzy.com"));

        startActivity(intent);
    }

    public void enableLink(View view) {

    }
}
```

The tasks performed by the *showWebPage()* method are very simple. First, a new intent object is created. Instead of specifying the class name of the intent, however, the code indicates the nature of the intent (to display something to the user) using the ACTION_VIEW option. The intent object also includes a URI containing the URL to be displayed. This indicates to the Android intent resolution system that the activity is requesting that a web page be displayed. The intent is then issued via a call to the *startActivity()* method.

Compile and run the application on either an emulator or a physical Android device, and once running, touch the *Show Web Page* button. When touched, a web browser view should appear and load the web page designated by the URL. A successful implicit intent has now been executed.

55.4 Adding a Second Matching Activity

The remainder of this chapter will demonstrate the effect of more than one activity installed on the device matching the requirements for an implicit intent. A second application will be created and installed on the device or emulator to achieve this. Begin by creating a new project within Android Studio with the application name set to *MyWebView*, using the same SDK configuration options used when creating the ImplicitIntent project earlier in this chapter and once again selecting an Empty Views Activity.

If you have a website to host a Digital Asset Links file and want to try out auto verification, use your website URL when specifying the package name. For example, if your website is hosted at *www.mycompany.com*, the package name needs to be set as follows:

```
com.mycompany.mywebview
```

If you do not have a website or do not plan on using auto verification, use the following package name:

```
com.ebookfrenzy.mywebview
```

Click Finish to create the project, then convert the project to use view bindings as outlined in section *11.8 Migrating a Project to View Binding*.

55.5 Adding the Web View to the UI

The user interface for the sole activity contained within the new *MyWebView* project will consist of an instance of the Android WebView widget. Within the Project tool window, locate the *activity_main.xml* file, which contains the user interface description for the activity, and double-click on it to load it into the Layout Editor tool.

With the Layout Editor tool in Design mode, select the default TextView widget and remove it from the layout using the keyboard delete key.

Drag and drop a WebView object from the *Widgets* section of the palette onto the existing ConstraintLayout view, as illustrated in Figure 55-2:

Figure 55-2

Before continuing, change the ID of the WebView instance to *webView1* and use the Infer constraints button to add any missing constraints.

Android Implicit Intents – A Worked Example

55.6 Obtaining the Intent URL

When the implicit intent object is created to display a web browser window, the web page URL will be bundled into the intent object within a Uri object. The task of the *onCreate()* method within the *MainActivity* class is to extract this Uri from the intent object, convert it into a URL string and assign it to the WebView object. To implement this functionality, modify the *MainActivity.java* file so that it reads as follows:

```java
package com.ebookfrenzy.mywebview;
.
.
import java.net.URL;
import android.net.Uri;
import android.content.Intent;
import android.webkit.WebView;

public class MainActivity extends AppCompatActivity {

    private ActivityMainBinding binding;

    @Override
    protected void onCreate(Bundle savedInstanceState) {
.
.
        handleIntent();
    }

    private void handleIntent() {
        Intent intent = getIntent();

        Uri data = intent.getData();
        URL url = null;

        try {
            url = new URL(data.getScheme(),
                    data.getHost(),
                    data.getPath());
        } catch (Exception e) {
            e.printStackTrace();
        }

        binding.webView1.loadUrl(url.toString());
    }
}
```

The new code added to the *onCreate()* method performs the following tasks:

- Obtains a reference to the intent which caused this activity to be launched

- Extracts the Uri data from the intent object

- Converts the Uri data to a URL object
- Loads the URL into the web view, converting the URL to a String in the process

The coding part of the MyWebView project is now complete. All that remains is to modify the manifest file.

55.7 Modifying the MyWebView Project Manifest File

A number of changes must be made to the MyWebView manifest file before it can be tested. In the first instance, the activity will need to seek permission to access the internet (since it will be required to load a web page). This is achieved by adding the appropriate permission line to the manifest file:

```
<uses-permission android:name="android.permission.INTERNET" />
```

Further, a review of the contents of the intent filter section of the *AndroidManifest.xml* file for the MyWebView project will reveal the following settings:

```
<intent-filter>
        <action android:name="android.intent.action.MAIN" />
        <category android:name="android.intent.category.LAUNCHER" />
</intent-filter>
```

In the above XML, the *android.intent.action.MAIN* entry indicates that this activity is the application's entry point when launched without data input - the *android.intent.category.LAUNCHER* directive, on the other hand, indicates that the activity should be listed within the application launcher screen of the device.

Since the activity is not required to be launched as the entry point to an application, cannot be run without data input (in this case, a URL), and is not required to appear in the launcher, neither the MAIN nor LAUNCHER directives are required in the manifest file for this activity.

The intent filter for the *MainActivity* activity does, however, need to be modified to indicate that it is capable of handling ACTION_VIEW intent actions for HTTP data schemes.

Android also requires that activities that handle implicit intents that do not include MAIN and LAUNCHER entries include the so-called *browsable* and *default* categories in the intent filter. The modified intent filter section should therefore read as follows where *<website url>* is replaced either by your website address or *www.ebookfrenzy.com*, depending on the package name you used when the MyWebView project was created:

```
<intent-filter android:autoVerify="true">
    <action android:name="android.intent.action.VIEW" />
    <category android:name="android.intent.category.BROWSABLE" />
    <category android:name="android.intent.category.DEFAULT" />
    <data android:scheme="https" />
    <data android:host="<website url>"/>
</intent-filter>
```

Bringing these requirements together results in the following complete *AndroidManifest.xml* file:

```
<?xml version="1.0" encoding="utf-8"?>
<manifest xmlns:android="http://schemas.android.com/apk/res/android"
    package="com.ebookfrenzy.mywebview">

    <uses-permission android:name="android.permission.INTERNET" />

    <application
```

Android Implicit Intents – A Worked Example

```
        android:allowBackup="true"
        android:icon="@mipmap/ic_launcher"
        android:label="@string/app_name"
        android:roundIcon="@mipmap/ic_launcher_round"
        android:supportsRtl="true"
        android:theme="@style/Theme.MyWebView">
        <activity
            android:name=".MainActivity"
            android:exported="true">
            <intent-filter android:autoVerify="true">
                <action android:name="android.intent.action.VIEW" />
                <category android:name="android.intent.category.BROWSABLE" />
                <category android:name="android.intent.category.DEFAULT" />
                <data android:scheme="https" />
                <data android:host="<website url>"/>
            </intent-filter>
        </activity>
    </application>

</manifest>
```

Load the *AndroidManifest.xml* file into the manifest editor by double-clicking on the file name in the Project tool window. Once loaded, modify the XML to match the above changes, remembering to enter the correct website URL.

Having made the appropriate modifications to the manifest file, the new activity is ready to be installed on the device.

55.8 Installing the MyWebView Package on a Device

Before the MyWebView main activity can be used as the recipient of an implicit intent, it must first be installed onto the device. This is achieved by running the application in the normal manner. Because the manifest file contains neither the *android.intent.action.MAIN* nor the *android.intent.category.LAUNCHER* settings, Android Studio must be instructed to install but not launch the app. To configure this behavior, select the *app -> Edit configurations…* menu from the toolbar as illustrated in Figure 55-3:

Figure 55-3

Within the Run/Debug Configurations dialog, change the Launch option located in the *Launch Options* section of the panel to *Nothing* and click on Apply followed by OK:

Figure 55-4

With this setting configured, run the app as usual. With this setting configured, run the app as usual. Note that the app is installed on the device but has yet to launch.

55.9 Testing the Application

With the MyWebView app installed, rerun ImplicitIntent and click the Show Web Page button. Note that the web page is still loaded into the Chrome browser instead of the main activity of the MyWebView app. This is because the MyWebView activity has not been verified or enabled to open the link contained in the launch intent. Some code must be added to the *enableLink()* method to enable the link manually.

55.10 Manually Enabling the Link

Within the *enableLink()* method, we need to create and launch an intent to display the Open by Default settings screen for the MyWebView app. Load the *MainActivity.java* file into the code editor and modify the *enableLink()* method so that it reads as follows, making sure to replace *<reverse domain>* with either com.ebookfrenzy or your own reverse domain depending on the package name you chose when creating the MyWebView project:

```
.
.
import android.provider.Settings;
.
.
public void enableLink(View view) {
    Intent intent = new Intent(
            Settings.ACTION_APP_OPEN_BY_DEFAULT_SETTINGS,
            Uri.parse("package:<reverse domain>.mywebview"));

    startActivity(intent);
}
.
.
```

Rerun the ImpicitIntent app and click on the Enable Link button to display the Open by Default settings screen for the MyWebView app:

Figure 55-5

Click on the Add Link button (marked A above), enable the checkbox next to your URL, and click the Add button:

Figure 55-6

Confirm that the link is now listed as being supported before clicking on the back arrow (marked B in Figure 55-5 above) to return to the ImplicitIntent app. Clicking the Open Web Page should now load the page into the MyWebView app instead of the Chrome browser:

Figure 55-7

55.11 Automatic Link Verification

If you chose to use your own website URL for the MyWebView package name, you can now take the additional step of using automatic link verification. Begin by uninstalling the MyWebView app from the device or emulator on which you have been testing. After placing the Digital Asset Links file on the website, we will reinstall the app to trigger the verification process.

Using the steps outlined in the chapter entitled *"An Overview of Android Intents"*, locate your *debug.keystore* file and obtain your SHA-256 certificate fingerprint using the *keytool* utility as follows:

```
keytool -list -v -keystore <path to debug.keystore file here>
```

Next, open the following page in a web browser:

https://developers.google.com/digital-asset-links/tools/generator

Once the page has loaded, enter your website URL into the *Hosting site domain* field, *com.<domain here>. mywebview* as the *App package name,* and your SHA-256 fingerprint into the *App package fingerprint (SHA256)* field:

Statement List Generator and Tester

Generate and save a statement file on your site to enable App Linking, or test an existing statement file.

Hosting site domain

www.yourcompany.com

App package name

com.ebookfrenzy.mywebview

App package fingerprint (SHA256)

78:EE:F3:C8:30:45:C1:EA:99:56:83:94:2A:4C:D2:EA:A0:69:88:96:D1:17:22:02:47:EC:AD:6E:3C:64:A9:29

[Generate statement]   or   [Test statement]

Figure 55-8

Click the *Generate statement* button to display the generated statement and place it in a file named *assetlinks.json* in a folder named *.well-known* on your web server. Return to the generator page and click on the *Test statement* button to verify that the file is valid and in the correct location.

Assuming a successful test, we are ready to try out the app link, reinstall the MyWebView app on your device or emulator and use the Settings app to navigate to the Open by Default page for MyWebView. The page should indicate that a link has been verified:

MyWebView

Allow web links to open in this app

Open supported links

Links to open in this app

☑ 1 verified link

Figure 55-9

Run the ImplicitIntent app again, click the Open Web Page button, and verify that the page content appears in the MyWebView app instead of the Chrome browser.

55.12 Summary

Implicit intents provide a mechanism by which one activity can request the service of another by specifying an action type and, optionally, the data on which that action is to be performed. To be eligible as a target candidate for an implicit intent, however, an activity must be configured to extract the appropriate data from the inbound intent object and be included in a correctly configured manifest file, including appropriate permissions and intent filters. The app containing the target activity must also be verified using a Digital Asset Links file or manually enabled by the user.

Within this chapter, an example was created to demonstrate both the issuing of an implicit intent, the creation of an example activity capable of handling such an intent, and the link verification process.

56. Android Broadcast Intents and Broadcast Receivers

In addition to providing a mechanism for launching application activities, intents are also used to broadcast system-wide messages to other components on the system. This involves the implementation of Broadcast Intents and Broadcast Receivers, both of which are the topic of this chapter.

56.1 An Overview of Broadcast Intents

Broadcast intents are Intent objects that are broadcast via a call to the *sendBroadcast()*, *sendStickyBroadcast()*, or *sendOrderedBroadcast()* methods of the Activity class (the latter being used when results are required from the broadcast). In addition to providing a messaging and event system between application components, broadcast intents are also used by the Android system to notify interested applications about key system events (such as the external power supply or headphones being connected or disconnected).

When a broadcast intent is created, it must include an action string, optional data, and a category string. As with standard intents, data is added to a broadcast intent using key-value pairs in conjunction with the *putExtra()* method of the intent object. The optional category string may be assigned to a broadcast intent via a call to the *addCategory()* method.

The action string, which identifies the broadcast event, must be unique and typically uses the application's package name syntax. For example, the following code fragment creates and sends a broadcast intent, including a unique action string and data:

```
Intent intent = new Intent();
intent.setAction("com.example.Broadcast");
intent.putExtra("MyData", 1000);
sendBroadcast(intent);
```

The above code would successfully launch the corresponding broadcast receiver on an Android device earlier than 3.0. On more recent versions of Android, however, the broadcast receiver would not receive the intent. This is because Android 3.0 introduced a launch control security measure that prevents components of *stopped* applications from being launched via an intent. An application is considered to be in a stopped state if the application has either just been installed and not previously launched or been manually stopped by the user using the application manager on the device. To get around this, however, a flag can be added to the intent before it is sent to indicate that the intent is to be allowed to start a component of a stopped application. This flag is FLAG_INCLUDE_STOPPED_PACKAGES and would be used as outlined in the following adaptation of the previous code fragment:

```
Intent intent = new Intent();
intent.addFlags(Intent.FLAG_INCLUDE_STOPPED_PACKAGES);
intent.setAction("com.example.Broadcast");
intent.putExtra("MyData", 1000);
sendBroadcast(intent);
```

56.2 An Overview of Broadcast Receivers

An application listens for specific broadcast intents by registering a *broadcast receiver*. Broadcast receivers are implemented by extending the Android BroadcastReceiver class and overriding the *onReceive()* method. The broadcast receiver may then be registered within code (for example, within an activity) or a manifest file. Part of the registration implementation involves the creation of intent filters to indicate the specific broadcast intents the receiver is required to listen for. This is achieved by referencing the *action string* of the broadcast intent. When a matching broadcast is detected, the *onReceive()* method of the broadcast receiver is called, at which point the method has 5 seconds to perform any necessary tasks before returning. It is important to note that a broadcast receiver does not need to run continuously. If a matching intent is detected, the Android runtime system automatically starts the broadcast receiver before calling the *onReceive()* method.

The following code outlines a template Broadcast Receiver subclass:

```
package com.example.broadcastdetector;

import android.content.BroadcastReceiver;
import android.content.Context;
import android.content.Intent;

public class MyReceiver extends BroadcastReceiver {

    public MyReceiver() {
    }

    @Override
    public void onReceive(Context context, Intent intent) {
        // Implement code here to be performed when
        // broadcast is detected
    }
}
```

When registering a broadcast receiver within a manifest file, a *<receiver>* entry must be added for the receiver.

The following example manifest file registers the above example broadcast receiver:

```
<?xml version="1.0" encoding="utf-8"?>
<manifest xmlns:android="http://schemas.android.com/apk/res/android"
    package="com.example.broadcastdetector.broadcastdetector"
    android:versionCode="1"
    android:versionName="1.0" >

    <uses-sdk android:minSdkVersion="17" />

    <application
        android:icon="@mipmap/ic_launcher"
        android:label="@string/app_name" >
        <receiver android:name="MyReceiver" >
        </receiver>
    </application>
```

```
</manifest>
```

When running on versions of Android older than Android 8.0, the intent filters associated with a receiver can be placed within the receiver element of the manifest file as follows:

```
<receiver android:name="MyReceiver" >
    <intent-filter>
        <action android:name="com.example.Broadcast" >
        </action>
    </intent-filter>
</receiver>
```

On Android 8.0 or later, the receiver must be registered in code using the *registerReceiver()* method of the Activity class together with an appropriately configured IntentFilter object:

```
IntentFilter filter = new IntentFilter("com.example.Broadcast");

MyReceiver receiver = new MyReceiver();
registerReceiver(receiver, filter);
```

When a broadcast receiver registered in code is no longer required, it may be unregistered via a call to the *unregisterReceiver()* method of the activity class, passing through a reference to the receiver object as an argument. For example, the following code will unregister the above broadcast receiver:

```
unregisterReceiver(receiver);
```

It is important to remember that some system broadcast intents can only be detected by a broadcast receiver if it is registered in code rather than in the manifest file. Check the Android Intent class documentation for a detailed overview of the system broadcast intents and corresponding requirements online at:

https://developer.android.com/reference/android/content/Intent

56.3 Obtaining Results from a Broadcast

When a broadcast intent is sent using the *sendBroadcast()* method, there is no way for the initiating activity to receive results from any broadcast receivers that pick up the broadcast. If return results are required, it is necessary to use the *sendOrderedBroadcast()* method instead. When a broadcast intent is sent using this method, it is delivered sequentially to each broadcast receiver with a registered interest.

The *sendOrderedBroadcast()* method is called several arguments, including a reference to another broadcast receiver (known as the *result receiver*) which is to be notified when all other broadcast receivers have handled the intent, together with a set of data references into which those receivers can place result data. When all broadcast receivers have been given the opportunity to handle the broadcast, the *onReceive()* method of the *result receiver* is called and passed the result data.

56.4 Sticky Broadcast Intents

By default, broadcast intents disappear once they have been sent and handled by interested broadcast receivers. A broadcast intent can, however, be defined as being "sticky". A sticky intent and the data contained therein remain in the system after it has completed. The data stored within a sticky broadcast intent can be obtained via the return value of a call to the *registerReceiver()* method using the usual arguments (references to the broadcast receiver and intent filter object). Many of the Android system broadcasts are sticky, a prime example being those broadcasts relating to battery level status.

A sticky broadcast may be removed at any time via a call to the *removeStickyBroadcast()* method, passing through as an argument a reference to the broadcast intent to be removed.

56.5 The Broadcast Intent Example

The remainder of this chapter will work through creating an Android Studio-based example of broadcast intents in action. In the first instance, a simple application will be created to issue a custom broadcast intent. A corresponding broadcast receiver will then be created to display a message on the display of the Android device when the broadcast is detected. Finally, the broadcast receiver will be modified to detect notification by the system that external power has been disconnected from the device.

56.6 Creating the Example Application

Select the *New Project* option from the welcome screen and, within the resulting new project dialog, choose the Empty Views Activity template before clicking on the Next button.

Enter *SendBroadcast* into the Name field and specify *com.ebookfrenzy.sendbroadcast* as the package name. Before clicking on the Finish button, change the Minimum API level setting to API 26: Android 8.0 (Oreo) and the Language menu to Java.

Once the new project has been created, locate and load the *activity_main.xml* layout file located in the Project tool window under *app -> res -> layout* and, with the Layout Editor tool in Design mode, replace the TextView object with a Button view and set the text property so that it reads "Send Broadcast". Once the text value has been set, follow the usual steps to extract the string to a resource named *send_broadcast*.

With the button still selected in the layout, locate the *onClick* property in the Attributes panel and configure it to call a method named *broadcastIntent*.

56.7 Creating and Sending the Broadcast Intent

Having created the framework for the *SendBroadcast* application, it is now time to implement the code to send the broadcast intent. This involves implementing the *broadcastIntent()* method specified previously as the *onClick* target of the Button view in the user interface. Locate and double-click on the *MainActivity.java* file and modify it to add the code to create and send the broadcast intent. Once modified, the source code for this class should read as follows:

```
package com.ebookfrenzy.sendbroadcast;

import androidx.appcompat.app.AppCompatActivity;
import android.os.Bundle;
import android.content.Intent;
import android.view.View;

public class MainActivity extends AppCompatActivity {
 .
 .
    public void broadcastIntent(View view)
    {
        Intent intent = new Intent();
        intent.setAction("com.ebookfrenzy.sendbroadcast");
        intent.addFlags(Intent.FLAG_INCLUDE_STOPPED_PACKAGES);
        sendBroadcast(intent);
    }
}
```

Note that in this instance, the action string for the intent is com.ebookfrenzy.sendbroadcast. When the broadcast

Android Broadcast Intents and Broadcast Receivers

receiver class is created in later sections of this chapter, the intent filter declaration must match this action string.

This concludes the creation of the application to send the broadcast intent. All that remains is to build a matching broadcast receiver.

56.8 Creating the Broadcast Receiver

To create the broadcast receiver, a new class needs to be created, which subclasses the BroadcastReceiver superclass. Within the Project tool window, navigate to *app -> java* and right-click on the package name. Select the *New -> Other -> Broadcast Receiver* menu option from the resulting menu, name the class *MyReceiver*, and ensure the Exported and Enabled options are selected. These settings allow the Android system to launch the receiver when needed and ensure that the class can receive messages sent by other applications. With the class configured, click on *Finish*.

Once created, Android Studio will automatically load the new *MyReceiver.java* class file into the editor, where it should read as follows:

```
package com.ebookfrenzy.sendbroadcast;

import android.content.BroadcastReceiver;
import android.content.Context;
import android.content.Intent;

public class MyReceiver extends BroadcastReceiver {

    @Override
    public void onReceive(Context context, Intent intent) {
        // TODO: This method is called when the BroadcastReceiver is receiving
        // an Intent broadcast.
        throw new UnsupportedOperationException("Not yet implemented");
    }
}
```

As seen in the code, Android Studio generated a template for the new class and a stub for the *onReceive()* method. Some changes now need to be made to the class to implement the required behavior. Remaining in the *MyReceiver.java* file, therefore, modify the code so that it reads as follows:

```
package com.ebookfrenzy.sendbroadcast;

import android.content.BroadcastReceiver;
import android.content.Context;
import android.content.Intent;
import android.widget.Toast;

public class MyReceiver extends BroadcastReceiver {

    @Override
    public void onReceive(Context context, Intent intent) {
        // TODO: This method is called when the BroadcastReceiver is receiving
        // an Intent broadcast.
        throw new UnsupportedOperationException("Not yet implemented");
```

```
            Toast.makeText(context, "Broadcast Intent Detected.",
                    Toast.LENGTH_LONG).show();
    }
}
```

The code for the broadcast receiver is now complete.

56.9 Registering the Broadcast Receiver

The project needs to publicize the presence of the broadcast receiver and must include an intent filter to specify the broadcast intents in which the receiver is interested. When the BroadcastReceiver class was created in the previous section, Android Studio automatically added a <receiver> element to the manifest file. All that remains, therefore, is to add code within the *MainActivity.java* file to create an intent filter and to register the receiver:

```
package com.ebookfrenzy.sendbroadcast;
.
.
import android.content.BroadcastReceiver;
import android.content.IntentFilter;
.
.
public class MainActivity extends AppCompatActivity {

    BroadcastReceiver receiver;

    @Override
    protected void onCreate(Bundle savedInstanceState) {
        super.onCreate(savedInstanceState);
        setContentView(R.layout.activity_main);

        configureReceiver();
    }

    private void configureReceiver() {
        IntentFilter filter = new IntentFilter();
        filter.addAction("com.ebookfrenzy.sendbroadcast");
        receiver = new MyReceiver();
        registerReceiver(receiver, filter);
    }
.
.
}
```

It is also important to unregister the broadcast receiver when it is no longer needed:

```
@Override
protected void onDestroy() {
    super.onDestroy();
    unregisterReceiver(receiver);
```

}
56.10 Testing the Broadcast Example

To test the broadcast sender and receiver, run the SendBroadcast app on a device or AVD and wait for it to appear on the display. Once running, touch the button, at which point the toast message reading "Broadcast Intent Detected." should pop up for a few seconds before fading away.

56.11 Listening for System Broadcasts

The final stage of this example is to modify the intent filter for the broadcast receiver to listen for the system intent that is broadcast when external power is disconnected from the device. That action is *android.intent. action.ACTION_POWER_DISCONNECTED*. Modify the *configureReceiver()* method in the *MainActivity.java* file to add this additional filter:

```
private void configureReceiver() {
    IntentFilter filter = new IntentFilter();
    filter.addAction("com.ebookfrenzy.sendbroadcast");
    filter.addAction(
            "android.intent.action.ACTION_POWER_DISCONNECTED");

    receiver = new MyReceiver();
    registerReceiver(receiver, filter);
}
```

Since the *onReceive()* method in the MyReceiver.java file will now be listening for two types of broadcast intent, it is worthwhile to modify the code so that the action string of the current intent is also displayed in the toast message. This string can be obtained via a call to the *getAction()* method of the intent object passed as an argument to the *onReceive()* method:

```
public void onReceive(Context context, Intent intent) {
    String message = "Broadcast intent detected "
                    + intent.getAction();

    Toast.makeText(context, message,
            Toast.LENGTH_LONG).show();
}
```

Test the receiver by re-installing the modified *SendBroadcast* package. Touching the button in the *SendBroadcast* application should now result in a new message containing the custom action string:

```
Broadcast intent detected com.ebookfrenzy.sendbroadcast
```

Next, remove the USB connector currently supplying power to the Android device, at which point the receiver should report the following in the toast message (the message may be truncated on devices in portrait orientation). If the app is running on an emulator, display the extended controls, select the *Battery* option and change the *Charger connection* setting to *None*.

```
Broadcast intent detected android.intent.action.ACTION_POWER_DISCONNECTED
```

To avoid this message appearing whenever the device is disconnected from a power supply, launch the Settings app and select the *Apps* option. Select the SendBroadcast app from the resulting list and tap the *Uninstall* button.

Android Broadcast Intents and Broadcast Receivers

56.12 Summary

Broadcast intents are a mechanism by which an intent can be issued for consumption by multiple components on an Android system. Broadcasts are detected by registering a Broadcast Receiver, which, in turn, is configured to listen for intents that match particular action strings. In general, broadcast receivers remain dormant until woken up by the system when a matching intent is detected. The Android system also uses broadcast intents to issue notifications of events such as a low battery warning or the connection or disconnection of external power to the device.

In addition to providing an overview of Broadcast intents and receivers, this chapter has also worked through an example of sending broadcast intents and implementing a broadcast receiver to listen for both custom and system broadcast intents.

57. Android Local Bound Services – A Worked Example

As outlined in the previous chapter, Bound services provide a mechanism for implementing communication between an Android service and one or more client components. This chapter builds on the overview of bound services provided in *"An Overview of Android Services"* before embarking on an example implementation of a *local* bound service.

57.1 Understanding Bound Services

Bound services are provided to allow applications to perform tasks in the background. Multiple client components may *bind* to a bound service and, once bound, interact with that service using various mechanisms.

Bound services are created as sub-classes of the Android Service class and must, at a minimum, implement the *onBind()* method. Client components bind to a service via a call to the *bindService()* method. The first bind request to a bound service will result in a call to that service's *onBind()* method (subsequent bind requests do not trigger an *onBind()* call). Clients wishing to bind to a service must also implement a ServiceConnection subclass containing *onServiceConnected()* and *onServiceDisconnected()* methods, which will be called once the client-server connection has been established or disconnected, respectively. In the case of the *onServiceConnected()* method, this will be passed an IBinder object containing the information needed by the client to interact with the service.

57.2 Bound Service Interaction Options

Two recommended mechanisms for implementing interaction between client components and a bound service exist. Suppose the bound service is local and private to the same application as the client component (in other words, it runs within the same process and is not available to components in other applications). In that case, the recommended method is to create a subclass of the Binder class and extend it to provide an interface to the service. An instance of this Binder object is then returned by the *onBind()* method and subsequently used by the client component to access methods and data held within the service directly.

When the bound service is not local to the application (in other words, it is running in a different process from the client component), interaction is best achieved using a Messenger/Handler implementation.

In the remainder of this chapter, an example will be created to demonstrate the steps involved in creating, starting, and interacting with a local, private bound service.

57.3 A Local Bound Service Example

The example application created in the remainder of this chapter will consist of a single activity and a bound service. The purpose of the bound service is to obtain the current time from the system and return that information to the activity, where it will be displayed to the user. The bound service will be local and private to the same application as the activity.

Select the *New Project* option from the welcome screen and, within the resulting new project dialog, choose the Empty Views Activity template before clicking on the Next button.

Enter *LocalBound* into the Name field and specify *com.ebookfrenzy.localbound* as the package name. Before

Android Local Bound Services – A Worked Example

clicking on the Finish button, change the Minimum API level setting to API 26: Android 8.0 (Oreo) and the Language menu to Java. Use the steps in section *11.8 Migrating a Project to View Binding* to migrate the project to view binding.

Once the project has been created, the next step is to add a new class to act as the bound service.

57.4 Adding a Bound Service to the Project

To add a new class to the project, right-click on the package name (located under *app -> java -> com.ebookfrenzy.localbound*) within the Project tool window and select the *New -> Service -> Service* menu option. Specify *BoundService* as the class name and make sure that both the *Exported* and *Enabled* options are selected before clicking on *Finish* to create the class. Android Studio will load the *BoundService.java* file into the editor, where it will read as follows:

```
package com.ebookfrenzy.localbound;

import android.app.Service;
import android.content.Intent;
import android.os.IBinder;

public class BoundService extends Service {
    public BoundService() {
    }

    @Override
    public IBinder onBind(Intent intent) {
        // TODO: Return the communication channel to the service.
        throw new UnsupportedOperationException("Not yet implemented");
    }
}
```

57.5 Implementing the Binder

As previously outlined, local bound services can communicate with bound clients by passing an appropriately configured Binder object to the client. This is achieved by creating a Binder subclass within the bound service class and extending it by adding one or more new methods the client can call. This usually involves implementing a method that returns a reference to the bound service instance. With a reference to this instance, the client can then access data and call methods within the bound service directly.

For this example, some changes are needed to the template *BoundService* class created in the preceding section. In the first instance, a Binder subclass needs to be declared. This class will contain a single method named *getService()* which will return a reference to the current service object instance (represented by the *this* keyword). With these requirements in mind, edit the *BoundService.java* file and modify it as follows:

```
package com.ebookfrenzy.localbound;

import android.app.Service;
import android.content.Intent;
import android.os.IBinder;
import android.os.Binder;

public class BoundService extends Service {
```

Android Local Bound Services – A Worked Example

```java
    private final IBinder myBinder = new MyLocalBinder();

    public BoundService() {
    }

    @Override
    public IBinder onBind(Intent intent) {
        // TODO: Return the communication channel to the service.
        throw new UnsupportedOperationException("Not yet implemented");
    }

    public class MyLocalBinder extends Binder {
        BoundService getService() {
            return BoundService.this;
        }
    }
}
```

Having made the changes to the class, it is worth taking a moment to recap the steps performed here. First, a new subclass of Binder (named *MyLocalBinder*) is declared. This class contains a single method to return a reference to the current instance of the *BoundService* class. A new instance of the *MyLocalBinder* class is created and assigned to the *myBinder* IBinder reference (since Binder is a subclass of IBinder, there is no type mismatch in this assignment).

Next, the *onBind()* method needs to be modified to return a reference to the *myBinder* object, and a new public method implemented to return the current time when called by any clients that bind to the service:

```java
package com.ebookfrenzy.localbound;

import java.text.SimpleDateFormat;
import java.util.Date;
import java.util.Locale;

import android.app.Service;
import android.content.Intent;
import android.os.IBinder;
import android.os.Binder;

public class BoundService extends Service {

    private final IBinder myBinder = new MyLocalBinder();

    public BoundService() {
    }

    @Override
    public IBinder onBind(Intent intent) {
```

Android Local Bound Services – A Worked Example

```java
        return myBinder;
    }

    public String getCurrentTime() {
        SimpleDateFormat dateformat =
                new SimpleDateFormat("HH:mm:ss MM/dd/yyyy",
                        Locale.US);
        return (dateformat.format(new Date()));
    }

    public class MyLocalBinder extends Binder {
        BoundService getService() {
            return BoundService.this;
        }
    }
}
```

At this point, the bound service is complete and is ready to be added to the project manifest file. Locate and double-click on the *AndroidManifest.xml* file for the *LocalBound* project in the Project tool window and, once loaded into the Manifest Editor, verify that Android Studio has already added a <service> entry for the service as follows:

```xml
<?xml version="1.0" encoding="utf-8"?>
<manifest xmlns:android="http://schemas.android.com/apk/res/android"
    package="com.ebookfrenzy.localbound.localbound" >

    <application
        android:allowBackup="true"
        android:icon="@mipmap/ic_launcher"
        android:label="@string/app_name"
        android:theme="@style/AppTheme" >
        <service
            android:name=".BoundService"
            android:enabled="true"
            android:exported="true" >
        </service>
        <activity
            android:name=".MainActivity" >
            <intent-filter>
                <action android:name="android.intent.action.MAIN" />

                <category android:name="android.intent.category.LAUNCHER" />
            </intent-filter>
        </activity>
    </application>

</manifest>
```

The next phase is writing the code within the activity to bind to the service and call the *getCurrentTime()* method.

57.6 Binding the Client to the Service

For this tutorial, the client is the *MainActivity* instance of the running application. As previously noted, to successfully bind to a service and receive the IBinder object returned by the service's *onBind()* method, it is necessary to create a ServiceConnection subclass and implement *onServiceConnected()* and *onServiceDisconnected()* callback methods. Edit the *MainActivity.java* file and modify it as follows:

```java
package com.ebookfrenzy.localbound;

import androidx.appcompat.app.AppCompatActivity;
import android.os.Bundle;
import android.os.IBinder;
import android.content.Context;
import android.content.Intent;
import android.content.ComponentName;
import android.content.ServiceConnection;
import com.ebookfrenzy.localbound.BoundService.MyLocalBinder;

public class MainActivity extends AppCompatActivity {

    BoundService myService;
    boolean isBound = false;

    @Override
    protected void onCreate(Bundle savedInstanceState) {
        super.onCreate(savedInstanceState);
        setContentView(R.layout.activity_main);
    }

    final private ServiceConnection myConnection = new ServiceConnection()
    {
        @Override
        public void onServiceConnected(ComponentName className,
                                       IBinder service) {
            MyLocalBinder binder = (MyLocalBinder) service;
            myService = binder.getService();
            isBound = true;
        }

        @Override
        public void onServiceDisconnected(ComponentName name) {
            isBound = false;
        }
    };
}
```

Android Local Bound Services – A Worked Example

The *onServiceConnected()* method will be called when the client binds successfully to the service. The method is passed as an argument the IBinder object returned by the *onBind()* method of the service. This argument is cast to an object of type MyLocalBinder. Then the *getService()* method of the binder object is called to obtain a reference to the service instance, which, in turn, is assigned to *myService*. A Boolean flag indicates that the connection has been successfully established.

The *onServiceDisconnected()* method is called when the connection ends and sets the Boolean flag to false.

Having established the connection, the next step is to modify the activity to bind to the service. This involves the creation of an intent and a call to the *bindService()* method, which can be performed in the *onCreate()* method of the activity:

```
@Override
public void onCreate(Bundle savedInstanceState) {
    super.onCreate(savedInstanceState);
    setContentView(R.layout.activity_main);
    Intent intent = new Intent(this, BoundService.class);
    bindService(intent, myConnection, Context.BIND_AUTO_CREATE);
}
```

57.7 Completing the Example

All that remains is to add a mechanism for calling the *getCurrentTime()* method and displaying the result to the user. As is now customary, Android Studio will have created a template *activity_main.xml* file for the activity containing only a TextView. Load this file into the Layout Editor tool and, using Design mode, select the TextView component and change the ID to *myTextView*. Add a Button view beneath the TextView and change the text on the button to read "Show Time", extracting the text to a string resource named *show_time*. On completion of these changes, the layout should resemble that illustrated in Figure 57-1. If any constraints are missing, click on the Infer Constraints button in the Layout Editor toolbar.

Figure 57-1

Complete the user interface design by selecting the Button and configuring the *onClick* property to call a method named *showTime*.

Finally, edit the *MainActivity.java* file code to implement the *showTime()* method. This method calls the *getCurrentTime()* method of the service (which, thanks to the *onServiceConnected()* method, is now available from within the activity via the *myService* reference) and assigns the resulting string to the TextView:

```
package com.ebookfrenzy.localbound;
.
.
import android.widget.TextView;

import com.ebookfrenzy.localbound.BoundService.MyLocalBinder;

public class MainActivity extends AppCompatActivity {

    BoundService myService;
    boolean isBound = false;

    public void showTime(View view)
    {
        String currentTime = myService.getCurrentTime();
        TextView myTextView = findViewById(R.id.myTextView);
        myTextView.setText(currentTime);
    }
.
.
}
```

57.8 Testing the Application

With the code changes complete, perform a test run of the application. Once visible, touch the button and note that the text view changes to display the current date and time. The example has successfully started and bound to a service and then called a method of that service to cause a task to be performed, and the results returned to the activity.

57.9 Summary

When a bound service is local and private to an application, components within that application can interact with the service without resorting to inter-process communication (IPC). In general terms, the service's *onBind()* method returns an IBinder object containing a reference to the running service instance. The client component implements a ServiceConnection subclass containing callback methods that are called when the service is connected and disconnected. The former method is passed the IBinder object returned by the *onBind()* method, allowing public methods within the service to be called.

Having covered the implementation of local bound services, the next chapter will focus on using IPC to interact with remote bound services.

58. Android Remote Bound Services – A Worked Example

In this final chapter dedicated to Android services, an example application will be developed to demonstrate the use of a messenger and handler configuration to facilitate interaction between a client and remote bound service of a messenger and handler configuration to facilitate interaction between a client and a remote bound service.

58.1 Client to Remote Service Communication

As outlined in the previous chapter, the interaction between a client and a local service can be implemented by returning to the client an IBinder object containing a reference to the service object. In the case of remote services, however, this approach does not work because the remote service is running in a different process and, as such, cannot be reached directly from the client.

In the case of remote services, a Messenger and Handler configuration must be created, which allows messages to be passed across process boundaries between client and service.

Specifically, the service creates a Handler instance that will be called when a message is received from the client. In terms of initialization, it is the job of the Handler to create a Messenger object which, in turn, creates an IBinder object to be returned to the client in the *onBind()* method. The client uses This IBinder object to create an instance of the Messenger object and, subsequently, to send messages to the service handler. Each time a message is sent by the client, the *handleMessage()* method of the handler is called, passing through the message object.

The example created in this chapter will consist of an activity and a bound service running in separate processes. The Messenger/Handler mechanism will send a string to the service, which will display in the Logcat output.

58.2 Creating the Example Application

Select the *New Project* option from the welcome screen and, within the resulting new project dialog, choose the Empty Views Activity template before clicking on the Next button.

Enter *RemoteBound* into the Name field and specify *com.ebookfrenzy.remotebound* as the package name. Before clicking on the Finish button, change the Minimum API level setting to API 26: Android 8.0 (Oreo) and the Language menu to Java.

58.3 Designing the User Interface

Locate the *activity_main.xml* file in the Project tool window and double-click on it to load it into the Layout Editor tool. With the Layout Editor tool in Design mode, right-click on the default TextView instance, choose the *Convert view...* menu option, select the Button view from the resulting dialog and click Apply. Change the button's text property to read "Send Message" and extract the string to a new resource named *send_message*.

Finally, configure the *onClick* property to call a method named *sendMessage*.

58.4 Implementing the Remote Bound Service

To implement the remote bound service for this example, add a new class to the project by right-clicking on the package name (located under *app -> java*) within the Project tool window and selecting the *New -> Service ->*

Android Remote Bound Services – A Worked Example

Service menu option. Specify *RemoteService* as the class name and make sure that both the *Exported* and *Enabled* options are selected before clicking on *Finish* to create the class.

The next step is to implement the handler class for the new service. This is achieved by extending the Handler class and implementing the *handleMessage()* method. This method will be called when a message is received from the client. It will be passed a Message object as an argument containing any data that the client needs to pass to the service. In this instance, this will be a Bundle object containing a string to be displayed to the user. The modified class in the *RemoteService.java* file should read as follows once this has been implemented:

```java
package com.ebookfrenzy.remotebound;

import android.app.Service;
import android.content.Intent;
import android.os.IBinder;
import android.os.Bundle;
import android.os.Handler;
import android.os.Looper;
import android.os.Message;
import android.os.Messenger;
import android.util.Log;

public class RemoteService extends Service {

    public RemoteService() {
    }

    static class IncomingHandler extends Handler {

        String TAG = "RemoteService";

        public IncomingHandler() {
            super(Looper.getMainLooper());
        }

        @Override
        public void handleMessage(Message msg) {
            Bundle data = msg.getData();
            String dataString = data.getString("MyString");
            Log.i(TAG, "Message = " + dataString);
        }
    }

    @Override
    public IBinder onBind(Intent intent) {
        // TODO: Return the communication channel to the service.
        throw new UnsupportedOperationException("Not yet implemented");
    }
```

}

With the handler implemented, the only remaining task in terms of the service code is to modify the *onBind()* method such that it returns an IBinder object containing a Messenger object which, in turn, contains a reference to the handler:

```
final Messenger myMessenger = new Messenger(new IncomingHandler());

@Override
public IBinder onBind(Intent intent) {
    return myMessenger.getBinder();
}
```

The first line of the above code fragment creates a new instance of our handler class and passes it through to the constructor of a new Messenger object. Within the *onBind()* method, the *getBinder()* method of the messenger object is called to return the messenger's IBinder object.

58.5 Configuring a Remote Service in the Manifest File

To accurately portray the communication between a client and remote service, it will be necessary to configure the service to run separately from the rest of the application. This is achieved by adding an *android:process* property within the <service> tag for the service in the manifest file. To launch a remote service, it is also necessary to provide an intent filter for the service. To implement this change, modify the *AndroidManifest.xml* file to add the required entry:

```
<?xml version="1.0" encoding="utf-8"?>
<manifest xmlns:android="http://schemas.android.com/apk/res/android"
    package="com.ebookfrenzy.remotebound" >

    <application
        android:allowBackup="true"
        android:icon="@mipmap/ic_launcher"
        android:label="@string/app_name"
        android:supportsRtl="true"
        android:theme="@style/AppTheme" >
        <service
            android:name=".RemoteService"
            android:enabled="true"
            android:exported="true"
            android:process=":my_process" >
        </service>

        <activity
            android:name=".MainActivity" >
            <intent-filter>
                <action android:name="android.intent.action.MAIN" />

                <category android:name="android.intent.category.LAUNCHER" />
```

```
            </intent-filter>
        </activity>
    </application>

</manifest>
```

58.6 Launching and Binding to the Remote Service

As with a local bound service, the client component needs to implement an instance of the ServiceConnection class with *onServiceConnected()* and *onServiceDisconnected()* methods. Also, in common with local services, the *onServiceConnected()* method will be passed the IBinder object returned by the *onBind()* method of the remote service, which will be used to send messages to the server handler. In the case of this example, the client is *MainActivity*, the code for which is located in *MainActivity.java*. Load this file and modify it to add the ServiceConnection class and a variable to store a reference to the received Messenger object together with a Boolean flag to indicate whether or not the connection is established:

```
package com.ebookfrenzy.remotebound;

import androidx.appcompat.app.AppCompatActivity;
import android.os.Bundle;
import android.os.IBinder;
import android.os.Message;
import android.os.Messenger;
import android.os.RemoteException;
import android.content.ComponentName;
import android.content.Context;
import android.content.Intent;
import android.content.ServiceConnection;
import android.view.View;

public class MainActivity extends AppCompatActivity {

    Messenger myService = null;
    boolean isBound;

    @Override
    protected void onCreate(Bundle savedInstanceState) {
        super.onCreate(savedInstanceState);
        setContentView(R.layout.activity_main);
    }

    final private ServiceConnection myConnection =
            new ServiceConnection() {
                public void onServiceConnected(
                        ComponentName className,
                                            IBinder service) {
                    myService = new Messenger(service);
                    isBound = true;
```

```
            }

            public void onServiceDisconnected(
                        ComponentName className) {
                myService = null;
                isBound = false;
            }
    };
}
```

Next, some code must be added to bind to the remote service. This involves creating an intent that matches the intent filter for the service as declared in the manifest file and then making a call to the *bindService()* method, providing the intent and a reference to the ServiceConnection instance as arguments. For this example, this code will be implemented in the activity's *onCreate()* method:

```
@Override
protected void onCreate(Bundle savedInstanceState) {
      super.onCreate(savedInstanceState);
      setContentView(R.layout.activity_main);

      Intent intent = new Intent(getApplicationContext(),
                      RemoteService.class);

      bindService(intent, myConnection, Context.BIND_AUTO_CREATE);
}
```

58.7 Sending a Message to the Remote Service

Before testing the application, all that remains is to implement the *sendMessage()* method in the MainActivity class, which is configured to be called when the user touches the button in the user interface. This method needs to check that the service is connected, create a bundle object containing the string to be displayed by the server, add it to a Message object, and send it to the server:

```
public void sendMessage(View view)
{
        if (!isBound) return;

     Message msg = Message.obtain();

     Bundle bundle = new Bundle();
     bundle.putString("MyString", "Message Received");

     msg.setData(bundle);

     try {
         myService.send(msg);
     } catch (RemoteException e) {
         e.printStackTrace();
     }
}
```

Android Remote Bound Services – A Worked Example

With the code changes complete, compile and run the application. Once loaded, open the Logcat tool window and enter the following into the filter field:

```
package:mine tag:RemoteServer
```

With the Logcat tool window still visible, tap the button in the user interface, at which point the log message should appear as follows:

```
Message = Message Received
```

58.8 Summary

To implement interaction between a client and remote bound service, an app must implement a handler/message communication framework. The basic concepts behind this technique have been covered in this chapter, together with the implementation of an example application designed to demonstrate communication between a client and a bound service, each running in a separate process.

59. A Basic Overview of Java Threads, Handlers and Executors

Threads are the cornerstone of any multitasking operating system and can be thought of as mini-processes running within a main process, the purpose of which is to enable at least the appearance of parallel execution paths within applications. In this chapter we will explore the importance of using threads in Android app development and demonstrate how they are created and managed.

59.1 The Application Main Thread

When an Android application is first started, the runtime system creates a single thread in which all application components will run by default. This thread is generally referred to as the main thread. The primary role of the main thread is to handle the user interface in terms of event handling and interaction with views in the user interface. Any additional components that are started within the application will, by default, also run on the main thread.

Any component within an application that performs a time consuming task using the main thread will cause the entire application to appear to lock up until the task is completed. This will typically result in the operating system displaying an "Application is not responding" warning to the user. Clearly, this is far from the desired behavior for any application. This can be avoided simply by launching the task to be performed in a separate thread, allowing the main thread to continue unhindered with other tasks.

59.2 Thread Handlers

Clearly, one of the key rules of Android development is to never perform time-consuming operations on the main thread of an application. The second, equally important, rule is that the code within a separate thread must never, under any circumstances, directly update any aspect of the user interface.

Any changes to the user interface must always be performed from within the main thread. The reason for this is that the Android UI toolkit is not thread-safe. Attempts to work with non-thread-safe code from within multiple threads will typically result in intermittent problems and unpredictable application behavior.

If the code executing in a thread needs to interact with the user interface, it must do so by synchronizing with the main UI thread. This is achieved by creating a handler within the main thread, which, in turn, receives messages from another thread and updates the user interface accordingly.

59.3 A Threading Example

The remainder of this chapter will work through some simple examples intended to provide a basic introduction to threads. The first step will be to highlight the importance of performing time-consuming tasks in a separate thread from the main thread.

Launch Android Studio, select the *New Project* option from the welcome screen and, within the resulting new project dialog, choose the Empty Activity template before clicking on the Next button.

Enter *ThreadExample* into the Name field and specify *com.ebookfrenzy.threadexample* as the package name. Before clicking on the Finish button, change the Minimum API level setting to API 26: Android 8.0 (Oreo) and the Language menu to Java. Convert the project to use view binding by following the steps in section *11.8*

Migrating a Project to View Binding.

59.4 Building the App

Load the *activity_main.xml* file for the project into the Layout Editor tool. Select the default TextView component and change the ID for the view to *myTextView* in the Properties tool window.

Add a Button view to the user interface positioned directly beneath the existing TextView object as illustrated in Figure 59-1. Once the button has been added, click on the Infer Constraints button in the toolbar to add the missing constraints.

Change the text to "Press Me" and extract the string to a resource named *press_me*. With the button view still selected in the layout, locate the onClick property and enter *buttonClick* as the method name.

Figure 59-1

Next, load the *MainActivity.java* file into an editing panel and add code for the *buttonClick()* method which will be called when the Button view is tapped by the user. Since the goal here is to demonstrate the problem of performing lengthy tasks on the main thread, the code will simply pause for 20 seconds before displaying different text on the TextView object:

.
.

```
public void buttonClick(View view) {

    long endTime = System.currentTimeMillis() + 20 * 1000;
    while (System.currentTimeMillis() < endTime) {
```

```
        synchronized (this) {
            try {
                wait(endTime - System.currentTimeMillis());
            } catch (Exception e) {
            }
        }
    }
    binding.myTextView.setText("Button Pressed");
}
```

·
·

With the code changes complete, run the application on either a physical device or an emulator. Once the application is running, tap the button, at which point the application will appear to freeze. It will, for example, not be possible to touch the button a second time and in some situations the operating system will report the application as being unresponsive as shown in Figure 59-2.

> ThreadExample isn't responding
>
> ✕   Close app
>
> 🕒 Wait

Figure 59-2

Clearly, anything that is going to take time to complete within the *buttonClick()* method needs to be performed within a separate thread.

59.5 Creating a New Thread

To create a new thread, the code to be executed in that thread needs to be placed within the *run()* method of a Runnable instance. A new Thread object then needs to be created, passing through a reference to the Runnable instance to the constructor. Finally, the *start()* method of the thread object needs to be called to start the thread running. To perform the task within the *buttonClick()* method, therefore, the following changes need to be made:

```
public void buttonClick(View view) {

    Runnable runnable = new Runnable() {
        public void run() {
            long endTime = System.currentTimeMillis() + 20 * 1000;
            while (System.currentTimeMillis() < endTime) {
                synchronized (this) {
                    try {
                        wait(endTime - System.currentTimeMillis());
                    } catch (Exception e) {
                    }
                }
            }
        }
```

A Basic Overview of Java Threads, Handlers and Executors

```
        }
        binding.myTextView.setText("Button Pressed");
    };
    Thread myThread = new Thread(runnable);
    myThread.start();
}
```

In fact, the runnable declaration can be simplified if desired by making use of a Java lambda expression. Making this change would result in the following declaration:

.
.
```
    Runnable runnable = () -> {
        long endTime = System.currentTimeMillis() + 20 * 1000;
            while (System.currentTimeMillis() < endTime) {
                synchronized (this) {
                    try {
                        wait(endTime - System.currentTimeMillis());
                    } catch (Exception e) {
                    }
                }
            }
    };
    Thread myThread = new Thread(runnable);
    myThread.start();
```
.
.

When the application is now run, touching the button causes the delay to be performed in a new thread leaving the main thread to continue handling the user interface, including responding to additional button presses. In fact, each time the button is touched, a new thread will be created, allowing the task to be performed multiple times concurrently.

A close inspection of the updated code for the *buttonClick()* method will reveal that the code to update the TextView has been removed. As previously stated, updating a user interface element from within a thread other than the main thread violates a key rule of Android development. To update the user interface, therefore, it will be necessary to implement a Handler for the thread.

59.6 Implementing a Thread Handler

Thread handlers are implemented in the main thread of an application and are primarily used to make updates to the user interface in response to messages sent by other threads running within the application's process.

Handlers are subclassed from the Android Handler class and can be used either by specifying a Runnable to be executed when required by the thread, or by overriding the *handleMessage()* callback method within the Handler subclass which will be called when messages are sent to the handler by a thread.

For the purposes of this example, a handler will be implemented to update the user interface from within the previously created thread. Load the *MainActivity.java* file into the Android Studio editor and modify the code to add a Handler instance to the activity:

.

```
import android.os.Handler;
import android.os.Message;
import android.os.Looper;

public class MainActivity extends AppCompatActivity {
.
.
    Handler handler = new Handler(Looper.getMainLooper()) {
        @Override public void handleMessage(Message msg) {
            binding.myTextView.setText("Message Received");
        }
    };
.
.
```

The above code changes have declared a handler and implemented within that handler the *handleMessage()* callback which will be called when the thread sends the handler a message. In this instance, the code simply displays a string on the TextView object in the user interface.

All that now remains is to modify the thread created in the *buttonClick()* method to send a message to the handler when the delay has completed:

```
public void buttonClick(View view) {

    Runnable runnable = () -> {
            long endTime = System.currentTimeMillis() + 20 * 1000;
            while (System.currentTimeMillis() < endTime) {
                synchronized (this) {
                    try {
                        wait(endTime - System.currentTimeMillis());
                    } catch (Exception e) {
                    }
                }
            }
            handler.sendEmptyMessage(0);
        }
    };
    Thread myThread = new Thread(runnable);
    myThread.start();
}
```

Note that the only change that has been made is to make a call to the *sendEmptyMessage()* method of the handler. Since the handler does not currently do anything with the content of any messages it receives it is sent an empty message object.

Compile and run the application and, once executing, touch the button. After a 20 second delay, the new text will appear in the TextView object in the user interface.

59.7 Passing a Message to the Handler

While the previous example triggered a call to the *handleMessage()* handler callback, it did not take advantage of the message object to send data to the handler. In this phase of the tutorial, the example will be further modified to pass data between the thread and the handler. First, the updated thread in the *buttonClick()* method will obtain the date and time from the system in string format and store that information in a Bundle object. A call will then be made to the *obtainMessage()* method of the handler object to get a message object from the message pool. Finally, the bundle will be added to the message object before being sent via a call to the *sendMessage()* method of the handler object:

```java
public void buttonClick(View view) {

    Runnable runnable = () -> {
        long endTime = System.currentTimeMillis() + 20 * 1000;
        while (System.currentTimeMillis() < endTime) {
            synchronized (this) {
                try {
                    wait(endTime - System.currentTimeMillis());
                } catch (Exception e) {
                }
            }
        }
        Message msg = handler.obtainMessage();
        Bundle bundle = new Bundle();
        bundle.putString("myKey", "Thread Completed");
        msg.setData(bundle);
        handler.sendMessage(msg);
    };
    Thread myThread = new Thread(runnable);
    myThread.start();
}
```

Next, update the *handleMessage()* method of the handler to extract the date and time string from the bundle object in the message and display it on the TextView object:

```java
Handler handler = new Handler(Looper.getMainLooper()) {
    @Override
    public void handleMessage(Message msg) {
        Bundle bundle = msg.getData();
        String string = bundle.getString("myKey");
        binding.myTextView.setText(string);
    }
};
```

Finally, compile and run the application and test that touching the button now causes the "Thread Complete" message to appear on the TextView object after the thread finishes.

59.8 Java Executor Concurrency

So far in this chapter we have looked exclusively at directly creating and managing Java threads. While acceptable for simple multi-threading tasks, this can prove to be inadequate when working with complex situations involving large number of threads. There is, for example, a system overhead involved in starting and stopping threads. An app that creates and destroys large number of threads is, therefore, at risk of exhibiting degraded performance. The basic threading API also does not provide pre-built options for scheduling or repeating task execution, or for returning results from a task.

The shortcomings of working directly with threads can be overcome by making use of the Executor classes of the Java Concurrent framework (part of the java.util.concurrent package). This framework allows for a pool of active threads to be created and manages how tasks are assigned to those threads. This allows existing threads to be reused for other tasks without the need to constantly create new threads.

This framework also provides additional functionality including the ability to return a result on completion of a task (referred to as a *Callable* task), check the status of a thread and to schedule tasks to run either after a timeout or at repeated time intervals.

59.9 Working with Runnable Tasks

The first step in exploring this framework is to modify the *buttonClicked()* method to use a concurrency framework Executor to run the task in a separate thread:

```java
.
.
import java.util.concurrent.ExecutorService;
import java.util.concurrent.Executors;
.
.
    public void buttonClick(View view) {

        ExecutorService executor = Executors.newSingleThreadExecutor();

        executor.submit(new Runnable() {
           public void run() {
               long endTime = System.currentTimeMillis() + 10 * 1000;
               while (System.currentTimeMillis() < endTime) {
                   synchronized (this) {
                       try {
                           wait(endTime - System.currentTimeMillis());
                       } catch (Exception e) {
                       }
                   }
               }
               Message msg = handler.obtainMessage();
               Bundle bundle = new Bundle();
               bundle.putString("myKey", "Button Pressed");
               msg.setData(bundle);
               handler.sendMessage(msg);
           }
        });
        executor.shutdown();
    }
```

When the above code is executed, the timeout will be performed on a separate thread as before. The changes made to the method, however, require some explanation. First, a reference to an ExecutorService instance is obtained from the system Executors instance:

```
ExecutorService executor = Executors.newSingleThreadExecutor();
```

In this case, a pool containing only one thread is requested. A pool with a specified number of threads could have been requested as follows:

```
ExecutorService executor = Executors.newFixedThreadPool(10);
```

Next, a Runnable task is started on the thread via a call to the *submit()* method of the executor service instance:

```
executor.submit(new Runnable() {
    public void run() {
        long endTime = System.currentTimeMillis() + 20 * 1000;
.
.
```

Note that the above declaration can be simplified by converting it to a lambda as follows:

```
executor.submit(() -> {
    long endTime = System.currentTimeMillis() + 20 * 1000;
.
.
```

From this point on, the task will run until completion. Once completed however, the executor service will continue to run. If you have no further use for the service, it should be shutdown.

59.10 Shutting down an Executor Service

ExecutorService provides a few techniques for initiating a shutdown. To notify the service that it should shutdown automatically after the currently running tasks have reached completion, a call to the *shutdown()* method should be made as follows:

```
executor.shutdown();
```

A call to the *shutdownNow()* method, on the other hand, stops all tasks running on the service and, cancels the processing of pending tasks:

```
executor.shutdownNow();
```

59.11 Working with Callable Tasks and Futures

As previously mentioned, the ExecutorService supports so called "Callable" tasks which are able to return a result after the task is completed. Tasks running on separate thread are typically expected to take some time to complete (otherwise they probably would not need to run on a separate thread in the first place). This raises the question of how the result is returned to the code in the thread from which the task was launched. This is achieved using the Future value type which represents a value which will be provided at some point in the future.

When a callable task is executed it returns a Future instance which may then be used by the app to obtain the result when the task completes. To see this in action, begin by editing the *activity_main.xml* file to add an additional button labeled "Status" with the onClick property configured to call method named *statusClick*:

A Basic Overview of Java Threads, Handlers and Executors

Figure 59-3

Next, modify the *buttonClick()* method to execute a Callable task configured to return a String value via a Future variable:

```
.
.
.
import java.util.concurrent.Callable;
import java.util.concurrent.Future;
.
.
public class MainActivity extends AppCompatActivity {

    Future<String> future;
.
.
   public void buttonClick(View view) {

        ExecutorService executor = Executors.newSingleThreadExecutor();

        future = executor.submit(new Callable<String>() {
            public String call() {
                long endTime = System.currentTimeMillis() + 10 * 1000;
                while (System.currentTimeMillis() < endTime) {
                    synchronized (this) {
                        try {
                            wait(endTime - System.currentTimeMillis());
                        } catch (Exception e) {
                        }
```

```
            }
        }
        return("Task Completed");
    }
});
executor.shutdown();
}
```

Note that in addition to importing the java.util.concurrent.Future package and declaring a Future variable for storing a string value, some changes have also been made to the way in which the task is launched:

```
future = executor.submit(new Callable<String>() {
        public String call() {
```

The key points here are that instead of submitting a Runnable task to the executor service, we are now passing through a Callable task (declared to return a String value). Note also that the result of the task is assigned to the Future variable. In addition, *call()* is used instead of the *run()* method used previously when submitting a Runnable task. Finally, a return statement has been added to return a string value:

```
return("Task Completed")
```

59.12 Handling a Future Result

The *buttonClick()* method is now configured to launch a Callable task with the return value assigned to the Future variable. The app now needs to know when the task is complete and the result available. One option is to call the *get()* method of the Future variable. Since this method is able to throw exceptions if the execution fails or is interrupted, this must be performed in a try/catch statement as follows:

```
String result = null;

try {
    result = future.get();
} catch (ExecutionException | InterruptedException e) {
    e.printStackTrace();
}
```

Unfortunately, the *get()* method will block the current thread until the task running in the thread completes, thereby defeating the purpose of running the task in a separate thread in the first place. Another option is to provide the *get()* method call with a timeout after which it will return control to the current thread. The following code, for example, will cause the *get()* call to timeout after 3 seconds:

```
result = future.get(3, TimeUnit.SECONDS);
```

A better alternative, however, is to call the *isDone()* method of the Future instance to check the status of the thread and only call the *get()* method once the task is complete. To implement this behavior, add the *statusClick()* method to the *MainActivity.java* file as follows:

```
import java.util.concurrent.ExecutionException;
import java.util.concurrent.TimeUnit;
import java.util.concurrent.TimeoutException;
```

```
public void statusClick(View view) {

    if ((future != null && future.isDone()) {
        String result = null;
        try {
            result = future.get(3, TimeUnit.SECONDS);
        } catch (ExecutionException | InterruptedException
                    | TimeoutException e) {
            e.printStackTrace();
        }
        binding.myTextView.setText(result);
    } else {
        binding.myTextView.setText("Waiting");
    }
}
```

With the changes made, run the app and click on the "Press Me" button. While the task is running, click on the Status button. As long as the task is still running, the "Waiting" message will be displayed in the TextView. Once the task completes, however, the *isDone()* method will return a true value, the *get()* method will be called and the string returned by the task ("Task Complete") displayed on the TextView.

59.13 Scheduling Tasks

The final area to be covered involves the use of ExecutorService to schedule task execution. This involves use of a ScheduledExecutorService instance on which the *schedule()* method needs to be called passing through the Runnable task to be executed together with a time delay. The *schedule()* call will return a ScheduledFuture instance which may be used to identify the remaining time before the task is due to start.

The following code, for example, schedules a task to run after a 30 second delay and accesses the remaining delay time:

```
ScheduledExecutorService executor = Executors.newScheduledThreadPool(1);

Runnable task = () -> {
        // Code to perform task here
};

ScheduledFuture<?> future = executor.schedule(task, 30, TimeUnit.SECONDS);
long delayRemaining = future.getDelay(TimeUnit.SECONDS);
```

Similarly, the ScheduledExecutorService may be used to execute a task repeatedly at regular intervals starting after an optional initial delay. The following code, for example, causes a task to be performed every 10 seconds after an initial 30 second delay:

```
executor.scheduleAtFixedRate(task, 30, 10, TimeUnit.SECONDS);
```

The *scheduleAtFixedRate()* method will launch the next instance of the task regardless of whether or not the previously scheduled task has completed. To specify a fixed period of time between the end of a task execution and the start of the next execution, use the *scheduleWithFixedDelay()* method. In the following example, the first task is scheduled after a 0 second delay, with each subsequent execution taking place 10 seconds after completion of the proceeding task:

```
executor.scheduleWithFixedDelay(task, 0, 10, TimeUnit.SECONDS);
```

59.14 Summary

The goal of this chapter was to provide an overview of threading within Android applications. When an application is first launched in a process, the runtime system creates a main thread in which all subsequently launched application components run by default. The primary role of the main thread is to handle the user interface, so any time consuming tasks performed in that thread will give the appearance that the application has locked up. It is essential, therefore, that tasks likely to take time to complete be started in a separate thread.

Because the Android user interface toolkit is not thread-safe, changes to the user interface should not be made in any thread other than the main thread. User interface changes can be implemented by creating a handler in the main thread to which messages may be sent from within other, non-main threads.

Threads can be created either directly, or using the executor services of the Java Concurrent framework. For more complex threading requirements, this framework provides automatic management of thread pools, returning of results from tasks and execution scheduling.

60. Making Runtime Permission Requests in Android

In a number of the example projects created in preceding chapters, changes have been made to the *AndroidManifest.xml* file to request permission for the app to perform a specific task. In a couple of instances, for example, internet access permission has been requested to allow the app to download and display web pages. In each case up until this point, adding the request to the manifest was all that was required for the app to obtain permission from the user to perform the designated task.

However, there are several permissions for which additional steps are required for the app to function when running on Android 6.0 or later. The first of these so-called "dangerous" permissions will be encountered in the next chapter. Before reaching that point, however, this chapter will outline the steps involved in requesting such permissions when running on the latest generations of Android.

60.1 Understanding Normal and Dangerous Permissions

Android enforces security by requiring the user to grant permission for an app to perform certain tasks. Before the introduction of Android 6, permission was always sought when the app was installed on the device. Figure 60-1, for example, shows a typical screen seeking a variety of permissions while installing an app via Google Play.

Figure 60-1

For many types of permissions, this scenario still applies to apps on Android 6.0 or later. These permissions are referred to as *normal permissions* and are still required to be accepted by the user at the point of installation. A second type of permission, called *dangerous permissions*, must also be declared within the manifest file in the same way as a normal permission but must also be requested from the user when the application is first launched. When such a request is made, it appears in the form of a dialog box, as illustrated in Figure 60-2:

Making Runtime Permission Requests in Android

Figure 60-2

The full list of permissions that fall into the dangerous category is contained in Table 60-1:

Permission Group	Permission
Calendar	READ_CALENDAR
	WRITE_CALENDAR
Camera	CAMERA
Contacts	READ_CONTACTS
	WRITE_CONTACTS
	GET_ACCOUNTS
Location	ACCESS_FINE_LOCATION
	ACCESS_COARSE_LOCATION
Microphone	RECORD_AUDIO
Notifications	POST_NOTIFICATIONS
Phone	READ_PHONE_STATE
	CALL_PHONE
	READ_CALL_LOG
	WRITE_CALL_LOG
	ADD_VOICEMAIL
	USE_SIP
	PROCESS_OUTGOING_CALLS
Sensors	BODY_SENSORS
SMS	SEND_SMS
	RECEIVE_SMS
	READ_SMS
	RECEIVE_WAP_PUSH
	RECEIVE_MMS

Making Runtime Permission Requests in Android

Storage	MANAGE_EXTERNAL_STORAGE
	READ_EXTERNAL_STORAGE
	WRITE_EXTERNAL_STORAGE

Table 60-1

The MANAGE_EXTERNAL_STORAGE permission gives the app access to all files on the device's external storage, including those belonging to other apps. Consequently, permission will only be enabled for your app once Google has verified during the review process that this level of access is needed. To test your app in advance of submitting it to the Google Play store, the following *adb* command can be executed to enable access for the app on the testing device temporarily:

```
adb shell appops set --uid <package name> MANAGE_EXTERNAL_STORAGE allow
```

This mode can be turned off as follows:

```
adb shell appops set --uid <package name> MANAGE_EXTERNAL_STORAGE default
```

60.2 Creating the Permissions Example Project

Select the *New Project* option from the welcome screen and, within the resulting new project dialog, choose the Empty Views Activity template before clicking on the Next button.

Enter *PermissionDemo* into the Name field and specify *com.ebookfrenzy.permissiondemo* as the package name. Before clicking on the Finish button, change the Minimum API level setting to API 26: Android 8.0 (Oreo) and the Language menu to Java.

60.3 Checking for a Permission

The Android Support Library contains several methods that can be used to seek and manage dangerous permissions within the code of an Android app. These API calls can be made safely regardless of the version of Android on which the app is running but will only perform meaningful tasks when executed on Android 6.0 or later.

Before an app attempts to use a feature that requires approval of a dangerous permission, and regardless of whether or not permission was previously granted, the code must check that the permission has been granted. This can be achieved via a call to the *checkSelfPermission()* method of the ContextCompat class, passing through as arguments a reference to the current activity and the requested permission. The method will check whether the permission has been previously granted and return an integer value matching *PackageManager.PERMISSION_GRANTED* or *PackageManager.PERMISSION_DENIED*.

Within the *MainActivity.java* file of the example project, modify the code to check whether permission has been granted for the app to record audio:

```
package com.ebookfrenzy.permissiondemoactivity;

import androidx.appcompat.app.AppCompatActivity;
import androidx.core.content.ContextCompat;
import androidx.annotation.NonNull;

import android.os.Bundle;
import android.Manifest;
import android.content.pm.PackageManager;
import android.util.Log;
```

505

Making Runtime Permission Requests in Android

```java
public class MainActivity extends AppCompatActivity {

    private static final String TAG = "PermissionDemo";

    @Override
    protected void onCreate(Bundle savedInstanceState) {
        super.onCreate(savedInstanceState);
        setContentView(R.layout.activity_permission_demo);

        setupPermissions();
    }

    private void setupPermissions() {
        int permission = ContextCompat.checkSelfPermission(this,
                Manifest.permission.RECORD_AUDIO);

        if (permission != PackageManager.PERMISSION_GRANTED) {
            Log.i(TAG, "Permission to record denied");
        }
    }
}
```

Edit the *AndroidManifest.xml* file (located in the Project tool window under *app -> manifests*) and add a line to request recording permission as follows:

```xml
<?xml version="1.0" encoding="utf-8"?>
<manifest xmlns:android="http://schemas.android.com/apk/res/android"
    package="com.ebookfrenzy.permissiondemoactivity" >

    <uses-permission android:name="android.permission.RECORD_AUDIO" />

    <application
        android:allowBackup="true"
        android:icon="@mipmap/ic_launcher"
        android:label="@sxtring/app_name"
        android:supportsRtl="true"
        android:theme="@style/AppTheme" >
        <activity android:name=".MainActivity" >
            <intent-filter>
                <action android:name="android.intent.action.MAIN" />

                <category
                    android:name="android.intent.category.LAUNCHER" />
            </intent-filter>
        </activity>
    </application>
</manifest>
```

Run the app on a device or emulator and open the Logcat tool window. Note that even though the permission has been added to the manifest file, the permission denied message appears. This is because Android requires that in addition to adding the request to the manifest file, the app must also request dangerous permissions at runtime.

60.4 Requesting Permission at Runtime

A permission request is made via a call to the *requestPermissions()* method of the ActivityCompat class. When this method is called, the permission request is handled asynchronously, and a method named *onRequestPermissionsResult()* is called when the task is completed.

The *requestPermissions()* method takes as arguments a reference to the current activity, the identifier of the requested permission, and a request code. The request code can be any integer value and will be used to identify which request has triggered the call to the *onRequestPermissionsResult()* method. Modify the *MainActivity.java* file to declare a request code and request recording permission if the permission check fails:

```
.
.
import androidx.core.app.ActivityCompat;
.
.
public class MainActivity extends AppCompatActivity {

    private static final String TAG = "PermissionDemo";
    private static final int RECORD_REQUEST_CODE = 101;
.
.

    @Override
    private void setupPermissions() {

        int permission = ContextCompat.checkSelfPermission(this,
                Manifest.permission.RECORD_AUDIO);

        if (permission != PackageManager.PERMISSION_GRANTED) {
            Log.i(TAG, "Permission to record denied");
            makeRequest();
        }
    }

    protected void makeRequest() {
        ActivityCompat.requestPermissions(this,
                new String[]{Manifest.permission.RECORD_AUDIO},
                RECORD_REQUEST_CODE);
    }
}
```

Next, implement the *onRequestPermissionsResult()* method so that it reads as follows:

```
@Override
public void onRequestPermissionsResult(int requestCode,
```

```
                   @NonNull String[] permissions, @NonNull int[] grantResults) {
    super.onRequestPermissionsResult(requestCode, permissions, grantResults);
    if (requestCode == RECORD_REQUEST_CODE) {
        if (grantResults.length == 0
                || grantResults[0] !=
                PackageManager.PERMISSION_GRANTED) {
            Log.i(TAG, "Permission has been denied by user");
        } else {
            Log.i(TAG, "Permission has been granted by user");
        }
    }
}
```

Compile and run the app on an emulator or device and note that a dialog seeking permission to record audio appears as shown in Figure 60-3:

Figure 60-3

Tap the *While using the app* button and check that the "Permission has been granted by user" message appears in the Logcat panel.

Once the user has granted the requested permission, the *checkSelfPermission()* method call will return a PERMISSION_GRANTED result on future app invocations until the user uninstalls and re-installs the app or changes the permissions for the app in Settings.

60.5 Providing a Rationale for the Permission Request

As evident from Figure 60-3, the user can deny the requested permission. In this case, the app will continue to request permission each time the user launches it unless the user selects the "Never ask again" option before clicking the Deny button. Repeated denials by the user may indicate that the user doesn't understand why the app requires permission. The user might, therefore, be more likely to grant permission if the reason for the requirements is explained when the request is made. Unfortunately, it is not possible to change the content of the request dialog to include such an explanation.

An explanation is best included in a separate dialog which can be displayed before the request dialog is presented

Making Runtime Permission Requests in Android

to the user. This raises the question of when to display this explanation dialog. The Android documentation recommends that an explanation dialog only be shown if the user has previously denied the permission and provides a method to identify when this is the case.

A call to the *shouldShowRequestPermissionRationale()* method of the ActivityCompat class will return a true result if the user has previously denied a request for the specified permission and a false result if the request has not previously been made. In the case of a true result, the app should display a dialog containing a rationale for needing permission, and once the dialog has been read and dismissed by the user, the permission request should be repeated.

To add this functionality to the example app, modify the *onCreate()* method so that it reads as follows:

.
.
.
```
import android.app.AlertDialog;
```
.
.
.
```
private void setupPermissions() {

    int permission = ContextCompat.checkSelfPermission(this,
            Manifest.permission.RECORD_AUDIO);

    if (permission != PackageManager.PERMISSION_GRANTED) {
        Log.i(TAG, "Permission to record denied");

        if (ActivityCompat.shouldShowRequestPermissionRationale(this,
                Manifest.permission.RECORD_AUDIO)) {
            AlertDialog.Builder builder =
                    new AlertDialog.Builder(this);
            builder.setMessage("Permission to access the microphone is required for this app to record audio.")
                    .setTitle("Permission required");

            builder.setPositiveButton("OK",
                    (dialog, id) -> makeRequest());

            AlertDialog dialog = builder.create();
            dialog.show();
        } else {
            makeRequest();
        }
    }
}
```

The method still checks whether or not the permission has been granted but now also identifies whether a rationale needs to be displayed. If the user has previously denied the request, a dialog is displayed containing an explanation and an OK button on which a listener is configured to call the *makeRequest()* method when the button is tapped. If the permission request has not previously been made, the code moves directly to seeking permission.

60.6 Testing the Permissions App

On the device or emulator session on which testing is being performed, launch the Settings app, select the *Apps* option, and scroll to and select the PermissionDemo app. On the app settings screen, tap the uninstall button to remove the app.

Rerun the app, and click on the *Don't allow* button when the permission request dialog appears. Stop and restart the app and verify that the rationale dialog appears. Tap the OK button, and tap the *While using the app* button when the permission request dialog appears.

Return to the Settings app, select the Apps option, and choose the PermissionDemo app again from the list. Once the settings for the app are listed, verify that the Permissions section lists the Microphone permission.

Return to the Settings app, select the Apps option, and choose the PermissionDemo app again from the list. Once the settings for the app are listed, verify that the Permissions section lists the *Microphone* permission:

Figure 60-4

60.7 Summary

Before the introduction of Android 6.0, the only step necessary for an app to request permission to access certain functionality was to add an appropriate line to the application's manifest file. The user would then be prompted to approve the permission when installing the app. This is still the case for most permissions, except for a set of permissions considered dangerous. Permissions that are considered dangerous usually have the potential to allow an app to violate the user's privacy, such as allowing access to the microphone, contacts list, or external storage.

As outlined in this chapter, apps based on Android 6 or later must now request dangerous permission approval from the user when the app launches and include the permission request in the manifest file.

Chapter 61

61. An Android Notifications Tutorial

Notifications provide a way for an app to convey a message to the user when the app is either not running or is currently in the background. For example, a messaging app might notify the user that a new message has arrived from a contact. Notifications can be categorized as being either local or remote. A local notification is triggered by the app itself on the device on which it is running. On the other hand, remote notifications are initiated by a remote server and delivered to the device for presentation to the user.

Notifications appear in the notification drawer that is pulled down from the screen's status bar, and each notification can include actions such as a button to open the app that sent the notification. Android also supports Direct Reply notifications, a feature that allows the user to type in and submit a response to a notification from within the notification panel.

This chapter outlines the implementation of local notifications within an Android app. The next chapter (*"An Android Direct Reply Notification Tutorial"*) will cover the implementation of direct reply notifications.

61.1 An Overview of Notifications

When a notification is initiated on an Android device, it appears as an icon in the status bar. Figure 61-1, for example, shows a status bar with several notification icons:

Figure 61-1

To view the notifications, the user makes a downward swiping motion starting at the status bar to pull down the notification drawer, as shown in Figure 61-2:

Figure 61-2

In devices running Android 8 or newer, performing a long press on an app launcher icon will display any pending notifications associated with that app, as shown in Figure 61-3:

An Android Notifications Tutorial

Figure 61-3

Android 8 and later also supports notification dots that appear on app launcher icons when a notification is waiting to be seen by the user.

A typical notification will display a message and, when tapped, launch the app responsible for issuing the notification. Notifications may also contain action buttons that perform a task specific to the corresponding app when tapped. Figure 61-4, for example, shows a notification containing two action buttons allowing the user to delete or save an incoming message:

Figure 61-4

It is also possible for the user to enter an in-line text reply into the notification and send it to the app, as is the case in Figure 61-5 below. This allows the user to respond to a notification without launching the corresponding app into the foreground:

Figure 61-5

The remainder of this chapter will work through creating and issuing a simple notification containing actions. The topic of direct reply support will be covered in the next chapter entitled *"An Android Direct Reply Notification Tutorial"*.

An Android Notifications Tutorial

61.2 Creating the NotifyDemo Project

Select the *New Project* option from the welcome screen and, within the resulting new project dialog, choose the Empty Views Activity template before clicking on the Next button.

Enter *NotifyDemo* into the Name field and specify *com.ebookfrenzy.notifydemo* as the package name. Before clicking on the Finish button, change the Minimum API level setting to API 33: Android 13 (Tiramisu) and the Language menu to Java.

61.3 Designing the User Interface

The main activity will contain a single button, the purpose of which is to create and issue an intent. Locate and load the *activity_main.xml* file into the Layout Editor tool and delete the default TextView widget.

With Autoconnect enabled, drag and drop a Button object from the panel onto the center of the layout canvas, as illustrated in Figure 61-6.

With the Button widget selected in the layout, use the Attributes panel to configure the onClick property to call a method named *sendNotification*.

Figure 61-6

Select the Button widget, change the text property in the Attributes tool window to "Notify" and extract the property value to a string resource.

61.4 Creating the Second Activity

In this example, the app will contain a second activity which will be launched by the user from within the notification. Add this new activity to the project by right-clicking on the *com.ebookfrenzy.notifydemo* package name located in *app -> java* and selecting the *New -> Activity -> Empty Views Activity* menu option to display the *New Android Activity* dialog.

Enter *ResultActivity* into the Activity Name field and name the layout file *activity_result*. Since this activity will not be started when the application is launched (it will instead be launched via an intent from within the notification), it is important to make sure that the *Launcher Activity* option is disabled before clicking on the Finish button.

Open the layout for the second activity (*app -> res -> layout -> activity_result.xml*) and drag and drop a TextView

An Android Notifications Tutorial

widget so that it is positioned in the center of the layout. Edit the text of the TextView so that it reads "Result Activity" and extract the property value to a string resource.

61.5 Creating a Notification Channel

Before an app can send a notification, it must create a notification channel. A notification channel consists of an ID that uniquely identifies the channel within the app, a channel name, and a channel description (only the latter two will be seen by the user). Channels are created by configuring a NotificationChannel instance and then passing that object through to the *createNotificationChannel()* method of the NotificationManager class. For this example, the app will contain a single notification channel named "NotifyDemo News". Edit the *MainActivity.java* file and implement code to create the channel when the app starts:

```java
.
.
import android.app.NotificationManager;
import android.app.NotificationChannel;
import android.content.Context;
import android.graphics.Color;

public class MainActivity extends AppCompatActivity {

    NotificationManager notificationManager;

    @Override
    protected void onCreate(Bundle savedInstanceState) {
        super.onCreate(savedInstanceState);
        setContentView(R.layout.activity_main);

        notificationManager =
                (NotificationManager)
                    getSystemService(Context.NOTIFICATION_SERVICE);

        createNotificationChannel(
                "com.ebookfrenzy.notifydemo.news",
                "NotifyDemo News",
                "Example News Channel");
    }

    protected void createNotificationChannel(String id, String name,
            String description) {

        int importance = NotificationManager.IMPORTANCE_LOW;
        NotificationChannel channel =
                new NotificationChannel(id, name, importance);

        channel.setDescription(description);
        channel.enableLights(true);
        channel.setLightColor(Color.RED);
```

```
            channel.enableVibration(true);
            channel.setVibrationPattern(
               new long[]{100, 200, 300, 400, 500, 400, 300, 200, 400});
            notificationManager.createNotificationChannel(channel);
       }
.
.
.
}
```

The code declares and initializes a NotificationManager instance and then creates the new channel with a low importance level (other options are high, max, min, and none) configured with the name and description properties. A range of optional settings are also added to the channel to customize how the user is alerted to the arrival of a notification. These settings apply to all notifications sent to this channel. Finally, the channel is created by passing the notification channel object through to the *createNotificationChannel()* method of the notification manager instance.

61.6 Requesting Notification Permission

Before testing the application, the appropriate permissions must be requested within the manifest file for the application. Specifically, the application will require permission to post notifications to the user. Within the Project tool window, locate and double-click on the *AndroidManifest.xml* file to load it into the editor and modify the XML to add the permission:

```
<?xml version="1.0" encoding="utf-8"?>
<manifest xmlns:android="http://schemas.android.com/apk/res/android"
    package="com.ebookfrenzy.audioapp" >

    <uses-permission android:name="android.permission.POST_NOTIFICATIONS" />
.
.
```

The above step will be adequate to ensure that the user enables notification permission when the app is installed on devices running versions of Android predating Android 6.0. Notification access is categorized in Android as a dangerous permission because it gives the app the potential to compromise the user's privacy. For the example app to function on Android 6 or later devices, code must be added to request permission at app runtime.

Edit the *MainActivity.java* file and begin by adding some additional import directives and a constant to act as request identification codes for the permission being requested:

```
.
.
import androidx.core.app.ActivityCompat;
import androidx.core.content.ContextCompat;
import androidx.annotation.NonNull;
import android.widget.Toast;
import android.Manifest;
import android.content.pm.PackageManager;
.
.
public class MainActivity extends AppCompatActivity {
```

An Android Notifications Tutorial

```
    private static final int NOTICATION_REQUEST_CODE = 101;
.
.
```

Next, a method needs to be added to the class, the purpose of which is to take as arguments the permission to be requested and the corresponding request identification code. Remaining with the *MainActivity.java* class file, implement this method as follows:

```
protected void requestPermission(String permissionType, int requestCode) {
    int permission = ContextCompat.checkSelfPermission(this,
            permissionType);

    if (permission != PackageManager.PERMISSION_GRANTED) {
        ActivityCompat.requestPermissions(this,
                new String[]{permissionType}, requestCode
        );
    }
}
```

Using the steps outlined in the *"Making Runtime Permission Requests in Android"* chapter of this book, the above method verifies that the specified permission has not already been granted before making the request, passing through the identification code as an argument.

When the request has been handled, the *onRequestPermissionsResult()* method will be called on the activity, passing through the identification code and the request results. The next step, therefore, is to implement this method within the *MainActivity.java* file as follows:

```
@Override
public void onRequestPermissionsResult(int requestCode,
            @NonNull String[] permissions, @NonNull int[] grantResults) {
    super.onRequestPermissionsResult(requestCode, permissions, grantResults);

    if (requestCode == NOTIFICATION_REQUEST_CODE) {
        if (grantResults.length == 0
                || grantResults[0] !=
                PackageManager.PERMISSION_GRANTED) {

            Toast.makeText(this,
                    "Notification permission required",
                    Toast.LENGTH_LONG).show();
        }
    }
}
```

The above code checks the request identifier code to identify which permission request has returned before checking whether or not the corresponding permission was granted. If permission is denied, a message is displayed to the user indicating that the app will not function and the record button is disabled.

Before testing the app, all that remains is to call the newly added requestPermission() method when the app launches. Remaining in the *MainActivity.java* file, modify the *onCreate()* method as follows:

```
@Override
```

```
protected void onCreate(Bundle savedInstanceState) {
    super.onCreate(savedInstanceState);
    setContentView(R.layout.activity_main);
    requestPermission(Manifest.permission.POST_NOTIFICATIONS,
            NOTIFICATION_REQUEST_CODE);
```

With the code changes complete, compile and run the app on a device or emulator running Android 13 or later. When the dialog shown in Figure 61-7 appears, click on the Allow button to enable notifications:

Figure 61-7

After launching the app, place it in the background and open the Settings app. Within the Settings app, select the *Apps* option, select the NotifyDemo project, and, on the subsequent screen, tap the *Notifications* entry. The notification screen should list the NotifyDemo News category as being active for the user:

Figure 61-8

Before proceeding, ensure that notification dots are enabled for the app.

An Android Notifications Tutorial

Although not a requirement for this example, it is worth noting that a channel can be deleted from within the app via a call to the *deleteNotificationChannel()* method of the notification manager, passing through the ID of the channel to be deleted:

```
String channelID = "com.ebookfrenzy.notifydemo.news";
notificationManager.deleteNotificationChannel(channelID);
```

61.7 Creating and Issuing a Notification

Notifications are created using the Notification.Builder class and must contain an icon, title, and content. Open the *MainActivity.java* file and implement the *sendNotification()* method as follows to build a basic notification:

```
.
.
import android.app.Notification;
import android.view.View;
.
.
public void sendNotification(View view) {

    String channelID = "com.ebookfrenzy.notifydemo.news";

    Notification notification =
            new Notification.Builder(MainActivity.this,
                                        channelID)
        .setContentTitle("Example Notification")
        .setContentText("This is an example notification.")
        .setSmallIcon(android.R.drawable.ic_dialog_info)
        .setChannelId(channelID)
        .build();
}
```

Once a notification has been built, it needs to be issued using the *notify()* method of the NotificationManager instance. The code to access the NotificationManager and issue the notification needs to be added to the *sendNotification()* method as follows:

```
protected void sendNotification(View view) {

    int notificationID = 101;

    String channelID = "com.ebookfrenzy.notifydemo.news";

    Notification notification =
            new Notification.Builder(MainActivity.this,
                            channelID)
        .setContentTitle("New Message")
        .setContentText("You've received new messages.")
        .setSmallIcon(android.R.drawable.ic_dialog_info)
        .setChannelId(channelID)
        .build();
```

An Android Notifications Tutorial

```
        notificationManager.notify(notificationID, notification);
}
```

Note that when the notification is issued, it is assigned a notification ID. This can be any integer and may be used later when updating the notification.

Compile and run the app and tap the button on the main activity. When the notification icon appears in the status bar, touch and drag down from the status bar to view the full notification:

Figure 61-9

Click and hold on the notification to view additional information:

Figure 61-10

Next, place the app in the background, navigate to the home screen displaying the launcher icons for all of the apps, and note that a notification dot has appeared on the NotifyDemo launcher icon as indicated by the arrow in Figure 61-11:

Figure 61-11

If the dot is not present, check the notification options for NotifyDemo in the Settings app to confirm that

An Android Notifications Tutorial

notification dots are enabled, as outlined earlier in the chapter. If the dot still does not appear, touch and hold over a blank area of the device home screen, select the *Home Settings* option from the resulting menu, and enable the *Notification dots* option.

Performing a long press over the launcher icon will display a popup containing the notification:

Figure 61-12

If more than one notification is pending for an app, the long press menu popup will contain a count of notifications (highlighted in the above figure). This number may be configured from within the app by making a call to the *setNumber()* method when building the notification:

```
Notification notification = new Notification.Builder(MainActivity.this, CHANNEL_ID)
        .setContentTitle("Example Notification")
        .setContentText("This is an  example notification.")
        .setSmallIcon(android.R.drawable.ic_dialog_info)
        .setChannelId(CHANNEL_ID)
        .setNumber(10)
        .build();
```

As currently implemented, tapping on the notification has no effect regardless of where it is accessed. The next step is configuring the notification to launch an activity when tapped.

61.8 Launching an Activity from a Notification

A notification should allow the user to perform some action, such as launching the corresponding app or taking another action in response to the notification. A common requirement is to launch an activity belonging to the app when the user taps the notification.

This approach requires an activity to be launched and an Intent configured to launch that activity. Assuming an app that contains an activity named ResultActivity, the intent would be created as follows:

```
Intent resultIntent = new Intent(this, ResultActivity.class);
```

This intent needs to then be wrapped in a PendingIntent instance. PendingIntent objects are designed to allow an intent to be passed to other applications, essentially granting those applications permission to perform the

An Android Notifications Tutorial

intent at some point in the future. In this case, the PendingIntent object is being used to provide the Notification system with a way to launch the ResultActivity activity when the user taps the notification panel:

```
PendingIntent pendingIntent =
    PendingIntent.getActivity(
    this,
    0,
    resultIntent,
    PendingIntent.FLAG_IMMUTABLE
);
```

All that remains is to assign the PendingIntent object during the notification build process using the *setContentIntent()* method.

Bringing these changes together results in a modified *sendNotification()* method, which reads as follows:

.
.
.
```
import android.app.PendingIntent;
import android.content.Intent;
import android.graphics.drawable.Icon;
.
.
.
protected void sendNotification(View view) {

    int notificationId = 101;

    Intent resultIntent = new Intent(this, ResultActivity.class);

    PendingIntent pendingIntent =
            PendingIntent.getActivity(
                this,
                0,
                resultIntent,
                PendingIntent.FLAG_IMMUTABLE
            );

    String CHANNEL_ID = "com.ebookfrenzy.notifydemo.news";

    Notification notification = new Notification.Builder(MainActivity.this,
                                                         CHANNEL_ID)
            .setContentTitle("Example Notification")
            .setContentText("This is an  example notification.")
            .setSmallIcon(android.R.drawable.ic_dialog_info)
            .setChannelId(channelID)
            .setContentIntent(pendingIntent)
            .build();
```

521

```
        notificationManager.notify(notificationId, notification);
}
```

Compile and rerun the app, tap the button, and display the notification drawer. This time, however, tapping the notification will cause the ResultActivity to launch.

61.9 Adding Actions to a Notification

Another way to add interactivity to a notification is to create actions. These appear as buttons beneath the notification message and are programmed to trigger specific intents when tapped by the user. The following code, if added to the *sendNotification()* method, will add an action button labeled "Open" which launches the referenced pending intent when selected:

```
final Icon icon = Icon.createWithResource(MainActivity.this,
            android.R.drawable.ic_dialog_info);

Notification.Action action =
        new Notification.Action.Builder(icon, "Open", pendingIntent)
               .build();

Notification notification = new Notification.Builder(MainActivity.this, CHANNEL_ID)
        .setContentTitle("Example Notification")
        .setContentText("This is an  example notification.")
        .setSmallIcon(R.drawable.ic_info_24dp)
        .setChannelId(channelID)
        .setContentIntent(pendingIntent)
        .setActions(action)
        .build();

notificationManager.notify(notificationId, notification);
```

Add the above code to the method and run the app. Issue the notification and note the appearance of the Open action within the notification (depending on the Android version, it may be necessary to pull down on the notification panel to reveal the Open action):

Figure 61-13

Tapping the action will trigger the pending intent and launch the ResultActivity.

61.10 Bundled Notifications

If an app tends to issue notifications regularly, there is a danger that those notifications will rapidly clutter both the status bar and the notification drawer providing a less-than-optimal experience for the user. This can be particularly true of news or messaging apps that send a notification every time a breaking news story or a new message arrives from a contact. Consider, for example, the notifications in Figure 61-14:

Figure 61-14

Now imagine if ten or even twenty new messages had arrived. To avoid this problem, Android allows notifications to be bundled into groups.

To bundle notifications, each notification must be designated as belonging to the same group via the *setGroup()* method, and an additional notification must be issued and configured as the *summary notification*. The following code, for example, creates and issues the three notifications shown in Figure 61-14 above but bundles them into the same group. The code also issues a notification to act as the summary:

```
final String GROUP_KEY_NOTIFY = "group_key_notify";

Notification.Builder builderSummary =
        new Notification.Builder(this, channelID)
                .setSmallIcon(android.R.drawable.ic_dialog_info)
                .setContentTitle("A Bundle Example")
                .setContentText("You have 3 new messages")
                .setGroup(GROUP_KEY_NOTIFY)
                .setGroupSummary(true);

Notification.Builder builder1 =
        new Notification.Builder(this, channelID)
                .setSmallIcon(android.R.drawable.ic_dialog_info)
                .setContentTitle("New Message")
                .setContentText("You have a new message from Kassidy")
                .setGroup(GROUP_KEY_NOTIFY);

Notification.Builder builder2 =
        new Notification.Builder(this, channelID)
                .setSmallIcon(android.R.drawable.ic_dialog_info)
                .setContentTitle("New Message")
                .setContentText("You have a new message from Caitlyn")
```

An Android Notifications Tutorial

```
                .setGroup(GROUP_KEY_NOTIFY);

Notification.Builder builder3 =
        new Notification.Builder(this, channelID)
                .setSmallIcon(android.R.drawable.ic_dialog_info)
                .setContentTitle("New Message")
                .setContentText("You have a new message from Jason")
                .setGroup(GROUP_KEY_NOTIFY);

int notificationId0 = 100;
int notificationId1 = 101;
int notificationId2 = 102;
int notificationId3 = 103;

notificationManager.notify(notificationId1, builder1.build());
notificationManager.notify(notificationId2, builder2.build());
notificationManager.notify(notificationId3, builder3.build());
notificationManager.notify(notificationId0, builderSummary.build());
```

When the code is executed, a single notification icon will appear in the status bar even though the app has issued four notifications. Within the notification drawer, a single summary notification is displayed listing the information in each of the bundled notifications:

Figure 61-15

Pulling further downward on the notification entry expands the panel to show the details of each of the bundled notifications:

Figure 61-16

61.11 Summary

Notifications provide a way for an app to deliver a message to the user when the app is not running or is currently in the background. Notifications appear in the status bar and notification drawer. Local notifications are triggered on the device by the running app, while remote notifications are initiated by a remote server and delivered to the device. Local notifications are created using the NotificationCompat.Builder class and issued using the NotificationManager service.

As demonstrated in this chapter, notifications can be configured to provide users with options (such as launching an activity or saving a message) by using actions, intents, and the PendingIntent class. Notification bundling provides a mechanism for grouping notifications to provide an improved experience for apps that issue more notifications.

Chapter 62

62. An Android Direct Reply Notification Tutorial

Direct reply is an Android feature that allows the user to enter text into a notification and send it to the app associated with that notification. This allows the user to reply to a message in the notification without launching an activity within the app. This chapter will build on the knowledge gained in the previous chapter to create an example app that uses this notification feature.

62.1 Creating the DirectReply Project

Select the *New Project* option from the welcome screen and, within the resulting new project dialog, choose the Empty Views Activity template before clicking on the Next button.

Enter *DirectReply* into the Name field and specify *com.ebookfrenzy.directreply* as the package name. Before clicking on the Finish button, change the Minimum API level setting to API 33: Android 13 and the Language menu to Java. Modify the project to support view binding using the steps outlined in section *11.8 Migrating a Project to View Binding*.

62.2 Designing the User Interface

Load the *activity_main.xml* layout file into the layout tool. With Autoconnect enabled, add a Button object beneath the existing "Hello World!" label, as shown in Figure 62-1. With the Button widget selected in the layout, use the Attributes tool window to set the onClick property to call a method named *sendNotification*. Use the Infer Constraints button to add any missing constraints to the layout if necessary. Before continuing, select the "Hello World!" TextView, change the id attribute to *textView*, and modify the text on the button to read "Notify":

Figure 62-1

An Android Direct Reply Notification Tutorial

62.3 Requesting Notification Permission

Within the Project tool window, locate and double-click on the *AndroidManifest.xml* file to load it into the editor and modify the XML to add the permission element:

```
<?xml version="1.0" encoding="utf-8"?>
<manifest xmlns:android="http://schemas.android.com/apk/res/android"
    package="com.ebookfrenzy.audioapp" >

    <uses-permission android:name="android.permission.POST_NOTIFICATIONS" />
.
.
.
```

Edit the *MainActivity.java* file and begin by adding some additional import directives and a constant to act as request identification codes for the permission being requested:

```
.
.
import androidx.annotation.NonNull;
import androidx.core.app.ActivityCompat;
import androidx.core.content.ContextCompat;
import android.widget.Toast;
import android.Manifest;
import android.content.pm.PackageManager;
.
.
public class MainActivity extends AppCompatActivity {

    private static final int NOTIFICATION_REQUEST_CODE = 101;
.
.
```

Next, a method needs to be added to the class, the purpose of which is to take as arguments the permission to be requested and the corresponding request identification code. Remaining with the *MainActivity.java* class file, implement this method as follows:

```
protected void requestPermission(String permissionType, int requestCode) {
    int permission = ContextCompat.checkSelfPermission(this,
            permissionType);

    if (permission != PackageManager.PERMISSION_GRANTED) {
        ActivityCompat.requestPermissions(this,
                new String[]{permissionType}, requestCode
        );
    }
}
```

When the request has been handled, the *onRequestPermissionsResult()* method will be called on the activity, passing through the identification code and the request results. The next step, therefore, is to implement this method within the *MainActivity.java* file as follows:

```
@Override
```

```
public void onRequestPermissionsResult(int requestCode,
            @NonNull String[] permissions, @NonNull int[] grantResults) {
    super.onRequestPermissionsResult(requestCode, permissions, grantResults);

    if (requestCode == NOTIFICATION_REQUEST_CODE) {
        if (grantResults.length == 0
                || grantResults[0] !=
                PackageManager.PERMISSION_GRANTED) {

            Toast.makeText(this,
                    "Notification permission required",
                    Toast.LENGTH_LONG).show();
        }
    }
}
```

Before testing the app, all that remains is to call the newly added *requestPermission()* method when the app launches. Remaining in the *MainActivity.java* file, modify the *onCreate()* method as follows:

```
@Override
protected void onCreate(Bundle savedInstanceState) {
    super.onCreate(savedInstanceState);
    binding = ActivityMainBinding.inflate(getLayoutInflater());
    View view = binding.getRoot();
    setContentView(view);

    requestPermission(Manifest.permission.POST_NOTIFICATIONS,
            NOTIFICATION_REQUEST_CODE);
}
```

62.4 Creating the Notification Channel

As with the example in the previous chapter, a channel must be created before a notification can be sent. Edit the *MainActivity.java* file and add code to create a new channel as follows:

```
.
.
import android.app.NotificationChannel;
import android.app.NotificationManager;
import android.content.Context;
import android.graphics.Color;
.
.
public class MainActivity extends AppCompatActivity {
.
.
    private NotificationManager notificationManager;
    private final String channelID = "com.ebookfrenzy.directreply.news";
```

```
    @Override
    protected void onCreate(Bundle savedInstanceState) {
.
.
        notificationManager =
                (NotificationManager)
                        getSystemService(Context.NOTIFICATION_SERVICE);

        createNotificationChannel(channelID,
                "DirectReply News", "Example News Channel");
    }

    protected void createNotificationChannel(String id,
            String name, String description) {

        int importance = NotificationManager.IMPORTANCE_HIGH;
        NotificationChannel channel =
                new NotificationChannel(id, name, importance);

        channel.setDescription(description);
        channel.enableLights(true);
        channel.setLightColor(Color.RED);
        channel.enableVibration(true);
        channel.setVibrationPattern(new long[]{100, 200, 300, 400,
                        500, 400, 300, 200, 400});

        notificationManager.createNotificationChannel(channel);
    }
.
.
}
```

62.5 Building the RemoteInput Object

The key element that makes direct reply in-line text possible within a notification is the RemoteInput class. The previous chapters introduced the PendingIntent class and explained how it allows one application to create an intent and then grant other applications or services the ability to launch that intent from outside the original app. In that chapter, entitled *"An Android Notifications Tutorial"*, a pending intent was created that allowed an activity in the original app to be launched from within a notification. The RemoteInput class allows a request for user input to be included in the PendingIntent object along with the intent. When the intent within the PendingIntent object is triggered, for example, launching an activity, that activity is also passed any input provided by the user.

The first step in implementing a direct reply within a notification is to create the RemoteInput object. This is achieved using the *RemoteInput.Builder()* method. To build a RemoteInput object, a key string is required that will be used to extract the input from the resulting intent. The object also needs a label string that will appear within the text input field of the notification. Edit the *MainActivity.java* file and add the *sendNotification()* method. Note also the addition of some import directives and variables that will be used later as the chapter

An Android Direct Reply Notification Tutorial

progresses:

```
package com.ebookfrenzy.directreply;
.
.
import android.app.PendingIntent;
import android.app.RemoteInput;
import android.content.Intent;
.
.
public class MainActivity extends AppCompatActivity {

    private static final int notificationId = 101;
    private static final String KEY_TEXT_REPLY = "key_text_reply";
    private NotificationManager notificationManager;
    private static final String channelID =
                    "com.ebookfrenzy.directreply.news";



    public void sendNotification(View view) {

        String replyLabel = "Enter your reply here";
        RemoteInput remoteInput =
           new RemoteInput.Builder(KEY_TEXT_REPLY)
                .setLabel(replyLabel)
                .build();
    }
.
.
}
```

Now that the RemoteInput object has been created and initialized with a key and a label string, it will need to be placed inside a notification action object. Before that step can be performed, however, the PendingIntent instance needs to be created.

62.6 Creating the PendingIntent

The steps to creating the PendingIntent are the same as those outlined in the *"An Android Notifications Tutorial"* chapter, except that the intent will be configured to launch MainActivity. Remaining within the *MainActivity.java* file, add the code to create the PendingIntent as follows:

```
public void sendNotification(View view) {

    String replyLabel = "Enter your reply here";
    RemoteInput remoteInput =
            new RemoteInput.Builder(KEY_TEXT_REPLY)
                .setLabel(replyLabel)
                .build();
```

531

```
        Intent resultIntent = new Intent(this, MainActivity.class);

        PendingIntent resultPendingIntent =
                PendingIntent.getActivity(
                        this,
                        0,
                        resultIntent,
                        PendingIntent.FLAG_MUTABLE
                );
    }
}
```

62.7 Creating the Reply Action

The in-line reply will be accessible within the notification via an action button. This action needs to be created and configured with an icon, a label to appear on the button, the PendingIntent object, and the RemoteInput object. Modify the *sendNotification()* method to add the code to create this action:

```
.
.
.
import android.graphics.drawable.Icon;
import android.app.Notification;
.
.
.
public void sendNotification(View view) {

    String replyLabel = "Enter your reply here";
    RemoteInput remoteInput =
            new RemoteInput.Builder(KEY_TEXT_REPLY)
            .setLabel(replyLabel)
            .build();

    Intent resultIntent = new Intent(this, MainActivity.class);

    PendingIntent resultPendingIntent =
            PendingIntent.getActivity(
                    this,
                    0,
                    resultIntent,
                    PendingIntent.FLAG_MUTABLE
            );

    final Icon icon =
            Icon.createWithResource(MainActivity.this,
                android.R.drawable.ic_dialog_info);

    Notification.Action replyAction =
```

```java
            new Notification.Action.Builder(
                    icon,
                    "Reply", resultPendingIntent)
                    .addRemoteInput(remoteInput)
                    .build();
}
```

.
.

At this stage in the tutorial, we have the RemoteInput, PendingIntent, and Notification Action objects built and ready to be used. The next stage is to build the notification and issue it:

```java
public void sendNotification(View view) {

    String replyLabel = "Enter your reply here";
    RemoteInput remoteInput =
            new RemoteInput.Builder(KEY_TEXT_REPLY)
                    .setLabel(replyLabel)
                    .build();

    Intent resultIntent = new Intent(this, MainActivity.class);

    PendingIntent resultPendingIntent =
            PendingIntent.getActivity(
                    this,
                    0,
                    resultIntent,
                    PendingIntent.FLAG_IMMUTABLE
            );

    final Icon icon =
        Icon.createWithResource(MainActivity.this,
            android.R.drawable.ic_dialog_info);

    Notification.Action replyAction =
            new Notification.Action.Builder(
                    icon,
                    "Reply", resultPendingIntent)
                    .addRemoteInput(remoteInput)
                    .build();

    Notification newMessageNotification =
            new Notification.Builder(this, channelID)
                    .setColor(ContextCompat.getColor(this,
                            android.R.color.holo_blue_dark))
                    .setSmallIcon(
                            android.R.drawable.ic_dialog_info)
```

```
            .setContentTitle("My Notification")
            .setContentText("This is a test message")
            .addAction(replyAction).build();

    NotificationManager notificationManager =
            (NotificationManager)
                    getSystemService(Context.NOTIFICATION_SERVICE);

    notificationManager.notify(notificationId,
            newMessageNotification);
}
```

With the changes made, compile and run the app, allow notifications, and test that tapping the button issues the notification successfully. When viewing the notification drawer, the notification should appear as shown in Figure 62-2:

> DirectReply
> **My Notification**
> This is a test message
>
> Reply

Figure 62-2

Tap the Reply action button so that the text input field appears, displaying the reply label embedded into the RemoteInput object when it was created.

> DirectReply
> **My Notification**
> This is a test message
>
> Enter your reply here   ➤

Figure 62-3

Enter some text and tap the send arrow button at the end of the input field.

62.8 Receiving Direct Reply Input

Now that the notification is successfully seeking input from the user, the app needs to do something with that input. This tutorial's objective is to have the text entered by the user into the notification appear on the TextView widget in the activity user interface.

When the user enters text and taps the send button, the MainActivity is launched via the intent in the PendingIntent object. Embedded in this intent is the text entered by the user via the notification. Within the *onCreate()* method of the activity, a call to the *getIntent()* method will return a copy of the intent that launched the activity. Passing this through to the *RemoteInput.getResultsFromIntent()* method will, in turn, return a Bundle object containing the reply text, which can be extracted and assigned to the TextView widget. This results in a modified *onCreate()* method within the *MainActivity.java* file, which reads as follows:

```
.
.
@Override
protected void onCreate(Bundle savedInstanceState) {
.
.
    createNotificationChannel(channelID, "DirectReply News",
                        "Example News Channel");

    handleIntent();
}

private void handleIntent() {

    Intent intent = this.getIntent();

    Bundle remoteInput = RemoteInput.getResultsFromIntent(intent);

    if (remoteInput != null) {

        String inputString = remoteInput.getCharSequence(
            KEY_TEXT_REPLY).toString();

        binding.textView.setText(inputString);
    }
}
.
.
```

After making these code changes build and run the app once again. Click the button to issue the notification and enter and send some text from within the notification panel. Note that the TextView widget in the MainActivity is updated to display the in-line text that was entered.

62.9 Updating the Notification

After sending the reply within the notification, you may have noticed that the progress indicator continues to spin within the notification panel, as highlighted in Figure 62-4:

An Android Direct Reply Notification Tutorial

Figure 62-4

The notification shows this indicator because it is waiting for a response from the activity confirming receipt of the sent text. The recommended approach to performing this task is to update the notification with a new message indicating that the reply has been received and handled. Since the original notification was assigned an ID when it was issued, it can be used again to perform an update. Add the following code to the *handleIntent()* method to perform this task:

```
private void handleIntent() {

    Intent intent = this.getIntent();

    Bundle remoteInput = RemoteInput.getResultsFromIntent(intent);

    if (remoteInput != null) {

        String inputString = remoteInput.getCharSequence(
                KEY_TEXT_REPLY).toString();

        binding.myTextView.setText(inputString);

        Notification repliedNotification =
                new Notification.Builder(this, channelID)
                        .setSmallIcon(
                                android.R.drawable.ic_dialog_info)
                        .setContentText("Reply received")
                        .build();

        notificationManager.notify(notificationId,
                repliedNotification);
    }
}
```

Test the app one last time and verify that the progress indicator goes away after the in-line reply text has been sent and that a new panel appears, indicating that the reply has been received:

```
         ┌──────────────────────────────────────────────┐
         │   ⓘ   DirectReply  🔔                    ⌄   │
         │       Reply received                         │
         └──────────────────────────────────────────────┘
```

Figure 62-5

62.10 Summary

The direct reply notification feature allows text to be entered by the user within a notification and passed via an intent to an activity of the corresponding application. Direct reply is made possible by the RemoteInput class, an instance of which can be embedded within an action and bundled with the notification. When working with direct reply notifications, it is important to let the NotificationManager service know that the reply has been received and processed. The best way to achieve this is to update the notification message using the notification ID provided when the notification was first issued.

Chapter 63

63. Foldable Devices and Multi-Window Support

Foldable devices are coming whether we are ready for them or not (or, in the case of the first Samsung Galaxy Fold, perhaps even before the devices themselves are ready). In preparation for this new category of device, it is important to be aware of some additional steps that should be taken to ensure that your app performs correctly when running on a foldable device.

Fortunately, much of the behavior for supporting foldable devices already exists on Android in the form of Multi-Window support.

63.1 Foldables and Multi-Window Support

When an app is running on a foldable device there is the potential that it will end up sharing the screen with other apps and encountering significant configuration changes (such as the size of the screen changing as the user folds or unfolds the display). If your app is already designed to handle device orientation changes, it will most likely also be able to handle changes caused by screen folding, though thorough testing is recommended.

Multi-window support was originally introduced with Android 7. Unlike previous versions of Android, multi-window support in Android 7 allowed more than one activity to be displayed on the device screen at one time.

Multi-window support in Android provides three different forms of window support. Split-screen mode, available on most phone, foldable and tablet devices, provides a split screen environment where two activities appear either side-by-side or one above the other. A movable divider is provided which, when dragged by the user, adjusts the percentage of the screen assigned to each of the adjacent activities:

Figure 63-1

Freeform mode provides a windowing environment on devices with larger screens and is currently enabled at the discretion of the device manufacturer. Freeform differs from split-screen mode in that it allows each activity to appear in a separate, resizable window and is not limited to two activities being displayed concurrently. Figure 63-2, for example, shows a device in freeform mode with the Calculator and a second app displayed in separate windows:

Foldable Devices and Multi-Window Support

Figure 63-2

Picture-in-picture support, as the name suggests, allows video playback to continue in a smaller window while the user performs other tasks, a topic that will be covered beginning with the chapter entitled *"Android Picture-in-Picture Mode"*.

63.2 Using a Foldable Emulator

Although at time of writing there are no foldable devices on the market with which to perform app testing, foldable emulators are included with the Android SDK. To create a foldable emulator, select the Android Studio *Tools -> AVD Manager* menu option, click on the Create Virtual Device button and, from the hardware selection screen, choose one of the Foldable options as highlighted in Figure 63-3 below:

Figure 63-3

After making a foldable selection, continue through the creation process, selecting Android 10 API 29 or newer as the system image.

Once the emulator is up and running, an additional button will appear in the toolbar allowing the emulator to be switched between folded and unfolded configurations:

Figure 63-4

63.3 Entering Multi-Window Mode

Split-screen mode can be entered by displaying the Overview screen, pressing and holding the app icon in the toolbar of a listed app and selecting the Split screen menu option as indicated in Figure 63-5:

Figure 63-5

Once in split-screen mode, the Overview button will change to display two rectangles (marked A in Figure 63-6), the current activity will fill part of the screen (B) and the Overview screen will appear in the adjacent part of the screen allowing the second activity to be selected for display (C):

Figure 63-6

Once the second app has been selected, the screen will be split evenly as illustrated previously in Figure 63-1

… above.

To exit split-screen mode, simply drag the divider separating the two activities to a far edge so that only one activity fills the screen, or press and hold the Overview button until it reverts to a single square.

63.4 Enabling and using Freeform Support

Although not officially supported on all devices, it is possible to enable freeform multi-window mode on large screen devices and emulators. To enable this mode, run the following adb command while the emulator is running, or the device is connected:

```
adb shell settings put global enable_freeform_support 1
```

After making this change, it may be necessary to reboot the device before the setting takes effect.

Once enabled, an additional option will appear within the Overview screen when performing a long press on the app icon as shown in Figure 63-7:

Figure 63-7

63.5 Checking for Freeform Support

As outlined earlier in the chapter, Google is leaving the choice of whether to enable freeform multi-window mode to the individual Android device manufacturers. Since it only makes sense to use freeform on larger devices, there is no guarantee that freeform will be available on every device on which an app is likely to run. Fortunately all of the freeform specific methods and attributes are ignored by the system if freeform mode is not available on a device, so using these will not cause the app to crash on a non-freeform device. Situations might arise, however, where it may be useful to be able to detect if a device supports freeform multi-window mode. Fortunately, this can be achieved by checking for the freeform window management feature in the package manager. The following code example checks for freeform multi-window support and returns a Boolean value based on the result of the test:

```
public Boolean checkFreeform() {
    return getPackageManager().hasSystemFeature(
            PackageManager.FEATURE_FREEFORM_WINDOW_MANAGEMENT);
}
```

63.6 Enabling Multi-Window Support in an App

The *android:resizableActivity* manifest file setting controls whether multi-window behavior is supported by an app. This setting can be made at either the application or individual activity levels. The following fragment, for example, configures the activity named MainActivity to support both split-screen and freeform multi-window modes:

```
<activity
    android:name=".MainActivity"
    android:resizeableActivity="true"
    android:label="@string/app_name"
    android:theme="@style/AppTheme.NoActionBar">
    <intent-filter>
        <action android:name="android.intent.action.MAIN" />

        <category android:name="android.intent.category.LAUNCHER" />
    </intent-filter>
</activity>
```

Setting the property to false will prevent the activity from appearing in split-screen or freeform mode and the corresponding buttons will not appear in the Overview menu for the app. Selecting an activity for which multi-window support is disabled as the second activity in a split-screen configuration will result in a message appearing indicating that the app may not support multi-window mode.

63.7 Specifying Multi-Window Attributes

A number of attributes are available as part of the <layout> element for specifying the size and placement of an activity when it is launched into a multi-window mode. The initial height, width and position of an activity when launched in freeform mode may be specified using the following attributes:

- **android:defaultWidth** – Specifies the default width of the activity.

- **android:defaultHeight** – Specifies the default height of the activity.

- **android:gravity** – Specifies the initial position of the activity (start, end, left, right, top etc.).

Note that the above attributes apply to the activity only when it is displayed in freeform mode. The following example configures an activity to appear with a specific height and width at the top of the starting edge of the screen:

```
<activity android:name=".MainActivity ">
    <layout android:defaultHeight="350dp"
        android:defaultWidth="450dp"
        android:gravity="start|end" />
</activity>
```

The following <layout> attributes may be used to specify the minimum width and height to which an activity may be reduced in either split-view or freeform modes:

- **android:minimalHeight** – Specifies the minimum height to which the activity may be reduced while in split-screen or freeform mode.

- **android:minimalWidth** - Specifies the minimum width to which the activity may be reduced while in split-screen or freeform mode.

When the user slides the split-screen divider beyond the minimal height or width boundaries, the system will stop resizing the layout of the shrinking activity and simply clip the user interface to make room for the adjacent activity.

The following manifest file fragment implements the minimal width and height attributes for an activity:

```
<activity android:name=".MainActivity ">
```

```
        <layout android:minimalHeight="400dp"
              android:minimalWidth="290dp" />
</activity>
```

63.8 Detecting Multi-Window Mode in an Activity

Situations may arise where an activity needs to detect whether it is currently being displayed to the user in multi-window mode. The current status can be obtained via a call to the *isInMultiWindowMode()* method of the Activity class. When called, this method returns a true or false value depending on whether or not the activity is currently full screen:

```
if (this.isInMultiWindowMode()) {
    // Activity is running in Multi-Window mode
} else {
    // Activity is not in Multi-Window mode
}
```

63.9 Receiving Multi-Window Notifications

An activity will receive notification that it is entering or exiting multi-window mode if it overrides the *onMultiWindowModeChanged()* callback method. The first argument passed to this method is true on entering multi-window mode, and false when the activity exits the mode. The new configuration settings are contained within the Configuration object passed as the second argument:

```
@Override
public void onMultiWindowModeChanged(boolean isInMultiWindowMode,
                                     Configuration newConfig) {
    super.onMultiWindowModeChanged(isInMultiWindowMode, newConfig);

    if (isInMultiWindowMode) {
        // Activity has entered multi-window mode
    } else {
        // Activity has exited multi-window mode
    }
}
```

As outlined in the chapter entitled *"Handling Android Activity State Changes"*, Android 10 and later allow multiple activities to be in the resumed state simultaneously (otherwise known as *multi-resume*). The activity with which the user most recently interacted is referred to as the topmost resumed activity. To track an activity as it gains and loses topmost resumed status, the *onTopResumedActivityChanged()* callback method may be implemented within the activity, for example:

```
@Override
public void onTopResumedActivityChanged(boolean isTopResumedActivity) {
    super.onTopResumedActivityChanged(isTopResumedActivity);

    if (isTopResumedActivity) {
        // Activity is now topmost resumed activity
    } else {
        // Activity is no longer topmost resumed activity
    }
}
```

It may also be possible to take advantage of multi-resume in an app on some devices running Android 9 by enabling the following property in the app manifest file:

```
<meta-data
android:name="android.allow_multiple_resumed_activities" android:value="true" />
```

63.10 Launching an Activity in Multi-Window Mode

In the *"Android Explicit Intents – A Worked Example"* chapter of this book, an example app was created in which an activity uses an intent to launch a second activity. By default, activities launched via an intent are considered to reside in the same *task stack* as the originating activity. An activity can, however, be launched into a new task stack by passing through the appropriate flags with the intent.

When an activity in multi-window mode launches another activity within the same task stack, the new activity replaces the originating activity within the split-screen or freeform window (the user returns to the original activity via the back button).

When launched into a new task stack in split-screen mode, however, the second activity will appear in the window adjacent to the original activity, allowing both activities to be viewed simultaneously. In the case of freeform mode, the launched activity will appear in a separate window from the original activity.

To launch an activity into a new task stack, the following flags must be set on the intent before it is started:

- Intent.FLAG_ACTIVITY_LAUNCH_ADJACENT

- Intent.FLAG_ACTIVITY_MULTIPLE_TASK

- Intent.FLAG_ACTIVITY_NEW_TASK

The following code, for example, configures and launches a second activity designed to appear in a separate window:

```
Intent i = new Intent(this, SecondActivity.class);

i.addFlags(Intent.FLAG_ACTIVITY_LAUNCH_ADJACENT|
        Intent.FLAG_ACTIVITY_MULTIPLE_TASK|
        Intent.FLAG_ACTIVITY_NEW_TASK);

startActivity(i);
```

63.11 Configuring Freeform Activity Size and Position

By default, an activity launched into a different task stack while in freeform mode will be positioned in the center of the screen at a size dictated by the system. The location and dimensions of this window can be controlled by passing *launch bounds* settings to the intent via the *ActivityOptions* class. The first step in this process is to create a *Rect* object configured with the left (X), top (Y), right (X) and bottom (Y) coordinates of the rectangle representing the activity window. The following code, for example, creates a Rect object in which the top-left corner is positioned at coordinate (0, 0) and the bottom-right at (100, 100):

```
Rect rect = new Rect(100, 800, 900, 700);
```

The next step is to create a basic instance of the ActivityOptions class and initialize it with the Rect settings via the *setLaunchBounds()* method:

```
ActivityOptions options = ActivityOptions.makeBasic();
ActivityOptions bounds = options.setLaunchBounds(rect);
```

Finally, the ActivityOptions instance is converted to a Bundle object and passed to the *startActivity()* method along with the Intent object:

```
startActivity(i, bounds.toBundle());
```

Combining these steps results in a code sequence that reads as follows:

```
Intent i = new Intent(this, SecondActivity.class);
i.addFlags(Intent.FLAG_ACTIVITY_LAUNCH_ADJACENT|
           Intent.FLAG_ACTIVITY_MULTIPLE_TASK|
           Intent.FLAG_ACTIVITY_NEW_TASK);

Rect rect = new Rect(100, 800, 900, 700);

ActivityOptions options = ActivityOptions.makeBasic();
ActivityOptions bounds = options.setLaunchBounds(rect);

startActivity(i, bounds.toBundle());
```

When the second activity is launched by the intent while the originating activity is in freeform mode, the new activity window will appear with the location and dimensions defined in the Rect object.

63.12 Summary

Android 7 introduced multi-window support, a system whereby more than one activity is displayed on the screen at any one time. This feature now forms the foundation of providing support for foldable devices. The three modes provided by multi-window support are split-screen, freeform and picture-in-picture. In split-screen mode, the screen is split either horizontally or vertically into two panes with an activity displayed in each pane. Freeform mode, which is only supported on certain Android devices, allows each activity to appear in a separate, movable and resizable window. As outlined in this chapter, a number of methods and property settings are available within the Android SDK to detect, respond to and control multi-window behavior within an app.

64. An Overview of Android SQLite Databases

Mobile applications that do not need to store at least some persistent data are few and far between. The use of databases is an essential aspect of most applications, ranging from almost entirely data-driven applications to those that need to store small amounts of data, such as the prevailing game score.

The importance of persistent data storage becomes even more evident when considering the transient lifecycle of the typical Android application. With the ever-present risk that the Android runtime system will terminate an application component to free up resources, a comprehensive data storage strategy to avoid data loss is a key factor in designing and implementing any application development strategy.

This chapter will cover the SQLite database management system bundled with the Android operating system and outline the Android SDK classes that facilitate persistent SQLite-based database storage within an Android application. Before delving into the specifics of SQLite in the context of Android development, however, a brief overview of databases and SQL will be covered.

64.1 Understanding Database Tables

Database *Tables* provide the most basic level of data structure in a database. Each database can contain multiple tables, each designed to hold information of a specific type. For example, a database may contain a *customer* table that contains the name, address, and telephone number of each of the customers of a particular business. The same database may also include a *products* table used to store the product descriptions with associated product codes for the items sold by the business.

Each table in a database is assigned a name that must be unique within that particular database. A table name, once assigned to a table in one database, may not be used for another table except within the context of another database.

64.2 Introducing Database Schema

Database Schemas define the characteristics of the data stored in a database table. For example, the table schema for a customer database table might define the customer name as a string of no more than 20 characters long and the customer phone number is a numerical data field of a certain format.

Schemas are also used to define the structure of entire databases and the relationship between the various tables in each database.

64.3 Columns and Data Types

It is helpful at this stage to begin viewing a database table as similar to a spreadsheet where data is stored in rows and columns.

Each column represents a data field in the corresponding table. For example, a table's name, address, and telephone data fields are all *columns*.

Each column, in turn, is defined to contain a certain type of data. Therefore, a column designed to store numbers would be defined as containing numerical data.

64.4 Database Rows

Each new record saved to a table is stored in a row. Each row, in turn, consists of the columns of data associated with the saved record.

Once again, consider the spreadsheet analogy described earlier in this chapter. Each entry in a customer table is equivalent to a row in a spreadsheet, and each column contains the data for each customer (name, address, telephone, etc.). When a new customer is added to the table, a new row is created, and the data for that customer is stored in the corresponding columns of the new row.

Rows are also sometimes referred to as *records* or *entries,* and these terms can generally be used interchangeably.

64.5 Introducing Primary Keys

Each database table should contain one or more columns that can be used to identify each row in the table uniquely. This is known in database terminology as the *Primary Key*. For example, a table may use a bank account number column as the primary key. Alternatively, a customer table may use the customer's social security number as the primary key.

Primary keys allow the database management system to uniquely identify a specific row in a table. Without a primary key, retrieving or deleting a specific row in a table would not be possible because there can be no certainty that the correct row has been selected. For example, suppose a table existed where the customer's last name had been defined as the primary key. Imagine the problem if more than one customer named "Smith" were recorded in the database. Without some guaranteed way to identify a specific row uniquely, ensuring the correct data was being accessed at any given time would be impossible.

Primary keys can comprise a single column or multiple columns in a table. To qualify as a single column primary key, no two rows can contain matching primary key values. When using multiple columns to construct a primary key, individual column values do not need to be unique, but all the columns' values combined must be unique.

64.6 What is SQLite?

SQLite is an embedded, relational database management system (RDBMS). Most relational databases (Oracle, SQL Server, and MySQL being prime examples) are standalone server processes that run independently and cooperate with applications requiring database access. SQLite is referred to as *embedded* because it is provided in the form of a library that is linked into applications. As such, there is no standalone database server running in the background. All database operations are handled internally within the application through calls to functions in the SQLite library.

The developers of SQLite have placed the technology into the public domain with the result that it is now a widely deployed database solution.

The developers of SQLite have placed the technology into the public domain with the result that it is now a widely deployed database solution.

SQLite is written in the C programming language, so the Android SDK provides a Java-based "wrapper" around the underlying database interface. This consists of classes that may be utilized within an application's Java or Kotlin code to create and manage SQLite-based databases.

For additional information about SQLite, refer to *https://www.sqlite.org*.

64.7 Structured Query Language (SQL)

Data is accessed in SQLite databases using a high-level language known as Structured Query Language. This is usually abbreviated to SQL and pronounced *sequel*. SQL is a standard language used by most relational database management systems. SQLite conforms mostly to the SQL-92 standard.

An Overview of Android SQLite Databases

SQL is a straightforward and easy-to-use language designed specifically to enable the reading and writing of database data. Because SQL contains a small set of keywords, it can be learned quickly. In addition, SQL syntax is more or less identical between most DBMS implementations, so having learned SQL for one system, your skills will likely transfer to other database management systems.

While some basic SQL statements will be used within this chapter, a detailed overview of SQL is beyond the scope of this book. However, many other resources provide a far better overview of SQL than we could ever hope to provide in a single chapter here.

64.8 Trying SQLite on an Android Virtual Device (AVD)

For readers unfamiliar with databases and SQLite, diving right into creating an Android application that uses SQLite may seem intimidating. Fortunately, Android is shipped with SQLite pre-installed, including an interactive environment for issuing SQL commands from within an adb shell session connected to a running Android AVD emulator instance. This is a useful way to learn about SQLite and SQL and an invaluable tool for identifying problems with databases created by applications running in an emulator.

To launch an interactive SQLite session, begin by running an AVD session. This can be achieved within Android Studio by launching the Android Virtual Device Manager (*Tools -> AVD Manager*), selecting a previously configured AVD, and clicking on the start button.

Once the AVD is up and running, open a Terminal or Command-Prompt window and connect to the emulator using the *adb* command-line tool as follows (note that the –e flag directs the tool to look for an emulator with which to connect, rather than a physical device):

```
adb -e shell
```

Once connected, the shell environment will provide a command prompt at which commands may be entered. Begin by obtaining superuser privileges using the *su* command:

```
Generic_x86:/ su
root@android:/ #
```

If a message indicates that superuser privileges are not allowed, the AVD instance likely includes Google Play support. To resolve this, create a new AVD and, on the "Choose a device definition" screen, select a device that does not have a marker in the "Play Store" column.

The data in SQLite databases are stored in database files on the file system of the Android device on which the application is running. By default, the file system path for these database files is as follows:

```
/data/data/<package name>/databases/<database filename>.db
```

For example, if an application with the package name *com.example.MyDBApp* creates a database named *mydatabase.db*, the path to the file on the device would read as follows:

```
/data/data/com.example.MyDBApp/databases/mydatabase.db
```

For this exercise, therefore, change directory to /data/data within the adb shell and create a sub-directory hierarchy suitable for some SQLite experimentation:

```
cd /data/data
mkdir com.example.dbexample
cd com.example.dbexample
mkdir databases
cd databases
```

With a suitable location created for the database file, launch the interactive SQLite tool as follows:

```
root@android:/data/data/databases # sqlite3 ./mydatabase.db
```

An Overview of Android SQLite Databases

```
sqlite3 ./mydatabase.db
SQLite version 3.8.10.2 2015-05-20 18:17:19
Enter ".help" for usage hints.
sqlite>
```

At the *sqlite>* prompt, commands may be entered to perform tasks such as creating tables and inserting and retrieving data. For example, to create a new table in our database with fields to hold ID, name, address, and phone number fields, the following statement is required:

```
create table contacts (_id integer primary key autoincrement, name text, address text, phone text);
```

Note that each row in a table should have a *primary key* that is unique to that row. In the above example, we have designated the ID field as the primary key, declared it as being of type *integer*, and asked SQLite to increment the number automatically each time a row is added. This is a common way to ensure that each row has a unique primary key. On most other platforms, the primary key's name choice is arbitrary. In the case of Android, however, the key must be named *_id* for the database to be fully accessible using all Android database-related classes. The remaining fields are each declared as being of type *text*.

To list the tables in the currently selected database, use the *.tables* statement:

```
sqlite> .tables
contacts
```

To insert records into the table:

```
sqlite> insert into contacts (name, address, phone) values ("Bill Smith", "123 Main Street, California", "123-555-2323");
sqlite> insert into contacts (name, address, phone) values ("Mike Parks", "10 Upping Street, Idaho", "444-444-1212");
```

To retrieve all rows from a table:

```
sqlite> select * from contacts;
1|Bill Smith|123 Main Street, California|123-555-2323
2|Mike Parks|10 Upping Street, Idaho|444-444-1212
```

To extract a row that meets specific criteria:

```
sqlite> select * from contacts where name="Mike Parks";
2|Mike Parks|10 Upping Street, Idaho|444-444-1212
```

To exit from the sqlite3 interactive environment:

```
sqlite> .exit
```

When running an Android application in the emulator environment, any database files will be created on the emulator's file system using the previously discussed path convention. This has the advantage that you can connect with adb, navigate to the location of the database file, load it into the sqlite3 interactive tool, and perform tasks on the data to identify possible problems occurring in the application code.

It is also important to note that while connecting with an adb shell to a physical Android device is possible, the shell is not granted sufficient privileges by default to create and manage SQLite databases. Therefore, database problem debugging is best performed using an AVD session.

64.9 The Android Room Persistence Library

As previously mentioned, SQLite is written in the C programming language, while Android applications are primarily developed using Java or Kotlin. To bridge this "language gap" in the past, the Android SDK included a set of classes that provide a layer on top of the SQLite database management system. Although available in the SDK, use of these classes still involved writing a considerable amount of code and did not take advantage of the new architecture guidelines and features such as LiveData and lifecycle management. The Android Jetpack Architecture Components include the Room persistent library to address these shortcomings. This library provides a high-level interface on top of the SQLite database system, making it easy to store data locally on Android devices with minimal coding while also conforming to the recommendations for modern application architecture.

The next few chapters will provide an overview and tutorial on SQLite database management using the Room persistence library.

64.10 Summary

SQLite is a lightweight, embedded relational database management system included in the Android framework and provides a mechanism for implementing organized persistent data storage for Android applications. When combined with the Room persistence library, Android provides a modern way to implement data storage from within an Android app.

This chapter provided an overview of databases in general and SQLite in particular within the context of Android application development. The next chapters will provide an overview of the Room persistence library, after which we will work through the creation of an example application.

Chapter 65

65. The Android Room Persistence Library

Included with the Android Architecture Components, the Room persistence library is designed to make it easier to add database storage support to Android apps in a way consistent with the Android architecture guidelines. With the basics of SQLite databases covered in the previous chapter, this chapter will explore the basic concepts behind Room-based database management, the key elements that work together to implement Room support within an Android app, and how these are implemented in terms of architecture and coding. Having covered these topics, the next two chapters will put this theory into practice with an example Room database project.

65.1 Revisiting Modern App Architecture

The chapter entitled *"Modern Android App Architecture with Jetpack"* introduced the concept of modern app architecture and stressed the importance of separating different areas of responsibility within an app. The diagram illustrated in Figure 65-1 outlines the recommended architecture for a typical Android app:

Figure 65-1

With the top three levels of this architecture covered in some detail in earlier chapters of this book, it is time to explore the repository and database architecture levels in the context of the Room persistence library.

65.2 Key Elements of Room Database Persistence

Before going into greater detail later in the chapter, it is first worth summarizing the key elements involved in working with SQLite databases using the Room persistence library:

The Android Room Persistence Library

65.2.1 Repository

As previously discussed, the repository module contains all of the code necessary for directly handling all data sources used by the app. This avoids the need for the UI controller and ViewModel to contain code directly accessing sources such as databases or web services.

65.2.2 Room Database

The room database object provides the interface to the underlying SQLite database. It also provides the repository with access to the Data Access Object (DAO). An app should only have one room database instance, which may be used to access multiple database tables.

65.2.3 Data Access Object (DAO)

The DAO contains the SQL statements required by the repository to insert, retrieve and delete data within the SQLite database. These SQL statements are mapped to methods which are then called from within the repository to execute the corresponding query.

65.2.4 Entities

An entity is a class that defines the schema for a table within the database, defines the table name, column names, and data types, and identifies which column is to be the primary key. In addition to declaring the table schema, entity classes contain getter and setter methods that provide access to these data fields. The data returned to the repository by the DAO in response to the SQL query method calls will take the form of instances of these entity classes. The getter methods will then be called to extract the data from the entity object. Similarly, when the repository needs to write new records to the database, it will create an entity instance, configure values on the object via setter calls, then call insert methods declared in the DAO, passing through entity instances to be saved.

65.2.5 SQLite Database

The SQLite database is responsible for storing and providing access to the data. The app code, including the repository, should never directly access this underlying database. All database operations are performed using a combination of the room database, DAOs, and entities.

The architecture diagram in Figure 65-2 illustrates how these different elements interact to provide Room-based database storage within an Android app:

Figure 65-2

The Android Room Persistence Library

The numbered connections in the above architecture diagram can be summarized as follows:

1. The repository interacts with the Room Database to get a database instance which, in turn, is used to obtain references to DAO instances.
2. The repository creates entity instances and configures them with data before passing them to the DAO for use in search and insertion operations.
3. The repository calls methods on the DAO passing through entities to be inserted into the database and receives entity instances back in response to search queries.
4. When a DAO has results to return to the repository, it packages them into entity objects.
5. The DAO interacts with the Room Database to initiate database operations and handle results.
6. The Room Database handles all low-level interactions with the underlying SQLite database, submitting queries and receiving results.

With a basic outline of the key elements of database access using the Room persistent library covered, it is time to explore entities, DAOs, room databases, and repositories in more detail.

65.3 Understanding Entities

Each database table will have associated with it an entity class. This class defines the schema for the table and takes the form of a standard Java class interspersed with some special Room annotations. An example Java class declaring the data to be stored within a database table might read as follows:

```java
public class Customer {

    private int id;
    private String name;
    private string address;

    public Customer(String name, String address) {
        this.id = id;
        this.name = name;
        this.address = address;
    }

    public int getId() {
        return this.id;
    }
    public String getName() {
        return this.name;
    }

    public int getAddress() {
        return this.address;
    }

    public void setId(int id) {
```

```
        this.id = id;
    }

    public void setName(String name) {
        this.name = name;
    }

    public void setAddress(int quantity) {
        this.address = address;
    }
}
```

As currently implemented, the above code declares a basic Java class containing several variables representing database table fields and a collection of getter and setter methods. This class, however, is not yet an entity. To make this class into an entity and to make it accessible within SQL statements, some Room annotations need to be added as follows:

```
@Entity(tableName = "customers")
public class Customer {

    @PrimaryKey(autoGenerate = true)
    @NonNull
    @ColumnInfo(name = "customerId")
    private int id;

    @ColumnInfo(name = "customerName")
    private String name;

    private String address;

    public Customer(String name, String address) {
        this.id = id;
        this.name = name;
        this.address = address;
    }

    public int getId() {
        return this.id;
    }

    public String getName() {
        return this.name;
    }

    public String getAddress() {
        return this.address;
    }
```

```
    public void setId(@NonNull int id) {
        this.id = id;
    }

    public void setName(String name) {
        this.name = name;
    }

    public void setAddress(int quantity) {
        this.address = address;
    }
}
```

The above annotations begin by declaring that the class represents an entity and assigns a table name of "customers". This is the name by which the table will be referenced in the DAO SQL statements:

`@Entity(tableName = "customers")`

Every database table needs a column to act as the primary key. In this case, the customer id is declared as the primary key. Annotations have also been added to assign a column name to be referenced in SQL queries and to indicate that the field cannot be used to store null values. Finally, the id value is configured to be auto-generated. This means the system automatically generates the id assigned to new records to avoid duplicate keys:

```
@PrimaryKey(autoGenerate = true)
@NonNull
@ColumnInfo(name = "customerId")
private int id;
```

A column name is also assigned to the customer name field. Note, however, that no column name was assigned to the address field. This means that the address data will still be stored within the database but is not required to be referenced in SQL statements. If a field within an entity is not required to be stored within a database, use the @Ignore annotation:

```
@Ignore
private String myString;
```

Finally, the setter method for the id variable is modified to prevent attempts to assign a null value:

```
public void setId(@NonNull int id) {
    this.id = id;
}
```

Annotations may also be included within an entity class to establish relationships with other entities using a relational database concept referred to as *foreign keys*. Foreign keys allow a table to reference the primary key in another table. For example, a relationship could be established between an entity named Purchase and our existing Customer entity as follows:

```
@Entity(foreignKeys = {@ForeignKey(entity = Customer.class,
        parentColumns = "customerId",
        childColumns = "buyerId",
        onDelete = ForeignKey.CASCADE,
        onUpdate = ForeignKey.RESTRICT})
public class Purchase {
```

The Android Room Persistence Library

```
    @PrimaryKey(autoGenerate = true)
    @ColumnInfo(name = "purchaseId")
    private int purchaseId;

    @ColumnInfo(name = "buyerId")
    private int buyerId;

}
```

Note that the foreign key declaration also specifies the action to be taken when a parent record is deleted or updated. Available options are CASCADE, NO_ACTION, RESTRICT, SET_DEFAULT, and SET_NULL.

65.4 Data Access Objects

A Data Access Object allows access to the data stored within a SQLite database. A DAO is declared as a standard Java interface with additional annotations that map specific SQL statements to methods that the repository may then call.

The first step is to create the interface and declare it as a DAO using the @Dao annotation:

```
@Dao
public interface CustomerDao {
}
```

Next, entries are added consisting of SQL statements and corresponding method names. The following declaration, for example, allows all of the rows in the customers table to be retrieved via a call to a method named *getAllCustomers()*:

```
@Dao
public interface CustomerDao {
    @Query("SELECT * FROM customers")
    LiveData<List<Customer>> getAllCustomers();
}
```

The *getAllCustomers()* method returns a List object containing a Customer entity object for each record retrieved from the database table. The DAO is also using LiveData so that the repository can observe changes to the database.

Arguments may also be passed into the methods and referenced within the corresponding SQL statements. Consider the following DAO declaration, which searches for database records matching a customer's name (note that the column name referenced in the WHERE condition is the name assigned to the column in the entity class):

```
@Query("SELECT * FROM customers WHERE name = :customerName")
List<Customer> findCustomer(String customerName);
```

In this example, the method is passed a string value which is, in turn, included within an SQL statement by prefixing the variable name with a colon (:).

A basic insertion operation can be declared as follows using the @Insert *convenience annotation*:

```
@Insert
void addCustomer(Customer customer);
```

This is referred to as a convenience annotation because the Room persistence library can infer that the Customer entity passed to the *addCustomer()* method is to be inserted into the database without the need for the SQL insert statement to be provided. Multiple database records may also be inserted in a single transaction as follows:

```
@Insert
public void insertCustomers(Customer... customers);
```

The following DAO declaration deletes all records matching the provided customer name:

```
@Query("DELETE FROM customers WHERE name = :name")
void deleteCustomer(String name);
```

As an alternative to using the @Query annotation to perform deletions, the @Delete convenience annotation may also be used. In the following example, all of the Customer records that match the set of entities passed to the *deleteCustomers()* method will be deleted from the database:

```
@Delete
public void deleteCustomers(Customer... customers);
```

The @Update convenience annotation provides similar behavior when updating records:

```
@Update
public void updateCustomers(Customer... customers);
```

The DAO methods for these types of database operations may also be declared to return an int value indicating the number of rows affected by the transaction, for example:

```
@Delete
public int deleteCustomers(Customer... customers);
```

65.5 The Room Database

The Room database class is created by extending the RoomDatabase class and acts as a layer on top of the actual SQLite database embedded into the Android operating system. The class is responsible for creating and returning a new room database instance and providing access to the database's associated DAO instances.

The Room persistence library provides a database builder for creating database instances. Each Android app should only have one room database instance, so it is best to implement defensive code within the class to prevent more than one instance from being created.

An example Room Database implementation for use with the example customer table is outlined in the following code listing:

```
import android.content.Context;
import android.arch.persistence.room.Database;
import android.arch.persistence.room.Room;
import android.arch.persistence.room.RoomDatabase;

@Database(entities = {Customer.class}, version = 1)
public class CustomerRoomDatabase extends RoomDatabase {

    public abstract CustomerDao customerDao();

    private static CustomerRoomDatabase INSTANCE;

    static CustomerRoomDatabase getDatabase(final Context context) {
        if (INSTANCE == null) {
```

```
            synchronized (CustomerRoomDatabase.class) {
                if (INSTANCE == null) {
                    INSTANCE = Room.databaseBuilder(
                            context.getApplicationContext(),
                                CustomerRoomDatabase.class, "customer_database")
                                .build();
                }
            }
        }
        return INSTANCE;
    }
}
```

Important areas to note in the above example are the annotation above the class declaration declaring the entities with which the database is to work, the code to check that an instance of the class has not already been created and the assignment of the name "customer_database" to the instance.

65.6 The Repository

The repository is responsible for getting a Room Database instance, using that instance to access associated DAOs, and then making calls to DAO methods to perform database operations. A typical constructor for a repository designed to work with a Room Database might read as follows:

```
public class CustomerRepository {

    private CustomerDao customerDao;
    private CustomerRoomDatabase db;

    public CustomerRepository(Application application) {
        db = CustomerRoomDatabase.getDatabase(application);
        customerDao = db.customerDao();
    }
    .
    .
    .
}
```

Once the repository can access the DAO, it can call the data access methods. The following code, for example, calls the *getAllCustomers()* DAO method:

```
private LiveData<List<Customer>> allCustomers;
allCustomers = customerDao.getAllCustomers();
```

When calling DAO methods, it is important to note that unless the method returns a LiveData instance (which automatically runs queries on a separate thread), the operation cannot be performed on the app's main thread. Attempting to do so will cause the app to crash with the following diagnostic output:

```
Cannot access database on the main thread since it may potentially lock the UI
for a long period of time
```

Since some database transactions may take a longer time to complete, running the operations on a separate thread avoids the app appearing to lock up. As will be demonstrated in the chapter entitled *"An Android Room Database and Repository Tutorial"*, this problem can be easily resolved by making use of Java threads (for more information or a reminder of how to use threads, refer back to the chapter entitled *"A Basic Overview of Java*

65.7 In-Memory Databases

The examples outlined in this chapter use a SQLite database that exists as a database file on the persistent storage of an Android device. This ensures that the data persists even after the app process is terminated.

The Room database persistence library also supports *in-memory* databases. These databases reside entirely in memory and are lost when the app terminates. The only change necessary to work with an in-memory database is to call the *Room.inMemoryDatabaseBuilder()* method of the Room Database class instead of *Room.databaseBuilder()*. The following code shows the difference between the method calls (note that the in-memory database does not require a database name):

```
// Create a file storage based database
INSTANCE = Room.databaseBuilder(context.getApplicationContext(),
                    CustomerRoomDatabase.class, "customer_database")
                    .build();


// Create an in-memory database
INSTANCE = Room.inMemoryDatabaseBuilder(context.getApplicationContext(),
                    CustomerRoomDatabase.class)
                    .build();
```

65.8 Database Inspector

Android Studio includes a Database Inspector tool window which allows the Room databases associated with running apps to be viewed, searched, and modified, as shown in Figure 65-3:

Figure 65-3

The Database Inspector will be covered in the chapter *"An Android Room Database and Repository Tutorial"*.

65.9 Summary

The Android Room persistence library is bundled with the Android Architecture Components and acts as an abstract layer above the lower-level SQLite database. The library is designed to make it easier to work with databases while conforming to the Android architecture guidelines. This chapter has introduced the elements that interact to build Room-based database storage into Android app projects, including entities, repositories, data access objects, annotations, and Room Database instances.

With the basics of SQLite and the Room architecture component covered, the next step is to create an example app that puts this theory into practice. Since the user interface for the example application will require a forms-based layout, the next chapter, entitled *"An Android TableLayout and TableRow Tutorial"*, will detour slightly from the core topic by introducing the basics of the TableLayout and TableRow views.

Chapter 66

66. An Android TableLayout and TableRow Tutorial

When the work began on the next chapter of this book (*"An Android Room Database and Repository Tutorial"*), it was originally intended to include the steps to design the user interface layout for the Room database example application. It quickly became evident, however, that the best way to implement the user interface was to use the Android TableLayout and TableRow views and that this topic area deserved a self-contained chapter. As a result, this chapter will focus solely on the user interface design of the database application to be completed in the next chapter, and in doing so, take some time to introduce the basic concepts of table layouts in Android Studio.

66.1 The TableLayout and TableRow Layout Views

The TableLayout container view allows user interface elements to be organized on the screen in a table format consisting of rows and columns. Each row within a TableLayout is occupied by a TableRow instance which, in turn, is divided into cells, with each cell containing a single child view (which may be a container with multiple view children).

The number of columns in a table is dictated by the row with the most columns, and, by default, the width of each column is defined by the widest cell in that column. Columns may be configured to be shrinkable or stretchable (or both) such that they change in size relative to the parent TableLayout. In addition, a single cell may be configured to span multiple columns.

Consider the user interface layout shown in Figure 66-1:

Figure 66-1

An Android TableLayout and TableRow Tutorial

From the visual appearance of the layout, it is difficult to identify the TableLayout structure used to design the interface. The hierarchical tree illustrated in Figure 66-2, however, makes the structure a little easier to understand:

Figure 66-2

The layout comprises a parent LinearLayout view with TableLayout, LinearLayout, and RecyclerView children. The TableLayout contains three TableRow children representing three rows in the table. The TableRows contain two child views, each representing the contents of a table column cell. The LinearLayout child view contains three Button children.

The layout shown in Figure 66-2 is the exact layout required for the database example that will be completed in the next chapter. Therefore, the remainder of this chapter will be used to work step by step through the design of this user interface using the Android Studio Layout Editor tool.

66.2 Creating the Room Database Project

Select the *New Project* menu option from the welcome screen and, within the resulting new project dialog, choose the Empty Views Activity template before clicking on the Next button.

Enter *RoomDemo* into the Name field and specify *com.ebookfrenzy.roomdemo* as the package name. Before clicking on the Finish button, change the Minimum API level setting to API 26: Android 8.0 (Oreo) and the Language menu to Java.

Migrate the project to view binding using the steps outlined in section *11.8 Migrating a Project to View Binding*.

66.3 Converting to a LinearLayout

Locate the *activity_main.xml* file in the Project tool window (*app -> res -> layout*) and double-click on it to load it into the Layout Editor tool. By default, Android Studio has used a ConstraintLayout as the root layout element in the user interface. This needs to be converted to a vertically oriented LinearLayout.

With the Layout Editor tool in Design mode, locate the ConstraintLayout component in the Component Tree panel, right-click on it to display the menu shown in Figure 66-3, and select the *Convert view...* option:

Figure 66-3

In the resulting dialog (Figure 66-4), select the option to convert to a LinearLayout before clicking on the Apply button:

Figure 66-4

By default, the layout editor will have converted the ConstraintLayout to a horizontal LinearLayout, so select the layout component in the Component Tree window, refer to the Attributes tool window, and change the orientation property to *vertical*:

Figure 66-5

With the conversion complete, select and delete the default TextView widget from the layout.

66.4 Adding the TableLayout to the User Interface

Remaining in the *activity_main.xml* file and referring to the Layouts category of the Palette, drag a TableLayout view to position it at the top of the LinearLayout canvas area.

Once these initial steps are complete, the Component Tree for the layout should resemble that shown in Figure 66-6.

```
Component Tree
 LinearLayout (vertical)
    TableLayout
        TableRow
        TableRow
        TableRow
        TableRow
```

Figure 66-6

Android Studio has automatically added four TableRow instances to the TableLayout. Since only three rows are required for this example, select and delete the fourth TableRow instance. Additional rows may be added to the TableLayout at any time by dragging the TableRow object from the palette and dropping it onto the TableLayout entry in the Component Tree tool window.

With the TableLayout selected, use the Attributes tool window to change the layout_height property to *wrap_content* and layout_width to *match_parent*.

66.5 Configuring the TableRows

From within the *Text* section of the palette, drag two TextView objects onto the uppermost TableRow entry in the Component Tree (Figure 66-7):

```
Component Tree
 LinearLayout (vertical)
    TableLayout
        TableRow
            Ab textView "@string/product_id"
            Ab productID "@string/not_assigned"
        TableRow
        TableRow
```

Figure 66-7

Select the left-most TextView within the screen layout and change the text property to "Product ID" in the Attributes tool window. Repeat this step for the rightmost TextView, changing the text to "Not assigned" and specifying an ID value of *productID*.

Drag and drop another TextView widget onto the second TableRow entry in the Component Tree and change the text on the view to read "Product Name". Locate the Plain Text object in the palette and drag and drop it to position it beneath the Product Name TextView within the Component Tree as outlined in Figure 66-8. Next,

An Android TableLayout and TableRow Tutorial

delete the "Name" string from the text property and set the ID to *productName*.

```
∨ ▭ TableRow
     Ab textView3 "@string/product_name"
     Ab productName (Plain Text)
  > ▭ TableRow
```

Figure 66-8

Drag and drop another TextView and a Number (Decimal) Text Field onto the third TableRow to position the TextView above the EditText in the hierarchy. Change the text on the TextView to "Product Quantity" and the ID of the EditText object to *productQuantity*.

Shift-click to select all of the widgets in the layout as shown in Figure 66-9 below, and use the Attributes tool window to set the textSize property on all of the objects to 18sp:

Figure 66-9

66.6 Adding the Button Bar to the Layout

The next step is to add a LinearLayout (Horizontal) view to the parent LinearLayout view, positioned immediately below the TableLayout view. Begin by clicking on the small disclosure arrow to the left of the TableLayout entry in the Component Tree so that the TableRows are folded away from view. Drag a *LinearLayout (horizontal)* instance from the *Layouts* section of the Layout Editor palette, drop it immediately beneath the TableLayout entry in the Component Tree panel, and change the layout_height property to *wrap_content*:

```
Component Tree                                    ⚙  —

  ▭ LinearLayout (vertical)
    > ▦ TableLayout
    > ▯ LinearLayout (horizontal)
```

Figure 66-10

Drag three Button objects onto the new LinearLayout and assign string resources for each button that read "Add", "Find" and "Delete" respectively. Buttons in this type of button bar arrangement should generally be displayed with a borderless style. Use the Attributes tool window for each button to change the *style* setting to *Widget.AppCompat.Button.Borderless* and the *textColor* attribute to *?attr/colorPrimary*. Change the IDs for the buttons to *addButton*, *findButton*, and *deleteButton*, respectively.

id	addButton	
style	opCompat.Button.Borderless ▼	
text	Widget.AppCompat.Button.Borderless	
textColor	Widget.AppCompat.Button.Borderless.Colored	
∨ Layout	Widget.AppCompat.Button.ButtonBar.AlertDialog	
layout_width	Widget.AppCompat.Button.Colored	
layout_height	Widget.AppCompat.Button.Small	
	Library	
layout_weight	Widget.Material3.Button	
visibility	Widget.Material3.Button.ElevatedButton	

Figure 66-11

With the new horizontal LinearLayout view selected in the Component Tree, change the gravity property to *center_horizontal* so that the buttons are centered horizontally within the display. Before proceeding, extract all of the text properties added in the above steps to string resources.

66.7 Adding the RecyclerView

In the Component Tree, click on the disclosure arrow to the left of the newly added horizontal LinearLayout entry to fold all the children from view.

From the Containers section of the Palette, drag a RecyclerView instance onto the Component Tree to position it beneath the button bar LinearLayout as shown in Figure 66-12. Ensure the RecyclerView is added as a direct child of the parent vertical LinearLayout view and not as a child of the horizontal button bar LinearLayout.

```
Component Tree
  LinearLayout (vertical)
  > TableLayout
  > LinearLayout (horizontal)
    productRecycler
```

Figure 66-12

With the RecyclerView selected in the layout, change the ID of the view to *product_recycler* and set the layout_height property to *match_parent*. Before proceeding, check that the hierarchy of the layout in the Component Tree panel matches that shown in the following figure:

An Android TableLayout and TableRow Tutorial

```
Component Tree
LinearLayout (vertical)
  TableLayout
    TableRow
      Ab textView "@string/product_id"
      Ab productID "@string/not_assigned"
    TableRow
      Ab textView3 "@string/product_name"
      Ab productName (Plain Text)
    TableRow
      Ab textView5 "@string/product_quantity"
      Ab productQuantity (Number (Decimal))
  LinearLayout (horizontal)
    addButton "@string/add_text"
    findButton "@string/find_text"
    deleteButton "@string/delete_text"
  productRecycler
```

Figure 66-13

66.8 Adjusting the Layout Margins

All that remains is to adjust some of the layout settings. Begin by clicking on the first TableRow entry in the Component Tree panel so that it is selected. Hold down the Cmd/Ctrl-key on the keyboard and click on the second and third TableRows, the horizontal LinearLayout, and the RecyclerView so that all five items are selected. In the Attributes panel, locate the *layout_margin* attributes category and, once located, change the value to 10dp as shown in Figure 66-14:

```
> layout_gravity
  layout_height    match_parent
∨ layout_margin   [10dp, ?, ?, ?, ?]
  layout_margin   10dp
  layout_margin...
  layout_margin...
```

Figure 66-14

With margins set, the user interface should appear as illustrated in Figure 66-1.

66.9 Summary

The Android TableLayout container view provides a way to arrange view components in a row and column configuration. While the TableLayout view provides the overall container, each row and the cells contained therein are implemented via instances of the TableRow view. In this chapter, a user interface has been designed in Android Studio using the TableLayout and TableRow containers. The next chapter will add the functionality behind this user interface to implement the SQLite database capabilities using a repository and the Room persistence library.

Chapter 67

67. An Android Room Database and Repository Tutorial

This chapter will combine the knowledge gained in *"The Android Room Persistence Library"* with the initial project created in the previous chapter to provide a detailed tutorial demonstrating how to implement SQLite-based database storage using the Room persistence library. In keeping with the Android architectural guidelines, the project will use a view model and repository. The tutorial will use all of the elements covered in *"The Android Room Persistence Library"* including entities, a Data Access Object, a Room Database, and asynchronous database queries.

67.1 About the RoomDemo Project

The user interface layout created in the previous chapter was the first step in creating a rudimentary inventory app to store product names and quantities. When completed, the app will provide the ability to add, delete and search for database entries while displaying a scrollable list of all products currently stored in the database. This product list will update automatically as database entries are added or deleted.

67.2 Modifying the Build Configuration

Launch Android Studio and open the RoomDemo project started in the previous chapter. Before adding any new classes to the project, the first step is to add some additional libraries to the build configuration, including the Room persistence library. Locate and edit the project level build.gradle.kts file (*app -> Gradle Scripts -> build.gradle.kts (Project :RoomDemo)*) as follows:

Next, make the following changes to the module level *build.gradle.kts* file (*app -> Gradle Scripts -> build.gradle.kts (Module :app)*):

```
dependencies {
    .
    .
    implementation("androidx.recyclerview:recyclerview:1.3.0")
    implementation("androidx.room:room-runtime:2.5.2")
    annotationProcessor("androidx.room:room-compiler:2.5.2")
    .
    .
}
```

67.3 Building the Entity

This project will begin by creating the entity defining the database table schema. The entity will consist of an integer for the product id, a string column to hold the product name, and another integer value to store the quantity.

The entity will consist of an integer for the product id, a string column to hold the product name, and another integer value to store the quantity. The product id column will serve as the primary key and will be auto-

An Android Room Database and Repository Tutorial

generated. Table 67-1 summarizes the structure of the entity:

Column	Data Type
productid	Integer / Primary Key / Auto Increment
productname	String
productquantity	Integer

Table 67-1

Add a class file for the entity by right-clicking on the *app -> java -> com.ebookfrenzy.roomdemo* entry in the Project tool window and selecting the *New -> Java Class* menu option. In the new class dialog, name the class *Product*, select the Class entry in the list, and press the keyboard return key to generate the file.

When the *Product.java* file opens in the editor, modify it so that it reads as follows:

```java
package com.ebookfrenzy.roomdemo;

public class Product {

    private int id;
    private String name;
    private int quantity;

    public Product(String name, int quantity) {
        this.name = name;
        this.quantity = quantity;
    }

    public int getId() {
        return this.id;
    }
    public String getName() {
        return this.name;
    }

    public int getQuantity() {
        return this.quantity;
    }

    public void setId(int id) {
        this.id = id;
    }

    public void setName(String name) {
        this.name = name;
```

```
    }

    public void setQuantity(int quantity) {
        this.quantity = quantity;
    }
}
```

The class now has variables for the database table columns and matching getter and setter methods. Of course, this class does not become an entity until it has been annotated. With the class file still open in the editor, add annotations and corresponding import statements:

```
package com.ebookfrenzy.roomdemo;

import androidx.room.ColumnInfo;
import androidx.room.Entity;
import androidx.room.PrimaryKey;

@Entity(tableName = "products")
public class Product {

    @PrimaryKey(autoGenerate = true)
    @ColumnInfo(name = "productId")
    private int id;

    @ColumnInfo(name = "productName")
    private String name;
    private int quantity;
    .
    .
}
```

These annotations declare this as the entity for a table named *products* and assign column names for the *id* and *name* variables. The id column is also configured to be the primary key and auto-generated. Since it will not be necessary to reference the quantity column in SQL queries, a column name has not been assigned to the *quantity* variable.

67.4 Creating the Data Access Object

With the product entity defined, the next step is to create the DAO interface. Referring again to the Project tool window, right-click on the *app -> java -> com.ebookfrenzy.roomdemo* entry and select the *New -> Java Class* menu option. In the new class dialog, enter *ProductDao* into the Name field and select *Interface* from the list as highlighted in Figure 67-1:

An Android Room Database and Repository Tutorial

New Java Class

- ProductDao
- © Class
- ⓘ Interface
- Ⓔ Enum
- @ Annotation

Figure 67-1

Press the Return key to generate the new interface and, with the *ProductDao.java* file loaded into the code editor, make the following changes:

```
package com.ebookfrenzy.roomdemo;

import androidx.lifecycle.LiveData;
import androidx.room.Dao;
import androidx.room.Insert;
import androidx.room.Query;

import java.util.List;

@Dao
public interface ProductDao {

    @Insert
    void insertProduct(Product product);

    @Query("SELECT * FROM products WHERE productName = :name")
    List<Product> findProduct(String name);

    @Query("DELETE FROM products WHERE productName = :name")
    void deleteProduct(String name);

    @Query("SELECT * FROM products")
    LiveData<List<Product>> getAllProducts();
}
```

The DAO implements methods to insert, find and delete records from the products database. The insertion method is passed a Product entity object containing the data to be stored, while the methods to find and delete records are passed a string containing the name of the product on which to perform the operation. The *getAllProducts()* method returns a LiveData object containing all of the records within the database. This method will be used to keep the RecyclerView product list in the user interface layout synchronized with the database.

67.5 Adding the Room Database

The last task before adding the repository to the project is implementing the Room Database instance. Add a new class to the project named *ProductRoomDatabase*, this time with the *Class* option selected.

Once the file has been generated, modify it as follows using the steps outlined in the *"The Android Room Persistence Library"* chapter:

```java
package com.ebookfrenzy.roomdemo;

import android.content.Context;

import androidx.room.Database;
import androidx.room.Room;
import androidx.room.RoomDatabase;

@Database(entities = {Product.class}, version = 1)
public abstract class ProductRoomDatabase extends RoomDatabase {

    public abstract ProductDao productDao();
    private static ProductRoomDatabase INSTANCE;

    static ProductRoomDatabase getDatabase(final Context context) {
        if (INSTANCE == null) {
            synchronized (ProductRoomDatabase.class) {
                INSTANCE =
                        Room.databaseBuilder(context.getApplicationContext(),
                                ProductRoomDatabase.class,
                                "product_database").build();
            }
        }
        return INSTANCE;
    }
}
```

67.6 Adding the Repository

Add a new class named *ProductRepository* to the project, with the *Class* option selected.

The repository class will be responsible for interacting with the Room database on behalf of the ViewModel. It must provide methods that use the DAO to insert, delete, and query product records. Except for the *getAllProducts()* DAO method (which returns a LiveData object), these database operations must be performed on separate threads from the main thread.

Remaining within the *ProductRepository.java* file, add the code for a handler to return the search results to the repository thread:

```java
package com.ebookfrenzy.roomdemo;

import android.os.Handler;
import android.os.Looper;
import android.os.Message;

import java.util.concurrent.ExecutorService;
import java.util.concurrent.Executors;
```

An Android Room Database and Repository Tutorial

```
import androidx.lifecycle.MutableLiveData;
import java.util.List;

public class ProductRepository {

    private final MutableLiveData<List<Product>> searchResults =
            new MutableLiveData<>();
    private List<Product> results;

    Handler handler = new Handler(Looper.getMainLooper()) {
        @Override public void handleMessage(Message msg) {
            searchResults.setValue(results);
        }
    };
}
```

The above declares a MutableLiveData variable named *searchResults* into which the results of a search operation are stored whenever an asynchronous search task completes (later in the tutorial, an observer within the ViewModel will monitor this live data object).

The repository class must now provide some methods the ViewModel can call to initiate these operations. However, the repository needs to obtain the DAO reference via a ProductRoomDatabase instance to do this. Add a constructor method to the ProductRepository class to perform these tasks:

.
.
```
import android.app.Application;
```
.
.
```
public class ProductRepository {

    private final MutableLiveData<List<Product>> searchResults =
                                             new MutableLiveData<>();
    private List<Product> results;
    private final ProductDao productDao;

    public ProductRepository(Application application) {
        ProductRoomDatabase db;
        db = ProductRoomDatabase.getDatabase(application);
        productDao = db.productDao();
    }
```
.
.

With a reference to DAO stored, the methods are ready to be added to the ProductRepository class file as follows:
```
public void insertProduct(Product newproduct) {
    ExecutorService executor = Executors.newSingleThreadExecutor();
```

```
        executor.submit(() -> productDao.insertProduct(newproduct));
        executor.shutdown();
}

public void deleteProduct(String name) {
        ExecutorService executor = Executors.newSingleThreadExecutor();
        executor.submit(() -> productDao.deleteProduct(name));
        executor.shutdown();
}

public void findProduct(String name) {
        ExecutorService executor = Executors.newSingleThreadExecutor();
        executor.submit(() -> {
            results = productDao.findProduct(name);
            handler.sendEmptyMessage(0);
        });
        executor.shutdown();
}
```

In the cases of the insertion and deletion methods, the appropriate new threads are created and used to perform the corresponding database operation. In the case of the *findProduct()* method, a message is sent to the handler indicating that new results are available.

One final task remains to complete the repository class. The RecyclerView in the user interface layout must keep up to date with the current list of products stored in the database. The ProductDao class already includes a method named *getAllProducts()* which uses a SQL query to select all of the database records and return them wrapped in a LiveData object. The repository needs to call this method once on initialization and store the result within a LiveData object that can be observed by the ViewModel and, in turn, by the UI controller. Once this has been set up, the UI controller observer will be notified each time a change occurs to the database table, and the RecyclerView can be updated with the latest product list. Remaining within the *ProductRepository.java* file, add a LiveData variable and call to the DAO *getAllProducts()* method within the constructor:

```
.
.
import androidx.lifecycle.LiveData;
.
.
public class ProductRepository {

    private final MutableLiveData<List<Product>> searchResults =
            new MutableLiveData<>();
    private List<Product> results;
    private final LiveData<List<Product>> allProducts;
    private final ProductDao productDao;

    public ProductRepository(Application application) {
        ProductRoomDatabase db;
        db = ProductRoomDatabase.getDatabase(application);
```

An Android Room Database and Repository Tutorial

```
        productDao = db.productDao();
        allProducts = productDao.getAllProducts();
    }
    .
    .
    .
}
```

To complete the repository, add methods that the ViewModel can call to obtain references to the *allProducts* and *searchResults* live data objects:

```
public LiveData<List<Product>> getAllProducts() {
    return allProducts;
}

public MutableLiveData<List<Product>> getSearchResults() {
    return searchResults;
}
```

67.7 Adding the ViewModel

The ViewModel is responsible for creating an instance of the repository and providing methods, and LiveData objects that the UI controller can utilize to keep the user interface synchronized with the underlying database. As implemented in *ProductRepository.java*, the repository constructor requires access to the application context to get a Room Database instance. To make the application context accessible within the ViewModel so it can be passed to the repository, the ViewModel needs to subclass AndroidViewModel instead of ViewModel.

Begin by locating the *com.ebookfrenzy.viewmodeldemo* entry in the Project tool window, right-clicking it, and selecting the *New -> Java Class* menu option. Next, name the new class MainViewModel and press the keyboard Enter key. Finally, edit the new class file to change the class to extend AndroidViewModel and implement the default constructor:

```java
package com.ebookfrenzy.roomdemo.ui.main;

import android.app.Application;
import androidx.lifecycle.AndroidViewModel;
import androidx.lifecycle.LiveData;
import androidx.lifecycle.MutableLiveData;
import com.ebookfrenzy.roomdemo.Product;
import com.ebookfrenzy.roomdemo.ProductRepository;
import java.util.List;

public class MainViewModel extends AndroidViewModel {
    final private ProductRepository repository;
    final private LiveData<List<Product>> allProducts;
    final private MutableLiveData<List<Product>> searchResults;

    public MainViewModel (Application application) {
        super(application);
        repository = new ProductRepository(application);
        allProducts = repository.getAllProducts();
```

```
        searchResults = repository.getSearchResults();
    }
}
```

The constructor creates a repository instance and then uses it to get references to the results and live data objects so that the UI controller can observe them. All that now remains within the ViewModel is to implement the methods that will be called from within the UI controller in response to button clicks and when setting up observers on the LiveData objects:

```
MutableLiveData<List<Product>> getSearchResults() {
    return searchResults;
}

LiveData<List<Product>> getAllProducts() {
    return allProducts;
}

public void insertProduct(Product product) {
    repository.insertProduct(product);
}

public void findProduct(String name) {
    repository.findProduct(name);
}

public void deleteProduct(String name) {
    repository.deleteProduct(name);
}
```

67.8 Creating the Product Item Layout

The name of each product in the database will appear within the RecyclerView list in the main user interface. This will require a layout resource file containing a TextView for each row in the list. Add this file now by right-clicking on the *app -> res -> layout* entry in the Project tool window and selecting the *New -> Layout Resource File* menu option. Name the file *product_list_item* and change the root element to a vertical LinearLayout before clicking on OK to create the file and load it into the layout editor. With the layout editor in Design mode, drag a TextView object from the palette onto the layout, where it will appear by default at the top of the layout:

Figure 67-2

With the TextView selected in the layout, use the Attributes tool window to set the ID of the view to *product_row* and the layout_height to 30dp. Select the LinearLayout entry in the Component Tree window and set the layout_height attribute to *wrap_content*.

67.9 Adding the RecyclerView Adapter

As outlined in detail in the chapter entitled *"Working with the RecyclerView and CardView Widgets"*, a RecyclerView instance requires an adapter class to provide the data to be displayed. Add this class by right-

An Android Room Database and Repository Tutorial

clicking on the *app -> java -> com.ebookfrenzy.roomdemo* entry in the Project tool window and selecting the *New -> Java Class* menu. In the dialog, name the class *ProductListAdapter* and choose *Class* from the list before pressing the keyboard Return key. With the resulting *ProductListAdapter.java* class loaded into the editor, implement the class as follows:

```
package com.ebookfrenzy.roomdemo.ui.main;

import android.view.LayoutInflater;
import android.view.View;
import android.view.ViewGroup;
import android.widget.TextView;
import com.ebookfrenzy.roomdemo.R;
import androidx.annotation.NonNull;
import androidx.recyclerview.widget.RecyclerView;
import com.ebookfrenzy.roomdemo.Product;

import java.util.List;

public class ProductListAdapter
        extends RecyclerView.Adapter<ProductListAdapter.ViewHolder> {

    private final int productItemLayout;
    private List<Product> productList;

    public ProductListAdapter(int layoutId) {
        productItemLayout = layoutId;
    }

    public void setProductList(List<Product> products) {
        productList = products;
        notifyDataSetChanged();
    }

    @Override
    public int getItemCount() {
        return productList == null ? 0 : productList.size();
    }

    @NonNull
    @Override
    public ViewHolder onCreateViewHolder(ViewGroup parent, int viewType) {
        View view = LayoutInflater.from(
                parent.getContext()).inflate(productItemLayout, parent, false);
        return new ViewHolder(view);
    }
```

```java
    @Override
    public void onBindViewHolder(final ViewHolder holder, final int listPosition) {
        TextView item = holder.item;
        item.setText(productList.get(listPosition).getName());
    }

    static class ViewHolder extends RecyclerView.ViewHolder {
        TextView item;
        ViewHolder(View iteview) {
            super(iteview);
            item = iteview.findViewById(R.id.product_row);
        }
    }
}
```

67.10 Preparing the Main Activity

The last remaining component to modify is the MainActivity class which needs to configure listeners on the Button views and observers on the live data objects in the ViewModel class. Before adding this code, some preparation work must be performed to add some imports and variables. Edit the *MainActivity.java* file and modify it as follows:

```java
.
.
import androidx.lifecycle.ViewModelProvider;
.
.
public class MainActivity extends AppCompatActivity {

    private ActivityMainBinding binding;
    private MainViewModel viewModel;
    private ProductListAdapter adapter;

    @Override
    protected void onCreate(Bundle savedInstanceState) {
        super.onCreate(savedInstanceState);
        binding = ActivityMainBinding.inflate(getLayoutInflater());
        View view = binding.getRoot();
        setContentView(view);
        viewModel = new ViewModelProvider(this).get(MainViewModel.class);

        listenerSetup();
        observerSetup();
        recyclerSetup();
    }
```

An Android Room Database and Repository Tutorial

At various stages in the code, the app will need to clear the product information displayed in the user interface. To avoid code repetition, add the following *clearFields()* convenience function:

```java
private void clearFields() {
    binding.productID.setText("");
    binding.productName.setText("");
    binding.productQuantity.setText("");
}
```

Before the app can be built and tested, the three setup methods called from the *onCreate()* method above need to be added to the class.

67.11 Adding the Button Listeners

The user interface layout for the main fragment contains three buttons, each needing to perform a specific task when clicked by the user. Edit the *MainActivity.java* file and add the *listenerSetup()* method:

```java
.
.
import com.ebookfrenzy.roomdemo.Product;
.
.
    private void listenerSetup() {

        binding.addButton.setOnClickListener(view -> {

            String name = binding.productName.getText().toString();
            String quantity = binding.productQuantity.getText().toString();

            if (!name.equals("") && !quantity.equals("")) {
                Product product = new Product(name,
                        Integer.parseInt(quantity));
                viewModel.insertProduct(product);
                clearFields();
            } else {
                binding.productID.setText("Incomplete information");
            }
        });

        binding.findButton.setOnClickListener(view ->
                viewModel.findProduct(binding.productName.getText().toString()
                )
        );

        binding.deleteButton.setOnClickListener(view -> {
            viewModel.deleteProduct(binding.productName.getText().toString());
            clearFields();
        });
    }
```

An Android Room Database and Repository Tutorial

}

The addButton listener performs some basic validation to ensure that the user has entered a product name and quantity and uses this data to create a new Product entity object (note that the quantity string is converted to an integer to match the entity data type). The ViewModel *insertProduct()* method is then called and passed the Product object before the fields are cleared.

The findButton and deleteButton listeners pass the product name to either the ViewModel *findProduct()* or *deleteProduct()* method.

67.12 Adding LiveData Observers

The user interface now needs to add observers to remain synchronized with the *searchResults* and *allProducts* live data objects within the ViewModel. Remaining in the *MainActivity.java* file, implement the observer setup method as follows:

```
.
.
import java.util.Locale;
.
.
    private void observerSetup() {

        viewModel.getAllProducts().observe(this,
                products -> adapter.setProductList(products));

        viewModel.getSearchResults().observe(this,
                products -> {
                    if (products.size() > 0) {
                        binding.productID.setText(String.format(Locale.US, "%d",
                                products.get(0).getId()));
                        binding.productName.setText(products.get(0).getName());
                        binding.productQuantity.setText(
                                String.format(Locale.US, "%d",
                                        products.get(0).getQuantity()));
                    } else {
                        binding.productID.setText("No Match");
                    }
                });
    }
.
.
}
```

The "all products" observer passes the current list of products to the *setProductList()* method of the RecyclerAdapter where the displayed list will be updated.

The "search results" observer checks that at least one matching result has been located in the database, extracts

An Android Room Database and Repository Tutorial

the first matching Product entity object from the list, gets the data from the object, converts it where necessary, and assigns it to the TextView and EditText views in the layout. If the product search fails, the user is notified via a message displayed on the product ID TextView.

67.13 Initializing the RecyclerView

Add the final setup method to initialize and configure the RecyclerView and adapter as follows:

```
.
.
import androidx.recyclerview.widget.LinearLayoutManager;
.
.
    private void recyclerSetup() {
        adapter = new ProductListAdapter(R.layout.product_list_item);
        binding.productRecycler.setLayoutManager(
                        new LinearLayoutManager(getContext()));
        binding.productRecycler.setAdapter(adapter);
    }
.
.
.
}
```

67.14 Testing the RoomDemo App

Compile and run the app on a device or emulator, add some products, and ensure they appear automatically in the RecyclerView. Perform a search for an existing product and verify that the product ID and quantity fields update accordingly. Finally, enter the name of an existing product, delete it from the database, and confirm that it is removed from the RecyclerView product list.

67.15 Using the Database Inspector

As previously outlined in *"The Android Room Persistence Library"*, the Database Inspector tool may be used to inspect the content of Room databases associated with a running app and to perform minor data changes. After adding some database records using the RoomDemo app, display the Database Inspector tool using the *View -> Tool Windows -> App Inspection* menu option:

From within the inspector window, select the running app from the menu marked A in Figure 67-3 below:

Figure 67-3

From the Databases panel (B), double-click on the *products* table to view the table rows currently stored in the database. Enable the *Live updates* option (C) and then use the running app to add more records to the database.

Note that the Database Inspector updates the table data (D) in real-time to reflect the changes.

Turn off Live updates so that the table is no longer read-only, double-click on the quantity cell for a table row, and change the value before pressing the keyboard Enter key. Return to the running app and search for the product to confirm that the change made to the quantity in the inspector was saved to the database table.

Finally, click on the table query button (indicated by the arrow in Figure 67-4 below) to display a new query tab (A), make sure that *product_database* is selected (B), and enter a SQL statement into the query text field (C) and click the Run button(D):

Figure 67-4

The list of rows should update to reflect the SQL query (E) results.

67.16 Summary

This chapter has demonstrated the use of the Room persistence library to store data in a SQLite database. The finished project used a repository to separate the ViewModel from all database operations. It demonstrated the creation of entities, a DAO, and a room database instance, including the use of asynchronous tasks when performing some database operations.

Chapter 68

68. Accessing Cloud Storage using the Android Storage Access Framework

Recent years have seen the wide adoption of remote storage services (otherwise known as "cloud storage") to store user files and data. Driving this growth are two key factors. One is that most mobile devices now provide continuous, high speed internet connectivity, thereby making the transfer of data fast and affordable. The second factor is that, relative to traditional computer systems (such as desktops and laptops) these mobile devices are constrained in terms of internal storage resources. A high specification Android tablet today, for example, typically comes with 128Gb of storage capacity. When compared with a mid-range laptop system with a 750Gb disk drive, the need for the seamless remote storage of files is a key requirement for many mobile applications today.

In recognition of this fact, Google introduced the Storage Access Framework as part of the Android 4.4 SDK. This chapter will provide a high level overview of the storage access framework in preparation for the more detail oriented tutorial contained in the next chapter, entitled *"An Android Storage Access Framework Example"*.

68.1 The Storage Access Framework

From the perspective of the user, the Storage Access Framework provides an intuitive user interface that allows the user to browse, select, delete and create files hosted by storage services (also referred to as *document providers*) from within Android applications. Using this browsing interface (also referred to as the *picker*), users can, for example, browse through the files (such as documents, audio, images and videos) hosted by their chosen document providers. Figure 68-1, for example, shows the picker user interface displaying a collection of files hosted by a document provider service:

Figure 68-1

Accessing Cloud Storage using the Android Storage Access Framework

Document providers can range from cloud-based services to local document providers running on the same device as the client application. At the time of writing, the most prominent document providers compatible with the Storage Access Framework are Box and, unsurprisingly, Google Drive. It is highly likely that other cloud storage providers and application developers will soon also provide services that conform to the Android Storage Access Framework.

In addition to cloud based document providers the picker also provides access to internal storage on the device, providing a range of file storage options to the application user.

Through a set of Intents, Android application developers can incorporate these storage capabilities into applications with just a few lines of code. A particularly compelling aspect of the Storage Access Framework from the point of view of the developer is that the underlying document provider selected by the user is completely transparent to the application. Once the storage functionality has been implemented using the framework within an application, it will work with all document providers without any code modifications.

68.2 Working with the Storage Access Framework

Android includes a set of Intents designed to integrate the features of the Storage Access Framework into Android applications. These intents display the Storage Access Framework picker user interface to the user and return the results of the interaction to the application via a call to the *onActivityResult()* method of the activity that launched the intent. When the *onActivityResult()* method is called, it is passed the Uri of the selected file together with a value indicating the success or otherwise of the operation.

The Storage Access Framework intents can be summarized as follows:

- **ACTION_OPEN_DOCUMENT** – Provides the user with access to the picker user interface so that files may be selected from the document providers configured on the device. Selected files are passed back to the application in the form of Uri objects.

- **ACTION_CREATE_DOCUMENT** – Allows the user to select a document provider, a location on that provider's storage and a file name for a new file. Once selected, the file is created by the Storage Access Framework and the Uri of that file returned to the application for further processing.

68.3 Filtering Picker File Listings

The files listed within the picker user interface when an intent is started may be filtered using a variety of options. Consider, for example, the following code to configure an ACTION_OPEN_DOCUMENT intent:

```
Intent intent = new Intent(Intent.ACTION_OPEN_DOCUMENT);
```

When launched, the above intent will cause the picker user interface to be displayed, allowing the user to browse and select any files hosted by available document providers. Once a file has been selected by the user, a reference to that file will be provided to the application in the form of a Uri object. The application can then open the file using the *openFileDescriptor(Uri, String)* method. There is some risk, however, that not all files listed by a document provider can be opened in this way. The exclusion of such files within the picker can be achieved by modifying the intent using the *CATEGORY_OPENABLE* option. For example:

```
Intent intent = new Intent(Intent.ACTION_OPEN_DOCUMENT);
intent.addCategory(Intent.CATEGORY_OPENABLE);
```

When the intent is now displayed, files which cannot be opened using the *openFileDescriptor()* method will be listed but not selectable by the user.

Another useful approach to filtering allows the files available for selection to be restricted by file type. This involves specifying the types of the files the application is able to handle. An image editing application might, for example, only want to provide the user with the option of selecting image files from the document providers.

Accessing Cloud Storage using the Android Storage Access Framework

This is achieved by configuring the intent object with the MIME types of the files that are to be selectable by the user. The following code, for example, specifies that only image files are suitable for selection in the picker:

```
intent.addCategory(Intent.CATEGORY_OPENABLE);
intent.setType("image/*");
```

This could be further refined to limit selection to JPEG images:

```
intent.setType("image/jpeg");
```

Alternatively, an audio player app might only be able to handle audio files:

```
intent.setType("audio/*");
```

The audio app might be limited even further in only supporting the playback of MP4 based audio files:

```
intent.setType("audio/mp4");
```

A wide range of MIME type settings are available for use when working with the Storage Access Framework, the more common of which can be found listed online at:

https://en.wikipedia.org/wiki/Internet_media_type#List_of_common_media_types

68.4 Handling Intent Results

Since we are launching intents which will return a result, the *registerForActivityResult()* method (covered in the chapter entitled *"Android Explicit Intents – A Worked Example"*) needs to be used to create a launcher and declare a lambda to handle the returned data, for example:

```
ActivityResultLauncher<Intent> startOpenForResult = registerForActivityResult(
        new ActivityResultContracts.StartActivityForResult(),
        new ActivityResultCallback<ActivityResult>() {
            @Override
            public void onActivityResult(ActivityResult result) {
                if (result.getResultCode() == Activity.RESULT_OK) {
                    Intent data = result.getData();
                    // Read file content from Uri here
                }
            }
        });
```

Once declared, the intent can be configured and launched as follows:

```
Intent intent = new Intent(Intent.ACTION_OPEN_DOCUMENT);
intent.addCategory(Intent.CATEGORY_OPENABLE);
intent.setType("text/plain");
startOpenForResult.launch(intent);
```

68.5 Reading the Content of a File

The exact steps required to read the content of a file hosted by a document provider will depend to a large extent on the type of the file. The steps to read lines from a text file, for example, differ from those for image or audio files.

An image file can be assigned to a Bitmap object by extracting the file descriptor from the Uri object and then decoding the image into a BitmapFactory instance. For example:

```
ParcelFileDescriptor pFileDescriptor =
            getContentResolver().openFileDescriptor(uri, "r");
```

```
FileDescriptor fileDescriptor =
        pFileDescriptor.getFileDescriptor();

Bitmap image = BitmapFactory.decodeFileDescriptor(fileDescriptor);

pFileDescriptor.close();

myImageView.setImageBitmap(image);
```

Note that the file descriptor is opened in "r" mode. This indicates that the file is to be opened for reading. Other options are "w" for write access and "rwt" for read and write access, where existing content in the file is truncated by the new content.

Reading the content of a text file requires slightly more work and the use of an InputStream object. The following code, for example, reads the lines from a text file:

```
InputStream inputStream = getContentResolver().openInputStream(uri);

BufferedReader reader = new BufferedReader(new InputStreamReader(
                inputStream));
String readline;

while ((readline = reader.readLine()) != null) {
        // Do something with each line in the file
}
inputStream.close();
```

68.6 Writing Content to a File

Writing to an open file hosted by a document provider is similar to reading with the exception that an output stream is used instead of an input stream. The following code, for example, writes text to the output stream of the storage based file referenced by the specified Uri:

```
try{
        ParcelFileDescriptor pFileDescriptor = this.getContentResolver().
                openFileDescriptor(uri, "w");

        FileOutputStream fileOutputStream =
                new FileOutputStream(pFileDescriptor.getFileDescriptor());

        String textContent = "Some sample text";
        fileOutputStream.write(textContent.getBytes());
        fileOutputStream.close();
        pFileDescriptor.close();
} catch (FileNotFoundException e) {
        e.printStackTrace();
} catch (IOException e) {
        e.printStackTrace();
}
```

First, the file descriptor is extracted from the Uri, this time requesting write permission to the target file. The file descriptor is subsequently used to obtain a reference to the file's output stream. The content (in this example, some text) is then written to the output stream before the file descriptor and output stream are closed.

68.7 Deleting a File

Whether a file can be deleted from storage depends on whether or not the file's document provider supports deletion of the file. Assuming deletion is permitted, it may be performed on a designated Uri as follows:

```
if (DocumentsContract.deleteDocument(getContentResolver(), uri))
        // Deletion was successful
else
        // Deletion failed
```

68.8 Gaining Persistent Access to a File

When an application gains access to a file via the Storage Access Framework, the access will remain valid until the Android device on which the application is running is restarted. Persistent access to a specific file can be obtained by "taking" the necessary permissions for the Uri. The following code, for example, persists read and write permissions for the file referenced by the *fileUri* Uri instance:

```
final int takeFlags = intent.getFlags()
            & (Intent.FLAG_GRANT_READ_URI_PERMISSION
            | Intent.FLAG_GRANT_WRITE_URI_PERMISSION);

getContentResolver().takePersistableUriPermission(fileUri, takeFlags);
```

Once the permissions for the file have been taken by the application, and assuming the Uri has been saved by the application, the user should be able to continue accessing the file after a device restart without the user having to reselect the file from the picker interface.

If, at any time, the persistent permissions are no longer required, they can be released via a call to the *releasePersistableUriPermission()* method of the content resolver:

```
final int releaseFlags = intent.getFlags()
            & (Intent.FLAG_GRANT_READ_URI_PERMISSION
            | Intent.FLAG_GRANT_WRITE_URI_PERMISSION);

getContentResolver().releasePersistableUriPermission(fileUri,
                            releaseFlags);
```

68.9 Summary

It is interesting to consider how perceptions of storage have changed in recent years. Once synonymous with high capacity internal hard disk drives, the term "storage" is now just as likely to refer to storage space hosted remotely in the cloud and accessed over an internet connection. This is increasingly the case with the wide adoption of resource constrained, "always-connected" mobile devices with minimal internal storage capacity.

The Android Storage Access Framework provides a simple mechanism for both users and application developers to seamlessly gain access to files stored in the cloud. Through the use of a set of intents and a built-in user interface for selecting document providers and files, comprehensive cloud based storage can now be integrated into Android applications with a minimal amount of coding.

Chapter 69

69. An Android Storage Access Framework Example

As previously discussed, the Storage Access Framework considerably eases the process of integrating cloud based storage access into Android applications. Consisting of a picker user interface and a set of new intents, access to files stored on document providers such as Google Drive and Box can now be built into Android applications with relative ease. With the basics of the Android Storage Access Framework covered in the preceding chapter, this chapter will work through the creation of an example application which uses the Storage Access Framework to store and manage files.

69.1 About the Storage Access Framework Example

The Android application created in this chapter will take the form of a rudimentary text editor designed to create and store text files remotely onto a cloud based storage service. In practice, the example will work with any cloud based document storage provider that is compatible with the Storage Access Framework, though for the purpose of this example the use of Google Drive is assumed.

In functional terms, the application will present the user with a multi-line text view into which text may be entered and edited, together with a set of buttons allowing storage based text files to be created, opened and saved.

69.2 Creating the Storage Access Framework Example

Select the *New Project* option from the welcome screen and, within the resulting new project dialog, choose the Empty Activity template before clicking on the Next button.

Enter *StorageDemo* into the Name field and specify *com.ebookfrenzy.storagedemo* as the package name. Before clicking on the Finish button, change the Minimum API level setting to API 26: Android 8.0 (Oreo) and the Language menu to Java. Follow the usual steps in section *11.8 Migrating a Project to View Binding* to add view binding support to the project.

69.3 Designing the User Interface

The user interface will need to be comprised of three Button views and a single EditText view. Within the Project tool window, navigate to the *activity_main.xml* layout file located in *app -> res -> layout* and double-click on it to load it into the Layout Editor tool. With the tool in Design mode, select and delete the *Hello World!* TextView object.

Drag and position a Button widget in the top left-hand corner of the layout so that both the left and top dotted margin guidelines appear before dropping the widget in place. Position a second Button such that the center and top margin guidelines appear. The third Button widget should then be placed so that the top and right-hand margin guidelines appear.

Change the text attributes on the three buttons to "New", "Open" and "Save" respectively. Next, position a Plain Text widget so that it is centered horizontally and positioned beneath the center Button so that the user interface layout matches that shown in Figure 69-1. Use the Infer Constraints button in the Layout Editor toolbar to add any missing constraints.

593

An Android Storage Access Framework Example

Select the Plain Text widget in the layout, delete the current text property setting, so the field is initially blank, and set the ID to *fileText*. Next, extract the string attributes to resource values named *string*, *open_string*, and *save_string*, respectively.

Figure 69-1

Using the Attributes tool window, configure the onClick property on the Button widgets to call methods named *newFile*, *openFile* and *saveFile* respectively.

69.4 Adding the Activity Launchers

Following the steps outlined in the chapter entitled *"Android Explicit Intents – A Worked Example"*, we need to begin by registering activity launchers to handle the creation, opening and saving of file content. Within the *MainActivity.java* file, add a launcher for each of the three actions as follows:

.
.

```
import androidx.activity.result.ActivityResult;
import androidx.activity.result.ActivityResultCallback;
import androidx.activity.result.ActivityResultLauncher;
import androidx.activity.result.contract.ActivityResultContracts;

import android.app.Activity;
import android.content.Intent;
import android.net.Uri;

import java.io.IOException;
```
.
.
```
    ActivityResultLauncher<Intent> startOpenForResult =
                            registerForActivityResult(
            new ActivityResultContracts.StartActivityForResult(),
            new ActivityResultCallback<ActivityResult>() {
                @Override
                public void onActivityResult(ActivityResult result) {
                    if (result.getResultCode() == Activity.RESULT_OK) {
                        Intent data = result.getData();
                        if (data != null) {
                            Uri currentUri = data.getData();
```

```java
                    try {
                        String content =
                                readFileContent(currentUri);
                        binding.fileText.setText(content);
                    } catch (IOException e) {
                        // Handle error here
                    }
                }
            }
        }
    });

ActivityResultLauncher<Intent> startSaveForResult =
                            registerForActivityResult(
    new ActivityResultContracts.StartActivityForResult(),
    result -> {
        if (result.getResultCode() == Activity.RESULT_OK) {
            Intent data = result.getData();
            if (data != null) {
                Uri currentUri = data.getData();
                try {
                    writeFileContent(currentUri);
                } catch (IOException e) {
                    // Handle error here
                }
            }
        }
    });

ActivityResultLauncher<Intent> startCreateForResult =
                            registerForActivityResult(
    new ActivityResultContracts.StartActivityForResult(),
    new ActivityResultCallback<ActivityResult>() {
        @Override
        public void onActivityResult(ActivityResult result) {
            if (result.getResultCode() == Activity.RESULT_OK) {
                Intent data = result.getData();
                if (data != null) {
                    binding.fileText.setText("");
                }
            }
        }
    });
```

An Android Storage Access Framework Example

69.5 Creating a New Storage File

When the New button is selected, the application will need to trigger an *ACTION_CREATE_DOCUMENT* intent configured to create a file with a plain-text MIME type. When the user interface was designed, the New button was configured to call a method named *newFile()*. It is within this method that the appropriate intent needs to be launched.

Remaining in the *MainActivity.java* file, implement this method as follows:

```
package com.ebookfrenzy.storagedemo;
.
.
public class MainActivity extends AppCompatActivity {
.
.
    public void newFile(View view)
    {
        Intent intent = new Intent(Intent.ACTION_CREATE_DOCUMENT);

        intent.addCategory(Intent.CATEGORY_OPENABLE);
        intent.setType("text/plain");
        intent.putExtra(Intent.EXTRA_TITLE, "newfile.txt");

        startCreateForResult.launch(intent);
    }
.
.
}
```

This code creates a new ACTION_CREATE_INTENT Intent object. This intent is then configured so that only files that can be opened with a file descriptor are returned (via the Intent.CATEGORY_OPENABLE category setting).

Next the code specifies that the file to be opened is to have a plain text MIME type and a placeholder filename is provided (which can be changed by the user in the picker interface).

When this method is executed and the intent has completed the assigned task, a call will be made to the *startCreateForResult()* lambda and passed the Uri of the newly created document.

69.6 Saving to a Storage File

Now that the application is able to create new storage based files, the next step is to add the ability to save any text entered by the user to a file. The user interface is configured to call the *saveFile()* method when the Save button is selected by the user. This method will be responsible for starting a new intent of type *ACTION_OPEN_DOCUMENT* which will result in the picker user interface appearing so that the user can choose the file to which the text is to be stored. Since we are only working with plain text files, the intent needs to be configured to restrict the user's selection options to existing files that match the text/plain MIME type. Having identified the actions to be performed by the *saveFile()* method, this can now be added to the *MainActivity.java* class file as follows:

```
public void saveFile(View view)
{
```

An Android Storage Access Framework Example

```
        Intent intent = new Intent(Intent.ACTION_OPEN_DOCUMENT);
        intent.addCategory(Intent.CATEGORY_OPENABLE);
        intent.setType("text/plain");

        startSaveForResult.launch(intent);
}
```

The lambda assigned to *startSaveForResult()* calls a method named *writeFileContent()*, passing through the Uri of the file to which the text is to be written. Remaining in the *MainActivity.java* file, implement this method now so that it reads as follows:

```
package com.ebookfrenzy.storagedemo;

import java.io.FileOutputStream;
import android.os.ParcelFileDescriptor;

public class MainActivity extends AppCompatActivity {
.
.
.
        private void writeFileContent(Uri uri) throws IOException
        {
            try{
                    ParcelFileDescriptor pfd =
                            this.getContentResolver().
                               openFileDescriptor(uri, "w");

                    FileOutputStream fileOutputStream =
                        new FileOutputStream(
                            pfd.getFileDescriptor());

                    String textContent =
                            binding.fileText.getText().toString();

                    fileOutputStream.write(textContent.getBytes());

                    fileOutputStream.close();
                    pfd.close();
            } catch (IOException e) {
                    e.printStackTrace();
            }
        }
.
.
}
```

The method begins by obtaining and opening the file descriptor from the Uri of the file selected by the user. Since the code will need to write to the file, the descriptor is opened in write mode ("w"). The file descriptor is then used as the basis for creating an output stream that will enable the application to write to the file.

An Android Storage Access Framework Example

The text entered by the user is extracted from the edit text object and written to the output stream before both the file descriptor and stream are closed. Code is also added to handle any IO exceptions encountered during the file writing process.

69.7 Opening and Reading a Storage File

Having written the code to create and save text files, the final task is to add some functionality to open and read a file from the storage. This will involve writing the *openFile()* onClick event handler method and implementing it so that it starts an ACTION_OPEN_DOCUMENT intent:

```
public void openFile(View view)
{
        Intent intent = new Intent(Intent.ACTION_OPEN_DOCUMENT);
        intent.addCategory(Intent.CATEGORY_OPENABLE);
        intent.setType("text/plain");
        startOpenForResult.launch(intent);
}
```

The next task is to implement the *readFileContent()* method called by the *startOpenForResult()* lambda:

```
package com.ebookfrenzy.storagedemo;
.
.
import java.io.BufferedReader;
import java.io.InputStream;
import java.io.InputStreamReader;
.
.
public class MainActivity extends AppCompatActivity {
.
.
        private String readFileContent(Uri uri) throws IOException {

            InputStream inputStream =
                        getContentResolver().openInputStream(uri);
            BufferedReader reader =
                new BufferedReader(new InputStreamReader(
                            inputStream));
            StringBuilder stringBuilder = new StringBuilder();
            String currentline;
            while ((currentline = reader.readLine()) != null) {
                stringBuilder.append(currentline).append("\n");
            }
            inputStream.close();
            return stringBuilder.toString();
        }
.
.
}
```

An Android Storage Access Framework Example

This method begins by extracting the file descriptor for the selected text file and opening it for reading. The input stream associated with the Uri is then opened and used as the input source for a BufferedReader instance. Each line within the file is then read and stored in a StringBuilder object. Once all the lines have been read, the input stream and file descriptor are both closed, and the file content is returned as a String object.

69.8 Testing the Storage Access Application

With the coding phase complete the app is ready to be tested. Compile and run the application and select the New button. The Storage Access Framework should subsequently display the Downloads user interface as illustrated in Figure 69-2:

Figure 69-2

Click the menu button highlighted above and select the *Drive* option followed by *My Drive* and navigate to a suitable location on your Google Drive storage into which to save the file. In the text field at the bottom of the picker interface, change the name from "newfile.txt" to a suitable name (but keeping the *.txt* extension) before selecting the *Save* option.

599

An Android Storage Access Framework Example

Figure 69-3

Once the new file has been created, the app should return to the main activity and a notification may appear within the notifications panel which reads "1 file uploaded".

Figure 69-4

At this point, it should be possible to log into your Google Drive account in a browser window and find the newly created file in the requested location. If the file is missing, make sure that the Android device on which the application is running has an active internet connection. Access to Google Drive on the device may also be verified by running the Google *Drive* app, which is installed by default on many Android devices, and available for download from the Google Play store.

Now that we have created a file, enter some text into the text area before clicking the "Save" button. Select the previously created text file from the picker to save the content to the file. On returning to the application, delete the text and select the "Open" button, once again choosing your saved file. When control is returned to the application, the text view should have been populated with the content of the text file.

It is important to note that the Storage Access Framework will cache storage files locally if the Android device lacks an active internet connection. Once connectivity is re-established, however, any cached data will be synchronized with the remote storage service. As a final test of the application, therefore, log into your Google Drive account in a browser window, navigate to the saved file and click on it to view the content which should, all being well, contain the text saved by the application.

69.9 Summary

This chapter has worked through the creation of an example Android Studio application in the form of a very rudimentary text editor designed to use cloud based storage to create, save and open files using the Android Storage Access Framework.

Chapter 70

70. Video Playback on Android using the VideoView and MediaController Classes

One of the primary uses for smartphones and tablets is to provide access to online content. Video is a key form of content widely used, especially on tablet devices.

The Android SDK includes two classes that make implementing video playback on Android devices extremely easy to implement when developing applications. This chapter will provide an overview of these two classes, VideoView and MediaController, creating a video playback application.

70.1 Introducing the Android VideoView Class

The simplest way to display video within an Android application is to use the VideoView class. This visual component provides a surface on which a video may be played when added to the layout of an activity. Android currently supports the following video formats:

- H.263
- H.264 AVC
- H.265 HEVC
- MPEG-4 SP
- VP8
- VP9

The VideoView class has a wide range of methods that may be called to manage video playback. Some of the more commonly used methods are as follows:

- **setVideoPath(String path)** – Specifies the video media path (as a string) to be played. This can be either a remote video file URL or a video file local to the device.
- **setVideoUri(Uri uri)** – Performs the same task as the *setVideoPath()* method but takes a Uri object as an argument instead of a string.
- **start()** – Starts video playback.
- **stopPlayback()** – Stops the video playback.
- **pause()** – Pauses video playback.
- **isPlaying()** – Returns a Boolean value indicating whether a video is playing.
- **setOnPreparedListener(MediaPlayer.OnPreparedListener)** – Allows a callback method to be called when the video is ready to play.

- **setOnErrorListener(MediaPlayer.OnErrorListener)** - Allows a callback method to be called when an error occurs during the video playback.

- **setOnCompletionListener(MediaPlayer.OnCompletionListener)** - Allows a callback method to be called when the end of the video is reached.

- **getDuration()** – Returns the duration of the video. Will typically return -1 unless called from within the *OnPreparedListener()* callback method.

- **getCurrentPosition()** – Returns an integer value indicating the current position of playback.

- **setMediaController(MediaController)** – Designates a MediaController instance allowing playback controls to be displayed to the user.

70.2 Introducing the Android MediaController Class

If a video is played using the VideoView class, the user will not be given any control over the playback, which will run until the end of the video is reached. This issue can be addressed by attaching an instance of the MediaController class to the VideoView instance. The MediaController will then provide a set of controls allowing the user to manage the playback (such as pausing and seeking backward/forwards in the video timeline).

The position of the controls is designated by anchoring the controller instance to a specific view in the user interface layout. Once attached and anchored, the controls will appear briefly when playback starts and may subsequently be restored at any point by the user tapping on the view to which the instance is anchored.

Some of the key methods of this class are as follows:

- **setAnchorView(View view)** – Designates the view to which the controller will be anchored. This designates the location of the controls on the screen.

- **show()** – Displays the controls.

- **show(int timeout)** – Controls are displayed for the designated duration (in milliseconds).

- **hide()** – Hides the controller from the user.

- **isShowing()** – Returns a Boolean value indicating whether the controls are currently visible to the user.

70.3 Creating the Video Playback Example

The remainder of this chapter will create an example application that uses the VideoView and MediaController classes to play an MPEG-4 video file.

Select the *New Project* option from the welcome screen and, within the resulting new project dialog, choose the Empty Views Activity template before clicking on the Next button.

Enter *VideoPlayer* into the Name field and specify *com.ebookfrenzy.videoplayer* as the package name. Before clicking on the Finish button, change the Minimum API level setting to API 33: Android 13 (Tiramisu) and the Language menu to Java. Use the steps in section *11.8 Migrating a Project to View Binding* to enable view binding for the project.

70.4 Designing the VideoPlayer Layout

The user interface for the main activity will consist solely of an instance of the VideoView class. Use the Project tool window to locate the *app -> res -> layout -> activity_main.xml* file, double-click on it, switch the Layout Editor tool to Design mode, and delete the default TextView widget.

From the Widgets category of the Palette panel, drag and drop a VideoView instance onto the layout to fill the available canvas area, as shown in Figure 70-1. Using the Attributes panel, change the layout_width and layout_height attributes to *match_constraint* and *wrap_content*, respectively. Also, remove the constraint connecting the bottom of the VideoView to the bottom of the parent ConstraintLayout. Finally, change the ID of the component to *videoView1*.

Figure 70-1

70.5 Downloading the Video File

The video that will be played by the VideoPlayer app is a short animated movie clip encoded in MPEG-4 format. Using a web browser, navigate to the following URL to play the video:

https://www.ebookfrenzy.com/android_book/demo.mp4

Staying within the browser window, right-click on the video playback, select the option to save or download the video to a local file, and choose a suitable temporary filesystem location, naming the file *demo.mp4*.

Within Android Studio, locate the *res* folder in the Project tool window, right-click on it, select the *New -> Directory* menu option, and enter *raw* into the name field before pressing the Return key. Using the filesystem navigator for your operating system, locate the *demo.mp4* file downloaded above and copy it. Returning to Android Studio, right-click on the newly created raw directory and select the Paste option to copy the video file into the project. Once added, the raw folder should match Figure 70-2 within the Project tool window:

```
∨ ⌷ res
    > ⌷ drawable
    > ⌷ layout
    > ⌷ mipmap
    ∨ ⌷ raw
          ⊜ demo.mp4
    > ⌷ values
```

Figure 70-2

70.6 Configuring the VideoView

The next step is configuring the VideoView with the video path to be played and then starting the playback. This will be performed when the main activity has initialized, so load the *MainActivity.java* file into the editor and

Video Playback on Android using the VideoView and MediaController Classes

modify it as outlined in the following listing:

```
package com.ebookfrenzy.videoplayer;

import androidx.appcompat.app.AppCompatActivity;
import android.os.Bundle;
import android.net.Uri;
.
.
public class MainActivity extends AppCompatActivity {

    private ActivityMainBinding binding;

    @Override
    protected void onCreate(Bundle savedInstanceState) {
        super.onCreate(savedInstanceState);
        binding = ActivityMainBinding.inflate(getLayoutInflater());
        View view = binding.getRoot();
        setContentView(view);
        configureVideoView();
    }

    private void configureVideoView() {

        binding.videoView1.setVideoURI(Uri.parse("android.resource://"
                + getPackageName() + "/" + R.raw.demo));

        binding.videoView1.start();
    }
}
```

This code obtains a reference to the VideoView instance in the layout, assigns to it a URI object referencing the movie file located in the raw resource directory, and then starts the video playing.

Test the application by running it on an emulator or physical Android device. After the application launches, there may be a short delay while video content is buffered before the playback begins (Figure 70-3).

Figure 70-3

This shows how easy it can be to integrate video playback into an Android application. Everything in this example has been achieved using a VideoView instance and three lines of code.

70.7 Adding the MediaController to the Video View

As the VideoPlayer application currently stands, there is no way for the user to control playback. As previously outlined, this can be achieved using the MediaController class. To add a controller to the VideoView, modify the *configureVideoView()* method once again:

```
package com.ebookfrenzy.videoplayer;
    .
    .
import android.widget.MediaController;

public class MainActivity extends AppCompatActivity {

    private ActivityMainBinding binding;
    private MediaController mediaController;
    .
    .
    private void configureVideoView() {

        binding.videoView1.setVideoURI(Uri.parse("android.resource://"
                + getPackageName() + "/" + R.raw.demo));

        mediaController = new MediaController(this);
        mediaController.setAnchorView(binding.videoView1);
        binding.videoView1.setMediaController(mediaController);

        binding.videoView.start();

    }
}
```

When the application is launched with these changes implemented, tapping the VideoView canvas will cause the media controls to appear over the video playback. These controls should include a Seekbar and fast forward, rewind, and play/pause buttons. After the controls recede from view, they can be restored anytime by tapping on the VideoView canvas again. With just three more lines of code, our video player application now has media controls, as shown in Figure 70-4:

Figure 70-4

70.8 Setting up the onPreparedListener

As a final example of working with video-based media, the activity will be extended further to demonstrate the mechanism for configuring a listener. In this case, a listener will be implemented that is intended to output the duration of the video as a message in the Android Studio Logcat panel. The listener will also configure video playback to loop continuously:

```
package com.ebookfrenzy.videoplayer;
.
.
import android.util.Log;

public class MainActivity extends AppCompatActivity {

    private ActivityMainBinding binding;
    private MediaController mediaController;
    String TAG = "VideoPlayer";

    private void configureVideoView() {

        binding.videoView1.setVideoURI(Uri.parse("android.resource://"
                + getPackageName() + "/" + R.raw.demo));

        MediaController mediaController = new
                MediaController(this);
        mediaController.setAnchorView(binding.videoView1);
        binding.videoView1.setMediaController(mediaController);
        binding.videoView1.setOnPreparedListener(mp -> {
            mp.setLooping(true);
            Log.i(TAG, "Duration = " +
                    binding.videoView1.getDuration());
        });
        binding.videoView.start();
    }
}
```

Now just before the video playback begins, a message will appear in the Android Studio Logcat panel that reads along the lines of the following, and the video will restart after playback ends:

```
2023-06-27 09:25:41.313 3050-3050 VideoPlayer com.ebookfrenzy.videoplayer
I  Duration = 25365
```

70.9 Summary

Android devices make excellent platforms for the delivery of content to users, particularly in the form of video media. As outlined in this chapter, the Android SDK provides two classes, namely VideoView and MediaController, which combine to make video playback integration into Android applications quick and easy, often involving just a few lines of Java code.

Chapter 71

71. Android Picture-in-Picture Mode

When multitasking in Android was covered in earlier chapters, Picture-in-picture (PiP) mode was mentioned briefly but not covered in any detail. Intended primarily for video playback, PiP mode allows an activity screen to be reduced in size and positioned at any location on the screen. While in this state, the activity continues to run, and the window remains visible regardless of any other activities running on the device. This allows the user to, for example, continue watching video playback while performing tasks such as checking email or working on a spreadsheet.

This chapter will provide an overview of Picture-in-Picture mode before Picture-in-Picture support is added to the VideoPlayer project in the next chapter.

71.1 Picture-in-Picture Features

As explained later in the chapter and demonstrated in the next chapter, an activity is placed into PiP mode via an API call from within the running app. When placed into PiP mode, configuration options may be specified that control the aspect ratio of the PiP window and also define the area of the activity screen to be included. Figure 71-1, for example, shows a video playback activity in PiP mode:

Figure 71-1

Figure 71-2 shows a PiP mode window after the user has tapped it. When in this mode, the window appears larger and includes a full-screen action in the center which, when tapped, restores the window to full-screen mode and an exit button in the top right-hand corner to close the window and place the app in the background. When displayed in this mode, any custom actions added to the PiP window will appear on the screen. In the case of Figure 71-2, the PiP window includes custom play and pause action buttons:

Figure 71-2

The remainder of this chapter will outline how PiP mode is enabled and managed from within an Android app.

71.2 Enabling Picture-in-Picture Mode

PiP mode is currently only supported on devices running API 26: Android 8.0 (Oreo) or newer. The first step in implementing PiP mode is to enable it within the project's manifest file. PiP mode is configured on a per-activity basis by adding the following lines to each activity element for which PiP support is required:

```xml
<activity android:name=".MyActivity"
    android:supportsPictureInPicture="true"
    android:configChanges=
        "screenSize|smallestScreenSize|screenLayout|orientation"
    <intent-filter>
        <action android:name="android.intent.action.MAIN" />
        <category android:name="android.intent.category.LAUNCHER" />
    </intent-filter>
</activity>
```

The *android:supportsPictureInPicture* entry enables PiP for the activity, while the *android:configChanges* property notifies Android that the activity can handle layout configuration changes. Without this setting, each time the activity moves in and out of PiP mode, the activity will be restarted, resulting in playback restarting from the beginning of the video during the transition.

71.3 Configuring Picture-in-Picture Parameters

PiP behavior is defined through the use of the PictureInPictureParams class, instances of which can be created using the Builder class as follows:

```
PictureInPictureParams params =
                new PictureInPictureParams.Builder().build();
```

The above code creates a default PictureInPictureParams instance with special parameters defined. The following optional method calls may also be used to customize the parameters:

- **setActions()** – Used to define actions that can be performed within the PiP window while the activity is in PiP mode. Actions will be covered in more detail later in this chapter.

- **setAspectRatio()** – Declares the preferred aspect ratio for the appearance of the PiP window. This method takes as an argument a Rational object containing the height width/height ratio.

- **setSourceRectHint()** – Takes as an argument a Rect object defining the area of the activity screen to be displayed within the PiP window.

The following code, for example, configures aspect ratio and action parameters within a PictureInPictureParams object. In the case of the aspect ratio, this is defined using the width and height dimensions of a VideoView instance:

```
Rational rational = new Rational(videoView.getWidth(),
                                 videoView.getHeight());

PictureInPictureParams params =
        new PictureInPictureParams.Builder()
                .setAspectRatio(rational)
                .setActions(actions)
                .build();
```

Once defined, PiP parameters may be set at any time using the *setPictureInPictureParams()* method as follows:

```
setPictureInPictureParams(params);
```

Parameters may also be specified when entering PiP mode.

71.4 Entering Picture-in-Picture Mode

An activity is placed into Picture-in-Picture mode via a call to the *enterPictureInPictureMode()* method, passing through a PictureInPictureParams object:

```
enterPictureInPictureMode(params);
```

If no parameters are required, create a default PictureInPictureParams object as outlined in the previous section. If parameters have previously been set using the *setPictureInPictureParams()* method, these parameters are combined with those specified during the *enterPictureInPictureMode()* method call.

71.5 Detecting Picture-in-Picture Mode Changes

When an activity enters PiP mode, it is important to hide unnecessary views so that only the video playback is visible within the PiP window. When an activity enters PiP mode, it is important to hide unnecessary views so that only the video playback is visible within the PiP window. When the activity re-enters full-screen mode, hidden user interface components must be reinstated. These and other app-specific tasks can be performed by overriding the *onPictureInPictureModeChanged()* method. When added to the activity, this method is called each time the activity transitions between PiP and full-screen modes and is passed a Boolean value indicating whether the activity is currently in PiP mode:

```
@Override
public void onPictureInPictureModeChanged(
                boolean isInPictureInPictureMode) {

    super.onPictureInPictureModeChanged(isInPictureInPictureMode);

    if (isInPictureInPictureMode) {
        // Acitivity entered Picture-in-Picture mode
    } else {
        // Activity entered full screen mode
    }
}
```

71.6 Adding Picture-in-Picture Actions

Picture-in-Picture actions appear as icons within the PiP window when the user taps it. Implementing PiP actions is a multi-step process that begins with implementing a way for the PiP window to notify the activity that an action has been selected. This is achieved by setting up a broadcast receiver within the activity and then creating a pending intent within the PiP action, which, in turn, is configured to broadcast an intent for which the broadcast receiver is listening. When the intent triggers the broadcast receiver, the data stored in the intent can be used to identify the action performed and to take the necessary action within the activity.

PiP actions are declared using the RemoteAction instances, initialized with an icon, a title, a description, and the PendingIntent object. Once one or more actions have been created, they are added to an ArrayList and passed through to the *setActions()* method while building a PictureInPictureParams object.

The following code fragment demonstrates the creation of the Intent, PendingIntent, and RemoteAction objects together with a PictureInPictureParams instance which is then applied to the activity's PiP settings:

```
final ArrayList<RemoteAction> actions = new ArrayList<>();

Intent actionIntent = new Intent("MY_PIP_ACTION");

final PendingIntent pendingIntent =
            PendingIntent.getBroadcast(MyActivity.this,
                    REQUEST_CODE, actionIntent, FLAG_IMMUTABLE);

final Icon icon = Icon.createWithResource(MyActivity.this,
                    R.drawable.action_icon);

RemoteAction remoteAction = new RemoteAction(icon,
                    "My Action Title",
                    "My Action Description",
                    pendingIntent);

actions.add(remoteAction);

PictureInPictureParams params =
        new PictureInPictureParams.Builder()
                .setActions(actions)
                .build();

setPictureInPictureParams(params);
```

71.7 Summary

Picture-in-Picture mode is a multitasking feature introduced with Android 8.0 designed specifically to allow video playback to continue in a small window while the user performs tasks in other apps and activities. Before PiP mode can be used, it must first be enabled within the manifest file for those activities that require PiP support.

PiP mode behavior is configured using instances of the PictureInPictureParams class and initiated via a call to the *enterPictureInPictureMode()* method from within the activity. When in PiP mode, only the video playback should be visible, requiring that any other user interface elements be hidden until full-screen mode is selected. These and other mode transition-related tasks can be performed by overriding the *onPictureInPictureModeChanged()* method.

PiP actions appear as icons overlaid onto the PiP window when the user taps it. When selected, these actions trigger behavior within the activity. The PiP window uses broadcast receivers and pending intents to notify the activity of an action.

72. An Android Picture-in-Picture Tutorial

Following the previous chapters, this chapter will take the existing VideoPlayer project and enhance it to add Picture-in-Picture support, including detecting PiP mode changes and adding a PiP action designed to display information about the currently running video.

72.1 Adding Picture-in-Picture Support to the Manifest

The first step in adding PiP support to an Android app project is to enable it within the project Manifest file. Open the *manifests -> AndroidManifest.xml* file and modify the activity element to enable PiP support:

```
<activity
    android:name=".MainActivity"
    android:supportsPictureInPicture="true"
    android:configChanges="screenSize|smallestScreenSize|screenLayout|orientation"
    android:exported="true">
    <intent-filter>
        <action android:name="android.intent.action.MAIN" />
        <category android:name="android.intent.category.LAUNCHER" />
    </intent-filter>
</activity>
```

72.2 Adding a Picture-in-Picture Button

As currently designed, the layout for the VideoPlayer activity consists solely of a VideoView instance. As currently designed, the layout for the VideoPlayer activity consists solely of a VideoView instance. A button will now be added to the layout to switch to PiP mode. Load the *activity_main.xml* file into the layout editor and drag a Button object from the palette onto the layout so that it is positioned as shown in Figure 72-1:

Figure 72-1

Change the text on the button to read "Enter PiP Mode" and extract the string to a resource named *enter_pip_mode*. Before moving on to the next step, change the ID of the button to *pipButton* and configure the onClick attribute to call a method named *enterPipMode*.

72.3 Entering Picture-in-Picture Mode

The *enterPipMode* onClick callback method must now be added to the *MainActivity.java* class file. Locate this file, open it in the code editor, and add this method as follows:

```
.
.
import android.app.PictureInPictureParams;
import android.util.Rational;
.
.
public void enterPipMode(View view) {

    Rational rational = new Rational(binding.videoView1.getWidth(),
            binding.videoView1.getHeight());

    PictureInPictureParams params =
            new PictureInPictureParams.Builder()
                    .setAspectRatio(rational)
                    .build();

    binding.pipButton.setVisibility(View.INVISIBLE);
    binding.videoView1.setMediaController(null);
    enterPictureInPictureMode(params);
}
```

The method begins by obtaining a reference to the Button view, then creates a Rational object containing the width and height of the VideoView. A set of Picture-in-Picture parameters is then created using the PictureInPictureParams Builder, passing through the Rational object as the aspect ratio for the video playback. Since the button does not need to be visible while the video is in PiP mode, it is invisible. The video playback controls are also hidden, so the video view will be unobstructed while in PiP mode.

Compile and run the app on a device or emulator running Android version 8 or newer and wait for video playback to begin before clicking on the PiP mode button. The video playback should minimize and appear in the PiP window as shown in :

Figure 72-2

Click in the PiP window, then click within the full-screen mode markers that appear in the center of the window.

An Android Picture-in-Picture Tutorial

Although the activity returns to full-screen mode, the button and media playback controls remain hidden.

Clearly, some code must be added to the project to detect when PiP mode changes occur within the activity.

72.4 Detecting Picture-in-Picture Mode Changes

As discussed in the previous chapter, PiP mode changes are detected by overriding the *onPictureInPictureModeChanged()* method within the affected activity. n this case, the method must be written to detect whether the activity is entering or exiting PiP mode and to take appropriate action to re-activate the PiP button and the playback controls. Remaining within the *MainActivity.java* file, add this method now:

```
@Override
public void onPictureInPictureModeChanged(boolean isInPictureInPictureMode) {
    super.onPictureInPictureModeChanged(isInPictureInPictureMode);

    if (isInPictureInPictureMode) {

    } else {
        binding.pipButton.setVisibility(View.VISIBLE);
        binding.videoView1.setMediaController(mediaController);
    }
}
```

When the method is called, it is passed a Boolean value indicating whether the activity is now in PiP mode. The code in the above method checks this value to decide whether to show the PiP button and to re-activate the playback controls.

72.5 Adding a Broadcast Receiver

The final step in the project is to add an action to the PiP window. The purpose of this action is to display a Toast message containing the name of the currently playing video. This will require some communication between the PiP window and the activity. One of the simplest ways to achieve this is to implement a broadcast receiver within the activity and use a pending intent to broadcast a message from the PiP window to the activity. Each time the activity enters PiP mode, these steps must be performed, so code must be added to the *onPictureInPictureModeChanged()* method. Locate this method now and begin by adding some code to create an intent filter and initialize the broadcast receiver:

```
    .
    .
import android.content.BroadcastReceiver;
import android.content.Context;
import android.content.Intent;
import android.content.IntentFilter;
import android.widget.Toast;
    .
    .
public class MainActivity extends AppCompatActivity {

    private BroadcastReceiver receiver;
    .
    .
```

An Android Picture-in-Picture Tutorial

```
    @Override
    public void onPictureInPictureModeChanged(
                boolean isInPictureInPictureMode) {
        super.onPictureInPictureModeChanged(isInPictureInPictureMode);

        if (isInPictureInPictureMode) {
            IntentFilter filter = new IntentFilter();
            filter.addAction(
                "com.ebookfrenzy.videoplayer.VIDEO_INFO");

            receiver = new BroadcastReceiver() {
                @Override
                public void onReceive(Context context,
                                      Intent intent) {
                    Toast.makeText(context,
                        "Favorite Home Movie Clips",
                            Toast.LENGTH_LONG).show();
                }
            };

            registerReceiver(receiver, filter, Context.RECEIVER_EXPORTED);

        } else {
            binding.pipButton.setVisibility(View.VISIBLE);
            binding.videoView1.setMediaController(mediaController);

            if (receiver != null) {
                unregisterReceiver(receiver);
            }
        }
    }
}
```

72.6 Adding the PiP Action

With the broadcast receiver implemented, the next step is to create a RemoteAction object configured with an image to represent the action within the PiP window.

For this example, an image icon file named *ic_info_24dp.xml* will be used. This file can be found in the *project_icons* folder of the source code download archive available from the following URL:

https://www.ebookfrenzy.com/retail/giraffejava/index.php

Locate this icon file and copy and paste it into the *app -> res -> drawables* folder within the Project tool window:

```
                    v  ⌐ res
                         v  ⌐ drawable
                                </> ic_info_24dp.xml
                                </> ic_launcher_background.xml
                                </> ic_launcher_foreground.xml
```

Figure 72-3

The next step is to create an Intent that will be sent to the broadcast receiver. This intent then needs to be wrapped up within a PendingIntent object, allowing the intent to be triggered later when the user taps the action button in the PiP window.

Edit the *MainActivity.java* file to add a method to create the Intent and PendingIntent objects as follows:

.
.
```
import android.app.PendingIntent;
import static android.app.PendingIntent.FLAG_IMMUTABLE;
.
.
public class MainActivity extends AppCompatActivity {

        private static final int REQUEST_CODE = 101;
.
.

        private void createPipAction() {
           Intent actionIntent =
                new Intent("com.ebookfrenzy.videoplayer.VIDEO_INFO");

           final PendingIntent pendingIntent =
                PendingIntent.getBroadcast(MainActivity.this,
                   REQUEST_CODE, actionIntent, FLAG_IMMUTABLE);
    }
.
.
}
```

Now that both the Intent object and the PendingIntent instance in which it is contained have been created, a RemoteAction object needs to be created containing the icon to appear in the PiP window and the PendingIntent object. Remaining within the *createPipAction()* method, add this code as follows:

.
.
```
import android.app.RemoteAction;
import android.graphics.drawable.Icon;
```

An Android Picture-in-Picture Tutorial

```
import java.util.ArrayList;
.
.
private void createPipAction() {

    final ArrayList<RemoteAction> actions = new ArrayList<>();

    Intent actionIntent =
            new Intent("com.ebookfrenzy.videoplayer.VIDEO_INFO");

    final PendingIntent pendingIntent = PendingIntent.getBroadcast(
        MainActivity.this,
            REQUEST_CODE, actionIntent, FLAG_IMMUTABLE);

    final Icon icon =
            Icon.createWithResource(MainActivity.this,
                    R.drawable.ic_info_24dp);
    RemoteAction remoteAction = new RemoteAction(icon, "Info",
            "Video Info", pendingIntent);

    actions.add(remoteAction);
}
```

Now a PictureInPictureParams object containing the action needs to be created and the parameters applied so that the action appears within the PiP window:

```
private void createPipAction() {

    final ArrayList<RemoteAction> actions = new ArrayList<>();

    Intent actionIntent =
            new Intent("com.ebookfrenzy.videoplayer.VIDEO_INFO");

    final PendingIntent pendingIntent =
        PendingIntent.getBroadcast(MainActivity.this,
            REQUEST_CODE, actionIntent, FLAG_IMMUTABLE);

    final Icon icon =
            Icon.createWithResource(MainActivity.this,
                    R.drawable.ic_info_24dp);
    RemoteAction remoteAction = new RemoteAction(icon, "Info",
            "Video Info", pendingIntent);

    actions.add(remoteAction);

    PictureInPictureParams params =
            new PictureInPictureParams.Builder()
```

```
            .setActions(actions)
            .build();

    setPictureInPictureParams(params);
}
```

The final task before testing the action is to make a call to the *createPipAction()* method when the activity enters PiP mode:

```
@Override
public void onPictureInPictureModeChanged(boolean isInPictureInPictureMode) {
    super.onPictureInPictureModeChanged(isInPictureInPictureMode);
.
.
        registerReceiver(receiver, filter);
        createPipAction();
    } else {
        binding.pipButton.setVisibility(View.VISIBLE);
        binding.videoView1.setMediaController(mediaController);
.
.
}
```

72.7 Testing the Picture-in-Picture Action

Rerun the app and place the activity into PiP mode. Tap on the PiP window so that the new action button appears, as shown in Figure 72-4:

Figure 72-4

Click on the action button and wait for the Toast message to appear, displaying the name of the video:

Figure 72-5

72.8 Summary

This chapter has demonstrated the addition of Picture-in-Picture support to an Android Studio app project, including enabling and entering PiP mode and implementing a PiP action. This included using a broadcast receiver and pending intents to implement communication between the PiP window and the activity.

73. Android Audio Recording and Playback using MediaPlayer and MediaRecorder

This chapter will provide an overview of the MediaRecorder class and explain how this class can be used to record audio or video. The use of the MediaPlayer class to play back audio will also be covered. Having covered the basics, an example application will be created to demonstrate these techniques. In addition to looking at audio and video handling, this chapter will also touch on saving files to the SD card.

73.1 Playing Audio

In terms of audio playback, most implementations of Android support AAC LC/LTP, HE-AACv1 (AAC+), HE-AACv2 (enhanced AAC+), AMR-NB, AMR-WB, MP3, MIDI, Ogg Vorbis, and PCM/WAVE formats.

Audio playback can be performed using either the MediaPlayer or the AudioTrack classes. AudioTrack is a more advanced option that uses streaming audio buffers and provides greater control over the audio. The MediaPlayer class, on the other hand, provides an easier programming interface for implementing audio playback and will meet the needs of most audio requirements.

The MediaPlayer class has associated with it a range of methods that can be called by an application to perform certain tasks. A subset of some of the key methods of this class is as follows:

- **create()** – Called to create a new instance of the class, passing through the Uri of the audio to be played.
- **setDataSource()** – Sets the source from which the audio is to play.
- **prepare()** – Instructs the player to prepare to begin playback.
- **start()** – Starts the playback.
- **pause()** – Pauses the playback. Playback may be resumed via a call to the *resume()* method.
- **stop()** – Stops playback.
- **setVolume()** – Takes two floating-point arguments specifying the playback volume for the left and right channels.
- **resume()** – Resumes a previously paused playback session.
- **reset()** – Resets the state of the media player instance. Essentially sets the instance back to the uninitialized state. At a minimum, a reset player will need to have the data source set again, and the *prepare()* method called.
- **release()** – To be called when the player instance is no longer needed. This method ensures that any resources held by the player are released.

In a typical implementation, an application will instantiate an instance of the MediaPlayer class, set the source of the audio to be played, and then call *prepare()* followed by *start()*. For example:

```
MediaPlayer mediaPlayer = new MediaPlayer();

mediaPlayer.setDataSource("https://www.yourcompany.com/myaudio.mp3");
mediaPlayer.prepare();
mediaPlayer.start();
```

73.2 Recording Audio and Video using the MediaRecorder Class

As with audio playback, recording can be performed using several different techniques. One option is to use the MediaRecorder class, which, as with the MediaPlayer class, provides several methods that are used to record audio:

- **setAudioSource()** – Specifies the audio source to be recorded (typically, this will be MediaRecorder.AudioSource.MIC for the device microphone).

- **setVideoSource()** – Specifies the source of the video to be recorded (for example MediaRecorder.VideoSource.CAMERA).

- **setOutputFormat()** – Specifies the format into which the recorded audio or video is to be stored (for example MediaRecorder.OutputFormat.AAC_ADTS).

- **setAudioEncoder()** – Specifies the audio encoder for the recorded audio (for example MediaRecorder.AudioEncoder.AAC).

- **setOutputFile()** – Configures the path to the file into which the recorded audio or video will be stored.

- **prepare()** – Prepares the MediaRecorder instance to begin recording.

- **start()** - Begins the recording process.

- **stop()** – Stops the recording process. Once a recorder has been stopped, it must be completely reconfigured and prepared before restarting.

- **reset()** – Resets the recorder. The instance will need to be completely reconfigured and prepared before being restarted.

- **release()** – Should be called when the recorder instance is no longer needed. This method ensures that all resources held by the instance are released.

A typical implementation using this class will set the source, output, encoding format, and output file. Calls will then be made to the *prepare()* and *start()* methods. The *stop()* method will then be called when the recording ends, followed by the *reset()* method. When the application no longer needs the recorder instance, a call to the *release()* method is recommended:

```
MediaRecorder mediaRecorder = new MediaRecorder();

mediaRecorder.setAudioSource(MediaRecorder.AudioSource.MIC);
mediaRecorder.setOutputFormat(MediaRecorder.OutputFormat.AAC_ADTS);
mediaRecorder.setAudioEncoder(MediaRecorder.AudioEncoder.AAC);
mediaRecorder.setOutputFile(audioFilePath);

mediaRecorder.prepare();
mediaRecorder.start();
```

```
mediaRecorder.stop();
mediaRecorder.reset();
mediaRecorder.release();
```

To record audio, the manifest file for the application must include the android.permission.RECORD_AUDIO permission:

```
<uses-permission android:name="android.permission.RECORD_AUDIO" />
```

As outlined in the chapter entitled *"Making Runtime Permission Requests in Android"*, access to the microphone falls into the category of dangerous permissions. To support Android 6, therefore, a specific request for microphone access must also be made when the application launches, the steps for which will be covered later in this chapter.

73.3 About the Example Project

The remainder of this chapter will create an example application to demonstrate the use of the MediaPlayer and MediaRecorder classes to implement the recording and playback of audio on an Android device.

When developing applications that use specific hardware features, the microphone being a case in point, it is important to check the feature's availability before attempting to access it in the application code. The application created in this chapter will, therefore, also include code to detect the presence of a microphone on the device.

Once completed, this application will provide a straightforward interface allowing the user to record and play audio. The recorded audio will be stored within an audio file on the device. That being the case, this tutorial will also briefly explore the mechanism for using SD Card storage.

73.4 Creating the AudioApp Project

Select the *New Project* option from the welcome screen and, within the resulting new project dialog, choose the Empty Views Activity template before clicking on the Next button.

Enter *AudioApp* into the Name field and specify *com.ebookfrenzy.audioapp* as the package name. Before clicking on the Finish button, change the Minimum API level setting to API 31: Android 12.0 and the Language menu to Java. Add view binding support to the project using the steps outlined in section *11.8 Migrating a Project to View Binding*.

73.5 Designing the User Interface

Once the new project has been created, select the *activity_main.xml* file from the Project tool window, and with the Layout Editor tool in Design mode, select the "Hello World!" TextView and delete it from the layout.

Drag and drop three Button views onto the layout. The positioning of the buttons is not paramount to this example, though Figure 73-1 shows a suggested layout using a vertical chain.

Configure the buttons to display string resources that read *Play*, *Record*, and *Stop* and give them view IDs of *playButton*, *recordButton*, and *stopButton*, respectively.

Select the Play button and, within the Attributes panel, configure the *onClick* property to call a method named *playAudio* when selected by the user. Repeat these steps to configure the remaining buttons to call methods named *recordAudio* and *stopAudio*, respectively.

Figure 73-1

73.6 Checking for Microphone Availability

Attempting to record audio on a device without a microphone will cause the Android system to throw an exception. It is vital, therefore, that the code checks for the presence of a microphone before making such an attempt. There are several ways of doing this, including checking for the physical presence of the device. An easier approach that is more likely to work on different Android devices is to ask the Android system if it has a package installed for a particular *feature*. This involves creating an instance of the Android PackageManager class and then calling the object's *hasSystemFeature()* method. *PackageManager.FEATURE_MICROPHONE* is the feature of interest in this case.

For this example, we will create a method named *hasMicrophone()* that may be called upon to check for the presence of a microphone. Within the Project tool window, locate and double-click on the *MainActivity.java* file and modify it to add this method:

```
package com.ebookfrenzy.audioapp;
.
.
import android.content.pm.PackageManager;
.
.
public class MainActivity extends AppCompatActivity {
.
.
    protected boolean hasMicrophone() {
        PackageManager pmanager = this.getPackageManager();
        return pmanager.hasSystemFeature(
                PackageManager.FEATURE_MICROPHONE);
    }
}
```

73.7 Initializing the Activity

The next step is to modify the activity to perform several initialization tasks. Remaining within the *MainActivity.java* file, modify the code as follows:

```
package com.ebookfrenzy.audioapp;

import java.io.File;
import java.io.IOException;

import androidx.annotation.NonNull;
import android.media.MediaRecorder;
import android.os.Environment;
import android.media.MediaPlayer;
.
.
public class MainActivity extends AppCompatActivity {

    private ActivityMainBinding binding;
    private static MediaRecorder mediaRecorder;
    private static MediaPlayer mediaPlayer;

    private static String audioFilePath;
    private boolean isRecording = false;

    @Override
    protected void onCreate(Bundle savedInstanceState) {
        super.onCreate(savedInstanceState);
        binding = ActivityMainBinding.inflate(getLayoutInflater());
        View view = binding.getRoot();
        setContentView(view);
        audioSetup();
    }

    private void audioSetup()
    {
        if (!hasMicrophone())
        {
            binding.stopButton.setEnabled(false);
            binding.playButton.setEnabled(false);
            binding.recordButton.setEnabled(false);
        } else {
            binding.playButton.setEnabled(false);
            binding.stopButton.setEnabled(false);
        }

        File audioFile = new File(this.getFilesDir(), "myaudio.3gp");
```

```
        audioFilePath = audioFile.getAbsolutePath();
    }
    .
    .
    .
}
```

The added code calls *hasMicrophone()* method to ascertain whether the device includes a microphone. If it does not, all the buttons are disabled; otherwise, only the Stop and Play buttons are disabled.

The next line of code needs a little more explanation:

```
File audioFile = new File(this.getFilesDir(), "myaudio.3gp");
audioFilePath = audioFile.getAbsolutePath();
```

This code creates a new file named *myaudio.3gp* within the app's internal storage to store the audio recording.

73.8 Implementing the recordAudio() Method

The *recordAudio()* method will be called when the user touches the Record button. This method will need to turn the appropriate buttons on and off and configure the MediaRecorder instance with information about the source of the audio, the output format and encoding, and the file's location into which the audio is to be stored. Finally, the *prepare()* and *start()* methods of the MediaRecorder object will need to be called. Combined, these requirements result in the following method implementation in the *MainActivity.java* file:

```
public void recordAudio (View view)
{
    isRecording = true;
    binding.stopButton.setEnabled(true);
    binding.playButton.setEnabled(false);
    binding.recordButton.setEnabled(false);

    try {
        mediaRecorder = new MediaRecorder(this);
        mediaRecorder.setAudioSource(MediaRecorder.AudioSource.MIC);
        mediaRecorder.setOutputFormat(
                MediaRecorder.OutputFormat.THREE_GPP);
        mediaRecorder.setOutputFile(audioFilePath);
        mediaRecorder.setAudioEncoder(MediaRecorder.AudioEncoder.AMR_NB);
        mediaRecorder.prepare();
    } catch (Exception e) {
            e.printStackTrace();
    }
    mediaRecorder.start();
}
```

73.9 Implementing the stopAudio() Method

The *stopAudio()* method enables the Play button, turning off the Stop button, and then stopping and resetting the MediaRecorder instance. The code to achieve this reads as outlined in the following listing and should be added to the *MainActivity.java* file:

```
public void stopAudio (View view)
{
```

```
      binding.stopButton.setEnabled(false);
      binding.playButton.setEnabled(true);

      if (isRecording)
      {
         binding.recordButton.setEnabled(false);
         mediaRecorder.stop();
         mediaRecorder.release();
         mediaRecorder = null;
         isRecording = false;
      } else {
         mediaPlayer.release();
         mediaPlayer = null;
         binding.recordButton.setEnabled(true);
      }
   }
}
```

73.10 Implementing the playAudio() method

The *playAudio()* method will create a new MediaPlayer instance, assign the audio file located on the SD card as the data source and then prepare and start the playback:

```
public void playAudio (View view) throws IOException
{
   binding.playButton.setEnabled(false);
   binding.recordButton.setEnabled(false);
   binding.stopButton.setEnabled(true);

   mediaPlayer = new MediaPlayer();
   mediaPlayer.setDataSource(audioFilePath);
   mediaPlayer.prepare();
   mediaPlayer.start();
}
```

73.11 Configuring and Requesting Permissions

Before testing the application, the appropriate permissions must be requested within the manifest file for the application. Specifically, the application will require permission to access the microphone. Within the Project tool window, locate and double-click on the *AndroidManifest.xml* file to load it into the editor and modify the XML to add the permission tags:

```
<?xml version="1.0" encoding="utf-8"?>
<manifest xmlns:android="http://schemas.android.com/apk/res/android"
    xmlns:tools="http://schemas.android.com/tools">

    <uses-permission android:name="android.permission.RECORD_AUDIO" />

    <application
    .
    .
```

Android Audio Recording and Playback using MediaPlayer and MediaRecorder

The above steps will be adequate to ensure that the user enables microphone access permission when the app is installed on devices running versions of Android predating Android 6.0. Microphone access is categorized in Android as being a dangerous permission because it allows the app to compromise the user's privacy. For the example app to function on Android 6 or later devices, code needs to be added to request permission at app runtime.

Edit the *MainActivity.java* file and begin by adding some additional import directives and a constant to act as request identification codes for the permissions being requested:

```
.
.
import androidx.core.app.ActivityCompat;
import androidx.core.content.ContextCompat;
import android.widget.Toast;
import android.Manifest;
.
.
public class MainActivity extends AppCompatActivity {

    private static final int RECORD_REQUEST_CODE = 101;
.
.
```

Next, a method needs to be added to the class, the purpose of which is to take as arguments the permission to be requested and the corresponding request identification code. Remaining with the *MainActivity.java* class file, implement this method as follows:

```
protected void requestPermission(String permissionType, int requestCode) {
    int permission = ContextCompat.checkSelfPermission(this,
                permissionType);

    if (permission != PackageManager.PERMISSION_GRANTED) {
        ActivityCompat.requestPermissions(this,
                new String[]{permissionType}, requestCode
        );
    }
}
```

Using the steps outlined in the *"Making Runtime Permission Requests in Android"* chapter of this book, the above method verifies that the specified permission has not already been granted before making the request, passing through the identification code as an argument.

When the request has been handled, the *onRequestPermissionsResult()* method will be called on the activity, passing through the identification code and the request results. The next step, therefore, is to implement this method within the *MainActivity.java* file as follows:

```
@Override
public void onRequestPermissionsResult(int requestCode,
            @NonNull String[] permissions, @NonNull int[] grantResults) {
    super.onRequestPermissionsResult(requestCode, permissions, grantResults);
```

```
    if (requestCode == RECORD_REQUEST_CODE) {
        if (grantResults.length == 0
                || grantResults[0] !=
                PackageManager.PERMISSION_GRANTED) {

            binding.recordButton.setEnabled(false);

            Toast.makeText(this,
                    "Record permission required",
                    Toast.LENGTH_LONG).show();
        }
    }
}
```

The above code checks the request identifier code to identify which permission request has returned before checking whether or not the corresponding permission was granted. If permission is denied, a message is displayed to the user indicating that the app will not function and the record button is disabled.

Before testing the app, all that remains is to call the newly added *requestPermission()* method for microphone access when the app launches. Remaining in the *MainActivity.java* file, modify the *audioSetup()* method as follows:

```
private void audioSetup(){
    binding.recordButton = findViewById(R.id.recordButton);
    binding.playButton = findViewById(R.id.playButton);
    binding.stopButton = findViewById(R.id.stopButton);

    if (!hasMicrophone())
    {
        stopButton.setEnabled(false);
        playButton.setEnabled(false);
        recordButton.setEnabled(false);
    } else {
        playButton.setEnabled(false);
        stopButton.setEnabled(false);
    }

    File audioFile = new File(this.getFilesDir(), "myaudio.3gp");
    audioFilePath = audioFile.getAbsolutePath();

    requestPermission(Manifest.permission.RECORD_AUDIO,
            RECORD_REQUEST_CODE);
}
```

73.12 Testing the Application

Compile and run the application on an Android device containing a microphone, allow microphone access, and tap the Record button. After recording, touch Stop followed by Play. At this point, the recorded audio should play back through the device speakers.

73.13 Summary

The Android SDK provides several mechanisms to implement audio recording and playback. This chapter has looked at two of these: the MediaPlayer and MediaRecorder classes. Having covered the theory of using these techniques, this chapter worked through creating an example application designed to record and then play back audio. While working with audio in Android, this chapter also looked at the steps involved in ensuring that the device on which the application is running has a microphone before attempting to record audio.

Chapter 74

74. Working with the Google Maps Android API in Android Studio

When Google introduced a map service many years ago, it is hard to say whether or not they ever anticipated having a version available for integration into mobile applications. When the first web-based version of what would eventually be called Google Maps was introduced in 2005, the iPhone had yet to ignite the smartphone revolution, and Google would not acquire the company that was developing the Android operating system for another six months. Whatever aspirations Google had for the future of Google Maps, it is remarkable to consider that all of the power of Google Maps can now be accessed directly via Android applications using the Google Maps Android API.

This chapter is intended to provide an overview of the Google Maps system and Google Maps Android API. The chapter will provide an overview of the different elements that make up the API, detail the steps necessary to configure a development environment to work with Google Maps, and then work through some code examples demonstrating some of the basics of Google Maps Android integration.

74.1 The Elements of the Google Maps Android API

The Google Maps Android API consists of a core set of classes that combine to provide mapping capabilities in Android applications. The key elements of a map are as follows:

- **GoogleMap** – The main class of the Google Maps Android API. This class is responsible for downloading and displaying map tiles and for displaying and responding to map controls. The GoogleMap object is not created directly by the application but is created when MapView or MapFragment instances are created. A reference to the GoogleMap object can be obtained within application code via a call to the *getMap()* method of a MapView, MapFragment, or SupportMapFragment instance.

- **MapView** - A subclass of the View class, this class provides the view canvas onto which the map is drawn by the GoogleMap object, allowing a map to be placed in the user interface layout of an activity.

- **SupportMapFragment** – A subclass of the Fragment class, this class allows a map to be placed within a Fragment in an Android layout.

- **Marker** – The purpose of the Marker class is to allow locations to be marked on a map. Markers are added to a map by obtaining a reference to the GoogleMap object associated with a map and then making a call to the *addMarker()* method of that object instance. The position of a marker is defined via Longitude and Latitude. Markers can be configured in various ways, including specifying a title, text, and an icon. Markers may also be "draggable" allowing the user to move the marker to different positions on a map.

- **Shapes** – Drawing lines and shapes on a map is achieved using the *Polyline*, *Polygon*, and *Circle* classes.

- **UiSettings** – The UiSettings class customizes which controls appear on a map. Using UiSettings, for example, the application can control whether or not the zoom, current location, and compass controls appear on a map. This class can also configure which touchscreen gestures are recognized by the map.

- **My Location Layer** – When enabled, the My Location Layer displays a button on the map which, when selected by the user, centers the map on the user's current geographical location. If the user is stationary, a blue

Working with the Google Maps Android API in Android Studio

marker represents this location on the map. If the user is in motion, the location is represented by a chevron indicating the user's direction of travel.

The best way to gain familiarity with the Google Maps Android API is to work through an example. The remainder of this chapter will create a Google Maps-based application while highlighting the key areas of the API.

74.2 Creating the Google Maps Project

Select the *New Project* option from the welcome screen and choose the No Activity template within the resulting new project dialog before clicking on the Next button.

Enter *MapDemo* into the Name field and specify *com.ebookfrenzy.mapdemo* as the package name. Before clicking on the Finish button, change the Minimum API level setting to API 26: Android 8.0 (Oreo) and the Language menu to Java.

Next, right-click on the *app -> java -> com.ebookfrenzy.mapdemo* entry in the Project tool window and select the *New -> Google -> Google Maps Views Activity* menu option. Finally, enable the Launcher Activity checkbox in the New Android Activity dialog before clicking the Finish button:

Figure 74-1

74.3 Creating a Google Cloud Billing Account

Before using the Google Map APIs, you must create a Google Cloud billing account (if you already have one, you can skip to the next section). To do this, open a browser and use the following link to navigate to the Google Cloud Console:

https://console.cloud.google.com/

Next, click on the menu button in the top left-hand corner of the console page and select the Billing entry as illustrated in Figure 74-2 below:

Working with the Google Maps Android API in Android Studio

Figure 74-2

On the Billing page, select the option to add a new billing account and then follow the steps to start a free trial. You must provide a credit card to open the account, but Google won't charge you when the free trial ends without your consent.

74.4 Creating a New Google Cloud Project

The next step is to create a Google Cloud project to be associated with the MapDemo app. To do this, return to the Google Cloud Console dashboard by using the following URL:

https://console.cloud.google.com/home/dashboard

Within the dashboard, click the *Select a project* button located in the top toolbar:

Figure 74-3

When the project selection dialog appears, click on the New Project button (highlighted in Figure 74-4):

Working with the Google Maps Android API in Android Studio

Figure 74-4

When the new project screen appears, provide a name for the project. The console will display a default id for the project beneath the project name field. If you don't like the default id, click the Edit button to change it:

Figure 74-5

Click the Create button, and after a brief pause, you will be returned to the dashboard where your new project will be listed.

74.5 Enabling the Google Maps SDK

Now that we have created a new Google Cloud project, the next step is to allow the project to use the Google Maps SDK. To enable Google Maps support, select your project in the Google Cloud Console, click the menu button in the top left-hand corner, and select the Google Maps Platform entry. Then, from the resulting menu, select the APIs option as shown in Figure 74-6:

Figure 74-6

Working with the Google Maps Android API in Android Studio

On the APIs screen, click on the *Maps SDK for Android* option and, on the resulting screen, click the Enable button:

Figure 74-7

Repeat the above steps to enable the Geocoding API credential, which will be needed later in the chapter to allow our app to display the user's current location.

Once you have enabled the credentials for your project, click the back arrow to return to the product details page in preparation for the next step.

74.6 Generating a Google Maps API Key

Before an application can use the Google Maps Android SDK, it must be configured with an API key to associate it with a Maps-enabled Google Cloud project. To generate an API key, select the Credentials menu option (marked A in Figure 74-8) followed by Create Credentials button (B):

Figure 74-8

After the credential is created, a dialog displaying the API key will appear:

635

Working with the Google Maps Android API in Android Studio

API key created

Use this key in your application by passing it with the `key=API_KEY` parameter.

Your API key
AIzaSyDS1tIV...

⚠ This key is unrestricted. To prevent unauthorized use, we recommend restricting where and for which APIs it can be used. Edit API key to add restrictions. Learn more

Figure 74-9

74.7 Adding the API Key to the Android Studio Project

Now that we have generated an API key allowing our app to use the Google Maps SDK, we must add it to our project. Return to Android Studio, edit the *manifests -> AndroidManifest.xml* file, and locate the API key entry, which will read as follows:

```
<meta-data
         android:name="com.google.android.geo.API_KEY"
         android:value="YOUR_API_KEY" />
```

Delete the text "YOUR_API_KEY" and replace it with the API key created in the Google Play Console.

Next, edit the *Gradle Scripts -> local.properties* file and add a new line that reads as follows (where the API key for your project replaces YOUR_API_KEY):

```
MAPS_API_KEY=YOUR_API_KEY
```

74.8 Testing the Application

Perform a test run of the application to verify that the API key is correctly configured. The application will run and display a map on the screen if the configuration is correct.

If a map is not displayed, check the following areas:

- If the application is running on an emulator, make sure that the emulator is running a version of Android that includes the Google APIs. The current operating system can be changed for an AVD configuration by selecting the *Tools -> Android -> AVD Manager* menu option, clicking on the pencil icon in the *Actions* column of the AVD, followed by the *Change...* button next to the current Android version. Select a target within the system image dialog that includes the Google APIs.

- Check the Logcat output for any areas relating to Google Maps API authentication problems. This usually means the API key was entered incorrectly. Ensure that the API key in the *AndroidManifest.xml* and *local.properties* files matches the key generated in the Google Cloud console.

- Verify within the Google API Console that *Maps SDK for Android* has been enabled in the Credentials panel.

74.9 Understanding Geocoding and Reverse Geocoding

It is impossible to talk about maps and geographical locations without first covering the subject of Geocoding. Geocoding converts a textual-based geographical location (such as a street address) into geographical coordinates expressed as longitude and latitude.

Geocoding can be achieved using the Android Geocoder class. For example, an instance of the Geocoder class can be passed a string representing a location, such as a city name, street address, or airport code. The Geocoder will attempt to find a match for the location and return a list of Address objects that potentially match the

Working with the Google Maps Android API in Android Studio

location string, ranked in order with the closest match at position 0 in the list. A variety of information can then be extracted from the Address objects, including the longitude and latitude of the potential matches.

The following code, for example, requests the location of the National Air and Space Museum in Washington, D.C.:

```
import java.io.IOException;
import java.util.List;

import android.location.Address;
import android.location.Geocoder;
.
.
.
double latitude;
double longitude;

List<Address> geocodeMatches = null;

try {
        geocodeMatches =
           new Geocoder(this).getFromLocationName(
                "600 Independence Ave SW, Washington, DC 20560", 1);
    } catch (IOException e) {
        // TODO Auto-generated catch block
        e.printStackTrace();
    }
}

if (!geocodeMatches.isEmpty())
{
        latitude = geocodeMatches.get(0).getLatitude();
        longitude = geocodeMatches.get(0).getLongitude();
}
```

Note that the value of 1 is passed through as the second argument to the *getFromLocationName()* method. This tells the Geocoder to return only one result in the array. Given the specific nature of the address provided, there should only be one potential match. For more vague location names, however, requesting more potential matches and allowing the user to choose the correct one may be necessary.

The above code is an example of *forward-geocoding* in that coordinates are calculated based on a text location description. *Reverse-geocoding*, as the name suggests, involves the translation of geographical coordinates into a human-readable address string. Consider, for example, the following code:

```
import java.io.IOException;
import java.util.List;

import android.location.Address;
import android.location.Geocoder;
.
.
.
```

637

```
List<Address> geocodeMatches = null;
String Address1;
String Address2;
String State;
String Zipcode;
String Country;

try {
        geocodeMatches =
            new Geocoder(this).getFromLocation(38.8874245, -77.0200729, 1);
} catch (IOException e) {
        // TODO Auto-generated catch block
        e.printStackTrace();
}

if (!geocodeMatches.isEmpty())
{
        Address1 = geocodeMatches.get(0).getAddressLine(0);
        Address2 = geocodeMatches.get(0).getAddressLine(1);
        State = geocodeMatches.get(0).getAdminArea();
        Zipcode = geocodeMatches.get(0).getPostalCode();
        Country = geocodeMatches.get(0).getCountryName();
}
```

The Geocoder object is initialized with latitude and longitude values via the *getFromLocation()* method. Once again, only a single matching result is requested. The text-based address information is then extracted from the resulting Address object.

The geocoding is not performed on the Android device but rather on a server to which the device connects when a translation is required, and the results are returned when the translation is complete. Geocoding can only occur when the device has an active internet connection.

74.10 Adding a Map to an Application

The simplest way to add a map to an application is to specify it in the user interface layout XML file for an activity. The following example layout file shows the SupportMapFragment instance added to the *activity_maps.xml* file created by Android Studio:

```
<fragment xmlns:android="http://schemas.android.com/apk/res/android"
    xmlns:tools="http://schemas.android.com/tools"
    android:layout_width="match_parent"
    android:layout_height="match_parent"
    android:id="@+id/map"
    tools:context=".MapsActivity"
    android:name="com.google.android.gms.maps.SupportMapFragment"/>
```

74.11 Requesting Current Location Permission

As outlined in the chapter entitled *"Making Runtime Permission Requests in Android"*, certain permissions are considered dangerous and require special handling for Android 6.0 or later. One set of permissions allows applications to identify the user's current location. Edit the *AndroidManifest.xml* file located under *app ->*

Working with the Google Maps Android API in Android Studio

manifests in the Project tool window and add the following permission lines:

```
<uses-permission
    android:name="android.permission.ACCESS_FINE_LOCATION" />

<uses-permission
    android:name="android.permission.ACCESS_COARSE_LOCATION" />
```

These settings will ensure that the app can provide permission to obtain location information when installed on older versions of Android. To support Android 6.0 or later, however, we need to add some code to the *MapsActivity.java* file to request this permission at runtime.

Begin by adding some import directives and a constant to act as the permission request code:

```
package com.ebookfrenzy.mapdemo;
.
.
import androidx.annotation.NonNull;
import androidx.core.content.ContextCompat;
import androidx.core.app.ActivityCompat;
import android.Manifest;
import android.widget.Toast;
import android.content.pm.PackageManager;
.
.
public class MapsActivity extends FragmentActivity implements OnMapReadyCallback
{
    private static final int LOCATION_REQUEST_CODE = 101;
    private GoogleMap mMap;
.
.
}
```

Next, a method must be added to the class to request a specified permission from the user. Remaining within the *MapsActivity.java* class file, implement this method as follows:

```
protected void requestPermission(String permissionType,
                                 int requestCode) {

    ActivityCompat.requestPermissions(this,
            new String[]{permissionType}, requestCode
    );
}
```

When the user has responded to the permission request, the *onRequestPermissionsResult()* method will be called on the activity. Remaining in the *MapsActivity.java* file, implement this method now so that it reads as follows:

```
@Override
public void onRequestPermissionsResult(int requestCode,
            @NonNull String[] permissions, @NonNull int[] grantResults) {

    super.onRequestPermissionsResult(requestCode, permissions, grantResults);
```

```
        if (requestCode == LOCATION_REQUEST_CODE) {
            if (grantResults.length == 0
                    || grantResults[0] !=
                    PackageManager.PERMISSION_GRANTED) {
                Toast.makeText(this,
                        "Unable to show location - permission required",
                        Toast.LENGTH_LONG).show();
            } else {

                SupportMapFragment mapFragment =
                        (SupportMapFragment) getSupportFragmentManager()
                                .findFragmentById(R.id.map);
                mapFragment.getMapAsync(this);
            }
        }
    }
}
```

If the user has not granted permission, the app displays a message indicating that the current location cannot be displayed. If, on the other hand, permission was granted, the map is refreshed to provide an opportunity for the location marker to be displayed.

74.12 Displaying the User's Current Location

Once the appropriate permission has been granted, the user's current location may be displayed on the map by obtaining a reference to the GoogleMap object associated with the displayed map and calling the *setMyLocationEnabled()* method of that instance, passing through a *true* value.

When the map is ready to display, the *onMapReady()* method of the activity is called. This method will also be called when the map is refreshed within the *onRequestPermissionsResult()* method above. By default, Android Studio has implemented this method and added some code to orient the map over Australia with a marker positioned over the city of Sidney. Locate and edit the *onMapReady()* method in the *MapsActivity.java* file to remove this template code and add code to check that the location permission has been granted before enabling the display of the user's current location. If permission has not been granted, a request is made to the user via a call to the previously added *requestPermission()* method:

```
@Override
public void onMapReady(GoogleMap googleMap) {
    mMap = googleMap;

    // Add a marker in Sydney and move the camera
    LatLng sydney = new LatLng(-34, 151);
    mMap.addMarker(new MarkerOptions().position(sydney).title("Marker in Sydney"));
    mMap.moveCamera(CameraUpdateFactory.newLatLng(sydney));

    if (mMap != null) {
        int permission = ContextCompat.checkSelfPermission(this,
                Manifest.permission.ACCESS_FINE_LOCATION);

        if (permission == PackageManager.PERMISSION_GRANTED) {
```

```
            mMap.setMyLocationEnabled(true);
    } else {
            requestPermission(
                Manifest.permission.ACCESS_FINE_LOCATION,
                    LOCATION_REQUEST_CODE);
        }
    }
}
```

When the app is now run, the dialog shown in Figure 74-10 will appear requesting location permission. If permission is granted, a blue dot will appear on the map indicating the device's location.

Figure 74-10

74.13 Changing the Map Type

The type of map displayed can be modified dynamically by making a call to the *setMapType()* method of the corresponding GoogleMap object, passing through one of the following values:

- **GoogleMap.MAP_TYPE_NONE** – An empty grid with no mapping tiles displayed.
- **GoogleMap.MAP_TYPE_NORMAL** – The standard view consisting of the classic road map.
- **GoogleMap.MAP_TYPE_SATELLITE** – Displays the satellite imagery of the map region.
- **GoogleMap.MAP_TYPE_HYBRID** – Displays satellite imagery with the road map superimposed.
- **GoogleMap.MAP_TYPE_TERRAIN** – Displays topographical information such as contour lines and colors.

The following code change to the *onMapReady()* method, for example, switches a map to Satellite mode:

.
.
```
if (mMap != null) {
```

Working with the Google Maps Android API in Android Studio

```
    int permission = ContextCompat.checkSelfPermission(
            this, Manifest.permission.ACCESS_FINE_LOCATION);

    if (permission == PackageManager.PERMISSION_GRANTED) {
       mMap.setMyLocationEnabled(true);
    } else {
       requestPermission(Manifest.permission.ACCESS_FINE_LOCATION,
             LOCATION_REQUEST_CODE);
    }
    mMap.setMapType(GoogleMap.MAP_TYPE_SATELLITE);
}
.
.
.
```

Alternatively, the map type may be specified in the XML layout file where the map is embedded using the *map:mapType* property together with a value of *none*, *normal*, *hybrid*, *satellite*, or *terrain*. For example:

```
<?xml version="1.0" encoding="utf-8"?>
<fragment xmlns:android="http://schemas.android.com/apk/res/android"
          xmlns:map="http://schemas.android.com/apk/res-auto"
          android:id="@+id/map"
          android:layout_width="match_parent"
          android:layout_height="match_parent"
          map:mapType="hybrid"
          android:name="com.google.android.gms.maps.SupportMapFragment"/>
```

74.14 Displaying Map Controls to the User

The Google Maps Android API provides several controls that may be optionally displayed to the user consisting of zoom-in and out buttons, a "my location" button, and a compass.

Whether or not the zoom and compass controls are displayed may be controlled programmatically or within the map element in XML layout resources. To programmatically configure the controls, a reference to the UiSettings object associated with the GoogleMap object must be obtained:

```
import com.google.android.gms.maps.UiSettings;
.
.
.
UiSettings mapSettings;
mapSettings = mMap.getUiSettings();
```

The zoom controls are turned on and off via the calls to the *setZoomControlsEnabled()* method of the UiSettings object. For example:

```
mapSettings.setZoomControlsEnabled(true);
```

Alternatively, the *map:uiZoomControls* property may be set within the map element of the XML resource file:

```
map:uiZoomControls="false"
```

The compass may be displayed via a call to the *setCompassEnabled()* method of the UiSettings instance or through XML resources using the *map:uiCompass* property. Note that the compass icon only appears when the map camera is tilted or rotated away from the default orientation.

Working with the Google Maps Android API in Android Studio

As outlined earlier in this chapter, the "My Location" button will only appear when My Location mode is enabled. The button may be prevented from appearing even in this mode via a call to the *setMyLocationButtonEnabled()* method of the UiSettings instance.

74.15 Handling Map Gesture Interaction

The Google Maps Android API can respond to various user interactions. These interactions can be used to change the map area displayed, the zoom level, and even the angle of view (such that a 3D representation of the map area is displayed for certain cities).

74.15.1 Map Zooming Gestures

Support for gestures relating to zooming in and out of a map may be turned on or off using the *setZoomGesturesEnabled()* method of the UiSettings object associated with the GoogleMap instance. For example, the following code turns off zoom gestures for our example map:

```
UiSettings mapSettings;
mapSettings = map.getUiSettings();
mapSettings.setZoomGesturesEnabled(false);
```

The same result can be achieved within an XML resource file by setting the *map:uiZoomGestures* property to true or false.

When enabled, zooming will occur when the user makes pinching gestures on the screen. Similarly, a double tap will zoom in, while a two-finger tap will zoom out. On the other hand, one-finger zooming gestures are performed by tapping twice but not releasing the second tap and then sliding the finger up and down on the screen to zoom in and out, respectively.

74.15.2 Map Scrolling/Panning Gestures

A scrolling or panning gesture allows the user to move around the map by dragging the map around the screen with a single-finger motion. Scrolling gestures may be enabled within code via a call to the *setScrollGesturesEnabled()* method of the UiSettings instance:

```
UiSettings mapSettings;
mapSettings = mMap.getUiSettings();
mapSettings.setScrollGesturesEnabled(true);
```

Alternatively, scrolling on a map instance may be enabled in an XML resource layout file using the *map:uiScrollGestures* property.

74.15.3 Map Tilt Gestures

Tilt gestures allow the user to tilt the map's projection angle by placing two fingers on the screen and moving them up and down to adjust the tilt angle. Tilt gestures may be turned on or off via the *setTiltGesturesEnabled()* method of the UiSettings instance, for example:

```
UiSettings mapSettings;
mapSettings = mMap.getUiSettings();
mapSettings.setTiltGesturesEnabled(true);
```

Tilt gestures may also be turned on and off using the *map:uiTiltGestures* property in an XML layout resource file.

74.15.4 Map Rotation Gestures

By placing two fingers on the screen and rotating them in a circular motion, the user may rotate the orientation of a map when map rotation gestures are enabled. This gesture support is turned on and off in code via a call to the *setRotateGesturesEnabled()* method of the UiSettings instance, for example:

Working with the Google Maps Android API in Android Studio

```
UiSettings mapSettings;
mapSettings = mMap.getUiSettings();
mapSettings.setRotateGesturesEnabled(true);
```

Rotation gestures may also be turned on and off using the *map:uiRotateGestures* property in an XML layout resource file.

74.16 Creating Map Markers

Markers notify the user of locations on a map and take the form of either a standard or custom icon. Markers may also include a title and optional text (called a *snippet*) and may be configured to be dragged to different locations on the map by the user. When the user taps a marker, an *info window* will appear, displaying additional information about the marker's location.

Markers are represented by instances of the Marker class and are added to a map via a call to the *addMarker()* method of the corresponding GoogleMap object. A MarkerOptions class instance containing the various options required for the marker, such as the title and snippet text, is passed through as an argument to this method. The location of a marker is defined by specifying latitude and longitude values, also included as part of the MarkerOptions instance. For example, the following code adds a marker, including a title, snippet, and a position to a specific location on the map:

```
import com.google.android.gms.maps.model.Marker;
import com.google.android.gms.maps.model.LatLng;
import com.google.android.gms.maps.model.MarkerOptions;
.
.
.
LatLng position = new LatLng(38.8874245, -77.0200729);
Marker museum = mMap.addMarker(new MarkerOptions()
                .position(position)
                .title("Museum")
                .snippet("National Air and Space Museum"));
```

When executed, the above code will mark the location specified, which, when tapped, will display an info window containing the title and snippet, as shown in Figure 74-11:

Figure 74-11

74.17 Controlling the Map Camera

Because Android device screens are flat and the world is a sphere, the Google Maps Android API uses the Mercator projection to represent Earth on a flat surface. The map's default view is presented to the user as though through a *camera* suspended above the map and pointing directly down at the map. The Google Maps Android API allows the *target, zoom, bearing,* and *tilt* of this camera to be changed in real time from within the application:

- **Target** – The location of the center of the map within the device display specified using longitude and latitude.

- **Zoom** – The zoom level of the camera specified in levels. Increasing the zoom level by 1.0 doubles the width of the amount of the map displayed.

- **Tilt** – The camera's viewing angle specified as a position on an arc spanning directly over the center of the viewable map area measured in degrees from the top of the arc (this being the nadir of the arc where the camera points directly down to the map).

- **Bearing** – The orientation of the map in degrees measured in a clockwise direction from North.

Camera changes are made by creating an instance of the CameraUpdate class with the appropriate settings. CameraUpdate instances are created by making method calls to the *CameraUpdateFactory* class. Once a CameraUpdate instance has been created, it is applied to the map via a call to the *moveCamera()* method of the GoogleMap instance. To obtain a smooth animated effect as the camera changes, the *animateCamera()* method may be called instead of *moveCamera()*.

A summary of CameraUpdateFactory methods is as follows:

- **CameraUpdateFactory.zoomIn()** – Provides a CameraUpdate instance zoomed in by one level.

- **CameraUpdateFactory.zoomOut()** - Provides a CameraUpdate instance zoomed out by one level.

- **CameraUpdateFactory.zoomTo(float)** - Generates a CameraUpdate instance that changes the zoom level to the specified value.

- **CameraUpdateFactory.zoomBy(float)** – Provides a CameraUpdate instance with a zoom level increased or decreased by the specified amount.

- **CameraUpdateFactory.zoomBy(float, Point)** - Creates a CameraUpdate instance that increases or decreases the zoom level by the specified value.

- **CameraUpdateFactory.newLatLng(LatLng)** - Creates a CameraUpdate instance that changes the camera's target latitude and longitude.

- **CameraUpdateFactory.newLatLngZoom(LatLng, float)** - Generates a CameraUpdate instance that changes the camera's latitude, longitude, and zoom.

- **CameraUpdateFactory.newCameraPosition(CameraPosition)** - Returns a CameraUpdate instance that moves the camera to the specified position. A CameraPosition instance can be obtained using CameraPosition.Builder().

The following code, for example, zooms in the camera by one level using animation:

```
mMap.animateCamera(CameraUpdateFactory.zoomIn());
```

The following code, on the other hand, moves the camera to a new location and adjusts the zoom level to 10 without animation:

Working with the Google Maps Android API in Android Studio

```
private static final LatLng position =
        new LatLng(38.8874245, -77.0200729);
```

```
mMap.moveCamera(CameraUpdateFactory.newLatLngZoom(position, 10));
```

Finally, the next code example uses *CameraPosition.Builder()* to create a CameraPosition object with changes to the target, zoom, bearing, and tilt. This change is then applied to the camera using animation:

```
import com.google.android.gms.maps.model.CameraPosition;
import com.google.android.gms.maps.CameraUpdateFactory;
.
.
CameraPosition cameraPosition = new CameraPosition.Builder()
     .target(position)
     .zoom(50)
     .bearing(70)
     .tilt(25)
     .build();
mMap.animateCamera(CameraUpdateFactory.newCameraPosition(
                         cameraPosition));
```

74.18 Summary

This chapter has provided an overview of the key classes and methods that make up the Google Maps Android API and outlined how to prepare both the development environment and an application project to use the API.

75. Printing with the Android Printing Framework

Android Printing Framework is used to print content from within Android applications. While subsequent chapters will explore in more detail the options for adding printing support to your applications, this chapter will focus on the various printing options now available in Android and the steps involved in enabling those options.

The chapter will then provide an overview of the various printing features available to Android developers to build printing support into applications.

75.1 The Android Printing Architecture

The Printing framework provides printing in Android. In basic terms, this framework consists of a Print Manager and a number of print service plugins.

It is the responsibility of the Print Manager to handle the print requests from applications on the device and to interact with the print service plugins installed on the device, thereby ensuring that print requests are fulfilled.

By default, many Android devices have print service plugins installed to enable printing using the Google Cloud Print and Google Drive services. Print Services Plugins for other printer types, if not already installed, may also be obtained from the Google Play store.

Print Service Plugins are currently available for HP, Epson, Samsung, and Canon printers, and plugins from other printer manufacturers will most likely be released in the future. However, the Google Cloud Print service plugin can print from Android to just about any printer type and model.

This book will use the HP Print Services Plugin as a reference example.

75.2 The Print Service Plugins

The purpose of the Print Service plugins is to enable applications to print to compatible printers that are visible to the Android device via a local area wireless network or Bluetooth.

The presence of the Print Service Plugin on an Android device can be verified by loading the Google Play app and performing a search for "Print Service Plugin".

Once the plugin is listed in the Play Store, and if it is not already installed, it can be installed by selecting the *Install* button. Figure 75-1, for example, shows the HP Print Service plugin within Google Play.

The Print Services plugins will automatically detect compatible printers on the network to which the Android device is currently connected and list them as options when printing from an application.

Printing with the Android Printing Framework

Figure 75-1

75.3 Google Cloud Print

Google Cloud Print is a service provided by Google that enables you to print content onto your printer over the web from anywhere with internet connectivity. Google Cloud Print supports many devices and printer models in both *Cloud Ready* and *Classic* printers. A Cloud Ready printer has technology built-in that enables printing via the web. Manufacturers that provide cloud-ready printers include Brother, Canon, Dell, Epson, HP, Kodak, and Samsung. To identify if your printer is both cloud-ready and supported by Google Cloud Print, review the list of printers at the following URL:

https://www.google.com/cloudprint/learn/printers.html

In the case of classic, non-Cloud Ready printers, Google Cloud Print provides support for cloud printing by installing software on the computer system to which the classic printer is connected (either directly or over a home or office network).

To set up Google Cloud Print, visit the following web page and log in using the same Google account ID that you use when logging in to your Android devices:

https://www.google.com/cloudprint/learn/index.html

Once printers have been added to your Google Cloud Print account, they will be listed as printer destination options when you print from within Android applications.

75.4 Printing to Google Drive

In addition to supporting physical printers, it is also possible to save printed output to your Google Drive account. When printing from a device, select the *Save to Google Drive* option in the printing panel. The content to be printed will then be converted to a PDF file and saved to the Google Drive cloud-based storage associated with the currently active Google Account ID on the device.

75.5 Save as PDF

The final printing option provided by Android allows the printed content to be saved locally as a PDF file on the Android device. Once selected, this option will request a name for the PDF file and a location on the device to which the document will be saved.

Both the Save as PDF and Google Drive options can be invaluable in terms of saving paper when testing the printing functionality of your own Android applications.

75.6 Printing from Android Devices

Google recommends that applications that can print content do so by placing the print option in the Overflow menu. Many applications bundled with Android now include "Print…" menu options. Figure 75-2, for example, shows the Print option accessed by selecting the "Share…" option in the Overflow menu of the Chrome browser application:

Figure 75-2

Once the print option has been selected from within an application, the standard Android print screen will appear, showing a preview of the content to be printed, as illustrated in Figure 75-3:

Figure 75-3

Tapping the panel along the top of the screen will display the full range of printing options:

Figure 75-4

The Android print panel provides standard printing options, such as paper size, color, orientation, and number of copies. Other print destination options may be accessed by tapping on the current printer or PDF output selection.

75.7 Options for Building Print Support into Android Apps

The Printing framework provides several options for incorporating print support into Android applications. These options can be categorized as follows:

75.7.1 Image Printing

As the name suggests, this option allows image printing to be incorporated into Android applications. When adding this feature to an application, the first step is to create a new instance of the PrintHelper class:

```
PrintHelper imagePrinter = new PrintHelper(context);
```

Next, the scale mode for the printed image may be specified via a call to the *setScaleMode()* method of the PrintHelper instance. Options are as follows:

- **SCALE_MODE_FIT** – The image will be scaled to fit within the paper size without cropping or changes to the aspect ratio. This will typically result in white space appearing in one dimension.

- **SCALE_MODE_FILL** – The image will be scaled to fill the paper size with cropping performed where necessary to avoid the appearance of white space in the printed output.

Without a scale mode setting, the system will default to SCALE_MODE_FILL. The following code, for example, sets scale to fit mode on the previously declared PrintHelper instance:

```
imagePrinter.setScaleMode(PrintHelper.SCALE_MODE_FIT);
```

Similarly, the color mode may also be configured to indicate whether the print output is to be in color or black and white. This is achieved by passing one of the following options through to the *setColorMode()* method of the PrintHelper instance:

- **COLOR_MODE_COLOR** – Indicates that the image is to be printed in color.

- **COLOR_MODE_MONOCHROME** – Indicates that the image will be printed in black and white.

The printing framework will default to color printing unless the monochrome option is specified as follows:

Printing with the Android Printing Framework

```
imagePrinter.setColorMode(PrintHelper.COLOR_MODE_MONOCHROME);
```

All that is required to complete the printing operation is an image to be printed and a call to the *printBitmap()* method of the PrintHelper instance, passing through a string representing the name to be assigned to the print job and a reference to the image (in the form of either a Bitmap object or a Uri reference to the image):

```
Bitmap bitmap = BitmapFactory.decodeResource(getResources(),
          R.drawable.oceanscene);
imagePrinter.printBitmap("My Test Print Job", bitmap);
```

Once the print job has been started, the Printing framework will display the print dialog and handle both the subsequent interaction with the user and the printing of the image on the user-selected print destination.

75.7.2 Creating and Printing HTML Content

The Android Printing framework also provides an easy way to print HTML-based content within an application. This content can either be HTML content referenced by the URL of a page hosted on a website or HTML content dynamically created within the application.

To enable HTML printing, the WebView class has been extended to include support for printing with minimal coding requirements.

When dynamically creating HTML content (as opposed to loading and printing an existing web page), the process involves the creation of a WebView object and associating with it a WebViewClient instance. The web view client is then configured to start a print job when the HTML has finished being loaded into the WebView. With the web view client configured, the HTML is loaded into the WebView, and the print process is triggered.

Consider, for example, the following code:

```
public void printContent()
{
        WebView webView = new WebView(this);
        webView.setWebViewClient(new WebViewClient() {

                public boolean shouldOverrideUrlLoading(WebView view,
                        String url)
                {
                        return false;
                }

                @Override
                    public void onPageFinished(WebView view, String url) {
                        createWebPrintJob(view);
                        myWebView = null;
                    }
        });

                String htmlDocument =
                    "<html><body><h1>Android Print Test</h1><p>"
                    + "This is some sample content.</p></body></html>";
```

Printing with the Android Printing Framework

```
            webView.loadDataWithBaseURL(null, htmlDocument,
                    "text/HTML", "UTF-8", null);

            myWebView = webView;
}
```

The code in this method begins by declaring a variable named *myWebView* in which will be stored a reference to the WebView instance created in the method. Within the *printContent()* method, an instance of the WebView class is created to which a WebViewClient instance is assigned.

The WebViewClient assigned to the web view object is configured to indicate that the loading of the HTML content is to be handled by the WebView instance (by returning *false* from the *shouldOverrideUrlLoading()*) method. More importantly, an *onPageFinished()* handler method is declared and implemented to call the *createWebPrintJob()* method. The *onPageFinished()* callback method will be called automatically when all HTML content is loaded into the web view. This ensures that the print job is not started until the content is ready, ensuring that all content is printed.

Next, a string is created containing some HTML to serve as the content. This is then loaded into the web view. Once the HTML is loaded, the *onPageFinished()* method will trigger. Finally, the method stores a reference to the web view object. Without this vital step, there is a significant risk that the Java runtime system will assume that the application no longer needs the web view object and will discard it to free up memory (a concept referred to in Java terminology as *garbage collection*), resulting in the print job terminating before completion.

All that remains in this example is to implement the *createWebPrintJob()* method as follows:

```
private void createWebPrintJob(WebView webView) {

        PrintManager printManager = (PrintManager) this
                .getSystemService(Context.PRINT_SERVICE);

        PrintDocumentAdapter printAdapter =
                webView.createPrintDocumentAdapter("MyDocument");
        String jobName = getString(R.string.app_name) + " Document";

        PrintJob printJob = printManager.print(jobName, printAdapter,
                new PrintAttributes.Builder().build());
}
```

This method obtains a reference to the PrintManager service and instructs the web view instance to create a print adapter. A new string is created to store the name of the print job (which, in this case, is based on the name of the application and the word "Document").

Finally, the print job is started by calling the *print()* method of the print manager, passing through the job name, print adapter, and a set of default print attributes. If required, the print attributes could be customized to specify resolution (dots per inch), margin, and color options.

75.7.3 Printing a Web Page

The steps involved in printing a web page are similar to those outlined above, with the exception that the web view is passed the URL of the web page to be printed in place of the dynamically created HTML, for example:

```
myWebView.loadUrl("https://developer.android.com/google/index.html");
```

It is also important to note that the WebViewClient configuration is only necessary if a web page is to automatically print as soon as it has loaded. If the printing is to be initiated by the user selecting a menu option after the page has loaded, only the code in the *createWebPrintJob()* method outlined above needs to be included in the application code. The next chapter, *"An Android HTML and Web Content Printing Example"*, will demonstrate such a scenario.

75.7.4 Printing a Custom Document

While the HTML and web printing features introduced by the Printing framework provide an easy path to printing content from within an Android application, it is clear that these options will be overly simplistic for more advanced printing requirements. The Printing framework also provides custom document printing support for more complex printing tasks. This allows content in the form of text and graphics to be drawn onto a canvas and then printed.

Unlike HTML and image printing, which can be implemented with relative ease, custom document printing is a more complex, multi-stage process which will be outlined in the *"A Guide to Android Custom Document Printing"* chapter of this book. These steps can be summarized as follows:

- Connect to the Android Print Manager
- Create a Custom Print Adapter sub-classed from the PrintDocumentAdapter class
- Create a PdfDocument instance to represent the document pages
- Obtain a reference to the pages of the PdfDocument instance, each of which has associated with it a Canvas instance
- Draw the content on the page canvases
- Notify the print framework that the document is ready to print

The custom print adapter outlined in the above steps must implement several methods that the Android system will call upon to perform specific tasks during printing. The most important of these are the *onLayout()* method, responsible for re-arranging the document layout in response to the user changing settings such as paper size or page orientation, and the *onWrite()* method which is responsible for rendering the pages to be printed. The chapter entitled *"A Guide to Android Custom Document Printing"* will cover this topic in detail.

75.8 Summary

The Android SDK can print content from within a running app. Print output can be directed to suitably configured printers, a local PDF file, or to the cloud via Google Drive. From the perspective of the Android application developer, these capabilities are available for use in applications by making use of the Printing framework. By far, the easiest printing options to implement are those involving content in the form of images and HTML. More advanced printing may, however, be implemented using the custom document printing features of the framework.

Chapter 76

76. An Android HTML and Web Content Printing Example

As outlined in the previous chapter, entitled *"Printing with the Android Printing Framework"*, the Android Printing framework can print both web pages and dynamically created HTML content. While there is much similarity between these two approaches to printing, there are also some subtle differences that need to be considered. This chapter will work through the creation of two example applications to bring some clarity to these two printing options.

76.1 Creating the HTML Printing Example Application

Select the *New Project* option from the welcome screen and, within the resulting new project dialog, choose the Empty Views Activity template before clicking on the Next button.

Enter *HTMLPrint* into the Name field and specify *com.ebookfrenzy.htmlprint* as the package name. Before clicking on the Finish button, change the Minimum API level setting to API 26: Android 8.0 (Oreo) and the Language menu to Java.

76.2 Printing Dynamic HTML Content

The first stage of this tutorial is to add code to the project to create some HTML content and send it to the Printing framework as a print job.

Begin by locating the *MainActivity.java* file (located in the Project tool window under *app -> java -> com.ebookfrenzy.htmlprint*) and loading it into the editing panel. Once loaded, modify the code so that it reads as outlined in the following listing:

```
package com.ebookfrenzy.htmlprint;

import androidx.appcompat.app.AppCompatActivity;
import android.os.Bundle;
import android.webkit.WebView;
import android.webkit.WebViewClient;
import android.webkit.WebResourceRequest;
import android.print.PrintAttributes;
import android.print.PrintDocumentAdapter;
import android.print.PrintManager;
import android.content.Context;

public class MainActivity extends AppCompatActivity {

    private WebView myWebView;

    @Override
    protected void onCreate(Bundle savedInstanceState) {
```

An Android HTML and Web Content Printing Example

```
        super.onCreate(savedInstanceState);
        setContentView(R.layout.activity_htmlprint);

        printWebView();
    }

    private void printWebView() {

        WebView webView = new WebView(this);
        webView.setWebViewClient(new WebViewClient() {
            public boolean shouldOverrideUrlLoading(WebView view,
                                   WebResourceRequest request)
            {
                return false;
            }

            @Override
            public void onPageFinished(WebView view, String url)
            {
                createWebPrintJob(view);
                myWebView = null;
            }
        });
        String htmlDocument =
            "<html><body><h1>Android Print Test</h1><p>"
             + "This is some sample content.</p></body></html>";

        webView.loadDataWithBaseURL(null, htmlDocument,
                "text/HTML", "UTF-8", null);
        myWebView = webView;
    }
}
```

The code changes begin by declaring a variable named *myWebView* in which will be stored a reference to the WebView instance used for the printing operation. Within the *printWebView()* method, an instance of the WebView class is created to which a WebViewClient instance is assigned.

The WebViewClient assigned to the web view object is configured to indicate that loading the HTML content is to be handled by the WebView instance (by returning *false* from the *shouldOverrideUrlLoading()* method). More importantly, an *onPageFinished()* handler method is declared and implemented to call the *createWebPrintJob()* method. The *onPageFinished()* method will be called automatically when all HTML content has been loaded into the web view. As outlined in the previous chapter, this step is necessary when printing dynamically created HTML content to ensure that the print job is only started once the content has fully loaded into the WebView.

Next, a String object is created containing some HTML to serve as the content and subsequently loaded into the web view. Once the HTML is loaded, the *onPageFinished()* callback method will trigger. Finally, the method stores a reference to the web view object in the previously declared *myWebView* variable. Without this vital step, there is a significant risk that the Java runtime system will assume that the application no longer needs the web

An Android HTML and Web Content Printing Example

view object and will discard it to free up memory resulting in the print job terminating before completion.

All that remains in this example is to implement the *createWebPrintJob()* method, which is currently configured to be called by the *onPageFinished()* callback method. Remaining within the *MainActivity.java* file, therefore, implement this method so that it reads as follows:

```
private void createWebPrintJob(WebView webView) {

        PrintManager printManager = (PrintManager) this
                .getSystemService(Context.PRINT_SERVICE);
        PrintDocumentAdapter printAdapter =
                webView.createPrintDocumentAdapter("MyDocument");

        String jobName = getString(R.string.app_name) + " Print Test";

        printManager.print(jobName, printAdapter,
                new PrintAttributes.Builder().build());
}
```

This method obtains a reference to the PrintManager service and instructs the web view instance to create a print adapter. A new string is created to store the name of the print job (in this case, based on the name of the application and the word "Print Test").

Finally, the print job is started by calling the *print()* method of the print manager, passing through the job name, print adapter, and a set of default print attributes.

Compile and run the application on a device or emulator running Android 5.0 or later. Once launched, the standard Android printing page should appear as illustrated in Figure 76-1.

Figure 76-1

An Android HTML and Web Content Printing Example

Print to a physical printer if you have one configured, save to Google Drive, or select the option to save to a PDF file. Once the print job has been initiated, check the generated output on your chosen destination. Note that the system will request a name and location for the PDF file when using the Save to PDF option. The Downloads folder makes a good option, the contents of which can be viewed by selecting the *Downloads* icon (renamed Files on Android 8) located amongst the other app icons on the device.

76.3 Creating the Web Page Printing Example

The second example application created in this chapter will provide the user an Overflow menu option to print the web page currently displayed within a WebView instance.

Select the *New Project* option from the welcome screen and, within the resulting new project dialog, choose the Basic Views Activity template before clicking on the Next button.

Enter *WebPrint* into the Name field and specify *com.ebookfrenzy.webprint* as the package name. Before clicking on the Finish button, change the Minimum API level setting to API 26: Android 8.0 (Oreo) and the Language menu to Java.

76.4 Removing the Floating Action Button

Selecting the Basic Views Activity template provided a context menu and a floating action button. Since the app does not require the floating action button, it can be removed before proceeding. Load the *activity_main.xml* layout file into the Layout Editor, select the floating action button, and tap the keyboard *Delete* key to remove the object from the layout. Edit the *MainActivity.java* file and remove the floating action button code from the onCreate method as follows:

```
@Override
protected void onCreate(Bundle savedInstanceState) {
    super.onCreate(savedInstanceState);

    binding = ActivityMainBinding.inflate(getLayoutInflater());
    setContentView(binding.getRoot());

    setSupportActionBar(binding.toolbar);
.
.
    binding.fab.setOnClickListener(new View.OnClickListener() {
        @Override
        public void onClick(View view) {
            Snackbar.make(view, "Replace with your own action",
                    Snackbar.LENGTH_LONG)
                    .setAction("Action", null).show();
        }
    });
}
```

76.5 Removing Navigation Features

As *"A Guide to the Android Studio Layout Editor Tool"* outlines, the Basic Views Activity template contains multiple fragments and buttons to navigate from one fragment to the other. These features are unnecessary for this tutorial and will cause problems later if not removed. Before moving ahead with the tutorial, modify the project as follows:

An Android HTML and Web Content Printing Example

1. Within the Project tool window, navigate to and double-click on the *app -> res -> navigation -> nav_graph.xml* file to load it into the navigation editor.

2. Within the editor, select the SecondFragment entry in the graph panel and tap the keyboard delete key to remove it from the graph.

3. Locate and delete the *SecondFragment.java (app -> java -> <package name> -> SecondFragment)* and *fragment_second.xml (app -> res -> layout -> fragment_second.xml)* files.

4. Locate the *FirstFragment.java* file, double-click on it to load it into the editor, and remove the code from the *onViewCreated()* method so that it reads as follows:

```
public void onViewCreated(@NonNull View view, Bundle savedInstanceState) {
    super.onViewCreated(view, savedInstanceState);

    binding.buttonFirst.setOnClickListener(new View.OnClickListener() {
        @Override
        public void onClick(View view) {
            NavHostFragment.findNavController(FirstFragment.this)
                    .navigate(R.id.action_FirstFragment_to_SecondFragment);
        }
    });
}
```

5. Edit the *MainActivity.java* file and remove the following navigation code:

```
@Override
protected void onCreate(Bundle savedInstanceState) {
    super.onCreate(savedInstanceState);

    binding = ActivityMainBinding.inflate(getLayoutInflater());
    setContentView(binding.getRoot());

    setSupportActionBar(binding.toolbar);

    NavController navController =
        Navigation.findNavController(this, R.id.nav_host_fragment_content_main);
    appBarConfiguration = new AppBarConfiguration.Builder(
        navController.getGraph()).build();
    NavigationUI.setupActionBarWithNavController(this, navController,
        appBarConfiguration);
}
.
.
@Override
public boolean onSupportNavigateUp() {
    NavController navController = Navigation.findNavController(this,
            R.id.nav_host_fragment_content_main);
    return NavigationUI.navigateUp(navController, appBarConfiguration)
```

An Android HTML and Web Content Printing Example

```
        || super.onSupportNavigateUp();
}
```

76.6 Designing the User Interface Layout

Load the *content_main.xml* layout resource file into the Layout Editor tool if it has not already been loaded and, in Design mode, select and delete the *nav_host_fragment_content_main* object. From the *Widgets* section of the palette, drag and drop a WebView object onto the center of the device screen layout. Click the Infer constraints toolbar button and, using the Attributes tool window, change the layout_width and layout_height properties of the WebView to *match constraint* so that it fills the entire layout canvas, as outlined in Figure 76-2 below.

Select the newly added WebView instance and change the ID of the view to *myWebView*.

Before proceeding to the next step of this tutorial, an additional permission must be added to the project to enable the WebView object to access the Internet and download a web page for printing. Add this permission by locating the *AndroidManifest.xml* file in the Project tool window and double-clicking on it to load it into the editing panel. Once loaded, edit the XML content to add the appropriate permission line, as shown in the following listing:

```xml
<?xml version="1.0" encoding="utf-8"?>
<manifest xmlns:android="http://schemas.android.com/apk/res/android"
    package="com.ebookfrenzy.webprint" >

    <uses-permission android:name="android.permission.INTERNET" />

    <application
        android:allowBackup="true"
.
.
</manifest>
```

Figure 76-2

76.7 Accessing the WebView from the Main Activity

As with the project in the chapter entitled *"An Android RecyclerView and CardView Tutorial"* we need to be able to use view binding to access a component (in this case *myWebView*) contained in the *content_main.xml* file from within the MainActivity class. To access views within the *content_main.xml* file, we again need to assign it an id at the point it is included. Edit the *activity_main.xml* file and modify the *include* element so that it reads

An Android HTML and Web Content Printing Example

as follows:

```
<include
    android:id="@+id/contentMain"
    layout="@layout/content_main" />
```

76.8 Loading the Web Page into the WebView

Before the web page can be printed, it must loaded into the WebView instance. For this tutorial, this will be performed by a call to the *loadUrl()* method of the WebView instance, which will be placed in a method named *configureWebView()* and called from within the *onStart()* method of the MainActivity class. Edit the *MainActivity.java* file, therefore, and modify it as follows:

```
package com.ebookfrenzy.webprint;
.
.
import android.view.Menu;
import android.view.MenuItem;
import android.webkit.WebView;
import android.webkit.WebViewClient;
import android.webkit.WebResourceRequest;

public class MainActivity extends AppCompatActivity {

    private WebView myWebView;
.
.
    @Override
    protected void onStart() {
        super.onStart();
        configureWebView();
    }

    private void configureWebView() {

        myWebView = findViewById(R.id.myWebView);
        myWebView.setWebViewClient(new WebViewClient(){
            @Override
            public boolean shouldOverrideUrlLoading(
                    WebView view, WebResourceRequest request) {
                return super.shouldOverrideUrlLoading(
                        view, request);
            }
        });
        myWebView.loadUrl(
```

661

```
            "https://www.answertopia.com");
    }
    .
    .
}
```

76.9 Adding the Print Menu Option

The option to print the web page will now be added to the Overflow menu using the techniques outlined in the chapter entitled *"Creating and Managing Overflow Menus on Android"*. The first requirement is a string resource to label the menu option. Within the Project tool window, locate the *app -> res -> values -> strings.xml* file, double-click on it to load it into the editor, and modify it to add a new string resource:

```
<resources>
    <string name="app_name">WebPrint</string>
    <string name="action_settings">Settings</string>
    <string name="print_string">Print</string>
    .
    .
</resources>
```

Next, load the *app -> res -> menu -> menu_main.xml* file into the menu editor, switch to Code mode, and replace the *Settings* menu option with the print option:

```
<menu xmlns:android="http://schemas.android.com/apk/res/android"
    xmlns:tools="http://schemas.android.com/tools"
    tools:context="com.ebookfrenzy.webprint.MainActivity" >
    <item
        android:id="@+id/action_settings"
        android:title="@string/action_settings"
        android:orderInCategory="100"
        app:showAsAction="never" />

    <item
        android:id="@+id/action_print"
        android:orderInCategory="100"
        app:showAsAction="never"
        android:title="@string/print_string"/>
</menu>
```

All that remains in terms of configuring the menu option is to modify the *onOptionsItemSelected()* handler method within the *MainActivity.java* file:

```
@Override
public boolean onOptionsItemSelected(MenuItem item) {
    int id = item.getItemId();
    if (id == R.id.action_print) {
        createWebPrintJob(myWebView);
        return true;
    }
    return super.onOptionsItemSelected(item);
```

An Android HTML and Web Content Printing Example

}

With the *onOptionsItemSelected()* method implemented, the activity will call a method named *createWebPrintJob()* when the print menu option is selected from the overflow menu. The implementation of this method is identical to that used in the previous HTMLPrint project and may now be added to the *MainActivity.java* file such that it reads as follows:

```
package com.ebookfrenzy.webprint;
.
.
.
import android.print.PrintAttributes;
import android.print.PrintDocumentAdapter;
import android.print.PrintManager;
import android.content.Context;

public class MainActivity extends AppCompatActivity {

    private WebView myWebView;
.
.
    private void createWebPrintJob(WebView webView) {

        PrintManager printManager = (PrintManager) this
                .getSystemService(Context.PRINT_SERVICE);

        PrintDocumentAdapter printAdapter =
                webView.createPrintDocumentAdapter("MyDocument");

        String jobName = getString(R.string.app_name) +
                " Print Test";

        printManager.print(jobName, printAdapter,
                new PrintAttributes.Builder().build());
    }
.
.
.
}
```

With the code changes complete, run the application on a physical Android device or emulator. Once successfully launched, the WebView should be visible with the designated web page loaded. Once the page has loaded, select the Print option from the Overflow menu and use the resulting print panel to print the web page to a suitable destination.

When building the project, you may encounter an error that reads in part:

```
Duplicate class kotlin.collections.jdk8.CollectionsJDK8Kt found in modules kotlin-stdlib
```

This error can be resolved by making the following changes to the *build.gradle.kts (Module: app)* file:

An Android HTML and Web Content Printing Example

```
dependencies {
.
.
    implementation(platform("org.jetbrains.kotlin:kotlin-bom:1.8.0"))
.
.
}
```

76.10 Summary

The Android Printing framework includes extensions to the WebView class that allow printing HTML-based content from within an Android application. This content can be HTML created dynamically within the application at runtime or a pre-existing web page loaded into a WebView instance. In the case of dynamically created HTML, it is important to use a WebViewClient instance to ensure that printing does not start until the HTML has been fully loaded into the WebView.

77. A Guide to Android Custom Document Printing

As we have seen in the preceding chapters, the Android Printing framework makes it relatively easy to build printing support into applications if the content is in the form of an image or HTML markup. More advanced printing requirements can be met by using the custom document printing feature of the Printing framework.

77.1 An Overview of Android Custom Document Printing

In simplistic terms, custom document printing uses canvases to represent the pages of the document to be printed. The application draws the content to be printed onto these canvases as shapes, colors, text, and images. The canvases are represented by instances of the Android Canvas class, providing access to a rich selection of drawing options. Once all the pages have been drawn, the document is then printed.

While this sounds simple enough, some steps need to be performed to make this happen, which can be summarized as follows:

- Implement a custom print adapter sub-classed from the PrintDocumentAdapter class.
- Obtain a reference to the Print Manager Service.
- Create an instance of the PdfDocument class to store the document pages.
- Add pages to the PdfDocument in the form of PdfDocument.Page instances.
- Obtain references to the Canvas objects associated with the document pages.
- Draw content onto the canvases.
- Write the PDF document to a destination output stream provided by the Printing framework.
- Notify the Printing framework that the document is ready to print.

This chapter will provide an overview of these steps, followed by a detailed tutorial designed to demonstrate the implementation of custom document printing within Android applications.

77.1.1 Custom Print Adapters

The role of the print adapter is to provide the Printing framework with the content to be printed and to ensure that it is formatted correctly for the user's chosen preferences (considering factors such as paper size and page orientation).

Much of this work is performed by the print adapters provided as part of the Android Printing framework and designed for these specific printing tasks when printing HTML and images. When printing a web page, for example, a print adapter is created for us when a call is made to the *createPrintDocumentAdapter()* method of an instance of the WebView class.

In the case of custom document printing, however, it is the responsibility of the application developer to design the print adapter and implement the code to draw and format the content in preparation for printing.

A Guide to Android Custom Document Printing

Custom print adapters are created by sub-classing the PrintDocumentAdapter class and overriding a set of callback methods within that class which will be called by the Printing framework at various stages in the print process. These callback methods can be summarized as follows:

- **onStart()** – This method is called when the printing process begins and is provided so that the application code can perform any necessary tasks to create the print job. Implementation of this method within the PrintDocumentAdapter sub-class is optional.

- **onLayout()** – This callback method is called after the call to the *onStart()* method and then again each time the user makes changes to the print settings (such as changing the orientation, paper size, or color settings). This method should adapt the content and layout to accommodate these changes. Once these changes are completed, the method must return the number of pages to be printed. Implementation of the *onLayout()* method within the PrintDocumentAdapter sub-class is mandatory.

- **onWrite()** – This method is called after each call to *onLayout()* and is responsible for rendering the content on the canvases of the pages to be printed. Amongst other arguments, this method is passed a file descriptor to which the resulting PDF document must be written once rendering is complete. A call is then made to the *onWriteFinished()* callback method passing through an argument containing information about the page ranges to be printed. Implementation of the *onWrite()* method within the PrintDocumentAdapter sub-class is mandatory.

- **onFinish()** – An optional method which, if implemented, is called once by the Printing framework when the printing process is completed, thereby providing the application the opportunity to perform any clean-up operations that may be necessary.

77.2 Preparing the Custom Document Printing Project

Select the *New Project* option from the welcome screen and, within the resulting new project dialog, choose the Empty Views Activity template before clicking on the Next button.

Enter *CustomPrint* into the Name field and specify *com.ebookfrenzy.customprint* as the package name. Before clicking on the Finish button, change the Minimum API level setting to API 26: Android 8.0 (Oreo) and the Language menu to Java.

Load the *activity_main.xml* layout file into the Layout Editor tool and, in Design mode, select and delete the "Hello World!" TextView object. Drag and drop a Button view from the Common section of the palette and position it in the center of the layout view. With the Button view selected, change the text property to "Print Document" and extract the string to a new resource. On completion, the user interface layout should match that shown in Figure 77-1.

When the button is selected within the application, it will be required to call a method to initiate the document printing process. Remaining within the Attributes tool window, set the *onClick* property to call a method named *printDocument*.

Figure 77-1

77.3 Creating the Custom Print Adapter

Most of the work involved in printing a custom document from within an Android application involves the implementation of the custom print adapter. This example will require a print adapter with the *onLayout()* and *onWrite()* callback methods implemented. Within the *MainActivity.java* file, add the template for this new class so that it reads as follows:

```
package com.ebookfrenzy.customprint;
.
.
import android.os.CancellationSignal;
import android.os.ParcelFileDescriptor;
import android.print.PageRange;
import android.print.PrintAttributes;
import android.print.PrintDocumentAdapter;
import android.content.Context;

public class MainActivity extends AppCompatActivity {

    public static class MyPrintDocumentAdapter extends PrintDocumentAdapter
    {
        Context context;

        MyPrintDocumentAdapter(Context context)
        {
            this.context = context;
        }
```

```
        @Override
        public void onLayout(PrintAttributes oldAttributes,
                            PrintAttributes newAttributes,
                            CancellationSignal cancellationSignal,
                            LayoutResultCallback callback,
                            Bundle metadata) {
        }

        @Override
        public void onWrite(final PageRange[] pageRanges,
                            final ParcelFileDescriptor destination,
                            final CancellationSignal
                                    cancellationSignal,
                            final WriteResultCallback callback) {
        }
    }
.
.
.
}
```

As the new class currently stands, it contains a constructor method to be called when a new class instance is created. The constructor takes the context of the calling activity as an argument, which is then stored so that it can be referenced later in the two callback methods.

With the class outline established, the next step is implementing the two callback methods, beginning with *onLayout()*.

77.4 Implementing the onLayout() Callback Method

Remaining within the *MainActivity.java* file, begin by adding some import directives that will be required by the code in the *onLayout()* method:

```
package com.ebookfrenzy.customprint;
.
.
.
import android.print.PrintDocumentInfo;
import android.print.pdf.PrintedPdfDocument;
import android.graphics.pdf.PdfDocument;

public class MainActivity extends AppCompatActivity {
.
.
.
}
```

Next, modify the MyPrintDocumentAdapter class to declare variables to be used within the *onLayout()* method:

```
public static class MyPrintDocumentAdapter extends PrintDocumentAdapter
{
        Context context;
        int pageHeight;
```

A Guide to Android Custom Document Printing

```java
    int pageWidth;
    PdfDocument myPdfDocument;
    int totalpages = 4;
    .
    .
}
```

Note that for this example, a four-page document will be printed. In more complex situations, the application will most likely need to dynamically calculate the number of pages to be printed based on the quantity and layout of the content in relation to the user's paper size and page orientation selections.

With the variables declared, implement the *onLayout()* method as outlined in the following code listing:

```java
@Override
public void onLayout(PrintAttributes oldAttributes,
                PrintAttributes newAttributes,
                CancellationSignal cancellationSignal,
                LayoutResultCallback callback,
                Bundle metadata) {

    myPdfDocument = new PrintedPdfDocument(context, newAttributes);

    pageHeight =
        Objects.requireNonNull(
            newAttributes.getMediaSize()).getHeightMils()/1000 * 72;
    pageWidth =
        newAttributes.getMediaSize().getWidthMils()/1000 * 72;

    if (cancellationSignal.isCanceled() ) {
        callback.onLayoutCancelled();
        return;
    }

    if (totalpages > 0) {
        PrintDocumentInfo.Builder builder = new PrintDocumentInfo
            .Builder("print_output.pdf").setContentType(
                PrintDocumentInfo.CONTENT_TYPE_DOCUMENT)
            .setPageCount(totalpages);

        PrintDocumentInfo info = builder.build();
        callback.onLayoutFinished(info, true);
    } else {
        callback.onLayoutFailed("Page count is zero.");
    }
}
```

This method performs quite a few tasks, each requiring some detailed explanation.

To begin with, a new PDF document is created as a PdfDocument class instance. One of the arguments passed

A Guide to Android Custom Document Printing

into the *onLayout()* method when the Printing framework calls it is an object of type PrintAttributes containing details about the paper size, resolution, and color settings the user selects for the print output. These settings are used when creating the PDF document, along with the context of the activity previously stored for us by our constructor method:

```
myPdfDocument = new PrintedPdfDocument(context, newAttributes);
```

The method then uses the PrintAttributes object to extract the height and width values for the document pages. These dimensions are stored in the object as thousandths of an inch. Since the methods that will use these values later in this example work in units of 1/72 of an inch, these numbers are converted before they are stored:

```
pageHeight = newAttributes.getMediaSize().getHeightMils()/1000 * 72;
pageWidth = newAttributes.getMediaSize().getWidthMils()/1000 * 72;
```

Although this example does not make use of the user's color selection, this property can be obtained via a call to the *getColorMode()* method of the PrintAttributes object, which will return a value of either COLOR_MODE_COLOR or COLOR_MODE_MONOCHROME.

When the *onLayout()* method is called, it is passed an object of type *LayoutResultCallback*. This object provides a way for the method to communicate status information back to the Printing framework via a set of methods. For example, the *onLayout()* method will be called if the user cancels the print process. The fact that the process has been canceled is indicated via a setting within the CancellationSignal argument. If a cancellation is detected, the *onLayout()* method must call the *onLayoutCancelled()* method of the *LayoutResultCallback* object to notify the Print framework that the cancellation request was received and that the layout task has been canceled:

```
if (cancellationSignal.isCanceled() ) {
        callback.onLayoutCancelled();
        return;
}
```

When the layout work is complete, the method is required to call the *onLayoutFinished()* method of the *LayoutResultCallback* object, passing through two arguments. The first argument is a PrintDocumentInfo object containing information about the document to be printed. This information consists of the name of the PDF document, the type of content (in this case, a document rather than an image), and the page count. The second argument is a Boolean value indicating whether or not the layout has changed since the last call made to the *onLayout()* method:

```
if (totalpages > 0) {
        PrintDocumentInfo.Builder builder = new PrintDocumentInfo
                .Builder("print_output.pdf")
                .setContentType(
                    PrintDocumentInfo.CONTENT_TYPE_DOCUMENT)
                .setPageCount(totalpages);

        PrintDocumentInfo info = builder.build();

        callback.onLayoutFinished(info, true);
} else {
        callback.onLayoutFailed("Page count is zero.");
}
```

If the page count is zero, the code reports this failure to the Printing framework via a call to the *onLayoutFailed()* method of the *LayoutResultCallback* object.

A Guide to Android Custom Document Printing

The call to the *onLayoutFinished()* method notifies the Printing framework that the layout work is complete, triggering a call to the *onWrite()* method.

77.5 Implementing the onWrite() Callback Method

The *onWrite()* callback method is responsible for rendering the pages of the document and then notifying the Printing framework that the document is ready to be printed. When completed, the *onWrite()* method reads as follows:

```
package com.ebookfrenzy.customprint;

import java.io.FileOutputStream;
import java.io.IOException;
 .
 .
 .
import android.graphics.pdf.PdfDocument.PageInfo;
 .
 .
 .
@Override
public void onWrite(final PageRange[] pageRanges,
                    final ParcelFileDescriptor destination,
                    final CancellationSignal cancellationSignal,
                    final WriteResultCallback callback) {

    for (int i = 0; i < totalpages; i++) {
        if (pageInRange(pageRanges, i))
        {
            PageInfo newPage = new PageInfo.Builder(pageWidth,
                    pageHeight, i).create();

            PdfDocument.Page page =
                    myPdfDocument.startPage(newPage);

            if (cancellationSignal.isCanceled()) {
                callback.onWriteCancelled();
                myPdfDocument.close();
                myPdfDocument = null;
                return;
            }
            drawPage(page, i);
            myPdfDocument.finishPage(page);
        }
    }

    try {
        myPdfDocument.writeTo(new FileOutputStream(
                destination.getFileDescriptor()));
    } catch (IOException e) {
```

```
            callback.onWriteFailed(e.toString());
            return;
    } finally {
            myPdfDocument.close();
            myPdfDocument = null;
    }

    callback.onWriteFinished(pageRanges);
}
```

The *onWrite()* method starts by looping through each page in the document. However, it is important to consider that the user may have requested that only some of the pages that make up the document be printed. The Printing framework user interface panel provides the option to specify specific pages or ranges of pages to be printed. Figure 77-2, for example, shows the print panel configured to print pages 1-4, page 9, and pages 11-13 of a document.

Figure 77-2

When writing the pages to the PDF document, the *onWrite()* method must take steps to ensure that only those pages specified by the user are printed. To make this possible, the Printing framework passes through as an argument an array of PageRange objects indicating the ranges of pages to be printed. In the above *onWrite()* implementation, the *pageInRange()* method is called for each page to verify that the page is within the specified ranges. The code for the *pageInRange()* method will be implemented later in this chapter.

```
for (int i = 0; i < totalpages; i++) {
        if (pageInRange(pageRanges, i))
        {
```

For each page that is within any specified ranges, a new PdfDocument.Page object is created. When creating a new page, the height and width values previously stored by the *onLayout()* method are passed through as arguments so that the page size matches the print options selected by the user:

```
PageInfo newPage = new PageInfo.Builder(pageWidth, pageHeight, i).create();

PdfDocument.Page page = myPdfDocument.startPage(newPage);
```

As with the *onLayout()* method, the *onWrite()* method is required to respond to cancellation requests. In this case, the code notifies the Printing framework that the cancellation has been performed before closing and de-referencing the myPdfDocument variable:

```
if (cancellationSignal.isCanceled()) {
```

```
        callback.onWriteCancelled();
        myPdfDocument.close();
        myPdfDocument = null;
        return;
}
```

As long as the print process has not been canceled, the method calls a method to draw the content on the current page before calling the *finishedPage()* method on the myPdfDocument object.

```
drawPage(page, i);
myPdfDocument.finishPage(page);
```

The *drawPage()* method is responsible for drawing the content onto the page and will be implemented once the *onWrite()* method is complete.

When the required number of pages have been added to the PDF document, the document is then written to the *destination* stream using the file descriptor, which is passed through as an argument to the *onWrite()* method. If, for any reason, the write operation fails, the method notifies the framework by calling the *onWriteFailed()* method of the *WriteResultCallback* object (also passed as an argument to the *onWrite()* method).

```
try {
        myPdfDocument.writeTo(new FileOutputStream(
                destination.getFileDescriptor()));
} catch (IOException e) {
                callback.onWriteFailed(e.toString());
                return;
} finally {
                myPdfDocument.close();
                myPdfDocument = null;
}
```

Finally, the *onWriteFinish()* method of the *WriteResultsCallback* object is called to notify the Printing framework that the document is ready to be printed.

77.6 Checking a Page is in Range

As previously outlined, when the *onWrite()* method is called, it is passed an array of PageRange objects indicating the ranges of pages within the document to be printed. The PageRange class is designed to store the start and end pages of a page range which, in turn, may be accessed via the *getStart()* and *getEnd()* methods of the class.

When the *onWrite()* method was implemented in the previous section, a call was made to a method named *pageInRange()*, which takes as arguments an array of PageRange objects and a page number. The role of the *pageInRange()* method is to identify whether the specified page number is within the ranges specified and may be implemented within the MyPrintDocumentAdapter class in the *MainActivity.java* class as follows:

```
public class MyPrintDocumentAdapter extends PrintDocumentAdapter {
.
.
.
        private boolean pageInRange(PageRange[] pageRanges, int page)
        {
                for (PageRange pageRange : pageRanges) {
                    if ((page >= pageRange.getStart()) &&
                        (page <= pageRange.getEnd()))
```

```
            return true;
        }
        return false;
    }
.
.
.
}
```

77.7 Drawing the Content on the Page Canvas

We have now reached the point where some code needs to be written to draw the content on the pages so that they are ready for printing. The content that gets drawn is completely application specific and limited only by what can be achieved using the Android Canvas class. In this example, however, some simple text and graphics will be drawn on the canvas.

The *onWrite()* method has been designed to call a method named *drawPage()* which takes as arguments the PdfDocument.Page object representing the current page, and an integer, representing the page number. Within the *MainActivity.java* file, this method should now be implemented as follows:

```
package com.ebookfrenzy.customprint;
.
.
.
import android.graphics.Canvas;
import android.graphics.Color;
import android.graphics.Paint;

public class MainActivity extends AppCompatActivity {
.
.
    public static class MyPrintDocumentAdapter extends
                            PrintDocumentAdapter
    {
.
.
        private void drawPage(PdfDocument.Page page,
                   int pagenumber) {
            Canvas canvas = page.getCanvas();

            pagenumber++; // Make sure page numbers start at 1

            int titleBaseLine = 72;
            int leftMargin = 54;

            Paint paint = new Paint();
            paint.setColor(Color.BLACK);
            paint.setTextSize(40);
            canvas.drawText(
                "Test Print Document Page " + pagenumber,
```

A Guide to Android Custom Document Printing

```
                            leftMargin,
                            titleBaseLine,
                            paint);

            paint.setTextSize(14);
            canvas.drawText("This is some test content to verify that
custom document printing works", leftMargin, titleBaseLine + 35, paint);

            if (pagenumber % 2 == 0)
                    paint.setColor(Color.RED);
            else
                paint.setColor(Color.GREEN);

            PageInfo pageInfo = page.getInfo();


            canvas.drawCircle(pageInfo.getPageWidth()/2f,
                            pageInfo.getPageHeight()/2f,
                            150,
                            paint);
        }
.
.
}
```

Page numbering within the code starts at 0. Since documents traditionally start at page 1, the method begins by incrementing the stored page number. A reference to the Canvas object associated with the page is then obtained, and some margin and baseline values are declared:

```
Canvas canvas = page.getCanvas();

pagenumber++;

int titleBaseLine = 72;
int leftMargin = 54;
```

Next, the code creates Paint and Color objects to be used for drawing, sets a text size, and draws the page title text, including the current page number:

```
Paint paint = new Paint();

paint.setColor(Color.BLACK);
paint.setTextSize(40);

canvas.drawText("Test Print Document Page " + pagenumber,
                                    leftMargin,
                                    titleBaseLine,
                                    paint);
```

675

A Guide to Android Custom Document Printing

The text size is then reduced, and some body text is drawn beneath the title:

```
paint.setTextSize(14);
canvas.drawText("This is some test content to verify that custom document
printing works", leftMargin, titleBaseLine + 35, paint);
```

The last task performed by this method involves drawing a circle (red on even-numbered pages and green on odd). Having ascertained whether the page is odd or even, the method obtains the height and width of the page before using this information to position the circle in the center of the page:

```
if (pagenumber % 2 == 0)
        paint.setColor(Color.RED);
else
        paint.setColor(Color.GREEN);

PageInfo pageInfo = page.getInfo();

canvas.drawCircle(pageInfo.getPageWidth()/2,
                pageInfo.getPageHeight()/2,
                150, paint);
```

Having drawn on the canvas, the method returns control to the *onWrite()* method.

With the completion of the *drawPage()* method, the MyPrintDocumentAdapter class is now finished.

77.8 Starting the Print Job

When the user touches the "Print Document" button, the *printDocument()* onClick event handler method will be called. All that now remains before testing can commence, therefore, is to add this method to the *MainActivity.java* file, taking particular care to ensure that it is placed outside of the MyPrintDocumentAdapter class:

```
package com.ebookfrenzy.customprint;
.
.
import android.print.PrintManager;
import android.view.View;

public class MainActivity extends AppCompatActivity {

        public void printDocument(View view)
        {
            PrintManager printManager = (PrintManager) this
                    .getSystemService(Context.PRINT_SERVICE);

            String jobName = this.getString(R.string.app_name) +
                    " Document";

            printManager.print(jobName, new
                    MyPrintDocumentAdapter(this),
                    null);
        }
```

.
.
}

This method obtains a reference to the Print Manager service running on the device before creating a new String object to serve as the job name for the print task. Finally, the *print()* method of the Print Manager is called to start the print job, passing through the job name and an instance of our custom print document adapter class.

77.9 Testing the Application

Compile and run the application on an Android device or emulator. When the application has loaded, touch the "Print Document" button to initiate the print job and select a suitable target for the output (the Save to PDF option is useful for avoiding wasting paper and printer ink).

Check the printed output, which should consist of 4 pages, including text and graphics. Figure 77-3, for example, shows the four pages of the document viewed as a PDF file ready to be saved on the device.

Experiment with other print configuration options, such as changing the paper size, orientation, and page settings within the print panel. The printed output should reflect each setting change, indicating that the custom print document adapter functions correctly.

Figure 77-3

77.10 Summary

Although more complex to implement than the Android Printing framework HTML and image printing options, custom document printing provides considerable flexibility in printing complex content within an Android application. Most of the work in implementing custom document printing involves the creation of a custom Print Adapter class that not only draws the content on the document pages but also responds correctly as the user changes print settings, such as the page size and range of pages to be printed.

78. An Introduction to Android App Links

As technology evolves, the traditional distinction between web and mobile content is beginning to blur. One area where this is particularly true is the growing popularity of progressive web apps, where web apps look and behave much like traditional mobile apps.

Another trend involves making the content within mobile apps discoverable through web searches and via URL links. In the context of Android app development, the App Links feature is designed to make it easier for users to discover and access content stored within an Android app, even if the user does not have the app installed.

78.1 An Overview of Android App Links

An app link is a standard HTTP URL that is an easy way to link directly to a particular place in your app from an external source such as a website or app. App links (also called *deep links*) are used primarily to encourage users to engage with an app and to allow users to share app content.

App link implementation is a multi-step process that involves the addition of intent filters to the project manifest, implementing link handling code within the associated app activities, and the use of digital asset links files to associate app and web-based content.

These steps can be performed manually by making changes within the project or automatically using the Android Studio App Links Assistant.

These steps can be performed manually by making project changes or automatically using the Android Studio App Links Assistant.

The remainder of this chapter will outline app links implementation in terms of the changes that must be made to a project. The next chapter (*"An Android Studio App Links Tutorial"*) will demonstrate the use of the App Links Assistant to achieve the same results.

78.2 App Link Intent Filters

An app link URL needs to be mapped to a specific activity within an app project. This is achieved by adding intent filters to the project's *AndroidManifest.xml* file designed to launch an activity in response to an *android.intent.action.VIEW* action. The intent filters are declared within the element for the activity to be launched and must contain the data outlining the scheme, host, and path of the app link URL. The following manifest fragment, for example, declares an intent filter to launch an activity named MyActivity when an app link matching *http://www.example.com/welcome* is detected:

```
<activity android:name="com.ebookfrenzy.myapp.MyActivity">

    <intent-filter android:autoVerify="true">
        <action android:name="android.intent.action.VIEW" />
        <category android:name="android.intent.category.DEFAULT" />
        <category android:name="android.intent.category.BROWSABLE" />
```

An Introduction to Android App Links

```
        <data
            android:scheme="http"
            android:host="www.example.com"
            android:pathPrefix="/welcome" />
    </intent-filter>
</activity>
```

The order in which ambiguous intent filters are handled can be specified using the *order* property of the intent filter tag as follows:

```
<application>
    <activity android:name=" com.ebookfrenzy.myapp.MyActivity">
        <intent-filter android:autoVerify="true" android:order="1">
.
.
```

The intent filter will cause the app link to launch the correct activity, but code must still be added to the target activity to handle the intent appropriately.

78.3 Handling App Link Intents

In most cases, the launched activity will need to gain access to the app link URL and take specific action based on how the URL is structured. Continuing from the above example, the activity will likely display different content when launched via a URL containing a path of */welcome/newuser* than one with the path set to */welcome/existinguser*.

When the link launches the activity, it is passed an intent object containing data about the action which launched the activity, including a Uri object containing the app link URL. Within the initialization stages of the activity, code can be added to extract this data as follows:

```
Intent appLinkIntent = getIntent();
String appLinkAction = appLinkIntent.getAction();
Uri appLinkData = appLinkIntent.getData();
```

Having obtained the Uri for the app link, the various components that make up the URL path can be used to decide the actions to perform within the activity. In the following code example, the last component of the URL is used to identify whether content should be displayed for a new or existing user:

```
String userType = appLinkData.getLastPathSegment();

if (userType.equals("newuser")) {
    // display new user content
} else {
    // display existing user content
}
```

78.4 Associating the App with a Website

Before an app link will work, an app link URL must be associated with the website on which the app link is based. This is achieved by creating a Digital Asset Links file named *assetlinks.json* and installing it within the website's *.well-known* folder. Note that digital asset linking is only possible for websites that are HTTPS based.

A digital asset links file comprises a *relation* statement granting permission for a target app to be launched using the website's link URLs and a target statement declaring the companion app package name and SHA-256 certificate fingerprint for that project. A typical asset link file might, for example, read as follows:

```
[{
    "relation": ["delegate_permission/common.handle_all_urls"],
    "target" : { "namespace": "android_app",
      "package_name": "<app package name here>",
                "sha256_cert_fingerprints": ["<app certificate here>"] }
}]
```

The *assetlinks.json* file can contain multiple digital asset links, allowing a single website to be associated with more than one companion app.

78.5 Summary

Android App Links allow app activities to be launched via URL links from external websites and other apps. App links are implemented using intent filters within the project manifest file and intent handling code within the launched activity. Using a Digital Asset Links file, it is also possible to associate the domain name used in an app link with the corresponding website. Once the association has been established, Android no longer needs to ask the user to select the target app when an app link is used.

79. An Android Studio App Links Tutorial

This chapter aims to provide a practical demonstration of both Android app links and the Android Studio App Link Assistant.

This chapter will add app linking support to an existing Android app, allowing an activity to be launched via an app link URL. In addition to launching the activity, the content displayed will be specified within the URL's path.

79.1 About the Example App

The project used in this chapter is named AppLinking and is a basic app designed to allow users to find information about landmarks in London. The app uses a SQLite database accessed through a standard Android content provider class. The app has an existing database containing records for some popular tourist attractions in London. In addition to the existing database entries, the app lets the user add and delete landmark descriptions.

Currently, the app allows the existing records to be searched and new records to be added and deleted.

The project consists of two activities named AppLinkingActivity and LandmarkActivity. AppLinkingActivity is the main activity launched at app startup. This activity allows the user to enter search criteria and add records to the database. When a search locates a matching record, LandmarkActivity launches and displays the information for the related landmark.

This chapter will enhance the app to support app linking so that URLs can be used to display specific landmark records within the app.

79.2 The Database Schema

The data for the example app is contained within a file named *landmarks.db* located in the *app -> assets -> databases* folder of the project hierarchy. The database contains a single table named *locations*, the structure of which is outlined in Table 79-1:

Column	Type	Description
_id	String	The primary index, this column contains string values that uniquely identify the landmarks in the database.
title	String	The name of the landmark (e.g., London Bridge).
description	String	A description of the landmark.
personal	Boolean	Indicates whether the record is personal or public. This value is set to true for all records added by the user. Existing records provided with the database are set to false.

Table 79-1

79.3 Loading and Running the Project

The project is contained within the *AppLinking* folder of the sample source code download archive located at the following URL:

An Android Studio App Links Tutorial

https://www.ebookfrenzy.com/retail/giraffejava/index.php

Having located the folder, open it within Android Studio and run the app on a device or emulator. Once the app is launched, the screen illustrated in Figure 79-1 below will appear:

Figure 79-1

If the "kotlin.collections.jdk8.CollectionsJDK8Kt" error appears, make the following change to the *build.gradle. kts (Module: app)* file, sync the project, and try again:

```
dependencies {
    .
    .
    implementation(platform("org.jetbrains.kotlin:kotlin-bom:1.8.0"))
    .
    .
}
```

As currently implemented, landmarks are located using the ID for the location. The default database configuration currently contains two records referenced by the IDs "londonbridge" and "toweroflondon". Test the search feature by entering *londonbridge* into the ID field and clicking the *Find* button. When a matching record is found, the second activity (LandmarkActivity) is launched and passed information about the record to be displayed. This information takes the form of extra data added to the Intent object. LandmarkActivity uses this information to extract the record from the database and display it to the user using the screen shown in Figure 79-2.

Figure 79-2

79.4 Adding the URL Mapping

Now that the app has been loaded into Android Studio and tested, we can add app link support. The objective is for the LandmarkActivity screen to launch and display information in response to an app link click. This is achieved by mapping a URL to LandmarkActivity. For this example, the format of the URL will be as follows:

```
http://<website domain>/landmarks/<landmarkId>
```

When all of the steps have been completed, the following URL should, for example, cause the app to display information about the Tower of London:

```
http://www.yourdomain.com/landmarks/toweroflondon
```

To add a URL mapping to the project, begin by opening the App Links Assistant using the *Tools -> App Links Assistant* menu option. Once open, the assistant should appear as shown in Figure 79-3:

An Android Studio App Links Tutorial

Figure 79-3

Click on the *Open URL Mapping Editor* button to map a URL to an activity. Within the mapping screen, click on the '+' button (highlighted in Figure 79-4) to add a new URL:

Figure 79-4

An Android Studio App Links Tutorial

In the Host field of the *Add URL Mapping* dialog, enter either the URL for your own website. If you do not have a website to use for this tutorial, you can still follow most of this chapter using *http://www.example.com,* though it will not be possible to test features that require the presence of a Digital Asset Links file.

The Path field (marked B in Figure 79-5 below) is where the path component of the URL is declared. The path must be prefixed with / so enter */landmarks* into this field.

The Path menu (B) provides the following three path-matching options:

- **path** – The URL must match the path component of the URL exactly to launch the activity. For example, if the path is set to /landmarks, *http://www.example.com/landmarks* will be considered a match. A URL of *http://www.example.com/landmarks/londonbridge*, however, will not be considered a match.

- **pathPrefix** – The specified path is only considered as the prefix. Additional path components may be included after the */landmarks* component (for example, *http://www.example.com/landmarks/londonbridge* will still be considered a match).

- **pathPattern** – Allows the path to be specified using pattern matching in the form of basic regular expressions and wildcards, for example, *landmarks/*/[l-L]ondon/**

Since the path in this example is a prefix to the landmark ID component, select the *pathPrefix* menu option.

Finally, use the Activity menu (C) to select LandmarkActivity as the activity to be launched in response to the app link:

Figure 79-5

After completing the settings in the dialog, click the *OK* button to commit the changes. Check that the URL is correctly formatted and assigned to the appropriate activity by entering the following URL into the *Check URL Mapping* field of the mapping screen (where *<your domain>* is set to the domain specified in the Host field above):

```
http://<your domain>/landmarks/toweroflondon
```

If the mapping is configured correctly, LandmarkActivity will be listed as the mapped activity:

Figure 79-6

An Android Studio App Links Tutorial

The latest version of Android requires that App Links be declared for HTTP and HTTPS protocols, even if only one is being used. Therefore, before proceeding to the next step, repeat the above steps to add the HTTPS version of the URL to the list.

The next step will also be performed in the URL mapping screen of the App Links Assistant, so leave the screen selected.

79.5 Adding the Intent Filter

As explained in the previous chapter, an intent filter is needed to launch the target activity in response to an app link click. In fact, when the URL mapping was added, the intent filter was automatically added to the project manifest file. With the URL mapping selected in the App Links Assistant URL mapping list, scroll down the screen until the intent filter Preview section comes into view. The preview should contain the modified *AndroidManifest.xml* file with the newly added intent filters included:

Preview

```
    </intent-filter>
    <intent-filter>
        <action android:name="android.intent.action.VIEW" />

        <category android:name="android.intent.category.DEFAULT" />
        <category android:name="android.intent.category.BROWSABLE" />

        <data android:scheme="https" />
        <data android:host="www.example.com" />
        <data android:pathPrefix="/landmarks" />
```

Open AndroidManfest.xml

Figure 79-7

Although App Links Assistant has added intent filters for us, it may not have included the autoVerify setting needed when working with app links. Open the *manifests -> AndroidManifest.xml* file and add this setting to the two intent filters as follows:

```
<intent-filter android:autoVerify="true">
.
.

    <data
        android:scheme="http"
        android:host="www.ebookfrenzy.com"
        android:pathPrefix="/landmarks" />
</intent-filter>
<intent-filter android:autoVerify="true">
.
.

    <data
        android:scheme="https"
        android:host="www.ebookfrenzy.com"
        android:pathPrefix="/landmarks" />
</intent-filter>
```

79.6 Adding Intent Handling Code

The steps taken so far ensure that the correct activity is launched in response to an appropriately formatted app link URL. The next step is to handle the intent within the LandmarkActivity class so that the correct record is extracted from the database and displayed to the user. Before making any changes to the code within the *LandmarkActivity.java* file, it is worthwhile reviewing some areas of the existing code. Open the *LandmarkActivity.java* file in the code editor and locate the *onCreate()* and *handleIntent()* methods which should currently read as follows:

```
@Override
protected void onCreate(Bundle savedInstanceState) {
    super.onCreate(savedInstanceState);

    binding = ActivityLandmarkBinding.inflate(getLayoutInflater());
    View view = binding.getRoot();
    setContentView(view);

    handleIntent(getIntent());
}

private void handleIntent(Intent intent) {
    String landmarkId =
        intent.getStringExtra(AppLinkingActivity.LANDMARK_ID);
    displayLandmark(landmarkId);
}
```

In its current form, the code expects to find the landmark ID within the extra data of the Intent bundle. Since the activity can now be launched by an app link, this code must be changed to handle both scenarios. Begin by deleting the call to *handleIntent()* in the *onCreate()* method:

```
@Override
protected void onCreate(Bundle savedInstanceState) {
    super.onCreate(savedInstanceState);

    binding = ActivityLandmarkBinding.inflate(getLayoutInflater());
    View view = binding.getRoot();
    setContentView(view);

    handleIntent(getIntent());
}
```

To add the initial app link intent handling code, return to the App Links Assistant panel and click on the *Select Activity* button listed under step 2. Within the activity selection dialog, select the LandmarkActivity entry before clicking on the *Insert Code* button:

An Android Studio App Links Tutorial

Figure 79-8

Return to the *LandmarkActivity.java* file and note that the following code has been inserted into the *onCreate()* method (note that you can manually add this code if Android Studio is unable to complete the request):

```
// ATTENTION: This was auto-generated to handle app links.
Intent appLinkIntent = getIntent();
String appLinkAction = appLinkIntent.getAction();
Uri appLinkData = appLinkIntent.getData();
```

This code accesses the Intent object and extracts the Action string and Uri. If the activity launch results from an app link, the action string will be set to *android.intent.action.VIEW*, which matches the action declared in the intent filter added to the manifest file. If, on the other hand, the activity was launched by the standard intent launching code in the *findLandmark()* method of the main activity, the action string will be null. By checking the value assigned to the action string, code can be written to identify how the activity was launched and take appropriate action:

.
.
```
import android.net.Uri;
```
.
.
```
@Override
protected void onCreate(Bundle savedInstanceState) {
    super.onCreate(savedInstanceState);
.
.
    // ATTENTION: This was auto-generated to handle app links.
    Intent appLinkIntent = getIntent();
    String appLinkAction = appLinkIntent.getAction();
    Uri appLinkData = appLinkIntent.getData();

    String landmarkId = appLinkData.getLastPathSegment();

    if (landmarkId != null) {
        displayLandmark(landmarkId);
    }
}
```

All that remains is to add some additional code to the method to identify the last component in the app link URL path and to use that as the landmark ID when querying the database:

```
@Override
protected void onCreate(Bundle savedInstanceState) {
.
.

    // ATTENTION: This was auto-generated to handle app links.
    Intent appLinkIntent = getIntent();
    String appLinkAction = appLinkIntent.getAction();
    Uri appLinkData = appLinkIntent.getData();

    if (appLinkAction != null) {

        if (appLinkAction.equals("android.intent.action.VIEW")) {
            String landmarkId = appLinkData.getLastPathSegment();

            if (landmarkId != null) {
                displayLandmark(landmarkId);
            }
        }
    } else {
        handleIntent(appLinkIntent);
    }
}
```

If the action string is not null, a check is made to verify that it is set to *android.intent.action.VIEW* before extracting the last component of the Uri path. This component is then used as the landmark ID when making the database query. If, on the other hand, the action string is null, the existing *handleIntent()* method is called to extract the ID from the intent data.

79.7 Testing the App

Run the app on a device or emulator and make sure it is still possible to search for the example landmarks. We have now successfully added app link support to the app. If you specified your own website URL for the app links, we can now take the example one step further by creating and installing a Digital Asset Links file.

79.8 Creating the Digital Asset Links File

As outlined in the chapter entitled *"An Overview of Android Intents"*, to fully support app links, we need to install a Digital Asset Links file on the website referenced in the app link. Begin by following the steps outlined in *"An Overview of Android Intents"* to locate your *debug.keystore* file and identify your SHA256 fingerprint.

Next, open the following page in a web browser:

https://developers.google.com/digital-asset-links/tools/generator

Once the page has loaded, enter your website URL into the *Hosting site domain* field, *com.ebookfrenzy.applinking* as the *App package name*, and your SHA256 fingerprint into the *App package fingerprint (SHA256)* field:

Statement List Generator and Tester

Generate and save a statement file on your site to enable App Linking, or test an existing statement file.

Hosting site domain
www.yourcompany.com

App package name
com.ebookfrenzy.applinking

App package fingerprint (SHA256)
78:EE:F3:C8:30:45:C1:EA:99:56:83:94:2A:4C:D2:EA:A0:69:88:96:D1:17:22:02:47:EC:AD:6E:3C:64:A9:29

[Generate statement]   or   [Test statement]

Figure 79-9

Click the *Generate statement* button to display the generated statement and place it in a file named *assetlinks.json* in a folder named *.well-known* on your web server. Return to the generator page and click on the *Test statement* button to verify that the file is in the correct location. On a successful test, output similar to the following will appear:

✓ Success! Host www.answertopia.com grants app deep linking to com.ebookfrenzy.applinking.

Figure 79-10

Assuming a successful test, we are now ready to try out the app link.

79.9 Testing the App Link

Test that the intent handling works by returning to the App Links Assistant panel and clicking on the *Test App Links* button. When prompted for a URL to test, enter the URL (using the domain referenced in the app link mapping) for the londonbridge landmark ID before clicking on the *Run Test* button:

App Links Assistant
④ **Test on Device or Emulator**

Enter a URL below and click 'Run Test' to simulate a user clicking the URL on a device with your app installed. A Run configuration will be automatically added to run with this URL so you can easily test it again.

URL
http://www.example.com/landmark/londonbridge   [Run Test]

Figure 79-11

Once the button has been clicked, the Landmark activity should launch on the device or emulator and display information about London Bridge.

79.10 Summary

This chapter has demonstrated the steps for implementing App Link support within an Android app project, including using the App Link Assistant in Android Studio, App Link URL mapping, intent filters, handling website association using Digital Asset Links file entries, and App Link testing.

Chapter 80

80. An Android Biometric Authentication Tutorial

Touch sensors are now built into many Android devices to identify the user and provide access to the device and application functionality, such as in-app payment options using fingerprint recognition. Fingerprint recognition is just one of several authentication methods, including passwords, PINs, and, more recently, facial recognition.

Although only a few Android devices currently on the market provide facial recognition, this will likely become more common in the future. In recognition of this, Google has begun to transition away from a fingerprint-centric approach to adding authentication to apps to a less specific approach called *biometric authentication*.

This chapter provides an overview of biometric authentication and a detailed, step-by-step tutorial demonstrating a practical approach to implementing biometric authentication within an Android app project.

80.1 An Overview of Biometric Authentication

The key biometric authentication component is the BiometricPrompt class. This class performs much of the work that previously had to be performed by writing code in earlier Android versions, including displaying a standard dialog to guide the user through the authentication process, performing the authentication, and reporting the results to the app. The class also handles excessive failed authentication attempts and enforces a timeout before the user can try again.

The BiometricPrompt class includes a companion Builder class that can be used to configure and create BiometricPrompt instances, including defining the text that is to appear within the biometric authentication dialog and the customization of the cancel button (also referred to as the *negative button*) that appears in the dialog.

The BiometricPrompt instance is also assigned a set of authentication callbacks that will be called to provide the app with the results of an authentication operation. A CancellationSignal instance is also used to allow the app to cancel the authentication while it is in process.

With these basics covered, the remainder of this chapter will implement fingerprint-based biometric authentication within an example project.

80.2 Creating the Biometric Authentication Project

Select the *New Project* option from the welcome screen and, within the resulting new project dialog, choose the Empty Views Activity template before clicking on the Next button.

Enter *BiometricDemo* into the Name field and specify *com.ebookfrenzy.biometricdemo* as the package name. Before clicking on the Finish button, change the Minimum API level setting to API 29: Android (Q) and the Language menu to Java.

An Android Biometric Authentication Tutorial

80.3 Configuring Device Fingerprint Authentication

Fingerprint authentication is only available on devices containing a touch sensor and on which the appropriate configuration steps have been taken to secure the device and enroll at least one fingerprint. For steps on configuring an emulator session to test fingerprint authentication, refer to the chapter *"Using and Configuring the Android Studio AVD Emulator"*.

Configure fingerprint authentication on a physical device by opening the Settings app and selecting the *Security* option. Within the Security settings screen, select the *Fingerprint* option. Tap the Next button on the resulting information screen to proceed to the Fingerprint setup screen. Before fingerprint security can be enabled, a backup screen unlocking method (such as a PIN) must be configured. If the lock screen is not secured, follow the steps to configure PIN, pattern, or password security.

With the lock screen secured, proceed to the fingerprint detection screen and touch the sensor when prompted lock screen secured, proceed to the fingerprint detection screen and touch the sensor when prompted (Figure 80-1), repeating the process to add additional fingerprints if required.

Figure 80-1

80.4 Adding the Biometric Permission to the Manifest File

Biometric authentication requires that the app request the *USE_BIOMETRIC* permission within the project manifest file. Within the Android Studio Project tool window, locate and edit the *app -> manifests -> AndroidManifest.xml* file to add the permission request as follows:

```xml
<?xml version="1.0" encoding="utf-8"?>
<manifest xmlns:android="http://schemas.android.com/apk/res/android"
    package="com.ebookfrenzy.biometricdemo">

    <uses-permission
        android:name="android.permission.USE_BIOMETRIC" />
```

An Android Biometric Authentication Tutorial

80.5 Designing the User Interface

To keep the example as simple as possible, the only visual element within the user interface will be a Button view. Locate and select the *activity_main.xml* layout resource file to load it into the Layout Editor tool.

Delete the sample TextView object, drag and drop a Button object from the *Common* category of the palette and position it in the center of the layout canvas. Using the Attributes tool window, change the text property on the button to "Authenticate" and extract the string to a resource. Finally, configure the onClick property to call a method named *authenticateUser*.

On completion of the above steps, the layout should match that shown in Figure 80-2:

Figure 80-2

80.6 Adding a Toast Convenience Method

At various points throughout the code in this example, the app will be designed to display information to the user via Toast messages. Rather than repeat the same Toast code multiple times, a convenience method named *notifyUser()* will be added to the main activity. This method will accept a single String value and display it to the user as a Toast message. Edit the *MainActivity.java* file now and add this method as follows:

```java
.
.
import android.widget.Toast;
.
.
    private void notifyUser(String message) {
        Toast.makeText(this,
                message,
                Toast.LENGTH_LONG).show();
    }
.
```

An Android Biometric Authentication Tutorial

80.7 Checking the Security Settings

Earlier in this chapter, steps were taken to configure the lock screen and register fingerprints on the device or emulator on which the app will be tested. It is important, however, to include defensive code in the app to ensure these requirements have been met before attempting to seek fingerprint authentication. These steps will be performed within the onCreate method residing in the *MainActivity.java* file, using the Keyguard and PackageManager manager services. Note that code has also been added to verify that the USE_BIOMETRIC permission has been configured for the app:

```java
package com.ebookfrenzy.biometricdemo;

import androidx.appcompat.app.AppCompatActivity;
import androidx.core.app.ActivityCompat;

import android.widget.Toast;
import android.Manifest;
import android.content.pm.PackageManager;

import android.app.KeyguardManager;

public class MainActivity extends AppCompatActivity {

    @Override
    protected void onCreate(Bundle savedInstanceState) {
        super.onCreate(savedInstanceState);
        setContentView(R.layout.activity_biometric_demo);
        checkBiometricSupport();
    }

    private void checkBiometricSupport() {

        KeyguardManager keyguardManager =
                (KeyguardManager) getSystemService(KEYGUARD_SERVICE);

        if (!keyguardManager.isKeyguardSecure()) {
            notifyUser("Lock screen security not enabled in Settings");
        }

        if (ActivityCompat.checkSelfPermission(this,
                Manifest.permission.USE_BIOMETRIC) !=
                PackageManager.PERMISSION_GRANTED) {

            notifyUser("Fingerprint authentication permission not enabled");
        }
    }
```

    }

The above code changes begin by using the Keyguard manager to verify that a backup screen unlocking method has been configured (in other words, a PIN or other authentication method can be used as an alternative to fingerprint authentication to unlock the screen). If the lock screen is not secured, the code reports the problem to the user and returns from the method.

The method then checks that the user has biometric authentication permission enabled for the app before using the package manager to verify that fingerprint authentication is available on the device.

80.8 Configuring the Authentication Callbacks

When the biometric prompt dialog is configured, it will need to be assigned a set of authentication callback methods that can be called to notify the app of the success or failure of the authentication process. These methods need to be wrapped in a BiometricPrompt.AuthenticationCallback class instance. Remaining in the *MainActivity.java* file, add a method to create and return an instance of this class with the appropriate methods implemented:

```java
.
.
import android.hardware.biometrics.BiometricPrompt;
.
.
    private BiometricPrompt.AuthenticationCallback getAuthenticationCallback() {

        return new BiometricPrompt.AuthenticationCallback() {
            @Override
            public void onAuthenticationError(int errorCode,
                                              CharSequence errString) {
                notifyUser("Authentication error: " + errString);
                super.onAuthenticationError(errorCode, errString);
            }

            @Override
            public void onAuthenticationHelp(int helpCode,
                                             CharSequence helpString) {
                super.onAuthenticationHelp(helpCode, helpString);
            }

            @Override
            public void onAuthenticationFailed() {
                super.onAuthenticationFailed();
            }

            @Override
            public void onAuthenticationSucceeded(
                    BiometricPrompt.AuthenticationResult result) {
                notifyUser("Authentication Succeeded");
```

```
                super.onAuthenticationSucceeded(result);
            }
        };
    }
    .
    .
    .
}
```

80.9 Adding the CancellationSignal

Once initiated, the biometric authentication process is performed independently of the app. To provide the app with a way to cancel the operation, an instance of the CancellationSignal class is created and passed to the biometric authentication process. This CancellationSignal instance can then be used to cancel the process if necessary. The cancellation signal instance may be configured with a listener, which will be called when the cancellation is completed. Add a new method to the activity class to configure and return a CancellationSignal object as follows:

```
.
.
import android.os.CancellationSignal;
.
.
    private CancellationSignal cancellationSignal;
.
.
    private CancellationSignal getCancellationSignal() {
        cancellationSignal = new CancellationSignal();
        cancellationSignal.setOnCancelListener(() ->
                notifyUser("Cancelled via signal"));
        return cancellationSignal;
    }
```

80.10 Starting the Biometric Prompt

All that remains is to add code to the *authenticateUser()* method to create and configure a BiometricPrompt instance and initiate the authentication. Add the *authenticateUser()* method as follows:

```
.
.
import android.view.View;
.
.
public void authenticateUser(View view) {
    BiometricPrompt biometricPrompt = new BiometricPrompt.Builder(this)
            .setTitle("Biometric Demo")
            .setSubtitle("Authentication is required to continue")
            .setDescription(
```

```
            "This app uses biometric authentication to protect your data.")
        .setNegativeButton("Cancel", this.getMainExecutor(),
            (dialogInterface, i) ->
                notifyUser("Authentication cancelled"))
        .build();

    biometricPrompt.authenticate(getCancellationSignal(), getMainExecutor(),
        getAuthenticationCallback());
}
```

The BiometricPrompt.Builder class creates a new BiometricPrompt instance configured with title, subtitle, and description text to appear in the prompt dialog. The negative button is configured to display text which reads "Cancel" and a listener is configured to display a message when this button is clicked. Finally, the *authenticate()* method of the BiometricPrompt instance is called and passed the AuthenticationCallback and CancellationSignal instances. The Biometric prompt also needs to know which thread to perform the authentication on. This is defined by passing through an Executor object configured for the required thread. In this case, the *getMainExecutor()* method is used to pass a main Executor object to the BiometricPrompt instance so that the authentication process occurs on the app's main thread.

80.11 Testing the Project

With the project now complete, run the app on a physical Android device or emulator session and click on the Authenticate button to display the BiometricPrompt dialog as shown in Figure 80-3:

Biometric Demo

Authentication is required to continue

This app uses biometric authentication to protect your data.

Touch the fingerprint sensor

CANCEL

Figure 80-3

Once running, either touch the fingerprint sensor or use the extended controls panel within the emulator to simulate a fingerprint touch as outlined in the chapter entitled *"Using and Configuring the Android Studio AVD Emulator"*. Assuming a registered fingerprint is detected, the prompt dialog will return to the main activity, where the toast message from the successful authentication callback method will appear.

Click the Authenticate button again, using an unregistered fingerprint to attempt the authentication. This time the biometric prompt dialog will indicate that the fingerprint was not recognized:

An Android Biometric Authentication Tutorial

Biometric Demo

Authentication is required to continue

This app uses biometric authentication to protect your data.

Not recognized

Figure 80-4

Verify that the error handling callback works by clicking on the activity outside the biometric prompt dialog. The prompt dialog will disappear, and the toast message will appear with the following message:

```
Authentication error: Fingerprint operation cancelled by user.
```

Check that canceling the prompt dialog using the Cancel button triggers the "Authentication Canceled" toast message. Finally, attempt to authenticate multiple times using an unregistered fingerprint and note that after several attempts, the prompt dialog indicates that too many failures have occurred and that future attempts cannot be made until later.

80.12 Summary

This chapter has outlined how to integrate biometric authentication into an Android app project. This involves using the BiometricPrompt class, which automatically handles most of the authentication process once configured with appropriate message text and callbacks.

81. Creating, Testing, and Uploading an Android App Bundle

Once the development work on an Android application is complete and tested on a wide range of Android devices, the next step is to prepare the application for submission to Google Play. Before submission can take place, however, the application must be packaged for release and signed with a private key. This chapter will work through obtaining a private key, preparing the Android App Bundle for the project, and uploading it to Google Play.

81.1 The Release Preparation Process

Up until this point in the book, we have been building application projects in a mode suitable for testing and debugging. On the other hand, building an application package for release to customers via Google Play requires additional steps. The first requirement is to compile the application in release mode instead of *debug mode*. Secondly, the application must be signed with a private key that uniquely identifies you as the application's developer. Finally, the application must be packaged into an *Android App Bundle*.

While these tasks can be performed outside of the Android Studio environment, the procedures can more easily be performed using the Android Studio build mechanism, as outlined in the remainder of this chapter. First, however, it is important to understand more about Android App Bundles.

81.2 Android App Bundles

When a user installs an app from Google Play, the app is downloaded in the form of an APK file. This file contains everything needed to install and run the app on the user's device. Before the introduction of Android Studio 3.2, the developer would generate one or more APK files using Android Studio and upload them to Google Play. Supporting multiple device types, screen sizes, and locales would require creating and uploading multiple APK files customized for each target device and locale or generating a large *universal APK* containing all of the different configuration resources and platform binaries within a single package.

Creating multiple APK files involved a significant amount of work that had to be repeated each time the app was updated, imposing a considerable time overhead on the app release process.

Creating multiple APK files involved a significant amount of work that had to be repeated each time the app needed to be updated imposing a considerable time overhead to the app release process.

The universal APK option, while less of a burden to the developer, caused an entirely unexpected problem. By analyzing app installation metrics, Google discovered that the larger an installation APK file becomes (resulting in longer download times and increased storage use), the fewer conversions the app receives. The conversion rate is calculated as a percentage of the users who completed the installation of an app after viewing that app on Google Play. Google estimates that the conversion rate for an app drops by 1% for each 6MB increase in APK file size.

Android App Bundles solve these problems by allowing the developer to create a single package from within Android Studio and have custom APK files automatically generated by Google Play for each individual supported configuration (a concept called *Dynamic Delivery*).

Creating, Testing, and Uploading an Android App Bundle

An Android App Bundle is a ZIP file containing all the files necessary to build APK files for the devices and locales for which support has been provided within the app project. The project might, for example, include resources and images for different screen sizes. When a user installs the app, Google Play receives information about the device, including the display, processor architecture, and locale. Using this information, the appropriate pre-generated APK files are transferred onto the user's device.

An additional benefit of Dynamic Delivery is the ability to split an app into multiple modules, referred to as *dynamic feature modules*, where each module contains the code and resources for a particular area of functionality within the app. Each dynamic feature module is contained within a separate APK file from the base module and is downloaded to the device only when the user requires that feature. Dynamic Delivery and app bundles also allow for the creation of *instant dynamic feature modules* which can be run instantly on a device without the need to install an entire app.

Although it is still possible to generate APK files from Android Studio, app bundles are now the recommended way to upload apps to Google Play.

81.3 Register for a Google Play Developer Console Account

The first step in the application submission process is to create a Google Play Developer Console account. To do so, navigate to *https://play.google.com/apps/publish/signup/* and follow the instructions to complete the registration process. Note that there is a one-time $25 fee to register. Once an application goes on sale, Google will keep 30% of all revenues associated with the application. After creating the account, the developer console can be accessed at *https://play.google.com/console*.

The next step is to gather together information about the application. To bring your application to market, the following information will be required:

- **Title** – The title of the application.

- **Short Description** - Up to 80 words describing the application.

- **Full Description** – Up to 4000 words describing the application.

- **Screenshots** – Up to 8 screenshots of your application running (a minimum of two is required). Google recommends submitting screenshots of the application running on a 7" or 10" tablet.

- **Language** – The language of the application (the default is US English).

- **Promotional Text** – The text that will be used when your application appears in special promotional features within the Google Play environment.

- **Application Type** – Whether your application is considered a *game* or an *application*.

- **Category** – The category that best describes your application (for example, finance, health and fitness, education, sports, etc.).

- **Locations** – The geographical locations into which you wish your application to be made available for purchase.

- **Contact Details** – Methods by which users may contact you for support relating to the application. Options include web, email, and phone.

- **Pricing & Distribution** – Information about the price of the application and the geographical locations where it is to be marketed and sold.

Having collected the above information, click the *Create app* button within the Google Play Console to begin the creation process.

81.4 Configuring the App in the Console

When the *Create app* button is first clicked, the app details and declarations screen will appear as shown in Figure 81-1 below:

Figure 81-1

Once the app entry has been fully configured, click on the *Create app* button (highlighted in the above figure) to add the app and display the dashboard screen. Within the dashboard, locate the *Initial setup* section and unfold the list of steps to configure the app store listing:

Figure 81-2

Creating, Testing, and Uploading an Android App Bundle

Work through the list of links and provide the requested information for your app, making sure to save the changes at each step.

81.5 Enabling Google Play App Signing

Until recently, Google Play uploads were signed with a release app signing key from within Android Studio and then uploaded to the Google Play console. While this option is still available, the recommended way to upload files is to use a process called *Google Play App Signing*. For a newly created app, this involves opting into Google Play App Signing and generating an *upload key* to sign the app bundle file within Android Studio. When the app bundle file generated by Android Studio is uploaded, the Google Play console removes the upload key and signs the file with an app signing key stored securely within the Google Play servers. For existing apps, some additional steps are required to enable Google Play Signing and will be covered at the end of this chapter.

Within the Google Play console, select the newly added app entry from the All Apps screen (accessed via the option located at the top of the left-hand navigation panel), unfold the Setup section (Marked A in Figure 81-3), and select the App Signing option (B).

Figure 81-3

Opt into Google Play app signing by clicking on the *Create release* button (C). The console is now ready to create the first release of your app for testing. Before doing so, however, the next step is to generate the *upload* key from within Android Studio. This is performed as part of the process of generating a signed app bundle. Leave the current Google Play Console screen loaded into the browser, as we will be returning to this later in the chapter.

81.6 Creating a Keystore File

To create a keystore file, select the Android Studio *Build -> Generate Signed Bundle / APK...* menu option to display the Generate Signed Bundle or APK Wizard dialog as shown in Figure 81-4:

Figure 81-4

Verify that the *Android App Bundle* option is selected before clicking the *Next* button.

704

If you have an existing release keystore file, click on the *Choose existing...* button on the next screen and navigate to and select the file. If you have not created a keystore file, click the *Create new...* button to display the *New Key Store* dialog (Figure 81-5). Click on the button to the right of the Key store path field and navigate to a suitable location on your file system, enter a name for the keystore file (for example, *release.keystore.jks*) and click the OK button.

The New Key Store dialog is divided into two sections. The top section relates to the keystore file. In this section, enter a strong password to protect the keystore file into both the *Password* and *Confirm* fields. The lower section of the dialog relates to the upload key that will be stored in the key store file.

Figure 81-5

Within the *Key* section of the New Key Store dialog, enter the following details:

- An alias by which the key will be referenced. This can be any sequence of characters, though the system uses only the first eight.

- A suitably strong password to protect the key.

- The number of years for which the key is to be valid (Google recommends a duration in excess of 25 years).

In addition, information must be provided for at least one of the remaining fields (for example, your first and last name or organization name).

Once the information has been entered, click the OK button to create the bundle.

81.7 Creating the Android App Bundle

The next step is instructing Android Studio to build the application app bundle file in release mode and sign it with the newly created private key. At this point, the *Generate Signed Bundle or APK* dialog should still be displayed with the keystore path, passwords, and key alias fields populated with information:

705

Creating, Testing, and Uploading an Android App Bundle

Figure 81-6

Ensure that the Export Encrypted Key option is enabled and, assuming the other settings are correct, click on the Next button to proceed to the app bundle generation screen (Figure 81-7). Within this screen, review the *Destination Folder:* setting to verify that the location into which the app bundle file will be generated is acceptable. If another location is preferred, click on the button to the right of the text field and navigate to the desired file system location.

Figure 81-7

Click the *Finish* button and wait for the Gradle system to build the app bundle. Once the build is complete, a dialog will appear providing the option to open the folder containing the app bundle file in an explorer window or to load the file into the APK Analyzer:

Figure 81-8

At this point, the application is ready to be submitted to Google Play. Click on the locate link to open a filesystem browser window. The file should be named *bundle.aab* and located in the project folder's *app/release* sub-directory unless another location is specified.

The private key generated as part of this process should be used when signing and releasing future applications and, as such, should be kept in a safe place and securely backed up.

81.8 Generating Test APK Files

An optional step at this stage is to generate APK files from the app bundle and install and run them on devices or emulator sessions. Google provides a command-line tool called *bundletool* designed specifically for this purpose which can be downloaded from the following URL:

https://github.com/google/bundletool/releases

At the time of writing, bundletool is provided as a .jar file which can be executed from the command line as follows (noting that the version number may have changed since this book was published):

```
java -jar bundletool-all-0.9.0.jar
```

Running the above command will list all of the options available within the tool. To generate the APK files from the app bundle, the *build-apks* option is used. The files will also need to be signed to generate APK files that can be installed onto a device or emulator. To achieve this, include the *--ks* option specifying the path of the keystore file created earlier in the chapter and the *--ks-key-alias* option specifying the alias provided when the key was generated.

Finally, the *--output* flag must be used to specify the path of the file (called the APK Set) into which the APK files will be generated. This file must not already exist and is required to have a *.apks* filename extension. Bringing these requirements together results in the following command line (allowing for differences in your operating system path structure):

```
java -jar bundletool-all-0.9.0.jar build-apks --bundle=/tmp/MyApps/app/release/bundle.aab --output=/tmp/MyApks.apks --ks=/MyKeys/release.keystore.jks --ks-key-alias=MyReleaseKey
```

When this command is executed, a prompt will appear requesting the keystore password before the APK files are generated into the specified APK Set file. The APK Set file is a ZIP file containing all the APK files generated from the app bundle.

To install the appropriate APK files onto a connected device or emulator, use a command similar to the following:

```
java -jar bundletool-all-0.9.0.jar install-apks --apks=/tmp/MyApks.apks
```

This command will instruct the tool to identify the appropriate APK files for the connected device and install them so that the app can be launched and tested.

It is also possible to extract the APK files from the APK Set for the connected device without installing them. The first step in this process is to obtain the specification of the connected device as follows:

```
java -jar bundletool-all-0.9.0.jar get-device-spec --output=/tmp/device.json
```

The above command will generate a JSON file similar to the following:

```
{
  "supportedAbis": ["x86"],
  "supportedLocales": ["en-US"],
  "screenDensity": 420,
  "sdkVersion": 27
```

Creating, Testing, and Uploading an Android App Bundle

}

Next, this specification file is used to extract the matching APK files from the APK Set:

```
java -jar bundletool-all-0.9.0.jar extract-apks --apks=/tmp/MyApks.apks --output-dir=/tmp/nexus5_apks --device-spec=/tmp/device.json
```

When executed, the directory specified via the *--output-dir* flag will contain the correct APK files for the specified device configuration.

The next step in bringing an Android application to market involves submitting it to the Google Play Developer Console o make it available for testing.

81.9 Uploading the App Bundle to the Google Play Developer Console

Return to the Google Play Console and select the *Internal testing* option (marked A in Figure 81-9) located in the *Testing* section of the navigation panel before clicking on the *Create new release* button (B):

Figure 81-9

On the resulting screen, click on the Continue button (marked A below) to confirm the use of Google Play app signing, then drag and drop the bundle file generated by Android Studio onto the upload drop point (B):

Figure 81-10

When the upload is complete, scroll down the screen and enter the release name and optional release notes. The release name can be any information you need to help you recognize the release, and it is not visible to users.

After the app bundle file is uploaded, Google Play will generate all the necessary APK files ready for testing. Once the APK files have been generated, scroll down to the bottom of the screen and click on the *Save* button. Once the settings have been saved, click on the *Review release* button.

81.10 Exploring the App Bundle

On the review screen, click on the arrow to the right of the uploaded bundle as indicated in Figure 81-11:

New app bundles and APKs

File type	Version	API levels	Target SDK	Screen layouts	ABIs	Required features	
Android App Bundle	1 (1.0)	29+	29	4	All	1	→

Release notes

Figure 81-11

In the resulting panel, click on the *Explore bundle* link to load the app bundle explorer. This provides summary information relating to the API levels, screen layouts, and platforms supported by the app bundle:

Details | Downloads

Details

Releases	1 release View ⌄
Supported Android devices	1,298 Go to device catalog
Localizations	85 localizations View ⌄
Permissions	android.permission.USE_BIOMETRIC
Features	android.hardware.faketouch
Screen layouts	small, normal, large, xlarge
Native platforms	No restrictions
API levels	29+
Target SDK	29
OpenGL ES versions	0.0+
OpenGL textures	No textures required

Figure 81-12

Clicking on the *Go to device catalog* link will display the devices that are supported by the APK file:

Figure 81-13

Currently, the app is ready for testing but can only be rolled out once some testers have been set up within the console.

81.11 Managing Testers

If the app is still in the Internal, Alpha, or Beta testing phase, a list of authorized testers may be specified by selecting the app from within the Google Play console, clicking on *Internal testing* in the navigation panel, and selecting the *Testers* tab as shown in Figure 81-14:

Figure 81-14

To add testers, click on the *Create email list* button, name the list, and specify the test users' email addresses manually or by uploading a CSV file.

The "Join on the web" URL may now be copied from the screen and provided to the test users so that they accept the testing invitation and download the app.

81.12 Rolling the App Out for Testing

Now that an internal release has been created and a list of testers added, the app is ready to be rolled out for testing. Remaining within the *Internal testing* screen, select the Releases tab before clicking on the Edit button for the recently created release:

Creating, Testing, and Uploading an Android App Bundle

Figure 81-15

On the review screen, scroll to the bottom and click on the *Start rollout to Internal testing* button. After a short delay while the release is processed, the app will be ready to be downloaded and tested by the designated users.

81.13 Uploading New App Bundle Revisions

The first app bundle file uploaded for your application will invariably have a version code of 1. If an attempt is made to upload another bundle file with the same version code number, the console will reject the file with the following error:

```
You need to use a different version code for your APK because you already have
one with version code 1.
```

To resolve this problem, the version code embedded into the bundle file needs to be increased. This is performed in the *module* level *build.gradle.kts* file of the project, shown highlighted in Figure 81-16:

Figure 81-16

This file will typically read as follows:

```
plugins {
    id("com.android.application")
}

android {
    namespace = "com.ebookfrenzy.biometricdemo"
    compileSdk = 33

    defaultConfig {
        applicationId = "com.ebookfrenzy.biometricdemo"
```

711

```
        minSdk = 29
        targetSdk = 33
        versionCode = 1
        versionName = "1.0"
```
.
.
.
}

To change the version code, change the number declared next to *versionCode*. To also change the version number displayed to users of your application, change the *versionName* string. For example:

```
versionCode 2
versionName "2.0"
```

After making these changes, rebuild the APK file and perform the upload again.

81.14 Analyzing the App Bundle File

Android Studio provides the ability to analyze the content of an app bundle file. To analyze a bundle file, select the Android Studio *Build -> Analyze APK...* menu option and navigate to and choose the bundle file to be reviewed. Once loaded into the tool, information will be displayed about the raw and download size of the package together with a listing of the file structure of the package as illustrated in Figure 81-17:

File	Raw File Size	Download Size	% of Total Download Size
classes.dex	9.1 MB	3.4 MB	85%
res	299.2 KB	291.6 KB	7.1%
resources.arsc	903.7 KB	196.4 KB	4.8%
classes2.dex	494.4 KB	112.1 KB	2.7%
kotlin	9.9 KB	9.9 KB	0.2%
classes3.dex	7.2 KB	3.4 KB	0.1%
AndroidManifest.xml	1.3 KB	1.3 KB	0%
DebugProbesKt.bin	777 B	777 B	0%
META-INF	400 B	482 B	0%

APK size: 11.4 MB, Download Size: 4 MB

com.ebookfrenzy.biometricdemo (Version Name: 1.0, Version Code: 1)

Figure 81-17

Selecting the *classes.dex* file will display the class structure of the file in the lower panel. Within this panel, details of the individual classes may be explored down to the level of the methods within a class:

This dex file defines **6061** classes with **47393** methods, and references **57837** methods.

Class	Defined Methods	Referenced Methods	Size
androidx	23159	25215	2.7 MB
com	9972	11084	986.5 KB
kotlin	9676	10709	1.1 MB
kotlinx	4501	4733	542.9 KB
android	62	4596	43.2 KB
java		1450	11.8 KB
org	23	45	2.9 KB

Figure 81-18

Similarly, selecting a resource or image file within the file list will display the file content within the lower panel. The size differences between two bundle files may be reviewed by clicking on the *Compare with previous APK...* button and selecting a second bundle file.

81.15 Summary

Once an app project is complete or ready for user testing, it can be uploaded to the Google Play console and published for production, internal, alpha, or beta testing. Before the app can be uploaded, an app entry must be created within the console, including information about the app and screenshots for use within the Play Store. A release Android App Bundle file is generated and signed with an upload key within Android Studio. After the bundle file has been uploaded, Google Play removes the upload key and replaces it with the securely stored app signing key, and the app is ready to be published.

The content of a bundle file can be reviewed at any time by loading it into the Android Studio APK Analyzer tool.

Chapter 82

82. An Overview of Android In-App Billing

In the early days of mobile applications for operating systems such as Android and iOS, the most common method for earning revenue was to charge an upfront fee to download and install the application. Another revenue opportunity was soon introduced by embedding advertising within applications. The most common and lucrative option is to charge the user for purchasing items from within the application after installing it. This typically takes the form of access to a higher level in a game, acquiring virtual goods or currency, or subscribing to premium content in the digital edition of a magazine or newspaper.

Google supports integrating in-app purchasing through the Google Play In-App Billing API and the Play Console. This chapter will provide an overview of in-app billing and outline how to integrate in-app billing into your Android projects. Once these topics have been explored, the next chapter will walk you through creating an example app that includes in-app purchasing features.

82.1 Preparing a Project for In-App Purchasing

Building in-app purchasing into an app will require a Google Play Developer Console account, details of which were covered previously in the *"Creating, Testing and Uploading an Android App Bundle"* chapter. You must also register a Google merchant account. These settings can be found by navigating to *Setup -> Payments profile* in the Play Console. Note that merchant registration is not available in all countries. For details, refer to the following page:

https://support.google.com/googleplay/android-developer/answer/9306917

The app must then be uploaded to the console and enabled for in-app purchasing. However, the console will not activate in-app purchasing support for an app unless the Google Play Billing Library has been added to the module-level *build.gradle.kts* file:

```
dependencies {
    .
    .
    implementation ("com.android.billingclient:billing:<latest version>")
    .
    .
}
```

Once the build file has been modified and the app bundle uploaded to the console, the next step is to add in-app products or subscriptions for the user to purchase.

82.2 Creating In-App Products and Subscriptions

Products and subscriptions are created and managed using the options listed beneath the Monetize section of the Play Console navigation panel, as highlighted in Figure 82-1 below:

An Overview of Android In-App Billing

Monetize

▼ 🛒 Products

App pricing

In-app products

Subscriptions

🏬 Promo codes

Figure 82-1

Each product or subscription needs an ID, title, description, and pricing information. Purchases fall into the categories of *consumable* (the item must be purchased each time it is required by the user, such as virtual currency in a game), *non-consumable* (only needs to be purchased once by the user, such as content access), and *subscription*-based. Consumable and non-consumable products are collectively referred to as *managed products*.

Subscriptions are useful for selling an item that needs to be renewed regularly, such as access to news content or the premium features of an app. When creating a subscription, a *base plan* specifies the price, renewal period (monthly, annually, etc.), and whether the subscription auto-renews. Users can also be given discount offers and the option of pre-purchasing a subscription.

82.3 Billing Client Initialization

Communication between your app and the Google Play Billing Library is handled by a BillingClient instance. In addition, BillingClient includes a set of methods that can be called to perform both synchronous and asynchronous billing-related activities. When the billing client is initialized, it will need to be provided with a reference to a PurchasesUpdatedListener callback handler. The client will call this handler to notify your app of the results of any purchasing activity. To avoid duplicate notifications, it is recommended to have only one BillingClient instance per app.

A BillingClient instance can be created using the *newBuilder()* method, passing through the current activity or fragment context. The purchase update handler is then assigned to the client via the *setListener()* method:

```java
private final PurchasesUpdatedListener purchasesUpdatedListener =
                            new PurchasesUpdatedListener() {
    @Override
    public void onPurchasesUpdated(BillingResult billingResult,
                            List<Purchase> purchases) {

        if (billingResult.getResponseCode() ==
                BillingClient.BillingResponseCode.OK
                && purchases != null) {

            // Purchase(s) successful

            for (Purchase purchase : purchases) {
                // Process purchases
```

```
            }
        } else if (billingResult.getResponseCode() ==
                BillingClient.BillingResponseCode.USER_CANCELED) {
            // User cancelled purchase
        } else {
            // handle errors here
        }
    }
};

private BillingClient billingClient = BillingClient.newBuilder(context)
    .setListener(purchasesUpdatedListener)
    .enablePendingPurchases()
    .build();
```

82.4 Connecting to the Google Play Billing Library

After successfully creating the Billing Client, the next step is initializing a connection to the Google Play Billing Library. A call must be made to the *startConnection()* method of the billing client instance to establish this connection. Since the connection is performed asynchronously, a BillingClientStateListener must be implemented to receive a callback indicating whether the connection was successful. Code should also be added to override the *onBillingServiceDisconnected()* method. This is called if the connection to the Billing Library is lost and can be used to report the problem to the user and retry the connection.

Once the setup and connection tasks are complete, the BillingClient instance will make a call to the *onBillingSetupFinished()* method, which can be used to check that the client is ready:

```
billingClient.startConnection(new BillingClientStateListener() {

    @Override
    public void onBillingSetupFinished(
            @NonNull BillingResult billingResult) {

        if (billingResult.getResponseCode() ==
                BillingClient.BillingResponseCode.OK) {
            // Connection successful
        } else {
            // Connection failed
        }
    }

    @Override
    public void onBillingServiceDisconnected() {
        // Existing connection lost
    }
});
```

An Overview of Android In-App Billing

82.5 Querying Available Products

Once the billing environment is initialized and ready to go, the next step is to request the details of the products or subscriptions available for purchase. This is achieved by making a call to the *queryProductDetailsAsync()* method of the BillingClient and passing through an appropriately configured QueryProductDetailsParams instance containing the product ID and type (ProductType.SUBS for a subscription or ProductType.INAPP for a managed product):

```
QueryProductDetailsParams queryProductDetailsParams =
    QueryProductDetailsParams.newBuilder()
        .setProductList(
            ImmutableList.of(
                QueryProductDetailsParams.Product.newBuilder()
                    .setProductId("one_button_click")
                    .setProductType(BillingClient.ProductType.INAPP)
                    .build()))
        .build();

billingClient.queryProductDetailsAsync(queryProductDetailsParams,
    new ProductDetailsResponseListener() {
        public void onProductDetailsResponse(
                @NonNull BillingResult billingResult,
                @NonNull List<ProductDetails> productDetailsList) {

            if (!productDetailsList.isEmpty()) {
                // Process list of matching products
            } else {
                // No product matches found
            }
        }
    }
);
```

The *queryProductDetailsAsync()* method is passed a ProductDetailsResponseListener handler which, in turn, is called and passed a list of ProductDetail objects containing information about the matching products. For example, we can call methods on these objects to get information such as the product name, title, description, price, and offer details.

82.6 Starting the Purchase Process

Once a product or subscription has been queried and selected for purchase by the user, the purchase process is ready to be launched. We do this by calling the *launchBillingFlow()* method of the BillingClient, passing through as arguments the current activity and a BillingFlowParams instance configured with the ProductDetail object for the purchased item.

```
BillingFlowParams billingFlowParams =
    BillingFlowParams.newBuilder()
        .setProductDetailsParamsList(
            ImmutableList.of(
                BillingFlowParams.ProductDetailsParams.newBuilder()
```

An Overview of Android In-App Billing

```
                    .setProductDetails(productDetails)
                    .build()
        )
    )
    .build();

billingClient.launchBillingFlow(this, billingFlowParams);
```

The success or otherwise of the purchase operation will be reported via a call to the PurchasesUpdatedListener callback handler outlined earlier in the chapter.

82.7 Completing the Purchase

When purchases are successful, the PurchasesUpdatedListener handler will be passed a list containing a Purchase object for each item. You can verify that the item has been purchased by calling the *getPurchaseState()* method of the Purchase instance as follows:

```
if (purchase.getPurchaseState() == Purchase.PurchaseState.PURCHASED) {
    // Purchase completed.
} else if (purchase.getPurchaseState() == Purchase.PurchaseState.PENDING) {
    // Payment is still pending
}
```

Note that your app will only support pending purchases if a call is made to the *enablePendingPurchases()* method during initialization. A pending purchase will remain so until the user completes the payment process.

When the purchase of a non-consumable item is complete, it must be acknowledged to prevent a refund from being issued to the user. This requires the *purchase token* for the item, which is obtained via a call to the *getPurchaseToken()* method of the Purchase object. This token is used to create an AcknowledgePurchaseParams instance and an AcknowledgePurchaseResponseListener handler. Managed product purchases and subscriptions are acknowledged by calling the BillingClient's *acknowledgePurchase()* method as follows:

```
AcknowledgePurchaseParams acknowledgePurchaseParams =
        AcknowledgePurchaseParams.newBuilder()
                .setPurchaseToken(purchase.getPurchaseToken())
                .build();

AcknowledgePurchaseResponseListener acknowledgePurchaseResponseListener =
                new AcknowledgePurchaseResponseListener() {

    @Override
    public void onAcknowledgePurchaseResponse(
                    @NonNull BillingResult billingResult) {
        billingClient.acknowledgePurchase(
                        acknowledgePurchaseParams,
                        acknowledgePurchaseResponseListener);

    }
};
```

For consumable purchases, you will need to notify Google Play when the item has been consumed so that it is available to be repurchased by the user. This requires a configured ConsumeParams instance containing a purchase token, a ConsumeResponseListener, and a call to the billing client's *consumeAsync()* method:

An Overview of Android In-App Billing

```java
ConsumeParams consumeParams =
    ConsumeParams.newBuilder()
            .setPurchaseToken(purchase.getPurchaseToken())
            .build();

ConsumeResponseListener listener = new ConsumeResponseListener() {
    @Override
    public void onConsumeResponse(BillingResult billingResult,
                                  @NonNull String purchaseToken) {
        if (billingResult.getResponseCode() ==
                BillingClient.BillingResponseCode.OK) {
            // Purchase consumed successfully
        }
    }
};

billingClient.consumeAsync(consumeParams, listener);
```

82.8 Querying Previous Purchases

When working with in-app billing, checking whether a user has already purchased a product or subscription is a common requirement. A list of all the user's previous purchases of a specific type can be generated by calling the *queryPurchasesAsync()* method of the BillingClient instance and implementing a PurchaseResponseListener. The following code, for example, obtains a list of all previously purchased items that have not yet been consumed:

```java
QueryPurchasesParams queryPurchasesParams =
        QueryPurchasesParams.newBuilder()
                .setProductType(BillingClient.ProductType.INAPP)
                .build();

billingClient.queryPurchasesAsync(queryPurchasesParams,
                    new PurchasesResponseListener() {
    @Override
    public void onQueryPurchasesResponse(@NonNull BillingResult billingResult,
                @NonNull List<Purchase> list) {
        // Process list of purchases
    }
});
```

To obtain a list of active subscriptions, change the ProductType value from INAPP to SUBS.

Alternatively, to obtain a list of the most recent purchases for each product, make a call to the BillingClient *queryPurchaseHistoryAsync()* method:

```java
QueryPurchaseHistoryParams queryPurchaseHistoryParams =
        QueryPurchaseHistoryParams.newBuilder()
                .setProductType(BillingClient.ProductType.INAPP)
                .build();

billingClient.queryPurchaseHistoryAsync(queryPurchaseHistoryParams,
```

```
                new PurchaseHistoryResponseListener() {

    @Override
    public void onPurchaseHistoryResponse(@NonNull BillingResult billingResult,
            @NonNull List<PurchaseHistoryRecord> list) {
        // Process purchase history
    }
});
```

82.9 Summary

In-app purchases provide a way to generate revenue from within Android apps by selling virtual products and subscriptions to users. This chapter explored managed products and subscriptions and explained the difference between consumable and non-consumable products. In-app purchasing support is added to an app using the Google Play In-app Billing Library. It involves creating and initializing a billing client on which methods are called to perform tasks such as making purchases, listing available products, and consuming existing purchases. The next chapter contains a tutorial demonstrating the addition of in-app purchases to an Android Studio project.

Chapter 83

83. An Android In-App Purchasing Tutorial

In the previous chapter, we explored how to integrate in-app purchasing into an Android project and also looked at some code samples that can be used when working on your own projects. This chapter will put this theory into practice by creating an example project demonstrating how to add a consumable in-app product to an Android app. The tutorial will also show how in-app products are added and managed within the Google Play Console and explain how to enable test payments to make purchases during testing without having to spend real money.

83.1 About the In-App Purchasing Example Project

The simple concept behind this project is an app in which an in-app product must be purchased before a button can be clicked. This in-app product is consumed each time the button is clicked, requiring the user to repurchase the product each time they want to be able to click the button. On initialization, the app will connect to the app store, obtain product details, and display the product name. Once the app has established that the product is available, a purchase button will be enabled, which will step through the purchase process when clicked. Upon completion of the purchase, a second button will be enabled so the user can click on it and consume the purchase.

83.2 Creating the InAppPurchase Project

The first step in this exercise is to create a new project. Launch Android Studio and select the *New Project* option from the welcome screen. Choose the Empty Views Activity template in the new project dialog before clicking the Next button.

Enter InAppPurchase into the Name field and specify a package name that uniquely identifies your app within the Google Play ecosystem (for example, *com.<your company>.InAppPurchase*). Before clicking on the Finish button, change the Minimum API level setting to API 26: Android 8.0 (Oreo) and the Language menu to Java. Once the project has been created, use the steps outlined in section *11.8 Migrating a Project to View Binding* to convert the project to use view binding.

83.3 Adding Libraries to the Project

Before writing code, some libraries must be added to the project build configuration, including the standard Android billing client library. Later in the project, we will also need to use the ImmutableList class, part of Google's Guava Core Java libraries. Add these libraries now by modifying the *Gradle Scripts -> build.gradle.kts (Module: app)* file with the following changes:

```
.
.
.
dependencies {
.
.
.
    implementation ("com.android.billingclient:billing:6.0.1")
    implementation ("com.google.guava:guava:24.1-jre")
    implementation ("com.google.guava:guava:27.0.1-android")
```

An Android In-App Purchasing Tutorial

•
•

Click on the *Sync Now* link at the top of the editor panel to commit these changes.

83.4 Designing the User Interface

The user interface will consist of the existing TextView and two Buttons. With the *activity_main.xml* file loaded into the editor, drag and drop two Button views onto the layout so that one is above and the other below the TextView. Select the TextView and change the id attribute to *statusText*.

Click on the *Clear all Constraints* button in the toolbar and shift-click to select all three views. Right-click on the top-most Button view and select the *Center -> Horizontally in Parent* menu option. Repeat this step once more, selecting *Chains -> Create Vertical Chain*. Change the text attribute of the top button so that it reads "Consume Purchase" and the id to *consumeButton*. Also, configure the onClick property to call a method named *consumePurchase*.

Select the bottom-most button and repeat the above steps, setting the text to "Buy Product", the id to *buyButton*, and the onClick callback to *makePurchase*. Once completed, the layout should match that shown in *Figure 83-1*:

Figure 83-1

83.5 Adding the App to the Google Play Store

Using the steps outlined in the chapter entitled *"Creating, Testing and Uploading an Android App Bundle"*, sign into the Play Console, create a new app, and set up a new internal testing track, including the email addresses of designated testers. Return to Android Studio and generate a signed release app bundle for the project. Once the bundle file has been generated, upload it to the internal testing track and roll it out for testing.

Now that the app is in the Google Play Store, we are ready to create an in-app product for the project.

An Android In-App Purchasing Tutorial

83.6 Creating an In-App Product

With the app selected in the Play Console, scroll down the list of options in the left-hand panel until the Monetize section appears. Within this section, select the *In-app products* option listed under *Products*, as shown in Figure 83-2:

Figure 83-2

On the In-app products page, click on the *Create product* button:

Figure 83-3

On the new product screen, enter the following information before saving the new product:

- **Product ID:** one_button_click
- **Name:** A Button Click
- **Description:** This is a test in-app product that allows a button to be clicked once.
- **Default price:** Set to the lowest possible price in your preferred currency.

83.7 Enabling License Testers

When testing in-app billing, it is useful to make test purchases without spending any money. This can be achieved by enabling license testing for the internal track testers. License testers can use a test payment card when making purchases so that they are not charged.

Within the Play Console, return to the main home screen and select the *Setup -> License testing* option:

An Android In-App Purchasing Tutorial

- Setup
- Email lists
- Pricing templates
- Game projects
- License testing
- Payments profile

Figure 83-4

Within the license testing screen, add the testers that were added for the internal testing track, change the *License response* setting to RESPOND_NORMALLY, and save the changes:

Figure 83-5

Now that the app and the in-app product have been set up in the Play Console, we can add code to the project.

83.8 Initializing the Billing Client

Edit the *MainActivity*.java file and make the following changes to begin implementing the in-app purchase functionality:

```
.
.
import androidx.annotation.NonNull;

import android.util.Log;
import com.android.billingclient.api.*;
.
.
public class MainActivity extends AppCompatActivity {
```

```java
    private ActivityMainBinding binding;
    private BillingClient billingClient;
    private ProductDetails productDetails;
    private Purchase purchase;

    static final String TAG = "InAppPurchaseTag";

    @Override
    protected void onCreate(Bundle savedInstanceState) {
        super.onCreate(savedInstanceState);
        binding = ActivityMainBinding.inflate(getLayoutInflater());
        View view = binding.getRoot();
        setContentView(view);
        billingSetup();
    }

    private void billingSetup() {

        billingClient = BillingClient.newBuilder(this)
                .setListener(purchasesUpdatedListener)
                .enablePendingPurchases()
                .build();

        billingClient.startConnection(new BillingClientStateListener() {

            @Override
            public void onBillingSetupFinished(
                    @NonNull BillingResult billingResult) {

                if (billingResult.getResponseCode() ==
                        BillingClient.BillingResponseCode.OK) {
                    Log.i(TAG, "OnBillingSetupFinish connected");
                    queryProduct();
                } else {
                    Log.i(TAG, "OnBillingSetupFinish failed");
                }
            }

            @Override
            public void onBillingServiceDisconnected() {
                Log.i(TAG, "OnBillingSetupFinish connection lost");
            }
        });
    }
```

When the app starts, the *onCreate()* method will now call *billingSetup()*, which will, in turn, create a new billing client instance and attempt to connect to the Google Play Billing Library. The *onBillingSetupFinished()* listener will be called when the connection attempt completes and output Logcat messages indicating the success or otherwise of the connection attempt. Finally, we have also implemented the *onBillingServiceDisconnected()* callback which will be called if the Google Play Billing Library connection is lost.

If the connection is successful, *queryProduct()* is called. This method and the purchasesUpdatedListener assigned to the billing client must be added.

83.9 Querying the Product

To make sure the product is available for purchase, we need to create a QueryProductDetailsParams instance configured with the product ID that was specified in the Play Console and pass it to the *queryProductDetailsAsync()* method of the billing client. This will require that we also add the *onProductDetailsResponse()* callback method, where we will check that the product exists, extract the product name, and display it on the status TextView. Now that we have obtained the product details, we can also safely enable the buy button. Within the *MainActivity.* file, add the *queryProduct()* method so that it reads as follows:

```
.
.
import com.google.common.collect.ImmutableList;

import java.util.List;
.
.
private void queryProduct() {

    QueryProductDetailsParams queryProductDetailsParams =
        QueryProductDetailsParams.newBuilder()
            .setProductList(
                ImmutableList.of(
                    QueryProductDetailsParams.Product.newBuilder()
                        .setProductId("one_button_click")
                        .setProductType(
                            BillingClient.ProductType.INAPP)
                        .build()))
            .build();

    billingClient.queryProductDetailsAsync(
        queryProductDetailsParams,
        new ProductDetailsResponseListener() {
            public void onProductDetailsResponse(
                @NonNull BillingResult billingResult,
                @NonNull List<ProductDetails> productDetailsList) {

                if (!productDetailsList.isEmpty()) {
                    productDetails = productDetailsList.get(0);
```

An Android In-App Purchasing Tutorial

```
                    runOnUiThread(() -> {
                        binding.buyButton.setEnabled(true);
                        binding.statusText.setText(productDetails.getName());
                    });
                } else {
                    Log.i(TAG, "onProductDetailsResponse: No products");
                }
            }
        }
    );
}
```

Much of the code used here should be familiar from the previous chapter. The listener code checks that at least one product matches the query criteria. The ProductDetails object is then extracted from the first matching product, stored in the *productDetails* variable, and the product name property is displayed on the TextView.

One point of note is that when we display the product name on the status TextView, we do so by calling *runOnUiThread()*. This is necessary because the listener is not running on the main thread, so it cannot safely make direct changes to the user interface. The *runOnUiThread()* method provides a quick and convenient way to execute code on the main thread without using coroutines.

83.10 Launching the Purchase Flow

When the user clicks the buy button, *makePurchase()* will be called to start the purchase process. We can now add this method as follows:

```
public void makePurchase(View view) {

    BillingFlowParams billingFlowParams =
        BillingFlowParams.newBuilder()
            .setProductDetailsParamsList(
                ImmutableList.of(
                    BillingFlowParams.ProductDetailsParams.newBuilder()
                        .setProductDetails(productDetails)
                        .build()
                )
            )
            .build();

    billingClient.launchBillingFlow(this, billingFlowParams);
}
```

83.11 Handling Purchase Updates

The results of the purchase process will be reported to the app via the PurchaseUpdatedListener assigned to the billing client during the initialization phase. Add this handler now as follows:

```
private final PurchasesUpdatedListener purchasesUpdatedListener = new
PurchasesUpdatedListener() {
    @Override
    public void onPurchasesUpdated(BillingResult billingResult,
                    List<Purchase> purchases) {
```

```
            if (billingResult.getResponseCode() ==
                        BillingClient.BillingResponseCode.OK
                    && purchases != null) {
                for (Purchase purchase : purchases) {
                    completePurchase(purchase);
                }
            } else if (billingResult.getResponseCode() ==
                    BillingClient.BillingResponseCode.USER_CANCELED) {
                Log.i(TAG, "onPurchasesUpdated: Purchase Canceled");
            } else {
                Log.i(TAG, "onPurchasesUpdated: Error");
            }
        }
    };
```

The handler will output log messages if the user cancels the purchase or another error occurs. However, a successful purchase results in a call to the *completePurchase()* method, which is passed the current Purchase object. Add this method as outlined below:

```
private void completePurchase(Purchase item) {

    purchase = item;

    if (purchase.getPurchaseState() == Purchase.PurchaseState.PURCHASED)
        runOnUiThread(() -> {
                binding.consumeButton.setEnabled(true);
                binding.statusText.setText("Purchase Complete");
        });
}
```

This method stores the purchase before verifying that the product has indeed been purchased and that payment is not still pending. The "consume" button is enabled, and the user is notified of the successful purchase. The buy button is also disabled to prevent the user from repurchasing before consuming the purchase.

83.12 Consuming the Product

With the user now able to click on the "consume" button, the next step is to ensure the product is consumed so that only one click can be performed before another button click is purchased. This requires that we now write the *consumePurchase()* method:

```
public void consumePurchase(View view) {
    ConsumeParams consumeParams =
            ConsumeParams.newBuilder()
                    .setPurchaseToken(purchase.getPurchaseToken())
                    .build();

    ConsumeResponseListener listener = new ConsumeResponseListener() {
        @Override
        public void onConsumeResponse(BillingResult billingResult,
```

```
                @NonNull String purchaseToken) {
        if (billingResult.getResponseCode() ==
                    BillingClient.BillingResponseCode.OK) {
            runOnUiThread(() -> {
                binding.consumeButton.setEnabled(false);
                binding.statusText.setText("Purchase consumed");
            });
        }
    }
};
billingClient.consumeAsync(consumeParams, listener);
}
```

This method creates a ConsumeParams instance and configures it with the purchase token for the current purchase (obtained from the Purchase object previously saved in the *completePurchase()* method). This is passed to the *consumePurchase()* method, which is launched within a coroutine using the IO dispatcher. If the product is successfully consumed, code is executed in the main thread to disable the consume button, enable the buy button, and update the status text.

83.13 Restoring a Previous Purchase

With the code added so far, we can purchase and consume a product within a single session. If we were to make a purchase and exit the app before consuming it, the purchase would be lost when the app restarts. We can solve this problem by configuring a QueryPurchasesParams instance to search for the unconsumed In-App product and passing it to the *queryPurchasesAsync()* method of the billing client together with a reference to a listener that will be called with the results. Add a new function and the listener to the *MainActivity.java* file as follows:

```
private void reloadPurchase() {

    QueryPurchasesParams queryPurchasesParams = QueryPurchasesParams.newBuilder()
            .setProductType(BillingClient.ProductType.INAPP)
            .build();

    billingClient.queryPurchasesAsync(
            queryPurchasesParams,
            purchasesListener
    );
}

private final PurchasesResponseListener purchasesListener = new
PurchasesResponseListener() {
    @Override
    public void onQueryPurchasesResponse(@NonNull BillingResult billingResult,
                        @NonNull List<Purchase> list) {
        if (!list.isEmpty()) {
            purchase = list.get(0);
            binding.consumeButton.setEnabled(true);
        } else {
            binding.consumeButton.setEnabled(false);
```

An Android In-App Purchasing Tutorial

```
        }
    }
};
```

If the list of purchases passed to the listener is not empty, the first purchase in the list is assigned to the *purchase* variable, and the consume button is enabled (in a more complete implementation, code should be added to check this is the correct product by comparing the product id and to handle the return of multiple purchases). If no purchases are found, the consume button is disabled until another purchase is made. All that remains is to call our new *reloadPurchase()* method during the billing setup process as follows:

```
private void billingSetup() {
.
.
            if (billingResult.getResponseCode() ==
                    BillingClient.BillingResponseCode.OK) {
                Log.i(TAG, "OnBillingSetupFinish connected");
                queryProduct();
                reloadPurchase();
            } else {
                Log.i(TAG, "OnBillingSetupFinish failed");
            }
.
.
}
```

83.14 Testing the App

Before we can test the app, we need to upload this latest version to the Play Console. As we already have version 1 uploaded, we need to increase the version number in the *build.gradle.kts (Module: app)* file:

```
.
.
defaultConfig {
    applicationId "com.ebookfrenzy.inapppurchase"
    minSdk 26
    targetSdk 32
    versionCode 2
    versionName "2.0"
.
.
```

Sync the build configuration, then follow the steps in the *"Creating, Testing and Uploading an Android App Bundle"* chapter to generate a new app bundle, upload it to the internal test track, and roll it out to the testers. Next, using the internal testing link, install the app on a device or emulator where one of the test accounts is signed in. To locate the testing link, select the app in the Google Play Console and choose the Internal testing option from the navigation panel followed by the Testers tab, as shown in Figure 83-6:

An Android In-App Purchasing Tutorial

Figure 83-6

Scroll to the "How testers join your test" section of the screen and click on *Copy link*:

Figure 83-7

Open the Chrome browser on the testing device or emulator, enter the testing link, and follow the instructions to install the app from the Play Store. After the app starts, it should, after a short delay, display the product name on the TextView. Clicking the buy button will begin the purchase flow, as shown in Figure 83-8:

Figure 83-8

Tap the buy button to complete the purchase using the test card and wait for the Consume Purchase button to be enabled. Before tapping this button, attempt to purchase the product again and verify that it is not possible because you already own the product.

Tap the Consume Purchase button and wait for the "Purchase consumed" message to appear on the TextView. With the product consumed, it should now be possible to purchase it again. Make another purchase, then terminate and restart the app. The app should locate the previous unconsumed purchase and enable the consume button.

83.15 Troubleshooting

If you encounter problems with the purchase, make sure the device is attached to Android Studio via a USB cable or WiFi, and select it from within the Logcat panel. Enter InAppPurchaseTag into the Logcat search bar and check the diagnostic output, adding additional Log calls in the code if necessary. For additional information about failures, a useful trick is to access the debug message from BillingResult instances, for example:

An Android In-App Purchasing Tutorial

```
        .
        .
} else if (billingResult.getResponseCode()
            == BillingClient.BillingResponseCode.USER_CANCELED) {
    Log.i(TAG, "onPurchasesUpdated: Purchase Canceled");
} else {
    Log.i(TAG, billingResult.getDebugMessage());
}
```

Note that as long as you leave the app version number unchanged in the module-level *build.gradle.kts* file, you should now be able to run modified versions of the app directly on the device or emulator without having to re-bundle and upload it to the console.

If the test payment card is not listed, ensure the device user account has been added to the license testers list. If the app is running on a physical device, try it on an emulator. If all else fails, you can enter a valid payment method to make test purchases and then refund yourself using the Order Management screen accessible from the Play Console home page.

83.16 Summary

In this chapter, we created a project demonstrating adding an in-app product to an Android app. This included the creation of the product within the Google Play Console and writing code to initialize and connect to the billing client, querying available products, and purchasing and consuming the product. We also explained how to add license testers using the Play Console to make purchases during testing without spending money.

84. Working with Material Design 3 Theming

The appearance of an Android app is intended to conform to a set of guidelines defined by Material Design. Google developed Material Design to provide a level of design consistency between different apps while also allowing app developers to include their own branding in terms of color, typography, and shape choices (a concept referred to as Material theming). In addition to design guidelines, Material Design also includes a set of UI components for use when designing user interface layouts, many of which we have used throughout this book.

This chapter will provide an overview of how theming works within an Android Studio project and explore how the default design configurations provided for newly created projects can be modified to meet your branding requirements.

84.1 Material Design 2 vs. Material Design 3

Before beginning, it is important to note that Google is transitioning from Material Design 2 to Material Design 3 and that Android Studio Giraffe projects default to Material Design 3. Material Design 3 provides the basis for Material You, a feature introduced in Android 12 that allows an app to automatically adjust theme elements to complement preferences configured by the user on the device. For example, dynamic color support provided by Material Design 3 allows the colors used in apps to adapt automatically to match the user's wallpaper selection.

84.2 Understanding Material Design Theming

We know that Android app user interfaces are created by assembling components such as layouts, text fields, and buttons. These components appear using default colors unless we specifically override a color attribute in the XML layout resource file or by writing code. The project's theme defines these default colors. The theme consists of a set of color slots (declared in *themes.xml* files) which are assigned color values (declared in the *colors.xml* file). Each UI component is programmed internally to use theme color slots as the default color for specific attributes (such as the foreground and background colors of the Text widget). It follows, therefore, that we can change the application-wide theme of an app by changing the colors assigned to specific theme slots. When the app runs, the new default colors will be used for all widgets when the user interface is rendered.

84.3 Material Design 3 Theming

Before exploring Material Design 3, we must consider how it is used in an Android Studio project. The theme used by an application project is declared as a property of the *application* element within the *AndroidManifest.xml* file, for example:

```
<?xml version="1.0" encoding="utf-8"?>
<manifest xmlns:android="http://schemas.android.com/apk/res/android"
    xmlns:tools="http://schemas.android.com/tools">

    <application
    .
    .
```

```
android:supportsRtl="true"
android:theme="@style/Theme.MyDemoApp"
tools:targetApi="31">
<activity
.
.
```

As previously discussed, all of the files associated with the project theme are contained within the *colors.xml* and *themes.xml* files located in the *res -> values* folder, as shown in Figure 84-1:

Figure 84-1

The theme itself is declared in the two *themes.xml* files located in the *themes* folder. These resource files declare different color palettes containing Material Theme color slots for use when the device is in light or dark (night) mode. Note that the style name property in each file must match that referenced in the *AndroidManifest.xml* file, for example:

```
<resources xmlns:tools="http://schemas.android.com/tools">
    <!-- Base application theme. -->
    <style name="Base.Theme.MyDemoApp" parent="Theme.Material3.DayNight.NoActionBar">
        <!-- Customize your light theme here. -->
        <!-- <item name="colorPrimary">@color/my_light_primary</item> -->
    </style>

    <style name="Theme.MyDemoApp" parent="Base.Theme.MyDemoApp" />
</resources>
```

These color slots (also referred to as *color attributes*) are used by the Material components to set colors when they are rendered on the screen. For example, the *colorPrimary* color slot is used as the background color for the Material Button component.

Color slots in MD3 are grouped as Primary, Secondary, Tertiary, Error, Background, and Surface. These slots are further divided into pairs consisting of a *base color* and an *"on" base color*. This generally translates to the background and foreground colors of a Material component.

Working with Material Design 3 Theming

The particular group used for coloring will differ between widgets. A Material Button widget, for example, will use the *colorPrimary* base color for the background color and *colorOnPrimary* for its content (i.e., the text or icon it displays). The FloatingActionButton component, on the other hand, uses *colorPrimaryContainer* as the background color and *colorOnPrimaryContainer* for the foreground. The correct group for a specific widget type can usually be identified quickly by changing color settings in the theme files and reviewing the rendering in the layout editor.

Suppose that we need to change *colorPrimary* to red. We achieve this by adding a new entry to the *colors.xml* file for the red color and then assigning it to the *colorPrimary* slot in the *themes.xml* file. The *colorPrimary* slot in an MD3 theme night, therefore, read as follows:

```
<resources xmlns:tools="http://schemas.android.com/tools">
    <!-- Base application theme. -->
    <style name="Base.Theme.MyDemoApp" parent="Theme.Material3.DayNight.NoActionBar">
        <item name="colorPrimary">@color/my_bright_primary</item>
    </style>

    <style name="Theme.MyDemoApp" parent="Base.Theme.MyDemoApp" />
</resources>
```

This color is then declared in the *colors.xml* file:

```
<?xml version="1.0" encoding="utf-8"?>
<resources>
.
.
    <color name="my_bright_primary">#FC0505</color>
</resources>
```

84.4 Building a Custom Theme

As we have seen, the coding work in implementing a theme is relatively simple. The difficult part, however, is often choosing complementary colors to make up the theme. Fortunately, Google has developed a tool that makes it easy to design custom color themes for your apps. This tool is called the Material Theme Builder and is available at:

https://m3.material.io/theme-builder#/custom

On the custom screen (Figure 84-2), make a color selection for the primary color key (A) by clicking on the color circle to display the color selection dialog. Once a color has been selected, the preview (B) will change to reflect the recommended colors for all MD3 color slots, along with example app interfaces and widgets. In addition, you can override the generated colors for the Secondary, Tertiary, and Neutral slots by clicking on the corresponding color circles to display the color selection dialog.

The area marked B displays example app interfaces, light and dark color scheme charts, and widgets that update to preview your color selections. Since the panel is longer than the typical browser window, you must scroll down to see all the information.

To incorporate the theme into your design, click the Export button (C) and select the Android View (XML) option. Once downloaded, the *colors.xml* and *themes.xml* files can be used to replace the existing files in your project. Note that the theme name in the two exported *themes.xml* files must be changed to match your project.

Working with Material Design 3 Theming

Figure 84-2

84.5 Summary

Material Design provides guidelines and components defining how Android apps appear. Individual branding can be applied to an app by designing themes that specify the colors, fonts, and shapes used when displaying the app. Google recently introduced Material Design 3, which replaces Material Design 2 and supports the new features of Material You, including dynamic colors. Google also provides the Material Theme Builder for designing your own themes, which eases the task of choosing complementary theme colors. Once this tool has been used to design a theme, the corresponding files can be exported and used within an Android Studio project.

Chapter 85

85. A Material Design 3 Theming and Dynamic Color Tutorial

This chapter will show you how to create a new Material Design 3 theme using the Material Theme Builder tool and integrate it into an Android Studio project. The tutorial will also demonstrate how to add support for and test dynamic theme colors to an app.

85.1 Creating the ThemeDemo Project
85.2

Select the *New Project* option from the welcome screen and, within the resulting new project dialog, choose the Empty Views Activity template before clicking on the Next button.

Enter *ThemeDemo* into the Name field and specify *com.ebookfrenzy.themedemo* as the package name. Before clicking on the Finish button, change the Minimum API level setting to API 26: Android 8.0 (Oreo) and the Language menu to Java.

85.3 Designing the User Interface

The main activity will consist of a simple layout containing some user interface components that will enable us to see the effects of the theming work performed later in the chapter. For information on MD3 components, refer to the following web page:

https://material.io/blog/migrating-material-3

The layout will be designed within the *activity_main.xml* file, which currently contains a single Text view. Open this file in the layout editor, delete the Text view, turn off Autoconnect mode (marked A in Figure 85-1), and click on the button to clear all constraints from the layout (B).

Figure 85-1

From the Buttons section of the Palette, drag Chip, CheckBox, Switch, and Button views onto the layout canvas. Next, drag a FloatingActionButton onto the layout canvas to position it beneath the Button component. When prompted to choose an icon to appear on the FloatingActionButton, select the *ic_lock_power_off* icon from within the resource tool window, as illustrated in Figure 85-2:

A Material Design 3 Theming and Dynamic Color Tutorial

Figure 85-2

Change the text attribute for the Chip widget to "This is my chip" and set the chipIcon attribute to @android:drawable/ic_btn_speak_now so that the layout resembles that shown to the left in Figure 85-3:

Figure 85-3

A Material Design 3 Theming and Dynamic Color Tutorial

To set up the constraints, select all the components, right-click on the Chip view, and select *Chains -> Create Vertical Chain* from the resulting menu. Repeat this step, this time selecting the *Center -> Horizontally in Parent* menu option.

Compile and run the app on a device or emulator and verify that the user interface matches that shown in Figure 85-3 above. The next step is to create a custom theme and apply it to the project.

85.4 Building a New Theme

Begin by opening a browser window and navigating to the following URL to access the builder tool:

https://m3.material.io/theme-builder#/custom

Once you have loaded the builder, select a wallpaper followed by the Custom button at the top of the screen, and then click on the Primary color circle in the Core Colors section to display the color selector. From the color selector, choose any color as the basis for your theme:

Figure 85-4

Review the color scheme in the Your Theme panel and make any necessary color adjustments using the Core colors settings until you are happy with the color slots. Once the theme is ready, click the Export button in the top right-hand corner and select the *Android Views (XML)* option. When prompted, save the file to a suitable location on your computer filesystem. The theme will be saved as a compressed file named *material-theme.zip*.

Using the appropriate tool for your operating system, unpack the theme file, which should contain the following folders and files in a folder named *material-theme*:

- **values/colors.xml** - The color definitions.
- **values/themes.xml** - The theme for the light mode.
- **values-night/themes.xml** - The theme for dark mode.

A Material Design 3 Theming and Dynamic Color Tutorial

Now that the theme files have been generated, they need to be integrated into the Android Studio project.

85.5 Adding the Theme to the Project

Before adding the new theme to the project, we first need to remove the old theme files. This is easier if the Project tool window is in Project Files mode. To switch mode, use the menu at the top of the tool Project tool window as shown below and select the Project Files option:

Figure 85-5

With Project Files mode selected, navigate to the *app -> src -> main -> res -> values* folder and select and delete the *colors.xml* and *themes.xml* files. Also, delete the *themes.xml* file located in the *values-night* folder.

Open the filesystem navigation tool for your operating system, locate the *colors.xml* and *themes.xml* files in the *values* folder of the new material theme, and copy and paste them into the *values* folder within the Project tool window. Repeat this step to copy the *themes.xml* file in the *values-night* folder, this time pasting it into the *values-night* folder.

Switch the Project tool window back to Android mode, at which point the value resource files section should match Figure 85-6:

Figure 85-6

Next, modify the light *themes.xml* file to match the current project as follows:

```
<resources>
    <style name="Base.Theme.ThemeDemo" parent="Theme.Material3.Light.NoActionBar">
        <item name="colorPrimary">@color/md_theme_light_primary</item>
        <item name="colorOnPrimary">@color/md_theme_light_onPrimary</item>
```

```xml
        </style>

        <style name="Theme.ThemeDemo" parent="Base.Theme.ThemeDemo" />

</resources>
```

Repeat these steps to make the same modifications to the *themes.xml (night)* file.

Return to the *activity_main.xml* file or rerun the app to confirm that the user interface is rendered using the custom theme colors.

85.6 Enabling Dynamic Color Support

The app will need to be run on a device or emulator running Android 12 or later with the correct Wallpaper settings to test dynamic colors. On the device or emulator, launch the Settings app and select *Wallpaper & style* from the list of options. On the wallpaper settings screen, click the option to change the wallpaper (marked A in Figure 85-7) and select a wallpaper image containing colors that differ significantly from the colors in your theme. Once selected, assign the wallpaper to the Home screen.

Return to the Wallpaper & styles screen and make sure that the *Wallpaper colors* option is selected (B) before choosing an option from the color scheme buttons (C). As each option is clicked, the wallpaper example will change to reflect the selection:

Figure 85-7

To enable dynamic colors, we need to call the *applyToActivitiesIfAvailable()* method of the DynamicColors class. To enable dynamic color support for the entire app, this needs to be called from within the *onCreate()* method of a custom Application instance. Begin by adding a new Java class file to the project under *app -> java -> com.ebookfrenzy.themedemo* named *ThemeDemoApplication*.java and modifying it so that it reads as follows:

```
package com.ebookfrenzy.themedemo;
```

A Material Design 3 Theming and Dynamic Color Tutorial

```java
import android.app.Application;
import com.google.android.material.color.DynamicColors;

public class ThemeDemoApplication extends Application {
    @Override
    public void onCreate() {
        super.onCreate();
        DynamicColors.applyToActivitiesIfAvailable(this);
    }
}
```

With the custom Application class created, we must configure the project to use this class instead of the default Application instance. To do this, edit the *AndroidManifest.xml* file and add an *android:name* element referencing the new class:

```xml
<?xml version="1.0" encoding="utf-8"?>
<manifest xmlns:android="http://schemas.android.com/apk/res/android"
    package="com.ebookfrenzy.themedemo">

    <application
        android:name=".ThemeDemoApplication"
        android:allowBackup="true"
```
.
.

Build and run the app and note that the layout uses a theme matching the wallpaper color. Place the ThemeDemo app into the background, return to the *Wallpaper & styles* settings screen, and choose a different wallpaper. Bring the ThemeDemo app to the foreground again. At this point, it will have dynamically adapted to match the new wallpaper.

85.7 Previewing Dynamic Colors

Dynamic color behavior can also be previewed within the Android Studio layout editor. To try this, open the *activity_main.xml* file, click on the theme menu, and select the More Themes option, as shown in Figure 85-8:

Figure 85-8

A Material Design 3 Theming and Dynamic Color Tutorial

Next, use the search field in the theme selection dialog to list dynamic themes:

Figure 85-9

Select the *Material3.DynamicColors.DayNight* theme before clicking on the OK button. On returning to the layout editor, select the System UI Mode menu and choose one of the wallpaper options as highlighted in Figure 85-10:

Figure 85-10

Once a wallpaper has been selected, the colors of the components in the layout will change accordingly.

85.8 Summary

In this chapter, we have used the Material Theme Builder to design a new theme and explained the steps to integrate the generated theme files into an Android Studio project. Finally, the chapter demonstrated how to implement and use the Material You dynamic colors feature.

86. An Overview of Gradle in Android Studio

Up until this point, it has been taken for granted that Android Studio will take the necessary steps to compile and run the application projects that have been created. Android Studio has been achieving this in the background using a system known as *Gradle*.

It is time to look at how Gradle is used to compile and package an application project's various elements and begin exploring how to configure this system when more advanced requirements are needed for building projects in Android Studio.

86.1 An Overview of Gradle

Gradle is an automated build toolkit that allows how projects are built to be configured and managed through a set of build configuration files. This includes defining how a project will be built, what dependencies need to be fulfilled to build successfully, and what the build process's end result (or results) should be.

The strength of Gradle lies in the flexibility that it provides to the developer. The Gradle system is a self-contained, command-line-based environment that can be integrated into other environments using plugins. In the case of Android Studio, Gradle integration is provided through the appropriately named Android Studio Plugin.

Although the Android Studio Plug-in allows Gradle tasks to be initiated and managed from within Android Studio, the Gradle command-line wrapper can still be used to build Android Studio-based projects, including on systems on which Android Studio is not installed.

The configuration rules to build a project are declared in Gradle build files and scripts based on the Groovy programming language.

86.2 Gradle and Android Studio

Gradle brings many powerful features to building Android application projects. Some of the key features are as follows:

86.2.1 Sensible Defaults

Gradle implements a concept referred to as *convention over configuration*. This means that Gradle has a predefined set of sensible default configuration settings that will be used unless settings in the build files override them. This means that builds can be performed with the minimum configuration required by the developer. Changes to the build files are only needed when the default configuration does not meet your build needs.

86.2.2 Dependencies

Another key area of Gradle functionality is that of dependencies. Consider, for example, a module within an Android Studio project which triggers an intent to load another module in the project. The first module has, in effect, a dependency on the second module since the application will fail to build if the second module cannot be located and launched at runtime. This dependency can be declared in the Gradle build file for the first module so that the second module is included in the application build, or an error flagged if the second module cannot be found or built. Other examples of dependencies are libraries and JAR files on which the project depends to compile and run.

An Overview of Gradle in Android Studio

Gradle dependencies can be categorized as *local* or *remote*. A local dependency references an item that is present on the local file system of the computer system on which the build is being performed. A remote dependency refers to an item that is present on a remote server (typically referred to as a *repository*).

Remote dependencies are handled for Android Studio projects using another project management tool named *Maven*. If a remote dependency is declared in a Gradle build file using Maven syntax, then the dependency will be downloaded automatically from the designated repository and included in the build process. The following dependency declaration, for example, causes the AppCompat library to be added to the project from the Google repository:

```
implementation("androidx.appcompat:appcompat:1.6.1")
```

86.2.3 Build Variants

In addition to dependencies, Gradle also provides *build variant* support for Android Studio projects. This allows multiple variations of an application to be built from a single project. Android runs on many different devices encompassing a range of processor types and screen sizes. To target as wide a range of device types and sizes as possible, it will often be necessary to build several variants of an application (for example, one with a user interface for phones and another for tablet-sized screens). Through the use of Gradle, this is now possible in Android Studio.

86.2.4 Manifest Entries

Each Android Studio project has associated with it an *AndroidManifest.xml* file containing configuration details about the application. Several manifest entries can be specified in Gradle build files which are then auto-generated into the manifest file when the project is built. This capability complements the build variants feature, allowing elements such as the application version number, application ID, and SDK version information to be configured differently for each build variant.

86.2.5 APK Signing

The chapter *"Creating, Testing, and Uploading an Android App Bundle"* covered creating a signed release APK file using the Android Studio environment. It is also possible to include the signing information entered through the Android Studio user interface within a Gradle build file to generate signed APK files from the command line.

86.2.6 ProGuard Support

ProGuard is a tool included with Android Studio that optimizes, shrinks, and obfuscates Java byte code to make it more efficient and harder to reverse engineer (the method by which others can identify the logic of an application through analysis of the compiled Java byte code). The Gradle build files allow you to control whether or not ProGuard is run on your application when it is built.

86.3 The Property and Settings Gradle Build File

The gradle build configuration consists of configuration, property, and settings files. The *gradle.properties* file, for example, contains mostly esoteric settings relating to the command-line flags used by the Java Virtual Machine (JVM), whether or not the project uses the AndroidX libraries and Kotlin coding style support. As a typical user, it is unlikely that you will need to change any of these settings in this file.

The *settings.gradle.kts* file, on the other hand, defines which online repositories are to be searched when the build system needs to download and install any additional libraries and plugins required to build the project and the project name. A typical *settings.gradle.kts* file will read as follows:

```
pluginManagement {
    repositories {
        google()
        mavenCentral()
```

```
        gradlePluginPortal()
    }
}
dependencyResolutionManagement {
    repositoriesMode.set(RepositoriesMode.FAIL_ON_PROJECT_REPOS)
    repositories {
        google()
        mavenCentral()
    }
}

rootProject.name = "ThemeDemo"
include(":app")
```

As with the *gradle.properties* file, it is unlikely that changes will need to be made to this file.

86.4 The Top-level Gradle Build File

A completed Android Studio project contains everything needed to build an Android application and consists of modules, libraries, manifest files, and Gradle build files.

Each project contains one top-level Gradle build file. This file is listed as *build.gradle.kts (Project: <project name>)* and can be found in the project tool window as highlighted in Figure 86-1:

Figure 86-1

By default, the contents of the top-level Gradle build file reads as follows:

```
// Top-level build file where you can add configuration options common to all sub-
projects/modules.
plugins {
    id("com.android.application") version "8.1.0-rc01" apply false
}
```

As it stands, all the file does is declare that remote libraries are to be obtained using the jcenter repository, and

An Overview of Gradle in Android Studio

that builds depend on the Android plugin for Gradle. In most situations, making any changes to this build file is unnecessary.

86.5 Module Level Gradle Build Files

An Android Studio application project is made up of one or more modules. Take, for example, a hypothetical application project named GradleDemo which contains modules named Module1 and Module2, respectively. In this scenario, each module will require its own Gradle build file. In terms of the project structure, these would be located as follows:

- Module1/build.gradle.kts

- Module2/build.gradle.kts

By default, the Module1 *build.gradle.kts* file would resemble that of the following listing:

```
plugins {
    id("com.android.application")
}

android {
    namespace = "com.example.gradlesample"
    compileSdk = 33

    defaultConfig {
        applicationId = "com.example.gradlesample"
        minSdk = 26
        targetSdk = 33
        versionCode = 1
        versionName = "1.0"

        testInstrumentationRunner = "androidx.test.runner.AndroidJUnitRunner"
    }

    buildTypes {
        release {
            isMinifyEnabled = false
            proguardFiles(
                getDefaultProguardFile("proguard-android-optimize.txt"),
                "proguard-rules.pro"
            )
        }
    }
    compileOptions {
        sourceCompatibility = JavaVersion.VERSION_1_8
        targetCompatibility = JavaVersion.VERSION_1_8
    }
}
```

```
dependencies {

    implementation("androidx.appcompat:appcompat:1.6.1")
    implementation("com.google.android.material:material:1.9.0")
    implementation("androidx.constraintlayout:constraintlayout:2.1.4")
    testImplementation("junit:junit:4.13.2")
    androidTestImplementation("androidx.test.ext:junit:1.1.5")
    androidTestImplementation("androidx.test.espresso:espresso-core:3.5.1")
}
```

As is evident from the file content, the build file begins by declaring the use of the Gradle Android application plug-in:

```
plugins {
    id("com.android.application")
}
```

The *android* section of the file declares the project namespace and then states the version of the SDK to be used when building Module1.

```
android {
    namespace = "com.example.gradlesample"
    compileSdk = 33
```

The items declared in the defaultConfig section define elements to be generated into the module's *AndroidManifest.xml* file during the build. These settings, which may be modified in the build file, are taken from the settings entered within Android Studio when the module was first created:

```
defaultConfig {
    applicationId = "com.example.gradlesample"
    minSdk = 26
    targetSdk = 33
    versionCode = 1
    versionName = "1.0"

    testInstrumentationRunner = "androidx.test.runner.AndroidJUnitRunner"
}
```

The buildTypes section contains instructions on whether and how to run ProGuard on the APK file when a release version of the application is built:

```
buildTypes {
    release {
        isMinifyEnabled = false
        proguardFiles(
            getDefaultProguardFile("proguard-android-optimize.txt"),
            "proguard-rules.pro"
        )
    }
}
```

An Overview of Gradle in Android Studio

As currently configured, ProGuard will not be run when Module1 is built. To enable ProGuard, the *minifyEnabled* entry must be changed from *false* to *true*. The *proguard-rules.pro* file can be found in the module directory of the project. Changes made to this file override the default settings in the *proguard-android.txt* file, which is located in the Android SDK installation directory under *sdk/tools/proguard*.

Since no debug buildType is declared in this file, the defaults will be used (built without ProGuard, signed with a debug key, and debug symbols enabled).

An additional section, entitled *productFlavors*, may also be included in the module build file to enable multiple build variants to be created.

Next, directives are included to specify the version of the Java compiler to be used when building the project:

```
compileOptions {
    sourceCompatibility JavaVersion.VERSION_1_8
    targetCompatibility JavaVersion.VERSION_1_8
}
```

Finally, the dependencies section lists any local and remote dependencies on which the module depends. The dependency lines in the above example file designate the Android libraries that need to be included from the Android Repository:

```
dependencies {

    implementation("androidx.appcompat:appcompat:1.6.1")
    implementation("com.google.android.material:material:1.9.0")
    .
    .
    .
}
```

Note that the dependency declarations include version numbers to indicate which library version should be included.

86.6 Configuring Signing Settings in the Build File

The *"Creating, Testing, and Uploading an Android App Bundle"* chapter of this book covered the steps involved in setting up keys and generating a signed release APK file using the Android Studio user interface. These settings may also be declared within a *signingConfigs* section of the *build.gradle.kts* file. For example:

```
    .
    .
    defaultConfig {
    .
    .
    }
    signingConfigs {
        release {
            storeFile file("keystore.release")
            storePassword "your keystore password here"
            keyAlias "your key alias here"
            keyPassword "your key password here"
        }
    }
```

An Overview of Gradle in Android Studio

```
    buildTypes {
    .
    .
    .
}
```

The above example embeds the key password information directly into the build file. An alternative to this approach is to extract these values from system environment variables:

```
signingConfigs {
    release {
        storeFile file("keystore.release")
        storePassword System.getenv("KEYSTOREPASSWD")
        keyAlias "your key alias here"
        keyPassword System.getenv("KEYPASSWD")
    }
}
```

Yet another approach is to configure the build file so that Gradle prompts for the passwords to be entered during the build process:

```
signingConfigs {
    release {
        storeFile file("keystore.release")
        storePassword System.console().readLine
                ("\nEnter Keystore password: ")
        keyAlias "your key alias here"
        keyPassword System.console().readLIne("\nEnter Key password: ")
    }
}
```

86.7 Running Gradle Tasks from the Command Line

Each Android Studio project contains a Gradle wrapper tool to invoke Gradle tasks from the command line. This tool is located in the root directory of each project folder. While this wrapper is executable on Windows systems, it may need to have execute permission enabled on Linux and macOS before it can be used. To enable execute permission, open a terminal window, change directory to the project folder for which the wrapper is needed, and execute the following command:

```
chmod +x gradlew
```

Once the file has execute permissions, the location of the file will either need to be added to your $PATH environment variable or the name prefixed by ./ to run. For example:

```
./gradlew tasks
```

Gradle views project building in terms of several different tasks. A full listing of tasks that are available for the current project can be obtained by running the following command from within the project directory (remembering to prefix the command with a ./ if running on macOS or Linux):

```
gradlew tasks
```

To build a debug release of the project suitable for device or emulator testing, use the assembleDebug option:

```
gradlew assembleDebug
```

Alternatively, to build a release version of the application:

```
gradlew assembleRelease
```

86.8 Summary

For the most part, Android Studio performs application builds in the background without any intervention from the developer. This build process is handled using the Gradle system, an automated build toolkit designed to allow how projects are built to be configured and managed through a set of build configuration files. While the default behavior of Gradle is adequate for many basic project build requirements, the need to configure the build process is inevitable with more complex projects. This chapter has provided an overview of the Gradle build system and configuration files within the context of an Android Studio project.

Index

Symbols

<application> 436

<fragment> 247

<fragment> element 247

<receiver> 470

<service> 436, 480, 487

Code Reformatting 79

.well-known folder 443, 466, 680

A

AbsoluteLayout 126

ACCESS_COARSE_LOCATION permission 504

ACCESS_FINE_LOCATION permission 504

acknowledgePurchase() method 719

ACTION_CREATE_DOCUMENT 596

ACTION_CREATE_INTENT 596

ACTION_DOWN 222

ACTION_MOVE 222

ACTION_OPEN_DOCUMENT intent 588

ACTION_POINTER_DOWN 222

ACTION_POINTER_UP 222

ACTION_UP 222

ACTION_VIEW 461

Active / Running state 100

Activity 87, 103

  adding views in Java code 203

  class 103

  creation 16

  Entire Lifetime 107

  Foreground Lifetime 107

  lifecycle methods 106

  lifecycles 97

  returning data from 440

  state change example 111

  state changes 103

  states 100

  Visible Lifetime 107

Activity Lifecycle 99

Activity Manager 86

ActivityResultLauncher 441

Activity Stack 99

Actual screen pixels 194

adb

  command-line tool 63

  connection testing 69

  device pairing 67

  enabling on Android devices 63

  Linux configuration 66

  list devices 63

  macOS configuration 64

  overview 63

  restart server 64

  testing connection 69

  WiFi debugging 67

  Windows configuration 65

  Wireless debugging 67

  Wireless pairing 67

addCategory() method 469

addMarker() method 644

addView() method 197

ADD_VOICEMAIL permission 504

android

  exported 437

  gestureColor 240

  layout_behavior property 419

  onClick 249

  process 437, 487

  uncertainGestureColor 240

Android

  Activity 87

  architecture 83

  events 215

  intents 88

  onClick Resource 215

Index

runtime 84
SDK Packages 6
android.app 84
Android Architecture Components 265
android.content 84
android.content.Intent 439
android.database 84
Android Debug Bridge. *See* ADB
Android Development
   System Requirements 3
Android Devices
   designing for different 125
android.graphics 84
android.hardware 84
android.intent.action 475
android.intent.action.BOOT_COMPLETED 437
android.intent.action.MAIN 461
android.intent.category.LAUNCHER 461
Android Libraries 84
android.media 85
Android Monitor tool window 36
Android Native Development Kit 85
android.net 85
android.opengl 84
android.os 85
android.permission.RECORD_AUDIO 623
android.print 85
Android Project
   create new 15
android.provider 85
Android SDK Location
   identifying 10
Android SDK Manager 8, 10
Android SDK Packages
   version requirements 8
Android SDK Tools
   command-line access 9
   Linux 11
   macOS 11
   Windows 7 10
   Windows 8 10
Android Software Stack 83

Android Storage Access Framework 588
Android Studio
   changing theme 61
   downloading 3
   Editor Window 56
   installation 4
   Linux installation 5
   macOS installation 4
   Navigation Bar 55
   Project tool window 56
   setup wizard 5
   Status Bar 56
   Toolbar 55
   Tool window bars 56
   tool windows 56
   updating 12
   Welcome Screen 53
   Windows installation 4
android.text 85
android.util 85
android.view 85
android.view.View 128
android.view.ViewGroup 125, 128
Android Virtual Device. *See* AVD
   overview 31
Android Virtual Device Manager 31
android.webkit 85
android.widget 85
AndroidX libraries 748
API Key 635
APK analyzer 712
APK file 705
APK File
   analyzing 712
APK Signing 748
APK Wizard dialog 704
App Architecture
   modern 265
AppBar
   anatomy of 417
appbar_scrolling_view_behavior 419
App Bundles 701

756

creating 705
overview 701
revisions 711
uploading 708
AppCompatActivity class 104
App Inspector 57
Application
  stopping 36
Application Context 89
Application Framework 85
Application Manifest 89
Application Resources 89
App Link
  Adding Intent Filter 688
  Digital Asset Links file 680, 443
  Intent Filter Handling 689
  Intent Filters 679
  Intent Handling 680
  Testing 692
  URL Mapping 685
App Links 679
  auto verification 442
  autoVerify 443
  overview 679
Apply Changes 211
  Apply Changes and Restart Activity 211
  Apply Code Changes 211
  fallback settings 213
  options 211
  Run App 211
  tutorial 213
applyToActivitiesIfAvailable() method 743
Architecture Components 265
ART 84
assetlinks.json , 680, 443
Attribute Keyframes 342
Audio
  supported formats 621
Audio Playback 621
Audio Recording 621
Autoconnect Mode 159
Automatic Link Verification 442, 465

autoVerify 443, 688
AVD
  cold boot 48
  command-line creation 31
  creation 31
  device frame 40
  Display mode 51
  launch in tool window 40
  overview 31
  quickboot 48
  Resizable 50
  running an application 34
  Snapshots 47
  standalone 37
  starting 33
  Startup size and orientation 34

B

Background Process 98
Barriers 152
  adding 171
  constrained views 152
Baseline Alignment 151
beginTransaction() method 248
BillingClient 720
  acknowledgePurchase() method 719
  consumeAsync() method 719
  getPurchaseState() method 719
  initialization 716, 726
  launchBillingFlow() method 718
  queryProductDetailsAsync() method 718
  queryPurchasesAsync() method 720
BillingResult 733
  getDebugMessage() 733
Binding Expressions 289
  one-way 289
  two-way 290
BIND_JOB_SERVICE permission 437
bindService() method 435, 477, 482
Biometric Authentication 693
  callbacks 697
  overview 693

Index

tutorial 693
Biometric Prompt 698
BitmapFactory 589
black activity 16
Blank template 129
Blueprint view 157
BODY_SENSORS permission 504
Bound Service 435, 477
   adding to a project 478
   Implementing the Binder 478
   Interaction options 477
BoundService class 479
Broadcast Intent 469
   example 472
   overview 88, 469
   sending 472
   Sticky 471
Broadcast Receiver 469
   adding to manifest file 474
   creation 473
   overview 88, 470
BroadcastReceiver class 470
BroadcastReceiver superclass 473
BufferedReader object 599
Build tool window 58
Build Variants , 58
   tool window 58
Bundle class 120
Bundled Notifications 523

C

Calendar permissions 504
CALL_PHONE permission 504
CAMERA permission 504
Camera permissions 504
CameraUpdateFactory class
   methods 645
CancellationSignal 698
Canvas class 674
CardView
   layout file 397
   responding to selection of 406

CardView class 397
CATEGORY_OPENABLE 588
C/C++ Libraries 85
Chain bias 180
chain head 150
chains 150
Chains
   creation of 177
Chain style
   changing 179
chain styles 150
CheckBox 125
checkSelfPermission() method 508
Circle class 631
Code completion 74
Code Editor
   basics 71
   Code completion 74
   Code Generation 77
   Code Reformatting 79
   Document Tabs 72
   Editing area 72
   Gutter Area 72
   Live Templates 80
   Splitting 74
   Statement Completion 76
   Status Bar 73
Code Generation 77
code samples
   download 1
cold boot 48
CollapsingToolbarLayout
   example 420
   introduction 420
   parallax mode 420
   pin mode 420
   setting scrim color 423
   setting title 423
   with image 420
Color class 675
COLOR_MODE_COLOR 650, 670
COLOR_MODE_MONOCHROME 650, 670

Index

Common Gestures 229
  detection 229
Component tree 20
Constraint Bias 149
  adjusting 163
ConstraintLayout
  advantages of 155
  Availability 156
  Barriers 152
  Baseline Alignment 151
  chain bias 180
  chain head 150
  chains 150
  chain styles 150
  Constraint Bias 149
  Constraints 147
  conversion to 175
  convert to MotionLayout 349
  deleting constraints 162
  guidelines 169
  Guidelines 152
  manual constraint manipulation 159
  Margins 148, 163
  Opposing Constraints 148, 165
  overview of 147
  Packed chain 151, 180
  ratios 155, 181
  Spread chain 150
  Spread inside 180
  Spread inside chain 150
  tutorial 185
  using in Android Studio 157
  Weighted chain 150, 180
  Widget Dimensions 151, 167
  Widget Group Alignment 173
ConstraintLayout chains
  creation of 177
  in layout editor 177
ConstraintLayout Chain style
  changing 179
Constraints
  deleting 162

ConstraintSet
  addToHorizontalChain() method 200
  addToVerticalChain() method 200
  alignment constraints 199
  apply to layout 198
  applyTo() method 198
  centerHorizontally() method 199
  centerVertically() method 199
  chains 199
  clear() method 200
  clone() method 199
  connect() method 198
  connect to parent 198
  constraint bias 199
  copying constraints 199
  create 198
  create connection 198
  createHorizontalChain() method 199
  createVerticalChain() method 199
  guidelines 200
  removeFromHorizontalChain() method 200
  removeFromVerticalChain() method 200
  removing constraints 200
  rotation 201
  scaling 200
  setGuidelineBegin() method 200
  setGuidelineEnd() method 200
  setGuidelinePercent() method 200
  setHorizonalBias() method 199
  setRotationX() method 201
  setRotationY() method 201
  setScaleX() method 200
  setScaleY() method 200
  setTransformPivot() method 201
  setTransformPivotX() method 201
  setTransformPivotY() method 201
  setVerticalBias() method 199
  sizing constraints 199
  tutorial 203
  view IDs 205
ConstraintSet class 197, 198
Constraint Sets 198

Index

ConstraintSets
  configuring 338
consumeAsync() method 719
ConsumeParams 731
ConsumeResponseListener 719
Contacts permissions 504
container view 125
Content Provider 86
  overview 89
Context class 89
CoordinatorLayout 126, 419
createPrintDocumentAdapter() method 665
Custom Attribute 339
Custom Document Printing 653, 665
Custom Gesture
  recognition 235
Custom Print Adapter
  implementation 667
Custom Print Adapters 665
Custom Theme
  building 737
Cycle Editor 367
Cycle Keyframe 347
Cycle Keyframes
  overview 363

D

dangerous permissions
  list of 504
Dark Theme 36
  enable on device 36
Data Access Object (DAO) 554
Data Access Objects (DAO) 558
Database Inspector 561, 584
  live updates 585
  SQL query 585
Database Rows 548
Database Schema 547
Database Tables 547
Data binding
  binding expressions 289
Data Binding 267

binding classes 288
  enabling 294
  event and listener binding 290
  key components 285
  overview 285
  tutorial 293
  with LiveData 267
DDMS 36
Debugging
  enabling on device 63
debug.keystore file 443, 465
DefaultLifecycleObserver 308, 311
deltaRelative 343
Density-independent pixels 193
Density Independent Pixels
  converting to pixels 208
Device Definition
  custom 143
Device File Explorer 58
device frame 40
Device Mirroring 69
  enabling 69
device pairing 67
Digital Asset Links file 680, 443, 443
Direct Reply Input 534
document provider 587
dp 193
Dynamic Colors
  applyToActivitiesIfAvailable() method 743
  enabling in Android 743
Dynamic State 105
  saving 119

E

Empty Process 99
Empty template 129
Emulator
  battery 46
  cellular configuration 46
  configuring fingerprints 48
  directional pad 46
  extended control options 45

Extended controls 45
fingerprint 46
location configuration 46
phone settings 46
Resizable 50
resize 45
rotate 44
Screen Record 47
Snapshots 47
starting 33
take screenshot 44
toolbar 43
toolbar options 43
tool window mode 50
Virtual Sensors 47
zoom 44
enablePendingPurchases() method 719
enabling ADB support 63
ettings.gradle file 748
Event Handling 215
   example 216
Event Listener 217
Event Listeners 216
Events
   consuming 219
explicit
   intent 88
explicit intent 439
Explicit Intent 439
Extended Control
   options 45

F

Files
   switching between 72
findPointerIndex() method 222
findViewById() 91
Fingerprint
   emulation 48
Fingerprint authentication
   device configuration 694
   permission 694

steps to implement 693
Fingerprint Authentication
   overview 693
   tutorial 693
FLAG_INCLUDE_STOPPED_PACKAGES 469
flexible space area 417
floating action button 16, 130
   changing appearance of 378
   margins 376
   removing 131
   sizes 376
Foldable Devices 108
   multi-resume 108
Foldable Emulator 540
Foldables 539
Foreground Process 98
Forward-geocoding 637
Fragment
   creation 245
   event handling 249
   XML file 246
FragmentActivity class 104
Fragment Communication 250
Fragments 245
   adding in code 248
   duplicating 386
   example 253
   overview 245
FragmentStateAdapter class 389
FrameLayout 126

G

Geocoder object 638
Geocoding 636
Gesture Builder Application 235
   building and running 235
Gesture Detector class 229
GestureDetectorCompat 232
   instance creation 232
GestureDetectorCompat class 229
GestureDetector.OnDoubleTapListener 229, 230
GestureDetector.OnGestureListener 230

Index

GestureLibrary 235
GestureOverlayView 235
   configuring color 240
   configuring multiple strokes 240
GestureOverlayView class 235
GesturePerformedListener 235
Gestures
   interception of 241
Gestures File
   creation 236
   extract from SD card 236
   loading into application 238
GET_ACCOUNTS permission 504
getAction() method 475
getDebugMessage() 733
getFromLocation() method 638
getId() method 198
getIntent() method 440
getPointerCount() method 222
getPointerId() method 222
getPurchaseState() method 719
getService() method 482
GNU/Linux 84
Google Cloud
   billing account 632
   new project 633
Google Cloud Print 648
Google Drive 588
   printing to 648
GoogleMap 631
   map types 641
GoogleMap.MAP_TYPE_HYBRID 641
GoogleMap.MAP_TYPE_NONE 641
GoogleMap.MAP_TYPE_NORMAL 641
GoogleMap.MAP_TYPE_SATELLITE 641
GoogleMap.MAP_TYPE_TERRAIN 641
Google Maps Android API 631
   Controlling the Map Camera 645
   displaying controls 642
   Map Markers 644
   overview 631
Google Maps SDK 631

API Key 635
   Credentials 635
   enabling 634
   Maps SDK for Android 635
Google Play App Signing 704
Google Play Console 724
   Creating an in-app product 724
   License Testers 725
Google Play Developer Console 702
Gradle
   APK signing settings 752
   Build Variants 748
   command line tasks 753
   dependencies 747
   Manifest Entries 748
   overview 747
   sensible defaults 747
Gradle Build File
   top level 749
Gradle Build Files
   module level 750
gradle.properties file 748
GridLayout 126
GridLayoutManager 395

H

Handler class 486
HP Print Services Plugin 647
HTML printing 651
HTML Printing
   example 655

I

IBinder 435, 479
IBinder object 477, 487
Image Printing 650
implicit
   intent 88
implicit intent 439
Implicit Intent 441
Implicit Intents
   example 457

importance hierarchy 97
in 193
INAPP 720
In-App Products 715
In-App Purchasing 723
    acknowledgePurchase() method 719
    BillingClient 716
    BillingResult 733
    consumeAsync() method 719
    ConsumeParams 731
    ConsumeResponseListener 719
    Consuming purchases 730
    enablePendingPurchases() method 719
    getPurchaseState() method 719
    launchBillingFlow() method 718
    Libraries 723
    newBuilder() method 716
    onBillingServiceDisconnected() callback 728
    onBillingServiceDisconnected() method 717
    onBillingSetupFinished() listener 728
    onProductDetailsResponse() callback 728
    Overview 715
    ProductDetail 718
    ProductDetails 729
    products 715
    ProductType 720
    ProductType.INAPP 720
    ProductType.SUBS 720
    Purchase Flow 729
    PurchaseResponseListener 720
    PurchasesUpdatedListener 719
    PurchaseUpdatedListener 729
    purchase updates 729
    queryProductDetailsAsync() 728
    queryProductDetailsAsync() method 718
    queryPurchasesAsync() 731
    queryPurchasesAsync() method 720
    runOnUiThread() 729
    subscriptions 715
    tutorial 723
In-Memory Database 561
Intent 88

explicit 88
implicit 88
Intent Availability
    checking for 446
Intent.CATEGORY_OPENABLE 596
Intent Filters 442
    App Link 679
Intents 439
    ActivityResultLauncher 441
    overview 439
    registerForActivityResult() 454
Intent Service 435
Intent URL 460

J

Java Native Interface 85
Jetpack 265
    overview 265
JobIntentService 435
    BIND_JOB_SERVICE permission 437
    onHandleWork() method 435

K

KeyAttribute 342
Keyboard Shortcuts 59
KeyCycle 363
    Cycle Editor 367
    tutorial 363
Keyframe 356
Keyframes 342
KeyFrameSet 372
KeyPosition 343
    deltaRelative 343
    parentRelative 343
    pathRelative 344
Keystore File
    creation 704
KeyTimeCycle 363
keytool 443
KeyTrigger 346
Killed state 100

Index

L

launchBillingFlow() method 718
layout_collapseMode
  parallax 422
  pin 422
layout_constraintDimentionRatio 182
layout_constraintHorizontal_bias 180
layout_constraintVertical_bias 180
layout editor
  ConstraintLayout chains 177
Layout Editor 19, 185
  Autoconnect Mode 159
  code mode 136
  Component Tree 134
  design mode 133
  device screen 134
  example project 185
  Inference Mode 159
  palette 134
  properties panel 134
  Sample Data 142
  Setting Properties 138
  toolbar 134
  user interface design 185
  view conversion 141
Layout Editor Tool
  changing orientation 20
  overview 133
Layout Inspector 58
Layout Managers 125
LayoutResultCallback object 670
Layouts 125
layout_scrollFlags
  enterAlwaysCollapsed mode 419
  enterAlways mode 419
  exitUntilCollapsed mode 419
  scroll mode 419
Layout Validation 144
libc 85
License Testers 725
Lifecycle
  awareness 307
  components 268
  owners 307
  states and events 309
  tutorial 311
Lifecycle-Aware Components 307
Lifecycle Methods 106
Lifecycle Observer 311
  creating a 311
Lifecycle Owner
  creating a 313
Lifecycles
  modern 268
LinearLayout 126
LinearLayoutManager 395
LinearLayoutManager layout 404
Linux Kernel 84
list devices 63
LiveData 266, 279
  adding to ViewModel 279
  observer 281
  tutorial 279
Live Templates 80
Local Bound Service 477
  example 477
Location Manager 86
Location permission 504
Logcat
  tool window 57
LogCat
  enabling 115

M

MANAGE_EXTERNAL_STORAGE 505
  adb enabling 505
  testing 505
Manifest File
  permissions 461
Maps 631
MapView 631
  adding to a layout 638
Marker class 631
Master/Detail Flow

Index

creation 426
   two pane mode 425
match_parent properties 193
Material design 375
Material Design 2 735
Material Design 2 Theming 735
Material Design 3 735
Material Theme Builder 737
Material You 735
MediaController
   adding to VideoView instance 605
MediaController class 602
   methods 602
MediaPlayer class 621
   methods 621
MediaRecorder class 621
   methods 622
   recording audio 622
Memory Indicator 73
Messenger object 487
Microphone
   checking for availability 624
Microphone permissions 504
mm 193
MotionEvent 221, 222, 243
   getActionMasked() 222
MotionLayout 337
   arc motion 342
   Attribute Keyframes 342
   ConstraintSets 338
   Custom Attribute 358
   Custom Attributes 339
   Cycle Editor 367
   Editor 349
   KeyAttribute 342
   KeyCycle 363
   Keyframes 342
   KeyFrameSet 372
   KeyPosition 343
   KeyTimeCycle 363
   KeyTrigger 346
   OnClick 341, 354

OnSwipe 341
overview 337
Position Keyframes 343
previewing animation 354
Trigger Keyframe 346
Tutorial 349
MotionScene
   ConstraintSets 338
   Custom Attributes 339
   file 338
   overview 337
   transition 338
moveCamera() method 645
multiple devices
   testing app on 35
Multiple Touches
   handling 222
multi-resume 108
Multi-Touch
   example 222
Multi-touch Event Handling 221
Multi-Window
   attributes 543
Multi-Window Mode
   detecting 544
   entering 541
   launching activity into 545
Multi-Window Notifications 544
multi-window support 108
Multi-Window Support
   enabling 542
My Location Layer 631

N

Navigation 317
   adding destinations 326
   overview 317
   pass data with safeargs 333
   passing arguments 322
   stack 317
   tutorial 323
Navigation Action

Index

triggering 321
Navigation Architecture Component 317
Navigation Component
   tutorial 323
Navigation Controller
   accessing 321
Navigation Graph 320, 324
   adding actions 329
   creating a 324
Navigation Host 318
   declaring 325
newBuilder() method 716
normal permissions 503
Notification
   adding actions 522
   Direct Reply Input 534
   issuing a basic 518
   launch activity from a 520
   PendingIntent 530
   Reply Action 532
   updating direct reply 535
Notifications
   bundled 523
   overview 511
Notifications Manager 86

O

Observer
   implementing a LiveData 281
onAttach() method 250
onBillingServiceDisconnected() callback 728
onBillingServiceDisconnected() method 717
onBillingSetupFinished() listener 728
onBind() method 436, 477
onBindViewHolder() method 403
OnClick 341
onClickListener 216, 217, 220
onClick() method 215
onCreateContextMenuListener 216
onCreate() method 98, 106, 436
onCreateView() method 107
onDestroy() method 106, 436

onDoubleTap() method 229
onDown() method 229
onFling() method 229
onFocusChangeListener 216
OnFragmentInteractionListener
   implementation 331
onGesturePerformed() method 235
onHandleWork() method 436
onKeyListener 216
onLayoutFailed() method 670
onLayoutFinished() method 671
onLongClickListener 216
onLongClick() method 219
onLongPress() method 229
onMapReady() method 640
onPageFinished() callback 656
onPause() method 106
onProductDetailsResponse() callback 728
onReceive() method 98, 470, 471, 473
onRequestPermissionsResult() method 507, 628, 516, 528
onRestart() method 106
onRestoreInstanceState() method 107
onResume() method 98, 106
onSaveInstanceState() method 107
onScaleBegin() method 241
onScaleEnd() method 241
onScale() method 241
onScroll() method 229
OnSeekBarChangeListener 260
onServiceConnected() method 477, 481, 488
onServiceDisconnected() method 477, 481, 488
onShowPress() method 229
onSingleTapUp() method 229
onStartCommand() method 436
onStart() method 106
onStop() method 106
onTouchEvent() method 229, 241
onTouchListener 216
onTouch() method 221
onViewCreated() method 107
onViewStatusRestored() method 107
openFileDescriptor() method 588

OpenJDK 3

P

Package Explorer 18
Package Manager 86
PackageManager class 624
PackageManager.FEATURE_MICROPHONE 624
PackageManager.PERMISSION_DENIED 505
PackageManager.PERMISSION_GRANTED 505
Package Name 16
Packed chain 151, 180
PageRange 672, 673
Paint class 675
parentRelative 343
parent view 127
pathRelative 344
Paused state 100
PdfDocument 653
PdfDocument.Page 665, 672
PendingIntent class 530
Permission
    checking for 505
permissions
    normal 503
Persistent State 105
Phone permissions 504
picker 587
Pinch Gesture
    detection 241
    example 241
Pinch Gesture Recognition 235
Position Keyframes 343
POST_NOTIFICATIONS permission 504, 528
PrintAttributes 670
PrintDocumentAdapter 653, 665
Printing
    color 650
    monochrome 650
Printing framework
    architecture 647
Printing Framework 647
Print Job
    starting 676
PrintManager service 657
Problems
    tool window 58
process
    priority 97
    state 97
PROCESS_OUTGOING_CALLS permission 504
Process States 97
ProductDetail 718
ProductDetails 729
ProductType 720
Profiler
    tool window 58
ProgressBar 125
proguard-rules.pro file 752
ProGuard Support 748
Project Name 16
Project tool window 18, 57
pt 193
PurchaseResponseListener 720
PurchasesUpdatedListener 719
PurchaseUpdatedListener 729
putExtra() method 439, 469
px 194

Q

queryProductDetailsAsync() 728
queryProductDetailsAsync() method 718
queryPurchaseHistoryAsync() method 720
queryPurchasesAsync() 731
queryPurchasesAsync() method 720
quickboot snapshot 48
Quick Documentation 79

R

RadioButton 125
ratios 181
READ_CALENDAR permission 504
READ_CALL_LOG permission 504
READ_CONTACTS permission 504
READ_EXTERNAL_STORAGE permission 505

Index

READ_PHONE_STATE permission 504
READ_SMS permission 504
RECEIVE_MMS permission 504
RECEIVE_SMS permission 504
RECEIVE_WAP_PUSH permission 504
Recent Files Navigation 60
RECORD_AUDIO permission 504
Recording Audio
   permission 623
RecyclerView 395
   adding to layout file 396
   GridLayoutManager 395
   initializing 404
   LinearLayoutManager 395
   StaggeredGridLayoutManager 395
RecyclerView Adapter
   creation of 402
RecyclerView.Adapter 396, 402
   getItemCount() method 396
   onBindViewHolder() method 396
   onCreateViewHolder() method 396
RecyclerView.ViewHolder
   getAdapterPosition() method 406
registerForActivityResult() method 440, 454
registerReceiver() method 471
RelativeLayout 126
releasePersistableUriPermission() method 591
Release Preparation 701
Remote Bound Service 485
   client communication 485
   implementation 485
   manifest file declaration 487
RemoteInput.Builder() method 530
RemoteInput Object 530
Remote Service
   launching and binding 488
   sending a message 489
Repository
   tutorial 571
Repository Modules 268
Resizable Emulator 50
Resource
   string creation 23
Resource File 25
Resource Management 97
Resource Manager , 57
result receiver 471
Reverse-geocoding 637
Reverse Geocoding 636
Room
   Data Access Object (DAO) 554
   entities 554, 555
   In-Memory Database 561
   Repository 554
Room Database 554
   tutorial 571
Room Database Persistence 553
Room Persistence Library 550, 553
root element 125
root view 127
Run
   tool window 57
Running Devices
   tool window 69
runOnUiThread() 729

S

safeargs
Sample Data 142, 409
   tutorial 409
Saved State 267, 301
   library dependencies 303
SavedStateHandle 302, 303
   contains() method 303
   keys() method 303
   remove() method 303
Saved State module 301
SavedStateViewModelFactory 302
ScaleGestureDetector class 241
Scale-independent 193
SDK Packages 6
Secure Sockets Layer (SSL) 85
SeekBar 253
sendBroadcast() method 469, 471

Index

sendOrderedBroadcast() method 469, 471
SEND_SMS permission 504
sendStickyBroadcast() method 469
Sensor permissions 504
Service
   anatomy 436
   launch at system start 437
   manifest file entry 436
   overview 88
   run in separate process 437
ServiceConnection class 488
Service Process 98
Service Restart Options 436
setAudioEncoder() method 622
setAudioSource() method 622
setBackgroundColor() 198
setCompassEnabled() method 642
setContentView() method 197, 203
setId() method 198
setMyLocationButtonEnabled() method 643
setOnClickListener() method 215, 217
setOnDoubleTapListener() method 229, 232
setOutputFile() method 622
setOutputFormat() method 622
setResult() method 441
setRotateGesturesEnabled() method 643
setScrollGesturesEnabled() method 643
setText() method 122
setTiltGesturesEnabled() method 643
settings.gradle.kts file 748
setTransition() 347
setVideoSource() method 622
setZoomControlsEnabled() method 642, 643
SHA-256 certificate fingerprint 443
shouldOverrideUrlLoading() method 656
SimpleOnScaleGestureListener 241
SimpleOnScaleGestureListener class 243
SMS permissions 504
Snackbar 375, 376, 377
Snapshots
   emulator 47
sp 193

Spread chain 150
Spread inside 180
Spread inside chain 150
SQL 548
SQLite 547
   AVD command-line use 549
   Columns and Data Types 547
   overview 548
   Primary keys 548
StaggeredGridLayoutManager 395
startActivity() method 439
startForeground() method 98
START_NOT_STICKY 436
START_REDELIVER_INTENT 436
START_STICKY 436
State
   restoring 122
State Change
   handling 101
Statement Completion 76
Status Bar Widgets 73
   Memory Indicator 73
Sticky Broadcast Intents 471
Stopped state 100
Storage Access Framework 587
   ACTION_CREATE_DOCUMENT 588
   ACTION_OPEN_DOCUMENT 588
   deleting a file 591
   example 593
   file creation 596
   file filtering 588
   file reading 589
   file writing 590
   intents 588
   MIME Types 589
   Persistent Access 591
   picker 587
Storage permissions 505
StringBuilder object 599
strings.xml file 27
Structure
   tool window 58

769

Index

Structured Query Language 548
Structure tool window 58
SUBS 720
subscriptions 715
SupportMapFragment class 631
Switcher 60
System Broadcasts 475
system requirements 3

T

TabLayout
  adding to layout 387
  app
    tabGravity property 393
    tabMode property 392
  example 384
  fixed mode 392
  getItemCount() method 383
  overview 383
TableLayout 126, 563
TableRow 563
Telephony Manager 86
Templates
  blank vs. empty 129
Terminal
  tool window 58
Theme
  building a custom 737
Theming 735
  tutorial 739
Time Cycle Keyframes 347
TODO
  tool window 59
ToolbarListener 250
tools
  layout 247
Tool window bars 56
Tool windows 56
Touch Actions 222
Touch Event Listener
  implementation 223
Touch Events

intercepting 221
Touch handling 221

U

UiSettings class 631
unbindService() method 435
unregisterReceiver() method 471
upload key 704
URL Mapping 685
USB connection issues
  resolving 66
USE_BIOMETRIC 694
user interface state 105
USE_SIP permission 504

V

Video Playback 601
VideoView class 601
  methods 601
  supported formats 601
view bindings
  enabling 92
  using 92
View class
  setting properties 204
view conversion 141
ViewGroup 125
View Groups 125
View Hierarchy 127
ViewHolder class 396
  sample implementation 403
ViewModel
  adding LiveData 279
  data access 276
  overview 266
  saved state 301
  Saved State 267, 301
  tutorial 271
ViewModelProvider 274
ViewModel Saved State 301
ViewPager
  adding to layout 387

example 384
Views 125
  Java creation 197
View System 86
Virtual Device Configuration dialog 32
Virtual Sensors 47
Visible Process 98

W

WebViewClient 651, 656
WebView view 459
Weighted chain 150, 180
Welcome screen 53
Widget Dimensions 151
Widget Group Alignment 173
Widgets palette 186
WiFi debugging 67
Wireless debugging 67
Wireless pairing 67
wrap_content properties 195
WRITE_CALENDAR permission 504
WRITE_CALL_LOG permission 504
WRITE_CONTACTS permission 504
WRITE_EXTERNAL_STORAGE permission 505

X

XML Layout File
  manual creation 193
  vs. Java Code 197

Printed by Amazon Italia Logistica S.r.l.
Torrazza Piemonte (TO), Italy